Hammer's German Grammar and Usage

SECOND EDITION

Revised by
Martin Durrell

Edward Arnold
A division of Hodder & Stoughton
LONDON NEW YORK MELBOURNE AUCKLAND

© 1971 and 1983   The Estate of A. E. Hammer

Revisions for the Second Edition © 1991 Edward Arnold

First published in Great Britain 1971
First paperback edition 1973
Reprinted with corrections and supplement 1983
Second edition published 1991
Reprinted with corrections 1991 (twice)
Reprinted 1992, 1993

Distributed in the USA by Routledge, Chapman and Hall, Inc.
29 West 35th Street, New York, NY 10001

British Library Cataloguing in Publication Data
Hammer, A. E.
   Hammer's German grammar and usage. – 2nd ed.
   1. German language. Grammar Secondary school texts
   I. Title   II. Durrell, M.   III. Hammer, A. E.
   438.2421

   ISBN 0–340–50128–6
   ISBN 0–340–50129–4 pbk

Library of Congress Cataloguing-in-Publication Data
Hammer, A. E. (Alfred Edward)
   [German grammar and usage]
   Hammer's German grammar and usage. — 2nd ed. / revised by
Martin Durrell.
   p.   cm.
   Includes bibliographical references and index.
   ISBN 0–340–50128–6 (c) : $65.00. — ISBN 0–340–50129–4 (p) :
$25.00
   1. German language—Grammar—1950-   2. German
language—Usage.   3. German language—Textbooks for foreign
speakers—English.
I. Durrell, Martin.   II. Title.
PF3105.H3   1991
438.2'421—dc20   90–23900
                                                  CIP

Typeset in Times 11/12pt by Anneset, Weston-super-Mare, Avon.
Printed and bound in Great Britain for Edward Arnold, a division of
Hodder and Stoughton Limited, Mill Road, Dunton Green,
Sevenoaks, Kent TN13 2YA by Clays Ltd, St Ives plc.

PREFACE to the first edition

This book is intended as a reference grammar for sixth form and university use, while teachers may also find it helpful. I have sought to test traditional rules and forms by current German practice, to avoid smoothing over the complications and vagaries of a living language and at the same time to present its complexities in as handy a form as possible. I hope the user may find that the book answers a good many of the questions.

No one writing a book on German grammar at this point of time starts from scratch or can avoid indebtedness to earlier workers in the field. My own great and principal debt is to the Dudenverlag in Mannheim and to the grey volumes of 'Der große Duden'. Volume 4, *Grammatik* (1966), has been invaluable as a sheer guide for the ground to be covered, as a reminder of many details which might have escaped inclusion (the paragraphs on the uses of the subjunctive may serve as an example) and for its exhaustive lists (e.g. of nouns with double genders, of adjectives used with the dative and of verbs with prepositional constructions). In the case of particularly helpful and perceptive sections of Duden, I have given specific references; factually, my chapter on word formation owes most to the *Grammatik*. Where I have used examples from Duden, I have frequently mentioned the fact, and always where the example is a quotation. I should, however, say that I have never accepted Duden as infallible, have frequently checked his rulings by reference to the layman and sometimes reached different conclusions. Exceptions to this are the chapters on orthography and punctuation, which are based more or less unquestioningly on the *Duden-Taschenbücher* listed in the Bibliography and especially on Vol. 3, from which my examples are largely taken. Finally, I cannot forbear mentioning a magic week's work, in August 1967, at the 'Sprachberatungsstelle' of the Dudenverlag in Mannheim, with Dr Wolfgang Mentrup as my untiring guide, philosopher and friend; he has been equally untiring in answering queries by letter.

My book owes much, too, to the Anglo-German dictionary of Muret-Sanders and to *Cassell's New German Dictionary* by Dr H. T. Betteridge, who very kindly gave me permission to draw on his admirable examples without individual acknowledgement, which, in the event, I have only sometimes presumed to do.

My indebtedness to the other items of the Bibliography has everywhere been specifically indicated. Beyond that, I owe something to the sound competence of F. R. H. McLennan's book and to J. A. Corbett's very full treatment of prepositions, while my section on the rendering of English prepositions in further contexts goes back to paragraph 296 in H. S. Beresford-Webb's *Practical German Grammar*; I also owe something to the treatment of prefixes in that book.

Some of my illustrative quotations are taken from papers set at Advanced Level by the Oxford and Cambridge Schools Examination Board and for Cambridge Scholarship Examinations; some of these come from works that I have not read.

I acknowledge with pleasure and sincere gratitude my debt to countless Germans of every age and calling, some of them complete strangers, who have willingly submitted to linguistic interrogations and have furthered my attempt to make this book at least an approximate reflection of current German usage. (As the late Professor Boyanus once observed, 'the native is always right'.) Even those who have, in addition, meticulously answered many pages of queries by letter are too numerous to mention by name. I must, however, make an exception in the case of my friend Dr Günther Deitenbeck, of the Zeppelin-Gymnasium, Lüdenscheid, and his family, who have helped me indefatigably over so many years.

Among those on this side of the North Sea who have kindly helped me in various ways, I would particularly like to thank Dr C. H. Good, of the University of East Anglia, who read the manuscript, correcting many points of detail and suggesting numerous, in some cases far-reaching improvements; Mr C. W. Oakley, Head of the Modern Languages Department, Selhurst Grammar School for Boys, Croydon, who checked the proofs and suggested various clarifications; and Mr J. A. Towers, sometime Senior Mathematics Master at Sedbergh School, who supplied the material from which 'some contemporary mathematical terms' (paragraph 259) were selected.

Finally, I gratefully remember the late Dr S. H. Steinberg and his ever ready collaboration in the production of a privately printed booklet of German Grammar Notes that formed the nucleus of the present volume.

A.E.H.

London
June, 1971

PREFACE to the second edition

Since the appearance of the first edition in 1971, Hammer's grammar has been an indispensable source of information about modern German grammar and usage for teachers and students of German. Its acknowledged strength lay above all in the wealth of well chosen examples, but also in its comprehensiveness and its sheer reliability. However, much has changed in the intervening twenty years, and it became clear that a thoroughgoing revision which retained the essential virtues of Mr Hammer's work had become necessary. For, if the basic structure of the language remains unaltered, the needs of language students and sixth-formers learning German are now rather different, as is the range of German with which they must cope and the methods by which they are taught, and it is these needs which this revised edition is intended to address.

In preparing the revision, I have attempted to bear a few central principles in mind, given that the work is intended to be a comprehensive descriptive grammar of standard German for the use of the foreign learner whose native or first language is English. First, if it is to be used by advanced learners of German in sixth forms and on university courses, it can no longer be taken for granted that they will be fully familiar with grammatical terminology and notions. I have thus added a certain amount of explanatory material to help the user to understand the points of grammar and usage being treated. In general, I have used familiar and traditional grammatical terminology where possible, and thus refer, for example, to 'subordinating conjunctions' rather than 'complementizers'. However, where I consider more recent and perhaps less familiar terms and ideas to be a help to the potential user in understanding the structures of the language, as is the case with 'determiners' (Chapter 5) or the 'valency' of verbs (Chapter 18), I have adopted them and explained them fully.

Secondly, I have retained the range of examples which constituted one of the principal strengths of the original edition. In practice, I have kept a large proportion of Mr. Hammer's examples, but checked them again with native speakers to confirm that they fully reflect current usage. Where I have substituted new examples, it has been with the aim of extending the range of registers covered (in particular to represent everyday spoken usage more fully) or updating the material.

Thirdly, it is taken as a basic principle that the work should be as comprehensive as possible and serve as a reference work which may be consulted on any point of grammar and usage. To this end, all the individual sections have been checked to confirm that the information is as full as necessary for the English learner and that it is as accurate as possible. A substantial body of research has been completed in the last twenty years which has increased our knowledge and understanding of current usage in German — there have, for example, been two completely new editions of the standard DUDEN grammar since 1971 — and this has been consulted at every stage. The reviser's debt to this original research on the modern language may be seen in the bibliography.

Fourthly, the changed needs of the present-day learner have been borne in mind by including information on all forms of the modern language. Thus, more attention has been paid to registers other than formal writing or literature and details given on spoken usage to reflect the greater emphasis paid to communicative skills in modern language teaching. Thus, where spoken and written usage diverge, this is clearly explained, as are forms which, though they may be regarded as grammatically 'correct', are felt to be stilted outside the most formal written registers. Similarly, forms which are frequently heard in everyday speech but widely thought of as substandard or incorrect are included here, as the foreign learner will encounter them every day, but with a clear indication of their status. In general, the foreign learner is counselled to avoid such forms as they sound particularly unacceptable when spoken with a foreign accent. Important regional variants within standard German are also included and marked accordingly, but purely dialectal forms have been ignored.

Finally, the structure of the work has been totally recast to simplify the user's task in finding his or her way to the required information. In practice, this has meant that the bulk of the text is quite new to this revised edition. Although the basic sequence of chapters is much the same as in the original edition, the layout has been simplified, longer chapters have been split up (that on verbs, which constituted almost a quarter of the whole book, has been divided into seven separate chapters), related information which was scattered in different parts has been brought together (even where this has involved a certain amount of repetition) and cross-references have been radically simplified and eliminated where unnecessary. The index has been expanded to include as many words and topics as possible, and to facilitate access to the material it has been divided into a German word-index, an English word-index and a topic index.

Acknowledgements

It is with sincere gratitude that I acknowledge the assistance I have been fortunate enough to receive during the preparation of the revised edition, first and foremost to those German speakers, unfortunately too numerous to mention, who have answered questions, given advice and, often unwittingly, provided me with examples and other linguistic data. I am especially indebted to those friends and colleagues in Britain who have been kind enough to comment on draft chapters, provide me with material, let me see their own notes resulting from their use of the first edition and advise me in other ways, in particular Dr. J.S. Barbour, Dr C. Beedham, Mr P. A. Coggle, Dr D. Duckworth, Dr J. L. Flood, Dr C. Hall, Mr W. Hanson, Mr P. Holgate, Mr D. H. R. Jones, Prof. W. J. Jones, Dr K. M. Kohl, Mr D. G. McCulloch, Dr G. D. C. Martin, Dr D. Rösler, Ms M. Schwab, Dr R. W. Sheppard, Prof. H. G. Siefken, Dr J. K. A. Thomaneck, Mrs A. Thompson, Dr B. Thompson, Mr M. R. Townson, Mr B. A. Watson, Dr J. West and Dr D. N. Yeandle. I must also express my thanks to the German Academic Exchange Service, who made it possible for me to spend a month at the Institut für deutsche Sprache in Mannheim, where I was able to check many aspects of usage and points of grammar in its computerised corpus of modern spoken and written German and use its inestimable library facilities. I am very grateful to all colleagues there for their help, particularly to Mr Tobias Brückner, Prof. U. Engel, Prof. G. Stickel, Mrs Eva Teubert, Prof. R. Wimmer and Dr Gisela Zifonun. Last not least, I must acknowledge my debt to Royal Holloway and Bedford New College, University of London, which granted me an invaluable term's leave of absence to work on this revision and to all my colleagues in the German Department at RHBNC for their continued support whilst I was engaged on this task.

Martin Durrell
1991

CONTENTS

xii *Contents*

POINTS FOR THE USER

1. Lists of words are in general alphabetical, though occasionally a deviation from this has seemed more helpful.
2. Where required, the plural of a noun is indicated in brackets after the noun, e.g. *das Lager* (–), i.e. *die Lager; der Hut* (¨e), i.e. *die Hüte*, etc. (–en, –en) or (–n, –n) indicates a weak masculine noun, cf. 1.3.2.
3. If necessary, the stressed syllable in a word is indicated by the mark ' placed before the stress syllable, e.g. *die Dok'toren, unter'schreiben*. Where required, a stressed word in context is shown by underlining, e.g. *Wie bist denn du gekommen?*

ABBREVIATIONS

In principle, abbreviations have been kept to a minimum in the revised edition. The following have been used where required by considerations of space:

A., acc.	accusative	medic.	medical
arch.	archaic	N., nom.	nominative
Austr.	Austria(n)	neut.	neuter
ch.	chapter	N. Ger.	north German
coll.	colloquial	obs.	obsolete
D., dat.	dative	occ.	occasionally
elev.	elevated	part.	participle
etw.	etwas	pej.	pejorative
fem.	feminine	pl.	plural
fig.	figurative	prep.	preposition
G., gen.	genitive	S. Ger.	south German
hist.	historical	sb.	somebody
indic.	indicative	sing.	singular
Konj.	Konjunktiv	sth.	something
lit.	literary	Switz.	Switzerland
masc.	masculine	techn.	technical

1 Nouns

1.1 Gender

Every German noun is assigned to one of the three genders: masculine, feminine or neuter.
Grammatical gender is distinct from natural gender, and this classification of nouns is in principle quite arbitrary. For this reason, it is recommended that each German noun should be learnt together with its gender, e.g. *der Tisch, die Wand, das Fenster*.

However, there are a number of useful clues to gender from the meaning or the form (or the plural, see 1.2) of many words and a knowledge of these, even if there are some exceptions, is a valuable assistance in learning genders and can help to eliminate random guesswork. We give below those clues to gender which have shown themselves to be most useful in practice.

1.1.1 The following nouns are <u>masculine</u> by meaning:

(a) Male persons and male animals (see also 1.1.4)
der Arzt, der Hengst *stallion*, der Ingenieur, der Kadett, der Löwe, der Schreiner *carpenter*, der Student, der Vater

(b) Seasons, months and days of the week
der Frühling, der Januar, der Mittwoch

EXCEPTIONS: the compounds das Frühjahr, die Jahreszeit

(c) Points of the compass and words referring to winds and kinds of weather
der Norden, Osten, Süden, Westen; der Föhn, der Passat *tradewind*; der Frost, der Hagel, der Nebel, der Orkan, der Schnee, der Sturm, der Tau *dew*, der Wind

EXCEPTIONS: die Brise, das Eis, das Gewitter (cf. 1.1.8c), das Wetter, die Witterung (cf. 1.1.6)

s and minerals
    nt, der Granit, der Lehm *loam*, der Quarz, der Ton *clay*

    Erz *ore*, die Kohle, die Kreide, das Mineral

1

(e) Alcoholic drinks
der Cocktail, der Drink, der Gin, der Schnaps, der Wein, der Wodka

EXCEPTION: das Bier

(f) Makes of car
der Audi, der BMW (but cf. 1.1.2b), der Citroën, der Mercedes, der Rolls-Royce

(g) Rivers outside Germany (cf. 1.1.2c for those within Germany)
der Euphrat, der Jordan, der Kongo, der Severn

EXCEPTIONS: those ending in *-a* or *-e* are feminine:
die Seine, die Themse *Thames*, die Wolga

1.1.2 The following nouns are <u>feminine</u> by meaning:

(a) Female persons and animals (see also 1.1.4)
die Frau, die Gans, die Henne, die Köchin, die Mutter, die Stute *mare*

EXCEPTIONS: das Weib, das Mädchen, das Fräulein (cf. 1.1.7).

(b) Aeroplanes, motor-bikes and ships
die Boeing, die Tu-154; die BMW, die Honda; die „Bismarck", die „Bremen"

EXCEPTIONS: der Starfighter, der Airbus. Some ship names retain the grammatical gender of the word, i.e.: das „Möwchen", der „Albatros".

(c) Native German names of rivers in Germany
die Donau, die Elbe, die Ems, die Maas, die Memel, die Ruhr, die Spree, die Weser, die Weichsel *Vistula*

EXCEPTIONS: der Inn, der Lech, der Main, der Neckar, der Rhein

(d) Names of numerals
die Eins, die Vier, die Tausend, die Million, die Milliarde

BUT note, as quantity expressions, das Dutzend, das Hundert, das Tausend, cf. 9.1.6.

1.1.3 The following nouns are <u>neuter</u> by meaning:

(a) Young persons and animals (see also 1.1.4)
das Baby, das Ferkel *piglet*, das Fohlen *foal*, das Junge *young* (of animal, cf. 1.1.12), das Kalb, das Kind, das Lamm

(b) Metals and chemical elements
das Aluminium, das Blei, das Eisen, das Gold, das Kupfer, das Messing *brass*, das Silber, das Uran, das Zinn *tin, pewter*

EXCEPTIONS: die Bronze, der Phosphor, der Schwefel *sulphur*, der Stahl ar
such as der Sauerstoff *oxygen*

(c) Physical units and entities
das Ampere, das Atom, das Elektron, das Molekül, das Pfund, das Watt

NB: *Liter* and *Meter* may be masculine or neuter, see 1.1.11b.

(d) Letters of the alphabet
das A, ein großes D, das Ypsilon

NB: these are masculine in Swiss usage, e.g.: der A

(e) Other parts of speech used as nouns
This includes verb infinitives, colours, languages and English *ing*-forms:
das Ach, das Blau des Himmels, das vertraute Du, das Inkrafttreten, das Jenseits, das Kommen, sein ewiges Nein, das moderne Spanisch, das Doping, das Meeting

(f) Hotels, Cafés, Restaurants and Cinemas
das Hilton, das „Kranzler", das „Roxy"

(g) Names of continents, countries, provinces and towns
das heutige Afrika, das viktorianische England, das alte Bayern, das zerstörte Frankfurt, das historische Neustadt (despite **die** Stadt)

NB: (i) A number of names of countries and provinces are feminine; they are always used
with the definite article, cf. 4.5.1. The commonest are:
die Lausitz   die Pfalz   die Schweiz
and all those in -a, -ei and -ie (except *China*), e.g.:
die Riviera   die Bretagne   die Türkei   die Normandie
(ii) A few are masculine; they are also used with the article:
der Irak   der Iran   der Jemen   der Kongo   der Libanon

1.1.4 Names of humans and animals: some special cases

(a) Professions, occupations, nationality, etc.
For many names denoting professions, occupations or nationality the basic designation is masculine, and a feminine may be formed from it with the suffix -*in*, or by replacing -*mann* with -*frau*:

der Koch	–	die Köchin,	der Lehrer	–	die Lehrerin,
der Kaufmann	–	die Kauffrau,	der Türke	–	die Türkin, etc.

However, the masculine form is often used in a general sense to refer to either sex, especially with titles and 'newer' professions, or when the profession itself is emphasized, e.g.: Frau Professor Dr. Hartmann, Frau Bundespräsident Rita Süßmuth (but, without the title *Frau*, usually: Bundespräsidentin Rita Süßmuth). Also:

Sie ist Ingenieur, Autoschlosser,   *She is an engineer, a car mechanic,*
    Informatiker   *an information technologist*

The feminine form is used if this is felt to be important in context:

Die neue Lehrerin scheint sehr beliebt zu sein	*The new teacher seems to be very popular*
Sie wurde die erste Professorin an einer deutschen Universität	*She became the first woman professor at a German university*

In practice usage is nowadays variable and uncertain, cf. Clyne (1984:168-173). In advertisements, both forms are now usually given:

Wir suchen ab sofort eine(n) Musiklehrer(in)	*We have an immediate vacancy for a music teacher*
Wir brauchen eine/n Mitarbeiter/in für Gemeinde- und Jugendarbeit	*We have a vacancy for a social and youth worker*

When no feminine form is available, the masculine must be used despite the clear anomaly, e.g.:

sie ist ein politischer Flüchtling; unser werter Gast, Frau Dr. Schilling.

(b) Animals

The names of species may be masculine, feminine or neuter, e.g.:

der Fisch, die Ratte, das Pferd, etc.

Many familiar or domesticated animals have distinct masculine and feminine forms, e.g.:

der Gänserich – die Gans   der Fuchs – die Füchsin   der Kater – die Katze

One of these is in most cases selected to designate the species and the other is only used if the sex is known or relevant in context.

In the absence of a specific term, male or female animals and birds may be indicated by *das -männchen* or *das -weibchen*, e.g.:

das Zebramännchen, das Froschweibchen.

(c) Anomalous genders of names of human beings

die Geisel *hostage*	das Mitglied *member*
das Genie *genius*	die Person *person*
das Haupt *head* (of state, family)	die Wache *sentry*
das Individuum *individual*	die Waise *orphan*
das Mannequin *mannequin*	das Weib *woman, wife* (pej. or arch.)

NB: (i) zum Waisen machen *to orphan*
      (ii) All nouns in *-chen* and *-lein* are neuter, irrespective of sex, e.g.: das Bübchen, das Fräulein, etc. (see 1.1.7).

1.1.5 Some nouns are masculine by form

(a) Nouns with the following endings are masculine:

-ant	der Passant	**-ast**	der Kontrast	**-ich**	der Teppich
-ig	der Honig	**-ismus**	der Idealismus	**-ling**	der Liebling
-or	der Motor	**-us**	der Rhythmus		

EXCEPTIONS: das Labor, das Genus, das Tempus *tense*

(b) Nouns formed from strong verbs without a suffix are masculine:
der Betrieb, der Biß, der Fall, der Gang, der Sprung, der Wurf, etc.

EXCEPTIONS: das Band, das Grab, das Leid *harm*, *sorrow*, das Maß *measurement*, das
Schloß, das Verbot

1.1.6 Nouns with the following endings are feminine:

-a	die Villa	-anz	die Eleganz	-ei	die Bücherei
-enz	die Existenz	-heit	die Gesundheit	-ie	die Biologie
-ik	die Panik	-in	die Freundin	-keit	die Heiterkeit
-schaft	die Botschaft	-sion	die Explosion	-sis	die Basis
-tion	die Revolution	-tät	die Universität	-ung	die Bedeutung
-ur	die Natur				

EXCEPTIONS: Words in *-ma* (see 1.1.7), chemical terms in *-in* (see 1.1.7) and the following:
das Sofa, der Papagei, das Genie, der Atlantik, der Katholik, das Mosaik,
der Pazifik, das Abitur, das Futur, das Purpur *crimson*

1.1.7 Nouns with the following endings are neuter:

-chen	das Mädchen	-icht	das Dickicht	-il	das Ventil
-it	das Dynamit	-lein	das Büchlein	-ma	das Schema
-ment	das Appartement	-tel	das Viertel	-tum	das Eigentum
-um	das Album				

and chemical terms in *-in:* das Benzin, das Protein

EXCEPTIONS: der Kontinent, der Profit, der Granit, die Firma,
der Zement, der Irrtum, der Reichtum, der Konsum

1.1.8 The endings of a number of other nouns give *some* clue to gender:

This is less clear than for those dealt with in 1.1.5 to 1.1.7. It is a matter of
tendencies rather than rules.

(a) Nouns in *-el*, *-er* and *-en*

(i) Nouns in *-er* (usually from verbs) denoting persons are masculine:
der Bäcker, der Bettler, der Lehrer, der Redner, etc.
(ii) All nouns from verb infinitives in *-en* are neuter (see 1.1.3e),
e.g.: das Essen, das Kaffeetrinken, das Kommen, etc.
(iii) Over 60% of other nouns in *-el*, *-en* and *-er* are masculine:
der Flügel, der Schatten, der Fehler, etc.
(iv) About a quarter (though **none** in *-en*) are feminine:
die Butter, die Regel, die Wurzel, etc.
(v) The rest (some 15%) are neuter:
das Fieber, das Segel, das Zeichen, etc.

(b) Nouns in -*e*

The vast majority of these (90%) are feminine:
die Blume, die Garage, die Liebe, etc.

EXCEPTIONS: (i) Names of male persons and animals:
der Bote, der Junge, der Lotse *pilot* (of ship), der Löwe, etc.
(ii) Eight irregular masculines (see 1.3.3):
der Buchstabe, der Friede, der Funke, der Gedanke, der Glaube, der Name,
der Same, der Wille
(iii) der Charme, der Käse
(iv) Most nouns with the prefix *Ge-* are neuter (cf. 1.1.8c):
das Gebirge, das Gebiet, etc.
(v) A few other neuters: das Auge, das Ende, das Erbe *inheritance*,
cf. 1.1.12, das Image, das Interesse, das Prestige, das Regime

(c) Nouns with the prefix *Ge*-[gə-]

The majority of these are neuter (90%):
das Gebäude, das Gebot, das Gespräch, etc.

EXCEPTIONS: (i) A few names of male or female humans:
der Gehilfe/ die Gehilfin *assistant*, der Gemahl/ die Gemahlin (elev.) *spouse*,
der Genosse/ die Genossin *comrade*, der Gevatter (arch.) *godfather*
(ii) Eleven other masculines:

der Gebrauch *use*	der Gedanke *thought*	der Gefallen *favour*
der Gehalt *content*	der Gehorsam *obedience*	der Genuß *enjoyment*
der Geruch *smell*	der Gesang *singing*	der Geschmack *taste*
der Gestank *stink*	der Gewinn *profit*	

NB: *Gefallen* and *Gehalt* are neuter in other meanings, cf. 1.1.12.
(iii) Eleven other feminines:

die Gebärde *gesture*	die Gebühr *fee*	die Geburt *birth*
die Geduld *patience*	die Gefahr *danger*	die Gemeinde *community*
die Geschichte *history*; *story*	die Geschwulst *tumour*	die Gestalt *figure*
die Gewähr *guarantee*	die Gewalt *force, violence*	

(d) Nouns with the suffixes -*nis* and -*sal*

These are mainly (about 70%) neuter:
das Bedürfnis, das Ereignis, das Scheusal, das Schicksal, etc.
About 30% are feminine, including:
(i) all those in -*nis* derived from adjectives, e.g.:
die Bitternis, die Finsternis
(ii) those derived from verbs denoting a state, e.g.:
die Besorgnis, die Betrübnis
(iii) Other common feminines:
die Erkenntnis, die Erlaubnis, die Kenntnis, die Mühsal, die Trübsal.

(e) Nouns with the following endings are usually neuter *if* they refer to things

If they refer to persons they are masculine, see 1.1.1

-al	das Lineal *ruler*	-an	das Organ	-ar	das Formular
-är	das Militär	-at	das Sekretariat	-ent	das Talent
-ett	das Etikett *label*	-ier	das Papier	-iv	das Adjektiv
-o	das Büro	-on	das Mikrophon		

EXCEPTIONS: der Kanal, die Moral, der Pokal, der Skandal, der Altar,
der Kommentar, der Apparat, der Automat, der Passat, der Salat,
der Senat, die Manier, der Sakko *jacket*, der Zoo, der Kanton,
die Person, die Saison,
and a number of grammatical terms, e.g.:
der Singular, der Plural, der Akkusativ, der Dativ, etc.,
der Imperativ, der Superlativ.

1.1.9 The gender of compound words and abbreviations

(a) Compound nouns have the gender of the last component:
der Fahrplan, die Bushaltestelle, das Hallenbad

EXCEPTIONS: (i) Some compounds of *der Mut* are feminine:
die Anmut, **die** Armut, **die** Demut, **die** Großmut, **die** Langmut,
die Sanftmut, **die** Schwermut, **die** Wehmut.
(ii) **die** Scheu BUT **der** Abscheu (cf. 1.1.11)
(iii) **das** Wort BUT **die** Antwort
(iv) **der** Grat BUT **das** Rückgrat

(b) The gender of abbreviations is determined by the basic word:
der HSV (der Hamburger Sportverein)
die CDU (die Christlich-Demokratische Union),
das BAFöG (das Bundesausbildungsförderungsgesetz)

(c) Shortened words have the gender of the full form:
der Akku (Akkumulator), der Krimi (Kriminalroman),
das Labor (Laboratorium), die Lok (Lokomotive), die Uni (Universität)
der Zoo (zoologischer Garten).

EXCEPTION: **das** Foto (despite: die Fotographie).
Note that in Switzerland *die Foto* is used.

1.1.10 The gender of recent English loan words

A detailed survey of the allocation of gender to English loans is given in
Gregor (1983)
   Recent imports from English are predominantly (60%) masculine:
der Boom, der Fallout, der Hit, der Jazz, der Job, der Pickup, der Sex, der
Showdown, der Streß, der Trend, etc.
   Otherwise, they are mainly neuter:
das Baby, das Bridge, das Cockpit, das Make-up, das Poster, das Puzzle
jig-saw, etc.
   However, some are feminine by analogy with a German word or
because the suffix 'looks' feminine:
die Bar, die City, die Compact Disc, die Party, die Show, die Story, etc.
   A considerable number show variation, especially between masculine

and neuter, because no gender has yet become firmly established, cf. also
1.1.11.

der/das Deal	der/das Go-slow	der/das Ketchup	der/das Looping
der/das Radar	der/das (coll. also: die) Joghurt		die/das Cola
	der/die Forehand	die/das Trademark, etc.	

1.1.11 Nouns with varying gender

The gender of a number of nouns is not absolutely fixed, although the
variation is often linked to regional or register differences.

(a) Some common examples

Abscheu *abhorrence*	**der** (obs. **die**)	Kompromiß *compromise*	**der** (esp. Austr. **das**)
Aperitif *aperitif*	**der** (Switz. **das**)	Match *match* (football)	**das** (Switz. **der**)
Barock *Baroque*	**der** or **das**	Meteor *meteor*	**der** or **das**
Dschungel *jungle*	**der** (occ. **das**, obs. **die**)	Pyjama *pyjamas*	**der** (Austr./Switz. **das**)
Filter *filter*	**der** (techn. **das**)	Radio *radio*	**das** (S.Ger. **der**)
Foto *photo*	**das** (Switz. **die**)	Sims (*window-*)*sill,*	**der** or **das**
Gelee *jelly*	**das** or **der**	*mantelpiece*	
Gischt *spray*	**der** or **die**	Spargel *asparagus*	**der** (Switz. **die**)
(from waves)		Taxi *taxi*	**das** (Switz. **der**)
Kehricht *sweepings*	**der** or **das**	NB: also common: die Taxe	
Keks *biscuit*	**der** (Austr. **das**)	Virus *virus*	**der** (medic. **das**)

(b) *Liter* and *Meter*
Both these words (and their compounds, e.g. *Zentimeter*) are 'officially'
neuter, i.e. *das Liter*, *das Meter*. However, they are regularly masculine in
colloquial speech, and not infrequently in print, i.e. *der Liter*, *der Meter*. In
Switzerland both are 'officially' masculine.

(c) *Teil*
Nowadays *Teil* is usually masculine, i.e. *der Teil*, in all meanings: dieser
Teil von Deutschland, er behielt den größten Teil für sich. However, it
may be neuter in a few set phrases:
ich für mein (*or* meinen) Teil, er hat sein (*or* seinen) Teil getan.
The neuter *das Teil* is also usual in technical language, to refer to a
detached part, cf. **das** *Einzelteil*, **das** *Ersatzteil*.
Compounds of *Teil* are mostly masculine, with the following exceptions:
das Abteil, **das** (*legal* der) Erbteil, **das** Einzelteil, **das** Ersatzteil,
das Gegenteil, **das/der** Oberteil, **das** Urteil

1.1.12 Double genders with different meanings

There are many words whose meanings are distinguished through having a
different gender. The following list gives the most common.

der Band (¨e) *volume, book*	das Band (¨er) *ribbon*
	das Band (-e) *bond, fetter*, cf. 1.2.7

NB also: die Band (-s) (pron. [bɛnt]) *band, (pop) group*

der Bulle (-n,-n) *bull*; *cop* (coll.)
der Bund ("e) *union*; *waistband*
der Erbe (-n,-n) *heir*
der Flur (-e) *entrance hall* (N.Ger.)
der Gefallen (-) *favour*
der Gehalt (-e) *content*
    (Austr. also = *salary*)
der Golf (-e) *gulf*
der Harz *Harz (mountains)*
der Heide (-n) *heathen*
der Hut ("e) *hat*

der Junge (-n,-n) *boy*
der Kiefer (-) *jaw*
der Kunde (-n,-n) *customer*
der Laster (-) *lorry* (coll.)
der Leiter (-) *leader*
der Mangel (") *lack*
die Mark (-) *mark* (coin)
die Marsch (-en) *fen* (N.Ger.)
der Mensch (-en,-en) *human being*
der Messer (-) *surveyor*; *gauge*
der Militär (-s) *military man* (coll.)
der Moment (-e) *moment*
der Otter (-) *otter*
    (also: der **Fisch**otter)
der Pack (-e *or* "e) *package*
der Pony (no pl.) *fringe* (of hair)
der Schild (-e) *shield*
der See (-n) *lake*
die Steuer (-n) *tax*
der Stift (-e) *pen*, *stripling* (coll.)

der Tau (no pl.) *dew*
der Tor (-en,-en) *fool* (lit.)
der Verdienst (no pl.) *earnings*
die Wehr (no pl.) *defence*

die Bulle (-n) (papal) *bull*
das Bund (-e) *bundle*, *bunch*
das Erbe (pl. die Erbschaften) *inheritance*
die Flur (-en) *meadow* (poet.)
das Gefallen (no pl.) *pleasure*
das Gehalt ("er) *salary*

das Golf (no pl.) *golf*
das Harz (no pl.) *resin*
die Heide (-n) *heath*
die Hut (no pl.) *guard*
    (e.g. auf der Hut sein *be on one's guard*)
das Junge (adj.) *young* (of animals)
die Kiefer (-n) *pine*
die Kunde (no pl.) *knowledge*, *news* (elev.)
das Laster (-) *vice*
die Leiter (-n) *ladder*
die Mangel (-n) *mangle*
das Mark (no pl.) *marrow* (bone)
der Marsch ("e) *march*
das Mensch (-er) *slut* (coll., pej.)
das Messer (-) *knife*
das Militär (no pl.) *the military*
das Moment (-e) (determining) *factor*
die Otter (-n) *adder*
    (also: die **Kreuz**otter)
das Pack (no pl.) *mob*, *rabble*
das Pony (-s) *pony*
das Schild (-er) *sign*, *plate*
die See (no pl.) *sea*
das Steuer (-) *steering-wheel*, *helm*
das Stift (-e) *foundation*,
    home (e.g. for aged)
das Tau (-e) *rope*, *hawser*
das Tor (-e) *gate*
das Verdienst (-e) *merit*
das Wehr (-e) *weir*

1.2 Noun plurals

There are seven ways in which German nouns form the plural.
The form which occurs with a particular noun is in principle as arbitrary as its gender, and recommended practice is to learn the plural formation of each noun separately. In practice, however, there are clear tendencies linking plural formation with the suffix of the noun (if any) and its gender, and it is worth being aware of these.
    The seven plural formations for German nouns are:

(a) No ending
der Deckel - die Deckel, das Fenster - die Fenster, etc.

(b) No ending, but with umlaut of the stressed vowel
der Garten - die Gärten, der Vater - die Väter, etc.

(c) Ending -*er*, with umlaut of the stressed vowel if possible
das Feld - die Felder, der Wald - die Wälder, etc.

(d) Ending -*e*
der Arm - die Arme, das Schaf - die Schafe, etc.

(e) Ending -*e*, with umlaut of the stressed vowel
die Luft - die Lüfte, der Stuhl - die Stühle, etc.

(f) Ending -(*e*)*n*
die Frau - die Frauen, die Schule - die Schulen, etc.

NB: -*n* is added if the word ends in -*e*,-*el* or -*er*, otherwise the ending is -*en*.

(g) Ending -*s*
das Baby - die Babys, der Streik - die Streiks, etc.

NB: This ending is mainly found with recent loan words from French or English, and is treated separately in 1.2.5.

1.2.1 Survey of plural formation according to gender

The table on p. 11 shows how the distribution of plural types (with the exception of (-s), which is a rather special case, see 1.2.5) correlates with gender. More details are given in paragraphs 1.2.2 to 1.2.4

1.2.2 The plural of masculine nouns

(a) Most masculine nouns ending in -*el*, -*en* or -*er* form their plural without an ending or umlaut:
der Onkel, der Schatten, der Bäcker, der Computer, der Lehrer, etc.

EXCEPTIONS: those dealt with in section (b) below and the following:

der Bauer (-n) *farmer, peasant*	der Pantoffel (-n) *slipper*
der Bayer (-n,-n) *Bavarian*	der Stachel (-n) *thorn; sting*
der Charakter (-e) *character*	der Vetter (-n) *cousin*
der Muskel (-n) *muscle*	

(b) About 20 masculine nouns in -*el*, -*en* or -*er* form their plural solely by umlauting the stressed vowel

These are:

der Acker	*field*	der Hafen	*harbour*	der Ofen	*stove*
der Apfel	*apple*	der Hammer	*hammer*	der Sattel	*saddle*
der Boden	*floor*	der Kasten	*box*	der Schnabel	*beak*
der Bogen	*arch*	der Laden	*shop; shutter*	der Schwager	*brother-in-law*
der Bruder	*brother*	der Magen	*stomach*	der Vater	*father*
der Faden	*thread*	der Mangel	*lack*	der Vogel	*bird*
der Garten	*garden*	der Mantel	*coat*		
der Graben	*ditch*	der Nagel	*nail*		

Table 1.2.1 Gender and plural in modern standard German

Plural / Gender	(-)	(¨)	(¨er)	(-e)	(¨e)	(-(e)n)
Masculine	most in *-el, -en, -er*	about 20 in *-el, -en, -er*	about 12	about 50% of those not in other groups	about 50% of those not in other groups	ALL those in *-e* and some others, mainly denoting male living beings
Feminine	NONE	2 *Mutter, Tochter*	NONE	only those in *-nis* and *-sal*	about 30 monosyllables	over 90%
Neuter	nearly all those in *-el, -en, -er* and all in *Ge - e, -chen* and *-lein*	2 *Kloster -wasser*	about 25% of those not in other groups	about 75% of those not in other groups	1 *Floß*	about 12

NB: (i) *der Bogen* and *der Kasten* may have the plural (-) in N.Ger.
The compounds *der Rundbogen* and *der Spitzbogen* always have (-).
(ii) *der Laden* sometimes has the plural (-) in N.Ger. usage in the
meaning 'shutter'.
(iii) In spoken S.Ger. *der Kragen* and *der Wagen* may have the
plural (¨). This is regarded as incorrect in written German.

(c) A few masculines have a plural in (-er) or (¨er)

der Bösewicht	*villain* (arch.)	der Geist	*spirit*	der Mund	*mouth*
der Vormund	*guardian*	der Gott	*god*	der Rand	*edge*
der Wald	*forest*	der Irrtum	*error*	der Reichtum	*wealth*
der Wiking	*viking*	der Leib	*body* (arch.)	der Ski	*ski*
der Wurm	*worm*	der Mann	*man*	der Strauch	*shrub*

NB: Compounds of *-mann* usually replace this by *-leute* in the plural when they refer to the
occupation as such or to the group as a whole:
der Fachmann - die Fachleute   der Kaufmann - die Kaufleute.
In cases where we think more in terms of individuals than a group, or where we are not
dealing with persons, the plural is in *-männer*:
die Ehrenmänner, Froschmänner, Schneemänner, Staatsmänner
In one or two cases both are used without any difference of meaning:
die Feuerwehrleute/-männer   die Kameraleute/-männer
However, the following should be noted:
die Ehemänner *husbands* (BUT: die Eheleute *married couples*),
die Seemänner *individuals* (BUT: die Seeleute *seafaring folk* (general)).

(d) The great majority of masculine nouns form their plural in (-e) or (¨e)
Umlaut is found in about half the cases where it would be possible:
der Stuhl (¨e) BUT der Punkt (-e).
The following list gives a selection of common masculines with the plural
(-e) where umlaut of the vowel would be possible:

der Aal	*eel*	der Huf	*hoof*	der Star	*starling*
der Arm	*arm*	der Hund	*dog*	der Stoff	*material*
der Beruf	*profession*	der Laut	*sound*	der Tag	*day*
der Besuch	*visit*	der Monat	*month*	der Takt	*beat (music)*
der Dolch	*dagger*	der Mond	*mouth*	der Thron	*throne*
der Dom	*cathedral*	der Ort	*place*	der Verlag	*publishing firm*
der Druck	*pressure*	der Pfad	*path*	der Verlust	*loss*
der Erfolg	*success*	der Punkt	*point*	der Versuch	*attempt*
der Grad	*degree*	der Ruf	*call*		
der Gurt	*belt*	der Schuh	*shoe*		

In general, no umlaut is found with nouns ending in stressed *-al*, *-an*, *-ar*,
-on or *-or*, with the following exceptions:

der Altar	–	die Altäre *altar*	der Kanal	–	die Kanäle *canal*
der Kardinal	–	diè Kardinäle *cardinal*			

NB: (i) *der General* and *der Kran* have either (¨e) or (-e).
(ii) *der Pastor* (usual pl. *-en*) may have (¨e) in N.Ger. usage.
(iii) The plural of *der Saal* is *die Säle*, cf. 23.4.2.

(e) A number of masculine nouns have the plural (-(e)n)
Depending on the declension of the singular, they fall into three groups:
(i) The so-called 'weak' masculines which have -(e)n in all the cases of the singular except the nominative as well as in the plural, e.g.:
der Affe, der Bär, der Mensch, der Polizist, der Student
Full details of these, with their declension, are given in section 1.3.2.
(ii) Eight irregular masculines which decline like *der Buchstabe* and *der Name.* Full details of these, with their declensions, are given in 1.3.3.
(iii) A small number of other masculines with a regular singular:

der Dorn	*thorn*	der See	*lake*
der Fasan	*pheasant*	der Staat	*state*
der Lorbeer	*laurel*	der Stachel	*prickle*
der Mast	*mast*	der Strahl	*ray*
der Muskel	*muscle*	der Typ	*bloke, chap, fellow*
der Pantoffel	*slipper*	der Vetter	*cousin*
der Schmerz	*pain*	der Zeh	*toe*

NB: (i) *der Bau* 'building' and *der Sporn* 'spur' belong to this group but have the irregular plural forms *die Bauten* and *die Sporen.*
(ii) *die Seen* is pronounced *See-en* [ze:ən] cf. 23.4.1.
(iii) *der Zeh* has the alternative (mainly N.Ger.) singular *die Zehe.*
(iv) Words in unstressed *-on* and *-or* belong to this group, with a shift of stress in the plural, e.g.:
der ′Dämon – die Dä′monen, der Pro′fessor - die Profes′soren, etc.

1.2.3 The plural of feminine nouns

(a) Over 90% of all feminine nouns have the plural (-(e)n):
die Arbeit, die Bühne, die Last, die Wiese, etc.

NB: (i) Feminine nouns in *-in* double the consonant in the plural:
die Studentin - die Studentinnen, etc.
(ii) *die Werkstatt* has an irregular plural with umlaut and the suffix *-en:*
die Werkstätten.

(b) About a quarter of feminine monosyllables have a plural in (¨e)
The following are the most common:

die Angst	*fear*	die Kraft	*strength*	die Not	*need, distress*
die Axt	*axe*	die Kuh	*cow*	die Nuß	*nut*
die Bank	*bench*	die Kunst	*art*	die Sau	*sow*
die Braut	*fiancée*	die Laus	*louse*	die Schnur	*string*
die Brust	*breast*	die Luft	*air; breeze*	die Stadt	*town, city*
die Faust	*fist*	die Lust	*desire*	die Wand	*wall*
die Frucht	*fruit*	die Macht	*power*	die Wurst	*sausage*
die Gans	*goose*	die Magd	*maid*	die Zunft	*guild*
die Gruft	*vault, tomb*	die Maus	*mouse*		
die Hand	*hand*	die Nacht	*night*		
die Haut	*skin*	die Naht	*seam*		

NB: Compounds of *-brunst, -flucht* and *-kunft* also have the plural (¨e), e.g.: die Feuersbrunst, die Ausflucht, die Auskunft.

(c) Only feminine nouns in *-nis* and *-sal* have the plural (-e)
Those in *-nis* double the consonant in the plural:
die Mühsale, die Kenntnisse, etc.

(d) Two feminine nouns have the plural (¨):

die Mutter *mother* (cf. 1.2.7)   die Tochter *daughter*

(e) *No* feminine nouns have plurals in (-) or (¨er)

1.2.4 The plural of neuter nouns

(a) Neuter nouns ending in *-el*, *-er*, diminutives in *-chen* and *-lein* and words in *Ge. . .e* have the plural (-):
das Segel, das Kissen, das Messer, das Mädchen, das Büchlein, das Gebäude, etc.

EXCEPTIONS: das Kloster (¨) and compounds of *-wasser*, e.g. das Abwasser *effluent*.

(b) About a quarter of neuter nouns have the plural (¨er)
The majority are monosyllabic:
das Blatt, das Dorf, das Kind, das Tal, etc.

A few polysyllabic neuters have this ending, i.e. all those in *-tum*, e.g.:
das Altertum (¨er) and the following:

das Gehalt	*salary*	das Gesicht	*face*
das Gemach	*chamber* (elev.)	das Gespenst	*ghost*
das Gemüt	*mood*	das Regiment	*regiment*
das Geschlecht	*sex, lineage*	das Spital	*hospice*

NB: (i) *das Roß* 'steed' (usual plural: (-e)) commonly has the regional plural (¨er) in the South-east, where it is the everyday word for 'horse'.
(ii) A number of words are used colloquially with an (-er) plural in a derogatory or facetious sense, e.g.: die Dinger, die Scheusäler.

(c) Roughly three-quarters of neuter nouns have the plural (-e):
das Bein, das Gefäß, das Jahr, das Schaf, das Ventil, das Verbot, etc.

This group includes most neuters of more than one syllable, especially foreign words, with the exceptions listed under other groups.

NB: (i) Neuters ending in *-nis* double the consonant in the plural:
das Zeugnis – die Zeugnisse, etc.
(ii) *das Knie* has the plural *die Knie*, pronunced *Knie-e* [kni:ə], cf. 23.4.1.

(d) *One* neuter noun has the plural (¨e):
das Floß *raft*

(e) A very few neuter nouns have the plural (-(e)n):

das Auge	*eye*		das Insekt	*insect*
das Bett	*bed*		das Interesse	*interest*
das Ende	*end*		das Juwel	*jewel*
das Fakt	*fact*		das Ohr	*ear*
das Hemd	*shirt*		das Statut	*statute*
das Herz	*heart*		das Verb	*verb*

NB: (i) Scientific terms in *-on* also belong to this group, with a shift of stress in the plural: *das E´lektron – die Elek´tronen, etc.*
   (ii) *das Herz* has an irregular singular: *das Herz, des Herzens, dem Herzen*, cf. 1.3.4.
   (iii) *das Kleinod* 'jewel' has the unusual plural *die Kleinodien*.

1.2.5 The plural ending (-s)

This has been frowned upon by purists, but it is increasingly common. It is current in the following cases:

(a) with most recent loans from English or French, e.g.:

das Atelier	der Balkon	der Chef	die Couch (pl.: Couches)
das Detail	das Hotel	der Karton	der Klub
das Labor	das Parfüm	der Park	der Scheck
der Streik	das Team	der Tunnel	der Waggon, etc.

NB: (i) Some of these words have an alternative 'native' plural. With the above nouns, *die Labore* and *die Tunnel* are common alternatives to the plural in *-s*. Others, e.g. *die Parke, die Schecke, die Streike* are scarcely encountered any more.
   (ii) English words in *-y* sometimes have a plural in *-ys*, e.g. *die Babys*, although the usual English plural spelling is also frequent with some words, e.g. *die Lobbies, die Partys* or *die Parties.*

(b) with words ending in a vowel other than *-e*, i.e. [ə]:

das Auto – die Autos	das Genie – die Genies
die Mutti – die Muttis	der Uhu – die Uhus, etc.

(c) with abbreviations and shortened words:
der PKW – die PKWs, die Lok – die Loks.
This ending is sometimes omitted with abbreviations in spoken German, i.e. die PKW.

(d) with some N.Ger. seafaring words, i.e.:
das Deck, das Dock, der Kai, das Wrack

(e) in colloquial N.Ger. usage with some words referring to persons, i.e.:
die Bengels, die Fräuleins, die Jungs or die Jungens, die Kerls, die Kumpels, die Mädels, die Onkels.
In written German these words have the usual plural forms, i.e.:
die Bengel, die Fräulein, die Kerle, etc.

(f) with family names: die Müllers, die Buddenbrooks, etc.

1.2.6 A number of words, particularly those borrowed into German from the classical languages, have retained unusual plural forms.

Some of the more unusual ones are restricted to the written language.

(a) Words in *-us* and *-um* replace this ending by *-en* in the plural:

der Genius	-	die Genien	das Album	-	die Alben (or: Albums)
der Organismus	-	Organismen	das Museum	-	die Museen
der Rhythmus	-	die Rhythmen	das Visum	-	Visen

EXCEPTIONS: die (Auto)busse, die Bonusse, die Zirkusse.

NB: also: der ´Kaktus – die Kak´teen (pron. Kaktee-en [kakteːən]), der Modus – die Modi.

(b) Words in *-ma* form the plural in *-men*:

das Drama - die Dramen	die Firma - die Firmen
das Dogma - die Dogmen	das Thema - die Themen

NB also: die Villa - die Villen, die Skala - die Skalen
EXCEPTIONS: das Komma - die Kommata (coll. die Kommas)
das Schema - die Schemata **or** die Schemen.

(c) Others:

das Adverb	-	die Adverbien
der Atlas	-	die Atlanten **or** (informal) Atlasse
das Epos	-	die Epen
das Examen	-	die Examina **or** (informal) Examen
das Fossil	-	die Fossilien
das Konto	-	die Konten **or** die Konti (coll. Kontos)
das Material	-	die Materialien
das Mineral	-	die Mineralien (occ. Minerale)
der Mythos	-	die Mythen
das Prinzip	-	die Prinzipien
das Reptil	-	die Reptilien
das Risiko	-	die Risiken (coll. Risikos)
das Tempo	-	die Tempi (also: Tempos)
das Textil	-	die Textilien

1.2.7 A few words have two plurals with different meanings.
The following are the most common:

der Abdruck	-	die Abdrucke *offprints*
		die Abdrücke *impressions*
das Band	-	die Bande *bonds*
		die Bänder *ribbons*
die Bank	-	die Bänke *benches*
		die Banken *banks*

der Block	-	die Blöcke *blocks* (i.e. large pieces, cf. Eisblöcke)
		die Blocks *blocks* (of houses); *pads* (of paper, etc.)
das Ding	-	die Dinge *things*
		die Dinger *things* (coll.); *girls* (coll.)
das Effekt	-	die Effekte *effects* (i.e. results)
		die Effekten *effects* (i.e. valuables)
der Mann	-	die Männer *men*
		die Mannen *vassals* (hist.)
die Mutter	-	die Mütter *mothers*
		die Muttern *nuts* (for bolts)
der Rat	-	die Räte *councils, officials*
		die Ratschläge *pieces of advice*
der Stock	-	die Stöcke *sticks*
		die Stockwerke *storeys* (sg. also: das Stockwerk)
der Strauß	-	die Strauße *ostriches*
		die Sträuße *bunches* (of flowers)
das Wort	-	die Wörter *words* (in isolation)
		die Worte *words* (connected words, i.e. sayings)

NB: In coll. speech *Wörter* tends to be used in both senses.

1.2.8 There are many instances where the most usual equivalent of a singular German word is an English plural, e.g.:

das Archiv *archives*
die Asche *ashes*
das Aussehen *looks*
das Benehmen *manners*
der Besitz *possessions*
der Bodensatz *dregs*
die Brille *spectacles*
der Dank *thanks*
das Fernglas *binoculars*
der Hafer *oats*
das Hauptquartier *headquarters*
die Hose *trousers*
der Inhalt *contents*
die Kaserne *barracks*
der Lohn *wages*
das Mittel *means*
das Mittelalter *the Middle Ages*

die Politik *politics*
das Protokoll *minutes* (of meeting)
der Pyjama *pyjamas*
der Reichtum *riches*
im Rückstand *in arrears*
der Schadenersatz *damages* (legal)
die Schere *scissors*
das Schilf *reeds*
die Treppe *(flight of) stairs, steps*
die Umgebung *surroundings*
die Waage *scales*
die Wahl *elections*
das Werk *works* (factory)
die Zange *tongs*
der Ziegenpeter *mumps*
der Zirkel *(pair of) compasses*

Naturally, many of these German words may also be used in the plural in appropriate contexts:

| Die meisten Löhne sind erhöht worden | *Most wages have been raised* |
| Er wohnt zwei Treppen hoch | *He lives on the second floor* |

1.2.9 Some German nouns are used only, or predominantly, in the plural

Most of these correspond to English plurals:
die Eltern *parents*, die Ferien *holidays*, die Leute *people*.

However, the following should be noted:

die Flitterwochen *honeymoon*	die Ränke *intrigue* (elev.)
die Kosten *cost(s)*	die Trümmer *rubble*
die Lebensmittel *food*	die Wirren *turmoil*
die Pocken *smallpox*	die Zinsen *interest* (on loan)

NB: The festivals *Ostern, Pfingsten* and *Weihnachten* are generally treated as plurals:
Frohe Weihnachten! Sie hat uns letzte Ostern besucht.
However, *Weihnachten* and *Ostern* may occur as neuter singulars, particularly with an indefinite article, e.g. *Wir haben ein stilles Weihnachten verbracht. Hast du ein schönes Ostern gehabt?*
All are followed by a verb in the singular:
Weihnachten steht vor der Tür   *Christmas is almost here*
Pfingsten fällt dieses Jahr spät   *Whitsun is late this year*.

1.2.10 Some English nouns have plurals, but their German equivalents usually do not.

In such cases a plural has to be expressed through other forms:

der Atem *breath*	die Atemzüge *breaths*
das Essen *meal*	die Mahlzeiten *meals* (occ. die Essen)
die Furcht *fear*	die Befürchtungen *fears*
der Käse *cheese*	die Käsesorten *cheeses*
der Kohl *cabbage*	die Kohlköpfe *cabbages*
die Liebe *love*	die Liebschaften *loves*
der Luxus *luxury*	die Luxusartikel *luxuries*
das Obst *fruit*	die Obstsorten *fruits*
der Rasen *lawn*	die Rasenflächen *lawns*
der Raub *robbery*	die Raubüberfälle *robberies*
der Sport *sport*	die Sportarten *sports*
der Tod *death*	die Todesfälle *deaths* (occ. die Tode)
das Unglück *accident*	die Unglücksfälle *accidents*

NB: The following words are used in the singular only in German:
der Kummer *care(s)* die Sehnsucht *longing(s)* der Verdacht *suspicion(s)*

1.2.11 Some German nouns have normal singular and plural forms which have no real correspondence in English:

die Auskunft *(piece of) information*	die Auskünfte *information*
das Brot *bread, loaf*	die Brote *loaves*
der Blitz *(flash of) lightning*	die Blitze *flashes of lightning*
der Fortschritt *advance*	die Fortschritte *progress*
die Hausaufgabe *(piece of) homework*	die Hausaufgaben *homework*
die Kenntnis *(piece of) knowledge*	die Kenntnisse *knowledge*
das Möbel *(piece of) furniture*	die Möbel *furniture*
die Nachricht *(piece of) news*	die Nachrichten *news*
der Rat *(piece of) advice*	die Ratschläge *(pieces of) advice*
der Schaden *damage*	die Schäden *(instances of) damage*

1.2.12 Masculine and neuter nouns denoting weight, measurement or value, preceded by a cardinal or by an adjective indicating number, do not take the form of the plural:

zwei Pfund Kirschen, zwei Sack Kartoffeln, drei Dutzend Eier, zwei Paar Schuhe, zehn Faß Wein, zwanzig englische Pfund, um ein paar Dollar mehr, ein, zwei, drei, mehrere Glas Bier

ein paar Schluck (Kaffee)	*a few mouthfuls (of coffee)*
Wir hatten zehn Grad Kälte	*We had ten degrees of frost*
zehn Schritt	*ten paces*
3 Schuß - eine Mark 50	*3 shots for one mark fifty*

NB: (i) The word *Stück* is much used in shopping to indicate the number of articles required:
Diese hier sind gerade das richtige. Geben Sie mir bitte drei Stück!
(ii) The singular is also typically used when ordering in cafés and restaurants:
Bringen Sie mir bitte drei Erdbeereis und zwei Glas Bier!
(iii) Masculine and neuter nouns of measurement **do** have the plural inflection if they are viewed as individual objects:
Auf dem Hof lagen zehn Fässer   *There were ten barrels in the yard*
(iv) Feminine nouns of measurement *do* take the plural form:
zehn Flaschen Wein   zwei Ladungen Holz   vier Tassen Kaffee

EXCEPTION: *die Mark* has **no** plural ending: zwanzig Mark.

1.3 Noun declension

1.3.1 The only regular case endings for the majority of nouns in modern German are the following:

(a) Masculine and neuter nouns add -*(e)s* **in the genitive singular:**
des Bahnhofs, des Busches, des Tal(e)s, des Fensters
For occasional exceptions and the use of -*s* and -*es* see 1.3.6 and 1.3.7

(b) -*n* **is added in the dative plural if possible,** i.e. if the nominative plural does not end in -*n* or -*s*:
den Kindern, den Stühlen, den Fenstern, den Hunden, etc.

BUT: den Gärten, den Frauen, den Autos, den Müllers, etc.

(c) This gives the following typical declensional paradigms for the three genders, with the definite article:

	Masc. Sg.	Masc. Pl.	Fem. Sg.	Fem. Pl.	Neut. Sg.	Neut. Pl.
Nom.	der Stuhl	die Stühle	die Frau	die Frauen	das Jahr	die Jahre
Acc.	den Stuhl	die Stühle	die Frau	die Frauen	das Jahr	die Jahre
Gen.	des Stuhles	der Stühle	der Frau	der Frauen	des Jahres	der Jahre
Dat.	dem Stuhl	den Stühlen	der Frau	den Frauen	dem Jahr	den Jahren

NB: (i) Nouns of measurement often lack the *-n* after numerals, e.g.: eine Entfernung von zweihundert Kilometer(n).
(ii) No *-n* is used in the phrase *aus aller Herren Länder.*
(iii) In some colloquial German, esp. in the south, this dative plural *-n* is sometimes omitted and one may even see notices such as *Eis mit Früchte*. However widespread, this is universally regarded as substandard.

Details on deviations from this pattern are given in the remainder of this section.

1.3.2 The so-called 'weak' masculine nouns have the ending *-(e)n* throughout the plural *and* in all the cases of the singular except the nominative:

	Sing.	Pl.	Sing.	Pl.
Nom.	der Affe	die Affen	der Mensch	die Menschen
Acc.	den Affen	die Affen	den Menschen	die Menschen
Gen.	des Affen	der Affen	des Menschen	der Menschen
Dat.	dem Affen	den Affen	dem Menschen	den Menschen

Most (but by no means all) of these 'weak' masculine nouns denote living beings. The following masculine nouns belong to this group:

(a) Those which end in *-e* in the nominative singular, e.g.: der Affe, der Bote, der Franzose, der Schwabe, etc.

EXCEPTIONS: (i) *der Käse* and *der Charme.*
(ii) the eight nouns which decline like *der Name* (see 1.3.3).

(b) A large number of foreign nouns,
in particular those ending in stressed *-and, -ant, -aph, -arch, -at, -ent, -et, -ist, -krat, -log, -nom,* e.g.:

der Diamant, der Monarch, der Automat, der Student, der Komet, der Komponist, der Demokrat, der Psycholog(e), der Astronom, der Dämon, etc.

Some have other endings:

der Barbar, der Chirurg, der Kamerad, der Katholik, der Tyrann, etc.

(c) Some native nouns not ending in *-e* in the nominative singular
The following are the most frequent:

der Bär	*bear*	der Mensch	*human being*
der Bauer	*peasant*	der Nachbar	*neighbour*
der Bayer	*Bavarian*	der Narr	*fool*
der Bub	*lad* (S.Ger.)	der Oberst	*colonel*
der Bursche	*chap*	der Ochs	*ox*
der Fink	*finch*	der Papagei	*parrot*
der Fürst	*prince*	der Pfau	*peacock*
der Graf	*count*	der Spatz	*sparrow*
der Held	*hero*	der Tor	*fool*
der Herr	*gentleman*	der Untertan	*subject*
der Hirt	*shepherd*		

NB: (i) There is a tendency, particularly in colloquial German, for these nouns to have a regular declension in the singular:
den Nachbar, des Nachbars, dem Nachbar.
In the written language, however, this usage is only acceptable and current in the case of *der Nachbar, der Spatz* and *der Untertan.*
(ii) *der Oberst, der Papagei* and *der Pfau* are commonly regular in the accusative and dative singular, e.g. *den Oberst, dem Oberst*, but have the 'weak' genitive singular, e.g. *des Obersten.*
(iii) *der Herr* has -*n* in the singular but -*en* in the plural, i.e.:
den Herrn, des Herrn, dem Herrn, plural: *die Herren*, etc.
(iv) All these nouns (except *der Herr*) have no ending in the singular cases if they are used without an article. This avoids any ambiguity between singular and plural:

Die Situation war für Arzt und Patient kritisch	*The situation was critical for doctor and patient alike*
Ich schrieb an Herrn Schulze, Präsident des Gesangvereins	*I wrote to Herr Schulze, the president of the choral society*
eine Herde ohne Hirt	*a flock without a shepherd*

NOTE: Adjectives which are used as nouns, e.g. *der Beamte, der Vorsitzende* etc., cf. 6.4, always keep their adjectival declensions. They should not be confused with 'weak' masculine nouns.

1.3.3 Eight masculine nouns with the plural (-n) have the ending -*n* in the accusative and dative singular, but -*ns* in the genitive singular, i.e.:

	Sing.	Pl.
Nom.	der Name	die Namen
Acc.	den Namen	die Namen
Gen.	des Namens	der Namen
Dat.	dem Namen	den Namen

These are:

der Buchstabe	*letter* (of alphabet)	der Glaube	*belief*
der Friede	*peace*	der Name	*name*
der Funke	*spark*	der Same	*seed*
der Gedanke	*thought*	der Wille	*will*

NB: *der Friede, der Funke* and *der Same* have alternative forms with -*n* in the nominative singular as well, i.e.:
der Frieden (no pl.), der Funken (-), der Samen (-)
These forms are the more common ones in modern German, particularly in the spoken language. Indeed, *der Same* is nowadays rare even in writing.

1.3.4 The neuter *das Herz* has the ending -*ens* in the genitive singular and -*en* in the dative singular, i.e.:

das Herz, des Herzens, dem Herzen.

1.3.5   Dative singular in *-e*

In older German, masculine and neuter nouns, particularly those of one syllable, regularly added *-e* in the dative singular, e.g.: dem Manne, dem Tale, etc. This has become obsolete; it is now found only occasionally in formal written language, and even there it tends to sound old-fashioned or facetious.

However, it is still usual or obligatory in a few fixed phrases, of which the following are the most common:

im Falle, daß	*if*
bis zu einem gewissen Grade	*to a certain extent*
im Grunde genommen	*basically*
jdm zum Halse heraushängen	*to be sick of sth*
jdm im Halse steckenbleiben	*to stick in one's throat*
aus vollem Halse	*at the top of one's voice*
nach Hause	*home*
zu Hause	*at home*
im Jahre 1989	*in 1989*
auf dem Lande	*in the country*
im Laufe des Tages	*in the course of the day*
in gewissem Maße	*to a certain extent*
jdn zu Rate ziehen	*consult sb.*
in diesem Sinne	*in this sense*
am Tage	*by day*
unter Tage arbeiten	*work below ground*
zu Werke gehen	*set to work*
(lit. for more usual: ans Werk gehen)	
jdn/etwas im Zaune halten	*to keep sb/sth in check*
(nicht) zum Zuge kommen	*(not) to get a look-in*

1.3.6   Genitive singular in *-es* or *-s*?

Masculine and neuter nouns have the ending *-s* or *-es* in the genitive singular. The choice between these most often depends on style, rhythm and ease of pronunciation. The ending *-es* is usually felt to be more formal and tends to be preferred with words of one syllable and those ending in more than one consonant. However, in some cases usage is more fixed:

(a) *-es* <u>must</u> be added to nouns ending in *-s, -sch, -ß, -st* or *-z*:
des Krebses, des Tisches, des Maßes, des Dienstes, des Kreuzes.

NB: Nouns in *-nis* have gen. sg. *-nisses*, e.g.: des Ereignisses

(b) *-s* is added
(i) to polysyllabic words ending in an unstressed syllable:
des Abends, des Königs, des Lehrers, des Schicksals, etc.
(ii) to words ending in a vowel (or vowel + *h*):
des Uhus, des Schnees, des Schuhs, etc.
(iii) to names and foreign words:
Schillers Dramen, des Hotels, des Klubs, etc.

1.3.7 Non-inflection in the genitive singular

There are a number of instances (apart from names, see 1.3.8) where the ending *-(e)s* is omitted in the genitive singular of masculine and neuter nouns. This is the case:

(a) Optionally, with nouns denoting languages, cf. 6.4.7a:
der Stil des modernen Deutsch(s)

(b) Frequently with the names of the months:
am Morgen des zehnten Januar(s)

The months in *-er* more often keep the *-s*:
in den ersten Tagen des Oktobers

(c) With the names of the days of the week. Here, although the *-s* is often omitted, it is considered 'incorrect' to do so:
am Morgen des folgenden Mittwoch(s)

(d) Often with names of artistic styles and epochs:
des Barock(s), des Empire(s), des Rokoko(s), etc.

(e) Optionally, with other parts of speech used as nouns and with abbreviations:
ein Stück des eignen Ich(s)   meines Gegunüber(s)
eines gewissen Jemand(s)   des Lkw(s)

(f) With certain foreign nouns (and a few native German words), e.g.:
der Dativ, der Dynamo, das Establishment, der Gulasch, der Holunder, das Interesse, der Islam, das Parlament, das Parterre, das Radar, der Test

NB: Duden (1984:§437) maintains that this usage, although it is by no means uncommon and clearly increasing, is 'incorrect' in written German, cf. the full account in Rowley (1987).

(g) Normally after prepositions when the noun has no accompanying adjective or article:

laut Bericht   wegen Schnee geschlossen   trotz Geldmangel

Cf. (illustrating the absence and presence of *-s* dependent on the absence or presence of article or adjective):

eine Agrar-Reform, die aber wegen   *an agricultural reform which is*
   Geldmangel und gebremsten Eifers   *only proceeding slowly because*
   nur langsam vorankommt (*Zeit*)   *of a lack of money and moderated*
                                                zeal

(h) Foreign nouns in *-s* and *-x* have no ending in the genitive:

des Atlas   des Index   des Globus   des Sozialismus   des Zirkus

EXCEPTION: des (Auto)busses.

1.3.8 Declension of proper names and titles

(a) Proper names without titles and geographical names add -*s* in the genitive singular (unless they end in a sibilant, see below), e.g.:

Helmut Kohls Politik   Elisabeths Buch   Goethes Werke
die Ermordung Cäsars   die Werke Johann Sebastian Bachs
der Tod Friedrichs des Großen
die Straßen Deutschlands   Deutschlands Straßen

NB: (i) Proper names ending in a sibilant, i.e. -*s*, -*ß*, -*x*, -*z* have a number of possible ways of
forming the genitive. In writing common practice is to use an apostrophe with personal
names, e.g:
Fritz' Hut Agnes' Schwester   Perikles' Tod   Marx' Einfluß
A construction with *von* is normal in speech and acceptable in writing except with
proper names, e.g.:
die Operetten von Johann Strauß   der Einfluß von Marx die Schwester von Agnes
With geographical names, only *von* is possible, e.g.:
die Straßen von Paris   die Geschichte von Florenz
(ii) In colloquial N.Ger., the generic names of members of the family are treated as
names, e.g.:
Tantes Haus   Mutters Kleid   Vaters Anzug

(b) Proper names rarely have the ending -*s* in the genitive singular if they are used with an article, e.g:

die Rolle des Egmont   die Werke eines Johann Sebastian Bach
die Siege des großen Napoleon   die Briefe dieses Schmidt.

(c) German geographical names used with an article
The ending -*(e)s* is optional in the genitive singular **unless** the article is part
of the name (as, for instance, with rivers), when the ending **must** be used,
e.g.:

eines vereinigten Europa(s)   des berühmten Frankfurt(s)
die Einwohner des geteilten Berlin(s) BUT: an den Ufern des Rheins

(d) Foreign geographical names usually lack the ending -*s* in the genitive singular, e.g.:

an den Ufern des Nil   die Berge des High Peak

(e) Proper names with titles
If there is no article, only the name is declined in the genitive singular, e.g:

König Heinrichs Politik   die Politik König Heinrichs
Onkel Roberts Haus   Regierungsrat Professor Pfeifers Rede

If there is an article, only the title is declined, e.g.:

die Siege des Kaisers Karl   die Hauptstadt des Landes Niedersachsen

NB: (i) *Herr* is always declined, and the title may then lack the -*s,* e.g.: der Vortrag des
Herrn Generaldirektor(s) Kramer.
(ii) *Doktor* and *Fräulein*, used as titles, are never declined:
die Erfolge unseres Doktor Meyer   die Mutter dieses Fräulein Lehmann

(f) Family names and geographical names form a plural in (-s)
This ending may be omitted with geographical names, e.g.:

Wir gehen heute abend zu Müllers   die beiden Deutschland(s)

(g) Titles and names of books, plays, newspapers, hotels, etc.
These are normally fully declined, e.g.:

ein Lied aus Brechts „kaukasischem Kreidekreis"
ein Artikel in der „Zeit"   ich wohne im „Goldenen Apostel"

A full title between quotation marks, remains in the nominative, e.g.:

in Brechts Schauspiel „Der kaukasische Kreidekreis"

A short title in the genitive with an article may drop the *-(e)s*, e.g.:

in der letzten Strophe des Erlkönig(s)

Names of companies should always be declined in full, e.g.:

der Überschuß bei der Süddeutschen Zucker-AG
die Verwaltung der Deutschen Bundesbahn.

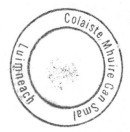

2 Case

German has four cases: nominative, accusative, genitive and dative.
They are indicated by inflections of the pronoun, noun or noun phrase.
The function of the cases is to indicate the role of these in the clause or
sentence and thus their relationship to other parts of the sentence. In
English, which has lost its cases (apart from the possessive in *-s* and some
pronouns like *I - me*, etc.), this is achieved in other ways, chiefly through
word order (e.g. *My brother* (subject) *gave his friend* (indirect object) *the
book* (direct object)) or by using prepositions (e.g. *My brother gave the
book **to** his friend*).

Case marking plays an essential part in showing the structure of a
German sentence; this becomes clear in particular in relation to verb
valency (cf. chapter 18) and word order (cf. chapter 21). Each of the
German cases has a number of uses; with the exception of the use after
prepositions (cf. chapter 20) these are all given below, with reference
where necessary to fuller details elsewhere in the book.

2.1 The nominative

2.1.1 The nominative is the neutral, unmarked case

As such it is used with nouns or pronouns in isolation:

Ein schöner Tag heute, nicht?
Aber der Uwe, den habe ich lange nicht mehr gesehen
Und dein Onkel, wann siehst du ihn wieder?

Similarly for persons and things addressed and in exclamations:

Was beunruhigt dich, mein Lieber?   Herr Müller, Telefon für Sie!
Ach du liebe Zeit!   Der unverschämte Kerl!

It is used in so-called absolute phrases, where the noun phrase seems to
hang in the air:

. . . als er an den Mann dachte, zu dem er jetzt gehen mußte, dieser Mann aus Röders Abteilung *(Seghers)*	. . . *when he thought of the man he now had to go to, that man from Röder's company*
Er saß am Feuer, der Hund zu seinen Füßen	*He sat by the fire, the dog at his feet*

26

The type of absolute phrase seen in the last example is found mainly in formal, especially literary German; other registers will tend to prefer a construction with *mit*, e.g.: mit dem Hund zu seinen Füßen.

2.1.2 The most important syntactic role of the nominative case is to mark the subject of the finite verb

As the subject is shown through the case marking it does not have to precede the verb, as it does in English, cf. chapter 21:

Der Zug war nicht pünktlich   Heute war **der Zug nicht** pünktlich
Heute war ausnahmsweise **der Mittagszug** nicht pünktlich

2.1.3 The nominative is used after the verbs *sein, werden, bleiben, heißen, scheinen* and with the passive of *nennen*: (cf. 18.8 for the constructions with these verbs)

Karl ist, wird, bleibt mein bester Freund   Ich will ein Schuft heißen
Er scheint ein großartiger Turner   Er wurde der Weise genannt
Das scheint mir der rechte Weg

2.2 The accusative

2.2.1 The main syntactic role of the accusative is to mark the direct object of transitive verbs, e.g.

Ich habe einen Stein geworfen   Die Frau hat den Fußboden gebohnert
Meine Schwester hat mir den Inhalt erklärt
Er hat die Tauben im Park vergiftet

Certain verbs, e.g. *kosten* and *lehren*, take two objects in the accusative, cf. 18.3.3.

2.2.2 Some otherwise intransitive verbs may be used with a 'cognate' accusative noun, i.e. a noun whose meaning is related to that of the verb and which thus repeats or explains more fully the idea expressed by the verb, e.g.:

Er starb einen schweren Tod   Sie schlief den Schlaf der Gerechten

2.2.3 Most conventional greetings and wishes are in the accusative:

Guten Morgen, Tag, Abend   Gute Nacht   Guten Rutsch (ins neue Jahr)
Schönen Sonntag   Besten Dank   Herzlichen Glückwunsch
Viel Vergnügen   Gute Besserung   Angenehme Reise.

In effect this is an elliptical construction, with a verb such as *wünschen* being understood.

2.2.4 A few adjectives are used with the accusative, e.g. *etwas gewohnt sein*. Details are given in section 6.5.3.

2.2.5 The accusative is used in a number of adverbial constructions

(a) To denote length of time or a point in time (cf. also 11.4), e.g.:

Es hat **den ganzen Tag** geschneit	Ich war **einen Monat** in Stuttgart
Ich sah ihn **letzten Freitag**	Er kommt noch **diesen Monat** zurück

Also in dates in letters: Essen, **den 4. August.**

(b) To express a measurement or value (esp. with adjectives of measurement)

Das ist **keinen Pfennig** wert	Der Tisch ist **ein(en) Meter** breit
Das Kind ist **vier Jahre** alt	Der Sack wiegt **einen Zentner**

(c) To express distance with verbs and adverbs denoting motion:

Ich bin **den ganzen Weg** zu Fuß gegangen	Sie kam **den Berg** herauf
Wir sind **die Straße** heruntergekommen	Die Sterne ziehen **ihre Bahn**

2.2.6 The accusative is sometimes used in so-called 'absolute' phrases without a verb

This usage is retricted to formal literary German. The accusative noun may be considered as the object of a participle such as *haltend* or *habend*, which is understood:

Der Polizist trat ins Zimmer, einen Revolver in der Hand	*The policeman came into the room, a revolver in his hand*
. . . und sagte, gemäßigten Vorwurf in der Stimme *(Goes)*	*. . . and said, with mild reproach in his voice*

This construction is not very common even in literary German, and a construction with *mit* is often used, as is usual also in other registers, i.e.

Der Polizist kam ins Zimmer mit einem Revolver in der Hand.

2.3 The genitive

In modern German the genitive case is mainly restricted to formal (especially written) registers.
This section gives an outline of its chief current uses with this general proviso. In a number of instances a prepositional phrase with *von* may be preferred, particularly in colloquial speech, cf. 2.4. For the use of the genitive of personal pronouns see 3.1.2; for the colloquial possessive dative see 2.5.10.

2.3.1 The main syntactic role of the genitive case in modern German is to link nouns or noun phrases

For this, English characteristically uses the preposition *of*. We can distinguish a number of different functions of this 'adnominal' genitive, chiefly:

(a) to express possession:	das Hause meines Bruders
(b) as a partitive:	die Hälfte des Kuchens
(c) for the subject of a verbal noun:	die Abfahrt des Zuges
(d) for the object of a verbal noun:	der Umbau des Hauses
(e) to qualify a noun:	ein Mann mittleren Alters
(f) to define a noun:	das Laster der Trunksucht

For the use of the genitive in measurement phrases, see 2.7.

2.3.2 In modern German the genitive usually follows the noun on which it depends, e.g.:

die Gefahr eines Erdbebens   das Rauschen der Bäume

The only exception to this is that proper names in the genitive may come first, e.g.:

Karls Freund   Manfreds Stereoanlage   Frau Benders Haus
Heinrich Bölls Werke   Deutschlands Grenzen

However, in written German, personal names without a title and geographical names may also follow, e.g.:

ein Freund Karls   die Werke Heinrich Bölls   die Grenzen Deutschlands

Otherwise, the order with the genitive first is restricted to rather old-fashioned literary style or set phrases:

seiner Vorfahren großes altes Haus   *the large old house of his ancestors*
Undank ist der Welt Lohn   *Never expect thanks for anything*

In other contexts it sounds facetious:

da wir des Postministers   *as we reject the post minister's*
   Kabelpläne verwerfen (*Zeit*)   *plans for cable television*

2.3.3 A few verbs still take an object in the genitive, e.g. *bedürfen, gedenken, sich ermächtigen*, see 18.5, where a full list is given. All are restricted to formal written German.

2.3.4 The genitive occurs as the predicate complement of the verb *sein*, chiefly in a few set expressions:

Wir sind gleichen Alters	*We are of the same age*
Ich bin der Ansicht, daß . . .	*I am of the view that . . .*
Ich bin der Auffassung, daß . . .	*I am of the opinion that . . .*
Hier ist meines Bleibens nicht (lit.)	*I cannot remain here*
Er ist guter Dinge	*He is in good spirits*
Wir waren guter Laune	*We were in a good mood*
Sie ist der Meinung, daß . . .	*She is of the opinion that . . .*
Er wurde anderen Sinnes (lit.)	*He changed his mind*
Dann sind wir des Todes	*Then we are doomed*
Sie sind der festen Überzeugung, daß . . .	*They are firmly convinced that . . .*
Das Wort ist griechischen Ursprungs	*The word is of Greek origin*

2.3.5 The genitive is found in a few fixed adverbial phrases

(a) to denote habitual or indefinite time (cf. also 11.5), e.g.:
eines Tages, eines schönen Sommers, eines Sonntagmorgens, montags, abends, wochentags, werktags.

(b) other adverbial genitives

unverrichteter Dinge	*without achieving anything*
letzten Endes	*after all*
meines Erachtens (m.E.)	*in my view*
allen Ernstes	*in all seriousness*
stehenden Fußes (lit.)	*immediately*
gesenkten/erhobenen Hauptes	*with one's head bowed/raised*
leichten/schweren Herzens	*with a light/heavy heart*
Er fährt erster Klasse	*He is travelling first class*
meines Wissens (m.W.)	*to my knowledge*

2.3.6 A few adjectives govern the genitive.

The most frequent English equivalent is a construction with *of*, e.g. *Er ist einer solchen Tat nicht fähig,* 'He is not capable of such a deed'. Full details are given in section 6.5.4.

2.4 Genitive or *von*?

A prepositional phrase with *von* is often used rather than a genitive.
Although the genitive is widely used in the written language, particularly in technical and non-literary registers, it tends to be avoided entirely in colloquial speech, except with names, e.g. *Antjes neuer Wagen, Jürgens Stereoanlage, Giselas Handtasche, Vaters alter Hut.* In other cases it is most often replaced in speech by a paraphrase with *von*, e.g. *das Dach vom Haus, der Ring von seiner Frau* (for written German: *das Dach des Hauses, der Ring seiner Frau*). In casual speech, a construction with the dative is used to show possession, cf. 2.5.10.
    However, there are occasions even in written German where the

genitive is not usual and where the paraphrase with *von* **must** be used or is a frequent and acceptable alternative to the genitive. Details are given in the following sections. In all other cases written German will almost invariably have a genitive, but colloquial German still uses the paraphrase with *von*.

2.4.1 The genitive is *not* used in formal written German in the following instances:

(a) If a noun stands by itself or is used with an indeclinable word
This reflects the rule that no German noun can be given a genitive inflection unless it has a preceding determiner or adjective.

der Bau von Kraftwerken	*the building of power stations*
die Wirkung von wenig Wein	*the effect of a little wine*
der Preis von fünf Fahrrädern	*the price of five bicycles*
ein Strahl von Hoffnung	*a ray of hope*

(b) With a descriptive phrase

eine Frau von deutscher Abstammung	*a woman of German descent*
ein Ereignis von weltgeschichtlicher Bedeutung	*an event of global historical significance*
Er war von bezaubernder Höflichkeit	*He was enchantingly courteous*

(c) With personal pronouns
The genitive forms of the pronouns are rarely used, see 3.1.2.

fünf von euch	*five of you*
ein Freund von ihr	*a friend of hers*

(d) In partitive constructions with *viel, wenig,* indefinites and numerals, etc.

viel/wenig von dem, was sie sagte	*much/little of what she said*
etwas von ihrem Charme	*something of her charm*
welches von diesen Büchern?	*which of those books?*
zwei von den Kindern	*two of the children*

2.4.2 The genitive is less common than a phrase with *von*, even in written German in the following instances:

(a) To avoid consecutive genitives in *-(e)s*:

Er klopfte an der Tür vom Schlafzimmer des Generals	*He knocked at the door of the general's bedroom*

(b) If a noun is qualified by an adjective alone:

der Bau von modernen Kraftwerken	*the building of modern power stations*
der Preis von sechs neuen Hemden	*the price of six new shirts*

(c) With nouns qualified by indefinites, etc.:

eine Dauer von mehreren Jahren	*a duration of several years*
die Ansicht von vielen Politikern	*the view of many politicians*
Bilder von anderen italienischen Malern	*pictures by other Italian artists*

2.4.3 In certain constructions a phrase with *von* may be used in written German, but the genitive is usually preferred

These are:

(a) Most partitive constructions
(with the exception of those listed under 2.4.1d above):

eines von den wenigen modernen Häusern (written: der modernen Häuser)	*one of the few modern houses*
viele von meinen Freunden (written: meiner Freunde)	*many of my friends*

(b) With geographical names which have no article

die Zerstörung von Dresden (written: Dresdens)	*the destruction of Dresden*
die Hauptstadt von Deutschland (written: die Hauptstadt Deutschlands *or* Deutschlands Hauptstadt)	*the capital of Germany*

2.5 The dative

The dative has the widest range of all the German cases.
In particular, it has many idiomatic uses, cf. the very detailed account in Wegener (1985). It marks the indirect or sole object of a verb (see 2.5.1 to 2.5.2) and it is also used as a so-called 'free dative' with other verbs where it is not usually a grammatical requirement (see 2.5.3 to 2.5.10). In both instances it typically marks a person (rather than a thing) who is in some way concerned or affected, if not necessarily very directly, by the verbal action or the event expressed in the verb. Finally, it is widely used with adjectives (see 2.5.11 to 2.5.13)

2.5.1 The main syntactic role of the dative is to mark the indirect object of transitive verbs

Further details are given in section 18.4.2. As such it is used principally with verbs of giving, receiving and the like, and it corresponds in the main to an English indirect object indicated by the word order or a phrase introduced by *to* or *for*:

Ich zeigte dem Polizisten meinen Führerschein.	*I showed the policeman my driving-licence/I showed my driving-licence to the policeman*
Ich habe meinem Freund ein Buch gebracht	*I brought my friend a book/ I brought a book to/for my friend*

2.5.2 Many verbs govern a sole object in the dative, e.g. *danken, dienen, folgen, gratulieren, helfen, schmeicheln.*

These are dealt with fully in 18.4.1.

2.5.3 The dative may indicate a person on whose behalf the action is done

This is sometimes referred to as the 'dative of advantage' or 'benefactive' dative and frequently corresponds to an English phrase with *for*:

Sie schrieb mir seine Adresse auf	*She wrote his address down for me*
Ich öffnete ihr die Tür	*I opened the door for her*
Er füllte meinem Vater das Glas	*He filled the glass for my father/my father's glass*
Er ebnete mir den Weg	*He smoothed my path for me*

In this 'benefactive' sense, a dative reflexive pronoun is common in idiomatic colloquial speech:

Ich muß (mir) einen neuen Stift kaufen	*I'll have to buy (myself) a new pen*
Ich will mir das Buch anschauen	*I want to go and look at that book*

A phrase with *für* is a frequent alternative to the dative in this sense, especially in spoken German:

Er will mir/für mich Blumen kaufen	*He's going to buy some flowers for me*
Ich habe ihm die Tür/die Tür für ihn geöffnet	*I opened the door for him*

This is naturally preferable if the dative could be ambiguous. Thus *Er hat seinem Vater einen Brief geschrieben* could mean 'to his father' or 'for his father', whereas *Er hat für seinen Vater einen Brief geschrieben* is quite clear.

2.5.4 The dative may also indicate a person who is disadvantaged in some way by the action

This is sometimes called the 'dative of disadvantage' and it is closely related to the 'dative of advantage'. Characteristically the person is affected by something undesirable happening to the person or thing which is the subject or object of the verb:

Der Schlüssel ist dem Kind ins Wasser gefallen	*The child let the key fall into the water*
Mir ist Großmutters Vase kaputtgegangen	*Grandmother's vase broke on me*
Dem Alten ist gerade die Frau gestorben	*The old man's wife has just died*
Sie haben uns das Haus niedergerissen	*They demolished our house*

2.5.5 The dative may mark a person from whose standpoint an action or event is judged or in respect of whom the statement holds good:

Mir verging die Zeit zu schnell	*As far as I was concerned, the time passed too quickly*
Er arbeitet dir wohl zu langsam	*You probably think he's working too slow*

A similar dative of the person concerned is frequently used with the verb *sein* and a noun. In such cases, English uses a phrase with *to* or *for*:

Das Wiedersehen mit dir war mir ein Vergnügen	*It was a pleasure for me to see you again*
Dem Schüler war diese Zensur eine Trost	*The mark was a consolation to/for the schoolboy*

2.5.6 The 'ethic dative' shows the speaker's emotional involvement

It is most common with the first person in commands or exclamations:

Du bist mir ein schöner Schwindler!	*You're a real con-man!*
Falle mir ja nicht hin!	*Be sure you don't fall, for my sake!*
Mach mir den Plattenspieler bloß nicht kaputt!	*Don't go and break my record-player!*

2.5.7 The dative of the person is often used in German to indicate possession

This is especially frequent with parts of the body or articles of clothing. The definite article is used rather than a possessive, cf. 4.7; the dative usually precedes the item possessed:

Das Blut schoß ihm ins Gesicht	*The blood rushed to his face*
Einem Mann ist das Bein gebrochen worden *(FR)*	*One man's leg was broken*
Mir muß der Mund offengeblieben sein *(Borst)*	*My mouth must have hung open*

If the possessor is the subject of the sentence, a reflexive pronoun in the dative is used. This is normally optional, cf.:

Ich wasche (mir) die Hände	*I am washing my hands*
Er wischte (sich) den Schweiß von der Stirn	*He wiped the sweat from his brow*
Willst du (dir) den grünen Pullover anziehen?	*Are you going to put your green pullover on?*

However, there are sentences where the possessive dative cannot be used and others where it must. Firm rules are difficult to give, but, broadly speaking, it is **not** used if no-one else could possibly do it to or for one, cf.:

Er machte die Augen auf	*He opened his eyes*
Sie hob den Arm	*She raised her arm*
Er nickte mit dem Kopf	*He nodded*

On the other hand, it **must be used** if the body part or article of clothing is used with a preposition (other than *mit*), cf.:

Ich habe mir in den Finger geschnitten	*I've cut my finger*
Die Mütze fiel mir vom Kopf	*The cap fell off my head*
Regen tropfte mir auf den Hut	*Rain was falling on my hat*

Where reference is not to the subject of the sentence, a possessive dative **must be used**, e.g.:

Die Mutter wusch ihm die Hände	*The mother washed his hands*
Wir zogen dem Verletzten die Hose aus	*We took the injured man's trousers off*

2.5.8 If the dative is used rather than a possessive construction (i.e. a possessive determiner or a genitive phrase), the person is seen as affected by the action as well

These other constructions may be grammatically possible, but will then often have a rather different meaning. Compare the following pairs of sentences:

Regen tropfte ihm auf den Hut	*(he was wearing it and getting wet)*
Regen tropfte auf seinen Hut	*(not explicitly clear that he was wearing it)*
Sie strich dem Jungen übers Gesicht	*(normal for 'she ran her hand over the boy's face')*
Sie strich über das Gesicht des Jungen	*(only possible if the boy is dead or unconscious)*
Er zog ihr die Jacke an	*He helped her on with her jacket*
Er zog sich ihre Jacke an	*He put her coat on*

2.5.9 With a few verbs the accusative of the person may be used rather than a dative

In effect, in such constructions the person is then seen as directly affected, rather than the body-part, e.g.:

Der Hund biß ihm/ihn ins Bein.   Ich klopfte ihm/ihn auf die Schulter

In practice, accusative and dative are equally common and usual with the following verbs:

beißen   küssen   stechen   stoßen   zwicken

With some verbs, the accusative is found, but the dative is more common, e.g.:

hauen   klopfen   schießen   schlagen   schneiden   treten

2.5.10 In colloquial speech a dative paraphrase may be used rather than a genitive to indicate possession

This construction, though very common, is universally regarded as substandard and is rarely found in written German:

Das ist meiner Mutter ihr Hut	*That's my mother's hat*
Meinem Onkel sein Garten ist ganz groß	*My uncle's garden is quite big*
Huck Finn sein Vater *(Andersch)*	*Huck Finn's father*

2.5.11 The dative is the most common case governed by adjectives,
e.g. *Er ist seinem Bruder sehr ähnlich*. Full details are given in section 6.5.1.

2.5.12 Adjectives qualified by *zu* or *genug* may govern a dative or a phrase with *für*

The latter may come before or after the adjective, whereas the dative always precedes:

Diese Uhr ist mir zu teuer/für mich	*This watch is too expensive*
zu teuer/zu teuer für mich	*for me*
Dieser Mantel ist mir nicht warm	*This coat is not warm enough*
genug/für mich nicht warm	*for me*
genug/nicht warm genug für mich	

2.5.13 A personal dative is used in impersonal constructions with *sein* and *werden* with certain adjectives expressing sensations

The person in the dative may be seen as experiencing the sensation; it corresponds to a simple subject in English: *Es ist mir kalt/Mir ist kalt* 'I am cold'. This construction occurs with the following adjectives:

bange	gut	heiß	kalt	schlecht	schwindlig
übel	warm	(un)wohl			

NB: For the omission of *es*, see 18.2.4e

2.6 Apposition

By 'apposition' we mean the use of a noun phrase to modify another one, e.g. *Wilhelm,* **der letzte deutsche Kaiser** and *Bonn,* **die Hauptstadt der Bundesrepublik.** There is usually no explicit linking word, but comparative phrases introduced by *als* and *wie* are also considered to be standing 'in apposition' to the noun they qualify, e.g. *ein Tag* **wie jeder andere**, *er gilt* **als großer Staatsmann**, *Jürgen ist größer als* **du.**

NB: Apposition in measurement phrases is dealt with in section 2.7.

2.6.1 The general rule in German is that a noun in apposition has the same case as the noun it modifies:

Es spricht Herbert Werner, der Vorsitzende des Vereins	*The speaker is Herbert Werner, the chairman of the society*
Ich sah meinen Freund, den Pfarrer	*I saw my friend, the parson*
Nach dem Tode meines Onkels, des früheren Bürgermeisters der Stadt	*After the death of my uncle, the former mayor of the city*
in Michelstadt, einem kleinen Städtchen im Odenwald	*in Michelstadt, a little town in the Odenwald*
für Heinrich Böll als gläubigen Katholiken	*for Heinrich Böll as a devout Catholic*
nach einem Tag wie diesem	*after a day like this*

2.6.2 There are few frequent exceptions to this rule

The only common ones are:

(a) After a genitive, an unqualified noun in apposition is usually in the nominative:

nach dem Tode meines Onkels, Bürgermeister der Stadt Krefeld	*after the death of my uncle, the mayor of the city of Krefeld*

(b) in dates a weekday introduced by *am* may be followed by the date in the dative *or* the accusative, e.g.: am Montag, dem 3. Juli 1989 *or* am Montag, den 3. Juli 1989

2.6.3 Occasionally other deviations from the general rule are encountered, both in spoken and written German:

(a) nominative or dative after a genitive noun:
nach dem Tode meines Onkels, der/dem früheren Bürgermeister dieser Stadt

(b) genitive after a phrase with *von*:
die Hauptstadt von Kalifornien, des reichsten Bundesstaates

However, these and similar deviations are neither common nor becoming more frequent, as the recent survey by Bergenholtz (1985) clearly shows. The rule given in 2.6.1 is followed in over 90% of cases in both spoken and written German.

2.6.4 In a number of instances German uses appositional constructions where English has *of*, e.g.: die Insel Malta, die Universität Heidelberg, die Stadt Bremen

BUT: die Schlacht bei Lützen   *the battle of Lützen.*

2.7 Measurement phrases: genitive, *von* or apposition?

Case usage in measurement phrases is a notoriously complex area and there is much variation and uncertainty, cf. DUDEN (1984:§1079) and Dückert/Kempcke (1984: 47–50). The survey in the following sections presents the most widely accepted current usage. For the use of singular nouns in measurement phrases, e.g. *zwei Pfund Kirschen*, see 1.2.12.

2.7.1 The most general rule is that nouns and phrases after a noun of measurement stand in apposition to it, i.e. in the same case:

eine Flasche Wein	*a bottle of wine*
eine Flasche deutscher Wein	*a bottle of German wine*
er kauft zwei Flaschen deutschen Wein	*he is buying two bottles of German wine*
für drei Tonnen hochwertigen Stahl	*for three tons of high-grade steel*
mit einer Tasse heißem Tee	*with a cup of hot tea*
von vier Kilo grünen Erbsen	*of four kilograms of green peas*

2.7.2 In formal written registers the genitive may be used, but then **only** in the sequence: noun of measurement + adj + noun:

ein Stück frostigen Winterhimmels (Plievier)	*a piece of frosty winter sky*
zehn Jahre treuer Mitarbeit	*ten years' faithful service*

Especially in the masculine and neuter singular this usage now sounds very stilted.

2.7.3 Usage with words of rather vague quantity, e.g. *die Anzahl, die Gruppe, der Haufen, die Schar, die Reihe, die Sorte.*

If the following noun has an adjective (or is an adjective used as a noun)

these are followed by a genitive or, especially in speech, by a phrase with *von*:

zwei Gruppen junger Arbeiter **or** zwei Gruppen von jungen Arbeitern
große Mengen neuer Platten **or** große Mengen von neuen Platten
eine Reihe ernsthafter Probleme **or** eine Reihe von ernsthaften Problemen
die wachsende Anzahl Ausreisewilliger **or** von Ausreisewilligen

If these words are followed by a single noun, normal usage is a phrase with *von*, although apposition is also possible, e.g.:

eine Art (von) Museum   eine Menge (von) Schallplatten
eine Anzahl (von) Touristen   zwei Gruppen von Schulkindern.

2.7.4 Usage with nouns of number, i.e. *das Dutzend, das Hundert, das Tausend, die Million, die Milliarde.*

When these are used in the plural, they are followed by a phrase with *von* or, if the following noun is qualified, a noun in apposition or a genitive:

Dutzende von Anfragen   Tausende von Arbeitern   Millionen von Jahren
Tausende von jungen Arbeitern **or** Tausende junge Arbeiter **or** Tausende junger Arbeiter

NB: If these nouns are used in the singular with an indefinite article ɔr in the plural with a
numeral, they are followed by a noun in apposition, e.g.:
ein Dutzend (weiße) Eier   eine Million deutsche Arbeiter,
zwei Millionen junge(r) Arbeiter

2.7.5 If the noun of measurement is in the dative the following alternative usages are encountered:

(a) Nouns of measurement in *-er*
e.g.: Zentner *hundredweight* (i.e. 500 kilos), Liter, Meter, etc. These may take a dative plural ending rather than the following noun, e.g.:
mit zwei Zentnern Äpfel **or** mit zwei Zentner Äpfeln.

(b) If the following noun is plural, it may be in the nominative:

mit einem Haufen Butterbrote(n)	*with a pile of sandwiches*
mit einem Dutzend Kühe(n)	*with a dozen cows*
mit einem Dutzend saure(n) Äpfel(n)	*with a dozen sour apples*

However, the dative should be used if the case is not otherwise clear from the measurement noun or its articles, etc.:

von drei Kilo Äpfeln	*of three kilos of apples*
mit zwei Tüten Nüssen	*with two bags of nuts*

(c) An adjective preceding the second noun may have the 'weak' adjective ending *-en*:

von einem Pfund gekochten Schinken $\Big\}$ *of a pound of cooked ham*
von einem Pfund gekochtem Schinken

2.7.6 Phrases with nouns of measurement in the genitive are generally avoided, even in written German

Thus: *der Preis von einem Pfund gekochtem/gekochten Schinken,* etc. is preferred to rather stilted constructions like *der Preis eines Pfundes gekochten Schinkens.*

3   Personal pronouns

3.1 The declension of the personal pronouns

3.1.1 Table of declensions

	First person Sing.	Pl.	Second person (familiar) Sing.	Pl.	Second person (polite) Sing. & Pl.
Nom.	ich	wir	du	ihr	Sie
Acc.	mich	uns	dich	euch	Sie
Gen.	meiner	unser	deiner	euer	Ihrer
Dat.	mir	uns	dir	euch	Ihnen

	Masc. sing.	Fem. sing.	Neut. sing.	Plural
Nom.	er	sie	es	sie
Acc.	ihn	sie	es	sie
Gen.	seiner	ihrer	seiner	ihrer
Dat.	ihm	ihr	ihm	ihnen

Notes on the above forms:

(a) In natural everyday speech, personal pronouns are weakly stressed and much reduced
Thus, one hears, for instance, *'ch soll's 'm geben* or *jetzt kannste'n sehen* rather than *ich soll es ihm geben* or *jetzt kannst du ihn sehen.*
These reductions are scarcely ever used in written German with the exception of *'s* for *es*, which is often found in written dialogue and poetry.

(b) In rapid colloquial speech, the subject pronouns *ich, du* and *es* are often omitted entirely:

(Ich) weiß es nicht   Kannst (du) morgen kommen?   (Es) scheint zu klappen

(c) In South Germany *mir* may be heard for *wir*
This usage, though very frequent, is universally regarded as substandard and best not imitated.

(d) Special forms of the genitive in *-(e)t-* are used in combination with the prepositions *wegen, um . . . willen* and *halber* (see also 20.4), e.g.:
meinetwegen,   deinetwegen,   um   ihretwillen,   um   unsertwillen, seinethalben.

3.1.2 The genitive forms of the personal pronoun sound stilted and archaic

They practically never occur in the spoken language and are infrequent even in formal registers. Their use may be avoided in the following ways:

(a) With verbs, an alternative construction or a different verb is used, e.g.:

Erinnern Sie sich an mich (NOT: meiner)
Er braucht mich nicht (NOT: Er bedarf meiner nicht).

(b) After the prepositions *wegen, statt* and *trotz*
The dative is used in colloquial speech and is no longer uncommon in writing:
wegen uns, trotz ihnen, statt ihm (or: an seiner Stelle)

(c) After the prepositions which have alternative constructions with *von* (cf. 20.4.2) the prepositional adverb *davon* (cf. 3.5) is used rather than a pronoun in the genitive, e.g.:
innerhalb davon, unweit davon, etc.

(d) After numerals, *von* is used:
sechs von ihnen, etc.

(e) In other cases, the genitive of the personal prounouns may be avoided by using alternative constructions:

was ihn betrifft, in bezug auf ihn (NOT: hinsichtlich seiner)	*with regard to him*
Wir sind alle eingeladen, du mit eingeschlossen *or* auch du (NOT: einschließlich deiner)	*We are all invited, including you*

3.1.3 The genitive of the third person pronouns may only refer to persons

To refer to things, the demonstratives *dessen* or *deren* are used, e.g.:

Ich war mir dessen bewußt   *I was conscious of it*

In some cases, adverbs or adverb phrases without pronouns are available, and these are used rather than a genitive pronoun, e.g.:
deswegen *because of it*, außerhalb, draußen *outside (it)*, diesseits, auf dieser Seite *on this side (of it)*, trotzdem *in spite of it*.

3.2 Reflexive and reciprocal pronouns

3.2.1 Forms of the reflexive pronoun

The reflexive pronoun *sich* is used for the third person, singular and plural, and for the 'polite' second person, in the accusative and dative cases. For the other persons and cases, the personal pronouns given in 3.1.1 are used reflexively.

To show the accusative and dative reflexives we give below the present tense and the imperative of the reflexive verbs *sich setzen* 'sit down' and *sich (etwas) einbilden* 'imagine (something)':

ich setze mich	ich bilde mir (etwas) ein
du setzt dich	du bildest dir (etwas) ein
er setzt sich	er bildet sich (etwas) ein
wir setzen uns	wir bilden uns (etwas) ein
ihr setzt euch	ihr bildet euch (etwas) ein
Sie setzen sich	Sie bilden sich (etwas) ein
sie setzen sich	sie bilden sich (etwas) ein
setze dich!	bilde dir (das) ein
setzt euch!	bildet euch (das) ein
setzen Sie sich!	bilden Sie sich (das) ein!

3.2.2 The genitive pronoun is very occasionally used reflexively in formal German

It mainly occurs in conjunction with certain adjectives (see 6.5.4.). To avoid ambiguity, it always occurs with *selbst*:

Er ist seiner selbst sicher	*He is sure of himself*
Sie war ihrer selbst nicht mehr mächtig	*She had lost control of herself*

3.2.3 The reflexive pronoun is used after a preposition to refer back to the subject of the sentence:

Er hatte kein Geld bei sich	*He had no money on him*
Sie schlossen die Tür hinter sich	*They closed the door behind them*

3.2.4 In infinitive constructions without *zu*, the reflexive pronoun refers back to the object of the finite verb:

Er hörte seinen Freund sich tadeln	*He heard his friend blaming himself*
Sie sah ihren Freund sich entfernen	*She saw her friend moving off*
Er ließ den Gefangenen sich ausziehen	*He made the prisoner get undressed*

A third person pronoun refers back to the subject of the sentence:

Er hörte seinen Freund ihn tadeln	*He heard his friend blaming him*
Er ließ den Gefangenen ihn ausziehen	*He made the prisoner undress him*

With prepositions, as only the reflexive is possible, ambiguities may arise, cf. Engel (1988: 665):

Er ließ den Patienten zu sich kommen	{ *He let the patient approach him* { *He let the patient come to*

3.2.5 In infinitive constructions with *zu*, the use of the reflexive or the personal pronoun depends on what is understood to be the subject of the infinitive

The following examples are taken from DUDEN (1984: §542):

Karl versprach Peter, sich zu entschuldigen (Karl is to apologize)
Karl versprach Peter, ihn zu entschuldigen (Karl is excusing Peter)
Karl bat Peter, sich zu entschuldigen (Peter should apologize)
Karl bat Peter, ihn zu entschudigen (Peter is asked to excuse Karl)

3.2.6 Emphatic 'myself', 'yourself', etc. is rendered by using the appropriate pronoun with the addition of *selbst* or *selber*

These are always stressed:

Ich habe selbst mit dem Minister darüber gesprochen	*I spoke to the minister about it myself*
Er hat selbst/selber den Brief gelesen	*He's read the letter himself*

NB: *selbst*, if unstressed, has the meaning 'even'. In this case it precedes the pronoun (or noun) which it qualifies:

Selbst er hat den Brief gelesen	*Even he has read the letter*
Selbst den Dom hat sie gesehen	*She even saw the cathedral*

3.2.7 The reciprocal pronoun ('each other')

The German equivalent is either the plural of the reflexive pronoun or *einander*. The latter is less common in speech than writing, but it is the only possible alternative after prepositions. In this case it is written together with the preposition (*durcheinander, miteinander*, etc.):

Sie sahen sich (*or* einander) oft	*They often saw each other*
Wir gehen uns (*or* einander) aus dem Wege	*We avoid each other*
Wir verlassen uns aufeinander	*We rely on each other*
Fünf Autos standen hintereinander	*Five cars were standing behind each other*
Sie sprachen voneinander	*They were talking about each other*
cf.: Sie sprachen von sich	*They were talking about themselves*

Where the reflexive pronoun might be ambiguous, *selbst* may be added to confirm that the sense is reflexive, or *gegenseitig* to show that it is reciprocal:

Sie widersprachen sich selbst	*They contradicted themselves*
Sie widersprachen sich gegenseitig (*or*: Sie widersprachen einander)	*They contradicted each other*

3.3　Pronouns of address

**For English 'you', German distinguishes between the 'familiar' pronouns
du and *ihr*, and the 'polite' pronoun *Sie*.**
Since the loss of *thou*, English has nothing comparable to this distinction,
and English-speaking learners of German are faced with the need to
establish which is appropriate.

Since the late 1960s the use of *du* and *Sie* (commonly referred to by the
verbs *duzen* and *siezen*) has shifted markedly with changing social attitudes
and conventions. The use of *du* has become more widespread, particularly
among younger people, though it is still less frequent than the use of first
names in English-speaking countries. The result is that Germans
sometimes feel rather insecure about which one to use in unfamiliar
surroundings. However, consciousness of the need to use the 'right' one is
as strong as ever.

Essentially, the use of *du* is a token of intimacy, affection and
solidarity. People who use *du* to one another are conscious of belonging to
the same group or standing together, whereas *Sie* signals a certain degree
of social distance (rather than 'politeness'). Thus, in the 'wrong' situation
du will sound too familiar and signal a lack of respect, whilst *Sie* in the
'wrong' situation will sound stand-offish or pompous. A detailed analysis
of current usage is given in Clyne (1984: 124–28).

Outside the confines of school or university, when addressing fellow
pupils or fellow students, it is advisable for non-native speakers to let
native speakers take the initiative in proposing the use of *du*.

3.3.1 The uses of the 'familar' pronoun *du*, its plural *ihr*, and the 'polite' pronoun *Sie* (which is used to address one or more than one person) may be summed up as follows:

(a) *du* is used:
(i) when speaking to children (up to about fourteen - in schools to the 10th
class), to animals and inanimate objects, to oneself and to God.
(ii) between relatives and close friends, between schoolchildren and
students, predominantly between blue-collar workmates, between non-
commissioned soldiers and between members of clubs, interest groups and
(especially left-wing) political parties.

**(b) *ihr* is commonly used to address a group of people at least one of whom is
addressed as *du* by the speaker,** e.g. (to a group of people at work, even
though one is not *per du* with all of them):

Ich will euch doch alle zum Kaffee einladen.

It is less common, but by no means rare, for *ihr* to be used to any group of
people, even if all would normally be addressed individually as *Sie*.
Indeed, *ihr* may often function as a kind of neutral compromise,

particularly if a group is present, to mask the speaker's uncertainty about whether to use *du* or *Sie*.

NB: *ihr* may still occasionally be heard in country districts, especially in the South, in addressing persons of standing in the village, e.g. the priest or the schoolteacher, but its use is more characteristic of dialect than standard German.

(c) Sie is used in all other cases
It is used especially to adult strangers and generally in middle class professions (e.g. to colleagues in an office or a bank).

Usually, the use of *du* is linked to that of first names, that of *Sie* to formal titles (Herr Engel, Frau Kallmeyer, etc.). However, parents may use *Sie* and first names to their older children's friends.

3.3.2 *du* and *ihr* and their associated forms (i.e. *dich, dein, euch,* etc.) are spelled with initial capitals in letter-writing (cf. 23.1.3b):

Ich danke **Dir** recht herzlich für **Deinen** Brief.

3.3.3 In older German the third person singular pronouns *Er* and *Sie* (spelled with capitals) were used to address people of a lower social standing

This usage is now obsolete (except facetiously), but was not unknown even in the early twentieth century, as is seen, for example, in Hofmannsthal's play *Der Schwierige*.

However, titles are still frequently employed in shops, restaurants, hotels, etc. to address customers, e.g.:

Was wünscht der Herr?   Was wollen die Herrschaften zu Mittagessen?

3.4 Third person pronouns

3.4.1 The third person singular pronouns agree in gender with the noun to which they refer

For things, *er, sie* or *es* may thus all correspond to the undifferentiated English *it*:

Dein Bleistift? Ach, **er** lag vorhin auf dem Tisch, aber ich muß **ihn** jetzt verloren haben

Your pencil? Oh, it was lying on the table a little while ago, but I must have lost it now

Er hörte meine Meinung und stimmte **ihr** bei

He heard my opinion and agreed with it

Darf ich Ihr Buch noch eine Woche behalten? Ich habe **es** noch nicht gelesen

May I keep your book another week? I haven't read it yet

3.4.2 There may sometimes be a conflict between grammatical and natural gender

This is especially the case with diminutives like *das Mädchen, das Bübchen*, etc., cf. 1.1.4c. In such cases, many Germans are uncertain whether the natural or the grammatical gender should determine the choice of pronoun. Especially in speech, the personal pronoun agrees with the natural gender:

Das junge Mädchen da ist gestern angekommen. **Sie** ist sehr liebenswürdig	*The young girl there arrived yesterday. **She** is very agreeable*
Sie stürzten sich auf das Mädchen, das in der Ecke stand, und drohten **ihr** mit Erschießen *(Quick)*	*They rushed upon the girl standing in the corner and threatened to shoot **her***

However, in formal written registers, strict grammatical agreement tends to be observed, particularly if the pronoun is close to the noun to which it refers or in the same sentence:

Bei diesem Unglück kam eines der vier Mädchen um, da **es** den herannahenden Lastzug nicht rechtzeitig erblickte	*One of the four girls died in the accident, as **she** failed to see the lorry approaching in time*

NB: In everyday speech in southern Germany the neuter pronoun is commonly used to refer to a younger girl. This is regarded as a mark of endearment.

3.4.3 In colloquial speech, forms of the demonstrative pronoun *der* (cf. 5.1.1d) are often used rather than a third person personal pronoun

This is often so when they need to be emphasized, e.g. *der kommt wohl nicht mehr* for *er kommt wohl nicht mehr*. This usage is generally avoided in written German, particularly when referring to people, but it may be found if there is a possible ambiguity or a need for emphasis, e.g.:

Sie hatte die Fernsehanstalten . . . massiv unter Druck gesetzt, als **die** sich in Gibraltar umtaten *(Zeit)*	*She had put massive pressure on the television companies, when they were nosing around in Gibraltar*

3.4.4 The third person pronoun is used in comparative clauses introduced by *wie*

In this way it is made clear what is being compared:

Hier gibt es keine Wälder, wie man **sie** in Deutschland findet	*Here, there are no forests such as you find in Germany*
Ein Kuchen, wie **ihn** deine Mutter backt, ist was Besonderes	*A cake like your mother makes is something special*

3.5 Third person pronoun or prepositional adverb?

3.5.1 After most prepositions the use of third person pronouns is limited

In many cases a form of the so-called 'prepositional adverb' (i.e. *da(r)* compounded with the preposition, e.g. *damit, daran, darüber*) is found instead. Modern usage may be summarized as follows:

(a) The pronoun *es* is <u>never</u> used after prepositions (except *ohne*, cf. 3.5.2):

Da steht mein neues Auto. Ich habe lange darauf (*not* auf es) warten müssen	*There's my new car. I had to wait a long time for it.*

(b) Prepositions <u>are</u> used with a following personal pronoun to refer to persons (but <u>not</u> groups of people, cf. 3.5.1d):

Du darfst nicht mit ihr spielen	*You mustn't play with her*
Ich kann mich nicht an ihn erinnern	*I can't remember him*

(c) When reference is to a specific concrete object (or objects), <u>either</u> preposition plus pronoun <u>or</u> the prepositional adverb may be used:

Ich habe diese Geschirrspülmaschine seit drei Wochen und bin sehr zufrieden damit **or** mit ihr	*I've had this dishwasher for three weeks and am very satisfied with it.*
Vor ihm lag die alte Brücke. Über sie **or** Darüber ging ein sehr starker Verkehr	*In front of him was the old bridge. There was very heavy traffic going over it*

(d) The prepositional adverb is <u>always</u> used to refer to abstracts and groups of people:

Die Ferien beginnen am 1. Mai. Ich freue mich schon darauf	*The holidays start on the first of May. I'm already looking forward to them*
Wie findest du den Vorschlag? Bist du damit einverstanden?	*What do you think of the suggestion? Do you agree with it?*
Ich erwarte zehn Gäste, darunter einige sehr alte Bekannte	*I am expecting ten guests, among them some very old acquaintances*

(e) The prepositional adverb is <u>always</u> used to refer to whole sentences or phrases:

Ihr Mann hat eine neue Stelle gekriegt. Darüber freut sie sich sehr.	*Her husband has got a new job. She's very pleased about it.*

(f) If motion is involved, separable prefixes with *hin-* or *her-* are used rather than the prepositional adverb:

Wir fanden eine Hütte und gingen hinein	*We found a hut and went into it*
Sie kam an einen langen Gang und eilte hindurch	*She came to a long passage and hurried through it*

3.5.2 A few prepositions do not form a prepositional adverb, i.e. *außer, gegenüber, ohne, seit*

These are used with pronouns with reference to people or things:

Außer ihm ist keiner gekommen	*Nobody came apart from him*
Vor uns ist das Rathaus, und ihm gegenüber liegt der Dom	*In front of us is the town hall and opposite it is the cathedral*
Ohne es wäre es nicht möglich gewesen	*Without it it wouldn't have been possible*

NB: (i) With reference to things, the pronoun is often omitted after *gegenüber* and *ohne*, e.g.:
(ihm) gegenüber liegt der Dom   ohne (es) wäre es nicht möglich gewesen
(ii) With reference to things, the adverbs *außerdem* and *seither* are more usual than the use of a pronoun with the corresponding preposition. In practice this means that *seit* is seldom found with a pronoun.
(iii) The prepositions which govern the genitive do not form prepositional adverbs. For the use of pronouns with them, see 3.1.2.

3.5.3 Further miscellaneous points on the use of the prepositional adverb

(a) In colloquial, especially North German speech, the prepositional adverb may be split:

Da weiß ich nichts von   Da kann ich nichts mit anfangen

(b) When the prepositional adverb replaces preposition plus pronoun, the preposition is usually stressed, e.g.: *da'mit, da'ran*, etc.
In spoken German the first syllable may be reduced, e.g.: *dran, drin*. If the prepositional adverb is a replacement for preposition plus demonstrative, (i.e. = 'with that', 'in that', etc., cf. 5.1.1k), the first syllable is heavily stressed, e.g.: *'damit, 'darin.*

(c) Some prepositional adverbs have idiomatic meanings
Details are given under the individual prepositions in chapter 20.

(d) The prepositional adverb is often used with verbs and adjectives to anticipate a following *daß*-clause or infinitive phrase
For details of this usage, see sections 6.6.2 and 18.6.

3.6 Special uses of the pronoun *es*

The pronoun *es* has an extended range of uses beyond simply referring back to a neuter noun.
A full account is given in Buscha (1988). These are all listed in this section, with indications where necessary to more extensive treatment elsewhere in this book. It should be noted that *es* cannot be heavily stressed. If emphasis is necessary the demonstrative *das* may replace it in the majority of uses given here, e.g.:

Sind das Ihre Handschuhe?   Das bist du.   Ich mache das schon.

3.6.1 *es* is used as an indeterminate subject with the verbs *sein* and *werden* followed by a noun or adjective

This usually corresponds to the English use of *it*:

Es ist der Briefträger, ein Polizist	*It's the postman, a policeman*
Es wurde spät	*It got late*
Es ist Mittag. Es ist Sonntag heute	*It's midday. It's Sunday to-day*

NB: *es* may be omitted in non-initial position in time phrases, e.g.:
     Jetzt ist (es) Mittag   Er weiß, daß heute Sonntag ist

Unlike English 'it', *es* can also be used with the plural verb:

Es sind Buchfinken	*They are chaffinches*
Sind es Ihre Handschuhe?	*Are they your gloves?*
Was sind es?	*What are they?*

es may be used, in this indeterminate function, to refer back to a non-neuter or plural noun:

Seine Mutter lebt noch. **Es/Sie** ist eine alte Frau	*His mother is still alive. She's an old woman*
Siehst du die Kinder dort? **Es/Sie** sind meine	*Do you see the children there? They're mine*

The construction of *es* with *sein* and a personal pronoun is quite different to the equivalent English construction:

Bist du es? Ich bin es	*Is it you? It's me*
Seid ihr es gewesen?	*Was it you?*
Sie werden es wohl sein	*It will be them*

3.6.2 *es* may refer back to a whole phrase, sentence or situation.

Willst du die Brötchen holen? Angela macht es schon	*Will you get the rolls? Angela is already doing it*
Ich weiß, daß sie gestorben ist, aber Uwe weiß es noch nicht	*I know that she is dead, but Uwe doesn't know it yet*

3.6.3 *es* may refer back to a noun or adjective complement of *sein*

In English nothing equivalent is required:

Er soll zuverlässig sein, und ich bin sicher, daß er es ist	*He is said to be reliable and I am sure he is*
Ist Jürgen ein guter Schwimmer? Ja, er ist es	*Is Jürgen a good swimmer? Yes, he is*

3.6.4 *es* is used in 'cleft sentence' constructions with relative clauses, cf. English 'it was you who rang the bell':

Er war es, der es mir sagte	*It was him who told me*
Du warst es also, der geklingelt hat	*So it was you who rang the bell*

Other cleft sentence constructions, corresponding to the frequent English type 'it was this morning that I saw her', are not usual in German, see section 21.2.5a.

3.6.5 *es* is often used as a 'dummy subject' in initial position in order to permit the 'real' subject to occur later in the sentence

The effect is to give greater emphasis to the 'real' subject as important new information, cf. 21.2.4d. With the verb *sein*, this corresponds to the 'existential' use of 'there' in English 'there is/are':

Es ist ein Brief für Sie da	*There's a letter for you*
Es waren viele Wolken am Himmel	*There were a lot of clouds in the sky*

This *es* is omitted in non-initial position, e.g.:

Viele Wolken waren am Himmel   Ich weiß, daß ein Brief für mich da ist

NB: For the difference between *es ist/sind* and *es gibt* as equivalents of English 'there is/ are', see 18.2.5.

In German, *es* may be used in this construction with <u>any</u> verb:

Es saß eine alte Frau am Fenster	*There was an old woman sitting at the window*
Es haben nur diejenigen das Wort ergriffen, die ihn für schuldig hielten	*Only those who considered him to be guilty spoke up*

This construction is particularly frequent with verbs of happening:

Es ist gestern ein schwerer Unfall passiert	*A serious accident happened yesterday*

In spoken German *da* is a common alternative to *es* in this function, e.g.:

Da hat eine alte Frau am Fenster gesessen

3.6.6 *es* is also used as a formal 'dummy' subject with a following *daß* clause or infinitive clause which is the real subject of the verb:

Es freut mich, daß du dein Examen bestanden hast	*I am pleased that you have passed your examination*
Es fällt mir ein, daß ich ihn schon gesehen haben muß	*It occurs to me that I must already have seen him*
Es war mir nicht möglich, früher zu kommen	*It wasn't possible for me to come earlier*
Es liegt mir fern, Schwierigkeiten zu machen	*The last thing I want is to make difficulties*

NB: If the clause precedes the verb there is no need for the *es*, e.g.:
Daß du dein Examen bestanden hast, freut mich.

With a number of verbs this 'dummy' *es* anticipating a subordinate clause or infinitive phrase can be omitted in non-initial position:

Dann fiel (es) auf, daß er kein weißes Hemd trug	*Then it was noticed that he wasn't wearing a white shirt*
Ihm steht (es) nicht zu, ein Urteil zu fällen	*It's not up to him to pass judgement*

Usage is variable on this point and there are no fixed rules for the omission of *es*. We can only identify the following general tendencies, which are based on the survey by Marx-Moyse (1983).

(a) *es* is regularly omitted with the following verbs before a following *daß*-clause or infinitive clause:

aufgehen	sich ergeben aus	sprechen für/gegen
bestehenbleiben	feststehen	(geschrieben) stehen
dazukommen	folgen aus	übrigbleiben
durchsickern	hervorgehen aus	verlauten aus
einfallen	hinzukommen	vorschweben

NB: *es* is usually also omitted with *gelten* in the sense 'be valid':

Grundsätzlich gilt, daß alle Einreisenden im Besitz eines gültigen Visums sein müssen	*In principle it is the case that everyone entering the country must be in possession of a valid visa*

(b) *es* is often omitted with the following verbs before a following *daß*-clause (but **not** before a following infinitive clause):

auffallen	einfallen	feststehen	hervortreten
aufgehen	einleuchten	gehören zu/in	sich zeigen
sich auswirken	nicht entgehen	herauskommen	
sich auszahlen	sich entscheiden	sich herausstellen	
sich bestätigen	sich erweisen	sich herumsprechen	

ALSO: *abhängen von* (with a following *ob*-clause) and the verbal phrases *ins Auge fallen*, *außer Zweifel stehen*.

(c) with many verbs *es* <u>may</u> be omitted, optionally, before a following *daß*-clause only, if the initial position in the clause is occupied by a pronoun (or

the prepositional adverb in the case of verbs taking a prepositional object), e.g.:

mich freut (es), daß Sie gekommen sind
Damit hängt (es) natürlich zusammen, daß er im Gefängnis sitzt.

This group is large, and contains many verbs expressing feelings and emotions. Only a selection of the most frequent can be given:

anmuten	empören	interessieren	stören
anstrengen	entmutigen	irritieren	überraschen
ärgern	ermutigen	kümmern	verärgern
aufregen	erregen	langweilen	verwirren
beeindrucken	erschüttern	passen	verwundern
beitragen zu	erstaunen	reuen	wundern
beruhigen	freuen	schmeicheln	zusammenhängen mit
deprimieren	imponieren	stimmen	von Interesse sein

(d) in constructions with *sein* and an adjective or noun complement, *es* may be omitted if the adjective or noun is in initial position:

Wichtig ist (es), daß er es weiß   *It's important for him to know it*
Ein Glück ist (es), daß du kommst   *It's fortunate you're coming*

NB: With a few adjectives, in particular *klar, leicht, möglich, schwer* and *wichtig, es* may be
     omitted, before a following *daß*-clause only, if another word, especially a pronoun, is
     in initial position, e.g.:
     Ihm war (es) völlig klar, daß er jetzt springen mußte.

3.6.7 *es* is used as the subject in a wide range of impersonal constructions

(a) with all kinds of impersonal verbs or verbs used in impersonal constructions (cf. 18.2.4.), e.g.:

es regnet   es klingelt   es fehlt mir an Geld   es bedarf noch einiger Mühe

(b) as an indefinite subject, communicating the idea of a vague, impersonal agent:

Plötzlich schüttelt es ihn in   *Suddenly a wild spasm shakes him*
     einem wilden Krampf (*Goes*)

Ringsum war alles still, dann   *Round about everything was quiet,*
     schrie es   *then there was a cry*
Ihn trieb es in die schottischen   *He felt a desire to go to the Highlands*
     Hochlande (*Zeit*)   *of Scotland*

(c) in impersonal reflexive constructions, often with the force of a passive (see also 15.4.3):

Es schreibt sich so leicht mit   *It's so easy to write with this*
     diesem Filzstift   *felt-tip pen*
Es lebt sich gut in dieser Stadt   *One can live well in this town*

NB: in this construction, *es* may be omitted in non-initial position, e.g.: eine Stadt, in der
     (es) sich gut lebt.

(d) as a 'dummy' subject in impersonal passive constructions and in passive constructions with verbs which do not govern the accusative (see also 15.1.5):

Es wurde in dieser Zeit viel gearbeitet	*A lot of work was done at this time*
Es wurde im Nebenzimmer geredet	*There was talking in the next room*
Es kann ihm doch nicht geholfen werden	*He can't be helped, though*
Es muß morgen darüber gesprochen werden	*It must be talked about tomorrow*

NB: This *es* is invariably omitted in non-initial position, e.g.:
In dieser Zeit wurde viel gearbeitet
Wir wissen doch, daß ihm nicht geholfen werden kann.

3.6.8 An accusative *es* is often used to anticipate a following infinitive phrase or an object clause (usually with *daß*):

Ich konnte es kaum ertragen, ihn so leiden zu sehen	*I could hardly endure to see him suffer like that*
Ich habe es erlebt, daß Riemann die beste Rede gehalten hat	*I have known Riemann to give the best speech*

The use of this 'anticipatory' *es* is variable and depends on the individual verb. In principle it is never absolutely essential, but in practice it is regular or possible with very many verbs, of which a selection of the most common is given below, following the survey by Ulvestad and Bergenholtz (1983):

(a) Verbs with which the anticipatory *es* is nearly always used:

ablehnen	danken	fügen	schätzen	versagen
abwarten	einrichten	genießen	übelnehmen	verschmähen
anrechnen	erleben	hassen	überlassen	vertragen
anstellen	ermöglichen	hinnehmen	überlegen	verübeln
aufgeben	erreichen	lassen	übernehmen	zeigen
aushalten	ersparen	leisten	verantworten	
begrüßen	ertragen	lieben	verdanken	
betrachten als	fassen	machen	verdenken	
dahinbringen	fertigbringen	schaffen	vergessen	

The complex verbal phrases *nicht erwarten können* and *nicht wahrhaben wollen* are also usually found with an anticipatory *es*, as is *finden* used with a following adjective, e.g.: ich finde es schön, daß du kommst.

(b) Verbs with which the anticipatory *es* is frequently used:

abgewöhnen	dulden	hindern	schaffen	versäumen
angewöhnen	durchsetzen	leiden	spüren	verzeihen
ansehen	erfahren	lernen	unterlassen	wagen
bedauern	erkennen	leugnen	verbieten	wollen
begreifen	gestehen	merken	verdienen	zutrauen
bemerken	gönnen	mögen	verhindern	zulassen
bereuen	halten für	riskieren	vermeiden	

The phrases *(es) gewohnt sein* and *(es) wert sein* also belong here, e.g.: Ich bin (es) nicht mehr gewohnt, am frühen Morgen aufzustehen.

(c) Verbs of saying, thinking and knowing, e.g.: *ahnen, denken, erzählen, fühlen, glauben, hören, sagen, wissen*

These are often used with an anticipatory *es* in conjunction with certain adverbs and particles, in particular *bereits, deutlich, doch, genug, ja, oft* and *schon*, or when there is an appeal to the listener's prior knowledge, e.g.:

Ich habe (es) ihm deutlich gesagt, daß er schreiben muß	*I've told him clearly enough that he's got to write*
Ich ahnte (es) schon, daß sie schwanger ist	*I already suspected she was pregnant*
Sie wissen (es) ja selber, daß die Ampel rot war	*You know yourself that the lights were red*

(d) Other verbs are occasionally found with an anticipatory *es*, e.g. *erlauben, klarmachen*, etc. These are used without *es* more frequently than with it. Some other verbs, e.g. *befürchten, beschließen*, are practically never used with *es*.

3.6.9 *es* corresponds to English 'so' as the object of a few verbs, especially *sagen* 'to say' and *tun* 'to do'

Er hat es gesagt	*He said so*
Warum hast du es getan?	*Why did you do so?*

However, *es* is not essential with *glauben* and *hoffen*:

Kommt sie? - Ja, ich glaube/hoffe (es)	*Is she coming? Yes, I think/hope so*

3.6.10 *es* is used as an object in a number of idiomatic verbal phrases

There are a large number of these and we give here a selection of the most frequent:

es auf etwas absehen	*to be after sth*
es auf etwas ankommen lassen	*to take a chance on sth*
es jdm antun	*to appeal to sb*
(e.g.: sie hat es ihm angetan)	*he fancies her*
es mit jdm/etwas aufnehmen können	*to be a match for sb/sth*
es bei etwas belassen	*to leave it at sth*
es weit bringen	*to go far*
es zu etwas bringen	*to attain sth* (esp. a position)
(e.g.: er hat es zum Oberst gebracht)	*(he got to be a general)*
es an etwas fehlen lassen	*to be lacking in sth*
es eilig haben	*to be in a hurry*
es gut/schlecht haben	*to be (un)fortunate*
es in sich haben	*to be a tough nut to crack*
es halten mit jdm/etwas	*to trust sb/sth*
es sich leicht/schwer, etc. machen	*to make it easy/difficult for o.s.*
es gut mit jdm meinen	*to mean well with sb*

es mit etwas genau nehmen	*to be punctilious with sth*
es mit jdm zu tun haben	*to have to deal with sb*
es sich mit jdm verdorben haben	*to have fallen out with sb*
es mit etwas versuchen	*to try (one's hand at) sth*

3.6.11 *es* is used with a number of adjectives in constructions with the verb(s) *sein* and/or *werden,*

in particular with adjectives which govern the genitive of nouns (cf. 6.5.4), e.g. *Ich bin es nun überdrüssig*. The following adjectives occur in this construction:

los   müde   satt   teilhaftig   überdrüssig   wert   würdig   zufrieden

NOTE ALSO: ich bin es gewohnt 'I am used to it'
ich wurde es gewahr (lit.) 'I became aware of it'

4 The articles

German, like English, has a definite and an indefinite article.
The articles belong to a limited set of words known as 'determiners', which are used with a noun to link it to a particular context or situation. Besides the articles, the determiners include all those words, like the demonstratives (*dieser, jener,* etc.), the possessives (*mein, sein,* etc.) and indefinites (*einige, etliche,* etc.) which are used to determine nouns and typically occur first in the noun phrase, before any adjectives. The articles differ from the other determiners in that they are only used in conjunction with a noun, whilst the other determiners are also used as pronouns. Because of this and their importance we deal with the articles in a separate chapter here; the other determiners are treated, in all their uses, in chapter 5.

4.1 Declension of the articles

4.1.1. Declension of the definite article:

	Masc.	Fem.	Neut.	Plural
Nom.	der	die	das	die
Acc.	den	die	das	die
Gen.	des	der	des	der
Dat.	dem	der	dem	den

Notes on the above forms

(a) In spoken German the definite article is relatively unstressed and reduced forms are usual, i.e.:

der: [dʌ]   *die*: [dɪ]   *das*: [d(ə)s] or [s]   *den*: [d(ə)n] or [n]
dem: [d(ə)m] or [m]   *des*: [d(ə)s]

These reductions are rarely reflected in writing except in the contractions used with some prepositions, cf. 4.1.1b. However, they are the norm in unaffected everyday speech, where using full forms, e.g. [de:m], would run the risk of possible confusion with the demonstrative pronoun *der*, cf. 5.1.1. Compare:

Ich habe 'n Tisch gekauft	*I bought the table*
Ich habe den [de: n] Tisch gekauft	*I bought that table*

(b) Contracted forms of the definite article are used with some prepositions
We may distinguish:
(i) Contractions which are usual in speech and writing, i.e.

ans < an+das	am < an+dem	beim < bei+dem	ins < in+das
im < in+dem	vom < von+dem	zum < zu+dem	zur < zu+der

With these the uncontracted forms are only used if the article needs to be relatively stressed. This often depends on style and sentence rhythm, but they tend to occur in particular to refer back to something recently mentioned to make it clear that it is the one meant, cf. Heidolph *et al.* (1981:371f.). Note the difference between:

Er ging zu der Hütte (i.e. the one we were just talking about)
Er ging zur Hütte (i.e. the one we all know about).

Where the force of *der* is essentially demonstrative (i.e. = 'that'), only the uncontracted form is possible, e.g.:

Einer der Affen war besonders lebhaft.   *One of the monkeys was particularly*
    Klaus wollte unbedingt eine   *active. Klaus really wanted to*
    Aufnahme von dem Affen machen   *take a picture of that monkey*

Similarly, where the noun is particularized, e.g. by a following relative clause, the uncontracted form is usual:

an dem Nachmittag, an dem sie anrief   *on the afternoon when she called*
Er geht zu der Schule, wo sein Vater   *He goes to the school where his*
    früher war   *father used to be*

On the other hand, only the contracted forms are used in set phrases and prepositional formulae, e.g.:

am Dienstag	am 10. Mai	im Frühling	zur Zeit	am einfachsten
im Freien	im Vertrauen	im Gang	zum Frühstück	
Ich nahm ihn beim Wort		Sie war beim Kochen		

Compare:

An dem Dienstag kam er spät zur Arbeit   *That Tuesday he came to work late*

(ii) Contractions which are common in speech and sometimes used in writing. These are:

aufs < auf+das	durchs < durch+das	fürs < für+das
übers < über+das	ums < um+das	unters < unter+das

By and large written German tends to prefer the uncontracted forms of these, using the contracted ones mainly in set phrases, e.g.:

aufs Land fahren	fürs Leben gern
übers Herz bringen	ums Leben kommen

(iii) Contractions which are usual in spoken German, but only very occasionally found in writing, usually in set phrases. These are:

außerm	hinterm	hintern	hinters	überm
übern	unterm	untern	vorm	vors

(iv) Other contractions are regular in everyday colloquial speech but not used in the written language, e.g.:

an'n   bei'n   durch'n   in'n   mit'm   nach'm   seit'm

4.1.2 Declension of the indefinite article

	Masc.	Fem.	Neut.
Nom.	ein	eine	ein
Acc.	einen	eine	ein
Gen.	eines	einer	eines
Dat.	einem	einer	einem

The indefinite article has no plural, as indefinite plural nouns are used without an article, as in English. The negative indefinite article *kein*, which declines like *ein* in the singular, has the plural forms nominative/accusative *keine*, genitive *keiner*, dative *keinen*, cf. 5.16.

In spoken German the indefinite article is relatively unstressed and reduced forms are frequent, i.e.:

ein: [n]   *eine*:[nə]   *einen*:[nən]
einem:[nəm]   *einer*: [nʌ]   *eines*:[nəs]

These reductions are rare in writing (except to render the flavour of colloquial dialogue) but they are the norm in unaffected speech, where the use of full forms, e.g. [aɪ], [aɪnən], etc., would risk possible confusion with the numeral *ein* 'one'. Compare:

Ich habe 'n Buch gekauft   *I bought a book*
Ich habe ein (aɪn) Buch gekauft   *I bought one book*

4.2 The uses of the articles: general

In most instances (85%) German and English agree in the use of definite, indefinite or no ('zero') articles with nouns.
However, given the frequency of the articles, the instances where the two languages do not correspond are by no means insignificant, in particular where German uses a definite article when English has none. In the remainder of this chapter an attempt is made to give general and simple indications of where usage differs in the two languages, principally on the basis of the excellent surveys by Grimm (1986, 1987). However, there is much idiomatic variation and it is impossible to give firm rules which will be valid in every case.

4.3 Use of the articles with abstract nouns

4.3.1 German commonly uses the definite article with abstract and similar nouns where English usually has no article

This is particularly the case where the reference is to a specific and definite whole, known and familiar to the speaker and listener, e.g.:

(a) abstract nouns

Er fürchtet das Alter	*He is afraid of old age*
Er liebte die Demokratie (*K. Mann*)	*He loved democracy*
Wir hängen von der Industrie ab	*We depend on industry*
Der Krieg brach aus	*War broke out*
Die Zeit vergeht	*Time passes*
ein Aufsatz über den Ehrgeiz	*an essay about ambition*
eine Schwäche wie die Eitelkeit	*a weakness such as vanity*
Die Erfahrung lehrte ihn, daß dies die Liebe sei (*Th. Mann*)	*Experience taught him that this was love*
Die Menschheit braucht nichts nötiger als den Frieden	*Humanity needs nothing more urgently than peace*

(b) infinitives used as nouns

Er hat das Schwimmen verlernt	*He has forgotten how to swim*
Das Kaffeetrinken kam im 17. Jahrhundert nach Europa	*Coffee-drinking came to Europe in the 17th century*
Vermeide das Spekulieren	*Avoid speculating*

4.3.2 Nevertheless, abstract nouns are used with no article in German in the following cases:

(a) Where the idea is referred to not as a whole, but in a vaguely general, indefinite and partial sense, which comes as a new idea in the context
In such contexts *some* or *any* may often be inserted in the English sentence without changing the meaning radically:

Zu dieser Aufgabe gehört Mut	*This task demands (some) courage*
Es war nicht das erstemal, daß Verrat seinen Lebensweg gekreuzt hatte (*Hermlin*)	*It was not the first time that (some) treachery had crossed his path*
Unentschlossenheit wäre jetzt verhängnisvoll	*(Any) indecision now would be fatal*
Bewegung ist gesund	*(Any) exercise is healthy*
Durch Feigheit kann man alles verlieren	*Through cowardice one may lose everything*
Es schien eine Stadt ohne Jugend und ohne Leben zu sein	*It seemed to be a town without (any) young people or life*

Compare:

Unter seinen Anhängern entstand Mißtrauen	*(Some) distrust arose among his followers*
Das Mißtrauen wächst unter seinen Anhängern	*Distrust is growing among his followers*

In the second sentence 'distrust' is a specific notion, already known and familiar from the context. In the first it is a new concept of a rather vague, general and indefinite nature.

In practice such a partial or indefinite sense will often arise when an abstract noun, particularly one denoting a human quality or emotion, is used with an adjective, e.g.:

Ich verachte kleinliche Eifersucht	*I despise petty jealousy*
Im Heer wuchs neuer Mut	*In the army new courage was growing*
Er neigt zu unnötiger Verschwendung	*He tends to unnecessary extravagance*

(b) In proverbs, sayings, set phrases and the like:

Alter schützt vor Torheit nicht	*There's no fool like an old fool*
Not kennt kein Gebot	*Necessity knows no law*
Stolz ist keine Tugend	*Pride is not a virtue*

(c) In a number of other cases, i.e.:
(i) in general statements, cf. 4.4.1.
(ii) in some constructions with the verbs *sein* and *werden*, cf. 4.9.2.
(iii) in pairs of words and enumerations, cf. 4.9.1.
(iv) in many phrasal verbs, cf. 4.3.3.

4.3.3. Article use with abstract nouns in phrasal verbs, e.g. *Abschied nehmen, in Erfahrung bringen.*

The use of a definite or zero article with these is often a matter of idiom, cf.:

zum Abschluß bringen	BUT zu Ende bringen
sich im Aufbau befinden	BUT sich in Betrieb befinden
den Vorzug geben	BUT Antwort geben

However, the following general rules usually apply:

(a) Infinitives as nouns have a definite article in phrasal verbs with prepositions, e.g.: ins Rollen kommen, zum Kochen bringen.

(b) Feminine nouns in phrasal verbs with *zu* have a definite article. e.g.: zur Kenntnis bringen, zur Verfügung stehen.

(c) All phrasal verbs with *außer* and *unter*, and most of those with *in*, have no article, e.g.:
außer Gefahr sein, jdn unter Druck setzen, jdn in Verlegenheit bringen

NB: Those with *in* plus an infinitive used as a noun have an article, cf. (a) above.

(d) Most phrasal verbs with *gehen, halten* and *setzen* have no article, e.g.:
in Erfüllung gehen, in Gang halten, in Brand setzen.

(e) Abstracts used with *haben* have no article, e.g.:
Aufenthalt haben, Angst haben, Durst haben, Geduld haben, Mut haben.

(f) Phrasal verbs consisting of a verb and an object noun as a unit usually have no article, e.g.:

Anspruch erheben, Antwort geben, Abschied nehmen, Rücksicht üben, Krieg führen, Not leiden, Zeit sparen.

NB: An article occurs with many phrasal verbs which customarily lack one when the noun is qualified, cf.:

jdn in Gefahr bringen	*lead sb into danger*
jdn in (eine) große Gefahr bringen	*lead sb into great danger*
jdn in die größte Gefahr bringen	*lead sb into the greatest danger*

4.3.4 The use of the article with some other groups of nouns is similar to that with abstract nouns:

(a) Names of substances

As general concepts, these are used with a definite article, but no article is used in an indefinite or partial sense:

Die Butter kostet sechs Mark das Pfund	*Butter costs six marks a pound*
Faraday hat die Elektrizität erforscht	*Faraday investigated electricity*
Frösche laichen im Wasser	*Frogs spawn in water*
Die Bauern bauen hier Roggen an	*The farmers are growing rye here*
Wir importieren Kaffee aus Afrika	*We are importing coffee from Africa*

NB: (i) A definite article also occurs in some set phrases, e.g.:
   beim Bier sitzen. Das steht nur auf dem Papier. Man kann nicht von der Luft leben.
   (ii) Usage is optional in generalizations, etc., cf. 4.4, e.g.:
   (Die) Elektrizität ist eine wichtige Energiequelle.

(b) Names of meals

A definite article is used if they are referred to as known quantities, but the article is optional if the reference is indefinite or partial:

Das Mittagessen wird um 13 Uhr eingenommen	*Lunch is taken at 1 p.m.*
Wir sollen uns vor dem Frühstück treffen	*We are to meet before breakfast*
Ich habe (das) Frühstück bestellt	*I have ordered breakfast*
Wann bekommen wir (das) Frühstück?	*When are we getting breakfast?*

(c) Names of sicknesses and diseases

These are used with a definite article when they are referred to in general as known quantities, but there is no article when they are referred to in an indefinite or partial sense, as a new idea in the context, particularly after *haben*:

Er ist an der Schwindsucht gestorben	*He died of consumption*
Sie ist an den Masern erkrankt	*She is ill with measles*
Die Grippe hat Tausende weggerafft	*Influenza carried off thousands*
Ich habe Kopfschmerzen, Gelbsucht	*I've got a headache, jaundice*

NB: Singular names of specific illnesses are used with the indefinite article to refer to a bout of that disease. This is in particular the case when the noun is modified by an adjective:

Er ist an einer Lungenentzündung gestorben	*He died of (a bout of) pneumonia*
Ich habe einen ekligen Rheumatismus	*I've got nasty rheumatism*
Er hat einen Schnupfen, eine Erkältung	*He's got a cold*

(d) Names of languages

These nouns from adjectives have two forms:

(i) an inflected one, always used with the definite article, which refers to the language in a general sense:

Das Spanische ist dem Portugiesischen sehr nahe verwandt	*Spanish is very closely related to Portuguese*
eine Übersetzung aus dem Russischen ins Deutsche	*a translation from Russian into German*

(ii) an uninflected form, which refers to the language in a specific context. With this, article use is similar to that in English:

das Deutsch des Mittelalters	*the German of the Middle Ages*
Luthers Deutsch	*Luther's German*
Sie kann, lernt, versteht Deutsch	*She knows, learns, understands German*

NB: Sie kann kein Deutsch   *She doesn't know any German*

Sie spricht ein akzentfreies Deutsch	*She speaks German without an accent*
Günther studiert Deutsch in Marburg	*Günther is studying German in Marburg*
eine Zusammenfassung in Deutsch	*a summary in German*
sein Deutsch ist mangelhaft	*his German is deficient*

4.3.5 A definite article is usual in German with some other groups of mainly abstract nouns which often lack an article in English, i.e.:

(a) Historical periods, literary and philosophical movements, religions

Marx begreift den Feudalismus als notwendige Stufe der historischen Entwicklung *(Knaur)*	*Marx sees feudalism as a necessary stage in the process of history*
der deutsche Expressionismus	*German Expressionism*
Diese Auffassung ist charakteristisch für den Islam	*This view is characteristic of Islam*

(b) Arts and sciences

Ich erwarte von der Literatur mehr Anregung als vom Leben *(Grass)*	*I expect more stimulus from literature than from life*
Darüber schweigt die Geschichte	*History is silent about that*
ein Lehrbuch der Astronomie	*a textbook of astronomy*
Sie liebt die Musik	*She loves music*

NB: no article is used for school or university subjects, e.g: Sie hat eine Zwei in Geschichte. Else studiert Astronomie in Göttingen.

(c) Institutions, company titles and buildings

Sie geht in die Schule	*She goes to school*
Er wurde ins Parlament gewählt	*He was elected to parliament*
Die Bundesrepublik gehört der NATO an	*The Federal Republic belongs to NATO*
Er arbeitet bei der BASF	*He works for BASF*
im Kölner Dom, das Ulmer Rathaus	*in Cologne cathedral, Ulm town hall*
die Paulskirche in Frankfurt	*St Paul's church in Frankfurt*

NB: No article is used with names of buildings with a proper name in apposition, e.g.: Schloß Sanssouci, Burg Gibichstein, Kloster Beuron.

4.4. Use of articles in generalizations

4.4.1 In general statements which are true for all members of a class, the definite article (sing. or pl.), the indefinite article (sing.) or no article (pl.) are often equally possible, e.g.:

(a) Die Tanne ist ein Nadelbaum	*The fir is a conifer*
(b) Die Tannen sind Nadelbäume	
(c) Eine Tanne ist ein Nadelbaum	*A fir is a conifer*
(d) Tannen sind Nadelbäume	*Firs are conifers*

In the main, type (a) above is more frequent in German than English, which has a clear preference for type (d), so that the following exemplifies a very common kind of equivalence:

Das Auto ist der Fluch der modernen Stadt *(Zeit)*	*Cars are the curse of modern cities*

Type (b) is not usual in English in generalizations with plural nouns, as in the example given and the following:

Die Beschwerden vermehren sich	*Complaints are increasing*
Die Steuern waren drückend *(Brecht)*	*Taxes were oppressive*

Nevertheless, there are words with which it is possible, e.g.:

Die Italiener lieben die Musik	*The Italians love music*

NB: English *man* in the sense 'human being' is usually found with no article, whilst *der Mensch,* with a definite article, is regular in German in general statements of type (a) above, e.g.:

Der Mensch ist ein seltsames Geschöpf	*Man is a strange animal*

4.4.2 In general statements with nouns which have no plural, the definite article and zero article are alternatives in German

This applies in particular to abstract nouns and names of substances:

(Der) Frieden ist das höchste Gut der Menschen	*Peace is man's greatest good*
(Das) Rauchen schadet der Gesundheit	*Smoking is injurious to health*
(Das) Eisen ist ein Metall	*Iron is a metal*

4.5 Use of articles with geographical and other proper names

4.5.1 Usage with geographical and astronomical names:

(a) With masculine names of countries the definite article is usual, but optional, e.g.:

(der) Libanon   (der) Iran   in/im Sudan.

NB: With masculine names of regions the use of the definite article is the norm, e.g.: der Balkan, der Bosporus.

(b) A definite article is the rule with feminine and plural names of countries and regions, e.g.:

die Schweiz   die Türkei   die Normandie   die Ukraine
die USA   die Niederlande

NB: no article for countries in addresses, e.g.:
Andreas Wernli, Kellergasse 7, 3000 Bern, Schweiz.

(c) With neuter names of countries and cities there is usually no article, e.g.:

Deutschland   Norwegen   Leipzig   Ulm

A few neuter names of regions always have the definite article, i.e.:

das Elsaß   das Engadin   das Ries   das Wallis *Valais*
das Rheinland   das Vogtland (and all others in *-land*)

NB: (i) Use of the article is optional with Tirol, cf. in/im Tirol.
(ii) The article is always used with the neuter nouns from adjectives for German regions which are frequent in colloquial German:
Jetzt kommen wir ins Bayrische. Das Dorf liegt im Thüringischen.

(d) The definite article is used with other geographical and astronomical names

This is so even where English has no article, e.g.:

der Bodensee *Lake Constance*   der Genfer See   der Mont Blanc
der Mars   der Venus   der Jupiter

(e) The definite article is used with street names:

Ich wohne in der Goethestraße   Wir treffen uns auf dem Schloßplatz
Der Alexanderweg ist die zweite Querstraße zur Humboldtstraße

NB: no article for street names in addresses:
Frau Gerlinde Haarmann, Weserstraße 7, 3500 <u>Kassel</u>.

4.5.2 In standard German there is usually no article with personal names

There are, however, some exceptions to this, i.e.:

(a) In colloquial speech a definite article is very frequent with personal names:

Ich sehe die Monika   Gestern war ich bei der Frau Schmidt

(b) to clarify case or gender (see also 4.8.1):

der Vortrag des Klaus Müller   Das hat Klaus dem Wolfgang Pedersen gesagt
Ich habe eben mit der Rupp (i.e. Mrs Rupp, not Mr Rupp) gesprochen

(c) to individualize the person concerned more strongly:

Der Lehmann hat einen ausgezeichneten Vortrag gehalten.

NB: The use of the article is almost regular with performing artists and other 'stars', e.g.:
die Callas, der Karajan, die Garbo.

(d) to refer to characters in plays:

Er hat in der vorigen Saison den Hamlet gespielt.

4.5.3 All geographical and proper names are used with a definite article when qualified by an adjective:

das heutige Deutschland   das viktorianische England
das zerstörte Dresden   der junge Heinrich
der alte Doktor Schulze

NB: This applies to saints' names: der heilige Franziskus *Saint Francis.*

4.6 Use of articles in time expressions

4.6.1 Names of months and seasons usually have the definite article:

Der April war verregnet   Wir fahren im August nach Italien
Der Frühling war dieses Jahr spät   Im Winter friert der Bach zu

NB: (i) no article after *sein* and *werden*, cf. 4.9.2c: Es ist, wird Sommer.
(ii) The names of the months have no article after prepositions other than *an, bis zu* and *in*, cf. 4.6.3, or after *Anfang, Mitte, Ende*:
Es war kalt für April   Der Fahrplan gilt von Mai bis September
Ende Februar hat es geschneit   Er kommt erst Anfang Mai
(iii) no article when the name is qualified by *nächsten, letzten, vorigen, vergangenen*:
nächsten Oktober, letzten Herbst.

4.6.2 The major festivals have no article, e.g.:

Weihnachten   Silvester   Neujahr   Pfingsten   Ostern

NOTE, however: der Heilige Abend *Christmas Eve*, der Karfreitag *Good Friday.*

4.6.3. All time nouns are used with the definite article after the prepositions *an, bis zu* and *in*:

am Tag *by day*   am Mittwoch   am 27. Januar   bis zum Montag
in der Nacht *at night*   im Jahre 1945   in der vorigen Woche
in der Gegenwart *at present*

After other prepositions in time expressions there is commonly no article:

ab 1. Mai   auf längere Zeit   bei Einbruch der Dunkelheit
binnen Jahresfrist   bis Ende März   gegen Abend
mit Beginn der Sommerzeit   nach Ablauf dieser Frist
seit Kriegsausbruch   von frühester Jugend an   vor Tagesanbruch
zu gleicher Zeit

Further details may be found under the individual prepositions (chapter 20) and with the time phrases, section 11.6.

4.7 Definite article or possessive?

4.7.1 The definite article is often used in German where English uses a possessive when referring to parts of the body and articles of clothing:

Hast du die Zähne geputzt?   *Have you cleaned your teeth?*
Sie hat das Bein gebrochen   *She has broken her leg*
Sie strich den Rock glatt   *She smoothed her skirt*
Das Mädchen . . . zog den rötlichen Kamm aus dem Haar, nahm ihn in den Mund
      und fing an, mit den Fingern die Frisur zurechtzuzupfen. *(Böll)*

A possessive dative is frequent in such constructions, and essential when the relevant person is not the subject of the verb, cf. 2.5.7, e.g.:

Sie nahm (sich) es in den Mund   *She put it in her mouth*
Die Mütze fiel mir vom Kopf   *The cap fell off my head*
Wir zogen dem Verletzten die Hose aus   *We took the injured man's trousers off*

NB: When referring to a number of people, the relevant noun is used in the singular if each
      individual only possesses one, cf.:
      Sie alle hoben die rechte Hand   *They all raised their right hands*
      Ihnen klopfte das Herz   *Their hearts were beating*

4.7.2 A possessive is used rather than the definite article:

(a) when the owner has been named in a previous sentence, or in other cases when the part of the body or article of clothing is the first element in the sentence:

Ein Fremder erschien. Seine Stirn   *A stranger appeared. His forehead*
      glänzte. Sein Anzug war altmodisch.   *glistened. His suit was old-fashioned*
Seine Hände konnte ich aber nicht sehen   *I wasn't able to see his hands, though*
Meine Beine sind nicht krumm *(Brecht)*   *My legs aren't crooked*
Dicht bei seinen Füßen lag ein Ring   *Right by his feet lay a ring*

(b) when the owner must be specified, but a possessive dative cannot be used in the particular sentence:

Ich erblickte eine Wespe auf meinem Ärmel	*I caught sight of a wasp on my sleeve*
Sie legte ihre Hand auf seine Hand (*Wendt*)	*She put her hand on his hand*

(c) to emphasize the owner or avoid ambiguity:

Langsam hob sie ihre rechte Hand	*Slowly, she raised her right hand*
Hast du deine Zähne geputzt?	*Have you cleaned your teeth?*
Zieh (dir) lieber deinen Mantel an!	*Put your coat on* (i.e. not mine!)
Ich zog mir seine Hose an	*I put his trousers on*

4.7.3 The definite article may be used rather than a possessive with some abstract nouns

This particularly applies to nouns denoting human attributes and emotions, which are thus seen as 'part' of the person concerned. A possessive dative may occur under the same conditions as with body parts:

Du mußt versuchen, die/deine Angst zu überwinden	*You must try to overcome your fear*
Er verlor den Mut	*He lost his courage*
Ich werde ihm die Faulheit austreiben	*I shall rid him of his laziness*
Der Appetit ist mir vergangen	*I've lost my appetite*

4.7.4 The definite or indefinite article, as appropriate, are commonly used rather than a possessive with the adjective *eigen*:

Er hat den/seinen eigenen Sohn erschlagen	*he has killed his own son*
Jetzt haben wir eine eigene Wohnung	*We've got our own flat/ a flat of our own now*

NB: (set phrase with no article):

Das haben wir mit eigenen Augen gesehen	*We saw it with our own eyes*

4.8 Miscellaneous uses of the definite article

4.8.1 The definite article may be used to make the case of a noun clear, even where it would not otherwise be required

This applies in particular in the dative and the genitive cases.

(a) With the genitive this reflects the rule that, aside from usage with names and after prepositions, no noun can be given a genitive ending unless it is preceded by a determiner or an adjective. Thus:

ein Ausdruck des Erstaunens	*an expression of surprise*

NB: If ambiguity could arise from the use of a definite article, then the paraphrase with *von* must be used, cf. 2.5. Thus 'the smell of seaweed' can only be *der Geruch von Seetang*, as *der Geruch des Seetangs* would mean 'the smell of the seaweed'.

The article is essential in the first of the following sentences to show the case clearly:

Sie bedarf der Ruhe	*She needs rest*
Sie braucht Ruhe	

(b) Examples of the use of the definite article to mark dative case:

Ich ziehe Kaffee dem Tee vor	*I prefer coffee to tea*
Dieses Metall gleicht dem Gold	*This metal resembles gold*
Er hat sich der Physik gewidmet	*He devoted himself to physics*

4.8.2 The definite article may be used in a distributive sense

Here English commonly uses the indefinite article or *per*:

Die Butter kostet sechs Mark das Pfund	*(The) butter costs six marks a pound*
Sie kommt zweimal die Woche	*She comes twice a week*

(OR: zweimal in der Woche)

Wir fuhren 80 Kilometer die Stunde	*We were doing 50 miles an hour*

pro or (with measurements) *je*, both without an article, are common alternatives to the definite article:

Wir zahlten 15 Pfennig pro/je Meter	*We paid 15 pfennigs a/per metre*
Es kostet 12 Mark pro Stunde	*It costs 12 marks an hour*

4.8.3 The definite article is always used with *meist*:

Er hat das meiste Geld	*He has (the) most money*
die meisten Jungen	*most of the boys*
die meisten meiner Freunde	*most of my friends*

4.9 Miscellaneous uses of the zero article

4.9.1 Nouns used in pairs or enumerations often lack the definite article even when a single noun in the same construction would require one

In many cases these are conventional or set phrases:

(in) Form und Inhalt	*(in) form and content*
Tag und Nacht	*day and night*
in Krieg und Frieden	*in war and peace*
(despite: im Krieg)	*(in wartime)*
mit Müh und Not	*with great difficulty*
Es geht um Leben und Tod	*It's a matter of life and death*
in Hülle und Fülle	*in plenty*

Rhein, Main und Donau sind schiffbare Flüsse	*The Rhine, the Main and the Danube are navigable rivers*
der Unterschied zwischen Stolz und Hochmut	*the difference between pride and arrogance*
Er haßt Lesen und Schreiben	*He detests reading and writing*
. . . die alten menschlichen Werte – ich möchte hier nur Pflicht, Gehorsam, Anstand, Autorität, Ordnung nennen (*Valentin*)	*. . . the old human values – I will mention here only duty, obedience, good manners, authority, order*

4.9.2 No article is used in some instances with the complement of the verbs *sein, werden, bleiben*

(a) With nouns denoting professions, nationality, origins or classes of people in general:

Er ist Arzt, Bäcker, Installateur	*He is a doctor, a baker, a plumber*
Ich bin Deutscher, Engländer, Schwede	*I am a German, an Englishman, a Swede*
Franz ist gläubiger Katholik	*Franz is a devout Catholic*
Helmut blieb Junggeselle	*Helmut remained a bachelor*
Danach wurde er Marxist	*After that he became a Marxist*

However, the indefinite article is used if the noun does not refer to a class:

Sie ist eine bekannte Anwältin	*She is a well-known lawyer*
Er ist ein richtiger Schauspieler	*He's a real actor*

NB: The indefinite article is used in descriptive constructions with professions and positions, e.g.: Er hatte die Stelle eines Untersuchungsrichters, den Titel eines Professors *He had the position of examining magistrate, the title of professor*.

(b) With certain nouns used mainly in formal writing,
i.e. *Bedingung, Fakt, Gegenstand, Grundlage, Sache, Schwerpunkt, Tatsache, Voraussetzung, Ziel*. These usually precede the verb:

Tatsache ist, daß . . .	*It is a fact that . . .*
Bedingung dafür ist, daß er den Vertrag unterschreibt	*The condition for this is that he signs the contract*
Grund meines Schreibens ist der Artikel ‚Unser Garten' (*HA*)	*The reason I am writing is the article 'Our Garden'.*

(c) With names of months and seasons, and abstract nouns used in a general sense:

Es war schon April	*It was already April*
Jetzt ist Sommer	*It's summer now*
Heute abend ist Tanz	*There's a dance on tonight*
Das ist Geschmackssache	*That is a matter of taste*
Donnerstags ist Sitzung	*On Thursdays there is a meeting*

4.9.3 The indefinite article is commonly lacking in phrases introduced by *als* 'as'

Ich kannte ihn als Junge	*I knew him when I was a boy*
Er sprach als Franzose	*He spoke as a Frenchman*
Er gab mir dies als Belohnung	*He gave me this as a reward*
die Bedeutung des Passes als wichtige(r) Handelstraße	*the significance of the pass as an important trade route*
Mir als Ungar traut er nicht	*He doesn't trust me, as a Hungarian*
Als überzeugter Demokrat kann ich das nicht gutheißen	*As a convinced democrat, I cannot approve of that*
Er gilt als bester Tenor der Neuzeit	*He is reckoned to be the best tenor of recent times*

NB: (i) With verbs followed by *als*, e.g. *ansehen, betrachten, fühlen, gelten*, the appropriate article is a permissible alternative, e.g.:
Er gilt als der beste Tenor der Neuzeit.
Sie betrachtet sich als (eine) fleißige Kontrolleurin.
(ii) The article is commonly used in the genitive, e.g.:
mit der Verhaftung des Generals als (des) eigentlichen Putschführers.

4.9.4 The article may be omitted in appositional phrases in formal German:

Zunächst kamen wir nach Florenz, (der) Hauptstadt der Toskana	*First we arrived at Florence, the capital of Tuscany*
Wir lernten Paul Fischer kennen, (den) Sohn des Bürgermeisters	*We met Paul Fischer, the son of the mayor*
dieses Zürich, Treffpunkt der Kaufleute *(Frisch)*	*this Zurich, the meeting place of businessmen*
Neil Armstrong, amerikanischer Astronaut, betrat als erster Mensch den Mond *(Zeit)*	*Neil Armstrong, the American astronaut, was the first man to set foot on the moon*

4.9.5 No article is used in a number of formulaic expressions referring to people

This usage is restricted to formal, especially official registers, e.g.:

Angeklagter hat gestanden, daß . . .	*The accused confessed that . . .*
Unterzeichneter bittet um rasche Entscheidung seiner Angelegenheit	*The undersigned requests a speedy decision in the matter concerning him*
Verfasser behauptet, das Problem gelöst zu haben	*The author claims to have solved the problem*

4.9.6 Articles are often omitted for stylistic effect in headlines and advertisements, etc.:

Verbrechen gestanden. Münchner Kaufmann vom Geschäftspartner erschlagen *(HA)*	*Crime admitted. Munich businessman killed by partner*
Wohnung mit Bad gesucht möglichst nahe Stadtzentrum	*Flat with bathroom required as close as possible to city centre*

4.9.7 The zero article is the most usual equivalent in German for the English indefinite determiners *some* or *any* (see also 5.5.10):

Ich möchte Suppe	*I should like some soup*
Brauchen Sie Marken?	*Do you need any stamps?*
Ich habe (rote) Äpfel gekauft	*I bought some (red) apples*
Wenn du noch Schwierigkeiten hast, . . .	*If you have any more difficulties*
Hast du Geld bei dir?	*Have you got any money on you?*

4.9.8 No article is used with adverbial genitives, e.g.: schweren Herzens *with a heavy heart*, cf. 2.3.5.

4.10   Article use with prepositions

Article use with prepositions is to a considerable degree idiomatic. Use in phrasal verbs and time phrases is dealt with in sections 4.3.3 and 4.6, and more detail, in particular concerning differences between German and English use of articles in set phrases with prepositions, may be found in chapter 20 under the individual prepositions. In this section, we deal with a few special cases where general rules can be stated.

4.10.1 The indefinite article is often omitted in adverbial or adjectival phrases consisting of preposition, adjective and noun

This is particularly common where a set phrase is extended by an adjective and is characteristic of formal registers:

. . .einen Virtuosen mit italienischem Namen *(Mann)*	*a virtuoso with an Italian name*
ein Anzug von altmodischem Schnitt	*a suit of an old-fashioned cut*
ein Mann, der solchem Rat nicht folgte und zu schrecklichem Ende kam *(Hildesheimer)*	*a man who failed to follow such advice and met a terrible end*
Wir erhielten den Betrag in frei konvertierbarer Währung	*We received the sum in a freely convertible currency*

NB: This usage is also the norm in phrases with *mit* which are alternatives to adverbial genitives, cf. 2.3.5b:

Sie ging mit schnellem Schritt (= schnellen Schrittes) über die Straße	*She crossed the road at a fast pace*

4.10.2 The definite article is often omitted in prepositional phrases where the following noun is qualified by a genitive or a further prepositional phrase

This is very frequent in set formulae in formal registers:

auf Anraten des Arztes	*on the advice of a doctor*
in Gegenwart von zwei Kollegen	*in the presence of two colleagues*
nach Empfang Ihres Schreibens vom 2.1.	*on the receipt of your letter of Jan. 2nd*
unter Ausnutzung aller Möglichkeiten	*by exploiting all possibilities*

4.10.3 A number of prepositions are used with a zero article in some or all of their uses

The most noteworthy (because of the differences from English) are:

(a) *mit* **is most often used with no article when a part-whole relationship is involved:**

ein Zimmer mit Bad	ein Hut mit breitem Rand
ein Opel mit Schiebedach	eine Suppe mit Wursteinlage

(b) *ohne* **is used with no article in German in cases where English has an indefinite article:**

Er geht gern ohne Hut   Sie trat ohne Brille auf
Ich übersetzte den Text ohne Wörterbuch, ohne Mühe
Wie hast du die Tür ohne Schlüssel aufgemacht?

(c) A number of other prepositions, mainly belonging to formal written registers, are used without a following article:

ab: ab ersten/erstem Mai, Preise ab Fabrik *ex works*, ab Bahnhof
gemäß: Die Angelegenheit wurde gemäß Verordnung entschieden
NB: an article is used when *gemäß* follows the noun, e.g.: den geltenden Verordnungen
       gemäß

infolge: Die Straße ist infolge schlechten Wetters gesperrt
kraft: Er handelte kraft Gesetzes
laut: Der Fahrer wurde laut Gesetz verurteilt
mangels: Der Angeklagte wurde mangels Beweises freigesprochen
per: per Einschreiben *by registered mail,* per Anhalter fahren *hitch-hike*
pro: pro Stück, der Preis pro Tag *per day*, pro männlichen Angestellten
von . . . wegen: Diese Angelegenheit muß von Amts wegen geklärt werden
zwecks: Junge Dame möchte netten, gebildeten Herrn zwecks Heirat kennenlernen *(FAZ)*

5   Other determiners and pronouns

Determiners are a limited ('closed') set of words used with nouns to relate them to a particular context or situation.
A characteristic feature of them in German is that they have a different set of endings to mark case, gender and number from that of a following adjective. The German determiners include the articles, which are dealt with in chapter 4, and a number of other words, such as the demonstratives (e.g. *dieser, jener*), possessives (e.g. *mein, unser*) and some indefinites (e.g. *einige, manche, viele*), all of which may also be used as pronouns. All these uses are treated in this chapter, together with those of the relative and other pronouns not covered in chapter 3.

NB: For the declension of adjectives after determiners, see 6.2.

5.1 Demonstratives

5.1.1. *der* 'that'
der is the most commonly used demonstrative in German. It may be used, like French *ce*, to point in a general way to something distant or something near at hand. It may thus be the equivalent of English *this* or *that*.

(a) *der*, when used as a determiner, has exactly the same written forms as the definite article, cf. 4.1.1.
However, it is always stressed and thus has full forms in spoken German, e.g. *den* [deːn], *der* [deːʁ] which differ from the typical spoken forms of the article, e.g. *'n, d'n* or *d'r*, etc., cf.:

Ich möchte ein Stück von d'r Wurst	*I would like a piece of the sausage*
Ich möchte ein Stück von der [deːʁ] Wurst	*I would like a piece of this/that sausage*

In written German the demonstrative force of *der* may sometimes be clear from the context, especially when a relative clause follows, e.g.:

Sie hatten das Buch nicht, das ich am Montag bestellt hatte	*They didn't have that book which I had ordered on Monday*

Otherwise, it may be awkward to distinguish the demonstrative *der* from the article in writing and *dieser* is commonly used in its stead (for both English *this* and *that*, cf.5.1.2.)

(b) The declension of the demonstrative *der* when used as a pronoun
Note the differences from the declension of the definitive article in the genitive and the dative plural.

	Masc.	Fem.	Neut.	Plural
Nom.	der	die	das	die
Acc.	den	die	das	die
Gen.	dessen	deren	dessen	deren
Dat.	dem	der	dem	denen

NB: *dessen* and *deren* are compounded with a following *-halben*, *-wegen* or *-willen* with a *-t* inserted, e.g. *dessentwegen, um derentwillen*.

(c) Typical examples of the use of *der* as a pronoun
Note that it often corresponds to English *the/this/that one*:

mein Wagen und der meines Bruders	*my car and my brother's*
Die Sache ist nämlich die: er ist schon verheiratet	*It's like this: he's already married*
Diese Seife ist besser als die, die ich gebrauche	*This soap is better than the one I use*
Wir können dem nicht so viel Bedeutung beimessen	*We cannot attach so much importance to that*
Die sind mir zu teuer	*Those are too dear for me*
Das kann ich nicht glauben	*That I can't believe*
Das Buch liegt auf dem Tisch. Ja, auf dem da drüben	*The book's lying on the table. Yes, on that one over there*

(d) Pronominal *der* is often used with little demonstrative force
It is then the equivalent of a third person pronoun, cf. 3.4.3, e.g.:

Ist der Teller kaputt? Ja, den hat Astrid fallen lassen	*Is the plate broken? Yes, Astrid dropped it*
Brauns? Ich glaube, die sind verreist	*Brauns? I think they're away*

This usage is chiefly colloquial, especially when used to refer to persons.

(e) *der*, whether used as a determiner or a pronoun, may be strengthened and the reference to something distant or near made more specific by the addition of *da* or *hier*, e.g.:

das Buch da *that book*, das Buch hier *this book*, das da *that one*, das hier *this one*.

This usage is principally colloquial.

(f) The genitive of pronominal *der* can be used for a possessive pronoun to avoid ambiguity, e.g.:

Karl sprach mit Heinrich, dann mit dessen Schwester	*Karl spoke with Heinrich, then with his (i.e. Heinrich's) sister*
Erboste Bauern nahmen britische LKW-Fahrer gefangen und plünderten deren Konvois (*Zeit*)	*Angry farmers held some British lorry-drivers captive and plundered their (i.e. the lorry-drivers') convoys*

In colloquial German, the genitive of *der* may appear instead of a possessive for reasons of emphasis, e.g.:

Ich kann deren Mann nicht leiden.

(g) As a pronoun referring forwards, especially with a following relative clause, *derer* is used rather than *deren* in the genitive plural:

die Zahl derer, die seit 1950 die Westzone verlassen haben *(ND)*	*the number of those who have left the Western zone since 1950*

(h) With the verb *sein*, pronominal *das* is used, like *es*, cf. 3.6.1, irrespective of the number or gender of the noun referred to, with a plural verb where necessary, e.g.:

Das sind meine Bücher	*Those are my books*
Das ist mein Arm, meine Hand, mein Knie	*That is my arm, my hand, my knee*

(i) *das* may be used generally as a stressed form of the pronoun *es*, cf. 3.6.

(j) *der und der* is used for English 'such and such (a one)':

Er nannte mir die und die Adresse	*He gave me such and such an address*
Er sagte, der und der hätte es getan	*He said, such and such a person had done it*

(k) A form of the prepositional adverb, cf. 3.5, is used rather than a preposition followed by the demonstrative pronoun, e.g.: ′damit *with that*, ′darin *in that*. The stress is on the first syllable:

′Damit kann man die Büchse nicht aufmachen	*You can't open the can with that*

To refer to something near, especially something just mentioned, a form with *hier* - may be used, e.g.: hiermit *with this*, hierin *in this*:

Hierüber läßt sich nichts mehr sagen	*There is nothing more to be said about this*

NB: The prepositional adverb is <u>not</u> used before a following relative clause, cf. 5.4.3c:

Ich richtete mein ganze Aufmerksamkeit auf das, was er erklärte	*I focused my whole attention on what he was saying*

5.1.2. *dieser* 'this'

dieser is declined as follows, as a determiner or a pronoun:

	Masc.	Fem.	Neut.	Plural
Nom.	dieser	diese	dieses	diese
Acc.	diesen	diese	dieses	diese
Gen.	dieses	dieser	dieses	dieser
Dat.	diesem	dieser	diesem	diesen

NB: The majority of other determiners have the same endings as *dieser*.

Notes on the use of *dieser*:

(a) As a determiner and a pronoun *dieser* principally refers to something near at hand, corresponding to English *this*
However, it may have a general demonstrative sense in sentences where the difference between something near and something distant is not crucial. In such cases it corresponds to English *that*. Such usage is most frequent in the written language, where *der*, which is the usual undifferentiated form in the spoken language, is ambiguous. As a determiner, it occurs in both spoken and written German, but as a pronoun it is mainly restricted to the written language. Examples of usage:

Diese Erklärung ist unbefriedigend	*This explanation is unsatisfactory*
Dieser Junge (spoken: der Junge (da)) arbeitet aber gut	*That boy really does work well*
Er kaufte den roten Wagen nicht, weil ihm dieser (spoken: der hier) viel besser gefiel	*He didn't buy the red car, because he liked this one much better*
Er unternahm noch einen Versuch. Durch diesen kam er zu dem Schluß, daß . . .	*He performed another experiment. Through this one he came to the conclusion that . . .*

(b) As a pronoun, the short neuter singular form *dies* is used rather than *dieses* to refer to something unspecific close by
It contrasts with *das*, which is used for unspecific distant or undifferentiated reference, and corresponds closely to English *this*, e.g.:

Dies geschieht nicht oft. Gerade dies hatte ich vergessen.

NB: (i) Like *das*, it may be used irrespective of gender or number, with a plural verb where appropriate, e.g.:
Dies sind meine Schwestern. Dies ist meine Frau.
(ii) *dies* is occasionally used in writing as a determiner in place of *dieses*, e.g.: Dies Werk malte Konrad Witz aus Basel (*Borst*).

5.1.3 *jener* 'that'

jener declines like *dieser*, cf. 5.1.2. It is largely restricted to certain special uses in formal written German only, i.e.:

(a) To contrast with *dieser*:

Herr Schröder wollte nicht dieses Bild verkaufen, sondern jenes	*Mr Schröder did not want to sell this picture, but that one*
Wir sprachen über dieses und jenes (more usual: über dies und das)	*We talked about this and that*

(b) to refer to something distant, but well-known:

Ich erinnere mich deutlich jenes Augenblickes (more usual: an diesen Augenblick)	*I recall that moment clearly*

(c) with a following relative clause:

. . . um Abschied von jener langen Anfangsphase zu nehmen, die die Beziehungen zwischen Washington und Moskau bislang kennzeichnete (*FR*)	. . . *to depart from that long initial phase which has so far been typical of relations between Washington and Moscow*

5.1.4 *derjenige* 'that'

derjenige is always written as one word, but both parts decline, i.e. *diejenige, dasjenige, denjenigen, demjenigen*, etc. It has strong demonstrative force, and is used, as a determiner or a pronoun, chiefly with a following restrictive relative clause, corresponding to English 'that (one), which/who'. It is no longer restricted to formal writing, being used increasingly in speech:

Wir wollen diejenigen Schüler herausfinden, die musikalisch begabt sind	*We want to find those pupils who are musically gifted*
Ich habe mit demjenigen gesprochen, der mir das Angebot gemacht hat	*I spoke with that man who made me the offer*

5.1.5 *derselbe* 'the same'

Like *derjenige*, both parts decline, e.g. *dieselbe, demselben, derselben*. However, unlike *derjenige*, it may be used with a contracted preposition, e.g. *am selben Tag, zur selben Zeit*. It corresponds to English 'the same':

Er gab mir dieselbe Antwort	*He gave me the same answer*
Er besucht dasselbe Gymnasium wie dein Bruder	*He goes to the same school as your brother*
Sind das dieselben?	*Are those the same?*
Sie wohnt im selben Hause	*She lives in the same house*
Es läuft auf (ein und) dasselbe hinaus	*It all comes to the same thing*

NB: The difference between *derselbe*, i.e. 'the very same' and *der gleiche*, i.e. 'one which is similar' (cf. *Er trägt den gleichen Hut* 'He is wearing the same (i.e. a similar) hat) is often ignored in spoken German, *derselbe* being used in both senses. However, it is widely felt that this distinction ought to be maintained, at least in writing.

5.1.6 *solch-* 'such'

solch- occurs in a number of forms, i.e.:
(i) inflected *solcher*, declining like *dieser*

EXCEPT: that in the genitive singular masculine and neuter it has the ending *-en*, not *-es* (which was once the norm), e.g. *Die Ursachen solchen Durcheinanders*.

(ii) endingless, usually followed by an indefinite article, e.g. *solch ein Unsinn*.

(iii) with the endings of an adjective after *ein*, e.g. *ein solches Buch*, or other determiners, e.g. *jeder solche Gedanke, alle solchen Gedanken.*

The usage of *solch-*, in these various forms, may be summarized as follows:

(a) The most usual variants in writing and speech are *ein solcher* in the singular and *solche* in the plural:

Einen solchen Wagen würde ich nie kaufen	*I would never buy a car like that*
Einem solchen Experten sollte das nicht passieren	*It shouldn't happen to an expert like him*
Solchen Leuten kann man alles erzählen	*You can tell people like that anything*
solche großen Häuser	*big houses like that*

NB: In everyday colloquial speech, *so ein* is more current in the singular than any form of *solch-*. In the plural, simple *so* may be used, too, but it is restricted to very colloquial registers, e.g.:
in so einer Stadt   so ein Geschenk   Das sind so Sachen

(b) Inflected *solcher* in the singular is found principally in formal, especially literary registers:

Solches Unglück wurde uns zuteil	*Such misfortune befell us*
Ich habe solchen Durst	*I have such a thirst*
bei solchem guten Wetter	*in such good weather*
ein Mann, der solchem Rat nicht folgte (*Hildesheimer*)	*a man who failed to follow such advice*

(c) When an adjective follows, the most usual equivalent in the singular with count nouns for English *such a* is *ein so* (more colloquial *so ein*):

ein so großes Haus }	*such a big house*
so ein großes Haus }	

In spoken German *so* is also used elsewhere, where the written language tends to prefer inflected *solcher*:

so große Häuser	*such big houses*
bei so gutem Wetter	*in such good weather*

In literary registers uninflected *solch*, followed by an adjective, is not uncommon. It also occurs in a few set phrases:

mit solch unermüdlichem Eifer	*with such tireless enthusiasm*
Der Westen ließ sich von solch verfehlter Ablehnung allen Verhandelns verleiten (*Zeit*)	*The West allowed itself to be misled into such mistaken rejection of any negotiations*
Solch dummes Gerede!	*Such stupid gossip*

(d) Uninflected *solch* may occur in formal registers with a <u>following</u> indefinite article

This is more emphatic in tone than if the article comes first:

Solch einem Experten sollte das nicht passieren	*That shouldn't happen to <u>such</u> an expert*

NB: Uninflected *solch* is also used occasionally without a following article before a neuter noun in the singular, e.g.: solch Wetter.

(e) In pronominal use, *solche* (pl.) and *so einer* (sing.) are the most usual variants:

Ich habe solche oft gesehen	*I've often seen ones like that*
So eines kann ich mir nicht leisten	*I can't afford one like that*

Singular *solcher* is used after *als*:

Der Fall als solcher interessiert mich	*The case as such interests me*

Singular *(k)ein solcher* is restricted to literary registers and sounds very stilted:

Sie hatte auch einen solchen	*She had one like that, too*
Leider haben wir keine solchen mehr	*I'm afraid we haven't got any more like that*

(f) The adjective *derartig* is a common, more emphatic alternative to *solch*

It is used with *ein* in the singular or a zero article in the plural:

Er fuhr mit einer derartigen Geschwindigkeit gegen die Mauer, daß . . .	*He drove into the wall at such a speed, that . . .*
Derartige Gerüchte hören wir oft	*We often hear rumours like those*

NB: Used with a following adjective, *derartig* may be left uninflected, e.g. *Er fuhr mit einer derartig(en) hohen Geschwindigkeit gegen die Mauer, daß* . . . In some contexts a difference in meaning may be perceived between, e.g. *ein derartig dummes Geschwätz*, i.e. 'gossip which is stupid to such an extent' and *ein derartiges dummes Geschwätz*, i.e. 'gossip like that which is stupid'.

5.2. Possessives

5.2.1 The German possessive forms are (with the personal pronoun to which they relate):

ich	-	**mein**	wir	-	**unser**
du	-	**dein**	ihr	-	**euer**
er, es	-	**sein**	Sie	-	**Ihr**
sie	-	**ihr**	sie	-	**ihr**

5.2.2 As determiners the possessives agree with the following noun for case, gender and number

They have the same set of endings as the indefinite article, cf. 4.1.2, i.e.:

	mein *my*				**unser** *our*			
	Masc.	**Fem.**	**Neut.**	**Plural**	**Masc.**	**Fem.**	**Neut.**	**Plural**
Nom.	mein	meine	mein	meine	unser	unsere	unser	unsere
Acc.	meinen	meine	mein	meine	unseren	unsere	unser	unsere
Gen.	meines	meiner	meines	meiner	unseres	unserer	unseres	unserer
Dat.	meinem	meiner	meinem	meinen	unserem	unserer	unserem	unseren

NB: (i) The *-er* of *unser* and *euer* is part of the stem and <u>not</u> an ending. As the table shows, the endings are attached to this stem. When *unser* and *euer* have an ending, the *-e-* of the stem is often dropped, e.g. *unsrer, unsren, eurer, euren.* Alternatively, the *-e-* of the endings *-en* or *-em* may be dropped, e.g. *unsern, unserm, euern, euerm.*

  With *unser*, the full forms, as given in the table, are the more usual ones in written German, although the reduced forms, which are the norm in speech, are quite permissible.

  With *euer*, the forms with no *-e-* in the stem, i.e. *euren, eurer, eures, eurem* are by far the most common in both spoken and written German.

  (ii) For the use of a definite article rather than a possessive, in particular with names of body parts and articles of clothing, cf. 4.7.

  (iii) For the use of the demonstrative for a third person possessive to avoid ambiguity, cf. 5.1.1f.

5.2.3 Used as pronouns, the possessives have the endings of *dieser*

(cf. 5.1.2), agreeing in case, gender and number to the noun to which they refer, i.e.:

	meiner *mine*				**unserer** *ours*			
	Masc.	**Fem.**	**Neut.**	**Plural**	**Masc.**	**Fem.**	**Neut.**	**Plural**
Nom.	meiner	meine	meines	meine	unserer	unsere	unseres	unsere
Acc.	meinen	meine	meines	meine	unseren	unsere	unseres	unsere
Gen.	meines	meiner	meines	meiner	unseres	unserer	unseres	unserer
Dat.	meinem	meiner	meinem	meinen	unserem	unserer	unserem	unseren

NOTE CAREFULLY: the endings in the nominative singular masculine and the nominative/accusative singular neuter, which differ from the endingless forms of the possessive determiner.

NB: (i) The *-e-* of the nominative/accusative neuter ending *-es* is often dropped in writing and almost always in speech, i.e. *meins, deins.* With *unseres* and *eueres* the *-e-* of the stem is dropped, i.e. *unsers, euers.* Otherwise, *unserer* and *euerer* may drop the *-e-* of the stem or the ending as with the possessive determiner, cf. 5.2.2 above.

  (ii) Endingless forms of the possessive, e.g.: Mein ist der Helm (*Schiller*), are now archaic except in set phrases, e.g.: Er kann mein und dein nicht unterscheiden.

5.2.4 Examples of the use of the possessives as pronouns

Hast du dein Fahrrad? Ich sehe mein(e)s nicht.
Unser Garten ist größer als Ihrer.
Er sprach mit meinen Eltern, ich mit seinen.
Ich nehme unsren Wagen. In seinem habe ich immer Angst.

5.2.5 Alternative forms of the possessive pronoun

Besides the possessives *meiner, unserer*, etc. given above, the following alternatives exist, with the possessive forms used as adjectives, with adjectival declensions:

(i) der meinige, der deinige, der uns(e)rige, etc.
(ii) der meine, der deine, der uns(e)re, etc.

These forms are less common than *meiner*, etc. and occur mainly in formal written German. Type (ii) is rather more emphatic than *meiner*, etc., whilst type (i) is current mainly in set phrases, e.g.: die Deinigen 'your people' (i.e. your family), ich habe das Meinige getan 'I've done my bit'.

5.2.6 Idiomatic differences between German and English in the use of the possessives:

Das gehört mir. Gehört das dir?	*That's mine. Is that yours?*
ein Freund von mir einer meiner Freunde	*a friend of mine*
Freunde von mir	*friends of mine*

5.3 Interrogatives

5.3.1 *welcher* 'which'

welcher declines like *dieser*, cf. 5.1.2, whether used as a determiner or a pronoun.

(a) Examples of the use of *welcher*:

Welches Bier willst du trinken?	*Which beer do you want to drink?*
Welchen Zug nehmen wir denn?	*Which train shall we take?*
Aus welchem Land kommt sie denn?	*Which country does she come from?*
Welcher berühmte Schriftsteller hat diesen Roman geschrieben?	*Which famous author wrote this novel?*
Hier sind zwei gute Romane. Welchen möchtest du zuerst lesen?	*Here are two good novels. Which one would you like to read first?*
Er fragte mich, welchen (Roman) ich zuerst lesen wollte	*He asked me which (novel) I wanted to read first*

NB: (i) Before an adjective, undeclined *welch* may be used as an alternative to the declined form, e.g.:
Welch berühmter Schriftsteller hat diesen Roman geschrieben?
Die Künstler zeigten, welch reiches Kulturgut sie mitbrachten *(MM)*
This usage is limited to the formal written language.
(ii) In the genitive singular masculine and neuter the determiner may have the ending *-en* rather than *-es*, e.g.:
Welchen/Welches Kindes Buch ist das? Welchen Weges erinnerst du dich?
This is only possible, though, if the noun itself has the genitive ending *-(e)s*. In practice the genitive is little used and other constructions preferred, e.g., for the above examples:
Welchem Kind gehört das Buch da? An welchen Weg erinnerst du dich?

(b) With the verb *sein*, **pronominal** *welcher*, **used in an indefinite sense, may have the neuter singular form** *welches* **irrespective of the gender and number of the noun it refers to,** e.g.:

Welches ist die jüngere Schwester?   Welches sind die besten Zeitungen?

Welche, in agreement with the following noun, would be equally possible in both these examples.

(c) *welcher* **may be used in exclamations,** e.g.:

Welcher Unterschied!   Welche Überraschung!   Welcher schöne Tag!
Welchen unglaublichen Unsinn hat er geredet!

In exclamations, undeclined *welch* also occurs, followed by *ein* or an adjective, e.g.:

Welch ein Unterschied!   Welch eine Überraschung!   Welch (ein) schöner Tag!
Welch unglaublichen Unsinn hat er geredet!

This exclamatory use of *welch* is mainly found in formal German; *was für (ein)*, cf. 5.3.2, is more current in the spoken register.

(d) Other uses of the form *welcher*
(i) For *welcher* as a relative pronoun (= 'who', 'which'), see 5.4.2.
(ii) For *welcher* as an indefinite ('some', 'any'), see 5.5.26.

5.3.2 *was für ein* 'what kind of (a)'

When this phrase is used as as determiner, *ein* has the declension of the indefinite article and is absent in the plural and before mass nouns in the singular. Used as a pronoun, *was für einer* 'what kind (of a one)', *einer* has the endings of pronominal *einer*, cf. 5.5.5, which are identical with those of *dieser*. The case of *ein(er)* depends on the role of the whole phrase in the sentence, i.e. it is not dependent on *für*.

(a) Examples of the use of *was für ein*:

Aus was für einer Familie stammt er?	*From what kind of a family does he come?*
Sie können sich denken, in was für einer schwierigen Lage ich mich befand	*You can imagine in what an awkward situation I found myself*
Was für ausländische Marken haben Sie?	*What kinds of foreign stamps do you have?*
Was für Käse soll ich kaufen?	*What kind of cheese shall I buy?*
Er hat sich ein Auto gekauft. – Was für ein(e)s?	*He has bought a new car. What kind?*

(b) *was* **is often separated from** *für (ein)*, **especially, but not only, in the spoken language,** e.g.:

Was hast du denn für ein Auto gekauft?   Was sind das für Vögel?

(c) *was für (ein)* is used in exclamations, where it is more common than *welcher*, especially in less elevated styles

In this usage the separated form is more frequent.

Was für eine Chance!	*What a chance!*
Was für herrliche Blumen!	*What lovely flowers!*
Er ist ein Schauspieler – und was	*He's an actor – and what an actor!*
für einer!	
Was sind das für wunderschöne Häuser!	*What lovely houses these are!*

NB: In full clauses the verb may alternatively be placed at the end, as in a subordinate clause, e.g. *Was für wunderschöne Häuser das sind!*

(d) In pronominal use *was für welche* is used in the plural, e.g.:

Ich habe ihr Blumen gebracht.   Was für welche?

NB: The use of *was für welcher* in place of *was für ein* in the singular belongs to colloquial North German, e.g.:
Er hat einen neuen Wagen gekauft. – Was für welchen?

(e) In colloquial speech *was für (ein)* is very commonly used instead of *welcher* 'which'

This usage is regarded as substandard:

Was für ein Kleid ziehst du an?   *Which dress are you going to wear?*

(f) *was für (ein)* is also used in concessive clauses, see 19.5.2c.

5.3.3 *wer, was* 'who', what'

(a) *wer* and *was* are only used as pronouns

wer, like English *who*, refers only to persons. It does not distinguish gender and has the following declension:

Nom.	wer
Acc.	wen
Gen.	wessen
Dat.	wem

was, like English *what*, refers only to things. Its only case form is the genitive *wessen*.

Both *wer* and *was* are singular in form, but may have singular or plural meaning. In the nominative, they are normally followed by a singular verb. However, with *sein* the appropriate singular or plural forms are usual:

Wer hat diesen Brief geschrieben?	*Who wrote this letter?*
Wen hast du heute gesprochen?	*Who(m) did you speak to today?*
Wem wollten sie vorhin helfen?	*Who(m) did they want to help just now?*
Mit wem hast du gespielt?	*Who(m) did you play with?*
Wessen Bücher sind das?	*Whose books are those?*
Wer sind diese Leute?	*Who are those people?*
Was bewegt sich dort im Gebüsch?	*What is moving there in the bushes?*

Was sind die längsten Flüsse der Welt?	*What are the longest rivers in the world?*
Ich kann Ihnen sagen, wer spielte	*I can tell you who was playing*
Weißt du, was er getan hat?	*Do you know what he did?*

NB: (i) *wessen*, as the genitive of *wer*, is by no means wholly obsolete in written German, but it is felt to be clumsy and tends to be avoided. For the example above, *Wem gehören diese Bücher?* would be more usual.

(ii) As the genitive of *was*, *wessen* is not unknown in literary German, but it is considered rather stilted and it is usually avoided by the use of alternative constructions, e.g. *Warum schämst du dich?* rather than *Wessen schämst du dich?*

(b) In standard German *was* does not occur with a preposition but is replaced by the form *wo(r)* + preposition

This compound is a form of the prepositional adverb, cf. 3.5:

Womit schreibst du?	*What are you writing with?*
Worauf soll ich mich setzen?	*What shall I sit on?*
Worüber sprechen Sie?	*What are you talking about?*
Ich habe gehört, worum er gebeten hat	*I heard what he asked for*

NB: (i) *wodurch, wonach, wovon* and *wozu* can only be used if there is no idea of movement involved, e.g.:

Wodurch weiß er das?	*How is that that he knows that?*
Wonach soll man sich denn richten?	*By what is one to be guided?*
Wovon sollen wir leben?	*What are we to live on?*
Wozu gebraucht man das?	*What is that used for?*

Cf.: *durch was?* 'through what?', *von wo?* or *woher?* 'where . . . from?', *wohin?* 'where . . . to?'.

(ii) The following prepositions do not form a prepositional adverb with *wo(r)*-: außer, gegenüber, hinter, neben, ohne, seit, zwischen.

(iii) In colloquial German *was* (irrespective of case) may frequently be heard with a preposition instead of *wo(r)*+preposition, e.g. *Von was sollen wir leben?* This usage is considered substandard.

(c) In constructions which would require the (non-existent) dative of *was*, a paraphrase must be found with a suitable noun and *welcher*, e.g.:

Welcher Ursache kann man seinen Erfolg zuschreiben?	*To what can one ascribe his success? (Literally: To what cause . . .?)*

(d) To indicate plurality with *wer* and *was*, *alles* may be added later in the sentence

This usage can no longer be regarded as purely colloquial:

Wer kommt denn alles?	*What people are coming?*
Wen kennen Sie hier alles?	*What people do you know here?*
Was hat er denn alles gefragt?	*What were the things he asked?*

(e) *wer* and *was* are common in exclamations:

Wer hätte so was erwartet!	*Who would have expected such a thing!*
Wem hat er nicht alles geholfen!	*Who(m) hasn't he helped!*
Was <u>haben</u> wir gelacht!	*How we laughed!*
Was er nicht alles tut!	*The things he does!*

(f) *was* may be combined with an adjective used as a noun, which has the neuter ending *-es*

It is separated from *was* and placed later in the sentence:

Was haben sie Wichtiges besprochen?	*What important matters did they discuss?*
Was ist Komisches dran?	*What's funny about it?*
Was gibt es hier Neues?	*What's new here?*
Ich möchte wissen, was hier Besseres geboten wird als bei uns	*I would like to know what is being offered here that's better than at home*
Was könnt ihr hier anderes erwarten? *(Fallada)*	*What else can you expect here?*

(g) *was* is used, in colloquial German only, in the sense of 'why?' or 'what for?', e.g.:

Was sitzt ihr darum?	*What are you doing just sitting around?*

(h) Idiomatic differences between German and English

Wie ist Ihr Name, bitte?	*What is your name, please?*
Wie heißt Ihr Bruder?	*What's your brother called?*
Wie ist das Buch?	*What's the book like?*

(j) Other uses of *wer* and *was*

(i) For the use of *wer* and *was* as relative pronouns, see 5.4.3. and 5.4.6.

(ii) For *wer* and *was* in concessive clauses (i.e. = 'whoever', 'whatever'), see 19.5.2.

(iii) For the colloquial use of *wer* as an indefinite (i.e. = 'someone'), see 5.5.27.

5.4 Relative pronouns

5.4.1 *der* 'who, which, that'

(a) *der* is the most commonly used relative pronoun in German
Its declension is identical to that of the demonstrative pronoun *der*, i.e.:

	Masc.	Fem.	Neut.	Plural
Nom.	der	die	das	die
Acc.	den	die	das	die
Gen.	dessen	deren	dessen	deren
Dat.	dem	der	dem	denen

It agrees in gender and number with the noun to which it refers (the 'antecedent'), and takes its case from its function within the clause which it introduces. Unlike English, the relative pronoun is <u>never</u> omitted in German:

Das Buch, das ich lese, ist recht interessant	*The book I am reading is very interesting*
Ich kannte den Rechtsanwalt, der gestern gestorben ist	*I knew the lawyer who died yesterday*
Mein Balkon, den ich endlich einmal nutzen konnte, erwies sich als sehr praktisch	*My balcony, which I was at last able to use, proved very convenient*
Der Mann, dem ich helfe, ist sehr alt	*The man I am helping is very old*
Mein Freund, dessen ältester Sohn krank ist	*My friend, whose eldest son is ill*
Wir kamen an die Straße, an deren anderem Ende er wohnt	*He came to the street, at the other end of which he lives*

(b) The genitive of *der*: notes on forms and usage

(i) The genitive of *der* corresponds to English 'whose' or 'of which':

der Mann, dessen Name ich immer vergesse	*the man whose name I always forget*
Sie blickten auf das Mietshaus gegenüber, in dessen Erdgeschoß sich eine Schreibwarenhandlung befand	*They looked out on the apartment house opposite, on the ground floor of which was a stationer's*

NB: Constructions of the type *one of whom, most of which, some of which* normally correspond to constructions with *von denen* in German, e.g.:
die Studenten, von denen ich einen nicht kenne
eine Anzahl Jungen, von denen ich die meisten kenne
viele Bilder, von denen einige ganz gut sind

(ii) In the genitive plural and the genitive singular feminine *derer* may occur rather than *deren* if no noun follows:

die Bilder, auf Grund derer wir urteilen, was getan werden muß *(Jaspers)*	*the images, on the basis of which we judge what must be done*
die ungewöhnliche Autorität, derer sich die katholischen Bischöfe in Polen erfreuen *(Spiegel)*	*the extraordinary authority which is enjoyed by the Catholic bishops in Poland*

This usage is still regarded as 'incorrect' by DUDEN (1984:§560), but *derer* is in practice more frequent in such cases than *deren*, especially in the plural. However, *deren* is always preferred with a following noun, e.g.:

die Frau, deren Tochter du kennst.

(iii) After prepositions, the shorter form *der* also occurs for *deren*:

eine lange Übergangszeit von sechs Jahren, innerhalb der die Länder die Juristenausbildung umstellen können *(Zeit)*	*a long transitional period of six years, within which the Länder can reorganize the training of lawyers*

(iv) It is incorrect (though a common mistake by Germans) to decline *dessen* and *deren*, i.e.: ein Mann, von dessen (NOT: dessem) Erfolg ich hörte.

(v) *dessen* and *deren* are compounded with -*halben*, -*wegen* and -*willen* with the insertion of a -*t*-, e.g. *derentwegen, um dessentwillen*:

das Außenhandelsgesetz, dessentwegen Nixon so lange mit dem Kongreß kämpft (*Welt*)	*The foreign trade bill, because of which Nixon has been battling so long with Congress*

5.4.2 *welcher* 'who, which, that'

welcher is used, sparingly, as a stylistic variant of *der* in formal written German. Like *welcher* used as an interrogative or as an indefinite, cf. 5.3.1, it has the same endings as *dieser*, cf. 5.1.2. However, it is not used in the genitive. It is most frequent, though never necessary, in order to avoid repetition of forms of *der*, e.g.:

der Präsident, welcher der Sitzung beiwohnte
die Stadt, in welcher der berühmte Maler wohnt
Die, welche zuletzt kamen, waren erschöpft

BUT compare, as perfectly acceptable, cf. 5.4.6b:

Die, die gingen, haben in der DDR mehr verändert, als die, die geblieben sind (FR).

However, *welcher* is used in formal German, like English *which,* before a noun referring back to part or whole of the preceding clause, e.g.:

Er wurde zum Stadtdirektor ernannt, welches Amt er gewissenhaft verwaltete	*He was appointed town-clerk, which office he administered conscientiously*
Er sagte ihr, sie müsse den Betrag sofort zurückzahlen, welcher Forderung sie dann auch nachging	*He told her she had to repay the amount immediately, which request she then complied with*

5.4.3 *was* is used as a relative pronoun in some constructions

In this usage it has no case forms, *dessen* normally being used rather than *wessen* if a genitive is required.

     was occurs:

(a) after neuter indefinites
i.e. *alles, einiges, etwas, folgendes, manches, nichts, vieles, weniges*:

Nichts, was er sagte, war mir neu	*Nothing (that) he said was new to me*
Ich bin mit allem zufrieden, was er tut	*I am satisfied with everything (that) he does*

NB: After *etwas, das* may be used if *etwas* refers to something specific:

Gerade in diesem Moment fiel ihr etwas ein, das sie erstarren ließ: Die Gasrechnung (*Baum*)	*Just then she remembered something that made her go rigid: the gas bill*

Ich erinnere mich an etwas Merkwürdiges, das er sagte	*I remember something strange that he said*

das is occasionally found after other indefinites, but this usage is regarded as incorrect, cf. DUDEN (1985:37).

(b) after a neuter adjective used as a noun referring to something indefinite
This usage is particularly frequent with superlatives:

Das Richtige, was man sich ansehen müßte, finden wir nie (*Fallada*)	*The right things* [in museums] *that one ought to look at, we never find*
Das Beste, was du tun kannst, ist nach Hause zu gehen	*The best thing you can do is to go home*
Das erste, was Evelyn sah, waren Mariannes Augen (*Baum*)	*The first thing Evelyn saw was Marianne's eyes*

NB: If the adjective refers to something specific, *das* may be used, e.g. *Das Gute, das er getan hat, wird ihn überdauern.* However, except with superlatives, where the use of *was* is general, the difference between the use of *das* and *was* is rarely clear cut and usage tends to be variable and uncertain.

(c) after the indefinite demonstrative *das*
Note that a dative or genitive of *das* must always be supplied as an antecedent, and in any case after a preposition, whereas in English only the relative *what* may be necessary, as in the last three examples below:

Eben das, was uns fehlte, hat er uns verweigert	*He denied us just what we were lacking*
Ich hörte nichts von dem, was er mir sagte	*I didn't hear anything of what he said to me*
seine Rede widerspricht dem, was in der Resolution der CDU festgehalten ist	*His speech contradicts what is set down in the CDU's resolution*
ein eifriger Leser dessen, was neu auf den Markt kommt (*Zeit*)	*a keen reader of what is new on the market*

(d) to refer back to a whole clause

Er hat sein Examen bestanden, was mich sehr erstaunt	*He passed his examination, which very much surprises me*
Er sagte, er hätte mich damals gesehen, was ich nicht glauben konnte	*He said he had seen me then, which I couldn't believe*

(e) in substandard usage for *das*, referring to a neuter noun, e.g.:
das Buch, was er mir geliehen hat.

5.4.4 Relative pronouns after prepositions

The predominant usage in modern German is the appropriate form of *der* after the preposition. The construction corresponds more closely to that of written English than that with a 'stranded' preposition typical of spoken English, cf. the alternative renderings for the first example:

die Frau, auf die Sie warten	{ *the woman for whom you are waiting* / *the woman you are waiting for*
der Stuhl, auf den du dich setzen wolltest	*the chair you wanted to sit down on*
der Stuhl, auf dem du sitzt	*the chair you are sitting on*
der Bleistift, mit dem sie schreibt	*the pencil she is writing with*
die Stadt, in der ich wohne	*the town I live in*

Referring to things, the form of the prepositional adverb with *wo(r)* (e.g. *worauf, woran, wovon,* cf. 5.3.3b) used to be a frequent alternative to preposition + *der*, e.g. *der Bleistift, womit sie schreibt*. This is now less usual even in formal written registers. The use of the prepositional adverb with *da(r)-* (e.g. *darauf, daran, davon,* cf. 3.5) as a relative to refer to things, e.g. *der Bleistift, damit sie schreibt,* is now archaic.

However, the prepositional adverb in *wo(r)-* is usual in those cases where the simple relative pronoun is *was*, cf. 5.4.3:

Das, woran du denkst, errate ich nie	*I'll never guess what you're thinking of*
das, wozu er berechtigt ist	*what he is entitled to*
Es ist das Einzige, wofür es sich lohnt, Richter zu sein (*Baum*)	*It is the only thing for which it is worthwhile being a judge*
Er hat sein Examen bestanden, worüber ich mich freue	*He has passed his examination, about which I am very pleased*

NB: After *etwas*, used with specific reference, preposition + *das* is a possible alternative to the prepositional adverb with *wo(r)*, e.g.: Ich spürte, daß noch etwas geschehen war . . . etwas, für das sich nur ein Anlaß ergeben hatte (*Lenz*)

5.4.5 Relative pronouns used after first and second person personal pronouns

Formal usage requires the pronoun to be repeated in the relative clause, e.g.:

du, der/die du ja nicht alles wissen kannst	ich, die/der ich mich oft irre

However, this construction is felt to be stilted and the alternative with a third-person verb, corresponding to the English equivalent, is nowadays the norm in speech and acceptable in writing, e.g.:

du, der/die nicht alles wissen kann	ich, die/der sich oft irrt

5.4.6 'the one who', 'that which', etc.

(a)*wer* and *was* may be used in generalizations as compound relatives:

wer viele Freunde hat, ist glücklich	*He who has many friends is happy*
Wer wagt, gewinnt	*Who dares wins*
Und was noch schlimmer ist, er merkt es selber nicht	*And what is worse, he doesn't realize it himself*
Was du sagst, stimmt nicht	*What you say is not right*

If there is a difference in case or construction between the two clauses, an appropriate form of the demonstrative is used to begin the main clause:

Wem du traust, der wird dir auch trauen	*Whom you trust will also trust you*
Was wir getan haben, darüber müssen wir auch Rechenschaft ablegen	*What we have done we shall also have to answer for*

(b) Where a demonstrative pronoun is followed by a relative pronoun, the following alternatives are found:

(i) demonstrative *der* followed by relative *der*:

Die, die gingen, haben in der DDR mehr verändert, als die, die blieben (*FR*)	*Those who left have changed more in the GDR than those who stayed*

This is the most usual alternative despite the repetition.

(ii) demonstrative *der* followed by relative *welcher*:

Die, welche ich kaufen wollte, waren mir zu teuer	*The ones I wanted to buy were too expensive for me*

This alternative is restricted to more elevated styles.

(iii) demonstrative *derjenige* followed by relative *der* or (in elevated style) *welcher*:

Diejenigen, die (welche) in den hinteren Reihen saßen, konnten nichts sehen	*Those who were sitting in the back rows couldn't see anything*

This is a more emphatic alternative, used in speech and writing.

(iv) demonstrative *jener* followed by relative *der* (or *welcher*):

Der deutsche Zug darf nicht aufgehalten werden von jenen, die sich hinter Europa verstecken, um Deutschland zu verhindern (*Brandt*)	*We cannot allow the train called Germany to be held up by people who are hiding behind Europe in order to prevent a (united) Germany*

This is infrequent, and regarded as incorrect by DUDEN (1985:370).

(v) *der* can be used as a compound relative (e.g. 'he who'):

Die hier leben, haben nichts mehr zu verlieren	*Those who live here have nothing more to lose*
Der da sitzt, ist mein Onkel	*The man sitting there is my uncle*

This alternative is common in spoken registers.

5.4.7 Other forms of the relative

(a) To refer to a place, *wo* is often used as a relative instead of *der* with a preposition:

die Stadt, wo (or: *in der*) ich wohne	*the town where I live*

If motion to or from a place is involved, *wohin* or *woher* are used:

die Stadt, wohin (or: *in die*) ich ging	*the town to which I went*
das Dorf, woher (or: *aus dem*) er kam	*the village from which he came*

The use of *wo* as a general relative pronoun to refer to people or things (e.g. *die Frau, wo jetzt kommt; der Tisch, wo die Blumen drauf liegen*) belongs to substandard regional speech, chiefly in South Germany.

(b) With time words, where English often uses *when* as a relative, the most generally acceptable alternative is to use a preposition with *der*:

Den Tag, an dem er ankam, werde ich nie vergessen	*I shall never forget the day when he arrived*
in einer Zeit, in der die Jugend immer unabhängiger wird	*at a time when youth is becoming more and more independent*

als (referring to past time) or *wenn* (referring to present or future time) are possible alternatives, and *da* is often used in formal (especially literary) German:

In dem Augenblick, als der Hund aufsprang, schrie er (*Valentin*)	*At the moment when the dog jumped up, he shouted*
an seinem nächsten Geburtstag, wenn er volljährig wird	*on his next birthday, when he comes of age*
Ach, wo sind die Zeiten, da Pinneberg sich für einen guten Verkäufer hielt? (*Fallada*)	*Oh, where are the days when Pinneberg considered himself a good salesman?*

The use of *wo* as a relative indicating time is very common, especially in speech. Although it is widely used in writing, many Germans continue to regard it as too colloquial for use in formal registers:

im Augenblick, wo er die Tür aufmachte	*at the moment when he opened the door*
Wir leben in einer Zeit, wo Verkaufen arm macht (*Remarque*)	*We live in times when selling makes one poor*
jetzt, wo ich das weiß	*now that I know that*

(c) *wie* is used to indicate manner, principally after *die Art*:

die Art, wie er zu mir sprach	*the manner in which he spoke to me*
so, wie ich es gewohnt bin	*just as I am used to*

(d) To indicate cause, chiefly after *der Grund*, *warum* (or, in formal registers, *weshalb*) is used:

der Grund, warum (weshalb) ich nach Breslau ging	*the reason why I went to Wrocław*

5.5 Indefinites, quantifiers and other miscellaneous determiners and pronouns

In this section we give full details on all the following determiners and pronouns:

aller, alle	irgend(-)	meinesgleichen
ander	jeder	nichts
beide(s)	jedermann	sämtlich
dergleichen/desgleichen	jedweder, jeglicher	unsereiner
einer	jemand, niemand	viel, viele,
ein wenig, ein bißchen	kein, keiner	wenig, wenige
ein paar	lauter	welcher
einiger, einige	man	wer
etliche	manch(-)	
etwas	mehrere	

5.5.1 *aller, alle* 'all (the)'

(a) *all-* **'all (the)', used as a determiner, has a number of alternative forms.**
(i) Fully inflected, with the endings of *dieser,* cf. 5.1.2:

ein Hotel mit allem modernen Komfort	*a hotel with all modern conveniences*
Alle Kinder spielen gern	*All children like playing*
Alle Schüler waren gekommen	*All the pupils had come*
mit allen denkbaren Mitteln	*with all conceivable means*
die Quelle allen Reichtums	*the source of all riches*

NB: (i) In the genitive singular masculine and neuter, the ending *-en* is more usual than *-es* if the noun has the genitive singular ending *-es*:
der Inbegriff alles Schlechten   *the epitome of everything bad*
(ii) Plural *alle* may correspond to English 'all' or 'all the', as shown in the examples above. Note that *alle* is <u>never</u> followed by a genitive, i.e. that *alle Schüler* is the equivalent of 'all the pupils' or 'all of the pupils'.

(ii) Inflected *all-* followed by the definite article:

alle die Bücher	*all the books*	alle die Mühe	*all the trouble*

(iii) Uninflected *all* followed by the definite article:

all das schlechte Wetter	*all the bad weather*
all die Schüler	*all the pupils*
mit all dem Geld	*with all the money*

In the plural inflected *alle*, i.e. alternative (i), is the commonest form, especially in the nominative and accusative, though both (ii) and (iii) are also current. Attempts to establish a consistent difference of meaning between the inflected and uninflected forms (e.g. DUDEN 1984:§336) are unconvincing.

In the singular, (iii) is the most usual alternative, though (ii) is not unknown with feminine nouns in the nominative and accusative, whilst (i) is restricted to set phrases and highly formal registers. Note that the most

idiomatic equivalent of English *all* with a singular noun is often a phrase
with *ganz*, cf. (g) below.

(b) *all-* is often used with another determiner
In the plural both inflected and uninflected forms are found, in the singular
only uninflected *all*, e.g.:

all mein Geld   von all diesem Brot   nach all ihrer Mühe   all/alle meine Brüder
mit all/allen diesen Schwierigkeiten

NB: Only the inflected form is used before *solch*, which then has the endings of an
adjective, e.g. *alle solchen Frauen*.

(c) *all-* used as a pronoun declines like *dieser* (cf. 5.1.2),
but it lacks genitive singular forms. The neuter singular *alles* is used for
'everything', the plural *alle* for 'everyone':

Alles ist bereit	*Everything is ready*
Ich bin mit allem einverstanden	*I agree to everything*
Alle waren anwesend	*Everybody was present*
Sind das alle?	*Is that all (of them)?*

NB: The missing genitive singular may be supplied by using *alles* together with a form of the
demonstrative *der*, e.g. *Ich erinnere mich alles dessen*. However, this sounds stilted and
is usually avoided by paraphrasing or using the endingless form, i.e. *all dessen*.

(d) *alle*, when used with a personal pronoun, normally follows it
Alternatively, mainly in the nominative, *alle* may be separated from the
pronoun, in which case it has slightly less emphasis:

Sie alle sind gekommen ⎫	
Sie sind alle gekommen ⎭	*They have all come*
Sie hat uns alle beleidigt	*She insulted us all*
Ich habe mit ihnen allen gesprochen	*I have spoken to all of them*
Das ist unser aller Hoffnung	*That is the hope of all of us*

(e) A preceding uninflected *all* is commonly used with the demonstrative pronouns *das* and *dies(es)*
Alternatively, inflected *alles* may precede or follow the demonstrative or,
with less emphasis, be separated from it:

Ich habe all das/alles das/das alles ⎫	
schon gesehen ⎭	*I've already seen all that*
Das habe ich alles schon gesehen	
Ich bin mit all dem/dem allen/	*I agree to all that*
allem dem einverstanden	
Mit all diesem werde ich nicht fertig	*I can't cope with all this*

NB: Note the inflection of a following *all-* in the dative singular, where the combinations
dem allen, diesem allen are nowadays at least as common as *dem allem, diesem allem*.

(f) An inflected *all-* may be used in conjunction with a noun, either immediately following it or separated from it
This usage is restricted to the nominative and accusative singular feminine
and neuter, mainly in colloquial spoken German, and the plural, where it

is found in all registers:

Das Brot ist alles trocken	Ich habe die Milch alle verschüttet.
Die Kinder spielen alle im Garten.	Die Semmeln sind alle trocken.

Singular *alles* is often used with a plural noun after the verb *sein* in the sense 'nothing but', e.g. *Das sind alles Lügen.*

(g) The use of *ganz* for English 'all'

In practice, the most idiomatic equivalent of English *all*, particularly with singular nouns, is given by the German adjective *ganz*, which has a much wider range of usage than English 'whole'. Thus, for English 'all my money', one may find the semantically equivalent phrases *mein ganzes Geld* and *all mein Geld*, with the former alternative being rather more frequent.

Cf. also:

Der ganze Wein war schlecht	*All the wine was bad*
diese ganze Unsicherheit	*all this uncertainty*
mit seiner ganzen jugendlichen Energie	*with all his youthful energy*

With collective nouns, time expressions and the names of continents, countries and towns, *ganz* is the only possible equivalent in German for English 'all':

Die ganze Familie kommt	*All of the family is coming*
in der ganzen Schule	*in all of the school*
den ganzen Tag (lang)	*all day*
Der ganze Januar war kalt	*All January it was cold*
ganz Europa, ganz Schweden, ganz München	*all (of) Europe, all (of) Sweden, all (of) Munich*
in der ganzen Schweiz	*in all of Switzerland*

NB: The use of *ganz* with a plural noun is purely colloquial, e.g. *Die ganzen Fenster waren nach dem Sturm kaputt.* In these cases, however, *sämtliche* is an acceptable and common alternative in writing, cf. 5.5.23, e.g. *Sämtliche Fenster waren nach dem Sturm kaputt.*

(h) 'all' with a relative pronoun, i.e. 'all of which'.

If possible, inflected *alles* or an appropriate form of *ganz* is used in the relative clause. Otherwise, especially in the masculine singular and the dative, a paraphrase must be used:

das Brot, das er alles gegessen hat	*the bread, all of which he has eaten*
die Stadt, deren Kirchen ich alle kenne	*the city, all of whose churches I know*
der Park, den Sie jetzt ganz gesehen haben	*the park, all of which you have now seen*
mein Freund, dessen ganzes Geld gut angelegt ist	*my friend, all of whose money is well invested*
der Wein, der ohne Ausnahme gut ist	*the wine, all of which is good*
der Garten, in dem überall Unkraut wächst	*the garden, in all parts of which there are weeds growing*

(j) Other miscellaneous uses of *all-*

(i) *alles* is often used to emphasize number with the interrogatives *wer* and *was*, cf.5.3.3d., e.g.:

Wer kommt denn alles?   Was hast du dort alles gekauft?

(ii) In the regional colloquial speech of the west and south-west, *all(e)s* (usually spelled *als*, although it is infrequently seen in writing) is used to emphasize the continuous nature of an action (= English 'keep on doing sth'.):

Er hat als geflucht   *He kept on cursing*

(iii) In colloquial North German speech *alle* is used in the sense of 'all gone', e.g.:

Die Butter ist jetzt alle.   Meine Geduld ist alle.

(iv) *alle* is compounded with the demonstrative pronoun in *bei alledem* 'for all that', *trotz alledem* 'in spite of all that'.

(v) *alles* is frequently combined with an adjective used as a noun, cf. 6.4.6. e.g. *alles Wichtige* 'all (the) important things'.

5.5.2 *ander* 'other'

ander is in most cases used as a normal adjective, but it has a number of special forms and uses which resemble those of a determiner or pronoun. When it has the ending *-e, -er* or *-es*, the *-e-* of the stem may be dropped, e.g. *and(e)re, and (e)rer, and (e)res*. With the other endings, the *-e-* of the ending or (less often) the *-e-* of the stem may be dropped, e.g. *ander(e)m, ander(e)n* (less common: *andrem, andren*). When used without a following noun, i.e. as a noun or pronoun, it differs from other adjectives in never being spelled with a capital letter:

der and(e)re Student	*the other student*
mein anderes Pferd	*my other horse*
der and(e)re	*the other one*
irgendein and(e)rer	*some/any other one*
kein and(e)rer als Müller	*no other than Müller*
die drei anderen	*the three others*
alle anderen	*all the others*
alles and(e)re	*everything else*

NB: (i) 'another cup of tea' = *noch eine Tasse Tee*
       (ii) For the adverb *anders* 'else', cf 7.4.2.

When *ander* is used without a preceding determiner, a following adjective has the same endings as those of *ander*, except that *-en* is the norm in the dative singular masculine and neuter, e.g.:

andere italienische Maler   aus anderem wertvollen Material

5.5.3 *beide* 'both' may be used as a determiner or a pronoun

In either case it has the same ending as the plural of *dieser*, cf. 5.1.2. It may also be used with the definite article (or another determiner), when it has the endings of an adjective and often corresponds to English 'two'.

Ich habe beide Bücher gekauft	*I bought both books*
Beide Brüder sind gekommen	*Both the brothers came*
Seine beiden Brüder sind gekommen⎤	
Seine Brüder sind beide gekommen ⎦	*Both his/His two brothers came*
Beide sind gekommen	*Both came*
Die beiden Brüder sind gekommen	*The two brothers came*
Welcher von (den) beiden gefällt dir?	*Which of the two do you like?*

NB: *beide*, used as a pronoun, may be strengthed by *alle:*
Alle beide sind gekommen　　　　　*The two of them came*

(a) Used with a personal pronoun, *beide* usually has the endings of *dieser*, e.g.:

wir beide, sie beide, von euch beiden, unser beider, etc.

However, *ihr beiden* is usual in isolation, e.g. *Ihr beiden, wollt ihr schon mitkommen?* Within a clause *ihr beide* or *ihr beiden* are alternatives, e.g. *Wollt ihr beide(n) schon mitkommen?*
　　wir beiden is a possible, if less frequent alternative to *wir beide* if used in isolation, but it is used if a noun follows, e.g. *wir beiden Freunde.*
　　If *beide* is separated from the pronoun, only the form in *-e* is possible, e.g.:

Wir wollen beide schon mitkommen.　　Ihr wollt wohl beide mitkommen, oder?

NB: Beide haben sie recht *They're both right.*

(b) The neuter singular *beides* is often used as a collective pronoun to refer back to two things:

Sie hatte einen Ring und eine Uhr und hat nun beides verloren	*She had a ring and a watch and now she has lost both*
Sprechen Sie Deutsch oder Englisch? – Beides	*Do you speak German or English? – Both*
Ich will beides tun	*I am going to do both things*
Beides ist möglich	*Either is possible*
Das Hotel und die Landschaft: beides gefällt mir	*The hotel and the scenery: I like both*

NB: (i) If *beides* is used as a subject of *sein*, either a singular or plural verb may be used:
Das Hotel und die Landschaft:　　*The hotel and the scenery: both*
　　beides ist/sind schön　　　　　*are lovely*

(ii) The use of *beides* to refer to people is purely colloquial, e.g.:
Ich habe mit den Brüdern Schmid zu Mittag gegessen. Beides ist/sind (written: Beide sind) Vegetarier.

(c) Miscellaneous uses of *beide* and other equivalents of 'both':

Einer von beiden könnte uns helfen	*One/Either of the two could help us*
An beiden Enden des Ganges hängt ein Bild	*At either end of the corridor there is a picture*
in beiden Fällen	*in either case*
Keiner von beiden ist gekommen	*Neither of them came*
Sowohl seine Frau als (auch) seine Tochter sind krank	*Both his wife and his daughter are sick*

5.5.4 *dergleichen* 'suchlike' and *desgleichen* 'likewise'

These do not decline.

(a) *dergleichen* is used with a following noun or as a pronoun meaning 'suchlike', 'of such a kind', e.g. *dergleichen Behauptungen* 'suchlike assertions', *nichts dergleichen* 'nothing of the kind', *und dergleichen mehr* (abbrev.: *u.dgl.m.*) 'and so forth':

Er hatte ein langes Messer oder dergleichen in der Tasche	*He had a long knife or something of the kind in his pocket*

(b) *desgleichen* is most commonly used in modern German as an adverb (= 'likewise', 'similarly'):

Zunächst wurden die Nummern eins bis zwölf aufgerufen, desgleichen einige höchst dringende Fälle	*The numbers one to twelve were called first, likewise a few really urgent cases*

5.5.5 *einer* 'one'

(a) *einer*, when used as a pronoun, declines like *dieser* or the possessive pronouns, cf. 5.1.2 and 5.2.3, i.e.:

	Masc.	Fem.	Neut.
Nom.	einer	eine	eines
Acc.	einen	eine	eines
Gen.	eines	einer	eines
Dat.	einem	einer	einem

NOTE CAREFULLY the difference from the declension of the indefinite article in the nominative singular masculine and the nominative/accusative singular neuter, cf. 4.1.2.

NB: (i) The neuter *eines* is usually pronounced, and may be written as *eins*.
(ii) The genitive is scarcely used (and Germans tend to make mistakes when they try to use it, cf. DUDEN 1985:204–5); in practice the paraphrase with *von*, cf. 2.4, is preferable. For the use of *eins* as a numeral, see 9.1.3.

(b) As a pronoun *einer* corresponds to English 'one', e.g.:

einer der Männer, eine der Frauen, eines der Kinder	*one of the men, one of the women one of the children*
einer, der ihn kannte	*a person/someone who knew him*
Ein Fenster war offen und ein(e)s war zu	*One window was open and one was shut*
Ich sprach mit einer der Damen	*I spoke to one of the ladies*
Sie kennt alle Hotels in dieser Stadt und wird Ihnen eines empfehlen können	*She knows all the hotels in this town and will be able to recommend one to you*
die Empfehlung von einem (elev.: eines) ihrer Bekannten	*the recommendation of one of her acquaintances*

NB: Unstressed *einer* has the negative *keiner*, cf. 5.5.16, stressed *einer* has the negative *nicht einer*, cf. *ich habe keinen gesehen* 'I haven't seen one', *Ich habe nicht einen gesehen* 'I haven't seen <u>one</u>'.

(c) *einer* is often used in the sense of 'someone, 'anyone':

Einer muß es getan haben	*Someone must have done it*
Mit einem wie dem will ich nichts zu tun haben	*I don't want anything to do with anyone like that*
Da kam einer durch die Glastür	*Then someone came through the glass door*

This is particularly common in the spoken language. It is often equivalent to *jemand*, cf. 5.5.15. although this more clearly refers to an indefinite 'somebody' whose identity is quite unknown, cf. Engel (1988:668–9). *jemand* is also generally more polite, where *einer* can convey a rather rude tone, particularly in the feminine, cf. *da war gerade eine mit sechs Kindern*. In colloquial German, *wer* is also used for 'someone', cf. 5.5.27. As a substitute for *man*, nominative *einer* is restricted to colloquial speech, cf. *und das soll einer wissen!* but the other masculine case forms of *einer* are quite normally used for those which *man* lacks, cf. 5.5.18.

(d) *ein-* may be used as an adjective with the definite article, demonstratives or possessives
It then has the 'weak' adjective endings:

Der eine deutsche Tourist beschwerte sich	*The one German tourist complained*
Das eine Gute ist, daß er Mut hat	*The one good thing is that he has courage*
das eine, das ich brauche	*the one thing I need*
Mein einer Sohn ist gestorben (coll.)	*One of my sons has died*
Mit dieser einen Hand konnte er Wunder tun	*With this one hand he could do wonders*

Particularly common is *der eine* linked to a following *der andere*, corresponding to English '(the) one . . . the other', etc. Note, though, that the definite article is usually present in German, whereas it may be lacking in English, and that the plural may occur, in the meaning 'some':

Mit der einen Hand wehrte er sich und mit der anderen suchte er in der Tasche nach seinem Schlüssel	*He defended himself with one hand, and with the other he hunted in his pocket for his key*

Das eine Buch habe ich gelesen, das andere aber noch nicht	*I've read one of the books, but not the other one yet*
Die einen sangen, die anderen spielten	*Some were singing, others were playing*

(e) Some idiomatic uses of *einer* and equivalents of English 'one':

Das ist einer!	*He's quite a lad*
Du bist mir einer!	*You're a nice one!*
Eins wollte ich noch sagen	*There's one more thing I wanted to say*
Trinken wir noch eins?	*Shall we have another?*
einen heben	*to have a drink*
Ich habe ihm eine gegeben/geklebt	*I gave him one* (i.e. a clout)
Es ist mir alles eins	*It's all the same to me*
Es läuft auf eins hinaus	*It all comes to the same*
Er redet in einem fort	*He talks without stopping*
Ich bin keiner, der sich leicht beklagt	*I'm not one to complain a lot*
Er ist mein einziger Freund	*He is my one* (i.e. only) *friend*

5.5.6 *ein wenig, ein bißchen* 'a little'

(a) *ein wenig* corresponds to English 'a little'

The *ein* is invariable, i.e. it does not decline, and the paraphrase with *von* is used rather than a genitive:

Ich hatte noch ein wenig deutsches Geld	*I still had a little German money*
Der Zug hatte sich ein wenig verspätet	*The train had got a little late*
Der Saal war ein wenig ruhiger geworden	*The room had become a little more quiet*
mit ein wenig weiblicher Eitelkeit	*with a little female vanity*

(b) *ein bißchen* is in many cases, as in all the above examples, a possible substitute for *ein wenig*

However, it is rather more colloquial, as is its south German variant *ein bisse(r)l*. However, it may, optionally, be declined in the dative singular, e.g. *mit ein(em) bißchen Geld,* and always is when used as a pronoun, e.g. *Mit einem bißchen wäre ich schon zufrieden.* It also has a wider range of uses than *ein wenig* in that it may be used with a preceding adjective:

ein winziges bißchen Käse	*a tiny little bit of cheese*
mit einem ganz kleinen bißchen gesunden Verstand	*with a very little bit of common sense*

(c) *bißchen* may also be used with a demonstrative, a possessive or *kein*:

mit dem bißchen Verstand, den sie hat	*with that little sense she has*
mit ihrem bißchen Talent	*with her bit of talent*
Er hat kein bißchen Humor	*He has not got the least sense of humour*

5.5.7 *ein paar* 'a few'

ein paar is invariable. A paraphrase with *von* is used rather than a genitive. It is very close in meaning to *einige*, cf. 5.5.8, but is rather more colloquial. The *ein* may be replaced by another determiner, which is then declined. Such combinations often have a rather pejorative undertone:

Ich habe ein paar gute Bücher gelesen	*I've read a few good books*
Ein paar Flaschen Wein haben wir noch im Keller	*We've still got a few bottles of wine in the cellar*
Willst du ein paar haben?	*Do you want a few?*
mit der Hilfe von ein paar alten Freunden	*with the help of a few old friends*
Was soll ich mit den paar Mark anfangen?	*What am I supposed to do with these paltry few marks?*
der Wert meiner paar Möbel	*the value of my few bits of furniture*
Die Straßenbahn kommt alle paar Minuten	*The tram comes every few minutes*

NB: *ein paar* 'a few' is not to be confused with *ein Paar* 'a pair' cf. *ein paar Schuhe* 'a few shoes' BUT *ein Paar Schuhe* 'a pair of shoes'.

5.5.8 *einiger, einige* 'some'

(a) *einig-* refers to a limited amount or number

It corresponds most closely to English unstressed 'some' (or 'a few', as it is very close in meaning to *ein paar*, which is rather more colloquial, cf. 5.5.7). It declines like *dieser*, except that the genitive singular masculine and neuter form (which is little used) is *einigen*.

(b) The use of the singular *einiger* is rather restricted

The reason is that there the most frequent German equivalents of English unstressed *some* are *etwas*, cf. 5.5.10, or, most commonly, the zero article, cf. 4.9.7, e.g. *Ich habe (etwas) Butter gekauft* 'I have bought some butter'. Where *einig-* occurs in the singular it tends to imply a rather unusual or unexpected quantity and hence often comes close to English 'no little'. It is most frequent with mass and abstract nouns (especially *Entfernung* and *Zeit*), adjectives used as nouns, and collectives:

Diese Schlangen, die ihr Gift spucken, zielen bis drei Meter weit noch mit einiger Treffsicherheit *(Grzimek)*	*These snakes which spit their venom can aim up to three metres away with some degree of accuracy*
mit einigem Glück	*with some degree of luck*
bei einigem guten Willen (*Th. Mann*)	*with a certain degree of good will*
vor ihm in einiger Entfernung	*some distance in front of him*
vor einiger Zeit schon	*some time ago now*
Er hat einiges Nützliche getan	*He did some useful things*
Inzwischen macht er das auch mit einigem Geschick	*Since then he has learnt to do it with no little skill*
nach einigem Überlegen	*after some consideration*

Although *einig-* is chiefly used as a determiner in the singular, the neuter singular *einiges* occurs as a collective indefinite pronoun:

Ich habe noch einiges zu tun	*I've still got a few things to do*
einiges davon	*some of it*

(c) The plural *einige* is widely used, both as a determiner and a pronoun:

In der Stadt gibt es einige Friseure	*There are a few hairdressers in the town*
Sie wollte einige Ansichtskarten von Rothenburg kaufen	*She wanted to buy some postcards of Rothenburg*
unter Verwendung einiger technischer Mittel	*by using some technical methods*
Einige mußten stehen	*Some/A few had to stand*
Sie hat schon einige mitgebracht	*She's already brought some/a few*

NB: (i) Referring to a quantity of articles, German frequently has a zero article where English uses unstressed *some*, e.g., as a common alternative to the above example: *Sie wollte Ansichtskarten von Rothenburg kaufen.*
(ii) *einige* is often used with numerals to mean 'a few', e.g. *einige tausend Bücher* 'a few thousand books'.

5.5.9 *etliche* 'some'

etliche is very similar in meaning to *einige*. However, it typically implies 'more than the expected number'. Hence it can approach the meaning of English 'several' or 'a number of'. It is used almost exclusively in the plural, as a determiner (less commonly as a pronoun), and it declines like *dieser*. It is by no means as obsolete or old-fashioned as some authorities maintain (e.g. Engel 1988:543), and is quite widely used, with its special meaning, in both spoken and written German:

Warum ist die Bahn so unpünktlich geworden? Da gibt es etliche Ursachen *(Spiegel)*	*Why have the railways become so unpunctual? There are a number of reasons for this.*
Etliche dieser Stücke sind auch für Anfänger relativ leicht zu bewältigen *(SWF)*	*Some/A number of these pieces are fairly easy to manage, even for beginners*

5.5.10 *etwas* 'something, anything'

etwas is used as an indefinite pronoun, to qualify nouns and as an adverb. It has no case forms and is not used in genitive constructions, the paraphrase with *von* being used if necessary:

(a) As an indefinite pronoun, *etwas* corresponds to English 'something' or 'anything'

In this use, it is commonly reduced to *was* in colloquial speech unless it occupies first place in the sentence:

Etwas störte mich	*Something disturbed me*
Ich habe etwas (coll.:was) für Sie	*I've got something for you*
Hast du etwas (coll.:was) gesagt?	*Did you say anything?*

It is very frequently used with a following adjective used as a noun, which has the strong endings, cf. 6.4.6.:

etwas (coll.:was) ganz Neues	*something quite new*
Er hat von etwas ganz Neuem gesprochen	*He spoke of something quite new*

It is common with *von* in partitive constructions, i.e. 'some (of)', although it may be omitted, as in the first example:

Ich möchte (etwas) von diesem Kuchen	*I would like some of this cake*
etwas von seinem Geld	*some of his money*

(b) Qualifying a noun, *etwas* has the sense of 'some, 'any' or a 'little'
It is used chiefly with mass and abstract nouns in the singular. Note that, as an equivalent to unstressed English 'some' or 'any', German very commonly uses the zero article as an alternative to *etwas*, as the first two examples show (cf. also 4.9.5). It would be equally possible to omit *etwas* in the other examples given below:

Ich brauche (etwas) frisches Fleisch	*I need some fresh meat*
Er hat kaum (etwas) Geld	*He has hardly any money*
Bringen Sie mir bitte etwas Brot	*Please bring me some bread*
Sie muß etwas Geduld haben	*She needs a little patience*
Hast du etwas Milch für mich?	*Have you got any/a little milk for me?*
Etwas mehr Aufmerksamkeit wäre nützlich gewesen	*A little more attentiveness would have been useful*
der Genuß von etwas frischem Obst	*the eating of some fresh fruit*

(c) In adverbial use, *etwas* means 'somewhat', 'a bit':

Er ist etwas nervös	*He is somewhat/rather/a bit nervous*
Es geht ihm etwas besser	*He is somewhat/ a bit better*
Er zögerte etwas	*He hesitated somewhat/ a bit*

5.5.11 *irgend*

(a) The principal use of *irgend* is to emphasize indefiniteness
It occurs in combination with a large number of indefinite pronouns, adverbs and determiners, giving them the sense of 'some . . . or other' or 'any . . . at all'. It is written as a separate word with *etwas*, *jemand* and *solche*, but compounded with other words, e.g. *irgendwer*, *irgendwas*, *irgendeiner*, *irgendwo*, etc.

(b) *irgend* is compounded with interrogative adverbs to form indefinite adverbs,

i.e. *irgendwann* 'sometime or other, any time', *irgendwie* 'somehow, anyhow', *irgendwo* 'somewhere, anywhere', *irgendwohin* '(to) somewhere, anywhere', *irgendwoher* 'from somewhere, anywhere':

Du mußt es irgendwie machen	*You'll have to do it somehow*
Er fährt heute nachmittag irgendwohin	*He's going somewhere this afternoon*
Gehst du heute abend irgendwohin?	*Are you going anywhere tonight?*

(c) Used with *einer, jemand* or *wer* (= 'somebody, anybody') and *(et)was* (= 'something, anything') *irgend* stresses indefiniteness

In practice *irgendeiner* and *irgendwer* are more frequent in the meaning 'somebody, anybody' than simple *einer* and *wer*, cf. 5.5.5 and 5.5.27:

Irgendwann wurden von irgendwem diese . . . Briefe aus dem Kasten genommen (*Böll*)	*At some time or other someone or other took these letters out of the letter box*
Versteht er irgend etwas vom Wein?	*Does he know anything at all about wine?*
irgend so etwas	*something/anything like this*
Irgendeiner soll es gesagt haben	*Someone or other is supposed to have said it*
Wollen Sie mit irgend jemandem sprechen?	*Do you want to talk to somebody?*

Compare: *Wollen Sie mit jemanden sprechen?* 'somebody in particular'

Hat denn irgend jemand angerufen?	*Did anybody phone?*

NB: With prepositions a compound form, using *irgend*, of the prepositional adverb with *wo(r)-*, is sometimes heard in spoken North German in place of *irgend etwas* with a preposition:

Ich habe mich irgendworan/ an irgend etwas gestoßen	*I knocked against something or other*

(d) *irgendein(er)* and *irgendwelcher* correspond to 'some (or other), any (whatsoever)', frequently with the sense of 'no matter which/who'

They may be used as determiners or pronouns:

(i) *irgendein*, when used as a determiner, has the endings of the indefinite article, cf. 4.1.2. It is used in the singular with countable nouns (i.e. those which can normally be used with an indefinite article):

Er zeigte mir irgendeine Broschüre	*He showed me some brochure or other*
Hat er irgendeine Bemerkung gemacht?	*Did he make any remark?*
Irgendein anderer antwortete	*Someone else answered*

(ii) The pronoun *irgendeiner*, which declines like *einer*, cf. 5.5.5, only has singular forms. It cannot be used to refer to mass or abstract nouns, i.e. those which cannot be used with an indefinite article. The masculine and feminine are used in the sense of 'somebody, anybody':

Irgendeiner muß dich gesehen haben	*Someone or other must have seen you*
Wenn du wirklich einen neuen Tisch suchst, mußt du hier im Geschäft irgendeinen gesehen haben, der dir gefällt	*If you're really looking for a new table, you must have seen one here in the shop which you like*
Ich habe ein paar Bücher über Berlin. Sie können irgendeins ausleihen	*I've got a few books on Berlin. You can borrow any one you like*
Ich suche einen Reiseführer. Können Sie mir irgendeinen empfehlen?	*I'm looking for a travel guide. Can you recommend one to me?*

(iii) *irgendwelcher*, which declines like *dieser*, is used as a determiner in the singular with mass and abstract nouns and in the plural. The genitive is rare in the singular:

Er zeigte mir irgendwelche neue Bücher	*He showed me some new books or other*
der Besuch irgendwelcher Verwandten	*the visit of some relatives or other*
irgendwelches mageres Vieh	*some lean cattle or other*
Haben wir irgendwelchen Käse im Haus?	*Have we got some cheese of any sort in the house?*
Wenn ich irgendwelche Angst hätte . . .	*If I felt any fear*
ohne irgendwelche Schwierigkeit	*without any difficulty at all*
die Folge von irgendwelchem unnötigen Zögern	*the consequence of some/any unnecessary hesitation*

Colloquially, it is often used for *irgendein*, e.g. *Er hat mir irgendwelche Broschüre gezeigt.*

(e) *irgend so ein* (plural: *irgend solche*) corresponds to English 'one/some of those', 'any/some such'
It usually has a pejorative tone:

Wer war es? – Es war irgend so ein Vertreter für Waschmittel	*Who was it? – It was one of those men who sell washing powder*
Er machte irgend solche komische Bemerkungen	*He made some such odd remarks*

(f) *irgend* may be used as an independent adverb with the sense of *irgendwie*,
i.e. 'somehow, anyhow, in some way':

Wenn es irgend geht, wäre ich froh	*If it's somehow possible, I would be happy*
wenn irgend möglich	*if at all possible*
Such ihn doch auf, wenn du irgend kannst	*Look him up, if at all possible*

5.5.12 *jeder* 'each, every'

(a) *jeder* is only used in the singular as a determiner (= English 'each, every') or a pronoun (= English 'everyone, everybody')
It declines like *dieser*, but *jeden* is as frequent as *jedes* in the genitive singular masculine and neuter if the following noun has the ending *-(e)s*, e.g. *am Ende jeden/jedes Abschnitts*. Pronominal *jeder* is not used in the genitive:

Sie hat jedem Kind einen Teddybären gegeben	*She gave each child a teddybear*
nach jedem solchen Versuch	*after each such attempt*
Er kam jeden Tag zur selben Zeit	*He came every day at the same time*
Leute in jedem Alter	*people of all ages*
In diesem kleinen Ort kennt jeder jeden	*In this little place everyone knows everybody else*

jeder can often have an individualizing sense (i.e. 'no matter which/who'), corresponding to English 'any':

Das weiß doch jeder gebildete Bürger	*Any/Every educated citizen knows that, though*
Jeder Versuch wäre zum Scheitern verurteilt	*Any/Every attempt would be doomed to failure*

NB: The neuter *jedes* can be used to refer back to both sexes:

Seine Eltern waren sehr tüchtig, jedes auf seine Weise	*His parents were very able, each in their own way*

(b) The combination *ein jeder* is more emphatic than *jeder*
It is used chiefly as a pronoun and is particularly frequent in the individualizing sense of stressed 'any', i.e. 'no matter which/who'. It usefully substitutes for the missing genitive of the pronoun *jeder*. In this combination, *jeder* has the endings of an adjective:

Ein jeder wollte was sagen	*Everyone wanted to say something*
Das könnte doch ein jeder machen	*Everybody/Anybody (at all) could do that*
Das kannst du doch nicht einem jeden erzählen	*But you can't tell that to just anybody*
Die Wünsche eines jeden wurden berücksichtigt	*The wishes of every individual were taken into account*

5.5.13 *jedermann* 'everybody, everyone'

jedermann is restricted in modern German to elevated, formal registers and set phrases. Its meaning is the same as that of *jeder*, which is much more commonly used. Its only case form is the genitive *jedermanns*:

Jedermann wußte, daß ihr Sohn im Krieg gefallen war	*Everyone knew that her son had fallen in the war*
Das ist nicht jedermanns Sache	*That's not everyone's cup of tea*

5.5.14 *jedweder, jeglicher* 'each, every'

jedweder and *jeglicher* are both alternatives to *jeder* as determiners or pronouns. Both are declined in the same way as *jeder* and are restricted largely to formal written language.

(a) *jedweder* is rather more emphatic than *jeder*
Though by no means totally obsolete, it has a rather old-fashioned ring and is used sparingly, even in very formal registers:

Er weist seine Sekundanten an, auf
    jedwede Bedingung der Gegenseite
    einzugehen

He instructs his seconds to agree to each and every condition of his opponent

(b) *jeglicher* stresses the individuality of the items in question and is thus most often used in the sense of stressed *any* (i.e. 'no matter who/what')
It is thus frequent in negative expressions and, unlike *jeder*, can also be used in the plural:

Verständlichkeitsstörungen, die
    jegliche Deutung nahezu jeglicher
    Szene zulassen *(HA)*
Ohne jegliches Gefühl für Schuld und
    Versagen drängten diejenigen wieder
    in Machtstellungen, die . . . *(Zeit)*

ohne jegliche Sicherheiten

lapses in intelligibility which allow any interpretation of almost every scene
Without any feelings of guilt or failure those people forced themselves again into positions of power who . . .

without any securities at all

5.5.15 *jemand* 'somebody, someone', *niemand* 'nobody, no-one'

(a) The indefinite pronouns *jemand* 'someone, somebody' and *niemand* 'no one, nobody' have the following declension:

Nom.	jemand	niemand
Acc.	jemand(en)	niemand(en)
Gen.	jemand(e)s	niemand(e)s
Dat.	jemand(em)	niemand(em)

In the accusative and dative, the endlingless forms are more common in both spoken and written German:

Ich habe niemand (less frequent: niemanden) gesehen
Ich habe jemand (less frequent: jemandem) das Paket gegeben

The genitive forms tend to be avoided by paraphrasing, e.g.:

Hat nicht jemand diese Aktentasche liegenlassen *rather than*: Ist das nicht jemands Aktentasche

NB: (i) In spoken German *einer* and *wer* are common alternatives to *jemand*, cf. 5.5.5 and 5.5.27. The use of *keiner* for *niemand*, though very frequent in colloquial speech, is regarded as substandard by many Germans.
(ii) The indefiniteness of *jemand* may be emphasized by combining it with *irgend*, cf. 5.5.11c.

(b) When *jemand* and *niemand* are used with a following adjective they normally do not have endings in the accusative and dative
The adjective is considered a noun and spelled with a capital letter (except *ander*, cf. 5.5.2). It usually has the ending *-es* in the nominative and *-es* or *-en* in the accusative, but *-em* in the dative, e.g.:

Jemand Fremdes ist gekommen   Ich habe jemand Fremdes/-en gesehen
Ich habe mit jemand Fremdem gesprochen

Some south German usage prefers the ending *-er* in the nominative, e.g. *jemand Bekannter*, but this is not regarded as good practice in standard German.

5.5.16   *kein, keiner* 'no, not . . . any, none'

(a) *kein* is the negative form of the indefinite article
It has a plural form and delines like *mein*, cf. 5.2.2. It is used primarily where the corresponding positive sentence has an indefinite or a zero article, corresponding to English 'not a', 'not . . . any' or 'no':

Es war ein angenehmer Anblick	Es war kein angenehmer Anblick
Kennst du einen Arzt?	Kennst du keinen Arzt?
Wir haben frische Brötchen	Wir haben keine frischen Brötchen
Ich habe Geld	Ich habe kein Geld

(b) *kein* or *nicht* in negation?
In some constructions it is not always an easy matter to decide whether to use *kein* or *nicht*, and the use of *nicht ein* instead of *kein* is a typical English learners' mistake in German. Some tricky cases are dealt with below:
(i) Phrasal verbs with nouns, e.g. *Atem holen, sich Mühe geben, Freude empfinden* and all those with *haben*, e.g. *Angst, Durst, Hunger haben*, etc. are generally negated with *kein*, e.g.:

Er hat sich keine Mühe gegeben	Ich habe keinen Durst
Dabei hat er keine Freude empfunden	Sie hatten keine Angst

(ii) However, *nicht* is used if the noun is felt to be the equivalent of a separable prefix, as it is so closely connected with the verb, cf. 22.5.4c, e.g.:

Er spielt nicht Klavier   Sie läuft nicht Schi   Sie haben in Berlin nicht Wurzel gefaßt
Er hält nicht Wort   Er kann nicht Auto fahren   Sie schreibt nicht Maschine
Similarly: *Schritt fahren, Gefahr laufen*, etc.

(iii) In a few cases either *kein* or *nicht* is possible, e.g.:

Er spricht kein/nicht Deutsch
Sie hat keinen/nicht Abschied von ihm genommen
Wir haben heute keinen/nicht Tennis gespielt

This is also general for phrasal verbs with *nehmen*, e.g.

Er hat keine/nicht Rücksicht auf mich genommen
Sie wollen keine/nicht Rache nehmen

(iv) *kein* or *nicht* are alternatives in the follolwing constructions:
– with the verbs *sein* and *werden*:

Er ist/wird kein/nicht Lehrer
Es ist/wird noch kein/nicht Sommer

NB: If *ein* would be used in the positive sentence, cf. 4.9.2, then *kein* is used for the
    negative, e.g.:
    Er ist ein Schauspieler   Er ist kein Schauspieler

– with prepositional phrases:

Sie geht in keine/nicht in eine Dorfschule
Ich fahre zu keinem/nicht zu einem Fest
Ich habe es mit keinem/nicht mit einem Bleistift geschrieben

In these cases, the negation with *nicht* is the general one, whilst that with
kein has to be understood as negating only the following noun. Thus *Sie
geht in keine Dorfschule* has the sense of 'It's not a <u>village</u> school she's
going to'.

(v) *nicht ein* is more usual than *kein* after *wenn* 'if':

Man hätte ihn kaum bemerkt, wenn ihm nicht ein Schnurrbart etwas
    Distinguiertes verliehen hätte

(vi) *nicht ein* and *kein* are alternatives in constructions with *sondern*:

Das ist nicht ein/kein Roman, sondern eine Biographie

(vii) *nicht ein* is used if *ein* is stressed, i.e. 'not one (single)':

Nicht <u>ein</u> Junge wußte die Antwort   *Not one (single) boy knew the answer*

(c) Some idiomatic uses of *kein* as a determiner:

Sie ist noch keine zehn Jahre alt   *She's not yet ten years old*
Es ist noch keine acht Uhr   *It's not eight o'clock yet*
keine zwei Stunden vor meiner Abreise   *Within two hours of my departure*
Es ist noch keine fünf Minuten her   *It is less than five minutes ago*
Sie ist schließlich kein Kind mehr   *After all, she's no longer a child*
keine Zeitungen und auch keine Bücher   *no newspapers or books*

(d) *keiner* 'none, not . . . any' is the pronominal form of *kein*
It declines like *einer*, with, similarly, the endings *-er* in the nominative
singular masculine and *-(e)s* in the nominative/accusative singular neuter,
cf. 5.5.5. In the plural it has the same endings as *dieser*. It is rarely used in

the genitive, and then only in the feminine singular or the plural:

Keiner im Dorf wollte was sagen   Keiner von uns hat es gewußt
Haben Sie einen Farbfernseher? – Nein, wir haben keinen
In keinem dieser neuen Häuser möchte ich wohnen
keins von beiden *neither of them*

NB: (i) The neuter form *kein(e)s* is used to refer to people of different sex:
Ich fragte meine Eltern, aber keins (von beiden) wußte es.
(ii) The use of the masculine singular form *keiner* in isolation instead of *niemand* in the meaning 'no one, nobody' is regarded as substandard by many Germans, although it is very frequent in the everyday spoken register.

5.5.17 *lauter* 'only, nothing but'

lauter is indeclinable. It is used only as a determiner before nouns:

Dort lag lauter Eis und Schnee   *Nothing but ice and snow lay there*
Es kamen lauter junge Leute   *Only young people came*
Er hat lauter solchen Unsinn geredet   *He only talked rubbish*
                                               like that

5.5.18 *man* 'one'

man is an indefinite pronoun. It corresponds to English 'one', but, unlike that, it is not restricted to formal registers or elevated speech. It thus corresponds to the general use of 'you' in spoken English, or, frequently, to 'they' or 'people'. Indeed, the overuse of *Leute* in German, where *man* would be appropriate, is very characteristic of English learners' German. It is also often used where English would most naturally use a general passive construction, e.g. *Man sagt* 'It is said', cf. 15.4.1.

The form *man* is only used in the nominative; in the accusative and dative *einen* and *einem* are used. It correlates where necessary with the possessive *sein* and the reflexive *sich*.

Als man sich zum Abendessen setzte,   *When they/we sat down to dinner*
    fehlte der alte Herr   *the old gentleman was missing*
Man weiß nie, ob er einen erkannt hat   *You never know whether he has*
                                               recognized you
So leid es einem tut, man muß   *However much you regret it, you*
    manchmal hart sein   *have to be hard sometimes*
Man sollte seinen Freunden helfen   *One ought to help one's friends*
Hier spricht man meistens Plattdeutsch   *People mainly speak Low German here*
    unter sich   *amongst themselves*

NB: (i) In standard German, *man* should never be referred back to with *er*, e.g. *Wenn man müde ist, muß man* (NOT: *er*) *sich setzen*.
(ii) The use of *einer* for *man* in the nominative singular is restricted to colloquial registers, cf. 5.5.5.
(iii) *man* is sometimes used, for reasons of politeness, to refer to the speaker, e.g. *Darf man fragen, wohin Sie fahren?* In certain situations this can acquire a note of sarcasm, and this is always so when the listener is meant, e.g. *Hat man schon wieder zu tief ins Glas geguckt?*

5.5.19 *manch* 'some, many a'

(a) *manch* always has the rather special sense of stressed 'some',
i.e. 'a fair number, but by no means all'. This is sometimes given in English by 'many a' and can in certain contexts come close to the sense of English 'several'. In formal registers *manch*, as a determiner or a pronoun, can be strengthened by a preceding *so* or *gar*: *so mancher Mann* 'so many a man', *gar manch ein König* 'so many a king'.

manch has a number of alternative forms, which are detailed in the sections below.

(b) As a determiner, *manch* is most often used in the inflected form,
i.e. with the endings of *dieser*. In the genitive singular masculine and neuter, the form *manchen* is occasionally found besides the more frequent *manches* if the following noun has the ending -*(e)s*.

Manch may be used in the singular or the plural. Although it could be said that the singular form (like English 'many a') puts more emphasis on the individual items, whilst the plural (like English stressed 'some') stresses the collectivity, in practical terms the difference between, for example, *mancher schöne Tag* and *manche schöne Tage* is rather slight.

Manches Reich ging dann unter	*Many an empire then came to an end*
Manchem Leser mag es wohl lächerlich erscheinen, daß . . .	*It may well appear ridiculous to some readers that . . .*
An manchen Tagen blieb er lange im Bett	*Some days he stayed in bed a long time*
Ich habe manche schöne Tage am Rhein verbracht	*I have spent several happy days on the banks of the Rhine*
manche Arbeiter und Angestellte (*Welt*)	*some workers and employees*

(c) Uninflected *manch* is not infrequently found as a determiner
The following cases are still current usage:
(i) before the indefinite article *ein*. This is a less common alternative to inflected *manch*, mainly used in formal written German, emphasizing the individual items rather more strongly:

Da gibt es mancherlei Grund zum Zweifeln – manch ein Zeitgenosse wird sagen: zum Verzweifeln (*Zeit*)	*There are many kinds of reasons for doubt – many a contemporary will say: for despair*

(ii) before an adjective, where the uninflected form is a widespread and frequent alternative to the inflected one, especially in the singular:

manch reiches Land	*many a rich kingdom*
Sie konnten dem Kanzler manch guten Tip geben (*MM*)	*They were able to give the Chancellor many a good tip*
. . . um neben manch Komischem auch etliches Entlarvende bieten zu können (*MM*)	*. . . to be able to present quite a few revealing things besides much that is comical*

(iii) before neuter nouns. This alternative sounds rather old-fashioned, but it has become rather fashionable recently, cf. Engel (1988:546):

manch Wörtchen der Verwunderung (Th. Mann)	*many a word of amazement*

(d) As a pronoun *mancher* declines like *dieser*

It is not used in the genitive:

Mancher hat es nicht geglaubt	*Not many believed it*
Das ist schon manchem passiert	*That has happened to quite a few people*
Manche trinken Tee, andere lieber Kaffee	*Some people drink tea, others prefer coffee*
manche meiner Bekannten	*some of my acquaintances*

manch einer is a not infrequent alternative to inflected *mancher*:

Manch einer mußte auf die Mittagspause verzichten (*MM*)	*Some had to give up their lunch hour*

5.5.20   *mehrere* 'several'

mehrere is used as a determiner or a pronoun in the plural only. It has the same endings as *dieser*:

Ich habe mehrere Bücher darüber gelesen	*I have read several books about it*
Im Hafen waren mehrere spanische Fischerboote	*There were several Spanish fishing boats in the harbour*
Wir haben mehrere solche Teppiche vorrätig	*We have several carpets like this in stock*
Mehrere standen draußen und warteten	*Several people were standing outside waiting*

5.5.21   *meinesgleichen* 'people like me'

meinesgleichen is an indeclinable pronoun. Parallel forms for the other persons are regularly formed, i.e. *deinesgleichen, seinesgleichen, ihresgleichen, unsresgleichen, euresgleichen*. They can have a rather old-fashioned ring in modern German:

Ich und meinesgleichen interessieren uns für so etwas nicht	*I and people like me aren't interested in things like that*
Euresgleichen hat es wirklich leicht	*People like you really have it easy*
Dieser Wagen hat nicht seinesgleichen	*This car has no equal*

5.5.22   *nichts* 'nothing'

nichts is an undeclinable pronoun. In colloquial speech it is almost invariably pronounced *nix*:

Aus nichts wird nichts (Proverb)	*Nothing comes of nothing*
Nichts gefiel ihr dort	*She didn't like anything there*
nichts als Schwierigkeiten	*nothing but difficulties*

nichts is frequently used with a following adjective used as a noun, which has the strong endings, cf. 6.4.6:

nichts Neues	*nothing new*
Er hat von nichts Neuem gesprochen	*He didn't speak of anything new*

It is also common with *von* in partitive constructions, i.e. 'nothing (of)':

Ich möchte nichts von dem Essen	*I don't want any of the food*
nichts von alledem	*nothing of all that*

5.5.23 *sämtlich* 'all (the)'

sämtlich is an emphatic alternative to *alle*. It is in very common use both as a determiner and as a pronoun, when it has the endings of *dieser*. It may be used with a preceding definite article, demonstrative or possessive, in which case it has the endings of an adjective:

Sämtliche neue Häuser wurden verkauft	*Every one of the new houses has been sold*
die Anschriften sämtlicher neuer/neuen Mitglieder	*the addresses of all the new members*
sämtliche politische Propaganda	*all political propaganda*
Meine sämtlichen Verwandten haben mir geschrieben	*All my relatives wrote to me*

NB: *sämtlich* is also used as an adverb, in the sense of 'without exception', e.g.:
Sie haben es sämtlich bestätigt   *They confirmed it without exception*

5.5.24 *unsereiner* 'someone like me, one of us'

unsereiner declines like *dieser*. There are parallel forms for the other persons, i.e. *eurereiner, ihrereiner*, although these are much less frequent. In the nominative and accusative, the neuter form *unsereins* is a common variant, used mainly in colloquial speech:

Unsereiner kann das nicht wissen	*Someone like me can't know that*
Mit unsereinem spricht sie nie	*She doesn't talk to the likes of me*

5.5.25 *viel* 'much', *viele* 'many', *wenig* 'a little', *wenige* 'a few'

(a) **The various forms and uses of the indefinites** *viel* **'much, many, a lot of' and** *wenig* **'(a) little, (a) few, not many' are broadly similar.**
They both have alternative uninflected and inflected forms, in the latter case with the endings of *dieser*. Both occur as a determiner, a pronoun or an adverb. In certain cases and uses the uninflected forms are more usual, in others the inflected. Differences in meaning between these have not been convincingly identified.

NB: (i) *ein wenig* 'a little' is invariable, cf. 5.5.6.
(ii) For the comparatives of *viel* and *wenig*, cf. 8.5.

(b) Used as pronouns, *viel* and *wenig* are most often uninflected in the singular, but inflected in the plural
They are not used in the genitive singular.

Er hat viel/wenig erzählt   Er will viel/wenig haben
Viel/Wenig von dem Kuchen   Sie hat nicht viel/wenig verraten
Ich bin mit viel/wenig von dem einverstanden, was du sagst
Viele/Wenige von diesen Büchern   Ich will doch viele/wenige

The inflected singular forms nominative/accusative *vieles*, dative *vielem* (very rarely: *weniges, wenigem*) are sometimes used, chiefly in formal writing:

Sie hat vieles versucht	*She has tried a lot of things*
Mit vielem bin ich nicht einverstanden	*There's a lot I don't agree with*

(c) Used as determiners, *viel* and *wenig* are usually uninflected in the singular, but inflected in the plural
The genitive singular is rarely used, the paraphrase with *von* being preferred:

Dazu ist viel Mut nötig	*Much courage is needed for that*
Ich trinke wenig Milch	*I don't drink much milk*
Er handelte mit viel Geschick	*He acted with a lot of skill*
Sie ist mit wenig Geld ausgekommen	*She managed with little money*
die Wirkung von wenig Wein	*the effect of not much wine*
der Genuß von viel Obst	*eating a lot of fruit*
Viele Probleme wurden besprochen	*Many problems were discussed*
Gestern waren wenige Zuschauer im Stadion	*There weren't many spectators at the ground yesterday*
Er hat viele/wenige Freunde	*He has a lot of/few friends*
die Reden vieler Politiker	*the speeches of a lot of politicians*
mit vielen/wenigen Ausnahmen	*with a lot of/few exceptions*

NB: The following exceptions to this general pattern apply:
(i) Inflected singular forms are not unusual in formal registers with a following adjective used as a noun, e.g. *Er hat vieles/weniges Interessante gesagt* for everyday *Er hat viel/wenig Interessantes gesagt.*
(ii) Inflected forms are quite common in the dative singular masculine and neuter, e.g. *Mit viel/vielem Zureden konnten wir einiges erreichen*
(iii) Uninflected forms in the plural are occasionally found, chiefly, though not exclusively, in colloquial language: *In Grunde interessieren mich furchtbar wenig Dinge außer meiner eigenen Arbeit (Langgässer).*
(iv) Inflected singular forms are used in a few set phrases, notably *vielen Dank.*

(d) *viel* and *wenig* may be used with a preceding definite article or other determiner
They then have the usual adjective endings:

Ich staunte über das viele Geld, das er ausgab	*I was amazed at the large amount of money that he spent*
der Mut dieser vielen/wenigen Frauen	*the courage of these many/few women*
Sie hat ihr weniges Geld verloren	*She lost her little bit of money*

Ich staunte über das viele, was er erledigt hatte	*I was amazed at the large number of matters that he had seen to*
die wenigen, die ihn erkannten	*the few who recognized him*
Er machte einige wenige solche Bemerkungen	*He made a few such remarks*

(e) *wenig* **in constructions like** *wenig gutes Fleisch* **is potentially ambiguous**
It could mean 'not much good meat' or 'not very good meat'. If the context does not resolve the ambiguity, the first meaning can be made clear by replacing *wenig* by *nicht viel*, i.e. *nicht viel gutes Fleisch*, the second by using *nicht sehr*, i.e. *nicht sehr gutes Fleisch*.

Similarly, *weniger gutes Fleisch* could mean 'meat which was less good' or 'a smaller amount of good meat' (English 'less good meat' shows similar ambiguity). This ambiguity may be also resolved if necessary by paraphrasing, i.e. *nicht so gutes Fleisch* or *nicht so viel gutes Fleisch*.

(f) The spelling of *soviel, wieviel, zuviel,* **etc.**
The following account follows the rulings given in DUDEN (1985), which may be taken as authoritative.
(i) *soviel, sowenig* are spelled as single words when these are used as adverbs or conjunctions, e.g.:

soviel ich weiß   sowenig du auch gelernt hast   soviel wie möglich
ich bin sowenig schuldig wie du

However, they are spelled as separate words if *so* is qualifying *viel* or *wenig* used as determiners or pronouns, i.e. in the meanings 'so much, so many', 'so little, so few', e.g.:

so viel Fleiß   so viele Schätze   so wenig Geld   so wenige Häuser

(ii) *wieviel* is always written as a single word, *wie viele* and *wie wenig* as two, e.g.:

Wieviel Birnen haben wir dieses Jahr? Wie viele Eier hast du?
Wie wenig er davon wußte!

(iii) *zuviel* and *zuwenig* are usually written as single words, e.g.:

Er gab mir zuviel/zuwenig von dem Fleisch
Im Kaffee ist zuviel/zuwenig Zucker

They are written as separate words if *zu* is particularly stressed or if *viel* or *wenig* is inflected, e.g.:

Sie haben für diese Stelle z<u>ú</u> wenig Erfahrung
er hat zu viele Eier gekauft

5.5.26 *welcher* 'some, any'

welcher is used as an indefinite pronoun in certain cases. It has the endings of *dieser* and is primarily typical of colloquial registers.
Although it may be found to a limited extent in formal written German,

other alternatives, i.e. *einige, manche, etwas,* will usually be preferred there.

It is used generally in the plural, but in the singular it can only refer to a mass noun. It is used to refer back to a noun which has just been mentioned or for 'some people' who are then identified by a following relative clause:

Hast du Käse? – Ja, ich habe welchen	*Have you got any cheese? Yes, I've got some*
Es gab ja nur wenig Tabak, aber das Mädchen beschaffte mir immer welchen	*As you know, there wasn't much tobacco, but the girl always got hold of some for me*
Ich brauche Marken. Kannst du mir welche geben?	*I need some stamps. Can you give me some/any?*
Es gibt welche, die froh sind, der Wirklichkeit ins Auge zu sehen	*There are some people who are happy to look reality in the face*

NB: For the use of *welcher* as an interrogative, cf. 5.3.1, as a relative pronoun, cf. 5.4.2.

5.5.27 *wer* 'someone, somebody'

wer is used as a pronoun in colloquial speech, where formal registers prefer *jemand*:

Dich hat wieder wer angerufen	*Someone's been on the phone for you again*
Die hat wohl wieder wen angelächelt	*It looks as if she's picked some bloke up again*
Hast du wenigstens wem Bescheid gesagt?	*Have you at least told someone about it?*

NB: For the use of *wer* as an interrogative pronoun, cf. 5.3.3.

6   Adjectives

6.1 Declension of adjectives

German adjectives are only inflected when they are used attributively, i.e.
when they qualify a following noun, e.g.:

ein guter Mensch   diese schönen Tage   reines Gold

In all other uses they have no endings, e.g.:

Der Mensch war gut   Mein Vater, in Hamburg tätig, . . .
Das Mädchen lag krank im Bett
Der Arzt, jung und unerfahren wie er war, . . .
Optimistisch wie immer, ließ sie sich von ihrem Vorhaben nicht abhalten
Vor dem Haus stand ein Mann, kahl, blaß und mager

NB: The use of an uninflected adjective after the noun is essentially poetic, e.g. *O Täler
weit, o Höhen* (*Eichendorff*). However, it has become quite frequent as a stylistic
device in advertising and technical language, cf. DUDEN (1984:§443.3), e.g.:
Henkel trocken   Schrankwand in Eiche rustikal oder Kiefer natur
Whisky pur   700 Nadelfeilen rund nach DIN 8342

6.1.1 There are two basic declensions for attributive adjectives in German.

These are usually referred to as the STRONG and WEAK declensions.

(a) The STRONG declension has the endings of *dieser,* **cf. 5.1.2, except that
the genitive singular masculine and neuter ending is** *-en*
The table below is arranged with the neuters next to the masculines in
order to show the overlap between the endings:

	Masc.	Neut.	Fem.	Plural
Nom.	-er	-es	-e	
Acc				
Gen.	-en	-er		
Dat.	-em	-en		

Full paradigms, with nouns, laid out in the usual way, with the neuters to the right of the feminines:

	Masc.		Fem.		Neut.		Plural	
Nom.	guter	Wein	gute	Suppe	gutes	Brot	gute	Weine
Acc.	guten	Wein	gute	Suppe	gutes	Brot	gute	Weine
Gen.	guten	Weines	guter	Suppe	guten	Brotes	guter	Weine
Dat.	gutem	Wein	guter	Suppe	gutem	Brot	guten	Weinen

NB: With weak masculine nouns which have the ending *-en* in the genitive singular, cf. 1.3.2, the strong adjective has the ending *-es*, e.g. *obiges Adressaten*. In practice this form scarcely ever occurs.

(b) The WEAK declension has the ending *-e* in the nominative singular of all genders and the accusative singular feminine and neuter, and elsewhere the ending *-en*

Cf. the following table:

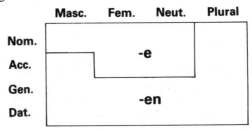

Full paradigms with the definite article:

	Masc.		Fem.		Neut.		Plural	
Nom.	der gute	Wein	die gute	Suppe	das gute	Brot	die guten	Weine
Acc.	den guten	Wein	die gute	Suppe	das gute	Brot	die guten	Weine
Gen.	des guten	Weines	der guten	Suppe	des guten	Brotes	der guten	Weine
Dat.	dem guten	Wein	der guten	Suppe	dem guten	Brot	den guten	Weinen

NOTE CAREFULLY: that the nominative and accusative plural have the ending *-en*.

6.2 The use of the strong and weak declensions

The underlying principle which governs the use of the strong and weak declensions is that the fuller 'strong' endings are used if there is no determiner preceding the adjective with an ending which indicates the case, gender or number of the noun as clearly as possible

If there is a determiner with an ending preceding the adjective, then the weak declension is used.

6.2.1 The STRONG declension is used, in line with the above principle:

(a) when no determiner precedes the adjective, e.g.:

frische Milch   frisches Obst   schöne Tage   durch genaue Beobachtung
mit neuem Mut   das Niveau französischer Filme   aus deutschen Landen

(b) when a determiner preceding the adjective is endingless:

ein älterer Herr	mein neues Kleid	unser kleines Kind
kein schöner Tag	manch reiches Land	viel indischer Tee
ein paar grüne Äpfel	lauter faule Äpfel	welch herrliches Wetter!
bei solch herrlichem Wetter	mit was für englischen Büchern	

NOTE CAREFULLY: that this means that the strong endings are used after the endingless forms of the indefinite articles *ein* and *kein* and after the possessives (i.e. *mein, dein, unser*, etc.) in the nominative singular masculine and the nominative/accusative singular neuter, as the relevant examples above show.

From this rule it follows that the strong endings are used after numerals (except declined *ein*) used on their own (including the genitives *zweier* and *dreier*, cf. 9.1.4a), after preceding genitives and after the genitive of the relative pronoun, since in all these cases the adjective is not preceded by a determiner with an ending, e.g.:

zwei schöne Pfirsiche	*two fine peaches*
Karls unermüdlicher Eifer	*Karl's tireless zeal*
in meines Vaters kleinem Arbeitszimmer	*in my father's little study*
mein Freund, dessen ältester Sohn krank war	*my friend, whose eldest son was ill*

6.2.2 The WEAK declension is used after most determiners with endings which clearly indicate the case, gender and number of the noun, e.g.:

die schönen Tage	auf diesem hohen Berg	vor einem blauen Himmel
für keine wilden Tiere	durch das tiefe Tal	bei jeder guten Gelegenheit
die alte Frau	trotz der alten Frau	mit der alten Frau
die alten Frauen	trotz der alten Frauen	mit den alten Frauen

This rule applies after all the major determiners, i.e.:

(a) the definite article and demonstrative *der*

(b) the indefinite articles *ein* and *kein* and the possessives if they have an ending, i.e. except in the nominative singular masculine and the nominative/accusative singular neuter.

(c) the demonstratives *dieser* and *jener*, the quantifier *jeder* (and its synonyms *jedweder* and *jeglicher*) and the interrogative *welcher*

6.2.3 The other determiners are most often followed by adjectives with weak endings, following the general principle given in 6.2

However, there are a number of exceptions:

(a) The weak endings are usual in the singular with those determiners which can be used in the singular, e.g.:

mit allem möglichen Fleiß   solches dumme Gerede   mancher brave Mann
von irgendwelchem puren Unsinn   mit folgender nachdrücklichen Warnung
einiges Interessante   mit einigem bühnentechnischen Aufwand (*Zeit*)
von vielem kalten Wasser   aus wenigem schlechten Wein

(b) In the plural there is some uncertainty and variation:
(i) After *alle* and *sämtliche* the weak endings are usual, e.g.:

alle fremden Truppen   samtliche schönen Bücher   alle Interessierten

In the genitive plural, the strong ending *-er* is sometimes found, but sounds rather old-fashioned. Modern usage prefers *aller fremden Truppen* to *aller fremder Truppen*, etc.
(ii) After *beide, irgendwelche* and *solche* either weak or strong endings are used. The weak endings are more frequent, e.g.:

beide alten (less common: alte) Frauen
irgendwelcher interessierten (less common: interessierter) Zuschauer
solche schönen (less common: schöne) Tage
(iii) After *manche* either weak or strong endings are used. The strong endings are rather more frequent, e.g.:

manche schöne (less common: schönen) Aussichten
(iv) After *einige, etliche, folgende, mehrere, viele, wenige* strong endings are the rule, e.g.:

einige neue Inter-City-Verbindungen   etliche fremde Besucher
folgende bezeichnende Beispiele   mehrere große Städte
vieler kleiner Zimmer

However, the weak ending is still occasionally found in the genitive plural, e.g. *einiger großen ausländischen Firmen* for (much more frequent) *einiger großer ausländischer Firmen*.

NB: (i) If one of these determiners is preceded by a definite or indefinite article, or by one of the demonstratives *dieser* or *jener*, or by one of the possessives *mein, dein*, etc., then they themselves will have a weak or strong adjective endings, as appropriate, as will any following adjective, e.g.:
eine solche interessante Nachricht   aller solchen guten Wünsche
mit der folgenden krassen Behauptung   diese vielen alten Dörfer
mit seinem wenigen deutschen Geld   mein sämtliches kleines Vermögen

(ii) Some of the above determiners have alternative endingless forms which are used under certain conditions cf. 5.5. These endingless forms are followed by adjectives with strong endings, following the principle explained in 6.2, e.g.:
viel deutsches Geld   manch schöner Tag   solch dummes Gerede
(iii) For use with *ander*, cf. 5.5.2.

6.2.4 A series of adjectives preceding a noun all have the same (weak or strong) ending:

dieser schöne, große Garten   mein lieber alter Vater   gutes bayrisches Bier
die Lösung wichtiger politischer Probleme

One occasional deviation from this rule is that in the dative singular masculine or neuter, a second (or subsequent) adjective may, optionally, have the ending *-en* rather than *-em* in the strong declension, e.g.:

mit dunklem bayrischem/bayrischen Bier
nach langem beunruhigendem/beunruhigenden Schweigen
mit unverantwortlichem individuellen Fehlverhalten (*Zeit*)

In general, *-en* is used less than *-em* in such cases in modern German. However, it is the norm with adjectives used as nouns, cf. 6.4.3a.

6.2.5 The adjective is still declined if the noun is understood

one is usually supplied in the equivalent English construction, e.g.

Welches Kleid hast du gewählt? – Das rote	*Which dress did you choose? – The red one*
Ich habe mein Taschenmesser verloren. Ich muß mir ein neues kaufen	*I've lost my penknife. I'll have to buy myself a new one.*
Deutsche Weißweine sind süßer als französische	*German white wines are sweeter than French*

6.2.6 In a few special cases an attributive adjective has no ending, i.e.

(a) In older German adjectives sometimes lacked the strong ending *-es* before a neuter singular noun in the nominative or accusative
This usage is retained in a few idioms and phrases, e.g.:

etwas auf gut Glück tun	*to take a chance*
sich lieb Kind machen	*to ingratiate oneself*
Gut Ding will Weile haben	*Nothing good is done in a hurry*
ruhig Blut bewahren!	*keep calm!*
Kölnisch Wasser	*eau de Cologne*
ein gehörig/gut Stück	*a substantial/good piece*
ein gut Teil	*a large proportion*
ein ander Mal	*another time*
(more usual: ein anderes Mal)	

(b) A number of colour adjectives from other languages ending in a vowel do not take endings, i.e., chiefly:
beige, lila, orange, rosa, e.g. *ein lila Mantel, die orange Farbe, ein rosa Kleid.*
    In writing a suffix such as *-farben* or *-farbig* is an acceptable

alternative, e.g. *ein rosafarbenes Kleid*. In substandard colloquial German, an *-n-* is often inserted to act as a base for the usual endings, e.g. *ein rosanes Kleid*.

(c) An adjective used adverbially before another adjective has no ending, cf. the difference between *ein unheilbarer, fauler Junge* 'an incurable lazy boy' and *ein unheilbar fauler Junge* an incurably lazy boy'.

This distinction is, however, not always clear-cut, and the first of a pair of adjectives is sometimes left uninflected even if the sense is not adverbial. This is a not uncommon stylistic device in modern prose writing, e.g.:

ein reingebürtiger Pole von traurig edler Gestalt (*Grass*)

Optionally, *einzig* regularly lacks inflections if it can be considered as qualifying a following adjective e.g. *die einzig(e) mögliche Lösung*. For similar usage with *derartig*, cf. 5.1.6.

(d) Adjectives from town names in *-er* do not inflect,
e.g. *die Leipziger Messe, die Lüneburger Heide, der Kölner Dom*.

(e) Adjectives from numerals in *-er* do not inflect,
e.g. *die neunziger Jahre* 'the nineties'.

(f) Uninflected adjectives are used with names of letters and numerals,
e.g. *groß 'A', klein 'z', römisch III, arabisch 4*.

(g) *halb* and *ganz* are not declined before geographical names used without an article,
e.g. *halb Berlin, ganz Deutschland, ganz Europa*

NB: See 9.3.2 for the use of *halb*.

6.2.7 The declension of adjectives after personal pronouns

The general rule is that an adjective after a personal pronoun has the strong endings, e.g.:

ich armer Deutscher   Wer hat dich dummen Kerl gesehen?
Wer konnte euch treulosen Verrätern helfen?
Wer kümmert sich um uns frühere Kollegen?

The following exceptions to this general rule apply:

(a) In the (rarely used) dative singular, weak and strong endings are alternatives in the masculine and neuter,
e.g. *mir mittellosem/mittellosen Mann*
     However, the feminine almost always has weak endings, e.g. *Er hat mir alten* (rarely: *alter*) *Frau geschmeichelt*.

(b) Weak endings are more usual in the nominative plural:
wir jungen Kollegen, ihr hilflosen Kerle, ihr Deutsche (less usual: *ihr*

Deutschen). However, exceptionally, *wir Deutsche* and *wir Deutschen* are equally common.

6.3 The spelling of certain adjectives

6.3.1 The spelling of inflected adjectives in *-el, -en, -er*

(a) Adjectives in *-el* always drop the *-e-* when the adjective is inflected, e.g. ein dunkler Wald, eine respektable Leistung.

NB: When used as a noun, *dunkel* drops the *-e-* of the ending, e.g. *im Dunkeln* 'in the dark'.

(b) Adjectives in *-en* may drop the *-e-* when the adjective is inflected
This is the norm in colloquial speech, but is less usual in writing: *eine metallene* (rarely written: *metallne*) *Stimme, ein seltener* (rarely written: *seltner*) *Schmetterling*.

(c) Adjectives in *-er*
Foreign adjectives and those with *au* or *eu* before the *r* always drop the *-e-*, whilst the others usually keep it in written German, e.g. *eine makabre Geschichte, mit teuren Weinen, durch saure Milch* BUT *eine muntere* (rarely written: *muntre*) *Frau*.

NB: (i) The *-e-* of the comparative ending *-er*, cf. 8.1 is rarely omitted in writing, e.g. *eine bessere* (rarely written: *beßre*) *Lösung*.
      (ii) For the spelling of declined *ander*, cf. 5.5.2.

(d) The *-e-* is frequently omitted in *-el-* or *-er-* when these are not at the end of the word, e.g. *neb(e)lige Tage, eine wäss(e)rige Suppe*.

6.3.2 *hoch* 'high'

When inflected, *hoch* has the special stem form *hoh-* to which the usual endings are added. Thus:

der Berg ist hoch BUT ein hoher Berg
die hohen Wolken   mit einem hohen Grad

6.3.3 A number of adjectives have alternative forms with or without final *-e-*,
e.g. *Er ist feig* or *feige* 'He is cowardly'. These have the same inflected forms, with the endings being added to the stem without *-e*, e.g. *ein feiger Junge*. Others are:

blöd(e)	bös(e)	fad(e)	irr(e)	leis(e)	mild(e)
müd(e)	öd(e)	träg(e)	trüb(e)	vag(e)	zäh(e)

With all except *blöd(e), mild(e)* and *zäh(e)* the alternative with *-e* is more common in written German. The form without *-e* tends to be more frequent in spoken German unless the adjective is stressed.

6.4 Adjectives used as nouns

6.4.1 All adjectives and participles can be used as nouns in German.

They are then usually written with a capital letter (but cf. 2.4.1), e.g.:

der Alte	*the old man*	die Alte	*the old woman*
das Alte	*old things*	die Alten	*the old people*

English does not share this facility of German for turning adjectives into nouns, except in a few restricted cases *(the young, the old, the Dutch, the good, the bad and the ugly,* etc.). Typically, in English we usually have to supply a dummy noun like *man, woman, thing(s), people* to be used with the adjective. The overuse of the corresponding German words like *Ding* or *Leute* is a characteristic feature of the German of English learners. Idiomatic German exploits fully the possibilities of concise expression offered by the fact that adjectives can readily be used as nouns. In particular, they are often used where full clauses would be needed in English, e.g.:

Der Gesang dieser Vögel war das für mich Interessante	*The song of these birds was what interested me*
Er hat sich über das Gesagte aufgeregt	*He got annoyed about what had been said*
Das Erschreckende an diesem Vorfall war seine scheinbare Unabwendbarkeit	*What was terrifying about this occurrence was its apparent inevitability*
Die gerade Eingestiegenen waren ein älterer Herr und eine elegante Dame	*the people who had just got in were an elderly man and an elegant lady*
ein Ort, wo das irgendwie zu denkende Konkrete unwiederbringlich in Abstraktes umschlägt	*a point where concrete reality, however it may be imagined, becomes irrevocably abstract*

6.4.2 Adjectives used as nouns usually decline in exactly the same way as adjectives preceding nouns,

i.e. they have the weak or strong endings according to the general rules given in 6.2. This also means that they have the same endings as any preceding adjective, e.g. *ein zuverlässiger Angestellter, von einer unbekannten Fremden.* As they are frequently confused with 'weak' masculine nouns, cf. 1.3.2, the declension of a typical masculine adjective used as a noun, *der Angestellte* 'employee', is given with the definite and indefinite articles:

	Singular	Plural
	the employee	*the employees*
Nom.	der Angestellte	die Angestellten
Acc.	den Angestellten	die Angestellten
Gen.	des Angestellten	der Angestellten
Dat.	dem Angestellten	den Angestellten

	Singular	**Plural**
	an employee	*employees*
Nom.	ein Angestell**ter**	Angestellte
Acc.	einen Angestell**ten**	Angestellte
Gen.	eines Angestell**ten**	Angestell**ter**
Dat.	einem Angestell**ten**	Angestell**ten**

NB: *der Angestellte* is naturally only used of a <u>male</u> employee. A female employee will be *die Angestellte, eine Angestellte*, with the appropriate endings, cf. 6.4.4.

6.4.3 Exceptions to the rule that adjectives used as nouns always decline in the same way as adjectives

(a) In the dative singular the adjective used as a noun usually has the ending *-en* if preceded by an adjective with the strong endings *-em* or *-er*:

Ich sprach mit Karls altem Bekannten, mit Helmuts englischer Bekannten

(b) In apposition, the weak ending is used in the dative singular even if there is no determiner:

Er sprach mit Karl Friedrichsen, Angestellten *(rarely:* Angestelltem) der BASF in Ludwigshafen.
Er sprach mit Heike König, Angestellten *(never:* Angestellter) der BASF in Ludwigshafen.

(c) The neuters *das Äußere, das Ganze* and *das Innere* may, optionally, have the weak or strong endings in the nominative/accusative singular after the indefinite article or the possessives <u>if</u> preceded by another adjective:

sein schlichtes Äußere(s)   ein einheitliches Ganze(s)
mein eigenes Innere(s)

6.4.4 Masculine and feminine adjectival nouns usually refer to people

The sex is indicated by using an appropriate article, e.g. *der Fremde* 'the (male) stranger, *die Fremde* 'the (female) stranger'. A large number of those in common use correspond to simple nouns in English, e.g.:

der Abgeordnete	*representative*	der Gesandte	*envoy*
der Angestellte	*employee*	der Heilige	*saint*
der Beamte	*civil servant*	der Industrielle	*industrialist*
der Bekannte	*acquaintance*	der Jugendliche	*young person*
der Deutsche	*German*	der Reisende	*traveller*
der Erwachsene	*adult*	der Verlobte	*fiancé*
der Freiwillige	*volunteer*	der Verwandte	*relative*
der Fremde	*stranger*	der Vorgesetzte	*superior*
der Gefangene	*prisoner*	der Vorsitzende	*chairman*
der Geistliche	*clergyman*		

Notes on some masculine and feminine adjectival nouns:

(a) A few with special meanings are always feminine, i.e.:

die Elektrische *tram* (mainly S. Germ.)　　die Gerade *straight line*
die Rechte, Linke *right, left* (hand); (political) *right, left*

(b) Some feminines are no longer treated as adjectival nouns, but as regular feminine nouns, i.e.: *die Horizontale* 'the horizontal' *die Parallele* 'the parallel (line)' and *die Vertikale* 'the vertical', cf. *aus der Horizontale* (no longer?: *Horizontalen*). After a numeral, though, one may still find *drei Parallele* as an alternative to the more usual *drei Parallelen*.

(c) *die Illustrierte* 'the magazine' is usually still treated as an adjectival noun, e.g.: *in dieser Illustrierten*.
In the plural, though, it may have the endings of an adjective or of a regular feminine noun, i.e. *Wir haben zwei Illustrierte (or Illustrierten) gekauft*.

(d) *die Brünette* and *die Kokette* have now become regular feminine nouns, e.g. *mit dieser Brünette* (no longer: *Brünetten*).

(e) Exceptionally, the feminine form corresponding to *der Beamte* is *die Beamtin*
This is treated as a regular feminine noun, with the plural *die Beamtinnen*, cf. 1.2.3a.

6.4.5　Neuter adjectival nouns usually denote abstract or collective ideas, e.g.:

Das Wahre ist wichtiger als das Schöne	*What is true is more important than what is beautiful*
Es ist schon Schlimmes passiert	*Bad things have certainly happened*
Er hat Hervorragendes geleistet	*He has achieved outstanding things*
der Schauer des Verbotenen und Versagten (*S. Zweig*)	*the frightening fascination of what is forbidden or denied*
. . . zugleich immer aufbauend auf das Erreichte (*Mercedes advert*)	*. . . at the same time always building on what has been achieved*

Especially in spoken German, the names of regions within the German-speaking countries often take the form of neuter adjectival nouns, e.g.:

Jetzt kommen wir ins Hessische. Hier sind wir im Thüringischen
Der Baron von Münchhausen kam im Braunschweigischen zur Welt. (*Kästner*)

6.4.6　Neuter adjectival nouns are frequently used after indefinites, e.g. *alles, nichts, viel(es), wenig,* cf. 5.5. They then have weak or strong endings as appropriate, i.e. depending on whether the indefinite has an ending, e.g.:

alles Gute　von allem Guten　nichts Neues　von nichts Neuem
viel/wenig Interessantes　von viel Interessantem
　　(BUT vieles Interessante, von vielem Interessanten, cf. 6.4.3a)
weiteres Interessante　folgendes Neue　lauter Neues

6.4.7 Words denoting languages and colours most often have the form of neuter adjectival nouns

(a) Names of languages

The usual form, used to refer to the language in a specific context or when another adjective precedes, is a neuter adjective which is most often not declined (though, optionally, -*s* may be added in the genitive, cf. 1.3.7).

Wir lernen Spanisch, Französisch, Russisch, Englisch
Die Aussprache des modernen Deutsch(s)

To refer to the language in a general sense, an inflected adjectival neuter noun is used. It is always accompanied by the definite article and can never be used with a preceding adjective, e.g.:

Das Englische ist dem Deutschen verwandt
eine Übersetzung aus dem Tschechischen
     BUT: eine Übersetzung aus dem amerikanischen Englisch

(b) Names of colours

These most usually take the form of a neuter adjectival noun which does not decline. The plural is also endingless in written German, though an -*s* may be used in the spoken language:

das Grün der Wiesen   von einem glänzenden Rot   in Schwarz gekleidet
eines häßlichen Gelb   die beiden Blau (spoken only: Blaus)

In a few set phrases with the definite article this adjectival noun is declined:

ins Grüne fahren   ins Schwarze treffen
das Blaue vom Himmel herunter versprechen

6.5 Cases with adjectives

6.5.1 The dative is the most common case governed by adjectives:

Er ist seinem Bruder sehr ähnlich	*He's very much like his brother*

Sie waren ihrem Freund beim Umzug
  behilflich
	*They helped their friend when he
	  moved house*

Dieses Gespräch war mir sehr nützlich	*This conversation was very useful for me*
Er war seinem Gegner überlegen	*He surpassed his opponent*
Ein ihr unbekannter Mann trat herein	*A man she didn't know walked in*

The following list gives a selection of frequently used adjectives which govern the dative. The adjective usually follows the noun (or pronoun) dependent on it, but those marked with an asterisk* in the following list may come first. Those marked with † may alternatively be used with *für* (before or after the noun), e.g. *Das war für mich unangenehm/ unangenehm für mich, böse* may also be used with *auf* or *mit*, cf. 6.6.:

ähnlich*	*like, similar*	günstig	*favourable*
angenehm†	*agreeable*	heilig	*holy, sacred*
begreiflich	*comprehensible*	hinderlich	*awkward*
behilflich	*helpful*	klar	*obvious*
bekannt	*known, familiar*	lästig†	*troublesome*
bequem	*comfortable*	leicht†	*easy*
bewußt	*known*	möglich†	*possible*
beschwerlich†	*arduous*	nahe*	*near, close*
böse	*angry*	nötig	*necessary*
dankbar	*grateful*	nützlich†	*useful*
eigen	*peculiar*	peinlich†	*embarrassing*
entbehrlich†	*unnecessary*	schädlich†	*injurious, harmful*
ergeben	*devoted, attached*	schuldig	*owing*
erwünscht	*desirable*	schwer	*difficult*
fern	*distant*	teuer	*expensive*
fremd	*strange*	treu*	*faithful*
gefährlich†	*dangerous*	überlegen	*superior*
gefällig	*obliging*	verhaßt	*hateful*
nicht geheuer	*scary*	verständlich†	*comprehensible*
gehorsam	*obedient*	wichtig†	*important*
geläufig	*familiar*	widerlich	*repugnant*
gemeinsam	*common*	willkommen	*welcome*
gerecht	*just*	zugänglich†	*accessible*
gesinnt	*inclined*	zuträglich	*beneficial*

(e.g.: sie war ihm freundlich gesinnt)
gewogen (lit.)   *well disposed*

6.5.2 A further group of adjectives which are constructed with the dative are only used predicatively, e.g.:

Sie ist mir zugetan   *She is well disposed towards me*

These are:

abhold (arch., lit.)	*ill-disposed*	untertan	*subordinate*
feind (arch., lit.)	*hostile*	zugetan	*well-disposed*
gram (lit.)	*angry* (with)	zuwider	*repugnant*
hold (arch., lit.)	*favourably disposed*		

To this group also belong the large number of adjectives meaning 'all the same', e.g.: *Das ist mir gleich* 'That's all the same to me', viz.: *einerlei, egal* (coll.;), *gleich, piepe* (coll.), *schnuppe* (coll.) *wurs(ch)t* (coll.).

6.5.3 A few adjectives are used with the accusative

They occur mainly in verbal constructions with *sein* or *werden*:

jdn/etwas *gewahr werden (lit.)   *to become aware of sth/sb*
   Wir wurden unseren Irrtum gewahr   *We realized our mistake*

etwas **gewohnt** sein	*to be used to sth*
Ich bin den Lärm nicht gewohnt	*I'm not used to the noise*
etwas/jdn **los** sein/werden	*to be/get rid of sth/sb*
Endlich bin ich den Schnupfen los	*At last I've got rid of the cold*
etwas/jdn **satt** sein/haben	*to be sick of sb/sth*
Er ist/hat es gründlich satt	*He's thoroughly sick of it*
jdm etwas **schuldig** sein	*to owe sb sth*
Sie ist ihm eine Erklärung schuldig	*She owes him an explanation*
etwas *****wert** sein	*to be worth sth*
Es ist das Papier nicht wert,	*It's not worth the paper*
auf dem es steht *(MM)*	*it's printed on*

NB: (i) The adjectives asterisked may be used with a genitive in formal registers, cf. 6.5.4; in the case of *satt* this is only possible in conjunction with *sein*, not with *haben*.
(ii) *schuldig* is used with a genitive in the sense of 'guilty', cf. *Er ist des Verbrechens schuldig* 'He is guilty of the crime'.

6.5.4 A few adjectives govern the genitive

The corresponding English construction often has *of*. In the main, they are limited to written German and a number have alternative constructions which are used in less formal registers. With the exception of *bar*, they follow the noun dependent on them. The following are relatively frequent in modern German:

bar devoid of	Seine Handlungsweise war bar aller Vernunft
	His action was devoid of all reason
bewußt *conscious of*	Ich war mir meines Irrtums bewußt
	I was conscious of my mistake
fähig *capable of*	Er ist einer solchen Tat nicht fähig
(or: with *zu* + noun)	*He is not capable of such a deed*
gewahr *aware of*	Wir wurden unseres Irrtums gewahr
(more often with acc.)	*We became aware of our mistake*
gewiß *certain*	Sie können meiner Unterstützung gewiß sein
	You can be certain of my support
mächtig *master of*	Sie ist des Deutschen absolut mächtig
	She has a complete command of German
müde *tired of*	Sie waren des langen Streites müde *(Döblin)*
(or, rarely, with acc.)	*They were tired of the long quarrel*
schuldig *guilty of*	Der Angeklagte ist des Hochverrats schuldig
(cf. 6.5.3)	*The accused is guilty of high treason*
sicher *sure of*	Du kannst seiner Freundschaft sicher sein
	You can be sure of his friendship
überdrüssig *tired of*	Er war des Herumhockens überdrüssig (*Pinkwart*)
(or, rarely, with acc.)	*He was tired of sitting around*
voll *full of*	Das Theater war voll aufmerksamer Zuschauer
(see note below)	*The theatre was full of attentive spectators*
wert *worthy of*	Er ist unseres Vertrauens wert
(often with acc.)	*He is worthy of our trust*
würdig *worthy of*	Er ist dieser Ehre nicht würdig
	He is not worthy of this honour

NB: *voll* is used with the genitive, as in the example given, only in formal written (mainly

literary) language. For English 'full of' the following other equivalents are the most common:
(i) With a noun standing alone, *voll* or *voller* with a nominative:
ein Korb voll(er) Obst, voll(er) Äpfel.
(ii) With a noun qualified by an adjective, *voll von*:
ein Korb voll von herrlichem Obst, roten Äpfeln
(iii) *voll mit* is also frequent, particularly in spoken registers:
ein Korb voll mit herrlichem Obst, roten Äpfeln

Some other adjectives governing the genitive are restricted to predicate use after *sein* and/or *werden* and used in the most formal (particularly legal) written German. They are:

ansichtig bedürftig eingedenk geständig gewärtig habhaft
(un)kundig ledig teilhaftig verdächtig verlustig

An example from official legal language:

Er ist der Bürgerrechte für verlustig   *He has been deprived of his*
    erklärt worden   *civic rights*

6.6 Adjectives with prepositions

A considerable number of adjectives are linked to a noun by means of prepositions, e.g.:

Das ist von dem Wetter abhängig   die um ihre Kinder besorgte Mutter
Er war mit meinem Entschluß einverstanden

Which preposition is used depends on the individual adjective; as with prepositions used in the prepositional object of some verbs, cf. 18.6, the preposition is used simply to form a link to a noun and it tends to retain little of its full lexical meaning, cf. Sommerfeldt/Schreiber (1977). We give below a selection of adjectives governing prepositional constructions, concentrating on those which are most frequently used and those with constructions which differ markedly from their usual English equivalents. Further details on the use of prepositions and their English equivalents are given in chapter 20.

The prepositional phrase may precede or follow the adjective. If it contains a noun it commonly comes first but may come second; if it contains a pronoun it almost invariably comes second, i.e.:

EITHER: Er ist über den neuen Lehrling verärgert
OR (rather less usual): Er ist verärgert über den neuen Lehrling
BUT ALWAYS: Er ist verärgert über ihn

However, *arm* and *reich* usually precede the phrase with *an*, even if it contains a noun, e.g. *Das Land ist arm/reich an Bodenschätzen.*

6.6.1 Frequently used adjectives governing prepositions

Note that *auf* and *über* always take the accusative when dependent on adjectives.

abhängig von — *dependent on*
angewiesen auf etwas/jdn sein — *to have to rely on sth/sb*
    Wir waren auf uns selber angewiesen
ärgerlich auf/über — *annoyed with*
arm an — *poor in*
aufmerksam auf — *aware of*
    Sie machte mich auf meinen Irrtum aufmerksam
begierig auf/nach — *eager, hungry for*
    Wir sind begierig auf seinen Besuch
begeistert von/über — *enthusiastic about*
berechtigt zu — *justified in*
    Sie sind zu diesem Vorwurf berechtigt
bereit zu — *ready for*
    Die Truppen waren zum Einsatz bereit
besorgt um — *anxious about*
bezeichnend für — *characteristic of*
blaß, bleich vor — *pale with*
    Er ist völlig blaß/bleich vor Entsetzen
böse auf/mit — *cross with*
    Bist du böse auf mich/mit mir? (Or: Bist du mir böse, cf. 6.5.1)
charakteristisch für — *characteristic of*
dankbar für — *grateful for*
    Ich war ihm für seine gütige Hilfe dankbar
durstig nach — *thirsty for*
eifersüchtig auf — *jealous of*
einverstanden mit — *in agreement with*
    Bist du mit diesem Vorschlag einverstanden?
empfänglich für — *susceptible, receptive to*
    Sie ist sehr empfänglich für Schmeichelei
empfindlich gegen — *sensitive to*
    Sie ist sehr empfindlich gegen Kälte
ersichtlich aus — *obvious, clear from*
    Das ist aus seiner letzten Bemerkung ersichtlich
fähig zu — *capable of*
    Sie ist zu einer solchen Tat nicht fähig (or genitive, cf. 6.5.4)
fertig mit etwas sein — *to have finished sth*
    Bist du mit dem Essen schon fertig?
geeignet für/zu — *suitable for*
    Er ist für diese/zu dieser Arbeit nicht geeignet
gefaßt auf — *ready, prepared for*
    Mach dich gefaßt auf seine Reaktion!
gespannt auf — *extremely curious about*
    Ich bin auf diesen Film sehr gespannt *I am dying to see that film*
gewöhnt an — *accustomed/used to*
    Ich bin jetzt an diesen Kaffee gewöhnt (i.e. *I have made myself accustomed to this coffee.* Compare: Ich bin diesen Kaffee gewohnt, cf. 6.5.3., *This is the coffee I am used to*)
gierig nach — *greedy for*
gleichgültig gegen/gegenüber — *indifferent to(wards)*

höflich zu/gegenüber	*polite to(wards)*
hungrig nach	*hungry for*
interessiert an	*interested in*
müde von	*tired from*

Er war müde von der schweren Arbeit

NB: *müde* governs an accusative or genitive in the sense 'tired of', cf. 6.5.4

neidisch auf	*envious of*
neugierig auf	*curious about*
reich an	*rich in*
scharf auf (coll.)	*keen on*

Er ist scharf auf seine Rechte

schuld an etwas sein/haben	*to be blamed for sth*

Wer war/hatte an dem Streit schuld?

sicher vor	*safe from*
stolz auf	*proud of*
typisch für	*typical of*
überzeugt von	*convinced of*
unabhängig von	*independent of*
verheiratet mit	*married to*
verliebt in	*in love with*

Sie ist in den Bruder ihrer Freundin verliebt

verschieden von	*different to/from*
versessen auf	*(very, mad) keen on*

Er ist versessen auf alte Sportwagen

verwandt mit	*related to*
vorbereitet auf	*prepared for*
wütend auf	*mad at, furious with*

Er war wütend auf seine Chefin

zornig auf	*angry with*
zuständig für	*responsible for*

In addition, *über* is used with many adjectives in the sense of 'about', cf. 20.3.12d, e.g. *aufgebracht* 'outraged', *beschämt* 'ashamed', *bestürzt*, *betroffen* 'full of consternation', *empört, entrüstet* 'indignant', *entzückt* 'delighted', *erbittert* 'bitter', *erbost* 'infuriated', *erfreut* 'delighted', *erstaunt* 'amazed', *froh* 'glad', *glücklich* 'happy', *traurig* 'sad', *verwundert* 'astonished'.

vor is used with a number of adjectives expressing a cause, cf. 20.3.15d., e.g. *angst* 'fearful', *elend* 'miserable', *starr* 'stiff', *stumm* 'speechless'.

6.6.2 Many adjectives governing prepositions may be used with a dependent clause or an infinitive clause with zu

In this case the clause is commonly anticipated by the prepositional adverb (i.e. *da(r)* + preposition, e.g. *daran, damit,* etc., cf. 3.5) as a correlating element, e.g.:

Er ist **davon** abhängig, daß ihm sein Bruder hilft	*He is dependent on his brother helping him*

Er ist **davon** abhängig, das Geld zu erhalten	*He is dependent on receiving the money*
Wir sind **dazu** bereit, Ihnen darüber Auskünfte zu geben	*We are prepared to give you some information about this*
Sie war **darüber** froh, daß sie ihn noch sehen würde	*She was pleased that she would still see him*

It is impossible to give clear rules for when the prepositional adverb is used in such constructions and when it is not. Usage is inconsistent and subject to variation. With a number of the adjectives given in section 6.6.1 it is quite optional and pairs of sentences like, e.g.:

Ich bin gewöhnt, jeden Tag eine Stunde zu üben
Ich bin daran gewöhnt, jeden Tag eine Stunde zu üben

can be equally acceptable and grammatical.

In particular the prepositional adverb is not obligatory with the following adjectives: *begierig, bereit, böse, einverstanden, gespannt, gewöhnt, neugierig, stolz, überzeugt, vorbereitet* and those with *über*. If it is used with these it tends to focus emphasis on the content of the dependent clause. In practice it is more commonly inserted than omitted, even where it is optional, especially in written German.

7 Adverbs

7.1 Adverbs: general

7.1.1 The traditional term 'adverb' covers a wide range of words with a great variety of uses

Typically, adverbs are words which do not inflect and which serve to express relations of time, place, manner and degree. They can qualify verbs, e.g. *Sie hat ihm **höflich** geantwortet*, cf.18.1.3, or adjectives, e.g. *ein **natürlich** eleganter Stil* and they very often relate to the sentence as a whole, e.g. ***Vielleicht** hat er ihr geholfen*. Their diversity means that it is not easy to define them simply and satisfactorily or distinguish them from adjectives on the one hand and other indeclinable words such as particles and verb prefixes on the other. It would go beyond the scope of this book to attempt a fully justified categorization of adverbs in German; a well presented recent account is to be found in Eisenberg (1986:195ff.). We shall concentrate in the following on those adverbs of German and their uses which present significant differences to their most usual English equivalents, in particular adverbs of place (7.2), of direction (7.3), of manner and cause (7.4), adverbs of degree (7.5) and interrogative adverbs (7.6). Adverbs of time are dealt with in chapter 11 with other time expressions and modal particles in chapter 10. The comparative and superlative forms of adverbs are treated in chapter 8.

7.1.2 Most adjectives (and participles) can be used as adverbs

The majority of these are adverbs of manner (cf. 7.4). In this case they have no ending, as German has no special suffix to mark adverbs comparable to the *-ly* of English:

Er hat die Sache überraschend schnell erledigt	*He settled the matter surprisingly quickly*
Ein Dokument zeigt doch, daß er mäßigend und bremsend zu wirken versuchte (*Zeit*)	*A document nevertheless shows that he tried to exercise a moderating and calming influence*

An adverb qualifying an adjective before a noun is marked as such by having no ending. Compare:

ein schön geschnitzter Schrank	*a beautifully carved cupboard*
ein schöner, geschnitzter Schrank	*a beautiful carved cupboard*

Such adjective-adverbs are very widely and flexibly used in German, often in a way which lacks a direct English equivalent:

Er hat mir brieflich mitgeteilt, daß er anderer Meinung sei	*He informed me by letter that he was of a different opinion*
Widerrechtlich geparkte Fahrzeuge werden kostenpflichtig abgeschleppt	*Illegally parked vehicles will be removed at the owner's expense*
Das Mitbringen von Hunden ist lebensmittelpolizeilich verboten	*Bringing dogs (into the shop) is forbidden by order of the food inspectorate*

7.2. Adverbs of place

7.2.1 *hier, dort, da*

(a) *hier* refers to a place close to the speaker (= English *here*), e.g.:

Ich habe deine Tasche **hier** im Schrank gefunden

(b) *dort* refers to a place away from the speaker (= English *there*), e.g.:

Ich sah ihn **dort** an der Ecke stehen

(c) *da* is most usually a less emphatic alternative to *dort* (and used more frequently), referring to a place away from the speaker, e.g.:

Ich sah ihn **da** an der Ecke stehen

However, *da* is often used to point in a rather general, unemphatic way when the difference between 'here' and 'there' is not crucial or obvious from the context. In such cases it may correspond to English *here*, cf.:

Herr Meyer ist im Moment nicht da	*Mr Meyer is not here at the moment*

7.2.2 *oben, unten*

German lacks specific noun equivalents for the English nouns 'top' and 'bottom' and most often uses phrases with the adverbs *oben* and *unten* where these nouns would be used in English, e.g.:

oben auf dem Turm	*at the top of the tower*
oben im Haus	*at the top of the house*
oben im/auf dem Baum	*at the top of the tree*
Sie stand ganz oben auf der Treppe	*She was standing right at the top of the stairs*
unten auf dem Bild	*at the bottom of the picture*

Bis unten sind es noch zwei Stunden zu Fuß	*It's another two hours' walk to the bottom*
Die Säule wird nach unten hin breiter	*The column broadens out towards the bottom*
Sein Name steht unten auf der Liste	*His name is at the bottom of the list*
ganz unten im Kasten	*right at the bottom of the chest*
auf Seite 90 unten	*at the bottom of page 90*
von oben bis unten	*from top to bottom*

7.2.3 *mitten*, usually followed by a preposition, most often corresponds to the English noun *middle*

Other English equivalents may be possible in certain contexts, e.g.:

Mitten im Garten ist ein Teich	*In the middle of the garden there is a pond*
Sie stellte die Vase mitten auf den Tisch	*She put the vase in the middle of the table*
mitten in der Nacht	*in the middle of the night*
mitten in der Aufregung	*in the midst of the excitement*
Er war mitten aus seinem Urlaub zu der Konferenz gekommen	*He had come back to the conference in the middle of his holidays*
Ich war mitten unter den Leuten auf der Straße (*Zuckmayer*)	*I was in the midst of the people in the street*
Er bahnte sich mitten durch die Menge einen Weg	*He forced his way through the middle of the crowd*
mitten auf der Leiter	*halfway up/down the ladder*

7.2.4 *außen, draußen, innen, drinnen*

In modern German *außen* and *innen* mean 'on the outside, inside', i.e. referring to the outer or inner surface of the object, whilst *draußen* and *drinnen* are used for 'outside' and 'inside', i.e. away from the object or contained within it:

Die Tasse ist außen schmutzig	*The cup is dirty on the outside*
Ich mußte draußen warten	*I had to wait outside*
Die Äpfel sind innen faul	*The apples are rotten inside*
Drinnen ist es aber schön warm	*Indoors it's nice and warm, though*
Dieses Fenster geht nach innen auf	*This window opens inwards*
Wir kommen von draußen	*We are coming from outside*
Er schloß die Tür von außen zu	*He shut the door from the outside*
von außen/innen gesehen	*seen from the outside/inside*

NB: The use of *außen* and *innen* for 'outside' and 'inside' is now archaic or regional (esp. Austrian).

7.2.5 Indefinite place adverbs

i.e. the equivalents of English 'somewhere, 'anywhere', 'everywhere', 'nowhere'.

(a) *irgendwo* corresponds to 'somewhere' or, in questions, 'anywhere':

Ich habe es irgendwo liegenlassen	*I've left it somewhere*
Hast du Paula irgendwo gesehen?	*Have you seen Paula anywhere?*

In spoken German *wo* is frequent if unstressed, e.g. *Ich habe ihn wohl wo liegenlassen.*

(b) *überall* corresponds to 'everywhere', or to 'anywhere' in the sense of 'no matter where':

Erika hat dich überall gesucht	*Erika was looking for you everywhere*
Sie dürfen hier überall parken	*You can park anywhere here*

(c) *nirgendwo, nirgends* correspond to 'nowhere', 'not . . . anywhere':

Er war nirgendwo/nirgends zu sehen	*He was nowhere to be seen*
Ich habe dich gestern nirgends gesehen	*I didn't see you anywhere yesterday*

(d) *anderswo, woanders* correspond to 'somewhere else', 'elsewhere' (in questions also = 'anywhere else'):

Sie müssen ihn anderswo/woanders suchen	*You'll have to look for him somewhere else*
Hast du ihn anderswo/woanders gesehen?	*Have you seen him somewhere/ anywhere else?*

7.3 Adverbs of direction: *hin* and *her*

German expresses direction away from or towards the speaker in a much more systematic and consistent way than is usual or possible in English by the use of the adverbs *hin* and *her*. This pair of adverbs (which are sometimes called 'direction particles') have a wide range of use and may occur alone or linked with another word. Broadly speaking, *hin* denotes motion away from the speaker (or the person concerned), *her* towards him or her.

7.3.1 Direction adverbs are formed in German by compounding the place adverbs with *hin* or *her*

In this way a consistent differentiation is maintained between 'rest', 'motion away from the speaker' and 'motion towards the speaker'. In all cases, German thus has three terms at its disposal which may be illustrated first by the interrogative adverbs, i.e.:

Wo wohnen Sie?	*Where do you live?*
Wohin gehen Sie?	*Where are you going (to)?*
Woher kommen Sie?	*Where are you coming from?*

Similarly with the other adverbs given in section 7.2.1 and 7.2.5, all of which form similar sets with *-hin* and *-her*:

Sie wohnt hier	*She lives here*
Sie kommt hierher	*She's coming here*
Leg das Paket hierhin!	*Put the parcel down here*
Da/Dort wohnt sie	*She lives there*
In den Ferien fahren wir dahin, wo wir auch voriges Jahr waren	*In the holidays we're going where we were last year again*
Daher kommt sie	*That's where she comes from*
Er stand dort an der Ecke	*He was standing there on the corner*
Wie wollen wir dorthin kommen?	*How are we going to get there?*
Er geht heute nachmittag irgendwohin	*He's going somewhere this afternoon*
Sie geht überallhin	*She goes everywhere*
Morgen fahren wir anderswohin	*We're going somewhere else tomorrow*

Notes on these forms:

(a) *wohin, woher, dahin, daher* are often split out, especially in spoken German, with *hin* and *her* occupying the position of a separable prefix, e.g.:

Wo kommt deine Mutter **her**?　　**Wo** gehört dieses Buch **hin**?
ein kleines, gutes Restaurant, **wo** keine Amerikaner **hin**kamen (*V. Baum*)
Da gehe ich praktisch nie **hin**　　**Da** kommt er doch nicht **her**, oder?

This is not possible when these words are being used in an extended sense, e.g. *woher* in *Woher weißt du das?* 'How do you know that?' and *daher* in the meaning 'that is why', e.g. *Daher hat sie sich aufgeregt.*

(b) *von wo* and *von da/dort* are often used as alternatives to *woher, daher/dorther,* e.g.:

Von wo kommt er? Er kommt von da/dort

(c) *dahin* is used with *sein* in the meaning 'finished, lost', e.g.:

Sein Leben ist dahin　　Mein ganzes Geld war dahin

7.3.2 *hin* and *her* combine with many verbs in the manner of a separable prefix to mark the direction of the movement

(a) They may then be used without a specific 'here' or 'there' element
With verbs other than those of going, coming, etc., they frequently

correspond to a range of adverbs or adverb phrase forms in English, which has no comparable means of indicating direction:

Heute ist eine Wahlversammlung, und ich gehe hin	*There's an election meeting today and I'm going there/to it*
Ich hielt ihm die Zeitung hin	*I held out the newspaper to him*
Ich hörte einen Ruf und sah hin	*I heard a cry and looked over in that direction*
Komm mal her!	*Come here*
Gib den Schlüssel her!	*Give me the key*
Er hat mich mit dem Auto hergefahren	*He drove me here*
Halt den Teller her!	*Hold out your plate*
Setz dich her zu mir!	*Come and sit down over here by me*

(b) Many verbs compounded with *hin-* and *her-* have a derived, abstract or figurative meaning

Those with *hin-* tend to retain a directional meaning, whilst those with *her* are chiefly purely idiomatic, e.g.:

sein Leben für etwas hingeben	*to sacrifice one's life for sth*
Er hat sich der Hoffnung hingegeben, daß . . .	*He cherished the hope that . . .*
Das wird schon hinhauen (coll.)	*It'll be OK in the end*
Nach dem Interview war ich völlig hin	*After the interview I was shattered*
Sie fielen über ihn her	*They attacked him*
Das Thema gibt doch nicht viel her	*There's not a lot to this topic*
Es ging recht lustig her	*It was good fun*
Ich weiß nicht, wo das herkommt	*I don't know the reason for that*
Sie hat ein Zimmer für ihn hergerichtet	*She got a room ready for him*

7.3.3 *hin* and *her* may be used to emphasize direction with a preceding prepositional phrase

(a) They are then usually optional, e.g.:

Wir wanderten bis zu den Bergen (hin)   der Hof ist zur Straße hin offen
Wir fuhren nach Süden (hin)   Er ging zum Fenster (hin)
Wir wanderten durch das Tal (hin)   Sie flogen über den Berg (hin)
der Weg führt an der Wiese hin   (*along the meadow*)
Eine Stimme kam von oben (her)   Sie kommt wohl von weit her
Rings um ihn (her) tobte der Sturm

(b) With *hinter, neben, vor* and *zwischen, her* is used to indicate movement in relation to another person or thing

Note that the preposition always takes the dative in this construction:

Er ging hinter ihr her	*He was walking behind her*
Der Hund lief neben mir her	*The dog was running beside me*
Ein deutscher Wagen fuhr vor ihm her	*A German car was driving in front of him*
Sie ging zwischen uns her	*She was walking between us*

The adverbs *hinterher* and *nebenher* (but not *vorher*, which means 'previously', cf. 11.7.4a) are used in a similar sense, e.g. *Er lief hinterher, nebenher* 'He was running behind, alongside'.

(c) Phrases with *auf* giving reasons or causes, cf. 20.3.5d., may be strengthened by adding *hin*, e.g.:

Das tat er auf meinen Vorschlag hin	*He did it at my suggestion*
auf die Gefahr hin, erkannt zu werden	*at the risk of being recognized*

7.3.4 *hin-* and *her-* combine with prepositions or adverbs to form directional adverbs, e.g. *hinab, herab, hinzu, herbei*, etc.

These are most often used as separable verb prefixes. In general they link the direction indicated by the preposition or adverb with the notion 'away from' or 'towards' the speaker.

(a) Six prepositions form pairs of compounds with *hin-* and *her-*:

hinab, herab	*down*	**hinein, herein**	*in*
hinauf, herauf	*up*	**hinüber, herüber**	*over*
hinaus, heraus	*out*	**hinunter, herunter**	*down*

Wir stiegen die Treppe hinauf	*We climbed up the stairs*
Wir kamen die Treppe herab/herunter	*We came down the stairs*
Er ging in das Haus hinein	*He went into the house*
Er kam in das Zimmer herein	*He came into the room*

NB: (i) *hin-, herab* and *hin-, herunter* have identical meanings. Those with *-unter* are more usual in spoken registers.
(ii) *hinaus* and *heraus* are used with a preceding phrase with *zu* to indicate movement or vision out of or through doors, windows etc., e.g.:

Er blickte zur Tür hinaus	*He glanced out at the door*
Sie warf es zum Fenster heraus	*She threw it out of the window*

(b) A few other prepositions or adverbs combine in modern usage with only one of *hin-* or *her-*:

With ***hin-*:**	**hindurch** *through*	**hinweg** *away*	**hinzu** *in addition*
With ***her-*:**	**heran** *along; up (to)*	**herbei** *along*	
	herum *round*	**hervor** *forth, out*	

The forms *hinan* 'upward', *hernieder* 'down' and *herzu* 'along' are rarely used in modern German.

Er drang durch die Menge hindurch	*He pushed through the crowd*
Die Rollbahn sauste unter uns hinweg	*The runway sped away beneath us*
Sie legte einige Papiere hinzu	*She added some papers to the pile*
Sie trat an den Tisch heran	*She stepped up to the table*
Einige Polizisten kamen herbei	*A few policemen came along*
Er kam um die Ecke herum	*He came round the corner*
Die Bücher lagen auf dem Tisch herum	*The books were lying around on the table*

Er zog einen Revolver unter dem Tisch
    hervor
	He pulled a revolver out from under
	    the table

NB: Formal German used to make a clear distinction between *herum* 'round in a circle' and *umher* 'criss-crossing; higgledy-piggledy'. *herum* is now commonly used in both senses in both spoken and written German.

(c) The adverb with *hin-* or *her-* often repeats the direction given by a previous preposition and may appear tautologous or unnecessary, e.g.:

Der Vogel flog **in** das Zimmer **hinein**   Er kam **um** die Ecke **herum**
Wir kamen **aus** dem Wald **heraus**   Sie gingen **durch** das Tal **hindurch**

If the adverb is omitted, the effect is usually that the verb is emphasized rather than the direction and it should thus be used unless the verb is to be stressed. Compare:

Der Vogel ist in das Zimmer ge'**flog**en (i.e. it flew rather than hopped)
Der Vogel ist in das Zimmer hin'**ein**geflogen (i.e. it didn't fly <u>out</u>)
Wir wollen die Truhe in dein Zimmer '**trag**en (i.e. carry, not push)
Wir wollen die Truhe in dein Zimmer hin'**über**tragen

However, if another word in the sentence is to bear the main stress, the adverb is optional, e.g.:

Der '**Vog**el ist in das Zimmer (hinein) geflogen
Wir wollen die '**Tru**he in dein Zimmer (hinüber) tragen

(d) Verbs with the simple prefixes, e.g. *ab-, an-, auf-*, etc. most often have a derived, extended or other non-literal sense, cf. also 22.5.2.
This is because direction is indicated by using the forms in *hin-* or *her-*, e.g.:

Er ist (in das Zimmer) hineingegangen	*He went in(to the room)*
Die Zeitung ist eingegangen	*The newspaper folded*
Er hat den Koffer hereingebracht	*He brought the suitcase in*
Das bringt nichts ein	*That's not worth it*
Er kam (aus dem Haus) heraus	*He came out (of the house)*
Mit 100 Mark kommen wir nicht aus	*We won't manage on 100 marks*
Ich ging zu ihm hinüber	*I went over to him*
Er ist zur SPD übergegangen	*He went over to the SPD*

(e) A few verbs with *hin-* and *her-* compounds have developed figurative or extended meanings, e.g.:

sich zu etwas herablassen	*to condescend to (do) sth*
Er gibt eine Zeitschrift heraus	*He edits a journal*
Es kommt auf dasselbe heraus	*It all comes to the same thing*
Er leierte die Predigt herunter	*He reeled off the sermon*
Die Verhandlungen zogen sich hinaus	*The negotiations dragged on*

(f) In colloquial German, especially in the North, both *hin-* and *her-* are often reduced to '*r-* in compound forms, irrespective of the direction involved, e.g.:

Wollen wir jetzt 'rausgehen (written: hinausgehen)
Wollen wir die Jalousien 'runterlassen? (written: herunterlassen)

7.3.5 Some special meanings and uses of *hin-* and *her-*

(a) *hin-* **often has the sense 'down', e.g.:**

Sie legte sich hin   Der Junge fiel hin   Er setzte den Stuhl hin

(b) *vor sich hin* **'to oneself', e.g.:**

Das murmelte er so vor sich hin   Sie las vor sich hin

(c) *hin und her* **'to and fro', 'back and forth'**

Er ging auf der Straße hin und her	*He was walking back and forth along the street*
Ich habe es hin und her überlegt	*I've considered it from every point of view*

(d) *hin und wieder* **'now and again'**

Hin und wieder sehe ich ihn in der Stadt

(e) *her* **is used in the sense of 'ago' in time phrases,** cf. 11.6.12:

Zwei Jahre her zogen wir nach Duisburg um   Das ist schon lange her
Wie lange ist es her, daß du in Gießen studiert hast?

7.4 Adverbs of manner

7.4.1 Adverbs of manner usually either answer the question 'how?' or can be used to answer a yes/no question,
e.g.: Kommt sie morgen? – **Vielleicht.**

Most adverbs from adjectives, cf. 7.1.2, fall into this category, but there are a number which are only adverbial. The following represent a selection of the most frequent from the more comprehensive lists in DUDEN (1984:§589–95). Some of them, e.g. *allerdings* and *freilich*, can also be used as modal particles, cf. chapter 10:

allerdings	*certainly; mind you*	mitnichten (lit.)	*by no means*
anders (cf. 7.4.3)	*else*	möglicherweise	*possibly*
anscheinend	*apparently*	rundheraus	*bluntly*
beinahe	*almost*	schlechthin	*absolutely*
ebenfalls	*likewise*	sicherlich	*surely*
einigermaßen	*to some extent*	sonst (cf. 7.4.4)	*otherwise*
freilich	*admittedly*	umsonst	*in vain*
gleichfalls	*likewise*	unversehens	*inadvertently*
größtenteils	*largely*	vergebens	*in vain*
hoffentlich	*hopefully*	vielleicht	*perhaps*
immerhin	*all the same*	vielmehr	*rather*
leider	*unfortunately*	zweifellos	*without doubt*

7.4.2 A large number of German adverbs, principally of manner, have a verb or a subordinate clause construction as their only or most natural idiomatic English equivalent.

Thus the most frequent equivalent of the English verb *to like* is to use the German adverb *gern* with *haben* or another appropriate verb, e.g. *Ich esse gern Käsekuchen* 'I like cheesecake', *Sie hat ihren Lehrer ganz gern* 'She quite likes her teacher'. A selection of these is given below. In some cases a construction with a verb is also possible in German; for instance, 'It must be admitted that it isn't easy' could correspond to *Man muß zugeben, daß es nicht einfach ist* as well as *Es ist freilich nicht einfach*. But, as general, the equivalents with adverbs often sound rather more idiomatic and concise:

Das Problem ist **allerdings** schwierig	*I must admit that the problem is difficult*
Er wurde **allmählich** rot im Gesicht	*He began to get red in the face*
Er hat **andauernd** gespielt	*He kept on playing*
Er ist **angeblich** arbeitslos	*He claims to be unemployed*
Er ist **anscheinend** nicht gekommen	*He seems not to have come*
Wir können Ihnen **bedauerlicherweise** nicht weiter behilflich sein	*We regret that we can be of no further assistance to you*
Er ist **bekanntlich** ein hervorragender Linguist	*Everyone knows that he is an outstanding linguist*
Hier können Sie **beliebig** lange bleiben	*You can stay here as long as you wish*
Am besten behalten Sie das für sich	*You'd better keep that to yourself*
Thomas kommt **bestimmt** mit	*I'm sure Thomas is coming with us/ Thomas is sure to be coming with us*
Es ist **freilich** nicht einfach	*It must be admitted that it isn't easy*
Gegebenenfalls kann man auch eine andere Taste wählen	*If the need should arise, another key may be selected*
Im Sommer spielt er **gern** Tennis	*He likes playing tennis in summer*
Hoffentlich erreichen wir die Hütte vor Sonnenuntergang	*I hope we shall reach the cabin before sunset*
Sie kann **leider** nicht kommen	*I'm afraid she can't come*
Im Winter spielt er **lieber** Fußball	*He prefers playing football in the winter*
Ich habe Reiten **lieber** als Radfahren	*I prefer riding to cycling*
Er kommt **möglicherweise** noch vor dem Abendessen	*It is possible that he will be coming before dinner*
Die Firma stellt diese Ersatzteile **nicht mehr** her	*The company has ceased/stopped making these spare parts*
Nimm dir **ruhig** noch etwas zu trinken	*Don't be afraid to help yourself to another drink*
Alle Insassen sind **vermutlich** ums Leben gekommen	*It is presumed that all the passengers lost their lives*
Er las **weiter**	*He continued to read/went on reading*
Ich habe sie **zufällig** in der Stadt gesehen	*I happened/chanced to see her in town*
Zweifellos wird auch dieses Jahr sehr wenig Schnee im Allgäu fallen	*There is no doubt that very little snow will fall in the Allgäu this year either*

7.4.3 *anders* 'else; differently'

In origin, *anders* is a genitive of the adjective *ander*, cf. 5.5.2. Although the spelling *anderes* is sometimes found, it usually has the written form *anders*, which differentiates it from the nominative/accusative singular neuter singular of *ander*, which is most often written *andres* or *anderes*. It is used as follows (cf. also *sonst*, 7.4.4):

(a) In the meaning 'else' with *jemand, niemand* and (colloquially) *wer*, e.g.:

Es ist jemand (coll.: wer) anders gekommen	*Somebody else came*
Der Schirm gehört jemand anders	*the umbrella belongs to somebody else*
Ich habe mit niemand anders gesprochen	*I didn't talk to anybody else*
Sie hat niemand anders als dich gesucht	*She wasn't looking for anyone else but you*

NB: In standard German, *jemand, niemand* do not normally inflect in combination with *anders*. In written and spoken South German usage, inflected forms of *ander* are sometimes found rather than the invariable *anders*, most commonly in the accusative and dative, e.g. *jemand/niemand anderer* (rare) *jemand/niemand anderen, jemand/niemand anderem*. The genitive is occasionally used, e.g. *mein oder jemand anderes Buch* 'my book or somebody else's'.

(b) *anders* is used in the meaning 'else' with *wo, wohin, woher, (n)irgendwo*, e.g.:

woanders/anderswo/irgendwo anders	*somewhere else/elsewhere*
Ich gehe irgendwo anders hin/ woandershin/anderswohin	*I'm going somewhere else*
Er kommt anderswoher, nicht aus Hamburg	*He comes from somewhere else, not from Hamburg*
nirgendwo anders	*nowhere else*
Ich gehe nirgendwo anders hin	*I'm not going anywhere else*

(c) *anders* also means 'different(ly)', 'in a different way'

Er ist ganz anders als sein Bruder	*He is quite different to his brother*
Du mußt es irgendwie anders anpacken	*You'll have to tackle it differently*
Es ist etwas anders	*It is rather different*
(Compare: Es ist etwas and(e)res	*It is something else)*
Das klingt jetzt anders	*That sounds different now*
Es ist nicht viel anders	*It is not very different*

7.4.4 *sonst* 'else', 'otherwise'

(a) In some of its uses *sonst* overlaps with *anders* 'else', cf. 7.4.3, and *ander* 'other', 'different', e.g.:

Kannst du etwas anderes/sonst etwas vorschlagen?	*Can you suggest anything else?*
War noch jemand anders/sonst noch jemand da?	*Was anyone else here?*

Niemand anders/Niemand sonst hat mir geholfen	*Nobody else helped me*
sonstwo/sonst irgendwo/irgendwo sonst/anderswo, etc.., cf. 7.2.5.	*somewhere/anywhere else*
Ich muß noch sonstwohin/anderswohin	*I've got to go somewhere else*
Wenn noch andere Probleme/sonst noch Probleme auftauchen, . . .	*If any other problems arise, . . .*
Wer anders kann es gesagt haben?/ (more common:) Wer kann es sonst gesagt haben?	*Who else can have said it?*

(b) However, if the meaning is clearly 'different' or 'other', then only *ander* or, where appropriate, *anders*, may be used
Compare:

Da ist Professor Niebaum und niemand anders	*That's Professor Niebaum and nobody else* (i.e. not a different person)
Da ist Professor Niebaum und sonst niemand	*That's Professor Niebaum and nobody else* (i.e. he's the only one there)

(c) If the meaning is clearly 'in addition', 'apart from that', 'otherwise', then only *sonst* is possible:

Wer kommt sonst noch?	*Who else is coming?*
Mit wem haben Sie sonst noch gesprochen	*Who else did you talk to?*
Was hat sie sonst noch gesagt?	*What else did she say?*
sonst irgendwann	*some/any other time*
Sonst geht alles gut	*Otherwise all is well*
Wir müssen uns beeilen, sonst verpassen wir den Zug	*We'll have to hurry, otherwise we'll miss the train*
länger als sonst	*longer than usual*

7.4.5 Adverbs in *-weise*

The suffix *-weise* is extremely productive for the formation of adverbs in modern German. It is most often added to nouns or adjectives.

(a) Adverbs formed from a noun or a verb + *weise* most often have the sense 'by way of', 'in the form of', etc., e.g.:

andeutungsweise	*by way of a hint*	pfundweise	*by the pound*
ausnahmsweise	*by way of exception*	probeweise	*on approval*
beispielsweise	*by way of example*	ruckweise	*by jerks*
beziehungsweise	*or, as the case may be*	schrittweise	*step by step*
bruchstückweise	*in the form of fragments*	stückweise	*piecemeal*
dutzendweise	*by the dozen*	stundenweise	*by the hour*
familienweise	*in families*	teilweise	*partly*
gruppenweise	*in groups*	versuchsweise	*tentatively*
massenweise	*on a massive scale*	zeitweise	*temporarily*
paarweise	*in pairs*	zwangsweise	*compulsorily*

Sein Sohn und seine Tochter sind 10 beziehungsweise (abbrev.: bzw.) 14 Jahre alt	*His son and daughter are 10 and 14 years old respectively*
Die Flüchtlinge strömten massenweise über die ungarische Grenze	*The refugees were flooding in hordes across the Hungarian border*
Sein neues Buch ist stellenweise ganz gut	*His new book is quite good in places*
Er wird stundenweise bezahlt	*He is paid by the hour*

These forms, which were originally exclusively adverbial, are more and more often used as adjectives as well, e.g.:

eine probeweise Anstellung	die teilweisen Verbesserungen
eine ruckweise Bewegung	eine stundenweise Bezahlung
der stückweise Verkauf	die stufenweisen Fortschritte
eine schrittweise Verminderung der Streitkräfte in Europa (*SZ*)	

However, there are restrictions on their use as adjectives. They can only be used in standard German with nouns which denote a process, chiefly those which are derived from verbs, as in the examples above, cf. Fleischer (1974:304). Thus, combinations like *der stückweise Preis* or *eine auszugsweise Urkunde* are not acceptable.

(b) Also very productive are adverbs formed from adjectives or participles with the suffix *-weise* and the linking element*-er-*,
e.g. *möglicherweise* from *möglich, bezeichnenderweise* from *bezeichnend*. Most of them convey the speaker's judgement of or attitude towards the event or action in question. Their meaning is thus different from the adjective-adverb without the suffix or the corresponding phrase with *Weise*, e.g.:

Er war merkwürdig müde	*He was strangely tired*
Er war merkwürdigerweise müde	*Strange to say, he was tired*
Er war in merkwürdiger Weise müde	*He was tired in an unusual way*
Er hat vernünftig geantwortet	*He replied sensibly*
Er hat vernünftigerweise geantwortet	*Sensibly enough, he replied*
Er hat auf vernünftige Weise geantwortet	*He replied in a sensible way*

Similarly:

bedauerlicherweise *regrettably*	liebenswürdigerweise *obligingly*
begreiflicherweise *understandably*	möglicherweise *possibly, perhaps*
dummerweise *foolishly*	natürlicherweise *of course*
erstaulicherweise *astonishingly*	normalerweise *normally*
fälschlicherweise *erroneously*	überflüssigerweise *superfluously*
glücklicherweise *fortunately*	unglücklicherweise *unfortunately*
interessanterweise *interestingly*	unnötigerweise *unnecessarily*
komischerweise *funnily*	unvermuteterweise *unexpectedly*

These adverbs in *-weise* from adjectives are never used as adjectives.

7.5 Adverbs of degree

7.5.1 Adverbs of degree (or 'intensifiers') are used to emphasize, amplify or tone down another part of speech

They principally (though not exclusively) modify adjectives or other adverbs. The following list gives a selection of the most frequent adverbs of degree of German. It is not an exhaustive list; many more occur, particularly in colloquial speech (e.g. *echt, enorm, ungeheuer, unheimlich, verdammt,* etc.):

außerordentlich	*extraordinarily*	mäßig	*moderately*
äußerst	*extremely*	nahezu	*virtually*
beinahe	*almost, nearly*	recht	*really*
besonders	*especially*	relativ	*relatively*
durchaus	*absolutely, thoroughly*	sehr (cf.7.5.3)	*very*
etwas	*a little*	überaus	*extremely*
fast	*almost, nearly*	verhältnismäßig	*relatively*
ganz	*quite*	völlig	*completely*
genug	*enough*	vollkommen	*completely*
geradezu	*absolutely, virtually*	wenig	*little*
höchst	*extremely, highly*	ziemlich	*fairly*
kaum	*hardly, scarcely*	zu	*too*

Some examples of use:

eine durchaus selbstkritische Einsicht	*a thoroughly self-critical understanding*
Der Kaffee ist etwas süß	*The coffee is a little sweet*
Er fährt schnell genug	*He's driving fast enough*
Das ist geradezu lächerlich	*That is a little short of ridiculous*
Die Suppe war nur mäßig warm	*The soup was (only) moderately warm*
eine nahezu optimale Lösung des Problems	*a virtually optimal solution to the problem*
Er arbeitet recht gut	*He works really well*
ein überaus ehrliches Geschäft	*a thoroughly honest transaction*
Dieser Schriftsteller ist wenig bekannt	*This author is little known*

NB: (i) *hoch* 'highly' is used with a limited number of mainly abstract adjectives with which it is compounded, e.g. *hochempfindlich, hochfrequent, hochinteressant, hochgeschätzt, hochqualifiziert.*
(ii) *lange* and *längst* usually preceded by *noch*, are used before a negative to indicate a considerable difference in degree:

Das ist noch lange nicht gut genug	*That is not nearly good enough*
Dieses Buch ist lange/längst nicht so gut wie sein letztes	*This book isn't nearly as good as his last one*

7.5.2 A number of adverbs of degree are used only or principally with adjectives in the comparative or superlative, i.e.:

bedeutend *significantly*:
Die Donau ist bedeutend länger als der Rhein

beträchtlich *considerably*:
   Die Zugspitze ist beträchtlich höher als die anderen Gipfel in den bayrischen Alpen
denkbar *possible*:
   Sie hat den denkbar schlechtesten Eindruck gemacht
entschieden *decidedly*:
   Er hat entschieden schlechter gespielt als vor einem Jahr
viel *much*:
   Diese Schule ist viel größer als meine
weit *far*:
   Der Wagen ist weit schneller, als ich dachte
bei weitem *(by) far*:
   Er ist bei weitem besser als Jochen
   Er ist bei weitem der beste in der Klasse
weitaus *(by) far*:
   Isabella ist weitaus reifer, als man ihrem Alter nach schließen dürfte
   Der neueren Geschichte ist das weitaus größte Gewicht beizumessen
wesentlich *substantially*:
   Er hat heute wesentlich besser gespielt

7.5.3 *sehr* is chiefly used as an adverb of degree (= 'very'), e.g.:

Er weiß es **sehr** gut. Das ist **sehr** nett von dir.

However, it has a wider range of use than English *very*:

(a) It may modify a verb or phrase, corresponding to English 'very much', e.g.

Ich bewundere sie sehr   Er ist sehr dafür   Das interessiert mich sehr
Das ist sehr nach meinem Geschmack   Er hat sich sehr verändert

(b) After *so, wie* or *zu*, it can denote degree, corresponding to English 'much', e.g.:

Nicht so sehr die Handlung wie der Stil hat mich gefesselt
Wie sehr ich es bedaure, daß sie durchgefallen ist!
Er hat es sich zu sehr zu Herzen genommen

7.6 Interrogative adverbs

7.6.1 The following are the main interrogative adverbs in German

They correspond to the '*wh*-words' of English:

(a) time

wann? 'when?': Wann kommt der Zug in Gelsenkirchen an?
bis wann? 'until when?', 'how long?': Bis wann bleibt ihr hier?
   'by when?': Bis wann seid ihr damit fertig?
seit wann? 'since when?, 'how long?': Seit wann spielen Sie Tennis?
wie lange? 'how long?': Wie lange wollt ihr heute noch spielen?
wie oft? 'how often?': Wie oft fährt ein Bus nach Eberbach?

(b) place and direction (cf. also 7.3.1)

wo? 'where?': Wo steckt die Angelika jetzt?
wohin? 'where (to)?': Wohin fahrt ihr heute?/Wo fahrt ihr heute hin?
woher? 'where from?': Woher kommt der Wagen?/Wo kommt der Wagen her?
von wo? 'where from?': Von wo kommt der Wagen?

(c) manner

wie? 'how?': Wie habt ihr das nur gemacht?

(d) cause

warum? 'why?': Warum wollt ihr nicht gehen?
wieso? (coll.) 'why?': Wieso wollt ihr nicht gehen?
weshalb? (formal) 'why?': Weshalb wollt ihr nicht gehen?
wozu? 'what . . . for?': Wozu benutzt man das?

NB: (i) All the above interrogative adverbs may be used to introduce indirect questions, e.g.:
Er hat mich gefragt, wann ich morgen komme
Ich habe dir doch gesagt, wie man das macht
(ii) For the interrogative pronouns *was* and *wer*, see 5.3.3. For the interrogative determiner *welcher*, see 5.3.1.

8 Comparison of adjectives and adverbs

By using the 'comparative' and 'superlative' forms of adjectives or adverbs we can indicate the degree to which a particular noun possesses the quality expressed by the adjective. Thus:

'positive' degree:	Mein Haus ist **groß**	*My house is big*
'comparative' degree:	Ihr Haus ist **größer**	*Your house is bigger*
'superlative' degree:	Sein Haus ist **das größte**	*His house is the biggest*

In English we can form comparatives and superlatives in two ways. With short adjectives, we use the endings *-er* and *-est*, with longer adjectives *more* and *most*. In German, the endings *-er* and *-st* are used irrespective of the length of the adjective (but cf. 8.1.8).

Naturally, some adjectives or adverbs, such as *einmalig* or *absolut* have a meaning which excludes the possibility of comparison, and there are a number of other ways of indicating degree, for instance by modifying the adjective or adverb by an adverb of degree, cf. 7.5. This chapter deals with the formation of the comparative and superlative degree and other various forms and uses of comparison in German.

NB: The comparative is normally used to compare two items, the superlative more than two, e.g.:
der größere der beiden Brüder
Von den zwei Büchern über Berlin hat er das billigere gekauft
der größte von acht Kindern
Von diesen vielen Büchern hat er das billigste gekauft
However, as in English, this rule is not universally observed in colloquial speech.

8.1 Formation of comparative and superlative

8.1.1 The comparative and superlative degree of adjectives is formed by adding the endings *-er* and *-st* to the 'positive' stem, e.g.:

Positive	Comparative	Superlative
langsam	langsam**er**	der/die/das langsam**ste**
schnell	schnell**er**	der/die/das schnell**ste**
tief	tie**fer**	der/die/das tie**fste**
unwiderstehlich	unwiderstehlich**er**	der/die/das unwiderstehlich**ste**

NB: (i) The superlative almost always occurs in an inflected form, with the definite article.

150

(ii) The superlative of adverbs is formed by using this stem with the contraction *am*, e.g. *am langsamsten, am schnellsten*, and this form is sometimes also used after *sein*, cf. 8.3.1b.

(iii) Comparative and superlative forms inflect in the same way as any adjective when used before a noun, e.g. *ein schnellerer Zug, der schellste Zug, in der tiefsten Schlucht der Erde.*

(iv) There are a number of exceptions and irregularities in the formation of comparatives and superlatives, cf. 8.1.2 to 8.1.8.

8.1.2 Adjectives in *-el, -en, -er* may drop the *-e-* of the stem in the comparative

(a) Those in -el *regularly drop the* -e-, e.g.:

dunkel – dunkler, edel – edler

(b) Those in *-en* and *-er* usually drop the *-e-* if they have an inflectional ending:

trocken – der trocknere Wein   bitter – ein bittrer Geruch

If there is no inflectional ending, the *-e-* is usually retained in writing, though it often drops in speech:

Dieser Wein ist trockener   Dieser Geruch war bitterer

If the *-er* is preceded by a diphthong, the *-e-* is always lost:

teuer – Diese Tasche ist teurer   die teurere Tasche

8.1.3 Some adjectives add *-est* in the superlative, i.e.:

(a) Those whose stem ends in *-haft, -s, -sk, -ß, -x* and *-z*:

boshaft – boshafteste   lieblos – der liebloseste
brüsk – der brüskeste   süß – der süßeste
fix – der fixeste   stolz – der stolzeste

(b) Those whose stem ends in *-d, -t* and *-sch* most often have *-est* <u>unless</u> they have more than one syllable and the last syllable is unstressed:

mild – der mildeste   sanft – der sanfteste
rasch – der rascheste   berühmt – der berühmteste
BUT usually: spannend – der spannendste, komisch – der komischste, etc.

(c) Those whose stem ends in a long vowel or diphthong sometimes have *-est* as an alternative to *-st*:

früh – der frühste/früheste   treu – der treuste/treueste

8.1.4 A number of frequently used adjectives and adverbs have Umlaut in the comparative and superlative,

e.g. *arm – ärmer – der ärmste.*

(a) The following always have this Umlaut:

alt	dumm	jung	krank	oft	schwarz
arg	grob	kalt	kurz	scharf	stark
arm	hart	klug	lang	schwach	warm

NB: (i) *groß, hoch* and *nah* always have Umlaut, but are otherwise irregular, cf. 8.1.5.
(ii) *am häufigsten* is more usual than *am öftesten* as the superlative of *oft*.

(b) The following have alternative forms with and without Umlaut,

e.g. *naß – nässer/nasser – der nässeste/nasseste*:

bang	fromm	glatt	krumm	schmal
blaß	gesund	karg	naß	

The forms without Umlaut are increasingly common in modern German, especially in writing. Nevertheless, Umlaut is still more usual with *fromm* and *gesund*.

8.1.5 Some adjectives and adverbs have irregular forms in the comparative and superlative, i.e.:

bald	eher	am ehesten	*soon*
gern	lieber	am liebsten	*willingly, gladly*
groß	größer	der größte	*big, large*
gut	besser	der beste	*good*
hoch	höher	der höchste	*high*
nah	näher	der nächste	*near*
viel	mehr	der meiste	*much, many*
wenig	weniger/ minder	der wenigste/ der mindeste	*little, few*
wohl	wohler/ besser	am wohlsten/ am besten	*well*

NB: (i) *mehr* and *weniger* do not inflect, e.g. *Er hat weniger Geld als ich, mehr Verstand als du, der Verlust von weniger Stunden.*
(ii) *minder* is restricted to formal written German. It is only used to qualify adjectives, e.g. *Er ist nicht minder begabt als sein Bruder. mindest* tends to be used for *least* in the sense 'slightest', e.g. *Er hatte nicht die mindesten Aussichten zu gewinnen.*
(iii) *wohl* has comparative and superlative *wohler* and *am wohlsten* in the meaning 'at ease, (physically) well', e.g. *sich wohler fühlen*, but *besser* and *am besten* when it is used in the meaning 'well', i.e. the adverb from *good*.
(iv) *böse* is not used in the comparative or superlative. If necessary *schlimmer* and *der schlimmste* are used.
(v) *nichts weniger als* normally means 'anything but' (= *alles andere als*), e.g. *Er ist nichts weniger als klug.* For 'nothing less than', German will most often use a positive statement, e.g. *Das ist wirklich katastrophal* 'That is nothing less than catastrophic'.

8.1.6 Eight adjectives denoting position only have comparative and, in most cases, superlative forms:

der äußere	*outer, external*	der äußerste	*outermost, utmost*
der innere	*inner, internal*	der innerste	*innermost*
der obere	*upper*	der oberste	*uppermost*
der untere	*lower*	der unterste	*lowest, bottom*
der vordere	*front*	der vorderste	*foremost, front*
der hintere	*back*	der hinterste	*back(most)*
der mittlere	*central, middle*	der mittelste	*central, middle*
der niedere	*low, inferior*	(superlative not used)	
(mainly of social rank)			

NB: (i) These adjectives are only used before a noun, e.g.:
seine äußere Erscheinung   mit der äußersten Höflichkeit
seine innersten Gedanken   in der vorderen, vordersten Reihe
(ii) *äußerlich* and *innerlich* are available as equivalents of English 'external(ly)' and 'internal(ly)' after *sein* or as adverbs, e.g.:
Seine Verletzungen sind nicht äußerlich, sondern innerlich
Äußerlich blieb er ganz ruhig

8.1.7 The comparative and superlative of compound adjectives

(a) In general compound adjectives are treated as single words and form their comparative and superlative in the usual way, e.g.:

altmodisch *old-fashioned* – altmodischer – der altmodischste
vielsagend *meaningful* – vielsagender – der vielsagendste
vielversprechend *promising* – vielversprechender – der vielversprechendste
weittragend *far-reaching* – weittragender – der weittragendste

(b) However, if both parts are considered to retain their original meaning, the first has the comparative or superlative form

In practice, there is a fair amount of variation in the forms actually used and a selection of the most frequent are given, following DUDEN (1985:713–14):

ein schwerverständlicher Text   *a text which is difficult*
                                                    to understand
    ein schwerer verständlicher Text – der am schwersten verständliche Text
eine dichtbevölkerte Stadt   *a densely populated city*
    eine dichter bevölkerte/dichterbevölkerte Stadt
    – die am dichtesten bevölkerte/dichtstbevölkerte Stadt
ein hochgelegener Ort   *a place situated high up*
    ein höhergelegener Ort – der höchstgelegene Ort
naheliegende Gründe   *obvious reasons*
    näherliegende Gründe – nächstliegende Gründe

(c) In one or two cases there is a choice between treating the compound as a single word or inflecting the first element, e.g.:

schwerwiegende Gründe   *serious, weighty reasons*
   schwerer wiegende Gründe **or** schwerwiegendere Gründe
   – die am schwersten wiegenden Gründe **or** die schwerwiegendsten Gründe
weitgehende Beschränkungen   *extensive limitations*
   weitergehende Beschränkungen (Austr.) **or** weitgehendere Beschränkungen
   – weitestgehende Beschränkungen **or** weitgehendsten Beschränkungen

8.1.8 The use of *mehr* and *meist* in comparison

A very few adjectives form their comparative and superlative by means of a preceding *mehr* or *am meisten*, e.g.:

Er verrichtet jetzt eine ihm mehr zusagende Tätigkeit	*He is now performing a job which appeals to him more*
Dresden ist die durch den Krieg am meisten zerstörte deutsche Stadt	*Dresden is the German city to have been most completely destroyed in the war*
Er ist mir noch mehr zuwider als sein Bruder	*He is even more repugnant to me than his brother*
Er ist der am meisten bemitleidens- werte Kranke	*He is the most to be pitied of all the patients*

This form of comparison is restricted to use with participles which are not normally used as adjectives, a few adjectives which are only used predicatively, like *zuwider*, cf. 6.5.2, and unusually long and complex adjectives like *bemitleidenswert*.

    With past participles a prefixed *meist* – may be used rather than *am meisten*, e.g. *die meistzerstörte Stadt, der meistgekaufte Geschirrspül – automat Deutschlands*.

NB: *mehr* is used if two qualities of the same object are being compared, in the sense 'rather', e.g. *diese Arbeit ist mehr langweilig als schwierig. eher* is an alternative in rather more formal German.

8.2 Other types of comparison

8.2.1 Equality is expressed by *so . . . wie* (= 'as . . . as'):

Peter ist so alt wie Thomas   Er arbeitet so fleißig wie ich
Mein neuer Wagen fährt nicht so schnell wie deiner
Er ist nur halb so alt wie seine Schwester

A number of variations of this construction are possible, i.e.:

(a) In colloquial German, *als* is sometimes used for *wie*, e.g. *Peter ist so alt als Thomas*. This is not usually acceptable in formal registers, but DUDEN

(1985:42) permits it in the following cases:
(i) 'as well as' may be *sowohl wie* or *sowohl als*, e.g.:

Ich will sowohl Anna als/wie (auch) Helga einladen

(ii) 'as soon/little as possible' may be *so bald/wenig wie möglich* or *so bald/ wenig als möglich.*
(iii) 'twice as . . . as' may be *doppelt so . . . wie* or *doppelt so . . . als*:

Die Ernte ist doppelt so groß als/wie im vorigen Jahr

(b) *so* may be omitted in certain commonly used phrases:

Er ist (so) hart wie Stahl   Er ist (so) schlau wie ein Fuchs.

(c) 'just as' is expressed by *ebenso . . . wie* or *genauso . . . wie*:

Peter ist ebenso/genauso alt wie Thomas
Dort können wir genauso gutes Fleisch kaufen

ebenso is also used to indicate equivalence between two qualities:

Er ist ebenso fleißig wie geschickt   *He is as industrious as he is*
                                             skilful

ebensosehr is used to indicate degree (= 'just as much'), e.g.:

Die Brücke ist ebensosehr ein Teil der   *The bridge is just as much part of*
    Landschaft wie der Fluß   *the scenery as the river*
NB: Er ist nicht so sehr dumm   *He is not so much stupid as lazy*
    wie faul

(d) *gleich* can be used to indicate equality:

Peter und Thomas sind gleich alt   Diese Städte sind gleich groß

8.2.2 Many compound adjectives involve a measure of comparison,

e.g. *blitzschnell, fuchsteufelswild, lammfromm,* etc. These tend to indicate a high degree of the quality in question and depend on equations of the kind *so schnell wie der Blitz,* etc. Further common examples:

baumlang	jammerschade	samtweich	spottbillig
bildschön	(kohl)rabenschwarz	schneeweiß	steinreich
blutjung	mäuschenstill	spatzenfrech	todsicher
eiskalt	nagelneu	spinnefeind	

Most of these are idiomatic, in that the elements are only used in those particular combinations, e.g. *klitzeklein, funkelnagelneu.* But certain prefix elements may be used more widely, with a range of adjectives, e.g.:

hochbegabt, hochkarätig, etc. (cf. 7.5.1)
hyperkorrekt, hypersensibel, etc.
leicht-/schwerverletzt, leicht/schwerverwundet, etc.
tiefbetrübt, tiefgefühlt, etc.
überempfindlich, überschlank, etc.

8.2.3 The comparative particle is usually *als* (= 'than'):

Peter ist älter als Thomas   Mein Wagen fährt schneller als deiner

The following variations are found:

(a) In colloquial speech *wie* may be used rather than *als*,
e.g. *Er ist größer wie du.* This is particularly common in spoken German in the south and east, but is regarded as unacceptable in formal registers.

(b) *denn* is sometimes found for *als*
Essentially *denn* is archaic, but it may be used in formal registers to avoid consecutive *als als,* e.g.:

Er ist als Kritiker bekannter denn   *He is better known as a critic than*
   als Dichter   *as a poet*

In informal German *wie als* is more common to avoid *als als*.

NB: *denn* is used in a couple of set phrases, i.e. *mehr denn je* 'more than ever', *Geben ist seliger denn nehmen* 'It is better to give than to receive'.

(c) Degree of difference is expressed by *um . . . als*, or simply by a noun in the accusative:

Eine Fahrt im TGV-Atlantique kann um   *A trip on the TGV-Atlantique can*
   bis zu 50 Prozent teurer kommen als in   *work out up to 50% more expensive*
   einem herkömmlichen Schnellzug *(FR)*   *than in an ordinary express train*
Er ist (um) einen Monat jünger als ich   *He is a month younger than me*

(d) A greater degree (= 'even') is expressed by using *noch* with the comparative:

London ist eine noch schmutzigere   *London is an even dirtier city*
   Stadt als Amsterdam   *than Amsterdam*
Er hat gestern noch weniger gearbeitet   *He worked even less yesterday*
Es regnete noch stärker   *It was raining even harder*

8.2.4 Lower degrees of comparison, i.e. = 'less tall than', 'least tall', etc. are expressed by using *weniger, am wenigsten*:

Er war weniger optimistisch als sein   *He was less optimistic than his*
   Bruder   *brother*
Er arbeitet weniger fleißig als ich   *He works less hard than me*
der am wenigsten talentierte Spieler   *the least talented player*
Er arbeitet am wenigsten fleißig von   *He works the least hard of all*
   allen

NB: In practice, *am wenigsten* is little used for 'least' and other constructions tend to be preferred wherever they are available, cf.:
   die uninteressanteste Rede   *the least interesting speech*
   der billigste/preiswerteste Wagen   *the least expensive car*
   die einfachste Methode   *the least difficult method*
   möglichst geringe Kosten   *the least possible expenditure*

8.2.5 The 'absolute comparative'

The comparative of a number of common adjectives or adverbs is used not to signal a direct comparison, but to indicate a fair degree of the relevant quality, e.g. *ein älterer Herr* 'an elderly gentleman', *eine größere Stadt* 'a fair-sized town'. This is possible with the comparative of the following adjectives or adverbs:

alt	dick	dünn	gut	jung	kurz	neu
bekannt	dunkel	groß	hell	klein	lang	oft

Further examples:

eine bessere Wohngegend	*a fairly good neighbourhood*
seit längerer Zeit	*for a longish time now*
ein neueres Modell	*a fairly new model*
Kommen Sie öfter (coll. also: öfters) hierher?	*Do you come here quite often?*

8.2.6 Progression (i.e. 'more and more') is expressed by using *immer* with the comparative:

Er lief immer schneller	*He ran faster and faster*
Das Benzin wird immer teurer	*Petrol is getting dearer and dearer*
Meine Arbeit wird immer schwieriger	*My work is getting more and more difficult*

NB: A construction like that of English, e.g. *Er lief schneller und schneller* is occasionally found, but is rather less common than that with *immer*.

8.2.7 Proportion (i.e. 'the more . . . the more') is expressed by using the subordinating conjunction *je,* with *um so* or (predominantly in written German) *desto* beginning the following main clause:

Je länger man Deutsch lernt, desto/um so leichter wird es	*The longer you learn German, the easier it gets*
Je älter er wird, desto/um so witzigere Reden hält er	*The older he gets, the wittier are the speeches he gives*
je eher, desto/um so besser	*the sooner the better*
Je besser das Wetter, desto/um so mehr können wir wandern	*The better the weather, the more we can go walking*

NB: (i) In older German, a second *je* was frequently used rather than *desto* or *um so*. This is nowadays infrequent, even in formal styles, except in set phrases such as *je länger, je lieber* and *je länger, je mehr*.
(ii) As an equivalent to 'all the more because', German uses *um so mehr, als/da/weil* . . . cf.19.3.3
(iii) In colloquial German it is not uncommon to hear *um so . . . um so*, e.g. *um so größer, um so besser* 'the bigger, the better'.

8.3 Types and uses of the superlative

8.3.1 The superlative form *am . . . sten* (cf. 8.1.1) is used in the following cases:

(a) always for adverbs:

Von allen Gästen sprach er am wenigsten	*Of all the guests he spoke least*
Ich arbeite am besten nachts	*I work best at night*
Am einfachsten schickst du es ihm per Eilboten	*The simplest thing is to send it to him by express mail*
Helmut läuft am schnellsten	*Helmut runs fastest*
Das hasse ich an den Schulmeistern am meisten (*T. Valentin*)	*That's what I hate most about schoolmasters*

(b) after the verb *sein*

Here both superlative forms are found, e.g. *Wer von euch ist am stärksten?* and *Wer von euch ist der stärkste*. The form with the article may be used if a noun is understood:

Diese Blume ist die schönste (i.e. Blume)	*This flower is the most beautiful*
Unter den deutschen Flüssen ist die Donau der längste (i.e. Fluß)	*Of the German rivers the Danube is the longest*

The form with *am* is also quite regularly used in such cases, e.g. *Diese Blume ist am schönsten . . . ist die Donau am längsten*.

The form with *am* is always used if there is no noun to be understood or if something is being compared with itself (= 'at its most . . .'):

Ein Mercedes wäre am teuersten	*A Mercedes would be the dearest*
Für meinen Geschmack ist eine Nelke schöner als eine Tulpe, aber eine Rose ist natürlich am schönsten	*For my taste a carnation is nicer than a tulip, but a rose is the nicest*
Hier ist der Rhein am tiefsten	*The Rhine is (at its) deepest here*
Der Garten ist am schönsten im Juni	*The garden is (at its) nicest in June*

8.3.2 Any superlative may be used in an absolute ('elative') sense, i.e. not as a comparison but in the sense 'extremely':

in höchster Erregung	*in great excitement*
mit größter Mühe	*with the greatest difficulty*
Es ist höchste Zeit, daß . . .	*It is high time that . . .*
Ich habe den ehrlichsten Respekt vor ihm	*I have the most genuine respect for him*
Es herrschte das rauheste Wetter	*The weather was extremely raw*
Modernste Kureinrichtungen stehen zu Ihrer Verfügung (*FAZ*)	*You will have the use of the most up-to-date spa treatment*

8.3.3 An adverbial absolute superlative is formed in *aufs . . . ste,* e.g. *aufs heftigste, aufs genaueste*, etc. It is widely used in formal written German:

Der große runde Tisch war aufs festlichste geschmückt (*Dürrenmatt*)	*The large round table was decorated in a most festive way*
Herr Naumann war aufs äußerste gereizt (*MM*)	*Mr Naumann was exceedingly irritated*
Sie protestierten aufs schärfste gegen die Verurteilung Max Reimanns (*ND*)	*they protested most strongly against the conviction of Max Reimann*
Der Vorfall hat mich aufs peinlichste berührt	*The incident made me feel most uncomfortable*

8.3.4 Some special adverbial superlatives are formed in -st, -stens and zu . . . st

In the main they have an absolute meaning, but only a few of each formation are still widely used, i.e.:

(a) The forms consisting simply of the superlative stem in -st have all developed distinct meanings
The following are still used:

äußerst *extremely*	längst *for a long time; a long time ago*
*eiligst *as quickly as possible*	meist *mostly*
*freundlichst *friendly*	möglichst *as . . . as possible*
gefälligst, *gütigst *kindly*	*schleunigst *as promptly as possible*
herzlichst *most cordially*	*sorgfältigst *most carefully*
höchst *highly, extremely*	tunlichst *absolutely*
*höflichst *respectfully*	unlängst *recently*

Those asterisked (*) are limited to use in very formal registers, often in formulaic idioms. They can sound rather stilted and some authorities, e.g. Götze and Hess-Lüttich (1989:244), advise against using them. Examples:

Ich danke Ihnen herzlichst	*I thank you most cordially*
Sie werden höflichst gebeten, diesen Irrtum ohne Verzug zu berichtigen	*You are kindly requested to rectify this mistake without delay*
Könnten Sie mir gefälligst eine Erklärung dafür geben?	*Could you be so kind as to give me an explanation for this?*
Wir bitten Sie, diesem Ersuchen schleunigst entgegenzukommen	*We ask you to accede to this request with all due speed*
Jeder Lärm ist tunlichst zu vermeiden	*Any noise is absolutely to be avoided*

The others are more widely used:

Sie zeigte sich äußerst dankbar	*She showed herself to be extremely thankful*
Die Situation ist höchst problematisch	*The situation is highly problematical*
Das weiß ich doch schon längst	*I've known that for a long time*
Er ist längst gestorben	*He died a long time ago*
Er kommt meist gegen Abend (more often: meistens)	*He mostly comes towards the evening*
Du mußt einen möglichst guten Eindruck machen	*You must make the best possible impression*

Komme möglichst früh am Morgen	*Come as early in the morning*
	as possible
Sie ist unlängst zurückgekehrt	*She got back recently*

NB: Some forms in *-st*, i.e. *best-, größt-, höchst-, kleinst-, kürzest-* may be compounded with *möglich* to mean 'the best possible', etc., e.g. *die bestmögliche Lösung, der größtmögliche Schaden, die kleinstmögliche Summe, der kürzestmögliche Weg.*

(b) Those in *-ens* which are still widely used:

bestens *very well*	schnellstens *as quickly as possible*
höchstens *at the most*	spätestens *at the latest*
meistens *mostly*	strengstens *strictly*
mindestens *at least*	wärmstens *most warmly*
nächstens *shortly, soon*	wenigstens *at least*

Selected examples in context:

Ich danke Ihnen bestens	*I thank you very much*
Es kommen höchstens dreißig Gäste	*At most thirty guests are coming*
Ich stehe meistens früh auf	*I mostly get up early*
(more formal: meist)	
Die Einwohner sind meistens Türken	*The inhabitants are mainly Turks*
Ich brauche mindestens tausend Mark	*I need at least a thousand marks*
für diese Reise	*for this trip*
Wir kommen spätestens um sechs an	*We'll arrive at six at the latest*
Rauchen ist strengstens verboten	*Smoking is strictly prohibited*
Ich kann das Buch wärmstens empfehlen	*I can recommend the book most warmly*
Er könnte wenigstens anrufen	*He might at least ring up*

NB: *wenigstens* and *mindestens* are often interchangeable, but *mindestens* emphasizes the idea of the absolute minimum possible rather more strongly. It is used less often when no actual figure is mentioned, in which case *zumindest* (cf. (c) below) is a possible, rather more emphatic alternative to *wenigstens*.

(c) A few forms in *zu . . . st* are still current:

zumindest at *(the very) least*	zutiefst *(very) deeply*
zunächst *at first, in the first place*	zuvorderst *(right) at the front*
zuoberst *(right) on top*	

Some examples of use in context:

Er hätte uns zumindest grüßen können	*He could at least have said hello*
Das Angebot sah zunächst verlockend	*The offer looked attractive at first*
aus	
Sie nahm des Buch, das zuoberst lag	*She took the book which was lying*
	on top
Ich war zutiefst davon beeindruckt	*I was deeply impressed by it*

9 Numerals

9.1 Cardinal numbers

9.1.1 The forms of the cardinal numbers:

0 null	10 zehn	20 zwanzig
1 eins	11 elf	21 einundzwanzig
2 zwei	12 zwölf	22 zweiundzwanzig
3 drei	13 dreizehn	23 dreiundzwanzig
4 vier	14 vierzehn	24 vierundzwanzig
5 fünf	15 fünfzehn	25 fünfundzwanzig
6 sechs	16 sechzehn	26 sechsundzwanzig
7 sieben	17 siebzehn	27 siebenundzwanzig
8 acht	18 achtzehn	28 achtundzwanzig
9 neun	19 neunzehn	29 neunundzwanzig

30 dreißig	70 siebzig
40 vierzig	80 achtzig
50 fünfzig	90 neunzig
60 sechzig	100 hundert

101 hundert(und)eins	1000 tausend
102 hundertzwei	1001 tausend(und)eins
151 hunderteinundfünfzig	1099 tausend(und)neunundneunzig
200 zweihundert	1100 tausendeinhundert/elfhundert

564 297 fünfhundertvierundsechzigtausendzweihundertsiebenundneunzig
1 000 000 eine Million
2 000 000 zwei Millionen
5 276 423 fünf Millionen zweihundertsechsundsiebzigtausendvierhundert-
dreiundzwanzig
1 000 000 000 eine Milliarde

9.1.2 Notes on the forms of the cardinal numbers

(a) Complex numbers are in practice never written out in full,
i.e. those with more than one element, like *zweiunddreißig*, *hundert-zwanzig*. In general, figures are used in written German rather more frequently than is customary in English.

(b) Numbers higher than a thousand are written with spaces every three digits,
i.e. **not** commas as in English, e.g. 564 297, not 564,297. The comma is used in German for the English decimal point, cf. 9.3.3.

(c) *hundert* **or** *einhundert***?**
A distinction is usually made between *hundert* 'a hundred', *tausend* 'a thousand' and *einhundert* '**one** hundred', *eintausend* '**one** thousand'. However, *ein* is normally inserted in complex numbers, e.g. 101 100 *hunderteintausendeinhundert*.

(d) *und* **may be used, optionally, between** *hundert* **and** *eins,*
e.g. *hundert(und)eins, zweihundert(und)eins* and between *tausend* and tens or units, e.g. *tausend(und)eins, viertausend(und)elf, zwanzigtausend(und) zweiunddreißig*

(e) *eine Million* **and** *eine Milliarde* **are treated as separate nouns**
They are always used with a plural ending where necessary, e.g.:

zwei Millionen   fünf Millionen vierhunderttausend

Numbers higher than *eine Milliarde* are not found in everyday use. *tausend Milliarden* is thus more usual than *eine Billion*.

(f) The old form *zwo* **is often heard for** *zwei* **to avoid the possibility of confusion with** *drei*
This usage is particularly frequent on the telephone, but it has become common in other spoken contexts and is extended to *2* in complex numbers, e.g. *zwounddreißig*, and the ordinal *der zwote*.

(g) The numbers from *2* **to** *12* **have alternative forms with an additional** *-e,*
e.g. *sechse, neune, elfe*. These are common in spoken colloquial German (especially in the south) for emphasis, particularly when stating the time, e.g. *Ich bin um fünfe aufgestanden*.

(h) Longer numbers are often stated in pairs,
e.g. *4711* (a brand of Eau de Cologne), spoken *siebenundvierzig elf*. This usage is regular with telephone numbers (but not the dialling code), e.g. *(0621) 54 87 23*, which will usually be given as *null sechs zwo eins – vierundfünfzig siebenundachtzig dreiundzwanzig*.

(j) Years are usually stated in hundreds,
e.g. *1988*: *neunzehnhundertachtundachtzig*.

(k) *beide* **is commonly used in contexts where English uses the numeral** *two*
This is particularly the case where it is a question of 'two and only two' of the relevant items, cf. 5.5.3, e.g. *Ich möchte diese beiden Hemden* 'I would like these two shirts'.

(l) *fünfzehn* **and** *fünfzig*
These are usually pronounced *fuffzehn* and *fuffzig* in informal colloquial speech.

(m) As an indefinite large number, corresponding to English *umpteen*, colloquial German uses *zig*:

Ich kenne sie schon zig Jahre	*I've known her umpteen years*
Die ist mit zig Sachen in die Kurve gefahren	*She took the bend at a fair old speed*

Cf. also the compounds *zigmal* 'umpteen times', *zigtausend* 'umpteen thousand', etc.

(n) Cardinal numbers used as nouns
Where these refer to the numeral as such, they are feminine and have a plural in *-en*, e.g.:

Die Sieben ist eine Glückszahl   In Mathe habe ich nie eine Fünf gehabt
Die Hundert ist eine dreistellige Zahl
Beim Abitur hat er drei Zweien und eine Eins gekriegt

NB: The feminine forms *die Hundert* and *die Tausend*, referring to the numbers as such, are to be distinguished from the neuters *das Hundert* and *das Tausend*, which refer to quantities, cf. 9.1.6b.

(o) The numeral 7 is usually written in handwriting with a stroke,
i.e. 7, to distinguish it from 1.

9.1.3 *eins, ein, einer* 'one'

(a) The form *eins* is used in isolation as a numeral,
i.e. in counting and the like, cf. also:

Wir müssen mit der (Linie) Eins zum Bahnhof fahren	*We've got to take the number one* (i.e. tram, bus) *to the station*

(b) The form *ein*, with the same endings as the indefinite article, cf. 4.1.2, is used with a following noun, e.g.:

ein Tisch *one table*   eine Kirche *one church*   ein Buch *one book*
durch einen Fehler *by one mistake*   aus einem Grund *for one reason*

The numerical sense of *ein* (i.e. 'one') is distinguished from the indefinite article (i.e. 'a, an') in speech by always being pronounced in full. In writing, if there is any likelihood of ambiguity in context, the numerical sense can be made clear by the use of an accent, italics, underlining or spacing, e.g.:

ein Buch   *ein* Buch   ein Buch   e i n Buch

In practice this is only necessary in exceptional cases.

NB: (i) After *hundert* and *tausend*, e.g. *301, 2001*, there is much uncertainty as to what constitutes correct or even acceptable usage. The combinations *hundertundeine Mark* '101 marks' and *Tausendundeine Nacht* 'The Arabian Nights' are well established idiomatically. However, few Germans are wholly sure whether this construction can be used with other nouns, i.e. *ein Buch mit dreihundertundeiner Seite?*. Equally, the alternative of undeclined *-ein*, with a plural noun, e.g. *ein Buch mit dreihundertein Seiten* , which is offered by DUDEN (1984:457), is felt by many to be unnatural.

(c) The form *einer*, with the same endings as *dieser*, is used as a pronoun (cf. also 5.5.5), e.g.:

Wir haben einen Rottweiler, und ihr habt auch **einen**, nicht?
einer der Männer *one of the men* **ein(e)s** der Häuser *one of the houses*

(d) After a determiner, e.g. *der eine*, *ein-* declines like an adjective, e.g.:

Das Dorf hatte bloß die eine Straße
Mit seinem einen Auge sieht er schlecht.

(e) Undeclined *ein* is used in a few constructions
(i) In *ein oder zwei, ein bis zwei, ein* is not declined, e.g.:

Ich pflückte ein oder zwei Rosen   Wir müssen ein bis zwei Tage warten
Er kam vor ein oder zwei Wochen   Ich sprach mit ein oder zwei anderen
BUT: with *Mark*: eine bis fünf Mark

(ii) When linked with *andere* or *derselbe*, the alternatives of using endings with *ein* or leaving it uninflected are equally acceptable. With *mehrere*, *ein* is more commonly inflected:

Ein(er) oder der andere machte eine   *One or other made a brief remark*
    kurze Bemerkung
An ein(em) und demselben Tag machten   *On one and the same day three*
    drei Firmen Pleite   *firms went bankrupt*
vor einem (rarely: ein) oder mehreren   *one or more months ago*
    Monaten

(iii) *ein* is not inflected in *ein Uhr* 'one o'clock'. Compare *eine Uhr* 'a/one clock'.

9.1.4 Inflection of cardinal numbers

Apart from *ein* 'one', which is declined as explained in section 4.1.2, cardinal numbers do not normally have any inflectional endings in German. Thus:

gegen sechs Kinder   mit sechs Kindern   wegen sechs Kindern
die sechs Kinder   mit den sechs Kindern   wegen der sechs Kinder

However, endings are found in one or two special uses:

(a) *zwei* and *drei* have the genitive forms *zweier* and *dreier*
These are quite frequent in formal written German, e.g.:

Der Taufe zweier Kinder aus der Ehe   *He agreed to the baptism of two*
    stimmte er zu (*MM*)   *children of the marriage*
die vielerlei Eindrücke dreier   *the various impressions*
    anstrengender Tage (*Zeit*)   *from three strenuous days*

Note that a following adjective has the 'strong' ending -*er*. In less formal German the paraphrase with *von* is used, e.g. *die Eindrücke von drei anstrengenden Tagen.*

(b) The numbers from *2* to *12* may have a dative in -*en* when used in isolation, e.g.:

Nur einer von zweien ist als gesund zu bezeichnen (*Zeit*)
als sich die Tür hinter den dreien geschlossen hatte (*Welt*)

This is not uncommon with the numbers 2, 3 and 4 in spoken German beside the endingless form, i.e. *einer von zwei*, etc. It is perhaps most frequent for emphasis and in set phrases such as *auf allen vieren* 'on all fours', *mit dreien* 'with three (Jacks)' (in the card game *Skat*) and in the formula *zu zweien, dreien, vieren* etc. 'in twos, threes, fours', e.g.:

dieser Spaziergang zu zweien (*Th. Mann*)

A rather more frequent alternative here is the form in -*t*, using the stem of the ordinal, cf. 9.2.1, e.g. *zu zweit, zu dritt, zu viert*. DUDEN (1984:458) points to a possible distinction between *zu zweien* 'in pairs' and *zu zweit* 'as a pair' (i.e. when there are only two), e.g.:

Sie gingen zu zweien über die Straße	*They crossed the road in pairs*
Sie gingen zu zweit über die Straße	*The two of them crossed the road together*

9.1.5 Cardinals have an adjectival form in -*er* which is used to denote value and measurement, or with reference to years

When used as nouns, they have the dative ending -*n*:

Ich habe zwei Zehner und einen Hunderter	*I've got two ten mark notes and a hundred mark note*
ein Zwanziger	*a twenty mark note*
zwei Fünfziger	*two fifty pfennig pieces* **or** *two fifty mark notes*
zehn neunziger Marken	*ten 90 pfennig stamps*
eine Neunziger	*a 90 pfennig stamp*
die Zehner und die Einer	*tens and units*
eine Sechserpackung	*a six-pack*
in den neunziger Jahren dieses Jahrhunderts	*in the nineties of this century*
ein Mann in den Vierzigern	*a man in his forties*
eine Mittfünfzigerin	*a woman in her mid-fifties*
ein Dreitausender	*a mountain (over) 3000 metres high*
ein neunundachtziger Heppenheimer Krötenbrunnen	*an '89 Heppenheimer Krötenbrunnen (i.e. a wine vintage 1989)*

9.1.6 hundert, tausend, Dutzend

(a) *hundert* and *tausend* are used as normal numerals

They are then not declined and may be preceded by quantifiers such as
einige, *mehrere*, *viele*, etc.:

hundert, zweihundert Häuser	*a hundred, two hundred houses*
viele hundert Kisten	*many hundreds of cases*
mit mehreren hundert Kisten	*with several hundred cases*
einige tausend Bücher	*a few thousand books*

(b) *das Hundert, das Tausend* and *das Dutzend* are used as nouns of quantity

They have a plural in *-e*, and, in the genitive plural, the ending *-er* if no
determiner precedes:

das zweite Dutzend	*the second dozen*
Hunderttausende von Menschen	*hundreds of thousands of people*
Die Menschen verhungerten zu Hunderten und Tausenden	*People were starving in hundreds and thousands*
die Beschwerden Dutzender von Touristen	*the complaints of dozens of tourists*
die Flucht Tausender DDR-Bewohner (*Spiegel*)	*the flight of thousands of inhabitants of the GDR*
die Ersparnisse vieler Tausende	*the savings of many thousands of people*

NB: (i) *Dutzend* does not take the plural ending when used as a measurement noun in
constructions such as *drei Dutzend (Eier)* 'three dozen (eggs)', cf. 1.2.12.
(ii) For the use of the genitive, apposition or a phrase with *von* after the nouns
Dutzend, Hundert, Tausend see 2.7.4.

9.1.7 Qualification of cardinal numbers

Numerals may be modified by a number of adverbs of degree, e.g.:

etwa, rund, ungefähr, circa/zirka (abbrev.: ca.) *approximately*
über *over*   unter *under*   zwischen *between*   knapp *barely*

NB also:

Es dauert gut drei Stunden	*It lasts a good three hours*
Er gab mir ganze fünf Mark	*He gave me all of five marks*

Some of these adverbs are identical with prepositions and the use of cases
with them may appear inconsistent:

(a) *an* (+ acc.) is used in the sense of 'getting on for', e.g.:

Da standen an siebenhundert deutsche Kriegsgefangene (*Plievier*)

(b) *an* and *um* 'about' are often followed by a definite article
A following adjective has strong endings, e.g.:

Im Hotel sind zur Zeit an die, um die vierzig ausländische Gäste

(c) *bis zu* 'up to', *gegen* 'about', *über, um, unter* and *zwischen* do not
influence the case of a following noun when used adverbially with a
numeral,
i.e. in cases where the sentence would still be grammatically correct if they
were omitted:

Bis zu zehn Kinder können mitfahren	*Up to ten children can come with us*
Sie ist zwischen 30 und 40 Jahre alt	*She is between 30 and 40 years old*

However, when used as prepositions, *gegen, über* and *um* take the
accusative, *bis zu, unter* and *zwischen* the dative. In such cases the sentence
ceases to be grammatically correct if they are omitted:

Kinder unter sieben Jahren zahlen die Hälfte	*Children under seven years old pay half-price*
Kinder über sechs Jahre zahlen voll	*Children over six years old pay the full price*
geeignet für Kinder zwischen sieben und zwölf Jahren	*suitable for children between the ages of seven and twelve*

9.2 Ordinal numbers

9.2.1 The formation of ordinal numbers

The majority of ordinal numbers are formed by adding the suffix *-te* to the
cardinals *2-19* and *-ste* to the cardinals from *20* upwards. The few
exceptions to this pattern are shown in bold print in the table below. All
ordinal numbers are used and declined as adjectives:

1 der **erste**	11 der elfte	30 der dreißigste
2 der zweite	12 der zwölfte	40 der vierzigste
3 der **dritte**	13 der dreizehnte	50 der fünfzigste
4 der vierte		
5 der fünfte	20 der zwanzigste	100 der hundertste
6 der sechste	21 der einundzwanzigste	101 der hundert(und)erste
7 der **siebte**	27 der siebenundzwanzigste	117 der hundertsiebzehnte
8 der **achte**		
9 der neunte		1000 der tausendste
10 der zehnte		1 000 000 der millionste
5473 der fünftausendvierhundertdreiundsiebzigste		

9.2.2 Notes on the forms and uses of the ordinals

(a) English 'to be the first to'
As an equivalent, German uses either *als erster*, or *der erste* followed by a relative clause:

Die Russen waren die ersten, die einen
   künstlichen Erdsatelliten um den
   Globus schickten; sie brachten als
   erste einen Menschen in den Weltraum
   (*Zeit*)

The Russians were the first to send an artificial satellite round the earth; they were the first to put a man into space

Ich war als erster an Ort und Stelle

I was the first to be on the spot

(b) *der x-te* (pronounced [ɪkstə]) and *der zigste*, cf. 9.1.2l, are used as indefinite ordinals,
i.e. as equivalents of English 'the umpteenth', e.g.:

Das war mein x-ter/zigster Versuch

(c) The ordinal stems may be compounded with superlatives, e.g.:

die zweitbeste Arbeit   die drittgrößte Stadt   der zweithöchste Berg

(d) Ordinal numbers are indicated in writing with a following full stop, e.g. *am 14. Mai, das 275. Regiment*.

9.2.3 For 'first(ly)', 'secondly' etc., German uses the stem of the ordinal with the suffix *-ens*,
e.g. *erstens* 'first(ly)', *zweitens* 'secondly', *drittens* 'thirdly', etc.

Alternatively, the forms *zum ersten, zum zweiten, zum dritten*, etc. are used.

9.3 Fractions

9.3.1 Fractions (*die Bruchzahlen*) are formed by adding *-el* to the ordinal stem
(with the exception of 'half', cf. 9.3.2), e.g.:

ein Drittel   ein Viertel   ein Fünftel   ein Achtel   ein Zehntel

Fractions are neuter nouns. They have an endingless plural, e.g. *zwei Drittel*, and often lack the *-n* in the dative plural, e.g.:

Die Prüfung wurde von vier Fünftel(n) der Schüler bestanden

When followed by a noun they are spelled with a small letter and an accompanying indefinite article takes its case and gender from the noun, e.g.:

mit einer drittel Flasche   mit einem viertel Liter

They are often written together with common measurement words, e.g. *ein Viertelliter*, *funf Achtelliter*, *vier Zehntelgramm* and (especially) *eine Viertelstunde*. The following alternative usages are thus possible:

Er verfehlte den Rekord um drei Zehntel einer Sekunde
Er verfehlte den Rekord um drei zehntel Sekunden
Er verfehlte den Rekord um drei Zehntelsekunden

dreiviertel is normally treated as a single word, e.g. *dreiviertel der Klasse*. It is compounded with *Stunde*, e.g. *in einer Dreiviertelstunde* 'in three-quarters of an hour'.

Used with full integers, they are read out as written, with no *und*, e.g.: $3^2/_5$ *drei zweifünftel*, $1^7/_{10}$ *eins siebenzehntel*

9.3.2 'half' corresponds to the German adjective *halb* and the noun *die Hälfte*

These are used as follows:

(a) 'half', used as a noun, is normally *die Hälfte*:

Er hat mir nur die Hälfte gegeben	*He only gave me half*
die größere Hälfte	*the bigger half*

However, the form *das Halb*, from the adjective, is used to refer to the number as such:

(Ein) Halb ist mehr als ein Drittel   *Half is more than a third*

(b) *half a*: the usual equivalent is the indefinite article plus *halb*:

Ich aß einen halben Apfel	*I ate half an apple*
ein halbes Dutzend	*half a dozen*
ein halbes Brot	*half a loaf*

(c) *half the/this/my*
The most frequent equivalent is *die Hälfte* with a following genitive, but the appropriate determiner may be used with *halb* when referring to a whole entity which can be divided cleanly in two:

Die Hälfte der Äpfel ist schlecht	*Half the apples are bad*
die Hälfte meines Geldes	*half my money*
Ich aß die Hälfte des Kuchens ⎫	
Ich aß den halben Kuchen ⎭	*I ate half the cake*

NB: The use of *halb* with a plural noun in such cases, e.g. *die halben Apfel* 'half the apples' is regarded as substandard colloquial usage.

(d) Adverbial *half* corresponds to *halb*:

halb angezogen	*half dressed*
Er weiß alles nur halb	*He only half knows things*

(e) *one and a half* is either *eineinhalb* or (in rather more informal usage) *anderthalb*. $2^1/_2$, $3^1/_2$ etc. are *zweieinhalb*, *dreieinhalb*, etc.

These forms are not declined:

Bis Walldürn sind es noch eineinhalb/ anderthalb Stunden	*It's another hour and a half to Walldürn*
Sie wollte noch sechseinhalb Monate bleiben	*She wanted to stay another six and a half months*

(f) Some other phrases and idioms:

Er hatte halb soviel wie ich	*He had half as much as me*
Kinder fahren zum halben Preis	*Children travel half price*
Er ist mir auf halbem Wege entgegen- gekommen	*He met me half-way (literal and figurative sense)*
Ich nehme noch ein Halbes	*I'll have another half*
Das ist nichts Halbes und nichts Ganzes	*That's neither flesh nor fowl*
Die Besucher waren zur Hälfte Deutsche	*Half the visitors were German*
nach der ersten Halbzeit	*after the first half* (sport)
halb Europa, halb München (cf.6.2.5g)	*half Europe, half Munich*

9.3.3 In German, decimals are written with a comma,
i.e. **not** with a point, e.g.:

3,426 *dreikommavierzweisechs*	0,7 *nullkommasieben*
4,75 *vierkommasiebenfünf*	109,1 *hundertneunkommaeins*

In colloquial speech, two places of decimals may be read out in terms of tens and units, e.g. 4,75 *vierkommafünfundsiebzig*.

9.4 Other numerical usages

9.4.1 Numerically equal distribution is expressed by *je*:

Ich gab den Jungen je zehn Mark	*I gave each of the boys ten marks*
A. und B. wurden zu je drei Jahren verurteilt	*A. and B. were each sentenced to three years*
Sie erhielten je fünf Kilo Reis	*They each received five kilograms of rice*

9.4.2 Multiples (i.e.'single', 'twofold', etc.) are expressed by suffixing -*fach* to the cardinal

e.g. *einfach*, *zweifach*, *dreifach*, etc.:

eine einfache Karte	*a single ticket*
ein dreifacher Sieg	*a threefold victory*
ein vierfacher Olympiasieger	*a fourfold gold-medal winner*
. . . stiegen die Grundstückspreise zunächst aufs Zehnfache(*Böll*)	*. . . the price of land went up tenfold in the first instance*

NB: (i) *zweifach* is sometimes interchangeable in meaning with *doppelt* 'double', but more often refers to two different things, whilst *doppelt* refers to two of the same, cf. DUDEN (1985:191), e.g.: *ein zweifaches Verbrechen* 'two kinds of crime' but *Der Koffer hat einen doppelten Boden* 'the suitcase has a double bottom'. *zweifach* has the variant form *zwiefach* in older literary usage.

(ii) *-fach* is also suffixed to a few indefinites, e.g. *vielfach* or *mehrfach* 'manifold', 'frequent(ly)', 'repeatedly', *mannigfach* 'varied', 'manifold'.

(iii) Parallel to the forms in *-fach* are rather less commonly used ones in *-fältig*, e.g. *zweifältig, dreifältig, vielfältig*, etc. Note, without Umlaut, *mannigfaltig*, which is rather more frequent than *mannigfach*, and *die (heilige) Dreifaltigkeit* 'the (Holy) Trinity'. *einfältig* most often has the meaning 'simple(-minded)'.

(iv) English *single*, in the meaning 'individual', 'separate' corresponds to *einzeln*, e.g. *Die Bände werden einzeln verkauft* 'The volumes are sold singly/separately'. In the sense 'sole', it corresponds to *einzig*, e.g. *Er hat keinen einzigen Freund* 'He hasn't got a single friend'.

9.4.3 German uses adverbs made up from *-mal* suffixed to the cardinals as equivalents of English *once, twice*, etc.,

e.g. *einmal, zweimal, dreimal, zehnmal, hundertmal*, etc., e.g.:

Ich habe ihn diese Woche dreimal gesehen	*I've seen him three times this week*
Ich habe es hundertmal bereut	*I've regretted it a hundred times*
Also, Herr Ober, zweimal Gulasch, bitte	*Right, waiter, goulash for two, please*
anderthalbmal so groß wie das erste	*one and a half times as big as the first*

Adjectives are formed from these adverbs by suffixing *-ig*, e.g. *einmalig, zweimalig*, etc.:

eine einmalige Gelegenheit	*a unique opportunity*
nach dreimaligem Durchlesen seines Briefes	*after reading his letter three times*

NB: Formed in a similar way is *mehrmalig* 'repeated'.

9.4.4 Forms and phrases with *Mal*

A number of phrases with *Mal* have variant spelling forms. In principle *Mal* (plural *Male*) is written, as a noun, separate from any preceding adjectives or determiners, e.g.:

das erste Mal, das ich ihn sah	Das letzte Mal war das schönste
kein einziges Mal	ein ums/über das andere Mal *time after time*
Ich werde es nächstes Mal tun	Das vorige Mal war es schöner
Das eine Mal zeigte er mir seine Sammlung	
Dieses Mal wird sie mich anders behandeln müssen	
Die letzten paar Male war sie nicht zu Hause	
Beide Male bin ich durchgefallen	viele (hundert) Male

However, there is a very commonly used alternative of compounding it, in the invariable form -*mal*, with the preceding adjective or determiner. This alternative is limited to the following set phrases:

als er das erstemal/letztemal hier war, . . .
Ich tue es heute zum erstenmal, zum zweitenmal, zum drittenmal
das nächstemal   das übernächstemal   das vorletztemal
zum wievieltenmal? diesmal jedesmal ein andermal ein paarmal
hundertemal   ein (halbes) dutzendmal   dutzendemal

NB: x-mal, zigmal *umpteen times*

These forms are used if *Mal* is hardly stressed and no longer really felt to be separate noun. Essentially they have become simple adverbs or set adverbial phrases.

   vielmals 'many times' is used in a few set constructions, i.e.:

Ich danke Ihnen vielmals/	*Many thanks*
Danke vielmals	
Ich bitte vielmals um Entschuldigung	*I do apologize*
Sie läßt Sie vielmals grüßen	*She sends you her kindest regards*

NB also: *erstmals* 'for the first time'

9.4.5 The suffix -*erlei* is added to the cardinals to give forms which mean 'x kinds of',

e.g. *zweierlei* 'two kinds of', *dreierlei* 'three kinds of', *vielerlei* 'many kinds of', etc. They can be used as nouns or adjectives and do not decline:

Ich ziehe zweierlei Bohnen	*I grow two kinds of beans*
Er hat hunderterlei Pläne	*He's got hundreds of different plans*
Ich habe ihm dreierlei vorgeschlagen	*I suggested three different things to him*

einerlei is most often used in the sense 'all the same' (i.e. = *egal*, *gleich*, etc, cf. 6.5.2), e.g. *Das ist mir alles einerlei.*

9.4.6 Mathematical terminology

The common arithmetic and mathematical functions are expressed as follows in German. In some cases the symbols used in Germany differ from those current in the English-speaking countries:

$4 + 5 = 9$	*vier und/plus fünf sind/gleich neun*
$8 - 6 = 2$	*acht weniger/minus sechs ist/gleich zwei*
$3 \times 4 = 12$ $3 \cdot 4 = 12$	*drei mal vier ist/gleich zwölf*
$8 : 2 = 4$	*acht (geteilt) durch zwei ist/gleich vier*
$3^2 = 9$	*drei hoch zwei ist/gleich neun*
$3^3 = 27$	*drei hoch drei ist/gleich siebenundzwanzig*
$\sqrt{9} = 3$	*Quadratwurzel/zweite Wurzel aus neun ist/gleich drei*
$5 > 3$	*fünf ist größer als drei*

9.5 Addresses

These are typically written in the following form:

Herrn	Frau
Dr. Ulrich Sievers	Maria Jellinek
Severinsstraße 17	Maximiliansgasse 34
5500 Trier	1084 Wien
Familie	Herrn und Frau
Karl (und Ute) Schuhmacher	Peter und Eva Specht
Königsberger Straße 36	Schloßbergweg 2½
6122 Erbach/Odw.	3550 Marburg/Lahn
Firma	An das
Eugen Spengel	Katasteramt Westfalen
Roßgasse 7-9	Bismarckallee 87
7802 Merzhausen	4400 Münster

When writing from outside the country, the appropriate country code, i.e. D (Germany), A (Austria), CH (Switzerland) is prefixed to the post code. The sender's name and address have up to now usually been written in a single line on the back of the envelope, preceded by *Abs.* (i.e. *Absender*), e.g.:

Abs.: Indermühle, Strohgasse 17, CH –8600 Düsendorf

Increasingly, though, the sender's address is put in the bottom left hand corner on the front of the envelope.

NB: In late 1990 the convention was introduced of using W- to prefix former West German post codes and O- for former East German ones, e.g. W-5500 Trier, O-7021 Leipzig, pending the reorganisation of the system.

10   Modal particles

Modal particles are words which express the speaker's attitude to what is being said.

These words, such as *aber*, *doch*, *ja*, *mal*, *schon*, etc., are a very characteristic feature of German, especially, if not exclusively, in everyday colloquial speech. By using them one may alter the tone of what is being said and, for example, appeal for agreement, express surprise or annoyance, soften a blunt question or statement or sound reassuring. They act as a kind of lubrication in dialogue, making sure that the speaker's intentions and attitudes are not misunderstood. German has a far richer repertoire of such words than English, which tends to use different means (notably intonation, tag questions like *isn't it?* and the like) to the same end.

There is no real agreement as to which words may be thought of as 'modal particles' in German. This chapter treats all those words which have some claim to being considered as such, but many of them have other uses. Thus, for instance, *aber* is a conjunction (= English 'but') as well as being a particle expressing, among other things, astonishment and surprise. But it is not always straightforward (or useful in practice) to determine which uses of these words can be considered under the heading 'modal particle', and so <u>all</u> the various uses of the words included are dealt with in this chapter.

A vast amount has been written on the meaning and use of the German modal particles. Two useful, practically orientated recent books are Helbig (1988) and Weydt *et al.* (1983). Much of the detail and many of the examples in this chapter are based on these accounts and they may be consulted with profit for further information.

The following modal particles are dealt with in this chapter, in alphabetical order:

aber	eh	halt	nun	übrigens
allerdings	eigentlich	immerhin	nur	vielleicht
also	einfach	ja	ohnehin	wohl
auch	erst	jedenfalls	ruhig	zwar
bloß	etwa	lediglich	schließlich	
denn	freilich	mal	schon	
doch	gar	man	sowieso	
eben	gleich	noch	überhaupt	

10.1 *aber*

10.1.1 In statements, *aber* expresses a surprised reaction to something unexpected:

Das war aber eine Reise!	*That was quite a journey, wasn't it?*
Der Film war aber gut!	*The film was good*
Der Kaffee ist aber heiß!	*Oh! The coffee is hot*
Heute kommst du aber spät!	*You are late today*

NB: (i) *aber* may be given greater emphasis by adding *auch*, cf.:
Das war aber auch eine Reise!   *That really was some journey!*
(ii) In this sense, *aber* can be replaced by *vielleicht*, cf. 10.34.2, e.g. *Der Tee ist vielleicht heiß!*
(iii) *ja* is also used to express surprise, cf. 10.19.3, but surprise resulting from a difference in kind, whereas *aber* indicates a difference in degree. Compare:
Der Kaffee ist aber heiß   (i.e. hotter than you had expected)
Der Kaffee ist ja kalt   (you had expected hot coffee)

10.1.2 *aber* can be used within a clause with much the same sense it would have at the beginning (i.e. = English 'but'), expressing a contradiction

This sense is very close to that of *doch*, cf. 10.7.2:

Mein Freund kam aber nicht	*My friend didn't come, though*
Sie muß uns aber gesehen haben	*But she must have seen us*
Jetzt kannst du etwas schneller fahren. . .Paß aber bei den Ampeln auf!	*You can go a bit quicker now… Look out at the lights, though!*

NB: Used with *oder*, *aber* has the sense of 'on the other hand':
Seine Befürwortung könnte der   *His support might help the cause or*
    Sache helfen oder aber (auch)   *on the other hand it might harm it*
    schaden

10.1.3 Used initially in exclamations, *aber* gives emphasis to the speaker's opinion

It may sound scolding, or, in some contexts, reassuring:

Hast du was dagegen? – Aber nein!	*Have you any objection? – Of course not!*
Aber Kinder! Was habt ihr schon wieder angestellt?	*Now, now, childen! What have you been doing?*
Aber, aber! Was soll diese Aufregung?	*Now! What's all the excitement about?*

10.1.4 *aber* is also used as a co-ordinating conjunction,
i.e. corresponding to English 'but', cf. 19.1.1.

10.2 *allerdings*

allerdings most often has a concessive sense, expressing reservations about what has just been said. It usually corresponds to English 'admittedly', 'of course', 'to be sure', 'all the same', etc. *freilich* has a very similar meaning, cf. 10.14.

10.2.1 Used within a sentence the concessive sense of *allerdings* comes close to that of *aber*, but it is rather less blunt:

Es ist ein gutes Buch, allerdings gefallen mir seine anderen etwas besser	*It's a good book. Even so, I like his others rather better*
Wir haben uns im Urlaub gut erholt, das Wetter war allerdings nicht sehr gut	*The holiday was a good rest for us. Admittedly, the weather wasn't very good, though*
Ich komme gern, allerdings muß ich zuerst der Rita Bescheid sagen	*I'd like to come. Of course I'll have to tell Rita first*

10.2.2 Used in isolation in answer to a question, it expresses a strong affirmative answer

There often tends to be a slight hint of a reservation or qualification of some kind which doesn't need to be made explicit:

Kennst du Angelika? – Allerdings!	*Do you know Angelika? – Of course! (I know what she's like, too!)*
Ist Helmut schon da? – Allerdings!	*Is Helmut here yet? – Oh, yes! (and you should see who he's come with!)*

10.3 *also*

also usually confirms something as the logical conclusion from what has just been said. It often corresponds to English 'so', 'thus' or 'then'.

10.3.1 *also* used within a sentence:

Du wirst mir also helfen können	*You're going to help me, then*
Wann kommst du also genau?	*So, when are you coming precisely?*
Sie meinen also, daß wir uns heute entscheiden müssen	*So you think we're going to have to make a decision today*

10.3.2 If *also* is used in isolation to introduce a statement or a question, it links it up with what has just been said:

Also, jetzt müssen wir uns überlegen, wie wir dahinkommen	*Well then, now we've got to think about how we're going to get there*

Also, besuchst du uns morgen?	*So, are you going to come to see us tomorrow?*
Also, gut!	*Well all right then!*
Also, so was!	*Well I never!*

10.4 *auch*

10.4.1 In statements, *auch* stresses the reasons why something is or is not the case

It can be used to correct a false impression and is often used with *ja*:

Günther sieht heute schlecht aus
  – Er ist (ja) auch lange krank gewesen
	Günther's not looking well today
	  – Well, he's been ill for a long time

Jetzt möchte ich schlafen gehen – Es ist (ja) auch spät	*I'd like to go to bed now – Well, after all, it is late*

Ich habe jetzt einen Mordshunger
  – Du hast auch lange nichts gegessen
	I'm absolutely famished –
	  Well, you know, you haven't eaten for a long time

Das hättest du nicht tun sollen
  – Ich habe es (ja) auch nicht getan
	You ought not to have done that
	  – But I didn't do it, you know

10.4.2 In yes/no questions, *auch* asks for confirmation of something which really ought to be taken for granted

The English equivalent is very often a tag question:

Kann ich mich auch darauf verlassen?	*I can rely on that, can't I?*
Hast du auch die Rechnung bezahlt?	*You did pay the bill, didn't you?*
Hörst du auch zu?	*You are listening, aren't you?*
Bist du auch glücklich mit ihm?	*You're happy with him, aren't you?*

10.4.3 In *w*-questions, *auch* turns them into rhetorical questions, confirming that nothing better could be expected:

Was kann man auch dazu sagen?	*Well, what can you say to that?*
Mir ist furchtbar kalt – Warum ziehst du dich auch so leicht an?	*I'm dreadfully cold – Well, why did you put such thin clothes on, then?*
Ich bin heute sehr müde – Warum gehst du auch immer so spät ins Bett?	*I'm very tired today – Well, what can you expect when you always go to bed so late?*

These questions can be turned into exclamations which emphasize the speaker's negative attitude:

Was war das auch für ein Erfolg!	*Well, what sort of success do you call that?!*
Wie konnte er auch so schnell abreisen!	*How could he have left as quickly as that?!*

10.4.4 *auch* is used to reinforce commands

This is similar to the use of English 'Be/Make sure . . .!':

Bring mir eine Zeitung und vergiß es auch nicht!	*Bring me a paper and be sure you don't forget!*
Sei auch schön brav!	*Be sure you behave!*

10.4.5 Other uses of *auch*

(a) Before a noun *auch* has the force of English 'even'
It is an alternative to *sogar*:

Auch der beste Arzt hätte ihr nicht helfen können	*Even the best doctor wouldn't have been able to help her*
Auch Manfred kann sich ab und zu mal irren	*Even Manfred can be wrong now and again*
NB: Und wenn auch!	*even so, no matter*

(b) As an adverb, *auch* has the meaning 'too', 'also', 'as well':

Auch Peter will mit	*Peter wants to come too*
Gisela ist auch nett	*Gisela's nice as well*
Ich kann auch schwimmen	*I can swim too*
In Potsdam sind wir auch gewesen	*We also went to Potsdam*

(c) The combination *auch nur* expresses a restriction
(= 'even', 'as little as', 'as few as'):

wenn ich auch nur zwei Freunde hätte	*if I only had just two friends*
ohne auch nur zu fragen	*without as much as asking*
Es war unmöglich, auch nur Brot zu kaufen	*You couldn't buy so much as a loaf of bread*
Ich war nicht imstande, die Szene auch nur zu schildern	*I was incapable of so much as describing the scene*

(d) *oder auch* has the sense 'or else', 'or even':

Du kannst Birnen kaufen oder auch Pfirsiche	*You can buy pears or else peaches*

(e) The combination *auch nicht* (*auch kein, auch nichts*) is the most usual German equivalent for 'nor', 'neither', etc, cf. 19.1.6b:

Ich habe nichts davon gewußt – Ich auch nicht	*I didn't know anything about it – Nor me/Neither did I*
Sie kann nicht nähen und stricken kann sie auch nicht	*She can't sew or knit*
Das wird ihm auch nichts helfen	*That won't help him either*
Er liest keine Zeitungen und auch keine Bücher	*He doesn't read any newspapers or books*

(f) For the use of *auch* in concessive constructions, e.g. *Wer es auch sein mag*, etc., see 19.5.2

10.5 *bloß*

bloß most often has a restrictive sense, corresponding to English 'only', 'simply', 'merely'
In all its uses it is a rather less formal alternative to *nur*, cf. 10.26:

Störe mich bloß nicht bei der Arbeit	You'd better not disturb me while I'm working
Wie spät ist es bloß?	How late is it really?
Wenn er bloß bald käme!	If only he would come soon!
Sie hatte bloß 100 Mark bei sich	She only had 100 marks on her
Sollen wir Tante Mia einladen? – Bloß nicht!	Shall we invite aunt Mia? Good heavens no!

10.6 *denn*

As a modal particle, *denn* is used exclusively in questions.

10.6.1 In most types of questions, *denn* refers back to what has just been said, or to the general context, and tones down the question, making it sound rather less blunt and more obliging

In practice it is almost automatic in *w*-questions:

Hast du denn die Renate gesehen?	Tell me, have you seen Renate?
Geht der Junge denn heute nicht in die Schule?	Isn't the boy going to school today, then?
Ach, der Bus hält. Sind wir denn schon da?	Oh, the bus is stopping. Are we already there, then?
Warum muß er denn in die Stadt?	Tell me, why has he got to go to town?
Wie bist denn du gekommen?	Tell me, how did you get here?
Wie geht es dir denn?	How are you then?

NB: In colloquial speech, *denn* is often reduced to '*n* and suffixed to the verb, e.g. *Hast'n du die Renate gesehen? Wie bist'n du gekommen?*

10.6.2 If there is an implicit or explicit negative element in the question, *denn* signals reproach and the question itself expects not an answer, but a justification:

Hast du denn keinen Führerschein?	Come on, haven't you got a driving licence?
Bist du denn blind?	Come on now, are you blind?
Wo bist du denn so lange geblieben?	Where on earth have you been all this time?
Was ist denn hier los?	What on earth's going on here?

10.6.3 *denn* may convert some *w*-questions into rhetorical questions, expecting a negative answer

The addition of *schon* makes it absolutely clear that the question is a rhetorical one:

Wer redet denn von nachgeben?	*Who's talking of giving in?*
	(prompting the answer: nobody!)
Was haben wir denn damit erreicht?	*And what have we achieved by that?*
	(prompting the answer: nothing!)
Was hat er denn schon damit gewonnen?	*And what did he gain by that?*
	(prompting the answer: nothing!)

10.6.4 Other uses of *denn*

(a) Yes/no questions with *denn* (often beginning with *so*) are used as exclamations of surprise:

Ist das Wetter denn nicht herrlich!	*How lovely the weather is!*
So hat er denn die Stellung erhalten!	*So he did get the job!*

(b) *denn noch* is used to recall a fact:

Wie heißt er denn noch?	*What is his name again?*

NB: The force of *denn noch* is very similar to that of *doch gleich*, cf. 10.7.5.

(c) The combination *es sei denn, (daß)* is used in formal German as a conjunction meaning 'unless', cf. 16.3.3d
In older literary German *denn* alone could be used with this force:

Sie kommt gegen ein Uhr, es sei denn, sie wird aufgehalten	*She'll be coming at about one o'clock unless she's held up*
„Ich lasse dich nicht fort", rief sie, „du sagst mir denn, was du im Sinn hast" (*Wiechert*)	*"I shan't let you go", she cried, "unless you tell me what you have in mind".*

(d) *geschweige denn* means 'let alone', 'not to mention', 'still less':

Er wollte mir kein Geld leihen, geschweige denn schenken	*He wouldn't lend me any money, let alone give me any*

(e) In north German speech, *denn* is often heard for the standard German time adverb *dann* 'then':

Na, denn geht es eben nicht	*Well, it just can't be done then*

(f) *denn* is used as a coordinating conjunction indicating a cause or reason
In this sense it corresponds to English 'for', cf. 19.1.2, e.g. *Er kann uns nicht verstehen, denn er spricht kein Deutsch.*

(g) *denn* is sometimes used in formal German and set phrases for *als* 'than'
Details of this usage are given in 8.2.3b.

10.7 *doch*

doch usually expresses a contradiction or disagreement of some kind, often corresponding to English 'though' or a tag question. This is more forceful if *doch* is stressed.

10.7.1 In statements, *doch* indicates a certain degree of disagreement with what has just been said

If it is stressed, it clearly contradicts, and its meaning is close to that of *dennoch* or *trotzdem*. If it is unstressed, it appeals politely for agreement or confirmation:

Gestern hat es <u>doch</u> geschneit	*All the same, it <u>did</u> snow yesterday*
Gestern hat es doch <u>geschneit</u>	*It snowed yesterday, didn't it?*
Ich habe <u>doch</u> recht gehabt	*Nevertheless, I <u>was</u> right*
Ich habe doch <u>recht</u> gehabt	*I was right, wasn't I?*
Wir müssen <u>doch</u> morgen nach Bremen	*All the same, we <u>have</u> got to go to Bremen tomorrow*
Ich habe ihm abgeraten, aber er hat es <u>doch</u> getan	*I advised him against it, but he did it all the same*
Du hast doch ge<u>sagt</u>, daß du kommst	*You <u>did</u> say you were coming, didn't you?*

In literary German *doch* may be used with the verb first in the clause:

War ich doch so durch den Lehrbetrieb beansprucht, daß ich keine Zeit dafür fand (*Grass*)	*After all, I was so busy with my lessons that I didn't have any time for it*

10.7.2 Unstressed *doch* may indicate, rather gently, a reason for disagreement

In this case it is interchangeable with *aber*, cf. 10.1.2:

Wir wollten doch/aber heute abend ins Theater gehen	*Surely we were going to go to the theatre tonight(, weren't we?)*
Die Ampel zeigt doch/aber rot, wir dürfen noch nicht gehen	*But the lights are red, we can't go yet*

10.7.3 The sense of unstressed *doch* means that it can have the effect of turning a statement into a question expecting a positive answer

It is then the equivalent of a following *oder?* or *nicht (wahr)?* and one of these may be used as well:

Den Wagen kann ich mir doch morgen abholen?	*I can collect the car tomorrow, can't I?*
Du kannst mir doch helfen(, oder)?	*You can help me, can't you?*
Du glaubst doch nicht, daß ich es getan habe?	*Surely you don't think I did it?*

10.7.4 In commands, *doch* may on the one hand add a note of impatience or urgency

In this case it can be strengthened by *endlich* or, in a negative sentence, by *immer*:

Reg dich doch nicht so auf!	*For heaven's sake, don't get so excited*
Bring den Wagen doch (endlich) in die Werkstatt!	*For goodness' sake, take the car to the garage*
Mach doch nicht (immer) so ein Gesicht!	*Don't keep making faces like that*
Freu dich doch!	*Do cheer up*

10.7.5 In *w*-questions, *doch* asks for confirmation of an answer or the repetition of information

It may be strengthened by adding *gleich*:

Wie heißt doch euer Hund?	*What did you say your dog is called?*
Wer war das doch (gleich)?	*Who was that again?*
Wohin fahrt ihr doch auf Urlaub?	*Where did you say you were going on holiday?*

10.7.6 In exclamations, *doch* emphasizes the speaker's surprise that something is the case

In such sentences *doch* is the equivalent of *ja*, cf. 10.19.3:

Wie winzig doch alles von hier oben aussieht!	*But how tiny everything looks from up here!*
Was war das doch für ein Spiel!	*What a game that was, though!*
Du bist doch kein kleines Kind mehr!	*You're not a baby any more, you know!*
Das ist doch die Höhe!	*That really is the limit!*

10.7.7 In exclamations with *Konjunktiv II* expressing a wish, *doch* emphasizes the urgency of the wish

In such sentences *doch* is the equivalent of *nur* and may be used together with it, cf. 10.26.2:

Wenn er doch jetzt käme!	*If only he would come now!*
Wäre ich doch zu Hause geblieben!	*If only I'd just stayed at home!*

10.7.8 In answer to a question, it contradicts a negative, emphasizes an affirmative reply or, used with *nein* or *nicht*, emphasizes a negative reply

Bist du nicht zufrieden? – Doch!	*Aren't you satisfied? – Yes, I am*
Kommt er bald? – Doch!	*Is he coming soon? – Oh, yes*

Mutti, kann ich ein Stück Schokolade haben? – Nein doch, du hast jetzt genug gegessen	*Mummy, can I have a piece of chocolate? – Certainly not, you've had enough to eat*

It can also be used in isolation to contradict a previous negative statement:

Er hat nie etwas für uns getan. – Doch, er hat mir einmal 100 Mark geliehen	*He's never done anything for us. – Oh, yes he has, he once lent me a hundred marks*

10.7.9 As a conjunction, *doch* is an alternative to *aber* 'but',

cf. 19.1.1, e.g. *Sie wollten baden gehen, doch es hat geschneit.*

10.8 *eben*

eben most often has the sense of a confirmation that something is precisely the case, often corresponding to English 'just'.

10.8.1 In statements, *eben* emphasizes an inescapable conclusion:

Das ist eben so	*But there, that's how it is*
Ich kann ihn nicht überreden. Er ist eben hartnäckig	*I can't convince him. He's just obstinate*
Karl hat angerufen. Er hat den Zug verpaßt. Also essen wir eben eine halbe Stunde später	*Karl rang up. He's missed his train. So we'll just have to eat half an hour later*
Er zeichnet ganz gut – Nun, er ist eben ein Künstler	*He draws quite well – Well, he is an artist*
Ich tue es, so gut ich eben kann	*I'll do it as well as I can (given the circumstances)*

10.8.2 In commands (often introduced by *dann*), *eben* emphasizes that there is no real alternative:

(Dann) bleib eben im Zug sitzen!	*Well, just stay on the train, then*
(Dann) fahr eben durch die Stadtmitte!	*Well, just drive through the town centre, then*

NB: In the uses given in 10.8.1 and 10.8.2, *halt* is a frequent alternative to *eben*. *halt* was originally a south German equivalent to the more north German *eben*, but both are now widely used.

10.8.3 Used before another word, or in response to a statement or a question, *eben* has the sense of 'exactly', 'precisely', 'just'

genau is a frequent alternative:

Eben dieses Haus hatte mir zugesagt	*It was just this house which attracted me*
Das wäre mir eben recht	*That would be just what I'd like*

Eben <u>daran</u> hatte ich nie gedacht	*That's the one thing I hadn't thought of*
In eben dieser Straße ist der Unfall passiert	*This was the street where the accident happened*
Jetzt muß er eine andere Stelle suchen. – Eben!	*Now he's got to look for another job. – Precisely!*
Das wird sie doch kaum schaffen. – Eben!	*She'll not manage it, will she? – Precisely!*

10.8.4 Other uses of *eben*

In (a) and (b), *gerade* is a common alternative to *eben*.

(a) Used with *nicht* before an adjective, *eben* lessens the force of the negative:

Sie ist nicht eben fleißig	*She's not exactly hard-working*
Der Zug war nicht eben pünktlich	*The train wasn't what you'd call on time*

(b) As an adverb, *eben* means 'just (now)':

Wir sind eben (erst) angekommen   Eben geht mir ein Licht auf
Mit zweitausend Mark im Monat kommen wir eben (noch) aus

(c) As an adjective, *eben* means 'level', e.g. *Die Straße ist hier nicht eben.*

10.9 *eh*

eh is used mainly in colloquial spoken German as an alternative to *ohnehin* or *sowieso* as an equivalent of English 'anyway'
It is predominantly south German, but its use is spreading in the north:

Ich kann dir leider nichts zu trinken anbieten – Ich habe eh keinen Durst	*I'm afraid I can't offer you anything to drink – I'm not thirsty anyway*
Gehst du eh heute einkaufen?	*Are you going shopping today anyway?*

10.10 *eigentlich*

eigentlich emphasizes that something is actually the case, even if it appears otherwise. It is often used to change the topic of conversation.

10.10.1 When used unstressed in questions, *eigentlich* tones the question down and makes it sound more casual

This comes close to the use of English 'actually'. It is frequently used in conjunction with *denn*:

Sind Sie eigentlich dieses Jahr schon in Urlaub gewesen?	*Tell me, have you been on holiday yet this year?*
Wohnt die Eva eigentlich schon lange in Hameln?	*Has Eva actually been living a long time in Hamelin?*
Wie spät ist es (denn) eigentlich?	*Tell me, what time is it actually?*

10.10.2 When used stressed in *w*-questions, it implies that the question has not yet been answered fully or satisfactorily and insists on the whole truth

It is close in meaning to *im Grunde genommen, tatsächlich* or *wirklich*, with the sense of 'at bottom', 'in actual fact', 'in reality':

Hast du eigentlich überhaupt keine Ahnung, wo sie ist?	*Do you really have absolutely no idea where she is?*
Wie heißt er eigentlich?	*What's his real name?*
Warum besuchst du mich eigentlich?	*Why, basically, did you come to visit me?*

10.10.3 In statements, *eigentlich* is used to indicate that something actually is the case, despite the appearances or what others might think

It often moderates a refusal, an objection or a contradiction by indicating how strong the reasons are:

Er scheint manchmal faul, aber er ist eigentlich sehr fleißig	*He appears lazy sometimes, but in actual fact he's quite hard-working*
Ich wollte eigentlich zu Fuß gehen	*In actual fact, I did want to walk*
Ich trinke eigentlich keinen Kaffee mehr	*Well, actually, I don't drink coffee now*

Sometimes *eigentlich* may signal that the question is still a little open:

Wir haben eigentlich schon zu	*Well, actually, we're already closed (hinting that an exception might not be entirely out of the question)*
Das darf man hier eigentlich nicht	*Strictly speaking, that's not allowed here (but, possibly,...)*
Das ist eigentlich mein Buch, aber es macht nichts	*Strictly speaking, that's my book, but never mind*

10.10.4 As an adjective, *eigentlich* means 'real', 'actual', 'fundamental':

Was ist die eigentliche Ursache?	Er nannte nicht den eigentlichen Grund

10.11 *einfach*

einfach **emphasizes that alternative possibilities are excluded**
It corresponds most often to English 'simply' or, especially in commands,
'just'. In commands it is frequently used in conjunction with *doch* and/or
mal and in exclamations with *ja*:

Ich bin einfach weggegangen	*I simply walked away*
Ich werde ihm einfach sagen, daß es nicht möglich ist	*I'll simply tell him it's not possible*
Warum gehst du nicht einfach ins Bett?	*Why don't you simply go to bed?*
Hat sie einfach die Geduld verloren?	*Did she simply lose patience?*
Leg dich (doch) einfach hin!	*Why don't you just go and lie down?*
Geh doch einfach mal zum Zahnarzt!	*Why not just simply go to the dentist?*
Heute ist das Wetter (ja) einfach herrlich!	*The weather is simply lovely today!*

NB: There is a clear difference in meaning between the particle *einfach* and the adverb
einfach, which has the full sense 'in an uncomplicated manner'. *einfach* has this full
meaning when it is stressed. Compare:

Sie macht es <u>ein</u>fach	*She is doing it simply* (i.e. in an uncomplicated manner)
Sie <u>macht</u> es einfach	*She's simply doing it* (i.e. 'just', without further ado)
Du mußt <u>ein</u>fach anfangen	*You have to begin simply*
Du mußt einfach <u>an</u>fangen	*You simply have to begin*

10.12 *erst*

10.12.1 Referring to time, *erst* implies that it is later than expected or desirable

It often corresponds to English 'only', 'not before', 'not until' or, in certain
contexts, 'as late as':

Er kommt erst (am) Montag	{ *He's not coming till Monday* { *He's only coming on Monday*
Es ist erst acht Uhr	*It's only eight o'clock*
Ich kam erst letzten Sommer nach Heidelberg	*I didn't get to Heidelberg until last summer*
erst wenn/als (cf. 19.2.2d)	*not until, only when*
wenn er erst zu Hause ist,…	*once he's home…*
Es hatte eben erst zu schneien aufgehört (*E. Jünger*)	*It had only just stopped snowing*
Ich kann den Wagen erst Anfang nächste Woche abholen	*I shan't be able to collect the car till the beginning of next week*
Erst im späten 19. Jahrhundert wurde in Rußland das Leibeigentum abgeschafft	*It wasn't until the late nineteenth century that serfdom was abolished in Russia*

10.12.2 Before a number or an expression of quantity, *erst* indicates that there are/were less or fewer than expected

In this sense it corresponds to English 'only'. Before other nouns the sense will be 'nothing less than':

Ich habe erst zehn Seiten geschrieben	*I've only written ten pages*
Er ist erst sieben Jahre alt	*He's only seven years old*
Ich habe erst die Hälfte fertig	*I've only got half of it finished*
Erst mit einer Stelle bei Braun wird er sich zufriedengeben	*He won't be satisfied with anything less than a job with Braun's*
Erst ein Hauptmann wäre ihr als Schwiegersohn recht	*She will accept nothing less than a captain as a son-in-law*

NB: (i) The opposite of *erst* 'only' as explained in 10.12.1 and 10.12.2 is *schon*, cf. 10.30.
(ii) *erst* 'only' should be carefully distinguished from *nur*, cf. 10.26.4 (although in practice this does not always happen in substandard colloquial speech). Whereas *erst* in time expressions has the sense 'not before', etc., *nur* means 'on that one occasion. Compare:

Sie ist erst Montag gekommen	*She only came on Monday* (i.e. not before Monday)
Sie ist nur Montag gekommen	*She only came on Monday* (i.e. on no other day)

With numbers, *erst* implies that more are to follow. In English this may be made clear by adding *as yet* to the sentence. *nur*, on the other hand, sets a clear limit, i.e. that number and no more. Compare:

Ich habe erst drei Briefe bekommen	*I've only received three letters (as yet)* (more are expected)
Ich habe nur drei Briefe bekommen	*I've only received three letters* (i.e. three and no more)

10.12.3 In statements and exclamations, *erst* has intensifying force

It implies that something really is the absolute limit and possibly more than expected or desirable. It is often strengthened by adding *recht*:

Dann ging es erst (recht) los	*Then things really got going*
Das konnte sie erst recht nicht	*That she really couldn't manage*
Das macht es erst recht schlimm	*That really does make it bad*
Sie hat schon Hunger, aber das Kind erst (recht)!	*She may be hungry, but that's nothing to how hungry the kid is*

10.12.4 *erst* can be used to intensify a wish

In these cases, *nur* or *bloß* are possible alternatives to *erst* (and are sometimes used with it):

Wäre er doch erst zu Hause! (*Fallada*)	*If only he were at home!*
Wenn er (bloß) erst wieder arbeiten könnte!	*If only he could start work again!*

10.13   *etwa*

10.13.1 In questions, *etwa* implies that something is undesirable and suggests that the answer ought to be *nein*

The English equivalent is usually a negative statement followed by a positive tag question or an exclamation beginning with *Don't tell me…*:

Hast du die Zeitung etwa schon weggeworfen?	*You've not thrown the paper away already, have you?*
Ist das etwa dein Wagen?	*That's not your car, is it?*
Habt ihr etwa geschlafen?	*Don't tell me you've been asleep!*

Such questions with *etwa* can be in the form of statements, in which case they always contain *doch nicht*:

Sie wollen doch nicht etwa nach Paderborn umziehen?	*You don't want to move to Paderborn, do you?*

10.13.2 In negative sentences, *etwa* can intensify the negation:

Sie müssen nicht etwa denken, daß ich ihn verteidigen will	*Now don't go and think I want to defend him*
Komm nicht etwa zu spät zum Flughafen!	*Make sure you don't get to the airport too late!*

10.13.3 In conditional sentences *etwa* stresses the idea of a possibility:

Wenn der Zug etwa verspätet sein sollte, so werden wir den Anschluß nach Offenbach verpassen	*If the train should be delayed we'll miss our connection to Offenbach*
Wenn das Wetter etwa umschlagen sollte, müssen wir die Wanderung verkürzen	*If the weather were to change, we'll have to shorten our walk*

10.13.4 Especially with a following number or expression of size or quantity, *etwa* expresses approximation:

Ich komme etwa um zwei	*I'll come at about two*
Es kostet etwa dreißig Mark	*It costs about thirty marks*
In etwa zwei Stunden sind wir in Passau	*We'll be in Passau in about two hours*
Er ist etwa so groß wie dein Vater	*He is about as tall as your father*
Wir haben es uns etwa so vorgestellt	*We imagined it to be something like that*

10.13.5 Before a noun or list of nouns, *etwa* suggests a possibility:

Er begnügte sich mit etwa folgender Antwort	*He was satisfied with, say, the following answer*

Bist du sicher, daß du den Jürgen gesehen hast, und nicht etwa seinen Bruder Thomas?	*Are you sure you saw Jürgen, and not perhaps his brother Thomas?*
Er hat viele Hobbys, (wie) etwa Reisen, Musik und Sport	*He has a lot of hobbies, for example travelling, music and sport*
Willst du etwa Sonntag kommen?	*You're not thinking of coming on Sunday, are you?*

10.14 *freilich*

freilich usually has a concessive sense and is a mainly South German alternative to *allerdings*, cf. 10.2. Note that it <u>never</u> means 'freely', which most often corresponds to *frei* in German.

10.14.1 Used within a sentence *freilich* corresponds to the concessive sense of English 'admittedly', 'all the same':

Es scheint freilich nicht ganz so einfach zu sein	*Admittedly, it doesn't appear to be that simple*
Wir nehmen ihn mit, freilich muß er pünktlich am Treffpunkt sein	*We'll take him with us, all the same he'll have to be at the meeting place on time*

10.14.2 Used in answer to a question, *freilich* emphasises that the answer is affirmative

It is often used in conjunction with *ja*. It lacks the hint that there is some kind of reservation or qualification to the answer which is present with *allerdings*:

Kennst du Angelika? - (Ja,) freilich (kenne ich sie)	*Do you know Angelika? - Of course (I know her)!*
Kannst du auch alles besorgen? (Ja,) freilich!	*Can you see to it all? Certainly I can*

10.15 *gar*

gar usually has an intensifying sense
Its most common use in modern German is to intensify a negative, when it is an alternative to *überhaupt*:

Davon hat er mir gar nichts erzählt	*He didn't tell me anything at all about that*
Ich habe doch heute gar keine Zeit	*I really haven't got any time at all today*

Rather less commonly, it can be used to intensify *so* or *zu* with an adjective. *allzu* is a more frequent alternative to *gar zu*:

Du darfst das nicht gar so ernst nehmen	*You really mustn't take that quite so seriously*
Es waren gar zu viele Leute auf der Straße	*There were far too many people in the street*

10.16 *gleich*

gleich is used as a particle in *w*-questions to politely request the repetition of information
It is often used with *doch*, cf. 10.7.5:

Wie war Ihr Name (doch) gleich?	*What was your name again?*
Was hast du gleich gesagt?	*What was it you said?*

NB: *gleich* is also used as a time adverb in the sense of 'immediately', e.g. *Ich werde ihn gleich fragen*, or to mean 'at once' or 'at the same time', e.g. *Er hat gleich zwei Hemden gekauft.*

10.17 *halt*

halt is a south German alternative to the northern *eben* in some senses, cf. 10.8.

10.18 *immerhin*

immerhin indicates that something might not have come up to expectations, but is acceptable at a pinch
It corresponds most often to English 'all the same' or 'even so' and can be used within a sentence or (very frequently) as a response:

Du hast immerhin tausend Mark gewonnen	*All the same, you won a thousand marks*
Wir haben uns immerhin ein neues Videogerät anschaffen können	*Even so, we were able to buy a new video recorder*
Das Wetter war miserabel, aber wir hatten ein schönes Zimmer – (Na,) immerhin!	*The weather was lousy, but we did have a nice room – Well, that was something, at least*

10.19 *ja*

10.19.1 In statements, *ja* confirms that both speaker and listener know something is correct or obvious

It may be used to appeal for agreement. A common English equivalent is the *do*-form of the verb:

Wir haben ja gestern davon gesprochen	*We did talk about that yesterday (you know)*

Ihr habt ja früher zwei Autos gehabt	*Of course, you did have two cars*
Ich komme ja schon	*It's all right, I'm on my way*
Wenn du den Brief gelesen hast, weißt du ja alles	*If you've read the letter, then of course you know everything*
Er ist ja schon längst im Ruhestand	*You know, of course, that he's been retired for a long time*

10.19.2 Distinctions of meaning between *ja* and *doch* used to appeal for agreement

Whilst *doch*, cf. 10.7.1, always suggests that there might be the possibility that the listener holds a different opinion, *ja* always presupposes that speaker and listener are agreed. Compare:

Du könntest dir ja Karls Rad leihen	*You could borrow Karl's bike, of course* (we both know you can)
Du könntest dir doch Karls Rad leihen	*Surely, you could borrow Karl's bike* (you might have thought you couldn't)
Das ist es ja eben	*Why, of course, that's the point*
Das ist es doch eben	*Don't you see, that's just the point*
Er kann unmöglich kommen, er ist ja krank	*He can't possibly come, he's ill, as you know*
er ist doch krank	*he's ill, don't you know*

10.19.3 In exclamations, *ja* expresses surprise at something the speaker has just noticed and which is in some way unexpected:

Heute ist es ja kalt!	*Oh, it is cold today!*
Er hat ja ein neues Auto!	*Why, he's got a new car!*
Das ist ja unerhört!	*That really is the limit!*
Da kommt ja der Arzt!	*Oh (good), here comes the doctor!*

NB: In contrast to *aber* or *vielleicht*, *ja* expresses surprise <u>that</u> something is the case at all, not at the extent of a quality, cf. 10.1.1 and 10.34.2. Thus *die Milch ist ja sauer!* would be said if the milk had been expected to be fresh, whilst *die Milch ist aber/vielleicht sauer* expresses surprise at <u>how</u> sour the milk is.

10.19.4 *ja* is used to intensify a command, often with an implied warning or threat:

Bleib ja hier!	*Be sure to stay here!*
Geht ja nicht auf die Straße!	*Just don't go out onto the street!*
Er soll <u>ja</u> nichts sagen	*He really must not say anything (or else)*

NB: *nur* is a possible alternative to *ja* to intensify commands and sound a note of warning, cf. 10.26.1.

10.19.5 In a string of nouns, verbs or adjectives, *ja* (sometimes in combination with *sogar*) emphasizes the importance of the one (usually the last) before which it is placed

This often corresponds to English *indeed*, *even* or *nay*:

Es war ein Erfolg, ja ein Triumph	*It was a success, indeed a triumph*
Es war ein unerwarteter, ja ein sensationeller Erfolg	*It was an unexpected, indeed a sensational success*
Sie konnte die Aussage bestätigen, ja (sogar) beeiden	*She was able to confirm the testimony, even on oath*

10.19.6 *ja* is also the affirmative particle,

i.e. corresponding to English *yes*, e.g.: Kommst du morgen? – Ja!
It can also be used as a tag, e.g.:

Es geht um acht los, ja?	*We're starting at eight, aren't we?*

10.20 *jedenfalls*

The phrases *auf jeden Fall* and *auf alle Fälle* are possible alternatives to the particle *jedenfalls*.

10.20.1 In statements *jedenfalls* marks the possible reason why something should be the case or why something is not as bad as it may seem

This usage is like that of English 'at least' or 'at any rate':

Vielleicht ist er krank, er sieht jedenfalls schlecht aus	*Perhaps he's ill, at least he doesn't look well*
Er ist nicht gekommen, aber er hat sich jedenfalls entschuldigt	*He didn't come, but at least he did apologize*

wenigstens or *zumindest*, cf. 8.3.4b, are possible further alternatives to *jedenfalls* in this meaning.

10.20.2 Especially in imperative sentences *jedenfalls* indicates that something should be done in any event

It corresponds to English 'anyhow' or 'in any case':

Bei schönem Wetter gehen wir morgen baden. Bring jedenfalls deinen Badeanzug mit	*If it's fine we'll go swimming tomorrow, but bring your costume anyhow*

10.21 *lediglich*

lediglich is used before another word to indicate a restriction or a limit
It is a more emphatic alternative to *nur* in the sense 'only', 'no more than'.

It is used predominantly in more formal registers and can often sound rather stilted:

Er hat lediglich zwei Semester in Münster studiert	*He only studied two terms in Münster*
Ich verlange lediglich mein Recht	*I am only asking for what's due to me*
Sie dürfen nicht lediglich nach dem Äußeren urteilen	*You mustn't judge simply by appearances*

10.22 *mal*

***mal* most often moderates the tone of a sentence, making it sound less blunt and more conciliatory**

It is particularly frequent in commands, requests and questions, suggesting the speaker doesn't see them as awfully important. It commonly corresponds to English *just* (though this is used far less often in practice than German *mal*):

Lies den Brief mal durch!	*Just read the letter through (will you?)*
Das sollst du mal probieren	*You just ought to try that*
Ich will sie schnell mal anrufen	*I just want to ring her up quickly*
Das wollen wir zur Abwechslung mal machen	*We just want to do that for a change*
Würden Sie mir bitte mal helfen?	*Could you just help me?*
Kannst du mir mal sagen, wie spät es ist?	*Can you just tell me the time?*
Hältst du mir mal die Tasche?	*Just hold my bag for me, will you?*

Especially with a verb on its own, *mal* is almost automatically added to a command in colloquial speech, e.g.:

Sieh mal her!   Hör mal zu!   Komm mal herüber!   Sag mal!

The tone of a request or a command may be moderated still further by using the combination *eben mal*:

Reich mir eben mal das Brot!	*Just pass me the bread, would you*
Lies den Brief eben mal durch!	*Won't you please just read the letter through?*

The combination *doch mal* makes a command sound rather casual:

Nimm doch mal ein neues Blatt!	*Why don't you get another piece of paper?*
Melde dich doch mal beim Chef!	*Why not just arrange to see the boss?*

NB: The particle *mal* is to be clearly differentiated from the adverb *einmal* 'once'. *einmal* cannot possibly replace *mal* in any of the uses explained above. However, *einmal* is sometimes shortened to *mal* in colloquial speech, especially in the following combinations:
(i) *noch einmal* '(once) again', 'once more':
Ich habe ihn noch (ein)mal gewarnt   *I warned him once again*

(ii) *nun einmal* 'just' (stressing the lack of alternatives; a rather more forceful equivalent to *eben* or *halt*, cf. 10.8.1):

Es wird nun (ein)mal lange dauern	*It's just going to take a long time*

(iii) *nicht einmal* 'not even':

Er hat sie nicht (ein)mal gegrüßt	*He didn't even say hello to her*

10.23 *man*

man is a purely colloquial north German equivalent to *mal* in commands and requests:

Geh du man vor!	*You just go ahead*
Er soll man nach Hause gehen!	*He just ought to go home*

10.24 *noch*

10.24.1 In relation to time, *noch* indicates that something is going on longer than expected

It may be strengthened by *immer* and corresponds to English *still* or *yet*:

Angela schläft noch	*Angela's still asleep*
Franz ist (immer) noch nicht gekommen	*Franz hasn't come yet/Franz still hasn't come*
Sie wohnen noch in Fritzlar	*They're still living in Fritzlar*
Ich habe sie noch nie gesehen	*I've never seen her (yet)*
Er arbeitete noch um 20 Uhr	*He was still working at 8 p.m.*
Sie ist doch noch jung	*She's still young, isn't she*

10.24.2 If a particular point in time is indicated, *noch* indicates that, contrary to expectations, an event took place or will take place by that time:

Ich habe ihn noch vor zwei Tagen gesehen	*I saw him only two days ago*
Noch im Mai hat sie ihre Dissertation abgegeben	*She managed to hand her thesis in by the end of May*
Ich werde heute noch den Arzt anrufen	*I'll ring the doctor this very day*

10.24.3 *noch* may indicate something additional:

Er hat noch drei Stunden geschlafen	*He slept another three hours*
Ich trinke noch eine Tasse Kaffee	*I'll have another cup of coffee*
Ich habe noch zwei Fragen an ihn	*I've got another two questions for him*
Haben Sie noch etwas gesehen?	*Did you see anything else?*
Das wird sich noch herausstellen	*That will remain to be seen, too*
Wer war noch da?	*Who else was there?*
Und es hat auch noch geregnet!	*And apart from that, it rained too*

10.24.4 Further uses of *noch*

(a) In *w*-questions, *noch* asks for the listener to jog the speaker's memory, suggesting that something has just slipped his/her mind:

Wie hieß er noch?   *Oh now, what <u>was</u> his name?*
Wann war das Spiel noch?   *Oh now, when <u>was</u> the game?*

(b) *noch* is used with comparatives in the sense of 'even', (cf. 8.2.3d), e.g.: Er ist noch größer als du.

(c) *noch* occurs in conjunction with *weder* as the equivalent of English 'neither...nor', cf. 19.1.6, e.g.: Er liest weder Bücher noch Zeitungen.

(d) *noch* is used with *so* and an adjective in a concessive sense, e.g.: Wenn sie (auch) noch so fleißig ist, sie wird die Prüfung doch nicht bestehen.

10.25 *nun*

10.25.1 *nun*, as an adverb of time, is rather less definite than *jetzt*

It is used less frequently to refer simply to time:

Nun wollen wir umkehren   *Now we'll turn back*
Nun hat er mehr Zeit als früher   *Now he's got more time than he used to have*

Geht es dir nun besser?   *Are you better now?*
als es nun Winter wurde, . . .   *now when it turned to winter . . .*

10.25.2 In questions, *nun* signals dissatisfaction with a previous answer and an insistence on the correct or complete information being provided:

Wann kommt der Zug nun an?   *When <u>does</u> this train get in, now?*
Stimmt es nun, daß sie verheiratet ist?   *Now, is it really true that she's married?*

NB: Simple *nun* is very commonly used as a question to push the listener to give more information, cf. *Nun?* 'Well?', *Nun...und?* 'And then what?'

10.25.3 In isolation at the beginning of a sentence, *nun* signals that the speaker considers the previous topic exhausted

It often corresponds to English 'well':

Nun, das ist alles schon wichtig, aber ich glaube, wir müssen zunächst das Wahlergebnis besprechen   *Well, of course that's all very important, but I think we've got to discuss the election results first*
Nun, natürlich hat er die besten Erfahrungen   *Well, of course he's got most experience*
Nun, wir werden ja sehen   *Well, we shall see*
Nun, meinetwegen!   *All right then/As far as I'm concerned*

10.26   *nur*

nur expresses a limitation or restriction and most often corresponds to English 'only', 'just', 'merely', 'simply'. *bloß*, cf. 10.5, is a frequent alternative to *nur* in all its uses except where indicated below; it tends to sound slightly more emphatic and more colloquial.

10.26.1 When used in a command, *nur* intensifies its basic meaning

Depending on the sense of the command, i.e. whether it is an urgent instruction or a request, it can make it sound, on the one hand, more of a threat or a warning or, on the other, more of a reassuring or tentative suggestion. The first sense, which is more common in negative commands or when *nur* is stressed, is similar to that of *ja*, cf. 10.19.4. The second sense is equivalent to that of *ruhig*, cf. 10.28.

(a) 'threatening' or 'warning' *nur*:

Komm nur nicht zu spät!	*You'd better not be late!*
Nimm dich nur in acht!	*You'd better be careful!*
Geh nur nicht in diesen Laden!	*Whatever you do, don't go into that shop!*
Sehen Sie nur, was Sie gemacht haben!	*Just look what you've done!*

NB: 'warning' *nur* (rarely *bloß*) can be used initially in a positive or negative command using the infinitive or with no verb at all:

Nur nicht so schnell laufen!	*Just don't run so fast!*
Nur aufpassen!	*Just be sure to look out!*
Nur immer schön langsam!	*Take it nice and slow!*

(b) 'reassuring' *nur*:

Laß ihn nur reden!	*Just let him speak, do!*
Kommen Sie nur herein!	*Do come in!*
Hab nur keine Angst!	*Don't be afraid, will you!*
Nur weiter!	*Just carry on!* (implying: *It's all right so far*)

NB: *bloß* is not used in this 'reassuring' sense, and commands with *bloß* tend always to have a 'warning' tone. Compare *Laß ihn bloß reden!* 'Just let him speak (and you'll suffer the consequences)' with the first example above.

10.26.2 *nur* intensifies *w*-questions and makes them sound more urgent or important

Wie kann er nur so taktlos sein?	*How on earth can he be so tactless?*
Was können wir nur tun, um ihr zu helfen?	*Whatever can we do to help her?*
Wo bleibt sie nur?	*Where on earth is she?*

NB: Such questions can be used as exclamations of reproach or astonishment, as no real answer is possible or expected:

Wie siehst du nur wieder aus?!	*What on earth do you look like?!*
Warum mußte er nur wegfahren?!	*Why on earth did he have to go away?!*

10.26.3 *nur* intensifies a wish in the form of a *wenn*-clause

Its force is similar to that of *doch*, cf. 10.7.7, and they are often used together to add an even greater intensity to the wish:

Wenn sie (doch) nur anrufen würde!	*If only she would ring up!*
Hätte ich nur mehr Zeit!	*If only I had more time!*
Wenn er mir nur geschrieben hätte!	*If only he had written to me!*

10.26.4 In all kinds of sentences *nur* can have the limiting sense of English *only,* expressing some kind of qualification to what is being said

lediglich, cf. 10.21, is a rather more formal alternative to *nur* in this sense:

Ich wollte nur Guten Tag sagen	*I only/just wanted to say Hello*
Die Mittelmeerküste ist sehr schön, sie ist leider nur etwas dreckig	*The Mediterranean coast is very nice, only I'm afraid it's rather dirty*
Man kann ihn nur bewundern	*You can only admire him*
Er geht nur bei schönem Wetter spazieren	*He only goes for a walk when it's fine*
Ich vermute nur, daß er gestern in Urlaub gefahren ist	*I only assume that he went on holiday yesterday*
Ich habe nur 100 Mark bei mir	*I've only got 100 marks on me*
Man kann es nur dort kaufen	*You can only buy it there*
Dort kann man nicht nur Bücher kaufen, sondern auch allerlei Zeitschriften	*You can not only buy books there, but also magazines of all kinds*

NB: (i) For the use of *erst* rather than *nur* as an equivalent of English 'only', cf. 10.12.2.

(ii) *nur daß* is used as the equivalent of the English conjunction 'only', cf. also 19.6.6:

Die Zimmer waren in Ordnung, nur daß die Duschen fehlten	*The rooms were OK, only they had no showers*

10.27 *ohnehin*

ohnehin indicates that something is correct irrespective of any other reasons given or implied and corresponds to English 'anyway' or 'in any case'
It is a more formal alternative to (southern) colloquial *eh*, cf. 10.9, or *sowieso*, cf. 10.31:

Er trinkt ohnehin zu viel	*He drinks too much anyway*
Der Zug hat ohnehin Verspätung	*The train's late anyway*
Du mußt sofort zum Arzt – Ich hätte ihn ohnehin morgen besucht	*You'll have to go to the doctor right away – I would have gone to see him tomorrow in any case*

10.28 *ruhig*

ruhig lends a reassuring tone to what the speaker is saying
This meaning is clearly linked to that of the adjective *ruhig* 'quiet'. It is

used in commands (where it is an alternative to *nur*, cf. 10.26.1), and in statements, especially with a modal auxiliary:

Bleib ruhig sitzen!	*Don't get up for me*
Arbeite ruhig weiter!	*Just carry on* (i.e. don't let me disturb you)
Auf dieser Straße kannst du ruhig etwas schneller fahren	*It's all right, you can go a bit faster on this road*
Sie dürfen ruhig hier im Zimmer bleiben	*You can stay here in this room, I don't mind*

10.29 *schließlich*

schließlich indicates that the speaker accepts the validity of a reason It usually corresponds to English 'after all':

Es liegt schließlich nicht genug Schnee auf der Piste	*After all, there's not enough snow on the piste*
Wir wollen ihn schließlich nicht zu sehr reizen	*We don't want to annoy him too much, after all*
Schließlich kann das einem jeden passieren	*After all, that can happen to anybody*

10.30 *schon*

10.30.1 In a temporal sense, *schon* indicates that something is happening or has happened rather sooner than expected or desirable, or that it has happened on some occasion

In this meaning, it is the opposite of *erst*, cf. 10.12.1, and sometimes corresponds to English 'already', but its range of use is far wider:

Er war schon angekommen	*He had already arrived*
schon am nächsten Tag	*the very next day*
Da bist du ja schon wieder	*There you are back again*
Sind Sie schon einmal in Köln gewesen?	*Have you been to Cologne before?*
Ich habe ihn auch schon in der Bibliothek gesehen	*I've sometimes seen him in the library*
Das habe ich schon 1960 geahnt	*I suspected that as early as 1960*
Es war schon 7 Uhr, als sie aufstand	*It was already 7 o'clock when she got up*

10.30.2 Before a number or an expression of quantity, *schon* indicates that this is more than expected or desirable at the particular point in time

erst is the opposite of *schon* in this meaning, cf. 10.12.2:

Sie hat schon drei Briefe bekommen	*She has already received three letters*
Ich habe schon die Hälfte des Buches gelesen	*I've already read half the book*
Er wartet schon eine Stunde auf dich	*He's been waiting for you for an hour*

10.30.3 With a noun (or, occasionally, another part of speech), *schon* expresses a restriction

allein is a frequent possible alternative in this meaning:

Schon dieses ‚good morning' war unvorsichtig genug (*Goes*)	*Even this 'good morning' was imprudent enough*
Schon der Gedanke ist mir unsympathisch	*The very thought is repugnant to me*
schon ihrer Kinder wegen	*if only because of their children*
Das geht schon daher nicht, weil . . .	*That's impossible, not least because . . .*
Schon vor dem Krieg war die Eisenbahn in Schwierigkeiten geraten	*Even before the war the railways had run into difficulties*

10.30.4 In statements referring to the future, *schon* expresses a fair expectation that something will happen

It usually sounds reassuring, but in some sentences it may take on a more threatening tone. English 'all right' has much the same force:

Er wird uns schon helfen	*He'll help us all right*
Es wird schon gehen	*It'll be all right, don't worry*
Ich krieg's schon hin	*I'll manage it all right*
Dem werde ich's schon zeigen!	*I'll show him all right!*

10.30.5 In statements, *schon* can express agreement or confirmation in principle, but tinged with a slight reservation

This sense is essentially concessive; it often has (or implies) a following *aber*, *nur* or the like, and *zwar* or, especially in north Germany, *wohl* are possible alternatives, cf. 10.35.3 and 10.36.1:

Das ist schon möglich(, aber . . .)	*That's quite possible (but . . .)*
Ich wollte schon kommen	*Well, I did want to come*
Das stimmt schon, aber es könnte auch anders kommen	*That may be true, but things might turn out differently*
Ja, ich glaube schon(, aber . . .)	*Well, I think so(, but . . .)*
Der Film hatte schon wunderschöne Aufnahmen, nur war er etwas langweilig	*The film may have had some lovely shots, only it was a bit boring*

NB: In a response, *schon* corrects what has just been said and indicates why it was wrong:

Niemand fährt über Ostern weg – Mutter schon!	*Nobody's going away over Easter – But mother is*
Heute waren keine deiner Freunde da – Der Kurt schon!	*None of your friends came today – But Kurt did*
Er hat da ein sehr schönes Haus gekauft – (Das) schon, aber . . .	*He's bought himself a nice house there – Well yes, but . . .*

10.30.6 In *w*-questions, *schon* gives persuasive force to a question which expects a negative answer or where the speaker has a negative attitude:

Was sagt die Regierung zu Ungarn? Nichts. Was sollen sie schon sagen? (*M. Horbach*)	*What does the government say about Hungary? Nothing. But then, what <u>are</u> they to say?*
Wer kann diesem Angebot schon widerstehen?	*Who can refuse this offer?* (i.e. 'nobody')
Warum kommt er schon wieder?	*What's he coming for again?* (implying: 'he's up to no good')
Na, und wenn schon?	*So what?*

10.30.7 In commands, *schon* adds an insistent note

The sentence often begins with *nun*:

(Nun,) beeile dich schon!	*Do hurry up(, then)!*
Fang schon an!	*Do make a start!*
Sag mir schon, was du denkst! Ich werde es dir nicht übelnehmen	*Do tell me what you think. I shan't take it amiss*

10.31 *sowieso*

sowieso indicates that something is correct irrespective of any other reasons given or implied
It usually corresponds to English 'anyway' or 'in any case' and is a more colloquial alternative to *ohnehin*, cf. 10.27:

Ich kann heute sowieso nicht arbeiten	*I can't work today anyway*
Der ist sowieso scharf auf sie	*He fancies her anyway*
Ich wäre sowieso nach Nürnberg gefahren	*I would have gone to Nuremberg in any case*

10.32 *überhaupt*

10.32.1 *überhaupt* makes statements and commands more general

The English equivalent is often 'at all' or 'anyhow':

Duisburg ist überhaupt eine gräßliche Stadt	*Duisburg is a dreadful city anyhow*
Das ist überhaupt eine gefährliche Angelegenheit	*That's a risky business in any case*
Er liebte die italienische Sprache, ja die Sprachen überhaupt (*Goes*)	*He loved the Italian language, indeed, languages in general*
Seinen Mut müßte man haben, dachte ich. Oder überhaupt Mut (*Walser*)	*One ought to have his courage, I thought. Or any courage at all*
Wir müssen uns beeilen, damit wir ihn überhaupt noch sehen	*We'll have to hurry if we want to see him at all*

Ich habe überhaupt noch einiges zu erklären	*In any case I've still got a few things to explain*
Wenn ich überhaupt komme, wird es nicht für lange sein	*If I come at all, it won't be for long*
Ihr sollt überhaupt besser aufpassen!	*You ought anyway to pay more attention*

10.32.2 In questions, *überhaupt* casts doubt on the basic assumption

In *w*-questions this can have the effect of changing the subject:

Er singt nicht besonders gut. – Kann er denn überhaupt singen?	*He doesn't sing particularly well. – Can he sing at all?*
Wie konntest du überhaupt so was tun?	*How could you do such a thing at all?*
Der Brief ist nicht da. Wo kann er überhaupt <u>sein</u>?	*The letter's not there. Wherever can it be?*
Was will er denn überhaupt?	*What the dickens does he want?*
Wo waren Sie überhaupt gestern?	*And where on earth were you yesterday?*

10.32.3 *überhaupt* intensifies a negative

gar is a frequent alternative, cf. 10.15:

Du hättest es überhaupt nicht tun sollen, und besonders jetzt nicht	*You ought not to have done it at all, and particularly not now*
Er ist überhaupt kein Dichter	*He isn't a poet at all*
Ich weiß überhaupt nichts von seinen Plänen	*I don't know anything about his plans*

10.33 *übrigens*

übrigens is used in statements and questions to indicate a casual remark which is incidental to the main topic of conversation
It corresponds to English 'by the way', etc.:

Ich habe übrigens erfahren, daß er eine neue Stelle bekommen hat	*By the way, I've found out he's got a new job*
Sie hat übrigens vollkommen recht	*Incidentally, she's perfectly right*
Wo wollt ihr übrigens dieses Jahr hin?	*By the way, where are you going this year?*

10.34 *vielleicht*

10.34.1 In all kinds of sentences, *vielleicht* can be used like English 'perhaps':

| Sie ist vielleicht 30 Jahre alt | *She is perhaps thirty years old* |
| Die Kiste ist vielleicht schwer | *Perhaps the case is heavy* |

Wird sie uns vielleicht morgen besuchen?	*Perhaps she'll come to see us tomorrow?*
Sie wird vielleicht morgen kommen	*She may come tomorrow* (cf. 17.3.3.)

NB: In requests in the form of a question, *vielleicht*, like English 'perhaps', expresses polite reserve on the part of the speaker:

Könnten Sie mir vielleicht sagen, wo es zum Bahnhof geht?	*Could you perhaps tell me the way to the station?*
Würden Sie mir vielleicht helfen?	*Would you mind helping me?*

10.34.2 In exclamations, which can have the form of statements or questions, unstressed *vielleicht* expresses surprise at something unusual or unexpected

In this sense it is often an alternative to *aber*, cf. 10.1.1:

Siehst du vielleicht schlecht aus!⎫ Du siehst vielleicht schlecht aus!⎭	*Oh, you really do look awful!*
Die Kiste ist vielleicht schwer!	*How heavy the crate is!*
Du bist vielleicht ein Idiot!	*You really are stupid!*
Das hat vielleicht gegossen!	*It really did pour!*
Ich habe vielleicht gestaunt!	*I wasn't half surprised!*

10.34.3 In yes/no questions, *vielleicht* signals that the speaker expects a negative answer

Its sense is thus close to that of *etwa*, cf. 10.13.1. The English equivalent is often an exclamation beginning with *Don't tell me . . .* or a negative statement followed by a positive tag question:

Willst du mir vielleicht erzählen, daß . . .?	*You don't mean to tell me that . . ., do you?*
Soll ich vielleicht bis 7 Uhr abends hier sitzen?	*I'm not supposed to sit here till seven at night, am I?*
Arbeitet er vielleicht?	*Don't tell me he's working?*

10.35 *wohl*

10.35.1 In statements, *wohl* signals a fair degree of probability

Its force is very similar to that of the future tense, cf. 14.4.2, and it is often used in conjunction with it. It corresponds to English 'I suppose', 'probably', the English future tense or a positive statement followed by a negative tag question:

Er ist noch nicht hier. Er hat wohl den Zug verpaßt	*He's not here yet. I suppose he's missed the train*
heute nicht, wohl aber morgen	*not today, but probably tomorrow*
Das wird wohl der Briefträger sein	*That'll be the postman*
Sie sind wohl neu hier	*You're new here, aren't you?*

Diese Probleme versteht er wohl nicht	*He probably doesn't understand these problems*
Sie hat wohl ihr Auto schon verkauft	*I suppose she's already sold her car*
Ich habe ihn nie gesprochen, wohl aber oft gesehen	*I've never spoken to him, but I have often seen him*

The combination *ja wohl* sounds rather more certain, corresponding to English '(pretty) certainly' or 'no doubt':

Sie wird ja wohl noch in Essen sein	*She's pretty certainly still in Essen*
Das weißt du ja wohl	*No doubt you know that*

The combination *wohl doch* (or, for some speakers, *doch wohl*) sounds rather less certain, though the speaker hopes that it is the case:

Er hat wohl doch noch einen Schlüssel	*Surely he's got another key, hasn't he?*
Die Antje wird doch wohl noch das Abitur schaffen	*Antje's surely going to get through her Abitur, isn't she?*

10.35.2 In questions which may have the form of a statement, *wohl* signals uncertainty and reserve on the part of the speaker, as if he/she is not sure the listener can give a clear answer:

Wer hat den Brief wohl geschrieben?	*Who can possibly have written the letter?*
Wie spät ist es wohl?	*I wonder what time it is*
Ist Peter wohl schon zu Hause?	*Peter is at home, isn't he?*
Darf ich wohl bei Ihnen telephonieren?	*Might I use your telephone?*
Horst ist wohl gestern abend angekommen?	*Horst arrived last night, didn't he?*

10.35.3 In statements, stressed *wohl* has a concessive sense, expressing agreement or confirmation in principle, but tinged with a slight reservation

It often has (or implies) a following *aber, nur* or the like, and *zwar* or, especially in southern Germany, *schon* are possible alternatives, cf. 10.30.5 and 10.36.1:

Er ist wohl mein Freund, aber ich kann ihm nicht helfen	*He may be my friend, but I can't help him*
Das ist wohl möglich(, aber . . .)	*That may be possible(, but . . .)*
Herbert ist wohl nach Basel gefahren, aber nur für eine Woche	*Herbert did go to Basle, but only for a week*

10.35.4 *wohl* intensifies a command, making it sound urgent, insistent and rather abrupt

It is often used with *werden* or *wollen*:

Hebst du wohl das Buch wieder auf!	*Pick that book up again right away!*

Wirst du wohl sofort wieder ins Bett gehen!	*Will you go straight back to bed!*
Wollt ihr wohl endlich still sein!	*Once and for all, will you be quiet!*

10.35.5 As an adverb, usually stressed, *wohl* has the sense 'well', 'fully', etc. It is very frequently used to strengthen an affirmative response, i.e. *jawohl!* 'yes, indeed':

Ich fühle mich wohl	*I feel well*
Er hatte es sich wohl überlegt	*He had considered it fully*
Er weiß sehr wohl, daß er unrecht hat	*He knows full well that he's wrong*
. . . und er war so geartet, daß er solche Erfahrungen wohl vermerkte (*Th. Mann*)	*. . . and his nature was such that he took full note of such experiences*
Schlaf wohl! Leb wohl!	*Sleep well! Farewell!*
wohl oder übel	*come what may/willy-nilly*

10.36 *zwar*

10.36.1 *zwar* may be used in a concessive sense, with a following *aber, nur* or the like, so that the combination *zwar . . . aber* can have the force of English '(al)though', cf. also 19.5.1d:

In north Germany *wohl* is a possible alternative in this concessive sense, cf. 10.35.3, whilst in southern and central Germany *schon* is often used, cf. 10.30.5:

Er ist zwar krank, aber er kommt heute abend noch mit	*Although he's ill, he's still coming with us tonight*
Es ist zwar ein gutes Buch, aber seine anderen haben mir viel besser gefallen	*It may be a good book, but I liked his others much better*

10.36.2 *und zwar* is used in the sense of English 'namely' to specify what has just been mentioned:

Ich habe ihn für heute abend eingeladen, und zwar für sieben Uhr	*I've invited him for this evening, (namely) for seven o'clock*
Ich habe die wichtigsten Museen besucht, und zwar das kunst-historische, das naturhistorische und die Albertina	*I visited the most important museums, namely the Museum of Art History, the Museum of Natural History and the Albertina*

11   Expressions of time

11.1 Times of the clock

In everyday speech the twelve-hour clock is the norm, but in official contexts the twenty-four-hour clock is used, i.e. for time-tables, television and radio programmes, theatrical performances, official meetings, business hours, etc. Even in conversation it is quite common for such 'official' times to be given using the twenty-four-hour clock. Thus one would say *Mein Zug fährt um 7.35* (i.e. *um sieben Uhr fünfunddreißig*), but it would be rather odd to say *Die Tante hat uns für fünfzehn Uhr dreißig zum Kaffee eingeladen*.

11.1.1 Clock times in everyday informal contexts:

1.00 Es ist ein Uhr/eins	*It is one (o'clock)*
3.00 Es ist drei (Uhr)	*It is three (o'clock)*
3.05 fünf (Minuten) nach drei	*five (minutes) past three*
3.07 sieben Minuten nach drei	*seven minutes past three*
3.10 zehn (Minuten) nach drei	*ten (minutes) past three*
3.15 Viertel nach drei Viertel vier (esp. S. & C. Ger.)	*quarter past three*
3.20 zwanzig nach drei zehn vor halb vier (not Switz.)	*twenty past three*
3.25 fünf vor halb drei	*twenty-five past two*
3.30 halb vier (sometimes written ½4)	*half past three*
3.35 fünf nach halb vier	*twenty-five to four*
3.40 zwanzig vor drei zehn nach halb drei (not Switz.)	*twenty to four*
3.45 Viertel vor vier drei Viertel vier (esp. S. & C. Ger.)	*quarter to four*
3.47 dreizehn Minuten vor vier	*thirteen minutes to four*
3.50 zehn (Minuten) vor vier	*ten (minutes) to four*
3.55 fünf (Minuten) vor vier	*five (minutes) to four*

11.1.2 The twenty-four-hour clock:

0.27 null Uhr siebenundzwanzig	*12.27 a.m.*
5.15 fünf Uhr fünfzehn	*5.15 a.m.*
10.30 zehn Uhr dreißig	*10.30 a.m.*

13.07 dreizehn Uhr sieben	*1.07 p.m.*
21.37 einundzwanzig Uhr siebenunddreißig	*9.37 p.m.*
24.00 vierundzwanzig Uhr	*12.00 midnight*

NB: In speech, *Uhr* may be omitted in giving the full hours between 1 a.m. and noon, e.g. *Ihr Zug kommt um 9.00 an* (spoken: *um neun (Uhr)*). Otherwise the full forms, with *Uhr,* are used, e.g. *Die Vorstellung beginnt um 20.00* (spoken: *um zwanzig Uhr*).

11.1.3 Other phrases with clock times:

Wieviel Uhr ist es? ⎫ Wie spät ist es? (coll.) ⎭	*What's the time?*
Wieviel Uhr haben Sie?	*What time do you make it?*
Um wieviel Uhr kommt sie?	*What time is she coming?*
Sie kommt um halb drei	*She's coming at half-past two*
um drei Uhr nachts	*at three in the morning*
um neun Uhr vormittags	*at nine in the morning*
um zwölf Uhr mittags	*at twelve noon*
um drei Uhr nachmittags	*at three in the afternoon*
um sieben Uhr abends	*at seven in the evening*
um Mitternacht	*at midnight*
Es ist Punkt/genau neun (Uhr)	*It is exactly nine (o'clock)*
Es ist gerade halb	*It is just half-past*
Es ist ungefähr neun (Uhr)	*It's about nine (o'clock)*
Es ist (schon) neun Uhr vorbei	*It's gone nine o'clock*
Er kommt ungefähr um neun Uhr	*He's coming at about nine o'clock*
Er kam gegen neun (Uhr) an	{ *He came at about nine* { *He came towards nine*

NB: *gegen* is ambiguous with clock times, cf. 11.6.6.

11.2 Days of the week, months and public holidays

11.2.1 The days of the week:

Sonntag	*Sunday*	Donnerstag	*Thursday*
Montag	*Monday*	Freitag	*Friday*
Dienstag	*Tuesday*	Samstag, Sonnabend	*Saturday*
Mittwoch	*Wednesday*		

NB: (i) As the equivalent for 'Saturday', *Samstag* was originally the southern word and *Sonnabend* northern. Since 1949 *Samstag* has come to be known and used more widely in the north, especially in West Germany.
(ii) For English 'on Sunday', etc. German uses **am** *Sonntag*, etc., cf. 4.6.3.

11.2.2 The months of the year:

Januar	*January*	Mai	*May*	September	*September*
Februar	*February*	Juni	*June*	Oktober	*October*
März	*March*	Juli	*July*	November	*November*
April	*April*	August	*August*	Dezember	*December*

NB: (i) In Austria, *Jänner* and *Feber* are commonly used in place of *Januar* and *Februar*.

(ii) *Juni* and *Juli* are sometimes pronounced *Juno* and *Julei* to avoid confusion, especially on the telephone.

(iii) For English 'in January', etc., German uses *im Januar*, etc., cf. 4.6.3.

11.2.3 The major public holidays and religious festivals:

Neujahr(stag)	*New Year's Day*
Rosenmontag	*Carnival Monday*
	(i.e. the day before Shrove Tuesday)
Aschermittwoch	*Ash Wednesday*
Gründonnerstag	*Maundy Thursday*
Karfreitag	*Good Friday*
Ostersonntag	*Easter Sunday*
Ostern	*Easter*
Ostermontag	*Easter Monday*
Fronleichnam	*Corpus Christi*
Pfingsten	*Whitsun*
Pfingstsonntag	*Whit Sunday*
Pfingstmontag	*Whit Monday*
(Christi) Himmelfahrt	*Ascension Day*
Mariä Himmelfahrt	*Assumption of the Virgin Mary*
	(15th August)
Allerheiligen	*All Saints' Day* (1st November)
Buß- und Bettag	*Day of Penitence and Prayer*
	(Wednesday before the last Sunday before Advent)
der Heilige Abend *or* Heiligabend	*Christmas Eve*
Weihnachten	*Christmas*
Erster Weihnachts(feier)tag	*Christmas Day*
Zweiter Weihnachts(feier)tag	*Boxing Day*
Silvester	*New Year's Eve*

11.3 Dates

Ordinal numbers are used for the days of the month, as in English. In practice numbers are always used for them in writing, i.e. they are never written out as words.

11.3.1 Dates are given as follows:

Der wievielte ist heute? ⎫ Den wievielten haben wir heute? ⎬	*What's the date today?*
Heute ist der 8. (spoken: achte) Mai ⎫ Wir haben heute den 8. (spoken: achten) Mai ⎬	*Today is the eighth of May*
Er kam am 5. (spoken: fünften) Juni, 1989 am 5.6.89	*He came on the fifth of June, 1989* *on 5.6.89*
(spoken: am fünften, sechsten, neunundachtzig)	

11.3.2 Usage where the day of the week precedes the date

There are three alternative possibilities. The day of the week and the date may be in the accusative, or the day of the week may be preceded by *am* followed by the date in the accusative or the dative, i.e.:

Wir kommen Montag, den 5. Juni(,) um 15.30 Uhr in Hamburg an
Wir kommen am Montag, den 5. Juni um 15.30 Uhr in Hamburg an
Wir kommen am Montag, dem 5. Juni, um 15.30 Uhr in Hamburg an

The last alternative given is the most formal. The use of commas in writing is given as prescribed by DUDEN (1985:174)

11.3.3 Usage in letter headings

In private correspondence (i.e. where the address is not printed on the notepaper), the writer's address is not usually written out in full at the head of the letter, as in usual English practice. Instead, just the town is given, followed by the date, which may be written in various ways, i.e.:

Siegen, (den) 5.6.89   Siegen, (den/d.) 5. Juni 1989
Siegen, am 5.6.89   Siegen, im Juni 1989

NB: When writing to an unknown person, especially for the first time, many Germans are tending nowadays to put their full name and address in the top <u>left</u>-hand corner of the letter <u>and</u> the town and date, as given above, in the top <u>right</u>-hand corner.

11.4 Accusative of time

A noun denoting time can be used in the accusative case, without a preposition, to express duration of time or a specific point in time or period of time.

11.4.1 The accusative can be used to indicate a length of time

The period of time lies entirely in the past, present or future, and the accusative here usually corresponds to the English preposition *for*, see also 11.6.5b. The word or phrase in the accusative may optionally be followed by *lang*, or, emphasizing the duration, *über* or *hindurch*:

Ich war einen Monat (lang) in Kassel	*I was in Kassel for a month*
drei Monate (lang)	*for three months*
viele Jahre (lang)	*for many years*
Jahre hindurch blieb er im Gefängnis von Santiago	*For years on end he remained in Santiago prison*
Ich bin jede Woche einen Tag (lang) in Kaiserslautern	*I am in Kaiserslautern one day every week*
den ganzen Tag (lang)	*all day (long), for the whole day*
Den ganzen Tag über lag er im Bett	*He lay in bed the whole day*

den ganzen Sommer (lang)	*all summer, for the whole of the summer*
den ganzen Winter hindurch/über	*throughout the winter*
sein ganzes Leben (lang)	*all his life*
Wo warst du die ganze Zeit?	*Where were you the whole time?*
Sie wohnte einige Zeit (lang) in Kiel	*She lived in Kiel for some time*
eine ganze Weile	*for quite a while*

Other words and phrases expressing a length of time:

Wie lang(e) bleibst du in Hamm?	*How long are you staying in Hamm?*
lang(e)	*for a long time*
stundenlang, monatelang	*for hours, months (on end)*
eine Zeitlang	*for a time*

11.4.2 The accusative can be used to indicate a specific time

(a) This is especially the case with words denoting periods of time, corresponding to English 'last week', 'next year', etc. It is also used with dates, cf. 11.3.2. In some cases a prepositional construction is a common alternative to the accusative:

Einen Augenblick zuvor hätte sie ihn noch retten können	*A moment before she could still have saved him*
Er kommt jeden Tag, jede Woche	*He comes every day, every week*
Sie fährt alle vierzehn Tage in die Schweiz	*She goes to Switzerland every fortnight*
alle paar Jahre	*every few years*
Jede halbe Stunde kommt ein Polizist vorbei	*Every half hour a policeman comes past*
Wir besuchen sie (am) nächsten Dienstag/ (am) kommenden Dienstag	*We are visiting her next Tuesday*
Wir besuchen sie kommende/nächste Woche/ in der kommenden/nächsten Woche	*We are visiting her next week*
Wir werden dieses Jahr/in diesem Jahr nicht verreisen	*We're not going away this year*
Sie ist 1987/im Jahre 1987 wieder zur Vorsitzenden des Vereins gewählt worden	*In 1987 she was elected chair of the society again*
Ich sah sie (am) letzten Freitag/ (am) vorigen Freitag/ (am) vergangenen Freitag	*I saw her last Friday*
Ich sah sie letzte/vorige/vergangene Woche/ in der letzten/vorigen/vergangenen Woche	*I saw her last week*

(b) *Anfang, Mitte* and *Ende*

Unlike their English equivalents, these are used without a preposition, i.e. in the accusative, in time phrases:

Er ist Anfang Januar, Mitte Januar, Ende Januar gestorben	*He died at the beginning of January, in the middle of January, at the end of January*
Ich fahre schon Anfang, Ende nächster Woche	*I'm leaving at the beginning, at the end of next week*
Anfang 1990 fanden in der DDR die ersten freien Wahlen statt	*At the beginning of 1990 the first free elections took place in the GDR*

(c) Especially in spoken German, the accusative is used in numerous phrases as an alternative to a construction with a preposition:

Ich bin Mittag (for: um Mittag) wieder zu Hause	*I'll be back home at noon*
Ich kann Montag (for: am Montag) leider nicht kommen	*I'm afraid I can't come on Monday*
Fährst du Ostern (for: zu Ostern) zu deinen Eltern?	*Are you going to your parents at Easter?*
Sind Sie das erste Mal (for: zum ersten Mal) hier?	*Is this the first time you've been here?*

11.5 Genitive of time

11.5.1 The genitive of nouns denoting time can be used to refer to indefinite or habitual time

In the main these are set expressions, and only in literary German are they commonly extended by adjectives:

eines Tages	*one day*
eines schönen Tages	*one fine day*
eines schönen Sommers (*Frisch*)	*one fine summer*
eines Sonntags	*one Sunday*
eines Morgens	*one morning*
eines Sonntagmorgens	*one Sunday morning*
eines nebligen Morgens (*A. Kolb*)	*one foggy morning*
eines Nachts	*one night*

NB: *eines Nachts* despite the fact that *die Nacht* is feminine.

A number of genitives have become simple adverbs, and they are written with a small initial letter:

morgens, vormittags	*in the mornings*
nachmittags, abends	*in the afternoons, in the evenings*
tags, nachts	*by day, at night*
dienstags, freitags	*on Thursdays, on Fridays*
wochentags, werktags	*on weekdays, on working days*
Donnerstag abends/donnerstags abends	*on Thurday evenings*
von morgens bis abends	*from morning till night*
morgens und abends	*morning and evening*

Notes relating to the use of the genitive of time:

(i) These adverbs can also be used to refer to single occasions, e.g.:

Nachmittags machten wir einen Spaziergang	*In the afternoon we went for a walk*

(ii) Genitive time phrases with the definite article or a demonstrative, e.g. *des Morgens, des Abends, dieser Tage.* These are the origin of the adverbs above and are used less frequently, chiefly in formal writing.

11.6 Time phrases with prepositions

This section deals with a selection of the most important prepositions used with nouns denoting time. A full account of the use of all prepositions is given in chapter 20.

11.6.1 *an* (+ dative) is used with nouns denoting days and parts of the day:

am Tag *in the daytime*	am Montag, Dienstag, etc.	an Wochentagen
an besonderen Tagen	am Abend am Nachmittag	an diesem Tag
am 31. Oktober (cf. 11.3)		

The following may be noted with regard to the use of *an*:

(a) *in* is used with *Nacht*, see 11.6.7a

(b) *an* is used with *Tag*, etc. even in cases where no preposition is needed in English:

am Tag nach seinem Tod	*the day after his death*
An diesem Morgen war er schlecht gelaunt	*That morning he was in a bad mood*

(c) In some cases an accusative of time may be used as an alternative to a phrase with *an*, see 11.4.2

(d) Other phrases with *an*:

am anderen Tag, am anderen Morgen am anderen Abend	*the next day, the next morning, the next evening*
Es ist an der Zeit, daß . . .	*It is about time that . . .*
am Anfang, am Ende	*at the beginning, at the end*
gleich am Anfang	*at the very beginning*

NB: No article is used with *Anfang* and *Ende* in extended time phrases, see 11.4.2b, or with prepositions other than *an*.

11.6.2 *auf* (= accusative) indicates a period of time extending from 'now'

It is thus as an equivalent of English 'for', and in this sense it is a rather less common alternative to *für*, cf. 11.6.5, found mainly in formal registers and set phrases:

Sie fährt auf vier Monate in die Schweiz	*She is going to Switzerland for three months*
auf unbestimmte Zeit	*indefinitely*
auf ewig, auf immer	*for ever, for good*

NB: *auf* is used idiomatically in *auf die Minute (genau)* '(precisely) to the minute'.

11.6.3 *bei* is used in a number of fixed time expressions

In such set phrases it occurs without an article and is usually the equivalent of English 'at':

Paris bei Tag, London bei Nacht	*Paris by day, London by night*
bei Tagesanbruch	*at daybreak*
bei Einbruch der Nacht	*at nightfall*
bei Sonnenuntergang	*at sunset*
bei Gelegenheit	*if the occasion arises*
bei Kriegsende (or: am Ende des Krieges)	*at the end of the war*

11.6.4 *bis* indicates an end-point in time

It marks the time <u>until</u> which something will continue or the time <u>by</u> which it will have happened. With a few simple time words, it is used on its own, without a following article. Otherwise it is followed by another appropriate preposition (especially *zu* in the meaning 'until'):

Bis 1945 lebte er in Wien	*Until 1945 he lived in Vienna*
Das Geschäft ist von 9 Uhr bis 18.30 Uhr durchgehend geöffnet	*The shop is open continuously from 9 a.m. until 6.30 p.m.*
Ich werde es bis heute abend, bis Montag fertig haben	*I'll have it finished by tonight, by Monday*
Bis (zum/am) kommenden Montag kannst du mich hier erreichen	*You can reach me here till next Monday*
bis vor kurzem	*until recently*
Bis vor zwei Wochen war er hier	*He was here until two weeks ago*
Ich arbeite bis gegen Mittag im Büro	*I'm working at the office until about noon*
Wir wollen es bis auf weiteres verschieben	*We'll postpone it for the present*
bis dahin/bis dann	*by then, till then*
Bis dahin bin ich längst zurück	*I'll be back long before then*
bis auf den heutigen Tag	*to this day*
bis zu seinem Tode	*until his death*
bis tief/spät in die Nacht hinein	*till late at night*
bis in den Herbst hinein	*right into autumn*

11.6.5 *für* and English 'for'

(a) *für* usually indicates a period of time extending from 'now'
In this sense, it corresponds to English 'for':

Ich habe das Haus für sechs Monate gemietet	*I've rented the house for six months*
Am nächsten Tag fuhren wir für einen Monat in den Schwarzwald	*The next day we went to the Black Forest for a month*

NB: (i) *auf* (= accusative) is a less common alternative in this meaning, used chiefly in formal registers and some set expressions, cf. 11.6.2
(ii) The use of *für* is idiomatic in *Tag für Tag* 'day by day'.

(b) English 'for' has the following German equivalents:
(i) an accusative phrase, used to denote a period of time lying entirely in the /past/or future, e.g. *Er blieb einen Monat (lang) in Berlin* 'He remained in Berlin for a month'. See 11.4.1 for further details.
(ii) *seit* to refer to a period of time which began in the past and extends up to the present, e.g. *Ich warte seit einer Stunde auf dich* 'I've been waiting for you for an hour'. See 11.6.9 for further details.
(iii) *für* (or more formal *auf*) to refer to a period of time extending the present, as illustrated above.

NB: In colloquial speech an accusative is sometimes used instead of *für* to refer to a period of time extending from the present, e.g. *Ich gehe eine halbe Stunde (lang) ins Café*. On the other hand, *für* is not unknown in the place of an accusative phrase, e.g. *Ich bin in Hannover für zehn Jahre in der Schule gewesen*.

11.6.6 *gegen* has the sense of 'about' or 'towards'

gegen can be ambiguous, especially with clock times, as some Germans understand *gegen zwei Uhr* to mean 'at about two o'clock', whilst others interpret it as 'getting on for two o'clock'. In other phrases it usually has the meaning 'towards'. It is most often used without an article in time expressions:

gegen Mittag, gegen Abend	*towards noon, towards evening*
gegen Monatsende	*towards the end of the month*
gegen Ende des Jahrhunderts	*towards the end of the century*

11.6.7 *in* can refer to a specific period of time or a length of time

(a) It is used with most words denoting periods of time
It is used with all such words except those with which *an* is used, cf. 11.6.1, i.e. the names of the months and seasons (always with a definite article, cf. 4.6.3), e.g. *im Juli* 'in July', *im Sommer* 'in the summer' and the following nouns:

der Augenblick	die Epoche	das Jahr	das Jahrhundert
die Minute	der Monat	die Nacht	die Woche
das Zeitalter			

Examples:

im Augenblick, im letzten Augenblick	*at the moment, at the last moment*
in der Frühe (S. Ger.)	*early in the morning*
im Jahre 1988 (*or, simply*: 1988)	*in 1988*
in dieser Jahreszeit	*in this season*
cf.: **zu** dieser Jahreszeit	*at this time of the year*
in den letzten paar Jahren	*in the last few years*
in letzter Minute	*at the last moment*
im Mittelalter	*in the Middle Ages*
in der Nacht	*at night*
in der Nacht von Sonntag auf Montag	*during the night from Sunday to Monday*
zweimal in der Woche	*twice a week*
in der Woche vor Weihnachten	*in the week before Christmas*
in der Vergangenheit	*in the past*
in Zukunft	*in future*

NB: (i) For the use of *in* or *zu* with *Zeit* and *Stunde*, see 11.6.13.

(ii) *im voraus* 'in advance'.

(b) *in* is used to indicate a period of time within which something happens:

Ich habe die Arbeit in zwei Stunden gemacht	*I did the work in two hours*
In zwei Jahren ist der Umsatz um 40% gestiegen	*In two years the turnover rose by 40%*
im Lauf(e) der Zeit	*in the course of time*
Das kann man in zwei Tagen schaffen	*You can do that in two days*

BUT: Das kann man **an** einem Morgen, Nachmittag, Abend schaffen

(c) *in* may indicate the time after which something happens or is done:

Er kommt in einer halben Stunde zurück	*He's coming back in half an hour*
heute in acht Tagen	*a week today, in a week's time*
Sie fliegt in ein paar Tagen nach Sydney	*She's flying to Sydney in a few days (time)*

NB: *in* is potentially ambiguous, as is English *in*. Thus, *in drei Tagen* can mean 'in the course of three days' or 'in three days time'.

11.6.8 *nach* usually corresponds to English 'after':

Nach vielen Jahren ließen sie sich scheiden	*After many years they got divorced*
Einen Monat nach seiner Verhaftung wurde er freigelassen	*A month after his arrest he was released*
Nach Ostern studiert sie in Erlangen Chemie	*After Easter she's going to study Chemistry in Erlangen*
bald nach Anfang des 17. Jahrhunderts	*soon after the beginning of the 17th century*
nach einer Weile	*after a while*
nach Wochen, Jahren	*weeks, years later*

11.6.9 *seit* is used to mark a period of time beginning in the past and continuing to the present or a more recent point in the past

It corresponds to English 'since' or 'for', cf. 11.6.5b:

Er ist seit drei Wochen hier	*He's been here for three weeks*
Ich wartete seit einer halben Stunde auf dem Marktplatz	*I had been waiting on the market-place for half an hour*
Erst seit heute weiß ich, daß . . .	*I've only learnt today that . . .*
Seit wann bist du wieder zu Hause?	*Since when have you been back home?*
Seit seiner Krankheit habe ich ihn nicht mehr gesehen	*I haven't seen him again since his illness*
Seit Anfang des Jahres spielt er wieder Fußball	*He's been playing football again since the beginning of the year*
Seit kurzem gibt es Sondertarife nach Spanien	*Recently there have been special fares to Spain*
Ich kenne ihn seit langem	*I've known him for a long time*
seit jeher	*for ages*

NB: (i) For the use of tenses with *seit* 'for', see 14.2.2 and 14.3.3.
(ii) An accusative phrase with *schon* is a possible alternative to *seit* 'for', e.g. *Er ist schon drei Wochen hier*, cf. 10.30.1.

11.6.10 *um* is used with clock times and to express approximation

(a) *um* corresponds to English 'at' with clock times,
e.g. *um vier Uhr* 'at four o'clock', etc., see 11.1.3.

(b) With other time words *um* expresses approximation
It corresponds to English 'around' or 'about' and is often used with *herum* following the noun:

um Mitternacht (herum)	*around midnight*
um Ostern (herum)	*round about Easter time*
um 1890 (herum)	*around 1890*
die Tage um die Sommersonnenwende (herum)	*the days either side of the summer solstice*

NB: *um diese Zeit* is ambiguous. It can mean 'at this time' or 'around this time'. Adding *herum*, i.e. *um diese Zeit herum*, makes it clear the second meaning is intended.

(c) Idiomatic time phrases with *um*:

Stunde um Stunde	*hour after hour*
einen Tag um den anderen	*one day after the other*

11.6.11 *von* indicates a starting-point in time

It corresponds to English 'from' and is often linked with a following *an*:

Von 1976 an lebte sie in Rottweil	*From 1976 she lived in Rottweil*
Von kommendem Montag an kostet das Benzin 10 Pfennig mehr pro Liter	*From next Monday petrol will cost 10 pfennigs a litre more*

von Anfang an	*(right) from the start*
von neun Uhr an	*from nine o'clock (on)*
von nun an	*from now on*
von der Zeit an	*from then onward*
von Anfang bis Ende	*from beginning to end*
von heute auf morgen	*from one day to the next, overnight*
von vornherein	*from the outset, from the first*
von jeher	
von alters her	*from time immemorial, always*
von Jugend auf	*from his (my, etc.) youth on*
von Zeit zu Zeit	*from time to time*

NB: *ab* can be used in the sense 'from' in time expressions, e.g. *ab Montag den/dem 5. August, ab nachste(r) Woche*, see also 20.2.10a.

11.6.12 *vor* corresponds to English 'ago' or 'before':

vor einem Jahr, vor mehreren Jahren	*a year ago, several years ago*
vor kurzem	*not long ago, recently* (cf. 11.7.5)
gestern vor acht Tagen	*a week ago yesterday*
die Verhältnisse vor der Krise	*the conditions before the crisis*

NB: In many contexts *her* can also be used in the sense of English 'ago', e.g. *Es ist schon lange, einen Monat her* 'It's a long time, a month ago'. *Wie lange ist es (schon) her?* 'How long ago is it?', see also 7.3.5e.

11.6.13 *zu* is used with a number of time words

(a) with the major festivals:

zu Weihnachten   zu Ostern   zu Pfingsten   zu Neujahr

NB: In south German, *an* is often used rather than *zu* with these festivals. In colloquial speech, there may be no preposition, e.g. *Sie kommt Weihnachten.*

(b) Both *zu* and *in* are used with *Zeit*
(i) *zu* occurs in contexts denoting one or more specific points or limited periods of time:

zur Zeit	*at present, at the moment, at the time*
zur Zeit der letzten Wahlen	*at the time of the last election*
zu der Zeit, zu dieser Zeit	*at that time*
zu der Zeit, als du hier warst	*at the time when you were here*
zu einer anderen Zeit	*at some other time*
zu jeder Zeit (or: jederzeit)	*at all times, at any time*
zu jeder Tageszeit	*at any time of the day*
zu gewissen Zeiten	*at certain times*
zur gewohnten Zeit	*at the usual time*
gerade noch zur rechten Zeit	*in the nick of time*
zu gleicher Zeit (or: zugleich, gleichzeitig)	*at the same time, simultaneously*
Zu meiner Zeit war das alles anders	*In my time that was all different*

NB also: *zu diesem Zeitpunkt* 'at this point in time'.

(ii) *in* is used to denote a period within or after which something occurs, or in phrases which are felt to denote duration rather than a point or limited period in time:

In all der Zeit (or: In der ganzen Zeit) haben wir sie nicht gesehen	*In all that time we didn't see her*
In kurzer Zeit war er wieder da	*In a short time he was back again*
In unserer Zeit tut man das nicht mehr	*In our times that is no longer done*
in einer Zeit, in der die Städte wachsen	*at a time when towns are growing*
in einer solchen Zeit wie heute	*at a time like the present*
in früheren Zeiten	*in earlier times*
in künftigen Zeiten	*in times to come*
in der ersten Zeit	*at first*

(c) The usage of *zu* or *in* with *Stunde* may be illustrated by the following examples:

zu dieser Stunde	*at this hour*
zu jeder Stunde	*at any time*
zur selben Stunde	*at the same hour*
zu später Stunde (lit.)	*at a late hour*
in ruhigen Stunden	*in peaceful hours*
in elfter Stunde	*at the eleventh hour*

(d) *zu* is used with *Mal*:

zum ersten Mal (zum erstenmal)   zum zehnten Mal, etc. (see 9.4.4)

11.7 Adverbs of time

11.7.1 A selection of commonly used adverbs of time.

Where indicated, further information on some of these words is given elsewhere.

anfangs	*initially*	heuer (S.Ger.)	*this year*
bald	*soon*	heute (11.7.2)	*today*
bisher	*up to now, hitherto*	heutzutage	*nowadays*
bislang	*up to now, hitherto*	immer	*always*
damals (11.7.3a)	*then*	indessen (form.)	*meanwhile*
danach (11.7.4b)	*after(wards)*	inzwischen	*meanwhile*
dann (11.7.3b)	*then*	irgendwann (5.5.11b)	*sometime*
demnächst	*soon*	jetzt	*now*
derzeit	*at present*	kürzlich (11.7.5)	*a short time ago*
ehedem (lit.)	*formerly*	lange	*(for) a long time*
ehemals (form.)	*formerly, previously*	längst (8.3.4a)	*(for) a long time, a long time ago*
einst	*once*		
fortan (form.)	*henceforth*	manchmal	*sometimes*
gestern (11.7.2)	*yesterday*	mittlerweile	*in the meantime*
gleich	*at once, immediately*	morgen (11.7.2)	*tomorrow*
gleichzeitig	*at the same time*	nachher (11.7.4b)	*after(wards)*
hernach (form.)	*after(wards)*	nächstens (8.3.4b)	*shortly, soon*

neulich (11.7.5)	*recently*	vorerst	*for the moment*
nun (10.25.1)	*now*	vorher (11.7.4a)	*before(hand)*
rechtzeitig	*in good time*	vorhin	*just now*
seinerzeit	*at the time*	vorläufig	*for the time being*
seitdem	*since then*	währenddessen	*in the meantime*
seither	*since then*	zeitweise	*at times*
selten	*seldom, rarely*	zuerst	*at first, to start*
soeben	*just (this moment)*	zugleich	*at the same time*
sofort	*at once, immediately*	zuletzt	*in the end*
sogleich	*at once, immediately*	zunächst (8.3.4c)	*first of all*
solange	*meanwhile*	zuvor (11.7.4a)	*before(hand)*
stets	*always*	zuweilen (form.)	*now and then*
unlängst (11.7.5)	*recently*	zwischendurch	*in between times*

11.7.2 *gestern, heute, morgen* are used in conjunction with words indicating periods of the day to give the equivalent of English 'last night', 'this afternoon', etc.:

gestern morgen	*yesterday morning*
gestern abend	*last night* (before bedtime)
vorgestern	*the day before yesterday*
heute nacht	{ *last night* (after bedtime)
	{ *tonight* (after bedtime)
heute morgen/heute früh	*this morning*
heute vormittag	*this morning* (after breakfast)
heute nachmittag	*this afternoon*
heute abend	*this evening*
morgen früh	*tomorrow morning*
morgen vormittag	*tomorrow morning* (after breakfast)
übermorgen	*the day after tomorrow*

11.7.3 German equivalents of English *then*

(a) *damals* is used with reference to past time, i.e. in the meaning 'at that time':

Sie war damals sehr arm	*She was very poor, then*
damals, vor dem großen Kriege (*Roth*)	*at that time, before the Great War*

(b) *dann* is used for other temporal meanings of *then*:

Dann fuhr er weg	*Then he left*
Erst bist du an der Reihe, dann ich	*First it's your turn, then mine*
Wenn er dir schreibt, dann mußt du es deiner Mutter sagen	*If he writes to you, then you'll have to tell your mother*
Und wenn sie kommt, was machst du dann?	*And if she comes, what then?*

NB: *dann* is not used after a preposition, cf.: *bis dahin* 'till then', *seither, seitdem* 'since then', *von da an* 'from then on', *vorher, zuvor* 'before then', cf. 11.7.4a.

(c) To intensify a question, the German equivalent is *denn*, cf 10.6:

Was ist denn daran so komisch?	*What's so funny about it, then?*

11.7.4 German equivalents of English *before* and *after*.

(a) *vorher* or *zuvor* are the most usual equivalents of 'before'
Both can be used with reference to past or future time:

Ich war ein Jahr vorher/zuvor da gewesen	*I had been there a year before*
Ich muß vorher/zuvor noch telephonieren	*I've got to make a phone call before then*
Er hatte uns am Tag vorher/zuvor besucht	*He had been to visit us the day before*
einige Zeit vorher/zuvor	*some time previously*

Referring to time up to the present moment, *früher* or *zuvor* are used (or, in a negative context, *noch*):

Sie hätten es mir früher/zuvor sagen sollen	*You ought to have told me before*
Ich habe sie nie zuvor/noch nie gesehen	*I've never seen her before*

(b) *danach* or *nachher* are the usual equivalents for 'after' (or 'later')
darauf is also often used after words expressing a period of time:

Ich habe sie einen Monat danach/nachher gesehen	*I saw her a month after/later*
lange danach/lange nachher	*a long time after*
kurz danach/kurz nachher/ kurz darauf	*a short time after/shortly afterwards*
Am Tag darauf/danach gingen wir ins Theater	*The day after we went to the theatre*
Das werde ich dir nachher erzählen	*I'll tell you that afterwards*

11.7.5 German equivalents for English *recent(ly)*

(a) The following are the main equivalents:

kürzlich/vor kurzem/unlängst	*a short time ago*
neulich	*the other day*
letzthin/in letzter Zeit/seit kurzem	*latterly* (i.e. during the last few weeks or months)

As the above are all adverbs, they have to be used in paraphrases, etc., to give German equivalents for the English adjective *recent*, e.g.:

auf der kürzlich stattgefundenen Konferenz	*at the recent conference*
bei unserer Begegnung neulich	*at our recent meeting*
als er vor kurzem krank war	*during his recent illness*
eine erst kürzlich eingeführte Neuerung	*a (very) recent innovation*
sein neuestes Buch	*his most recent book*

(b) Other phrases and renderings

bis vor kurzem	*until recently*
Ich habe ihn noch später gesehen als Sie	*I have seen him more recently than you*
Kurt hat sie zuletzt gesehen	*Kurt has seen her most recently/ just recently*

12   Verbs: Conjugation

12.1 Verb conjugation

12.1.1 The various forms of the verb express different grammatical ideas, known as 'grammatical categories'. All the forms of a particular verb constitute its 'conjugation'

German verbs are given in most dictionaries in the 'infinitive' form, ending in *-en* or *-n*, e.g. *kaufen, singen, wandern*. By deleting this *-(e)n*, we obtain the basic core of the verb, which is called the 'stem', e.g. **kauf-, sing-, wander-**. The stem carries the essential 'lexical' meaning of the verb. By altering this stem, i.e. by adding 'affixes' (i.e. prefixes or endings) or changing the vowel (and in a few cases the consonants, too) we can:

(a) indicate the person and number of the subject of the verb, e.g.:

ich kaufe	du singst	er/sie/es wandert
wir kaufen	ihr singt	sie/Sie wandern

We usually say that, through these changes, the verb 'agrees' with the subject for person (i.e. first, second or third person) and number (i.e. singular or plural).

(b) indicate the time of the action, process or event expressed by the verb, e.g.:

ich kaufe	(present)	–	ich kaufte	(past)
du singst	(present)	–	du sangst	(past)
er wandert	(present)	–	er wanderte	(past)

The various forms of the verb which express time relationships are known as the 'tenses' of the verb. German, like English, has two simple (i.e. one-word) tenses, the 'present' and the 'past' tense. The other tenses are 'compound' tenses, formed by using one of the 'auxiliary' verbs *haben, sein* or *werden* with the past participle or the infinitive, e.g.:

ich habe gekauft, ich habe gesungen, ich bin gewandert (perfect)
er hatte gekauft, er hatte gesungen, er war gewandert (pluperfect)
sie werden kaufen, sie werden singen, sie werden wandern (future)

The use of the tenses in German is treated in chapter 14.

(c) show whether we are dealing with a fact, a possibility or a command

The difference between these is shown by the 'mood' of the verb. German has three moods:

(i) The 'indicative' mood states a fact:

ich kaufe   du sangst   sie sind gewandert

(ii) The 'subjunctive' mood indicates a possibility or a report:

er kaufe   er sänge   er würde wandern

(iii) The 'imperative' mood expresses a command:

kaufe!   singt!   wandern Sie!

The use of the subjunctive mood in German is dealt with in chapter 16.

(d) change the relationship between the elements in the sentence

The use of a different 'voice' of the verb, i.e. the 'active' or 'passive' voice permits different elements to appear as the subject of the verb, e.g.:

active voice: er kaufte das Buch
passive voice (with *werden*):   das Buch wurde gekauft
passive voice (with *sein*):   das Buch war gekauft

German has two forms of the passive, both of which are compound, using one of the auxiliary verbs *werden* or *sein* and the past participle. Their uses are dealt with in chapter 15.

(e) construct the 'non-finite' forms of the verb

The non-finite forms of the verb in German are the 'infinitive', e.g. *kaufen, singen, wandern*, the 'present participle', e.g. *kaufend, singend, wandernd* and the 'past participle', e.g. *gekauft, gesungen, gewandert*.

These non-finite forms are used in conjunction with other verbs, or combined with auxiliary verbs to form the compound tenses and the passive voice.

Other uses of the infinitive and the participles are treated in chapter 13.

12.1.2 The conjugation of a particular verb depends on whether it belongs to the 'weak' or 'strong' class

The main difference between these classes is the way in which the past tense is formed:

(a) WEAK **verbs form their past tense by adding** -*te* **to the stem**, e.g.:

kauf-en – kaufte   mach-en – machte   wander-n – wanderte

(b) STRONG **verbs form their past tense by changing the vowel of the stem**, e.g.:

beiß-en – biß   fließ-en – floß   sing-en – sang

The great majority of German verbs are 'weak', and we may consider them as the 'regular' verbs of the language. Although there are relatively few 'strong' verbs, many of them are very common. There is no way of telling from the infinitive of a verb whether it is 'weak' or 'strong'. This means that there is no practical alternative for the foreign learner to knowing <u>which</u> verbs are 'strong' and learning their main forms, which are given in 12.6.

12.1.3 In addition, there are a small number of 'irregular' verbs

These fall into four main groups:

(a) A few irregular weak verbs with vowel changes (and sometimes also consonant changes) in the past tense:

kenn-en – kannte   renn-en – rannte   bring-en – brachte

The main forms of these verbs are given in 12.6.

(b) A few irregular strong verbs, with consonant changes as well as vowel changes in the past tense:

geh-en – ging   leid-en – litt   steh-en – stand   zieh-en – zog

The main forms of these verbs are given in 12.6.

(c) The 'modal auxiliary' verbs and *wissen*
These verbs, i.e. the six modal auxiliary verbs *dürfen, können, mögen, müssen, sollen, wollen* and the verb *wissen* 'to know' have an irregular present tense with no -*t* in the third person singular and, in most cases, a different vowel in the singular and plural of the present tense, e.g.:

dürfen – er darf, wir dürfen   können – er kann, wir können
müssen – er muß, wir müssen   wissen – er weiß, wir wissen

The forms of these verbs are given in 12.2.3.

(d) The verbs *haben, sein* and *werden*
These three verbs are wholly irregular. Aside from their basic meanings, i.e. *haben* 'to have', *sein* 'to be', *werden* 'to become', they are used as auxiliaries to form the compound tenses and the passives. All the forms of these verbs are given in 12.2.4.

12.2 Simple tenses and non-finite forms

In this section paradigms are given for the simple forms of the various classes of verb, i.e. the infinitive, the present and past participles, the present and past indicative tenses and the imperative.

12.2.1 Weak and strong verbs

Weak and strong verbs differ principally in the formation of the past tense and the past participle. Weak verbs have the ending *-te* in the past tense and *-t* in the past participle, whilst strong verbs change the vowel of the stem in the past tense and have the ending *-en* (sometimes with a further change of vowel) in the past participle. Otherwise, weak and strong verbs have similar endings.

The weak verb *kaufen* 'buy' (stem *kauf-*) and the strong verb *singen* 'sing' (stem *sing-*) are conjugated as follows:

Infinitive	kaufen	singen
Present participle	kaufend	singend
Past participle	gekauft	gesungen
Present tense:		
	ich kaufe	ich singe
	du kaufst	du singst
	es kauft	es singt
	wir kaufen	wir singen
	ihr kauft	ihr singt
	sie kaufen	sie singen
Past tense:		
	ich kaufte	ich sang
	du kauftest	du sangst
	es kaufte	es sang
	wir kauften	wir sangen
	ihr kauftet	ihr sangt
	sie kauften	sie sangen
Imperative:		
singular	kaufe!	singe!
plural (familiar)	kauft!	singt!
plural (polite)	kaufen Sie!	singen Sie!

NB: (i) The form of the 'polite' second person (with the pronoun *Sie*) is not given separately, as the ending of the verb is always the same as that of the third person plural, cf. *Sie kaufen – sie kaufen.*

(ii) The third person singular of the verb always has the same ending irrespective of the gender of the subject, i.e. whether it is *er*, *sie* or *es*. The pronoun *es* is used throughout this section.

(iii) The vowel changes for the individual strong verbs in the past tense and past participle are given in section 12.6.

(iv) The irregular weak and strong verbs, e.g. *kennen*, *bringen*, *gehen*, *ziehen*, etc. have the same endings as *kaufen* and *singen*. Their irregularities consist in the changes to their stem in the past tense and the past participle; these are given in 12.6.

(v) In spoken German, the pronoun is occasionally added for emphasis in the singular and familiar plural of the imperative, e.g.: *Nimm du das Messer! Geht ihr schon vor!*

12.2.2 Variations on the basic conjugation pattern of weak and strong verbs

(a) Verbs with stems ending in -d or -t, or in -m or -n preceded by a consonant other than l or r
These add a linking -e- before the personal endings -t, -st and, in the case of weak verbs, the -te of the past. Thus, for the weak verb *arbeiten* 'work':

Present tense:	du arbeitest, er arbeitet, ihr arbeitet
Imperative:	arbeitet!
Past tense:	ich arbeitete, du arbeitetest, er arbeitete, etc.
Past participle:	gearbeitet

Relevant forms of the strong verb *finden* 'find':

Present tense:	du findest, er findet, ihr findet
Imperative:	findet!
Past tense:	du fandest, ihr fandet

Other examples:

regnen *rain*:	es regnet, es regnete, geregnet, etc.
atmen *breathe*:	du atmest, sie atmet, ihr atmet, ich atmete, geatmet, etc.

NB: (i) Verbs with *l* or *r* before *m* or *n* do not need the linking -e-: er filmt *he films*, sie lernt *she learns*.
(ii) Strong verbs with a vowel change do not add -t in the third person singular, cf. (e) and (f) below.

(b) Verbs with stems ending in -s, -ß, -x or -z
In the present, these have the ending -t in the second person singular, e.g.:

rasen *race*	–	du rast	grüßen *greet*	–	du grüßt
mixen *mix*	–	du mixt	setzen *put*	–	du setzt

NB: The older ending -est with such verbs, e.g. *du setzest*, is no longer current.

In the past, the strong verbs have a linking -e- in the second person singular, e.g.:

du lasest *you read*   du ließest *you let*   du wuchsest *you grew*

NB: The insertion of an -e- in the second person plural of these strong verbs, e.g. *ihr laset, ihr aßet*, is elevated and rather old-fashioned. The usual forms are *ihr last, ihr aßt*, etc.

(c) Verbs with stems ending in -el and -er
These verbs have the following variations on the general pattern of endings:
(i) In the infinitive and the first and third person plural of the present they have the ending -n, e.g.:

klingeln *ring*:   wir klingeln, sie klingeln
wandern *wander*:   wir wandern, sie wandern

(ii) In the first person singular, the -e- of the stem is always lost with verbs in *-el* and occasionally with verbs in *-er* (more commonly in speech than in writing), e.g.:

ich klingle, ich wand(e)re
Similarly in the imperative singular:
klingle!, wand(e)re!, cf. (g) below.

NB: In speech one also hears forms where the *-e-* of the stem is kept, but the *-e* of the ending dropped, e.g. *ich klingel, ich wander*, etc.

(d) Verbs with stems ending in a vowel
Note the following:
(i) The present tense of *tun* 'do':
ich tue, du tust, es tut, wir tun, ihr tut, sie tun

(ii) The present tense of *knien* [kni:n] 'kneel':
ich knie [kni:ə], du kniest [kni:st], es kniet [kni:t],
wir knien [kni:ən], ihr kniet, sie knien:

The past tense of the strong verb *schreien* 'shout, scream' is similar, i.e. *ich/es schrie, wir/sie schrien* [ʃri:n]. The past participle is *geschrieen* or *geschrien*.

(iii) Other verbs whose stem ends in a long vowel or diphthong generally lose the *-e-* of the ending *-en* in spoken German, and these forms are occasionally found in writing, e.g *schaun, gehn, gesehn* for *schauen, gehen, gesehen*, etc.

(e) In the second and third person singular of the present, and in the imperative singular most strong verbs with *-e-* in their stem change this to *-i-* or *-ie-*
In general verbs in short *-e-* change this to *-i-*, whilst those in long *-i-* change this to *-ie-*. Note that such verbs lack the ending *-e* in the imperative, e.g:

essen *eat*:	du ißt, es ißt, iß!
helfen *help*:	du hilfst, es hilft, hilf!
lesen *read*:	du liest, es liest, lies!
stehlen *steal*:	du stiehlst, es stiehlt, stiehl!

There are some exceptions and further irregularities with these verbs. Full details are given under the individual verbs in section 12.6, but the following should be noted:
(i) The following strong verbs in *-e-* do not change the vowel:

bewegen	*induce*	gehen	*go*	genesen	*recover*	heben	*lift*
melken	*milk*	scheren	*shear*	stehen	*stand*	weben	*weave*

(ii) erlöschen 'go out' (of lights, fires) changes *-ö-* to *-i-*, e.g. *es erlischt*
(iii) Three strong verbs in long *-e-* change this to *-i-*, i.e.:

geben	*give*	– du gibst, es gibt, gib!
nehmen	*take*	– du nimmst, es nimmt, nimm!
treten	*step*	– du trittst, es tritt, tritt!

(iv) Verbs with this vowel change whose stem ends in *-d* or *-t* do not add *-et* in the third person singular, e.g.:

gelten – es **gilt**   schelten – es **schilt**   treten – es **tritt**

(v) In non-standard colloquial speech, a regular imperative, without the vowel change, is common, e.g. *eß!, geb!, nehm!*

(f) Most strong verbs with -a- or -au- in their stem have Umlaut in the second and third person singular of the present:

fahren *go*: du fährst, es fährt   lassen *let*: du läßt, es läßt
wachsen *grow*: du wächst, es wächst   laufen *run*: du läufst, es läuft

A few exceptions and further irregularities may be noted in this context. Full details are given in 12.6, but the following may be noted here:

(i) *stoßen* 'push' has Umlaut of *-o-*, e.g.: stoßen *push* – du stößt, es stößt
(ii) *schaffen* 'create' does **not** have Umlaut, i.e.: du schaffst, es schafft.
(iii) Verbs in this group whose stem ends in *-t* or *-d* do not add *-et* in the third person singular, e.g.:

halten – es **hält**   laden – es **lädt**   raten – es **rät**

NB: In spoken south German, Umlaut tends not to be used with these verbs, and one hears, for instance, *er schlaft* instead of *er schläft*. This is considered substandard.

(g) The ending -e of the singular imperative is generally dropped in spoken German, e.g.:

Komm in den Garten!   Setz dich!   Stör mich nicht!

This is by no means unusual in written German, too.

However, a few verbs always retain the *-e*, i.e. those whose stems end in *-d*, *-t*, *-ig*, and *-m* or *-n* preceded by a consonant other then *-r*, e.g.:

Antworte mir sofort!   Rede nicht so laut!   Entschuldige bitte!
Atme stärker!   Segne mich!

Verbs in *-el* drop the *-e-* of the stem, but always retain the ending, e.g. *Klingle laut!* This is also an option with verbs in *-er*, e.g. *Wand(e)re!*

Verbs which change *-e-* to *-i-* or *-ie-* do **not** have the ending *-e*, e.g. *Gib her! Nimm es doch!* However, the form *Siehe!* is used in the (biblical) set phrase *Siehe da!* 'Behold!' and in giving references in books, e.g. *s.S.90* (= *siehe Seite 90*).

(h) A number of verbs lack the prefix *ge-* in the past participle

All these are verbs which are not stressed on the first syllable of the stem, i.e.:
(i) Verbs with inseparable or double prefixes, cf. 22.4 and 22.5.1d, e.g.:

bedeuten *mean*	– bedeutet	erfinden *invent*	– erfunden
gelingen *succeed*	– gelungen	mißlingen *fail*	– mißlungen
zerbrechen *smash*	– zerbrochen	überlegen *consider*	– überlegt
unterdrücken *suppress*	– unterdrückt	anvertrauen *entrust*	– anvertraut

(ii) Verbs in *-ieren*, e.g.:

gratulieren *congratulate* – gratuliert   studieren *study* – studiert

(iii) A few others which are not stressed on the first syllable, e.g.:

froh'locken *rejoice* – froh'lockt   offen'baren *reveal* – offen'bart
   (also: ge'frohlockt)   (also: ge'offenbart)
prophe'zeien *prophesy* – prophe'zeit   po'saunen *bellow* – po'saunt
schma'rotzen *sponge* – schma'rotzt

(j) Separable verbs

These verbs are conjugated in the same way as the simple verbs from which they are derived.

(i) In finite forms in main clauses, the prefix is detached from the verb and takes up the final position in the clause, i.e. it becomes the final part of the 'verbal bracket' construction, cf. 21.1.2, e.g.:

ankommen *arrive*:   Ich komme morgen um zwei Uhr **an**
ausgehen *go out*:   Sie geht heute abend **aus**
nachahmen *imitate*:   Sie ahmten seine Bewegungen **nach**
totschlagen *kill*:   Er schlug das Tier mit einer Keule **tot**

(ii) The prefix remains joined with the verb in the non-finite forms, with the *ge-* of the past participle being inserted after the prefix, e.g.:

ankommen – ankommend – angekommen   ausgehen – ausgehend – ausgegangen

In cases where the basic verb has no *ge-* in the past participle, it is also lacking in corresponding separable verbs, e.g.:

einstudieren *rehearse* – einstudiert   anerkennen *recognize* – anerkannt

(iii) In subordinate clauses, the prefix rejoins the finite verb in final position and is written together with it, e.g.:

Ich weiß, daß sie heute abend **ausgeht**
Er sah, wie sie seine Bewegungen **nachahmten**

12.2.3 The modal auxiliary verbs and *wissen*

The six 'modal auxiliary' verbs *dürfen, können, mögen, müssen, sollen, wollen* and the verb *wissen* 'know' are wholly irregular in their present tenses, with no *-e* in the first person singular and no *-t* in the third person singular and, in most cases, vowel changes between the singular and plural of the present tense. They form their past tenses with *-te*, like weak verbs, but, again, in most cases there are vowel changes.

   The meanings and uses of the modal auxiliary verbs are explained in chapter 17.

(a) Present tense:

	dürfen	können	mögen	müssen	sollen	wollen	wissen
ich	darf	kann	mag	muß	soll	will	weiß
du	darfst	kannst	magst	mußt	sollst	willst	weißt
es	darf	kann	mag	muß	soll	will	weiß
wir	dürfen	können	mögen	müssen	sollen	wollen	wissen
ihr	dürft	könnt	mögt	müßt	sollt	wollt	wißt
sie	dürfen	können	mögen	müssen	sollen	wollen	wissen

(b) Past tense:

ich	durfte	konnte	mochte	mußte	sollte	wollte	wußte
du	durftest	konntest	mochtest	mußtest	solltest	wolltest	wußtest
es	durfte	konnte	mochte	mußte	sollte	wollte	wußte
wir	durften	konnten	mochten	mußten	sollten	wollten	wußten
ihr	durftet	konntet	mochtet	mußtet	solltet	wolltet	wußtet
sie	durften	konnten	mochten	mußten	sollten	wollten	wußten

(c) Non-finite and imperative forms
(i) Past participle:

gedurft gekonnt gemocht gemußt gesollt gewollt gewußt

Note that the past participle of the modal auxiliaries is rarely used, as when these verbs are used in the perfect tenses in conjunction with a main verb, the infinitive is used rather than the past participle, e.g.:

Ich habe es machen **müssen**	Sie hatte es sehen **können**
Wir haben ihn lehren **sollen**	Sie hatten es uns sagen **wollen**

Details about this are given in 13.3.2a.

(ii) The present participle and imperative of the modal auxiliaries do not occur in practice. *wissen* has the following forms:

Present participle: wissend
Imperative: wisse! wißt! wissen Sie!

12.2.4 The irregular verbs *sein, haben, werden*

(a) Present tense:

	sein	haben	werden
ich	bin	habe	werde
du	bist	hast	wirst
es	ist	hat	wird
wir	sind	haben	werden
ihr	seid	habt	werdet
sie	sind	haben	werden

NB: In colloquial speech the final *-t* of *ist* is often lost, and one hears *es is* for *es ist*.

(b) Past tense:

ich	war	hatte	wurde
du	warst	hattest	wurdest
es	war	hatte	wurde
wir	waren	hatten	wurden
ihr	wart	hattet	wurdet
sie	waren	hatten	wurden

NB: The older form *ich/es ward* was sometimes used for *ich/es wurde* in elevated styles into the present century. It is still occasionally encountered in archaicizing (especially biblical) contexts.

(c) Non-finite forms and imperatives:

Infinitive:	sein	haben	werden
Present participle:	seiend	habend	werdend
Past participle:	gewesen	gehabt	geworden
Imperative:	sei!	habe!	werde!
	seid!	habt!	werdet!
	seien Sie!	haben Sie!	werden Sie!

NB: The past participle of *werden* has no *ge-* when used as an auxiliary to form the passive, cf. 12.4, e.g.: Er ist gelobt worden. BUT compare: Er ist Schauspieler **ge**worden.

12.2.5 Reduction of endings in colloquial German

Some verb endings are regularly reduced in everyday speech. Such forms are regarded as colloquial and seldom used in the written language.

(a) The ending -*e* tends to be lost in everyday spoken German,
e.g. *ich kauf, ich fall, ich/es sucht* for standard German *ich kaufe, ich falle, ich/es suchte.*
    This loss of *-e* is particularly frequent in the imperative singular, cf. 12.2.2g.

(b) The ending -*en* tends to be reduced to -*n* in everyday spoken German,
e.g. *wir kaufn, sie falln, wir kauftn, sie botn, getretn* for standard German *wir kaufen, sie fallen, wir kauften, sie boten, getreten.*
    This reduction is particularly common in verbs with a stem ending in a long vowel or diphthong, cf. 12.2.2d.

NB: In the spoken German of the west and southwest, the *-n* of the ending *-en* is lost, e.g. *mir kaufe, sie falle.* This is a non-standard regionalism.

12.3 The compound tenses: perfect and future

The perfect tenses are formed using the past participle and the auxiliary *haben* or *sein*. The future is constructed with the auxiliary *werden* and the infinitive.
    The non-finite parts of these compound tenses are placed at the end of

the clause in main clauses, i.e. they constitute the final part of the 'verbal bracket', cf. 21.1, e.g. *Ich* **habe** *sie gestern in der Stadt* **gesehen**.

In subordinate clauses the auxiliary usually follows the non-finite part at the end of the clause, cf. 21.1.3, e.g. *Sie wissen, daß ich sie gestern in der Stadt* **gesehen habe**.

The uses of these tenses are explained in detail in chapter 14.

12.3.1 The conjugation of the compound perfect and future tenses

The full forms are given for the weak verb *kaufen* 'buy' and the strong verb *singen* 'sing', which form their perfect tenses with the auxiliary *haben*, and the strong verb *bleiben* 'remain' which forms its perfect tenses with the auxiliary *sein*.

(a) Perfect:

ich habe	gekauft	habe	gesungen	bin	geblieben
du hast	gekauft	hast	gesungen	bist	geblieben
es hat	gekauft	hat	gesungen	ist	geblieben
wir haben	gekauft	haben	gesungen	sind	geblieben
ihr habt	gekauft	habt	gesungen	seid	geblieben
sie haben	gekauft	haben	gesungen	sind	geblieben

(b) Pluperfect:

ich hatte	gekauft	hatte	gesungen	war	geblieben
du hattest	gekauft	hattest	gesungen	warst	geblieben
es hatte	gekauft	hatte	gesungen	war	geblieben
wir hatten	gekauft	hatten	gesungen	waren	geblieben
ihr hattet	gekauft	hattet	gesungen	wart	geblieben
sie hatten	gekauft	hatten	gesungen	waren	geblieben

(c) Future:

ich werde	kaufen	werde	singen	werde	bleiben
du wirst	kaufen	wirst	singen	wirst	bleiben
es wird	kaufen	wird	singen	wird	bleiben
wir werden	kaufen	werden	singen	werden	bleiben
ihr werdet	kaufen	werdet	singen	werdet	bleiben
sie werden	kaufen	werden	singen	werden	bleiben

(d) Future perfect:

ich werde	gekauft haben	werde	gesungen haben	werde	geblieben sein
du wirst	gekauft haben	wirst	gesungen haben	wirst	geblieben sein
es wird	gekauft haben	wird	gesungen haben	wird	geblieben sein
wir werden	gekauft haben	werden	gesungen haben	werden	geblieben sein
ihr werdet	gekauft haben	werdet	gesungen haben	werdet	geblieben sein
sie werden	gekauft haben	werden	gesungen haben	werden	geblieben sein

12.3.2 *haben* or *sein* in the perfect?

(a) The following groups of verbs form their perfect with *sein*. All are intransitive, i.e. they do not have an object in the accusative case
(i) Intransitive verbs of motion:

Ich **bin** in die Stadt gegangen   Wir **sind** aus dem Haus entkommen
Sie **war** zum Boden gefallen   Ihr **wart** auf die Mauer geklettert
Um die Zeit werden wir schon angekommen **sein**

NB: A few verbs of motion take *sein **or** haben* in different contexts,cf. 12.3.2c.

(ii) Intransitive verbs expressing a change of state.
This group includes a large number of verbs which point to the beginning or end of a process, notably those with the prefixes *er-* and *ver-*, cf.22.4.

Sie **ist** schon eingeschlafen   Die Bombe **ist** um zwei Uhr explodiert
Das Licht **ist** ausgegangen   Mein Buch **ist** verschwunden
Die Glocke **ist** erklungen   Die Blumen **sind** verwelkt
Der Reifen **war** geplatzt   Der Schnee **war** schon geschmolzen
Sie werden gleich danach ertrunken **sein**

NB: In colloquial North German, *anfangen* and *beginnen* are included in this group and
     form their perfect with *sein*. One thus hears *ich bin angefangen, begonnen* for standard
     German *ich habe angefangen, begonnen*.

(iii) Most verbs meaning 'happen', 'succeed', 'fail', i.e.:

begegnen *meet* (by chance)	glücken *succeed*	vorgehen *happen*
fehlschlagen *fail*	mißglücken *fail*	vorkommen *occur*
gelingen *succeed*	mißlingen *fail*	zustoßen *happen*
geschehen *happen*	passieren *happen*	

Ich **bin** ihr gestern begegnet   Der Plan **ist** fehlgeschlagen
Es **war** mir gelungen, ihn zu überzeugen Das **war** schon einmal vorgekommen
Was wird mit ihr passiert **sein**?

EXCEPTION: The colloquial verb *klappen* 'succeed' takes *haben*, e.g. *Hat's mit den Karten*
             geklappt? 'Did you manage to get the tickets?'
(iv) The verbs *bleiben* and *sein*:

Sie **ist** früher Lehrerin gewesen   Wir **sind** in Dessau geblieben
War er mal Diplomat gewesen?   Sie wird dort geblieben **sein**

(b) All other verbs form their perfect tenses with *haben*
This set includes the majority of German verbs. The most important fall into the following groups:
(i) Transitive verbs, i.e. those which take an accusative object:

Ich **habe** sie gesehen   Sie **hat** ihn geschlagen   Er **hat** die Wohnung geputzt
Der Hund **hatte** die Mülltonne umgeworfen
Ich werde den Brief bis morgen früh geschrieben **haben**

EXCEPTIONS – a few compounds of *gehen* and *werden*, e.g.:
       Er ist die Strecke abgegangen   *He paced the distance*
       Sie ist die Arbeit mit dem Schüler   *She went through the work with*
          durchgegangen   *the pupil*

Er ist die Wette eingegangen	*He made the bet*
Ich bin ihn endlich losgeworden	*I have finally got rid of him*

(ii) Reflexive verbs

Sie **hat** sich sehr gefreut	Ich **habe** mich schon erholt
Ich **hatte** mich aus dem Zimmer gestohlen	Ich **hatte** mir alles eingebildet
Sie wird sich müde gelaufen **haben**	

EXCEPTIONS: verbs which otherwise take *sein*, used with a reciprocal reflexive pronoun in the dative (= 'each other', cf. 3.2.7), e.g.:

Sie sind sich ausgewichen	*They avoided each other*
Wir sind uns in der Stadt begegnet	*We met (each other) in town*

(iii) Intransitive verbs which do not express motion or a change of state, cf. 12.3.3 (a) above. Most of these verbs denote a continuous action, e.g.:

Ich **habe** gestern lange gearbeitet	**Hast** du in der Nacht gut geschlafen?
Dort **hat** jemand auf der Bank gesessen	Oben **hat** vorhin das Licht gebrannt
Sie **hatte** dabei gepfiffen	Sie **hatten** in Münster studiert
Sie wird dort lange gewartet **haben**	

NB: The verbs *liegen*, *sitzen* and *stehen* belong to this group and form their perfect tenses with *haben* in standard German. Thus: *ich habe gelegen, gesessen, gestanden*. However, in South German, *sein* is commonly used (i.e. *ich bin gelegen*, etc.) and this usage is accepted in writing in Austria and Switzerland.

(iv) Most impersonal verbs:

Es **hat** geregnet, geschneit, gehagelt	An der Tür **hat** es geklopft
Es **hatte** nach Benzin gerochen	Da **hatte** es einen Krach gegeben

EXCEPTIONS: Impersonal expressions with verbs which usually form their perfect tenses with *sein*, e.g.:

Es **ist** mir kalt geworden	Wie **war** es Ihnen in Berlin gegangen?

(v) The modal auxiliaries:

Ich **habe** es hinnehmen müssen	Sie **hat** ihn besuchen wollen
Wir **haben** es nicht gekonnt	

(c) The use of *haben* and *sein* with the same verb

The choice of *haben* or *sein* depends on meaning, i.e. it is not an automatic feature of a particular verb irrespective of meaning. Thus, a fair number of verbs which have more than one meaning, or which can be used transitively or intransitively, can be used with *haben* and *sein* in the perfect as their meaning varies between the categories explained in (a) and (b) above.

In this way, *fahren*, used as an intransitive verb of motion, forms its perfect with *sein*, e.g.:

Sie **ist** nach Stuttgart gefahren	Wir **sind** zu schnell gefahren

But when it is used transitively, it takes *haben*, e.g.:

Sie **hat** einen neuen Porsche gefahren	Ich **habe** ihn nach Hause gefahren

Selected further examples:

Ich **habe** einen Brief bekommen	*I have received a letter*
Das Essen **ist** mir gut bekommen	*The meal agreed with me*
Er **hat** das Rohr gebrochen	*He has broken the pipe*
Das Rohr **ist** gebrochen	*The pipe has broken*
Sie **hat** auf Zahlung gedrungen	*She has pressed for payment*
Wasser **ist** in das Haus gedrungen	*Water has penetrated into the house*
Er **hat** ihr gefolgt	*He has obeyed her*
Er **ist** ihr gefolgt	*He has followed her*
Es **hat** in der Nacht gefroren	*There was a frost in the night*
Der See **ist** gefroren	*The lake has frozen*
Da **haben** Sie sich geirrt	*You have made a mistake*
Er **ist** durch die Straßen geirrt	*He roamed through the streets*
Sie **hat** ihn zur Seite gestoßen	*She pushed him to one side*
Ich **bin** an den Schrank gestoßen	*I bumped into the cupboard*
Du **hast** mir den Spaß verdorben	*You have spoilt my fun*
Das Fleisch **ist** verdorben	*The meat has gone bad*

A few verbs of motion take *sein* if they express movement from one place to another, but may have *haben* if they just refer to the activity as such, without any mention of the destination, e.g.:

Ich **habe** als junger Mann viel getanzt	*I danced a lot when I was a young man*
Er **ist** aus dem Zimmer getanzt	*He danced out of the room*
Sie **hat** den ganzen Morgen gesegelt	*She's been sailing the whole morning*
Sie **ist** über den See gesegelt	*She sailed across the lake*

This usage is restricted to a very small number of verbs in modern German, i.e. *paddeln* 'paddle', *reiten* 'ride', *rudern* 'row', *schwimmen* 'swim', *segeln* 'sail', *tanzen* 'dance', *treten* 'step'.

12.4 The passive

German has two passive forms, using one of the auxiliary verbs *werden* or *sein* and the past participle. The uses of these two forms are dealt with fully in chapter 15.

As in other compound verb forms, the participle is normally placed at the end of the clause in main clauses and at the end, before the auxiliary, in subordinate clauses, cf. 21.1, e.g.:

Das Haus wurde voriges Jahr **gebaut**
Ich weiß, daß das Haus voriges Jahr **gebaut** wurde

12.4.1 The *werden*-passive of *loben* 'praise':

Present		Past		Perfect		
ich werde	gelobt	wurde	gelobt	bin	gelobt	worden
du wirst	gelobt	wurdest	gelobt	bist	gelobt	worden
es wird	gelobt	wurde	gelobt	ist	gelobt	worden
wir werden	gelobt	wurden	gelobt	sind	gelobt	worden
ihr werdet	gelobt	wurdet	gelobt	seid	gelobt	worden
sie werden	gelobt	wurden	gelobt	sind	gelobt	worden

Pluperfect	Future	Future Perfect
ich war gelobt worden	werde gelobt werden	werde gelobt worden sein
du warst gelobt worden,	wirst gelobt werden,	wirst gelobt worden sein,
etc.	etc.	etc.

Notes on the formation of the *werden*-passive:

(i) The form of the past participle of *werden* without *ge-*, i.e. *worden*, is used in the perfect tenses

(ii) Imperative forms of the *werden*-passive, e.g. *werde gelobt!* are rarely used. If a passive imperative is needed, the form with *sein* is used, cf. 12.4.2.

12.4.2 The *sein*-passive of *verletzen* 'injure'

Present	Past
ich bin verletzt	war verletzt
du bist verletzt	warst verletzt
es ist verletzt	war verletzt
wir sind verletzt	waren verletzt
ihr seid verletzt	wart verletzt
sie sind verletzt	waren verletzt

Other tenses of the *sein*-passive, e.g. the perfect (*ich bin verletzt gewesen*, etc.), the future (*ich werde verletzt sein*, etc.) are in practice rather uncommon. On the other hand, the imperative does occur regularly, e.g.:

Sei gegrüßt   Seid gegrüßt   Seien Sie gegrüßt!

12.5 The subjunctive

We follow the practice of most recent German grammars in distinguishing two major forms of the subjunctive, i.e. 'Konjunktiv I' and 'Konjunktiv II', each of which has a basic form and various compound forms constructed with auxiliary verbs. These terms are preferable to the traditional terms 'present subjunctive', 'past subjunctive', etc., because the difference between the uses of these forms has nothing to do with time or tense, as is explained in chapter 16.

12.5.1 The basic form of 'Konjunktiv I' (the 'present subjunctive')

This is regular for all verbs with the sole exception of *sein* 'be'. There are no vowel changes with any strong or irregular verbs:

	kaufen	singen	geben	dürfen	werden	haben	sein
ich	kaufe	singe	gebe	dürfe	werde	habe	sei
du	kaufest	singest	gebest	dürfest	werdest	habest	sei(e)st
es	kaufe	singe	gebe	dürfe	werde	habe	sei
wir	kaufen	singen	geben	dürfen	werden	haben	seien
ihr	kaufet	singet	gebet	dürfet	werdet	habet	seiet
sie	kaufen	singen	geben	dürfen	werden	haben	seien

Notes on these forms:

(i) The second person singular and plural forms in *-est* and *-et* are widely felt to be artificial and are seldom used. This means in practice that, for most verbs except *sein*, the only difference between Konjunktiv I and the present indicative is in the third person singular.

(ii) The verbs with a stem in *-el* (cf. 12.2.2c) usually drop the *-e-* of the stem before the ending *-e*, e.g. *es segle, es lächle*, etc.

12.5.2 Compound forms of Konjunktiv I

Perfect, future and passive forms of Konjunktiv I are constructed using the auxiliary verbs *haben, sein* or *werden* linked with the past participle or the infinitive, as in the indicative. These are illustrated below for the third person, which are the most commonly used of these forms and where the difference from the indicative is clear:

Perfect (with *haben*):	es habe gekauft, etc.
Perfect (with *sein*):	es sei geblieben, etc.
Future:	es werde kaufen, etc.
***werden*-passive present:**	es werde gekauft, etc.
***werden*-passive perfect:**	es sei gekauft worden, etc.
***werden*-passive future:**	es werde gekauft werden, etc.
***sein*-passive present:**	es sei gekauft, etc.

12.5.3 Konjunktiv II has alternative basic forms

(a) the simple form (traditionally called the 'past subjunctive')

For weak verbs, this is identical with the past indicative, e.g. *ich kaufte, du kauftest*, etc.

For most strong verbs, it is formed by taking the form of the past indicative, umlauting the vowel if possible, and adding personal endings as illustrated below:

Verb:		**geben**	**fliegen**	**bleiben**	**gehen**
Past indicative:		gab	flog	blieb	ging
Konjunktiv II:	ich	gäbe	flöge	bliebe	ginge
	du	gäbest	flögest	bliebest	gingest
	er	gäbe	flöge	bliebe	ginge
	wir	gäben	flögen	blieben	gingen
	ihr	gäbet	flöget	bliebet	ginget
	sie	gäben	flögen	blieben	gingen

NB: In practice, the *-e* of these endings is often dropped in speech.

Some irregular verbs also have Umlaut, or a change of vowel, in the simple Konjunktiv II. Full details are given with the individual verbs in 12.6.:

sein:	ich wäre	haben:	ich hätte	werden:	ich würde
dürfen:	ich dürfte	können:	ich könnte	mögen:	ich möchte
müssen:	ich müßte	wissen:	ich wüßte	bringen:	ich brächte
denken:	ich dächte	brennen:	ich brennte	kennen:	ich kennte, etc.

NB: In colloquial (especially South German) speech, *brauchen* 'need' also often has a

Konjunktiv II form with Umlaut, e.g. *ich bräuchte*, etc. DUDEN (1985:145) considers this usage to be substandard, but it is widespread and not infrequently encountered in writing.

A few strong verbs have an irregular Konjunktiv II form with a different vowel from the past indicative. Full details are given under the individual verbs in 12.6. In practice, only the following are at all current nowadays:

helfen: hülfe (less common: hälfe)   stehen: stünde (less common: stände)
sterben: stürbe

(b) the compound form (traditionally called the 'conditional')
This is formed with the Konjunktiv II of the auxiliary *werden* and the infinitive, e.g.:

ich	würde	kaufen	
du	würdest	kaufen	
er	würde	kaufen	

wir	würden	kaufen	
ihr	würdet	kaufen	
sie	würden	kaufen	

12.5.4 The use of the simple and compound forms of Konjunktiv II
There is no difference in meaning between these forms. In principle, *ich käme* and *ich würde kommen*, for example, could replace each other in any context. Which is used depends on the individual verb involved and on register. The use of the simple forms is often encouraged as a mark of good formal written style, cf. Berger (1982:65ff.), but a fair number are felt to be stilted or archaic and avoided. Indeed, many Germans are ignorant of some of the less frequent forms. The following summary of current usage is based on the details given by Bausch (1979):

(a) With weak verbs the simple form may be used in formal written German if the subjunctive meaning is otherwise clear from the context
For instance, where there is a distinctive subjunctive form in the other half of a conditional sentence, e.g.:

Wenn ich das Fenster **aufmachte**, 　　*If I opened the window, we would*
　　hätten wir ein bißchen frische Luft　*have some fresh air in the room*
　　im Zimmer

In spoken German, the compound form will normally be used, e.g.

Wenn ich das Fenster **aufmachen würde**, hätten wir ein bißchen frische Luft.

The compound form is normally used, even in writing, in cases where the subjunctive meaning is not otherwise clear from the context, e.g.:

In diesem Fall **würde** ich das Fenster　*In that case I would open the*
　　aufmachen　　　　　　　　　　　*window*

(b) With the common irregular verbs only the simple form is usual
This applies in particular to the modal auxiliaries, with which the compound form is never used, only *könnte, müßte*, etc.

With *sein, werden* and *haben*, the simple forms *wäre, würde* and *hätte* are more frequent than the compound forms *würde sein/werden/haben*, whether these verbs are used as auxiliaries or in isolation.

(c) The simple forms of a few other strong or irregular verbs are roughly as frequent as the compound forms in writing, i.e.:

finden	geben	gehen	halten	heißen
kommen	lassen	stehen	tun	wissen

Of these, only the simple forms of *kommen, tun* and *wissen* (i.e. *käme, täte, wüßte*) are at all current in everyday spoken German.

(d) The simple forms of the other strong or irregular verbs are restricted to formal written German
However, even there they tend to be less frequent than the compound forms. Several, in particular most of the irregular ones and others in -ö- and -ü- (e.g. *begönne, flösse, verdürbe*) are felt to be archaic and stilted and they are generally avoided even in writing. The verbs to which this applies are indicated in the table of strong and irregular verbs in 12.6

12.5.5 Other forms of Konjunktiv II

Perfect and passive forms of Konjunktiv II are constructed with the auxiliaries *haben, sein* or *werden* and the past participle, e.g.:

Pluperfect (with *haben*):	es hätte gekauft, etc.
Pluperfect (with *sein*):	es wäre geblieben, etc.
***werden*-passive:**	es würde gekauft (werden), etc.
***werden*-passive pluperfect:**	es wäre gekauft worden, etc.
***sein*-passive:**	es wäre gekauft, etc.

12.6 Principal parts of strong and irregular verbs

In the following tables we give the principal parts of all the strong and irregular verbs which are widely used in modern German, with the exception of the wholly irregular verbs, i.e. the modal auxiliaries and *wissen*, and the verbs *sein, haben* and *werden*. The forms of these are given in detail in 12.2.3 and 12.2.4.

The third person singular of the present tense is given for those verbs which have vowel changes (cf. 12.2.2e/f). The simple form of Konjunktiv II (cf. 12.5.3) is also given for all verbs listed, **but it is enclosed in square brackets if it is felt to be stilted and thus rarely used** (cf. 12.5.4d). The auxiliary used to form the perfect tenses (cf. 12.3.2) is indicated by *hat* or *ist* alongside the past participle.

Less common alternative forms are given in brackets after the more common ones; in general little used or archaic verbs and forms have been omitted. In principle, simple forms of the verbs (i.e. without prefixes) are given if they exist, even though some of these simple verbs are less common than their derivatives with prefixes. As a rule, compound verbs conjugate in the same way as the simple verb from which they are derived; apparent exceptions to this are noted. Where appropriate, notes on the form are given below the verb.

Infinitive 3rd sing. pres.	Past indic. Konj. II	Past part.
backen *bake* es bäckt (backt)	**backte** (buk) [büke]	hat **gebacken**

es backt is frequent in speech. *buk* is still quite common in writing.
backen 'stick' (of snow) is wholly weak, i.e. *backte, gebackt*.

befehlen *command* es befiehlt	**befahl** [beföhle (befähle)]	hat **befohlen**

   empfehlen 'recommend' has similar forms. *fehlen* 'lack' is weak, i.e. *fehlte, gefehlt*.

beginnen *begin*	**begann** [begänne (begönne)]	hat **begonnen**
beißen *bite*	**biß** bisse	hat **gebissen**
bergen *rescue; hide* es birgt	**barg** [bärge]	hat **geborgen**
bersten *crack, burst* es birst (berstet)	**barst** [bärste]	hat **geborsten**
bewegen *induce*	**bewog** [bewöge]	hat **bewogen**

      bewegen 'move' is weak, i.e. *bewegte, bewegt*

biegen *bend; turn*	**bog** [böge]	hat/ist **gebogen**
bieten *offer*	**bot** [böte]	hat **geboten**
binden *bind*	**band** bände	hat **gebunden**
bitten *ask, request*	**bat** bäte	hat **gebeten**
blasen *blow* es bläst	**blies** [bliese]	hat **geblasen**
bleiben *stay, remain*	**blieb** bliebe	ist **geblieben**
braten *fry, roast* es brät	**briet** [briete]	hat **gebraten**
brechen *break* es bricht	**brach** bräche	hat/ist **gebrochen**
brennen *burn*	**brannte** [brennte]	hat **gebrannt**
bringen *bring*	**brachte** brächte	hat **gebracht**
denken *think*	**dachte** dächte	hat **gedacht**
dreschen *thresh* es drischt	**drosch** [drösche]	hat **gedroschen**

dringen *penetrate*   **drang**   hat/ist **gedrungen**
          [dränge]
empfehlen *recommend* has the same forms as *befehlen*, q.v.

erkiesen *choose, elect* **erkor**   hat **erkoren**
          [erköre]
  In practice only the past tense and past participle forms are used, in elevated styles.

erlöschen *go out* (of lights) **erlosch**   ist **erloschen**
 es erlischt   [erlösche]
  The transitive verb *löschen* 'extinguish' is weak, i.e. *löschte, gelöscht.*

erschrecken *be startled* **erschrak**   ist **erschrocken**
 es erschrickt   [erschräke]
  The transitive verb *erschrecken* 'frighten' is weak, i.e. *erschreckte, erschreckt.*

essen *eat*   **aß**   hat **gegessen**
 es ißt   äße
fahren *go, drive*   **fuhr**   ist/hat **gefahren**
 es fährt   führe
fallen *fall*   **fiel**   ist **gefallen**
 es fällt   fiele
fangen *catch*   **fing**   hat **gefangen**
 es fängt   finge
fechten *fight, fence* **focht**   hat **gefochten**
 es ficht   [föchte]
finden *find*   **fand**   hat **gefunden**
          fände
flechten *plait, braid* **flocht**   hat **geflochten**
 es flicht   [flöchte]
fliegen *fly*   **flog**   ist/hat **geflogen**
          flöge
fliehen *flee*   **floh**   ist **geflohen**
          [flöhe]
fließen *flow*   **floß**   ist **geflossen**
          [flösse]
fragen *ask*   **fragte** (frug)   hat **gefragt**
 er fragt (frägt)   fragte
  In standard German *fragen* is normally weak. *frägt* is colloquial South German. *frug* is
  occasional in literary registers.

fressen *eat* (of animals) **fraß**   hat **gefressen**
 es frißt   [fräße]
frieren *freeze*   **fror**   hat/ist **gefroren**
          [fröre]
gären *ferment*   **gor/gärte**   hat/ist **gegoren/**
          [göre/gärte]   **gegärt**
  The strong forms are more usual when the verb is used in a literal sense, the weak ones
  when it is used figuratively.

gebären *give birth*   **gebar**   hat **geboren**
 es gebärt (gebiert) [gebäre]
geben *give*   **gab**   hat **gegeben**
 es gibt   gäbe
gedeihen *thrive*   **gedieh**   ist **gediehen**
          [gediehe]

gehen *go*	**ging**	ist **gegangen**
	ginge	
gelingen *succeed*	**gelang**	ist **gelungen**
	gelänge	

mißlingen 'fail' has similar forms.

gelten *be valid*	**galt**	hat **gegolten**
es gilt	[gälte (gölte)]	
genesen *recover* (elev.)	**genas**	ist **genesen**
	[genäse]	
genießen *enjoy*	**genoß**	hat **genossen**
	[genösse]	
geschehen *happen*	**geschah**	ist **geschehen**
es geschieht	geschähe	
gewinnen *win*	**gewann**	hat **gewonnen**
	[gewänne/gewönne]	
gießen *pour*	**goß**	hat **gegossen**
	[gösse]	
gleichen *resemble*	**glich**	hat **geglichen**
	gliche	
gleiten *glide, slide*	**glitt**	ist **geglitten**
	[glitte]	

begleiten 'accompany' is weak, i.e. *begleitete, begleitet.*

glimmen *glimmer*	**glomm/glimmte**	hat **geglommen/**
	[glömme/glimmte]	**geglimmt**

The verb is restricted to formal literary language. Strong and weak forms are equally common.

graben *dig*	**grub**	hat **gegraben**
es gräbt	[grübe]	
greifen *grab*	**griff**	hat **gegriffen**
	griffe	
halten *hold; stop*	**hielt**	hat **gehalten**
es hält	hielte	

The compound verbs *beinhalten* 'comprise' and *haushalten* 'be economical' are weak.

hängen *hang* (intrans.)	**hing**	hat **gehangen**
	hinge	

The transitive verb *hängen* 'hang' is weak, i.e. *hängte, gehängt.*

hauen *hew, cut*	**haute** (hieb)	hat **gehauen** (gehaut)
	[haute (hiebe)]	

The strong past form *hieb* is used, in formal literary German only, in the meaning 'hew, cut (with a sword)'. The weak past participle *gehaut* is regional and colloquial.

heben *lift*	**hob** (hub)	hat **gehoben**
	[höbe (hübe)]	

The alternative forms *hub* and *hübe* are archaic, but still occasionally used in formal literary registers, with the compound *anheben* 'commence'.

heißen *be called*	**hieß**	hat **geheißen**
	hieße	
helfen *help*	**half**	hat **geholfen**
es hilft	[hülfe (hälfe)]	
kennen *know*	**kannte**	hat **gekannt**
	kennte	

klimmen *climb*   **klomm** (klimmte)   hat **geklommen**
                         [klömme]   (geklimmt)
The simplex is nowadays scarcely used, but the compound *erklimmen* 'scale', which only has the strong forms, is still found in literary registers.

klingen *sound*   **klang**   hat **geklungen**
                         klänge

kneifen *pinch*   **kniff**   hat **gekniffen**
                         kniffe

kommen *come*   **kam**   ist **gekommen**
                         käme

kriechen *creep, crawl*   **kroch**   ist **gekrochen**
                         [kröche]

laden *load; invite*   **lud**   hat **geladen**
es lädt (ladet)   [lüde]
ladet is regional, and only used in the sense 'invite', or with the compound *einladen*.

lassen *leave; let* **ließ**   hat **gelassen**
es läßt   ließe
Note that *veranlassen* 'cause' is weak, i.e. *veranlaßte, veranlaßt*.

laufen *run*   **lief**   ist/hat **gelaufen**
es läuft   liefe

leiden *suffer*   **litt**   hat **gelitten**
                         litte
The verb *verleiden* 'spoil' is weak, i.e. *verleidete, verleidet*.

leihen *lend; borrow*   **lieh**   hat **geliehen**
                         liehe

lesen *read*   **las**   hat **gelesen**
es liest   [läse]

liegen *lie*   **lag**   hat **gelegen**
                         [läge]

mahlen *grind*   **mahlte**   hat **gemahlen**
                         mahlte

meiden *avoid*   **mied**   hat **gemieden**
                         miede

melken *milk*   **melkte** (molk)   hat **gemolken**
es melkt (milkt)   melkte   (gemelkt)

messen *measure*   **maß**   hat **gemessen**
es mißt   [mäße]

nehmen *take*   **nahm**   hat **genommen**
es nimmt   nähme

nennen *name, call* **nannte**   hat **genannt**
                         [nennte]

pfeifen *whistle*   **pfiff**   hat **gepfiffen**
                         pfiffe

preisen *praise*   **pries**   hat **gepriesen**
                         priese

quellen *gush, well up*   **quoll**   ist **gequollen**
es quillt   [quölle]

raten *advise*   **riet**   hat **geraten**
es rät   riete

rieben *rub*   **rieb**   hat **gerieben**
                         riebe

reißen *tear*	**riß** risse	hat/ist **gerissen**
reiten *ride* (a horse)	**ritt** ritte	hat/ist **geritten**
rennen *run*	**rannte** [rennte]	hat/ist **gerannt**
riechen *smell*	**roch** [röche]	hat **gerochen**
ringen *wrestle*	**rang** [ränge]	hat **gerungen**
rinnen *flow, trickle*	**rann** [ränne (rönne)]	ist **geronnen**
rufen *call, cry*	**rief** riefe	hat **gerufen**
salzen *salt*	**salzte** salzte	hat **gesalzen** (gesalzt)

In a figurative sense, only the form *gesalzen* is used, e.g. *gesalzene Preise.*

saufen *drink* (of animals), *booze*	**soff**	hat **gesoffen**
säuft	[söffe]	
saugen *suck*	**saugte/sog** [saugte/söge]	hat **gesaugt/gesogen**

In technical language only the weak forms are used, esp. in the compound *staubsaugen* 'vacuum'.

schaffen *create*	**schuf** [schüfe]	hat **geschaffen**

schaffen is weak (i.e. *schaffte, geschafft*) in the meaning 'manage, work'.

scheiden *separate; depart*	**schied** schiede	hat/ist **geschieden**
scheinen *seem; shine*	**schien** schiene	hat **geschienen**
scheißen *shit* (vulgar)	**schiß** [schisse]	hat **geschissen**
schelten *scold* es schilt	**schalt** [schölte]	hat **gescholten**
scheren *shear, clip*	**schor** [schöre]	hat **geschoren**

scheren is weak (i.e. *scherte, geschert*) in the meaning 'concern', as is the reflexive *sich scheren* 'bother about; clear off'.

schieben *push, shove*	**schob** [schöbe]	hat **geschoben**
schießen *shoot*	**schoß** [schösse]	hat/ist **geschossen**
schinden *flay, ill-treat*	–	hat **geschunden**

In practice, no past tense forms of this verb are used.

schlafen *sleep* es schlaft	**schlief** schliefe	hat **geschlafen**
schlagen *hit, beat* es schlägt	**schlug** schlüge	hat **geschlagen**
schleichen *creep*	**schlich** schliche	ist **geschlichen**

schleifen *grind, sharpen*   **schliff**   hat **geschliffen**
                                     schliffe
schleifen is weak (i.e. *schleifte, geschleift*) in the meaning 'drag'.

schließen *shut*   **schloß**   hat **geschlossen**
                                     schlösse
schlingen *wind, wrap*   **schlang**   hat **geschlungen**
                                     [schlänge]
schmeißen *chuck* (coll.)   **schmiß**   hat **geschmissen**
                                     schmisse
schmelzen *melt*   **schmolz** (schmelzte)   hat/ist **geschmolzen**
   es schmilzt (schmelzt)   [schmölze]   (geschmelzt)
The weak forms are only used with transitive *schmelzen*, and are less frequent even
then.

schneiden *cut*   **schnitt**   hat **geschnitten**
                                     schnitte
schreiben *write*   **schrieb**   hat **geschrieben**
                                     schriebe
schreien *shout, scream*   **schrie**   hat **geschrie(e)n**
                                     [schriee]
schreiten *stride*   **schritt**   ist **geschritten**
                                     schritte
schweigen *be silent*   **schwieg**   hat **geschwiegen**
                                     schwiege
schwellen *swell*   **schwoll**   ist **geschwollen**
   es schwillt   [schwölle]
schwellen is weak (i.e. *schwellte, geschwellt*) when used transitively.

schwimmen *swim*   **schwamm**   ist/hat **geschwommen**
                                     [schwömme (schwämme)]
schwinden *disappear*   **schwand**   ist **geschwunden**
                                     schwände
schwingen *swing*   **schwang**   hat **geschwungen**
                                     [schwänge]
schwören *swear*   **schwor** (schwur)   hat **geschworen**
                                     [schwüre (schwöre)]
schwur is only found in old-fashioned literary German.

sehen *see*   **sah**   hat **gesehen**
   es sieht   sähe
senden *send*   **sendete/sandte**   hat **gesendet/gesandt**
                                     sendete
Only the regular forms (*sendete, gesendet*) are used in technical senses, (i.e. =
broadcast'). Otherwise the irregular forms are commoner, but NB that *schicken* is the
commoner equivalent for English 'send'.

sieden *boil*   **siedete/sott**   hat **gesotten**
                                     [siedete (sötte)]   (gesiedet)
kochen is the commoner equivalent for English 'boil'; *sieden* is mainly formal and South
German.

singen *sing*   **sang**   hat **gesungen**
                                     sänge
sinken *sink*   **sank**   ist **gesunken**
                                     [sänke]

sinnen *meditate* (elev.)	**sann** [sänne (sönne)]	hat **gesonnen**
sitzen *sit*	**saß** säße	hat **gesessen**
spalten *split, cleave*	**spaltete** spaltete	hat/ist **gespaltet** (gespalten)

The strong past participle *gespalten* is used mainly as an adjective, e.g. *das gespaltene Deutschland.*

speien *spit, spew* (elev.)	**spie** [spiee]	hat **gespie(e)n**
spinnen *spin; be stupid*	**spann** [spönne (spänne)]	hat **gesponnen**
sprechen *speak* es spricht	**sprach** spräche	hat **gesprochen**
sprießen *sprout* (elev.)	**sproß** [sprösse]	ist **gesprossen**
springen *jump*	**sprang** spränge	ist **gesprungen**
stechen *prick, sting* es sticht	**stach** [stäche]	hat **gestochen**
stehen *stand*	**stand** stünde (stände)	hat **gestanden**
stehlen *steal* es stiehlt	**stahl** [stähle (stöhle)]	hat **gestohlen**
steigen *climb; rise*	**stieg** stiege	ist **gestiegen**
sterben *die* es stirbt	**starb** stürbe	ist **gestorben**
stieben *fly up* (like dust) (elev.)	**stob** (stiebte) [stöbe]	ist **gestoben** (gestiebt)
stinken *stink*	**stank** [stänke]	hat **gestunken**
stoßen *bump; push* es stößt	**stieß** stieße	ist/hat **gestoßen**
streichen *stroke*	**strich** striche	ist/hat **gestrichen**
streiten *quarrel*	**stritt** stritte	hat **gestritten**
tragen *carry; wear* es trägt	**trug**	hat **getragen** trüge

The verbs *beantragen* 'apply' and *beauftragen* 'commission' are weak.

treffen *meet; hit* es trifft	**traf** träfe	hat **getroffen**
treiben *drive; drift*	**trieb** triebe	ist/hat **getrieben**
treten *step* es tritt	**trat** träte	ist/hat **getreten**
trinken *drink*	**trank** tränke	hat **getrunken**
trügen *deceive*	**trog** [tröge]	hat **getrogen**
tun *do*	**tat** täte	hat **getan**

verderben *spoil*	**verdarb**	hat/ist **verdorben**
es verdirbt	[verdürbe]	
verdrießen *vex* (elev.)	**verdroß**	hat **verdrossen**
	[verdrösse]	
vergessen *forget*	**vergaß**	hat **vergessen**
es vergißt	vergäße	
verlieren *lose*	**verlor**	hat **verloren**
	verlöre	
verziehen *excuse*	**verzieh**	hat **verziehen**
	verziehe	
wachsen *grow*	**wuchs**	ist **gewachsen**
es wächst	wüchse	
wägen *weigh* (one's words)	**wog/wägte**	hat **gewogen/gewägt**
	[wöge]	

Simple *wägen* is rather archaic. The more frequent compound *erwägen* 'consider' only has strong forms, i.e. *erwog, erwogen*.

waschen *wash*	**wusch**	hat **gewaschen**
es wäscht	[wüsche]	
weben *weave*	**webte** (wob)	hat **gewebt** (gewoben)
	webte	

Usually weak, but the strong forms are used in literary German in figurative senses.

weichen *yield, give way*	**wich**	ist **gewichen**
	wiche	

There is a weak verb *weichen* (*weichte, geweicht*) meaning 'soften', with the compounds *einweichen* 'soak' and *aufweichen* 'make soft'.

weisen *point*	**wies**	hat **gewiesen**
	wiese	
wenden *turn*	**wandte/wendete**	hat **gewandt/gewendet**
	wendete	

The forms *wandte, gewandt* are generally more frequent, except in the sense 'turn over, turn round' (e.g *das Auto, den Braten, das Heu wenden*) and in the compounds *entwenden* and *verwenden*.

werben *recruit; advertise*	**warb**	hat **geworben**
es wirbt	[würbe]	
werfe *throw*	**warf**	hat **geworfen**
es wirft	[würfe]	
wiegen *weigh*	**wog**	hat **gewogen**
	[wöge]	

wiegen is weak (i.e. *wiegte, gewiegt*) in the meaning 'rock' (cradle, etc.).

winden *wind, twist* (elev.)	**wand**	hat **gewunden**
	[wände]	
winken *wave*	**winkte**	hat **gewinkt**
	winkte	(gewunken)

The widely used past participle *gewunken* is regional and colloquial.

wringen *wring* (clothes)	**wrang**	hat **gewrungen**
	[wränge]	
ziehen *pull; move*	**zog**	hat/ist **gezogen**
	zöge	
zwingen *force*	**zwang**	hat **gezwungen**
	[zwänge]	

13   The infinitive and the participles

This chapter deals with the main uses of the infinitive and the present and past participles, aside from the formation of compound tenses and the passive (see 12.3 and 12.4.).

    Unlike the finite forms these non-finite forms do not have endings to show agreement with the subject for person and number, or to express other categories of the verb such as tense and mood. The non-finite forms are used in a number of constructions which depend on an element in a full clause with a finite verb, from which their subject must be understood. Despite some similarities, German differs quite markedly from English in respect of some such constructions and their use, especially with the present participle.

13.1   Forms of the infinitive

13.1.1   The simple infinitive

The simple infinitive is the basic form under which verbs are usually listed in dictionaries, cf. 12.1. For most verbs it ends in -*en*, but a few verbs have an infinitive ending in -*n*, i.e. *sein*, *tun* and verbs whose stem ends in -*el* and -*er*, cf. 12.2.2c.

13.1.2   The compound infinitive

The infinitive of the auxiliary verbs *haben, sein* and *werden* can be combined with the past participle of a verb to form compound infinitives, e.g.:

perfect (with *haben* or *sein*, cf. 12.3):	gesehen haben, angekommen sein
passive (with *werden* or *sein*, cf. 12.4):	verletzt werden, verletzt sein
perfect passive:	verletzt worden sein

NB: (i) Like its English counterpart (e.g. *to have seen*, etc.), the German perfect auxiliary is used to denote that an action took place before that of the main verb. Compare:

Sie muß das Buch **lesen**	*She must* **read** the book
Sie muß ihn **gesehen haben**	*She must* **have seen** *him*

(ii) The use of *werden* or *sein* in the passive infinitive follows the same rules as for the use of these auxiliaries in other passive constructions. Full details are given in chapter 15.

13.1.2 The infinitive with and without *zu*

In a number of constructions in German, the infinitive is accompanied by
the particle *zu*, whilst in others a 'bare' infinitive is used, without *zu*, e.g.:

Ich riet ihr, zum Arzt **zu gehen**	*I advised her to go to the doctor*
Ich konnte nicht zum Arzt **gehen**	*I couldn't go to the doctor*

Most constructions with the infinitive have the *zu*, and these are dealt with
in 13.2. Constructions with the bare infinitive are treated in 13.3.

The uses of the German infinitive are very fully treated in Buscha/
Zoch (1988), which has a good range of examples and exercises for the
foreign learner.

13.1.3 The form of the infinitive with *zu*

The particle *zu* is placed immediately before simple verbs and verbs with
inseparable prefixes, e.g.:

Sie fing an **zu schreiben**	Ich war bereit **zu verhandeln**
Es gefiel mir, mich mit ihr **zu unterhalten**	

It is placed between a separable prefix and the main verb, the whole being
written as a single word, e.g.:

Sie hatte vor, ihn **anzurufen**	Es war schön, euch **wiederzusehen**
Es freut mich, Sie **kennenzulernen**	

This also applies to verbs with a separable prefix preceding an inseparable
one, e.g.:

Es fällt mir nicht ein, mich ihm **anzuvertrauen**

EXCEPTION: Although *mißverstehen* is inseparable, the *zu* is placed after the prefix, i.e
mißzuverstehen. This is an alternative, if less frequent, possibility with a few
other verbs with the prefix *miß-*, e.g. *zu mißachten* or (less commonly)
mißzuachten, cf. also 22.6.3b.

Note the position of *zu* in complex infinitives, e.g.:

Er verleugnet es, sie betrogen **zu** haben	*He denies having deceived her*
Ihr gefällt es nicht, betrogen **zu** werden	*She doesn't like being deceived*
Sie behauptete, betrogen worden **zu** sein	*She claims to have been deceived*
Es freut mich, Sie hier begrüßen **zu** dürfen	*It is a pleasure to be able to welcome you here*

The infinitive with *zu* most commonly occurs in a reduced clause, called in
German the *Infinitivsatz*, depending on a noun, verb or adjective in a full

clause within the same sentence, e.g.:

Er fing an, heftig zu weinen	*He began to cry bitterly*
Er gab mir die Erlaubnis, in Berlin zu bleiben	*He gave me permission to stay in Berlin*
Es ist nicht schwer, eine fremde Sprache zu lernen	*It is not difficult to learn a foreign language*

The infinitive with *zu* comes at the end of its clause, cf. 21.1.1c. In most cases the infinitive clause is quite separate from the rest of the sentence, and in writing it is typically marked off by commas (but see 23.5.2 for exceptions to this).

13.2 The use of the infinitive with *zu*

13.2.1 An infinitive clause with *zu* may function as the subject of a verb

If it comes first in the sentence, there is no comma, cf. 23.5.2c:

So etwas zu erlauben ist unerhört	*To allow that kind of thing is outrageous*
Ihr Ziel ist einen Roman zu schreiben	*Her aim is to write a novel*

The following should be noted concerning the use of an infinitive clause as the subject of a verb:

(a) A German infinitive clause often corresponds to an English clause with an *ing*-form as the subject of the verb:

Ihn zu überzeugen wird nicht leicht sein	*Convincing him won't be easy*

(b) If a subject infinitive clause is short, it may, optionally, lack *zu*
This is most frequent with the verb *sein* and in set phrases:

Früh auf(zu)stehen ist etwas Schreckliches	*Getting up early is horrible*
Lange Auto (zu) fahren ist sehr anstrengend	*Driving a car for long periods is very strenuous*
Irren ist menschlich	*To err is human*

(c) An infinitive clause placed after the main verb is often anticipated by *es* in the main clause:

Es war mir nicht möglich, früher zu kommen	*It wasn't possible for me to come earlier*
Ihm steht (es) nicht zu, ein Urteil zu fällen	*It's not up to him to pass judgement*

Full details of this use of *es* are given in 3.6.6 and 3.6.7.

13.2.2 Many verbs may have an infinitive clause with *zu* as their object

The English equivalent may be an infinitive or the *ing*-form, depending on the individual verb used. The subject of the verb is understood as the subject of the infinitive:

Ich hoffe, dich bald wiedersehen zu können	*I hope to be able to see you again soon*
Ich gebe zu, das gesagt zu haben	*I admit having said that*
Ich habe vor, sie morgen zu besuchen	*I intend to visit them/visiting them tomorrow*

The following points are to be noted concerning the use of an infinitive clause as the object of a verb:

(a) An infinitive clause can be used in German with a number of verbs denoting mental processes

The English equivalents usually require a *that*-clause:

Er behauptete (glaubte, meinte, war überzeugt), mich gesehen zu haben	*He maintained (believed, thought, was convinced) that he had seen me*
. . . da er uns zusicherte, uns nochmals einen Zahlungsaufschub zu gewähren	*. . . as he assured us that he would grant us another extension of credit*

This construction is more usual in writing than in speech, where a subordinate clause will frequently be preferred, e.g. *Er meinte, er hätte mich gesehen/daß er mich gesehen hätte.*

(b) A following object infinitive may be anticipated by *es*:

Ich konnte es kaum ertragen, ihn so leiden zu sehen	*I could hardly bear to see him suffer like that*
Sie hat (es) versäumt, die Miete zu zahlen	*She failed to pay the rent*

Details of the use of this anticipatory *es* are given in 3.6.9.

(c) Some German verbs allow their (accusative or dative) object to be understood as the subject of a following infinitive clause:

Karl bat Ulrike, ihn mitzunehmen	*Karl asked Ulrike to take him with her*
Sie hat ihm geraten, die Ausstellung zu besuchen	*She advised him to see the exhibition*

This construction is not possible with as many verbs in German as in English. In particular, it cannot be used with verbs of wishing, desiring, saying, knowing, thinking and the like. In all these cases a subordinate clause is required in German:

Sie will, daß ich mit ihr gehe	*She wants me to go with her*
Ich möchte nicht, daß es irgendein Mißverständnis gibt	*I don't want there to be any misunderstanding*
Ich erwarte, daß sie bald nach Flensburg umzieht	*I expect her to move to Flensburg soon*
Mir wäre es lieber, wenn Sie hier nicht rauchen würden	*I would prefer you not to smoke here*
Sage ihm doch, daß er warten soll	*Tell him to wait, though*
Ich wußte, daß es ein Irrtum war	*I knew it to be a mistake*

(d) When verbs which take a prepositional object are followed by an infinitive clause, it is usually anticipated by a prepositional adverb (i.e. *da(r)* + preposition):

Ich verlasse mich **darauf**, ihn zu Hause zu finden	*I am relying on finding him at home*
Ich erinnere mich (**daran**), sie voriges Jahr in Bremen gesehen zu haben	*I remember having seen her in Bremen last year*
Ich werde meine Freundin **davor** warnen, das zu tun	*I shall warn my friend against doing that*

With some verbs (like *sich erinnern* in the second example above), the prepositional adverb is optional. Details are given in 18.6.14.

(e) Conflation of infinitive clause and main clause

If there is only the finite verb and its subject in the main clause, the infinitive clause may be conflated with the main clause by placing the object of the infinitive within it, e.g.:

Das bleibt noch **abzuwarten**	*That remains to be seen*
Den Betrag bitten wir auf unser Konto **zu überweisen**	*We request you to transfer the amount to our account*
Er wagte **die Reise** aus diesem Grunde nicht **abzubrechen**	*He didn't dare to break his journey for this reason*
Diesen Vorgang wollen wir **zu erklären** versuchen	*We want to try to explain this series of events*

A similar conflation is also possible in relative clauses, where the infinitive may be enclosed within the clause in German. Alternatively, it may be placed at the end, as in English:

ein Mann, **den** ich **zu töten** versuchte ⎫ ein Mann, **den** ich versuchte **zu töten** ⎭	*a man whom I tried to kill*

13.2.3 Infinitive clauses with 'semi-auxiliary' verbs

Some verbs have a closer link with a following infinitive clause than others. Like the modal auxiliaries, their main role is to modify the meaning of the

infinitive in some way, and they may thus be termed 'semi-auxiliaries'.
An important characteristic of these semi-auxiliaries is that they always
enclose the infinitive in dependent clauses or compound tenses, e.g.:

. . . da er den eben Angekommenen **zu erkennen schien**
. . . als das Boot **zu kentern drohte**
Sie hat uns **zu verstehen gegeben**, daß sie morgen kommt

The semi-auxiliaries are also often conflated with their dependent
infinitive phrase, cf. 13.2.2e, and the infinitive is often not marked off by
commas in writing, cf. 23.5.2d.

NB: English has a far wider range of semi-auxiliary verbs than German.
     The natural German equivalent to many of these English verbs is a construction with
     an adverb, e.g. *Ich spiele* **gern** *Tennis* 'I like to play tennis', *Ich sah sie* **zufällig** *in der
     Stadt* 'I happened to see her in town'. A selection of such equivalences is given in 7.4.2.
     The most important verbs which can be used as semi-auxiliaries in German are listed
     below with examples. Many of them have other uses and meanings besides those given
     here:

bekommen 'get':

Und wenn ich dich zu fassen bekomme . . . *And if I lay hands on you,* . . .

belieben 'like, wish'. Nowadays archaic except in an ironic sense:

Sie belieben zu scherzen   *You must be joking*

bleiben 'remain'. The following infinitive has a passive sense:

Die Gesetzesvorlage bleibt noch zu   *The draft bill still remains to
   diskutieren   be discussed*

NB: For the use of *bleiben* with a bare infinitive, see 13.3.1f.

brauchen 'need'. As a semi-auxiliary it is only used in the negative (or with
nur). In practice, it is the most common negative to *müssen*, cf. 17.5.1c:

Du brauchst nur anzurufen, und ich   *You only need to call and I'll come
   komme sofort   straight away*
Du wirst dieses Fenster nie   *You'll never need to open this
   aufzumachen brauchen   window*

NB: (i) In colloquial speech, *brauchen* is commonly used without *zu*, e.g. *Ich brauche nicht
     hingehen.*
     (ii) The infinitive is used rather than the past participle in the perfect tenses, e.g. *Du
     hättest nicht hinzugehen brauchen.*

drohen 'threaten'

Die Brücke drohte einzustürzen   *The bridge threatened to collapse*

geben 'give'. Used mainly with *verstehen, erkennen, denken*:

. . . weil sie uns zu verstehen gab, daß   *. . . because she gave us to understand
   sie bald kommen würde   that she would be coming soon*

gedenken 'propose'. It is restricted to elevated, formal registers:

Sie hatte das Kabinett umzubilden gedacht	*She had proposed a cabinet reshuffle*

gehen expresses a possibility and is restricted to colloquial speech. The infinitive has passive meaning:

Die Uhr geht zu reparieren	*The clock can be repaired*

NB: For the use of *gehen* with a bare infinitive, see 13.3.1e.

haben 'have' expresses necessity or obligation. It is a (rather less frequent) alternative to *müssen* or *sollen*:

Was habe ich zu bezahlen?	*What have I got to pay?*
Ich habe mehrere Briefe zu schreiben	*I have several letters to write*

With many verbs (especially with *tun*), the use of *haben* is idiomatic and there is little sense of obligation or necessity:

Das hat mit dieser Sache nichts zu tun	*That's got nothing to do with this matter*
Ich will nichts mehr mit ihr zu tun haben	*I don't want anything more to do with her*
Das hat wenig zu bedeuten	*That doesn't mean very much*
Sie haben hier nichts zu suchen	*You have no business here*

NB: For the use of *haben* with a bare infinitive, see 13.3.1f.

kommen 'come' expresses a (chance) result.

Es war nicht meine Absicht, daß wir auf dieses Thema zu sprechen kamen	*It was not my intention for us to get onto this subject*
Wir arrangierten es so, daß ich neben ihr zu sitzen kam	*We arranged it so that I came to sit next to her*

NB: For the use of *kommen* with a bare infinitive, see 13.3.1e.

pflegen 'to be accustomed to' is restricted to literary registers:

Oft pflegte er im Garten zu sitzen	*He often used to sit in the garden*

scheinen 'seem'

. . . als er endlich zu sich zu kommen schien	*. . . when he finally seemed to come round*
Ihm schien es zu gefallen	*He seemed to like it*

NB: *zu sein* is often omitted after *scheinen*, especially in written registers, e.g. *sie scheint ganz glücklich (zu sein).*

sein 'be' expresses possibility (or, less frequently, necessity). It is thus the equivalent of *können* (or sometimes *müssen* or *sollen*). The following infinitive has a passive meaning:

Das Buch ist nicht zu haben	*The book is not to be had*
Ist der Direktor heute zu sprechen?	*Can I see the manager today?*
Die Fahrausweise sind auf Verlangen	*The tickets are to be shown on*
vorzuzeigen	*demand*
Das Haus ist zu verkaufen	*The house is for sale*

NB: (i) In formal written (especially official) German, this construction can be turned into an extended adjective using a present participle, e.g. *eine nicht zu vermeidende Schwierigkeit*, cf. 13.5.2.
(ii) For the use of *sein* with a bare infinitive, see 13.3.1e.

stehen expresses necessity, like *sein*, and the following infinitive has passive meaning. It is used only with verbs of expecting and the like:

Es steht zu erwarten, daß er	*It is to be expected that he will*
bald nachgibt	*soon give in*

suchen 'try, seek':

Er sucht die Erinnerung festzuhalten	*He is trying to retain the memory*

vermögen 'be able, be capable' is a rather formal alternative to *können:*

Sie hätte den Unfall nur mit großer	*She would only have been able to*
Mühe zu verhindern vermocht	*prevent the accident with*
	great difficulty

versprechen 'promise'. As a semi-auxiliary, *versprechen* always refers to an involuntary action and indicates that something desirable is in store:

Das Wetter verspricht schön zu werden	*The weather promises to be nice*
Wir sind froh, weil das Unternehmen	*We are happy because the enterprise*
zu gedeihen verspricht	*promises to prosper*

NB: As a full verb, in the sense of 'make a promise', *versprechen* is used with a separated infinitive clause, e.g. *Der Arzt versprach, sofort zu kommen.*

wissen 'know'. With an infinitive clause it is the equivalent of English 'know how to':

Er weiß mit den Leuten umzugehen	*He knows how to deal with people*
Ihre Mutter hätte es zu erklären	*Her mother would have known how*
gewußt	*to explain it*

NB: *verstehen* is a common alternative to *wissen* in this use as a semi-auxiliary, with essentially the same meaning, e.g. *Ihre Mutter hätte es zu erklären verstanden.*

13.2.4 The infinitive with *zu* after adjectives

In some infinitive constructions after *sein* followed by an adjective the subject of *sein* has to be understood as the object of the infinitive. Compare:

Diese Aufgabe ist einfach zu lösen	*This problem is simple to solve*
Er ist leicht zu überzeugen	*He is easy to convince*
Diese Frage ist schwer zu beantworten	*This question is difficult to answer*

This construction is only possibly in German with a few adjectives, i.e. *einfach, interessant, leicht, schwer, schwierig*, and then only if the verb used in the infinitive clause governs an accusative. In other cases another construction has to be used, e.g.:

Es war schön, sie zu kennen	*She was nice to know*
(i.e. NOT *Sie war schön zu kennen*)	
Meiner Schwester zu helfen war schwierig	*My sister was difficult to help*
(i.e. NOT *Meine Schwester war schwierig zu helfen*)	
Zum Trinken war der Kaffee zu heiß	*The coffee was too hot to drink*
(i.e. NOT *Der Kaffee war zu heiß zu trinken*)	

Similarly, in German an infinitive cannot depend on an adjective used with a noun. Compare:

Diese Frage zu beantworten ist schwer	} *That is a hard question to answer*
Das ist eine schwer zu beantwortende Frage	
Es ist ein leicht erreichbarer Ort	*It's an easy place to reach*
Es war dumm, diese Frage gestellt zu haben	*That was a silly question to have asked*

13.2.5 The infinitive with *zu* after prepositions

An infinitive clause can only be used after very few prepositions, i.e. *um, ohne, (an)statt* and (to a more limited extent) *außer*. Such constructions are in effect the equivalent of adverbial clauses.

(a) The construction *um . . . zu* has a number of different uses:
(i) It can express purpose, often corresponding to English 'in order to'. It is the equivalent of a clause introduced by *damit*, cf. 19.4.1a.:

Ich konnte nichts tun, um ihn zu beruhigen	*I couldn't do anything to reassure him*
Er zündete das Haus an, um die Versicherung zu kassieren	*He set fire to the house (in order) to collect on the insurance*
Da war kein Wasser, um das Feuer zu löschen	*There was no water to put the fire out*

NB: The *um* is sometimes omitted, especially in elevated registers, e.g. *Ich konnte nichts tun, ihn zu beruhigen*.

(ii) It is used after an adjective qualified by *zu* or *genug*:

Er ist zu jung, um alles zu verstehen	*He is too young to understand everything*
Er ist alt genug, um alles zu verstehen	*He is old enough to understand everything*

NB: (i) The *um* is sometimes omitted, especially in colloquial speech, e.g. *Er ist zu jung, alles zu verstehen*.

(ii) With a change of subject, the conjunction *als daß* is used after *zu* or negated *genug*, cf.19.4.3. After simple *genug*, *daß* is used, e.g.:

Er ist zu jung (nicht alt genug), als daß wir es ihm erklären könnten
Er ist alt genug, daß man es ihm erklären kann

(iii) A infinitive noun with *zum* is often a possible alternative with adjectives qualified by *zu* or *genug*, cf. 13.4.3b, e.g.:

Der Kaffee ist zu heiß (kalt genug) zum Trinken	*The coffee is too hot (cold enough) to drink*

(iii) It can be used simply to link clauses, as an equivalent to *und*:

Er betrat die Gaststätte, um sie nach kurzer Zeit wieder zu verlassen	*He went into the restaurant, only to leave it again after a short time*

NB: This construction is limited to formal written registers. It cannot be used if *um . . . zu* might be understood to imply purpose.

(b) *ohne . . . zu*

This corresponds to English *without* followed by an *ing*-form:

Er verließ das Haus, ohne gesehen zu werden	*He left the house without being seen*

With a change of subject, the conjunction *ohne daß* (cf. 19.6.7) is used, e.g. *Er verließ das Haus, ohne daß ich ihn sah.*

(c) *(an)statt...zu*

This corresponds to English *instead of* followed by an *ing*-form:

Er hat gespielt, (an)statt zu arbeiten	*He played instead of working*

A subordinate clause with *(an)statt daß*, e.g. *Er hat gespielt, (an)statt daß er gearbeitet hat* is an alternative to the infinitive construction. No change of subject is possible with either construction.

(d) *außer . . . zu*

This corresponds to English *except* or *besides* with an infinitive:

Was könnten sie tun, außer zu protestieren?	*What could they do except protest?* (*Zeit*)

NB: The use of *außer* with an infinitive is a relatively recent development in German. A frequent alternative is the preposition *außer* with an infinitive noun, e.g *Sie tat nichts außer Schlafen*. With a change in subject, the conjunction *außer daß* is used, e.g.:

Alle Folgen des Unwetters waren beseitigt, außer daß bei ihnen noch Wasser im Keller stand	*All the effects of the storm had been cleared away, except that they still had water in their cellar*

(e) German equivalents for other English prepositions used with the infinitive

(i) English *for* + noun/pronoun + infinitive

In some cases this may correspond to a noun with *für* or a noun in the dative in the main clause in German:

Es ist Zeit für uns loszugehen	*It is time for us to leave*
Es war ihm unmöglich, das auch nur zu verstehen	*It was impossible for him even to understand that*

However, the most usual German equivalent is a construction with a subordinate clause, with the conjunction used depending on the sense:

Ihr lag es sehr daran, daß er die Stelle annahm	*She was very keen for him to take the job*
Es ist üblich, daß Hüte so getragen werden	*It is usual for hats to be worn like that*
Hier sind ein paar Formulare, die Sie ausfüllen sollen	*Here are a few forms for you to fill in*
Er wartete darauf, daß sie ankam	*He was waiting for her to arrive*
Sie bringt die Fotos, damit wir sie uns ansehen können	*She's bringing the photographs for us to see*
Sie muß schon sehr krank sein, wenn ihre Mutter ein Telegramm schickt	*She must be very ill for her mother to send a telegram*

(ii) English *with* + noun/pronoun + infinitive

Depending on the sense, the German equivalent for this will be a subordinate clause with *da* or *weil*, a separate clause with *und*, or a relative clause:

Da ich so viele Aufsätze schreiben muß, werde ich Sie wohl nicht besuchen können	*With so many essays to write, I probably shan't be able to visit you*
Sie waren nur auf der Durchreise in München und konnten dort nur ein paar Stunden verbringen	*They were just passing through Munich, with no more than an hour or two to spend*
Auch der Sonntag, an dem sie nicht ins Büro gehen konnte, verging irgendwie	*Even Sunday, with no office to go to, passed somehow*

13.2.6 Other uses of the infinitive with *zu*

(a) in comparative phrases

zu may (less commonly) be omitted in these, e.g.:

Du kannst nichts Besseres tun, als zu Hause (zu) bleiben
Man sollte lieber erst alles gründlich besprechen, als sofort (zu) streiten

(b) in exclamations, as in English

Und zu denken, daß es ihr nichts bedeutet hat!	*And to think it didn't anything to her!*
So schnell so viel Bier zu trinken!	*To drink so much beer so quickly!*
Ach, immer hier zu bleiben!	*Oh, to stay here for ever!*

(c) in small ads

Zwei-Zimmer-Wohnung ab 1. Mai zu vermieten	*Two-room-flat to let from May 1st.*

13.2.7 English uses infinitives in a number of constructions where an infinitive with *zu* cannot be used in German.

Aside from those instances dealt with in 13.2.2 and 13.2.4, the following should be noted:

(a) English infinitives in indirect questions
e.g. *He told me **how to do** it.* In German a subordinate clause (often with *sollen, müssen* or *können*) is used:

Er sagte mir, wie ich es machen soll	*He told me how to do it*
Ich weiß nicht, was ich tun soll/muß	*I don't know what to do*
Woher weiß man, welchen Knopf man drücken soll?	*How do you tell which button to press?*

(b) English infinitives used as attributes,
e.g. *the person **to apply to**.* In German, a relative clause is used:

Er war der Mann, an den man sich wenden mußte	*He was the man to apply to*
Ich möchte ein Paar Handschuhe, die zu meinem Wintermantel passen	*I want a pair of gloves to go with my winter coat*
das einzige, was man tun kann	*the only thing to do*

Such constructions are particularly common after superlatives:

Er war der erste (der letzte, der beste Redner), der gekommen ist	*He was the first (the last, the best speaker) to come*

13.3 The infinitive without *zu*

13.3.1 The infinitive without *zu* is used after a limited number of verbs

Such infinitives normally come at the end of the clause, cf. 21.1, e.g. *Sie will diese Briefe morgen **schreiben**.* They are enclosed in subordinate clauses and compound tenses, cf. 21.1.3, e.g. *Ich weiß, daß sie diese Briefe morgen **schreiben** will* or *Sie hat diese Briefe heute **schreiben** wollen.*
    The infinitive without *zu* is used after the following verbs:

(a) the modal auxiliaries
i.e. *dürfen, können, mögen, müssen, sollen, wollen,* e.g.:

Sie **darf** heute nicht **ausgehen**	Er wird mir nicht **helfen wollen**

Full details on the meaning and use of these verbs is given in chapter 17.

NB: There is a tendency in colloquial German to treat *brauchen* as a modal auxiliary and use it with a bare infinitive, e.g. *Sie brauchen heute nicht hingehen.* However, accepted written usage requires an infinitive with *zu* after *brauchen*, cf. 13.2.3.

(b) a few verbs of perception
i.e. *fühlen, hören, sehen, spüren, e.g.*:

Ich **sah** ihn ins Zimmer **kommen**	*I saw him come into the room*
Sie **hörte** das Kind **weinen**	*She heard the child crying*
Er **fühlte** sein Herz **klopfen**	*He felt his heart beat(ing)*
Ich **spürte** seinen Einfluß **wachsen**	*I sensed how his influence was growing*

With these verbs, a clause with *wie* is an alternative to the infinitive construction, e.g.

Ich hörte, wie das Kind weinte	Ich spürte, wie sein Einfluß wuchs
Ich sah, wie der Polizist sich nach dem alten Mann umsah	

This tends to be more frequent than the infinitive construction in colloquial registers, with the verbs *fühlen* and *spüren*, or if the sentence is long or complex.

(c) *lassen*
lassen with a bare infinitive has two principle meanings, i.e.:
(i) 'let, allow':

Er ließ mich das Buch behalten	*He let me keep the book*
Laß sie doch hereinkommen!	*Do let her come in!*

Particularly frequent is the use of reflexive *lassen*, with an inanimate subject, as an alternative to the passive, cf. 15.4.7:

Das läßt sich leicht ändern	*That can easily be changed*

(ii) 'cause, make':

Sie ließ den Schlosser die Tür reparieren	*She had the locksmith fix the door*
Die Nachricht ließ ihn erblassen	*The news made him turn pale*
Er ließ sich die Haare schneiden	*He had his hair cut*

NB: (i) In both meanings the infinitive after *lassen* may have passive force, e.g.:
Er ließ sich sehen	*He allowed himself to be seen*
Er ließ die Brücke von den Gefangenen bauen	*He had the bridge built by the prisoners*

lassen is never followed by a passive infinitive.
(ii) A number of combinations with *lassen* have developed into separable compounds with a number of verbs, e.g. *fallenlassen* 'drop', *stehenlassen, liegenlassen* 'leave behind'.

(d) *tun*
tun is frequently used with a bare infinitive for emphasis in colloquial German (especially in the North):

Er tut ja immer noch essen	*He's still eating*
Tust du mich auch verstehen?	*Do you understand me?*
Ich täte gern ins Kino gehen	*I would like to go to the cinema*

This usage is generally considered substandard and usually unacceptable in writing. It is, however, permissible in written German to use *tun* in order to allow an emphasized verb to be placed first in the sentence:

Bewundern tu ich ihn nicht, aber er imponiert mir doch	*I don't admire him, but he does impress me*
Aber schmerzen tat es darum nicht weniger (*G.Reuter*)	*But it was no less painful for all that*

(e) certain verbs of motion
i.e. *fahren, gehen, kommen, schicken*. The verb used in the infinitive expresses the purpose of going:

Ich gehe jetzt schlafen	*I'm going to bed*
Kommst du heute schwimmen?	*Are you coming swimming today?*
Er fährt immer vormittags einkaufen	*He always goes shopping in the mornings*
Sie hat den Großvater einkaufen geschickt	*She sent grandfather shopping*

NB: (i) With *schicken*, a long infinitive clause may be separated out and used with *zu*, e.g. *Sie hat den Großvater geschickt, Kartoffeln und Gemüse zu kaufen.*
(ii) *spazieren* forms separable compounds with *gehen* and *fahren*, i.e. *spazierengehen, spazierenfahren.*
(iii) In colloquial speech, the past tenses of *sein* are often used with a bare infinitive in the sense of 'go':

Ich war heute morgen schwimmen	*I went swimming this morning*
Er ist einkaufen gewesen	*He went/has been shopping*

For the use of *sein* with *zu* + infinitive, see 13.2.3.

(f) *bleiben, finden* and *haben* followed by a verb of place

Er blieb im Zimmer sitzen	*He stayed sitting in the room*
Sie ist an den Ampeln stehengeblieben	*She stopped at the lights*
Er hat sein Auto vor der Tür stehen	*He's got his car at the door*
Sie hat einen Bruder in Köln wohnen	*She's got a brother living in Cologne*
Sie fand das Buch auf dem Boden liegen	*She found the book lying on the floor*

NB: (i) *stehenbleiben* 'stop' and *sitzenbleiben* 'repeat a year (at school)' have become separable compounds.
(ii) For the use of *finden* with the present participle, see 13.7.5c.
(iii) *haben* is also used with a bare infinitive in a few set constructions with adjectives, i.e. *Du hast gut/leicht reden* 'It's all very well for you to talk'.
For the use of *haben* with *zu* + infinitive, see 13.2.3.

(g) *heißen, helfen, lehren, lernen*
These verbs may be followed by a bare infinitive **or** an infinitive with *zu*:

Sie hieß ihn schweigen	*She bade him be silent*
Er hieß seine Truppen, die Burg bis zum letzten Mann zu verteidigen	*He ordered his troops to defend the castle to the last man*
und jetzt hilf mir anpacken (*Remarque*)	*and now give me a hand*

Er half Carla, die Weinflaschen zu öffnen (*M. Horbach*)	*He helped Carla to open the wine-bottles*
Sie lehrte mich kochen	*She taught me to cook*
Sie lehrte mich, Suppe zu kochen	*She taught me how to make soup*
Ich habe gelernt, schneller zu schwimmen	*I have learnt to swim faster*

NB: (i) The above sense of *heißen*, i.e. 'command', is restricted to older literary language. In the sense 'mean', *heißen* is followed by an infinitive complement without *zu*, cf. (h) below.

(ii) *kennenlernen* 'meet, get to know' has become a distinct separable compound.

In general, the construction with *zu* tends to be used with longer and more complex infinitive clauses. Nevertheless, as the following example shows, the bare infinitive will naturally be preferred if the alternative is an awkward construction:

Es geht darum, die seit vierzig Jahren geforderte Freiheit der osteuropäischen Völker verwirklichen zu helfen (*FR)* (i.e. NOT *zu* *verwirklichen zu helfen*)	*It is a matter of helping the peoples of Eastern Europe to realise the freedom which has been demanded for forty years*

(h) a few other verbs in certain constructions or idioms

(i) In modern German, the bare infinitive is used after *machen* only in the idioms *von sich reden machen* 'become a talking point' and *jemanden etwas glauben machen* 'convince someone of something'.

(ii) A bare infinitive is used as the complement of *heißen* 'be (the equivalent of), mean' and *nennen* 'call', e.g.:

Das heißt lügen	*That amounts to lying*
Das hieße wieder von vorne anfangen	*That would mean starting fom scratch again*
Das nennst du höflich sein!	*You call that being polite!*

NB: For infinitive constructions after *heißen* in the meaning 'order', see (g) above.

(iii) *legen* is followed by a bare infinitive in *sich schlafen legen* 'go to bed', e.g. *Ich legte mich schlafen.*

13.3.2 The use of the infinitive for a past participle

An infinitive is used rather than a past participle in the perfect tenses of some verbs used with a bare infinitive, e.g. *Sie hat kommen* **wollen** (not: *gewollt*). The past participle of these verbs is used only if they have no dependent infinitive, e.g. *Sie hat es nicht* **gewollt**. This applies to the following verbs:

(a) the modal auxiliaries
(see chapter 17 for further details on these verbs)

Er hat heute ausgehen **dürfen**	Wir hätten Ihnen helfen **können**
Er hat ihn sehen **müssen**	Sie hätte es machen **sollen**
Karl hatte Sie sehen **wollen**	

NB: The semi-auxiliary *brauchen* also forms its perfect tenses with the infinitive rather than the past participle, whether used with an infinitive with or without *zu* (cf. 13.2.3 and 13.3.1a), e.g.: *Wir haben nicht (zu) warten brauchen.*

(b) *lassen*

Sie hat sich in die Irre führen **lassen**	*She let herself be led astray*
Ich habe ihn zu mir kommen **lassen**	*I sent for him*

NB: In the meaning 'let, allow', cf. 13.3.1c, the past participle is occasionally found, but it is less common than the infinitive, e.g. *Ich habe meinen Schirm irgendwo liegen(ge)lassen.*

(c) *sehen* and *hören*

Ich habe sie hereinkommen **sehen**	*I have seen her come in*
Sie hatte ihn nicht kommen **hören**	*She hadn't heard him come*

NB: In colloquial speech, the past participle is occasionally used with these verbs, e.g. *Sie hatte ihn nicht kommen gehört.* This is usually regarded as substandard, but it is encountered in writing, cf. Eggeling (1961:10).

(d) In subordinate clauses the auxiliary precedes these double infinitives cf. also 17.1.2e and 21.1.3c:

Er sagte, daß sie es **hätte** machen sollen	*He said that she ought to have done it*

13.3.3 Other uses of the bare infinitive

(a) in commands, in place of an imperative

The use of the infinitive with the force of a command is particularly frequent in official language and instructions of all kinds:

Nicht rauchen! Bitte anschnallen!	*No smoking. Fasten seat-belts*
Erst gurten, dann starten (official advice to motorists)	*Fasten your safety-belt before setting off*
Bitte einsteigen und die Türen schließen! (railway announcement)	*Please get in and close the doors*
4 Eiweiß zu sehr steifem Schnee schlagen (cooking instruction)	*Beat 4 egg-whites until stiff*

With reflexive verbs, the reflexive pronoun is usually omitted, e.g.:

Nicht hinauslehnen! (*sich hinauslehnen* 'lean out')	*Do not lean out of the window*

(b) in isolation, especially in elliptical questions, wishes and the like

Wie? Alles vergessen und vergeben?	*What? (Am I supposed to) forgive and forget?*

Wozu sich weiter bemühen?	*Why (should we) bother further?*
Was möchtest du jetzt? – Schlafen bis Mittag!	*What would you like to do now? – Sleep till lunchtime!*

13.4 Infinitival nouns

13.4.1 The infinitive of almost any verb may be used as a noun in German

It often corresponds to the use of the English *ing*-form as a noun. Such nouns from infinitives are neuter, cf. 1.1.3e, and they are spelled with a capital letter. As they simply express the action denoted by the verb, they cannot normally be used in the plural (but cf. 13.3.4):

Ich hörte das laute Bellen eines Hundes	*I heard the loud barking of a dog*
Nach monatelangem Warten erhielt er die Nachricht von seinem Erfolg	*After waiting for months he received news of his success*
Das Mitnehmen von Hunden ist polizeilich verboten	*Bringing dogs in is forbidden by law*
die Kunst des Schreibens	*the art of writing*

With reflexive verbs, the pronoun *sich* is usually omitted, e.g. *das Benehmen* 'behaviour' (from *sich benehmen* 'behave'), but it may be included if it is needed for the sense, e.g. *die Kunst des Sichäußerns* 'the art of expressing oneself', where *das Äußern* could clearly not have the intended meaning.

13.4.2 The extensive use of such nouns from infinitives is a very typical feature of modern written German

They are often compounded with the object of the verb or another part of the clause, e.g. *das Zeitunglesen* 'reading the newspaper', *das Rückwärtsfahren* 'reversing', *das Schlafengehen* 'going to bed'.

They are especially frequent in technical registers, e.g.:

In der Bundesrepublik beginnt sich diese Basis humanen **Miteinanderlebens, Untereinanderaussprechens** und **Miteinanderwirkens** aufzulösen (*FAZ*)	*In the Federal Republic this foundation of humane living together, freely exchanging ideas and cooperating is beginning to dissolve*

But they are used widely in literary prose, too, e.g.:

Dann kam das Schiff, und ich beobachtete, wie so viele Male schon, das vorsichtige **Längsfahren**, **Stoppen**, **Zurückweichen** in dem **Sprudeln** und **Rauschen** und **Räderklatschen**, das **Taueschleudern** und **Festbinden** (*Emil Strauß*).

13.4.3 Infinitival nouns used with prepositions

(a) *beim* + infinitive

This is often an equivalent for English *on* with an *ing* form, or a clause with *when* or *as*:

Beim Verlassen des Zimmers bemerkte sie einen roten Schein in der Ferne	*On leaving the room/As she left the room she noticed a red glow in the distance*
Beim Lesen dieses Buches sollten Sie vor allem auf den eigentümlichen Stil des Autors aufpassen	*When you read this book you should pay particular attention to the author's curious style*

(b) *zum* + infinitive

This combination expresses purpose. It often corresponds to English *for* with an *ing*-form or an infinitive with *to*:

Zum Fußballspielen ist der Garten viel zu klein	*The garden is much too small for playing football in*
Ich gebrauche das Messer zum Kartoffelschälen	*I use the knife for peeling potatoes*
Er machte sich zum Ausgehen fertig	*He got ready to go out*
Der Kaffee ist zu heiß zum Trinken	*The coffee is too hot to drink*

A number of combinations of infinitives with *zum* are essentially idiomatic, e.g.:

Das ist doch zum Lachen, zum Kotzen, zum Verrücktwerden	*But that's laughable, enough to make you sick, enough to drive you mad*

zum + infinitive is used with *bringen* to form phrasal verbs expressing the completion of an action, e.g.:

zum Halten bringen	*bring to a stop*
zum Kochen bringen	*bring to the boil*

(c) *ins* + infinitive

This combination is frequent with *geraten* or *kommen* to form phrasal verbs denoting the beginning of an action, e.g.:

Der Ball geriet/kam ins Rollen	*The ball started rolling*
Der Turm kam/geriet ins Schwanken	*The tower started to sway*
Der Wagen kam ins Schleudern	*The car went into a skid*

13.4.4 Some infinitival nouns have extended meanings.

Many of these have, in effect, become independent nouns, isolated from the verb they come from and no longer merely expressing the action denoted by it. The following is a selection of the most frequent:

das Andenken	*souvenir*	das Leben	*life*
das Benehmen	*behaviour*	das Schrecken	*terror*

das Dasein	*existence*	das Unternehmen	*enterprise*
das Einkommen	*income*	das Verbrechen	*crime*
das Essen	*meal*	das Vergnügen	*pleasure*
das Gutachten	*reference*	das Vermögen	*wealth*
das Guthaben	*credit balance*	das Versprechen	*promise*
		das Vorhaben	*intention*

NB: Such nouns are not infrequently used in the plural, and plural forms of all the above nouns except *das Benehmen* and *das Dasein* may be encountered.

13.5 The present and past participles

Aside from the use of the past participle to form the perfect tenses and the passive, cf. 12.3 and 12.4, the German participles are chiefly employed as adjectives or in participial clauses. The formation of the participles is dealt with in 12.2.

13.5.1 The names and meanings of the participles

The two participles of German are usually called the 'present participle' (e.g. *lesend, überwältigend*, etc.), and the 'past participle' (e.g. *gestellt, geworfen*, etc.). These traditional terms are not very satisfactory, as the two participles do not necessarily refer to present or past time (hence, in German, they are commonly termed 'das erste Partizip' and 'das zweite Partizip' respectively).

(a) The present participle usually indicates an action simultaneous with that of the finite verb, e.g.:

Den Schildern **folgend**, fanden sie das Krankenhaus (*Walser*)
Following the signs, they found the hospital

(b) The meaning of the past participle differs according to the meaning of the verb:
(i) With intransitive verbs, the past participle has an active (i.e. not passive) sense, and refers to an action which has taken place prior to that indicated by the main verb, e.g.:

Der neue Lehrer, in Freiburg **angekommen**, suchte das Humboldt-Gymnasium auf
Having arrived in Freiburg, the new teacher went to the Humboldt Secondary School

(ii) With transitive verbs, the past participle has a passive sense. If the verb denotes a continuous action, the participle refers to an action simultaneous with that of the main verb, e.g.:

Der Zug, von zwei Lokomotiven **gezogen**, fuhr in den Bahnhof ein
The train, which was being pulled by two engines, came into the station

With verbs which denote a momentary action, the past participle refers to an action which has taken place before that of the main verb, e.g.:

Der Flüchtling, von seinen Freunden **gewarnt**, verließ sein Versteck

The fugitive, who had been warned by his friends, left his hiding-place

13.5.2 The adjectival use of the participles

Most German present and past participles may be employed as adjectives, and this is their most frequent role aside from the use of the past participle in compound tenses and the passive.

die **schreienden** Vögel
mein **verlorener** Schirm

das **kochende** Wasser
der **gehaßte** Feind

Like other adjectives, cf. 6.4, they can be used as nouns:

die **Streikenden** *the people on strike*
die **Gehaßte** *the woman who is detested*

der **Sterbende** *the dying man*
das **Hervorragende** *the outstanding thing*

ein bitterer Kampf zwischen **Habenden** und Habenichtsen, zwischen **Überfütterten** und **Zukurzgekommenen** (*Zeit*)

a bitter struggle between the haves and the have-nots, between people who are overfed and people who have come off badly

Many such adjectival participles used as nouns have taken on special meanings, e.g. *der/die Abgeordnete* 'member of parliament', *der/die Vorsitzende* 'chairperson', etc. More of these are given in 6.4.4.

In common with other adjectives, cf. 7.1.2, they may be used adverbially:

Er hat die Sache **überraschend** schnell erledigt
Sie antwortete **lächelnd**
Die alte Frau ging **gebückt** zum Rathaus hin

He settled the matter surprisingly quickly
She answered with a smile
The old woman was walking with a stoop towards the town-hall

They are often compounded, especially in written German. Such compounds may also be used as nouns or adverbs in the same way as simple participles:

Vancouver ist eine Stadt von **atemberaubender** Schönheit
die **Arbeitssuchenden**
ein **weichgekochtes** Ei
Tiefgefrorenes

Vancouver is a breathtakingly beautiful city
the people looking for work
a soft-boiled egg
frozen food

The present participle may be used adjectivally with an accompanying *zu*, e.g. *das **abzufertigende** Gepäck* 'the baggage for checking'. This is the adjectival form of the construction with *sein* and an infinitive with *zu* expressing possibility or necessity, cf. 13.2.3. The participle has passive force. This construction is particularly common in official written registers, but is scarcely used in informal speech. Further examples:

ein nicht **zu übersehender** Fehler	*a mistake which cannot be overlooked*
ihre **anzuerkennende** Leistung	*her achievement which must be acknowledged*
ein **Auszubildender**	*a trainee*

13.5.3 Lexicalization of participles used as adjectives

Many participles used as adjectives have been lexicalized, i.e. they have developed a meaning distinct from that of the original verb and come to be felt as independent adjectives rather than as participles. A clear indication of this is that, if their meaning permits is, such lexicalized participles can be used with the usual comparative and superlative endings, e.g. *spannender, am spannendsten* 'more, most exciting', whereas with true participles, *mehr* and *meist* are used, cf. 8.1.8. Similarly, some can be used with the adjective prefix *un-* to give the opposite meaning, e.g. (*un*)*bedeutend* '(in)significant', (*un*)*angebracht* '(in)appropriate', etc.

(a) Lexicalized present participles
The following is a selection of those most frequently used:

abstoßend	*repulsive*	beruhigend	*reassuring*	rührend	*touching*
abwesend	*absent*	dringend	*urgent*	spannend	*exciting*
ansteckend	*infectious*	drückend	*oppressive*	überraschend	*surprising*
anstrengend	*strenuous*	einleuchtend	*reasonable*	überzeugend	*convincing*
anwesend	*present*	empörend	*outrageous*	umfassend	*extensive*
auffallend	*conspicuous*	entscheidend	*decisive*	verblüffend	*amazing*
aufregend	*exciting*	glühend	*glowing*	verlockend	*tempting*
bedeutend	*significant*	reizend	*charming*	wütend	*furious*

A notable feature of these is that they can be used not only before a noun, but also after the verb *sein*, cf.:

ein spannender Film	*an exciting film*
der Film war spannend	*the film was exciting*

True present participles cannot be used in this way, and English speakers must beware of equating such participial adjectives with forms of the English progressive tenses, cf:

die brennenden Lichter	*the burning lights*
die Lichter brennen	*the lights are burning*

i.e. **not**: *die Lichter sind brennend*! The German present participle cannot be used with the auxiliary *sein* to form progressive tenses as can the English *ing*-form.

(b) Lexicalized past participles

The following is a selection from the large number in common use:

angebracht	*appropriate*	ausgezeichnet	*excellent*	gelehrt	*scholarly*
angesehen	*respected*	bekannt	*famous*	geschickt	*clever*
aufgebracht	*outraged*	belegt	*occupied*	verliebt	*in love*
aufgeregt	*excited*	erfahren	*experienced*	verrückt	*insane*

A very few lexicalized past participles from transitive verbs have an active meaning, against the usual pattern, cf. 13.5.1, e.g.: ein **Bedienter** (arch.) *a servant* (i.e. one who serves, not one who is served), ein **gelernter** Arbeiter *a skilled worker* (i.e. one who has learned).

Some lexicalized past particles are archaic forms which are no longer used as the past participate of the verb in question, e.g.:

erhaben *illustrious* (from *erheben* 'raise', modern p.p. *erhoben*)
gediegen *solid, upright* (from *gedeihen* 'prosper', modern p.p. *gediehen*)
verhohlen *secret* (from *verhehlen* 'conceal', modern p.p. *verhehlt*)
verworren *confused* (from *verwirren* 'confuse', modern p.p. *verwirrt*)

A number of adjectives with the form of past participles are in fact not from verbs at all, e.g. *beleibt* 'portly' and *benachbart* 'neighbouring', which are derived directly from the nouns *der Leib* 'body' and *der Nachbar* 'neighbour', there being no such verbs as *beleiben* or *benachbaren*.

13.5.4 The extended participial phrase

In German, a participle used with a noun may be expanded leftwards by adding objects and/or adverbs and adverbial phrases. Essentially what in English would be a phrase or subordinate clause placed **after** the noun can appear in German as an extended adjectival phrase placed **before** the noun, e.g.:

Die **um ihre eigenen Arbeitsplätze fürchtenden** Stahlarbeiter wollten nicht streiken (*Zeit*)	*The steelworkers who were afraid for their own jobs did not want to strike*
Ich habe dieses **von meinem Vetter warm empfohlene** Buch mit Genuß gelesen	*I enjoyed reading this book which was strongly recommended to me by my cousin*
Wegen Überproduktion entlassene Arbeiter demonstrierten im Fabrikhof	*Workers who had been laid off on account of overproduction were demonstrating in the factory yard*
eine **von allen echten Demokraten zu begrüßende** Entwicklung	*a development which must be welcomed by all true democrats*

NB: (i) The order of elements within such extended phrases is the same as in a subordinate clause, cf. 21.1.1.
(ii) Such extended adjectival phrases may be made into nouns, e.g. *das wirklich Entscheidende* 'what is really decisive', *die soeben Angekommenen* 'the people who have just arrived', etc.

This construction is very typical of formal written German, especially in non-literary registers (journalism, officialese, non-fiction, etc.). It is not used in everyday spoken language. As the following example shows, such extended phrases may result in there being a quite considerable distance between the article and the noun:

Zwar gilt **der** in den vergangenen vier Jahren auf der Basis einer deutsch-amerikanischen Regierungsvereinbarung für bislang 552 Millionen Mark **entwickelte Panzer** als Spitzenmodell seiner Klasse (*Spiegel*)

NB: Although such constructions are most characteristically encountered with participles, they are not infrequent with other adjectives, e.g.:
Er hielt **eine** von rhetorischen Effekten **freie** Rede

13.6 Participial clauses

13.6.1 Both participles are used to construct non-finite clauses

These may have adjectival force, qualifying a noun or pronoun, or adverbial, giving the circumstances of the action. The participle is normally the last element in the clause, but, exceptionally, it may be placed earlier for emphasis:

Ich putzte **auf dem Brett stehend** das Fenster von außen (*Spiegel*)

I was cleaning the window from the outside, standing on the plank

eine ständige Verbesserung des Automobils nach den Möglichkeiten der Zeit, **doch zugleich immer aufbauend auf das Erreichte** (*Mercedes advert*)

a continuous improvement of the car according to the possibilities of the time, but at the same time always building on what has been achieved

Zwar hatte dieses Mal der Dolch, **durch ein seidenes Unterkleid abgelenkt**, das Opfer nicht sogleich tödlich getroffen (*Heyse*)

Although this time the dagger, deflected by a silk petticoat, had not immediately wounded the victim fatally

Von der Wucht seiner Rede hingerissen, brachen die Zuhörer immer wieder in Beifall aus

Carried away by the force of his speech, the audience continually broke out into applause

Da saß eine zarte Dame mit einem zarten Gesicht, **umrahmt von einem blonden Pagenkopf**

There sat a delicate lady with a delicate face, which was framed by blond hair cut in the page-boy style

Such participial clauses tend to be restricted to the most formal written registers in German. In particular, those with present participles are far less widely employed than clauses with *ing*-forms in English, and English learners of German are best advised to avoid them entirely and use instead one of the alternative equivalents detailed in 13.7.

Nevertheless, a few constructions with past participles have become established idioms, and are widely used both in writing and speech, e.g.:

offen gesagt/offen gestanden	*to be frank*
nebenbei gesagt/bemerkt	*incidentally*
gesetzt den Fall(, daß . . .)	*assuming (that)*
wohl gemerkt	*mind you*
strenggenommen	*strictly speaking*
Bedienung inbegriffen	*service included*

13.6.2 Comparative clauses may be formed with the past participle and the conjunction *wie*:

eine Betonburg, wie von einem anderen Stern in diesen Wald gefallen (*Walser*)	*a castle made of concrete, as if it had fallen into this forest from another planet*

This construction is also essentially literary, but, again, some have become fixed idioms and are more widely used, e.g.:

Also, wie ausgemacht: Wir treffen uns um acht	*Well, then, as arranged, we'll meet at eight o'clock*
wie gesagt, wie erwartet, wie vorausgesehen	*as I said, as expected, as foreseen*
wie gehabt (coll.)	*as before, as usual*

13.6.3 A clause with a past participle can be introduced by the conjunction *obwohl*

This is similar to the English construction with (*al*)*though*:

Obwohl von seinen Kollegen geachtet, war er nicht sehr beliebt	(*Al*)*though respected by his colleagues, he was not very popular*

No other conjunction can be used to introduce a participial clause in German.

13.7 German equivalents of English constructions with the *ing*-form

The English *ing*-form has a far wider and less restricted range of application than the German present participle, which is found mainly as an adjective, cf. 13.5. In other cases, German uses different constructions, details of which are given in this section.

In particular, as explained in 13.6.1, the German present participle is only found to a very limited extent in participial clauses, chiefly in rather formal writing. Because of these limitations, it is advisable for English learners to use the German present participle **only** as an adjective and to use the equivalents explained below for all other constructions with the English *ing*-form.

13.7.1 English *ing*-form used as a noun

The usual German equivalents will be one of the following constructions. In many cases more than one alternative is possible.

(a) an infinitive used as a noun, or another noun derived from a verb:

Aufmerksames **Zuhören** ist wichtig	*Attentive listening is important*
die Freuden des **Skilaufens**	*the pleasures of skiing*
Warum hat man die **Eröffnung** der neuen Schule aufgeschoben?	*Why has the opening of the new school been delayed?*
Er ist einer solchen **Tat** nicht fähig	*He is not capable of doing such a thing*

(b) an infinitive clause with *zu*:

Es ist wichtig, **aufmerksam zuzuhören**	*Attentive listening is important*
Er gab zu, **das Fenster zerbrochen zu haben**	*He admitted having broken the window*
Ich verlasse mich darauf, **ihn zu Hause zu finden**	*I rely on finding him at home*

(c) a *daß*-clause:

Es ist wichtig, **daß man aufmerksam zuhört**	*Attentive listening is important*
Er gab zu, **daß er das Fenster zerbrochen hatte**	*He admitted having broken the window*
Ich verlasse mich darauf, **daß ich ihn zu Hause finde**	*I rely on finding him at home*

This alternative **must** be used where the English *ing*-form has a different subject from that of the main verb:

Ich kann es mir nicht vorstellen, **daß sie ihren Ring verkauft**	*I can't imagine her selling her ring*
Ich verlasse mich darauf, **daß er alles arrangiert**	*I rely on his/him arranging everything*

NB: After verbs (or nouns and adjectives) governing a preposition, the infinitive clause or *daß*-clause of alternatives (b) and (c) above is usually anticipated by a prepositional adverb (e.g. *darauf*), as the relevant examples show. This prepositional adverb is sometimes optional, e.g. *Ich erinnere mich (daran), ihn gesehen zu haben* 'I remember having seen him', cf. 6.6.2 and 18.6.14.

(d) a finite verb:

Wer **kocht** bei Ihnen zu Hause?	*Who does the cooking at your house?*

Note that the impersonal passive, cf. 15.1.5, can be used for an English *ing*-form after *there is/are*:

Überall **wurde** laut **gesungen**	*There was loud singing everywhere*

For *there is/are* followed by *no* and an *ing*-form, a construction with *sich lassen*, cf. 15.4.7, is often possible, e.g.:

Das **läßt sich** nicht leugnen   *There's no denying that*

13.7.2 The English *ing*-form after prepositions

(a) *by* (or *through*) + *ing*-form
This construction usually corresponds to a clause with *dadurch, daß* or *indem*, or to *durch* followed by an infinitival noun:

Er rettete sich dadurch, daß er
   aus dem Fenster sprang
Er rettete sich, indem er aus dem   *He escaped by jumping out of*
   Fenster sprang   *the window*
Er rettete sich durch einen Sprung
   aus dem Fenster
Er erreichte sein Ziel dadurch, daß   *He attained his goal through our*
   wir ihm geholfen haben   *having helped him*

(b) *for* + *ing*-form
The commonest equivalents are (*um*)...*zu*, cf. 13.2.5a, or *zum* followed by a infinitival noun, cf. 13.4.3b:

Sie hat keine Zeit mehr, (um)   *She no longer has any time*
   zu üben   *for practising*
Sie hat keine Zeit mehr zum Üben
Es ist zu kalt zum Schwimmen   *It's too cold for swimming*

(c) *instead of* + *ing*-form
For this, (*an*)*statt* . . . *zu* or (*an*)*statt daß* is used, cf. 13.2.5c:

Er spielte, { anstatt zu arbeiten   *He was playing instead of working*
        { anstatt daß er arbeitete

(d) *on* + *ing*-for
This usually corresponds to a clause with *als* or *wenn*, or *beim* followed by an infinitival noun, cf. 13.4.3a:

Als sie den Brief las, wurde sie rot
Beim Lesen des Briefes wurde sie rot   *On reading the letter, she blushed*

(e) *with* + *ing*-form
This construction has a variety of possible equivalents in German, similar to those for clauses with *ing*-forms, cf. 13.7.3:

Wenn der Berg nur als ein   *If the hill only appears as an*
   unbestimmtes Gebilde erscheint, wobei   *indefinite shape with the groups*
   sich die Baumgruppen bloß als blasse   *of trees showing only as faint*
   Schatten zeigen, . . .   *shadows, . . .*
Es ist schön hier, wenn die Sonne   *It's lovely here with the sun*
   durch die Bäume scheint   *shining through the trees*

Wir sahen die alte Stadt, über die die zerfallene Burg emporragte	*We could see the old town with the ruined castle towering above it*
Da der Fluß rasch stieg, mußten Notmaßnahmen getroffen werden	*With the river rising rapidly, emergency measures had to be taken*
Der Bürgermeister eröffnete die Sitzung unter Ausschluß der Offentlichkeit	*The mayor opened the meeting, with the public being excluded*
Sie eilte durch die Stadt, und dabei wehten ihre Haare nach hinten	*She raced through the town with her hair streaming behind her*

(f) *without* + *ing*-form

This corresponds to *ohne . . . zu* or *ohne daß*, cf. 13.2.5b:

Der Zug fuhr durch, ohne zu halten	*The train went through without stopping*
Er bot uns seine Hilfe an, ohne daß wir ihn darum bitten mußten	*He offered us his help without our/us having to ask him for it*

(g) Other prepositions followed by *ing*-forms

For these, German can normally use subordinate clauses with an appropriate conjunction or an appropriate preposition with an infinitival noun, e.g.:

Nach seiner Ankunft/Nachdem er angekommen war, ging er sofort zum Rathaus	*After arriving he went straight to the town hall*
Vor dem Einschlafen/ Bevor er einschlief las er schnell die Zeitung	*Before going to sleep he read the newspaper quickly*
Trotz seiner Hilfe/Obwohl er mir geholfen hatte, kam ich zu spät an	*In spite of his/him having helped me, I arrived late*

(h) *ing*-forms after prepositions governed by nouns, verbs or adjectives,

e.g. *I rely on finding him at home*. These are dealt with in 13.7.1.

13.7.3 Adverbial clauses with *ing*-forms

Such constructions are very frequent in English, but, as explained in 13.6.1, their use is limited in German. The German equivalent will depend on the sense of the clause.

(a) The participial clause and the main verb refer to consecutive or simultaneous actions

The simplest German equivalent is to use main clauses joined by *und*, possibly with *dabei* in the second to emphasise the simultaneity of the actions:

Sie öffnete die Schublade und nahm das Testament heraus	*Opening the drawer, she took out the will*
Ich saß an seinem Tisch und schrieb einen Brief	*I was sitting at his table writing a letter*
Er erzählte seine Geschichte und machte (dabei) nach jedem Satz eine Pause	*He told his story, pausing after each sentence*

NB: Despite what is said in some English handbooks, a clause with *indem* **cannot** be employed as an equivalent of such English participial clauses in modern German. For the use of *indem*, see 19.6.3. However, a clause introduced by *wobei* is often a useful possible alternative with simultaneous actions, e.g. *Er erzählte seine Geschichte, wobei er nach jedem Satz eine Pause machte*.

If the participial clause comes before the main clause in English, a clause with *als*, *wenn* or *nachdem* may be possible in German:

Als wir zum Fenster hinausschauten, sahen wir einen Polizeiwagen heranfahren	*Looking out of the window, we saw a police-car approaching*
Wenn man oben auf dem Kirchturm steht, sieht man das ganze Dorf	*Standing on the church tower, you can see the whole village*
Nachdem ich die Briefe beantwortet hatte, ging ich spazieren	*Having answered the letters, I went for a walk*

(b) Participial clauses which give a reason or cause
In German, a subordinate clause with *da* may be used:

Da es schon spät war, gingen wir nach Hause	*It being late, we went home*
Da ich wußte, daß sie verreist war, habe ich sie nicht angerufen	*Knowing that she was away, I didn't call her*

(c) Participial clauses introduced by a conjunction
Subordinate clauses with the appropriate conjunction are used in German:

Während ich auf dich wartete, habe ich einen schweren Unfall gesehen	*While waiting for you, I saw a bad accident*

13.7.4 Clauses with *ing*-forms used to qualify nouns

These correspond in German to a relative clause or, especially in formal written German, to an extended participial phrase, cf. 13.5.4:

Er sah ein in entgegengesetzter Richtung kommendes Auto Er sah ein Auto, das in entgegengesetzter Richtung kam	*He saw a car coming in the opposite direction*
Einige Minuten später eilte der Arzt, der einen kleinen Koffer trug, zum Krankenhaus hin	*A few minutes later the doctor, carrying a small suitcase, was hurrying towards the hospital*

13.7.5 English *ing*-forms after some verbs

As explained in 13.7.1, the usual German equivalent of English *ing*-forms after verbs is an infinitive with *zu* or a clause. One or two verbs, however, are special cases:

(a) verbs of perception

i.e. *see*, *hear*, *feel*. The English *ing*-form corresponds to a bare infinitive or a clause with *wie* in German, cf. 13.3.1b, e.g.:

Ich hörte die Vögel laut singen Ich hörte, wie die Vögel laut sangen }	*I heard the birds singing loudly*

(b) verbs of motion

e.g. *go, come, send*, etc. If the *ing*-form expresses purpose, an bare infinitive is used in German, cf. 13.3.1e, e.g.:

Wir gehen heute schwimmen	*We're going swimming today*
Kommst du heute mit schwimmen?	*Are you coming swimming with us today?*
Sie schickte ihn einkaufen	*She sent him shopping*

After *kommen*, though, the <u>past</u> participle is used to indicate manner:

Er kam ins Zimmer gelaufen	*He came running into the room*
Sie kam herbeigeeilt	*She came hurrying along*

(c) *ing*-form expressing position,

i.e. *standing, sitting*, etc. after *find, have, leave, remain, stay*. German can use a bare infinitive after *bleiben, finden, haben* and *lassen*, cf. 13.3.1, e.g.:

Sie blieb neben dem Ofen sitzen	*She remained sitting by the stove*
Ich fand ihn am Fenster stehen	*I found him standing by the window*
Haben Sie einen Mantel in der Garderobe hängen?	*Have you got a coat hanging in the wardrobe?*
Sie ließ ihre Sachen herumliegen	*She left her things lying about*

finden can also be used with the present participle of a large number of verbs, e.g. *Sie fand ihn schlafend. Er fand sie Pilze suchend im Wald.* This construction is also possible with verbs of place, as an alternative to the infinitive, e.g. *Sie fand das Buch auf dem Boden liegend.*

(d) *keep* + *ing*-form

A frequent possible equivalent is *lassen* with a bare infinitive, cf. 13.3.1:

Sie ließ uns warten	*She kept us waiting*

(e) *need, want* + *ing*-form

These most often correspond to *müssen*, cf. 17.5.1b:

Das muß noch erklärt werden	*That still needs/wants explaining*
Man muß sich um sie kümmern	*She needs/wants looking after*

(f) *can't help* + *ing*-form

einfach müssen is the commonest German equivalent, see also 17.3.7, e.g.:

Sie mußte einfach lachen	*She couldn't help laughing*

13.8   Miscellaneous uses of the German participles

13.8.1   Elliptical use of the past participle

The past participle is sometimes used in isolation, usually as an exclamation or a depersonalised command. Many such forms have become idiomatic, e.g.:

Verdammt! Verflucht (noch mal)!	*Blast!*
Abgemacht!	*Agreed!*
Frisch gewagt!	*Let's get on with it!*
Aufgepaßt!	*Watch out!*
Stillgestanden!	*Attention!* (military command)

13.8.2   The past participle after *finden*

This corresponds closely to the English construction:

Ich fand sie vor dem Ofen zusammengesunken	*I found her slumped in front of the stove*
Du wirst ihn dort aufgebahrt finden	*You will find him laid out there*

NB: For the use of *finden* with a present participle, see 13.7.5c.

13.8.3   Some participles are used as conjunctions or prepositions

The following are in common use:
ausgenommen '*excepting*'. It usually precedes a noun, which has the same case as the word it refers to, e.g.:

Alle waren da, ausgenommen mein Bruder	*Everyone was there except my brother*
Allen begegnete sie, ausgenommen dem Lehrer	*She met everyone except the teacher*

NB: *außer*, cf. 20.2.2a, is a more widely used equivalent for 'except'.

betreffend 'concerning', (off.) see 20.1.7b. It governs the accusative and may precede or follow a noun:

Der Bericht betreffend den Unfall liegt auf meinem Schreibtisch	*The report concerning the accident is on my desk*

eingerechnet 'including' (comm.). It follows a noun in the accusative, cf.20.1.7:

meine Unkosten eingerechnet	*including my expenses*

eingeschlossen 'including'. It follows a noun which has the same case as the noun referred to:

Sie hat alle eingeladen, meinen Bruder eingeschlossen	*She invited everyone, including my brother*

entsprechend 'in accordance with' governs a preceding or following noun in the dative, cf. 20.2.10e:

entsprechend meinem Vorschlag/   *in accordance with my proposal*
    meinem Vorschlag entsprechend

vorausgesetzt(, daß) 'provided (that)', cf.16.3.3d, e.g.:

Wir wollen baden gehen, vorausgesetzt   *We want to go swimming, provided*
    (, daß) die Sonne scheint   *(that) the sun shines*

14   The uses of the tenses

This chapter deals with the uses of the tenses of the indicative in German. German and English agree in many features of tense usage, and, in the main, full details are only given here for those where German usage differs in such a way from English as to present difficulties for English learners.

A great deal has been written on the German tenses. Ballweg (1988) is a comprehensive recent survey of a theoretical kind, and Dieling and Kempter (1989) give full and useful details for the foreign learner from a practical point of view.

14.1 The German tenses: general

Standard German has six tenses in the indicative mood of the active voice, i.e. two simple tenses, the present and the past, and four compound tenses formed with auxiliaries, the perfect, the pluperfect, the future and the future perfect. Full details on the formation of the tenses are presented in chapter 12, but by way of illustration we give below examples of the six tenses with the verbs *machen* and *bleiben* in the first person singular:

Present	ich mache	ich bleibe
Past	ich machte	ich blieb
Perfect	ich habe gemacht	ich bin geblieben
Pluperfect	ich hatte gemacht	ich war geblieben
Future	ich werde machen	ich werde bleiben
Future Perfect	ich werde gemacht haben	ich werde geblieben sein

NB: (i) The *werden*-passive has the same range of tenses as the active, but in the *sein*-passive, only the present and past are commonly used. Full details are given in 15.2.1.

(ii) There is a rather different range of tenses in the subjunctive. Details are given in 16.1.

(iii) There are no progressive tenses in German, and *ich bleibe*, for instance, usually corresponds both to English *I stay* and *I am staying*, etc. However, the difference in meaning between these English forms may sometimes be rendered in a different way in German, cf. 14.6.2.

(iv) What we call the 'past tense' in German is sometimes referred to as the 'imperfect tense'. However, unlike the 'imperfect tense' of some other languages (e.g. French or Latin), but like the English 'past tense', this German tense does not necessarily convey the idea of an incomplete or continuous action and the less misleading term 'past tense' is to be preferred.

278

14.2 The present tense

14.2.1 The present tense is used to relate present, habitual or 'timeless' actions or events

This corresponds to the use of the present tense (simple or progressive) in English:

Sie singt gut	*She sings/is singing well*
Ich lese die Zeitung von gestern	*I'm reading yesterday's newspaper*
Dankend bestätigen wir den Empfang Ihres Schreibens vom 30. Juni	*We gratefully acknowledge receipt of your letter of June 30th.*
Ursula spricht ein wenig Spanisch	*Ursula speaks a little Spanish*
In Irland regnet es viel	*It rains a lot in Ireland*

14.2.2 The present tense is commonly used to relate an action or state which began in the past and is still going on at the moment of speaking

Such sentences usually contain an adverb (*schon* or *bisher*), an adverbial phrase with *seit* or an adverbial clause with *seit*(*dem*) or *solange* expressing the idea of 'up to now'.

(a) In such 'up-to-now' sentences the German present tense usually corresponds to an English perfect, most often a perfect progressive:

Ich stehe schon lange hier vor dem Bahnhof	*I've been standing in front of the station for a long time*
Obwohl wir bisher mit diesem alten Gerät arbeiten, sind wir zufrieden	*Although we've been working up to now with this old equipment, we're satisfied*
Ich arbeite seit sieben Uhr	*I've been working since seven o'clock*
Seit wann wohnen Sie in Rendsburg?	*How long have you been living in Rendsburg?*
Das Haus gehört unserer Familie seit mehreren Generationen	*The house has belonged to our family for several generations*
Seitdem ich die Tabletten nehme, fühle ich mich besser	*Since I've been taking the tablets I've been feeling better*
Er wohnt in Hamburg, solange ich ihn kenne	*He's been living in Hamburg as long as I've known him*

(b) In some 'up-to-now' sentences German uses the perfect rather than the present, i.e.:
(i) In negative statements:

Ich habe ihn seit Jahren nicht gesehen	*I haven't seen him for years*
Seitdem ich ihn kenne, haben wir uns nie gestritten	*Since I've known him, we have never quarrelled*

Nevertheless, the present tense is used in cases of clear continuity:

Seit Weihnachten arbeitet er nicht mehr	*He hasn't worked since Christmas*
Seitdem ich im Dorf wohne, bin ich nie einsam	*Since I've been living in the village, I've never been lonely*

(ii) When referring to a series of actions or states:

Er ist seit Weihnachten mehrmals krank gewesen	*He's been ill several times since Christmas*
Seit ihrer Erkrankung hat sie viele Bücher gelesen	*Since she's been ill, she has read a lot of books*

However, the present tense is used when referring to a continuing habit (notice the difference in tense in English to the previous example):

Seit ihrer Erkrankung liest sie viele Bücher	*Since she's been ill, she's been reading a lot of books*

NB: As the examples show, the rules given in (a) and (b) above only affect the tense of the verb in the main clause in sentences with a *seit(dem)* clause. The verb in the *seit(dem)* clause is always in the present tense.

(c) In a similar way, the present of *kommen* is often used to refer to the immediate past, whereas English normally uses the perfect:

Ich komme, die Miete zu bezahlen	*I've come to pay the rent*

14.2.3 The present tense used to refer to future time

(a) German uses the present tense with future reference much more than is possible in English
A present tense is often quite usual in German where a future (whether with *will/shall* or *be going to*) is required in English, e.g.:

In zwei Stunden bin ich wieder da	*I'll be back in two hours*
Wir finden es nie	*We're never going to find it*

In practice, the present is more frequent than the future in German as long as it is clear from the context that the reference is to the future. It is especially common with verbs of motion, with verbs denoting a momentary action or when the time reference is given by an adverb:

Er holt uns von der Bahn ab	*He's going to meet us at the station*
Ich erwarte, daß sie kommt	*I expect she'll come*
Weitere Einzelheiten erteilt Ihnen unser Fachpersonal	*Our specialist staff will give you further information*
Vielleicht sage ich es ihm	*Perhaps I'll tell him*
Ich schreibe den Brief heute abend	*I'll write the letter tonight*
Morgen um diese Zeit bin ich in Wien	*This time tomorrow I'll be in Vienna*

(b) The German future tense, if used in sentences like those in (a), tends to emphasize the idea of a prediction or a possibility or stress intention or

determination
(see also 14.4.2 for further details on the use of the future tense).

Nächstes Jahr wird alles besser sein	*Next year everything will be better*
Da wird er sich wundern!	*He will be surprised!*
Ich <u>werde</u> den Brief heute abend schreiben	*I <u>am</u> going to write the letter tonight*

(c) In practice, we only need to use the future in German to express future time if the present tense could be taken simply to refer to the present
This is shown by the following pairs of sentences:

Er wird wieder bei der Post arbeiten	*He's going to work for the post-office again*
Er arbeitet wieder bei der Post	*He's working for the post-office again*
Ich werde viel lesen	*I'm going to read a lot*
Ich lese viel	*I'm reading a lot*
Ich werde auf euch warten	*I'll be waiting for you*
Ich warte auf euch	*I'm waiting for you*

14.2.4 The present tense is sometimes used to refer to the past

This so-called 'historic present' is much more frequent in German than English. It has the effect of making the past seem more immediate and is a common stylistic device in narrative prose, both in fiction and historical writing:

Mit zuckenden Nerven marschieren sie näher, noch immer versuchen sie sich gegenseitig zu täuschen, so sehr sie alle schon die Wahrheit wissen: daß die Norweger, daß Amundsen ihnen zuvorgekommen ist. Bald zerbricht der letzte Zweifel . . . (*Stefan Zweig*)

Similarly in newspaper headlines:

40-Tonner zermalmt Trabi – 2 starben (*BILD*)	*Forty-ton lorry squashes Trabi – two dead*

It is also a very typical feature of colloquial speech:

Denk dir, gestern abend geh' ich ins Café und seh' den Horst Brunner dort an der Theke sitzen	*Just think, last night I went into the pub and saw Horst Brunner sitting there at the bar*

14.3 The past and the perfect

In English there is a clear difference in meaning and usage between the past and the perfect tenses, so that *I have broken my leg* and *I broke my leg* are quite distinct and hardly ever interchangeable in context. The deceptively similar German forms *Ich habe mir das Bein gebrochen* and *Ich brach mir das Bein*, on the other hand, are much less clearly differentiated and may often replace one another in context. Significantly, Germans learning English find it very difficult to use the English tenses correctly and often produce sentences like 'I have broken my leg last year', because *Ich habe mir voriges Jahr das Bein gebrochen* is perfectly good German.

The use of the past and perfect tenses in German is thus rather different to the use of the past and perfect in English. It is not simply a matter of hard and fast grammatical rules, but rather of tendencies, as there is a great deal of stylistic and regional variation. The following sections attempt to sketch as simply as possible the main features of current written and spoken usage, following the very detailed account in Latzel (1977), as it would be impractical, and potentially confusing, to try to cover all the numerous possibilities.

14.3.1 The use of the perfect and past tenses to refer to a past action or event which has continuing relevance in the present

(a) The perfect tense is normally used in both spoken and written German to indicate a past action or event whose effect is still felt at the moment of speaking
This linking up of the past with the present is the typical function of the perfect, and, broadly speaking, English and German agree in using the perfect in such cases. Thus, we find the perfect in German:
(i) Where the result of an action or event is still evident at the moment of speaking:

Es hat in der Nacht geschneit	*It has snowed in the night*
(there's snow on the ground)	
Sie hat sich das Bein gebrochen	*She's broken her leg*
(her leg is still in plaster)	
Meine Tante ist gestern angekommen	*My aunt arrived last night*
(and she's still here)	

NB: As the last example above shows, the perfect may be used in German to refer to the present result of a past action even if there is a past time expression in the sentence, as in the last example above. In such cases English always uses the past tense.

(ii) to refer to something which happened in the immediate past:

Jetzt hat Breitner den Ball eingeworfen	*Breitner has just thrown the ball in*
Damit haben wir diese kleine Führung beendet	*With this we have come to the end of this short guided tour*

(iii) To refer to states or repeated actions which have lasted up to the moment of speaking:

Ich habe immer gefunden, daß es nützlich ist, viel zu wissen	*I've always found it useful to know a lot*
Ich habe ihm wiederholt gesagt, daß er ihr schreiben sollte	*I've told him repeatedly that he ought to write to her*
Das Paket ist noch nicht angekommen	*The parcel hasn't arrived yet*

NB: The present tense is used to refer to activities or states which began in the past and continue into the present, i.e. in cases where English typically uses a perfect progressive, cf. 14.2.2.

(b) The past tense may sometimes substitute for the perfect to indicate a past action or event which has relevance for the present,
i.e. in the cases listed under (a) above. This use of the past tense in these typically 'perfect' meanings is chiefly found in written German, especially in the following cases:

(i) In newspaper headlines and short announcements. In such cases the one-word form of the past tense has the stylistic merit of greater brevity:

Lastwagenfahrer gaben Blockade am Brenner nach einer Woche auf (*FR*)	*Lorry drivers have given up their blockade on the Brenner pass after a week*
Sie sahen soeben einen Bericht von unserem Korrespondenten in Moskau	*You have just been watching a report from our Moscow correspondent*

(ii) With common verbs, especially the auxiliaries, and in the passive:

In der letzten Zeit war sie sehr krank	*She has been very ill recently*
Er mußte heute kommen	*He has had to come today*
Noch nie wurde ein Auto so oft gebaut (*VW advert*)	*No car has ever been produced in such numbers*

(iii) In relative clauses:

Das sind die ersten Bilder der Unruhen in Peking, die uns erreichten	*These are the first pictures to reach us of the disturbances in Peking*

14.3.2 The use of the past and perfect tenses when recording actions or events which belong wholly to the past and without reference to the present

In English, we typically use the past tense to indicate that an action or event occurred entirely before the moment of speaking. In German, however, whilst the past tense is the norm in such contexts in the written language, the perfect predominates in everyday spoken language, especially in South Germany (roughly as far north as Frankfurt/Main), where the past tense is unknown in everyday speech. Thus, whilst we may read in Böll's novel *Billiard um halb zehn*:

Aber ich **hatte** Angst, **wartete**, bis auch die Putzfrau **ging**, und **ließ** mich in die Schule einschließen; es **gelang** mir nicht immer, denn meistens **warf** mich die Putzfrau hinaus, bevor sie **abschloß**, aber wenn es mir **gelang**, eingeschlossen zu werden, **war** ich froh.

what we might have heard in the corresponding spoken narrative would perhaps have run as follows:

Aber ich **habe** Angst **gehabt**, **habe gewartet**, bis auch die Putzfrau **gegangen ist**, und **habe** mich in die Schule einschließen **lassen**; es **ist** mir nicht immer **gelungen**, denn meistens **hat** mich die Putzfrau **hinausgeworfen**, bevor sie **abgeschlossen hat**, aber wenn es mir **gelungen ist**, eingeschlossen zu werden, **bin** ich froh **gewesen**.

The general tendency for the past tense to be used in writing and the perfect in speech is subject to certain qualifications, i.e.:

(a) The past tense is not uncommon in the spoken language of North and Central Germany in the following cases:
(i) With some frequently used verbs, i.e. with *sein, haben, bleiben, gehen, kommen* and *stehen*, with the modal auxiliaries, with verbs of saying, thinking and feeling and in the passive voice. In practice, the following alternatives are equally likely to be heard in this region:

Ich war vorige Woche in Bremen Ich bin vorige Woche in Bremen gewesen	*I was in Bremen last week*
Sie konnte gestern nicht kommen Sie hat gestern nicht kommen können	*She couldn't come yesterday*
Was sagten Sie? Was haben Sie gesagt?	*What did you say?*
Das alte Haus wurde abgerissen Das alte Haus ist abgerissen worden	*The old house was demolished*

The past tense of other verbs may occasionally be heard in spoken North and Central German, but, in general, rather less frequently than the perfect.
(ii) In subordinate clauses introduced by *als* or *wie*, and in any clause with the adverb *damals*:

Ich habe sie bemerkt, als sie aus der Straßenbahn ausstieg	*I noticed her when she got out of the tram*
Ich habe gehört, wie sie die Treppe herunterkam	*I heard her coming down the stairs*
Damals mußten wir alle Ersatzkaffee trinken	*At that time we all had to drink coffee substitute*

(iii) To record a state, or a habitual or repeated action in the past:

Die Rechnung lag auf dem Balkon	*The bill was lying on the balcony*
Bei uns in der alten Heimat dauerten die Sommerferien länger als hier	*In our old homeland the summer holidays used to last longer than they do here*
Ich habe gewußt, daß sein Vater trank	*I knew his father used to drink*

(b) There is a clear tendency for a longer narrative to start with a perfect, and then continue in the past
The perfect is used to set the scene, as it were. This usage is not only found in spoken north and central German, but also in writing, especially in newspaper reports, e.g.:

10 Tage nach der Jumbo-Katastrophe in Japan **ist** schon wieder eine Boeing **explodiert**. 54 Urlauber **starben** gestern in einem flammenden Inferno auf dem Flughafen Manchester (England). Als ihr Jet nach Korfu (Griechenland) starten **wollte**, **wurde** das linke Triebwerk krachend zerfetzt. Sofort **brannte** die Maschine wie eine Riesenfackel. Im Rumpf eingeschlossene Urlauber **trampelten** andere tot. (*BILD*)

(c) The perfect is sometimes used as a narrative tense in written German
The perfect may be used deliberately to lend a rather more colloquial tone to a passage, but, particularly outside the realm of fiction, it is quite

regularly treated as a simple alternative to the past and used for personal reasons relating to style, emphasis and sentence rhythm, as in the following text from a feature article, cited by Lockwood (1987:239):

In Wolfenbüttel **hat** ein Herzog namens Julius, der von 1568 bis 1589 sein Herzogtum **regierte**, den Grundstock für eine weltberühmte Bibliothek **gelegt**. Julius, der in Köln und Löwen **studiert hat**, **sammelte** seit frühester Jugend Bücher.

In practice, the past could be substituted for any of the perfect tenses in this passage, or vice-versa, without any significant change in meaning.

NB: It is for such stylistic reasons that the *du* and *ihr* past tense forms of many verbs tends to be avoided, since they can sound rather unwieldy. Thus, *du hast gearbeitet, du hast geschossen, ihr habt gebadet* will usually be preferred to *du arbeitetest, du schossest* and *ihr badetet*, etc.

14.3.3 Further uses of the past tense

In these, the past is not interchangeable with the perfect.

(a) To relate a state or activity which began in the past and is still in progress at a more recent point in the past

This is the equivalent in past time of the use of the present with *seit* phrases and the like, cf. 14.2.2. In English the pluperfect (especially the pluperfect progressive) is used in such sentences:

Seitdem ich ihn kannte, besuchte ich ihn jeden Sonntag	*Since I had known him, I had been visiting him every Sunday*
Ich wartete schon zwei Stunden auf sie ⎫ Ich wartete seit zwei Stunden auf sie ⎭	*I had been waiting for her for two hours*

Similar exceptions to those for the present apply here, too, in that the pluperfect, not the past, is used in negative statements or when referring to a series of actions or states:

Seitdem ich ihn kannte, hatten wir uns nie gestritten	*Since I had known him, we had never quarrelled*
Ich hatte ihm seit Jahren zugeredet, sein Haus zu verkaufen	*I had been urging him for years to sell his house*

(b) With the sense of a future-in-the-past

Here, the past is a (much less frequently used) alternative to the *würde*-form of 'Konjunktiv II', (the so-called 'conditional'), in the same way that the present may be used with a future meaning, cf. 14.2.3:

Die Felsennase raste auf mich zu. Sekunden noch, dann überrollte und begrub uns die Lawine (*Mundstock*) (more usual: *dann würde uns die Lawine überrollen und begraben*)	*The sharp crag was rushing towards us. A few more seconds and the avalanche would roll over us and bury us*

(c) To refer to the present

This usage is chiefly restricted to a few set phrases, where information already given in the past is recalled:

Wie war ihr Name doch gleich?	*What was your name again?*
Wer erhielt das Eisbein?	*Who is getting the knuckle of pork?*
Herr Ober, ich bekam noch ein Bier	*Waiter, I did order another beer*

14.3.4 Further uses of the perfect

In the following uses, the past cannot substitute for the perfect.

(a) As an alternative to the future perfect
The perfect is very commonly used in the sense of a future perfect, as long as the time reference is clear from the context, in the same way that the present can be employed to refer to the future, cf. 14.2.2:

Bis morgen um diese Zeit habe ich alles geregelt	*By this time tomorrow I shall have settled everything*
Bald habe ich den Brief geschrieben	*I'll have written the letter soon*

If the future perfect is used in such sentences, e.g. *Bis morgen um diese Zeit werde ich alles geregelt haben*, there tends to be an additional sense of a prediction, a supposition or a possibility, cf. 14.4.2.

NB: The perfect is normal in subordinate time clauses with future reference in both English and German, e.g.:

Wenn ich von ihm gehört habe, werde ich dir schreiben	*When I've heard from him, I shall write to you*

<u>Very</u> occasionally, a future perfect is found in such sentences in German, e.g.:

Ich will fortgehen, wenn ich genug gelesen haben werde (*Andersch*)	*I intend to leave when I have read enough*

(b) To indicate a characteristic state
Because the perfect is often used to signal the present result of a past action, it can be used in German to indicate an action whose completion can be taken to define a particular person or thing. This usage, which has no direct equivalent in English, is particularly common in technical and legal language:

Ein Unglück ist schnell geschehen	*Accidents happen quickly* (i.e. they are finished before you've realized it)
Ein Akademiker hat studiert	*A graduate is a person who has completed a course of studies*
Die Mannschaft, die zuerst 50 Punkte erreicht hat, ist Sieger	*The first team to reach 50 points is the winner*

14.4 The future and the future perfect

14.4.1 Both the future and the future perfect are used less frequently in German than in English simply to refer to future time
As long as the time reference is clear from the context, German tends to prefer the present tense to the future and the perfect to the future perfect, cf. 14.2.3 and 14.3.4a.

14.4.2 When the future and future perfect tenses are used in German, they usually convey the idea of a prediction, an intention, a supposition or a probability
This is inevitably so when the future tense is employed with reference to the present and the future perfect to the past, as is frequently the case, as with the corresponding English tenses. But these senses are usually also present even when these tenses are used with future reference:

Morgen wird es bestimmt schneien	*It will definitely snow tomorrow*
Ich werde es heute abend noch erledigen	*I am going to finish it tonight*
Sie wird bereits zu Hause sein	*She'll be home already*
Astrid wird auch noch kommen wollen	*Astrid will want to come too*
Unsere Mannschaft wird in Hamburg gewinnen	*Our team will win in Hamburg*
Er ist nicht gekommen. Er wird wieder zu viel zu tun haben	*He hasn't come. He'll have too much to do again*
Morgen wird er die Arbeit beendet haben	*He'll (probably) have finished the work tomorrow*
Sie wird den Zug verpaßt haben	*She'll have missed the train*
Sie wird sich gestern einen neuen Hut gekauft haben	*She'll have bought a new hat yesterday*

When used to express a probability, these tenses are very often used with the particle *wohl*, cf. 10.35.1, e.g.:

Sie wird wohl bereits zu Hause sein	*She'll most likely already be at home*
Astrid wird wohl auch noch kommen wollen	*Astrid will (probably) want to come too*
Sie wird wohl schon nach München gefahren sein	*She'll (probably) already have left for Munich*

NB: This sense of the future and future perfect is very similar to the meaning of *dürfte*, cf. 17.2.2, so that *Sie wird wohl bereits zu Hause sein* and *Sie wird wohl schon nach München gefahren sein* have much the same meaning as *Sie dürfte bereits zu Hause sein* and *Sie dürfte schon nach München gefahren sein*.

14.5   The pluperfect

14.5.1 The pluperfect is chiefly used in German to indicate a past within the past

This usage corresponds closely to that of the English pluperfect:

Wir warteten, bis der Zug abgefahren war	*We waited until the train had left*
Sie kamen zu spät, denn das Hochwasser hatte den Damm schon überflutet	*They came too late, as the high water had already flooded over the embankment*
Das bemerkte man erst, nachdem man Platz genommen hatte (*Morgner*)	*You only noticed that after you had sat down*

NB: (i) The perfect is occasionally used in written German where one would expect a pluperfect in order to emphasize the immediacy of a state or an action. The effect is rather similar to that of the 'historic present', cf. 14.2.4, e.g.:

Dann seufzte sie auf eine Weise, die mir deutlich machte, wie alt sie geworden ist (*Böll*)	*Then she sighed in a way which made it clear to me how old she had become*

(ii) In literary German the past is occasionally used for an expected pluperfect, for stylistic reasons, e.g.:

. . . doch ergab der Befund jene hoffnungslose Krankheit, die man vermutete (*Dürrenmatt*)	*. . . but the investigation revealed the terminal disease which had been suspected*

14.5.2 The pluperfect is sometimes used in colloquial German simply to refer to the past,

i.e. the pluperfect occurs where a simple past or perfect would be expected:

Eva hatte dich gesucht	*Eva was looking for you*
Wer war das gewesen?	*Who was that?*

This 'pseudo-pluperfect', as Lockwood (1987:241) calls it, is a fairly recent development, but it seems increasingly common in everyday speech. DUDEN (1984:§240) considers it to be substandard.

14.5.3   Complex pluperfect forms

In South Germany, where the forms of the simple past tense have been lost in the spoken language, the pluperfect is commonly formed with the perfect of the auxiliary verb *haben*, and one hears, for example, *Ich habe ihn gesehen gehabt* for standard German *Ich hatte ihn gesehen*.

NB: Similar constructions with verbs which take *sein* (e.g. *Ich bin nach Zürich gefahren gewesen* for *Ich war nach Zürich gefahren*), though not unknown, are markedly less frequent outside dialect.

Forms like this have now spread and they are to be heard in the spoken language everywhere. They are most common where emphasis is needed on the fact that an action has been completed, being used instead of an expected perfect or pluperfect, e.g.:

Ich habe es ihm gesagt gehabt	*I (really) have told him*
Sie hatte den Schlüssel vergessen gehabt	*She had forgotten her key*

Although primarily colloquial, generally regarded as non-standard, e.g. by DUDEN (1985:283), and best avoided by the foreign learner, they are by no means unknown in written prose:

Er dachte: Du kannst jetzt nichts gesehen haben, du kannst wegdrücken...und **hast** bloß den Anschluß **verloren gehabt** und bist kein Jäger (*Gaiser*)
Wir **haben** uns alle schon daran **gewöhnt gehabt**, daß nichts geschieht, aber immer etwas geschehen soll (*Musil*)

14.6 German equivalents for the English progressive tenses

14.6.1 There are no progressive tenses in German,

i.e. none which correspond to the English tenses with *be* and an *ing*-form. Thus, we cannot express the distinction between, say, the progressive *He is singing well* and the habitual *He sings well* in terms of different forms of the verb. In many cases this distinction can be ignored in German and we can simply use *Er singt gut* for both these English sentences.

NB: The English perfect progressive is often used to indicate that an action beginning in the past is still going on at the moment of speaking, e.g. *I have been waiting here for an hour*. In this 'up-to-now' sense German uses the simple present tense, e.g. *Ich warte schon eine Stunde hier*, as explained in 14.2.2.
In similar contexts with reference to past time, German uses the simple past tense for the English pluperfect progressive, cf. 14.3.3a.

14.6.2 Ways of indicating continuous action in German

There are nevertheless occasions where it is desirable to indicate in German that we are dealing with a continuous action. For instance, an English sentence like *He was reading 'War and Peace' yesterday* implies that he didn't finish reading it, whereas to say in German *Gestern las er ‚Krieg und Frieden'* or *Gestern hat er ‚Krieg und Frieden' gelesen* could naturally be taken to mean that he did finish it. In such cases, a number of possibilities are available in German, depending on the context and the individual verb used, i.e.:

(a) By using an appropriate adverb,
especially *eben* or *gerade*, e.g.:

Ich schreibe **eben** Briefe	*I'm writing letters*
Er rasiert sich **gerade**	*He's shaving*

With verbs of motion, *schon* or *gleich* can often be used, e.g.:

Ich fahre **schon**	*I'm leaving*
Sie kommt **gleich**	*She's coming*

Other adverbs may serve in other contexts, e.g.:

Ich habe ihn **letzthin** zweimal in der Woche gesehen	*I've been meeting him twice a week (recently)*
Ich kümmere mich **eben mal** darum	*I'm seeing to it now*

NB: The sense of habitual or repeated action expressed by a simple present tense in English may also be indicated by an adverb in German, e.g.:

Damals stand ich **immer** um sechs auf	*In those days I got up at six*
Sie spielt **meistens** gut	*She (usually) plays well*

(b) By using (*gerade/eben*) *dabei sein* followed by an infinitive with *zu*:

Ich bin **gerade dabei**, das Zimmer ein bißchen aufzuräumen	*I'm just tidying the room up a bit*
Gestern war er **gerade dabei**, ‚Krieg und Frieden' zu lesen	*He was reading 'War and Peace' yesterday*

(c) By using *beim* with an infinitive noun:

Als seine Frau zurückkam, war er **beim Kochen**	*When his wife returned, he was cooking*
Wir waren **beim Kartenspielen**, als er klingelte	*We were playing cards when he rang the bell*

This construction cannot be used if the verb has an adverb or an object with it, unless, as in the second example, a compound is possible.

In the north-west and the Rhineland, *am* is often used with an infinitive noun, e.g.:

Wir sind **am Arbeiten**	*We're working*
In Köln ist es immer **am Regnen**	*It's always raining in Cologne*

This form is regional and colloquial. DUDEN (1985:44) considers it non-standard.

(d) By using a noun with a prepositional phrase:

Wir sind an der Arbeit	*We're working*
Er liest in der Zeitung	*He's reading the newspaper*
Sie strickte an einem Strumpf	*She was knitting a stocking*

(e) By using a different verb

A number of German verbs, particularly those with prefixes, imply the completion of an action. Others, especially those without prefixes, do not necessarily imply that the action has finished and may in certain contexts correspond more closely to the sense of an English progressive, e.g.:

Sie erkämpften die Freiheit ihres Landes (i.e. they were successful)	*They fought for their country's freedom*
Sie kämpften für die Freiheit ihres Landes	*They were fighting for their country's freedom*
Wir aßen die Würste auf	*We ate the sausages (up)*
Wir aßen die Würste	*We were eating the sausages*
Sie erstiegen den Berg	*They climbed the mountain*
Sie stiegen auf den Berg	*They were climbing the mountain*

    (i.e. in the process of climbing, or only part of the way)

15   The passive

The active and passive voices differ in the perspective from which an action or state is viewed. Using the passive allows us to talk about an activity without mentioning who is doing it (the 'agent'). In an active sentence like *Er liest das Buch* we are told clearly who is doing what, whereas in a passive sentence like *Das Buch wird gelesen* we are informed about what is going on without the agent being identified.

There are two passives in German, using the auxiliary verbs *werden* or *sein* together with the past participle. The conjugation of both is given in full in 12.4. The use of the *werden*-passive is explained in 15.1. It expresses a process and is more closely related in meaning to the corresponding active voice. The use of the *sein*-passive is explained in 15.2. It is more restricted in use (the *werden*-passive is four times more frequent) and expresses a state.

German also has a wide range of alternative ways of expressing passives. Many of these are very common, and they are treated in detail in 15.4.

15.1 The *werden*-passive

15.1.1 The *werden*-passive has the same range of tense and mood forms as the active voice

The full conjugation of these in the indicative is given in 12.4.1, in the subjunctive in 12.5.

(a) In the main, the use of the tenses in the passive is the same as in the active, i.e. as explained in chapter 14, with the following qualifications:
(i) The future tense is uncommon in practice, and the present tense tends to be preferred unless there is a serious risk of being misunderstood, cf. 14.2.3, e.g.:

Das Buch wird nächste Woche gelesen   *The book will be read next week*

The future form (e.g. *Das Buch wird gelesen werden*) is only needed if

292

there is nothing else in the context which points unambiguously to the future.

(ii) The future perfect is virtually never used, the perfect (cf. 14.3.4a) or another construction (cf. 15.4) being used in its place, e.g.:

Bis sieben Uhr wird man mich von dem Ergebnis benachrichtigen	*I shall have been informed of the result by seven o'clock*

(iii) The past tense is quite commonly used rather than a perfect in both written and spoken German, cf. 14.3.1b and 14.3.2a.

(b) Imperative forms of the *werden*-passive are scarcely ever used
Thus, we rarely encounter, for example, *Werde gelobt!* On the other hand, the imperative of the *sein*-passive is by no means unusual, cf. 15.2.1.

15.1.2 The *werden*-passive can be formed from most transitive verbs,

i.e those which govern a direct object in the accusative case, cf. 18.3.1. The direct object of the active verb becomes the subject in the corresponding passive construction:

Mein Vater liest **das Buch**	*My father is reading the book*
→ **Das Buch** wird (von meinem Vater) gelesen	*The book is being read (by my father)*
Der starke Verkehr hielt **mich** auf	*The heavy traffic held me up*
→ **Ich** wurde (durch den starken Verkehr) aufgehalten	*I was held up (by the heavy traffic)*
Meine Schwester hat **diesen Brief** geschrieben	*My sister has written this letter*
→ **Dieser Brief** ist (von meiner Schwester) geschrieben worden	*This letter has been written (by my sister)*

NB: For the use of *von* or *durch* for English 'by', see 15.3.

15.1.3 Only the accusative object of an active verb can become the subject of the corresponding passive construction in German

This is an important restriction which does not apply in English, where we have no cases. It means that the dative object, the genitive object or the prepositional object of a verb in the active can <u>never</u> become the subject of the corresponding passive. Thus:

(a) If verbs which take a dative, a genitive or a prepositional object are used in the passive, these objects remain in <u>the same form</u>
The passive is then 'subjectless', and the verb has the endings of the third person singular:

Die Zigeuner können **Ihnen** helfen	*The gypsies can help you*
→ **Ihnen** kann geholfen werden	*You can be helped*

Er hat **mir** empfohlen, eine Kur zu nehmen	*He has recommended me to take a of treatment at a spa*
→ **Mir** ist empfohlen worden, eine Kur zu nehmen	*I have been recommended to take a course of treatment at a spa*
Sie gedachten **der Toten**	*They remembered the dead*
→ **Der Toten** wurde gedacht	*The dead were remembered*
Meine Mutter sorgt **für die Kinder**	*My mother is taking care of the children*
→**Für die Kinder** wird gesorgt	*The children are being taken care of*

The pronoun *es* is inserted as a 'dummy subject' (cf. 3.6.7d) if no other element (e.g. the dative, genitive or prepositional object, or an adverb or adverb phrase) occupies the first position in a main clause, e.g.:

Es kann Ihnen geholfen werden
Es ist ihm empfohlen worden, eine Kur zu nehmen
Es wurde der Toten gedacht

NB: (i) This construction which is used with verbs which do not govern an accusative is essentially the same as the 'subjectless' passive which may be formed from any intransitive verb, cf. 15.1.5.
(ii) In practice, *gedenken* is the only verb which governs the genitive which can be used in the passive in modern German.

(b) With verbs which take a direct (accusative) and an indirect (dative) object, the indirect object must similarly remain in the dative in the passive in German.

In such cases, it is again the direct object of the active which must become the subject in the passive. This is different to English, where either the direct or the indirect object may become the subject of the passive:

Er gab dem alten Mann ein Paar Schuhe	*He gave the old man a pair of shoes*
→**Dem alten Mann** wurde ein Paar Schuhe gegeben	*The old man was given a pair of shoes*
Seine Eltern hatten **ihm** ein neues Fahrrad versprochen	*His parents had promised him a new bike*
→**Ihm** war ein neues Fahrrad versprochen worden	*He had been promised a new bike*

NB: An indirect object may become the subject of a passive construction with *bekommen* or *kriegen*, cf. 15.4.2.

(c) It is usually impossible to use infinitive clauses containing the passive infinitive of a verb governing the dative

The (understood) subject of an infinitive with *zu* must normally be the same as that of the verb in the main clause, cf. 13.2.2. This precludes the use of 'subjectless' passive infinitives. Thus:

Er konnte nicht hoffen, daß ihm geholfen wurde	*He could not hope to be helped*
Er besteht darauf, daß ihm geantwortet wird	*He insists on being answered*

A sentence like *Er konnte nicht hoffen, geholfen zu werden* is impossible, as the infinitive clause must have the same subject as the main clause.

15.1.4 A few transitive verbs cannot be used in the *werden*-passive

In most cases, similar restrictions apply in English, but the following should be noted:

(a) No passive is possible in German with verbs of knowing, containing, possessing and receiving, i.e.: *bekommen, besitzen, enthalten, erhalten, haben, kennen, kriegen, wissen.* Recourse must be had to paraphrases to give German equivalents for English passives with such verbs, e.g.:

Dieses Schloß gehört dem Grafen von Libowitz (i.e. NOT *wird . . . besessen*)	*This palace is owned by Count von Libowitz*
Ihr Brief traf gestern ein (i.e. NOT *wurde . . . erhalten*)	*Your letter was received yesterday*
Man wußte nicht, wie viele Kinder kommen würden	*It was not known how many children would come*

NB: *enthalten* may, however, be used in the *sein*-passive, e.g.:

Wieviel Essig ist in diesem Gefäß enthalten?	*How much vinegar is contained in this receptacle?*

(b) No passive can be formed directly from verbs which are constructed with a bare infinitive (cf. 13.3.1).
An alternative construction is required in German, e.g.:

Man hörte ihn singen	*He was heard singing*
Ein Vorbeigehender sah ihn in das Haus einbrechen	*He was seen breaking into the house by a passer-by*

(c) Reflexive verbs cannot be used in the passive

15.1.5 In German the *werden*-passive may be used without a grammatical subject to denote an activity in general

The agent is unspecified, i.e. there is no indication at all of who is doing it. The verb has the third person singular endings. This 'subjectless' passive construction is very widely used in both spoken and written German. Nothing comparable exists in English:

Sie hörten, wie im Nebenzimmer geredet wurde	*They heard someone talking in the next room*
Hier darf nicht geraucht werden	*Smoking is not allowed here*
Vor Hunden wird gewarnt	*Beware of dogs*
Heute ist mit den Bauarbeiten begonnen worden (*ARD*)	*They started building today*

(a) If no other element appears in first position in a main clause, the pronoun *es* is added as a 'dummy subject' (cf. 3.6.7d):

Es wurde auf den Straßen getanzt	*There was dancing in the streets*
Es wird besonders rücksichtslos geparkt (*ARD*)	*People are parking in a particularly inconsiderate way*

(b) A subjectless passive can also be formed from intransitive verbs
These form a notable exception to the general rule, which is valid for English, that the passive is restricted to use with transitive verbs:

Dann wurde auf den Straßen getanzt	*Then there was dancing in the streets*
An dem Abend wurde viel gesungen	*There was a lot of singing that evening*
Hier wird gelegen, gestöhnt, geliebt, gestorben (*Goes*)	*Here men lie, moan, love, die*

NB: This is essentially the same construction as that which must be used with verbs which do not govern a direct object in the accusative case, (and which, strictly speaking, are also intransitive), cf. 15.1.2.

(c) The subjectless passive is often used to give commands:

Jetzt wird gearbeitet!	*Let's get down to work now*
Jetzt wird nicht gelacht!	*No laughing now!*

15.2 The *sein*-passive

15.2.1 Forms of the *sein*-passive

The conjugation of verbs in the *sein*-passive is detailed in 12.4.2. In practice, only a restricted range of tenses and moods is in common use, i.e.:

Present	ich **bin** verletzt	**Past**	ich **war** verletzt
Konjunktiv I	ich **sei** verletzt	**Konjunktiv II**	ich **wäre** verletzt
Imperative	**Sei** gegrüßt!		

The future tense (e.g. *Die Bilder* **werden** morgen entwickelt **sein**) is infrequent, not least because we rarely have cause to refer to a state in the future, and, in any case, the present may be used to refer to the future unless there is a serious possibility of being misunderstood, cf. 14.2.3. The past tends to be used rather than the perfect, although the perfect is sometimes heard in spoken German and may occasionally be encountered in writing, e.g.:

Nicht selten **bin** ich versucht **gewesen**, einen Essay zu beginnen „Über die Grenzen des Wissenswerten" (*Hildesheimer*)	*I have not infrequently been tempted to begin an essay "On the limits of what is worth knowing"*

15.2.2 The *sein*-passive is used to indicate the <u>state</u> which the subject of the verb is in as the <u>result</u> of a previous action

This is reflected in the usual German term of *Zustandspassiv*. The *werden*-passive, on the other hand, is used to relate an action or process, hence the German term *Vorgangspassiv*. The following sentence, taken from Andersen (1990:196), illustrates the difference between the two passives:

Als ich um fünf kam, **war** die Tür **geschlossen**, aber ich weiß nicht, wann sie **geschlossen wurde**	*When I came at five the door was shut, but I don't know when it was shut*

In the first case, someone had already shut the door by the time I arrived, i.e. it was in a shut **state**, and thus we find the *sein*-passive. In the second case I am referring to the time when the **action** of shutting the door occurred, and the *werden*-passive has to be used.

Compare the following further examples:

Der Tisch wird gedeckt	*The table is being laid*
(i.e. someone is performing the action of laying the table)	
Der Tisch ist gedeckt	*The table is laid*
(i.e. someone has already laid it)	
Das Pferd wird an den Baum gebunden	*The horse is being tied to the tree*
(i.e. someone is carrying out the action at this moment, or does it regularly)	
Das Pferd ist an den Baum gebunden	*The horse is tied to the tree*
(i.e. someone has tied the horse to the tree)	
Die Stadt wurde 1944 zerstört	*The town was destroyed in 1944*
(i.e. the action took place in 1944)	
Die Stadt war zerstört	*The town was destroyed*
(i.e. someone had already destroyed it)	
Die Stadt wurde allmählich von Truppen umringt	*The town was gradually (being) surrounded by troops*
(i.e. the troops were in the process of surrounding it)	
Die Stadt war von Truppen umringt	*The town was surrounded by troops*
(i.e. the troops are already in position round the town)	

NB: As with the *werden*-passive, cf.15.1.2a, only the object of a transitive verb can become the subject of a *sein*-passive. With verbs which take a dative, genitive or prepositional object, a 'subjectless' construction must be used in the *sein*-passive, too, e.g.:

Damit ist dem Kranken nicht geholfen	*The patient has not been helped by that*
Für die Verletzten ist gesorgt	*The wounded are taken care of*

A major difficulty for English learners is that the English passive, which uses the auxiliary *be*, <u>looks</u> confusingly like the less common *sein*-passive. But, as the examples above show, the two German passives have quite distinct meanings and are very rarely interchangeable in standard German (although the difference is not always consistently maintained in substandard colloquial speech).

The following remarks are helpful in establishing whether it is appropriate to use the *sein*-passive:

(a) The *werden*-passive often corresponds to an English progressive form, whilst this is never the case with the *sein*-passive
As the above examples show, this is especially the case in the present tense.

(b) As the *sein*-passive relates the state resulting from a previous action, its meaning is very close to that of the perfect tense (cf. 14.3.1.)
This means, for example, that the difference in meaning between the following pairs of sentences may be very slight:

Das Haus ist gebaut	–	Das Haus ist gebaut worden
Die Stadt war zerstört	–	Die Stadt war zerstört worden

For this reason, the idiomatic English equivalent of a German *sein*-passive is quite often a perfect or pluperfect rather than a present or a past, e.g.:

Ihre Fotos sind entwickelt	*Your photos have been developed*
Das Gesetz war schon am 8. Februar	*The law had already been passed*
verabschiedet	*on the 8th of February*

(c) In the *sein*-passive, the past participle is essentially descriptive,
i.e. it is used with the force of an adjective describing the state of the subject of the verb. Thus *geöffnet* in the sentence *Die Tür ist geöffnet* is being used with much the same function as *offen* in *Die Tür ist offen*. Compare also:

Der Brief ist geschrieben	–	Der Brief ist fertig
Die Stadt war zerstört	–	Die Stadt war kaputt

(d) As the *sein*-perfect expresses a state resulting from a previous action, it can only be used with verbs whose action produces a clear result of some kind,
e.g. *verletzen, zerstören*, etc. Cf. the following examples:

Meine Hand ist verletzt	*My hand is injured*
(and you can see the resulting injury)	
Mein Wagen ist beschädigt	*My car is damaged*
(and you can see the resulting damage)	

By contrast, verbs whose action does not involve some kind of tangible or visible result, like *bewundern* or *zeigen*, cannot be used in the *sein*-passive at all, as admiring or showing do not produce a result. Other common verbs which similarly cannot be used in the *sein*-passive are:

anbieten	*offer*	bemerken	*notice*	brauchen *need*		erinnern	*remind*
loben	*praise*	schmeicheln	*flatter*	schulden	*owe*	schicken	*send*

NB: the *sein*- and *werden*-passive are used with *geboren* as follows:
   Ich bin geboren is used when no other circumstances or only the place of birth are mentioned, e.g.:
   Wann sind Sie geboren?   Ich bin in Hamburg geboren

Ich wurde geboren is used if further circumstances, or the date, are mentioned, e.g.:
Ich wurde im Jahre 1965 in Hamburg geboren.
Als ich geboren wurde, schneite es.
Referring to people who are dead, either passive may be used, e.g.:
Goethe wurde/war im Jahre 1749 in Frankfurt geboren.

15.2.3 The *sein*-passive may also be used to indicate a continuing state:

Diese Insel ist von Kannibalen bewohnt	*The island is inhabited by cannibals*
Die Stadt ist von Bergen umgeben	*The town is surrounded by hills*
Die Häuser sind nur durch einen Drahtzaun von der Müllverbrennungsanlage getrennt	*The houses are only separated from the incinerating plant by a wire fence*
Das Eßzimmer ist von einem großen Kronleuchter beleuchtet	*The dining-room is lit by a large chandelier*
Die Bücher in der alten Bibliothek sind mit Staub bedeckt	*The books in the old library are covered with dust*

Here we are not dealing with the result of a process, but with a lasting state, often a permanent one. In such sentences, and <u>only</u> in such sentences, the *werden*-passive and the *sein*-passive may freqently be interchangeable. Thus, the following are possible alternatives to the first four examples above:

Diese Insel wird von Kannibalen bewohnt   Die Stadt wird von Bergen umgeben
Die Häuser werden nur durch eine Drahtzaun von der Müllverbrennungsanlage
    getrennt
Das Eßzimmer wird von einem großen Kronleuchter beleuchtet

But <u>not</u>, however, *Die Bücher in der alten Bibliothek* **werden** *mit Staub bedeckt*, as that would suggest someone is covering them with dust!

15.3 *von* or *durch* with the passive

A major motivation for the use of the passive rather than the active is to leave the agent of the action (i.e. the subject of the active verb) unspecified. However, if required, the agent may be included in a prepositional phrase introduced by *von* or *durch*, corresponding to English *by*. These occur chiefly with the *werden*-passive; with the *sein*-passive they are only employed when it is a matter of a continuing state, as in 15.2.3.

(a) *von* is used to indicate the doer or agent of the action
This is most often a person, less commonly a thing:

Ich war von meinem Onkel gewarnt worden	*I had been warned by my uncle*
Sie wurde von zwei Polizeibeamten verhaftet	*She was arrested by two police-officers*
Die Brücke wird von vier Betonpfeilern getragen	*The bridge is supported by four concrete pillars*

(b) *durch* **indicates the means by which the action is carried out**
This is most often a thing, which is the involuntary cause of the occurrence, but it may be a person acting as an intermediary:

Die Ernte wurde durch den Hagel vernichtet	*The crop was destroyed by hail*
Ich wurde durch den starken Verkehr aufgehalten	*I was held up by the heavy traffic*
Ich wurde durch einen Boten benachrichtigt	*I was informed by a messenger*

(the messenger was an intermediary for someone else's message)

Die Provinz wurde durch Flüchtlinge neu besiedelt	*The province was resettled by refugees*

(*durch* can be used because it was ultimately some other, unnamed person(s) who instigated the resettlement of the province)

NB: *durch*, not *von*, is used after a noun with verbal force:

die Entdeckung Amerikas durch Kolumbus	*the discovery of America by Columbus*
der Ersatz der Muskelkraft durch die Maschine	*the replacement of muscle power by machines*

(c) The difference between *von* and *durch* is most clear when both are used in the same sentence:

Ich war von meinem Onkel durch seinen Sohn gewarnt worden	*I had been warned by my uncle through his son*

(My uncle is doing the warning, his son is the intermediary)

Die Kaserne wurde von Terroristen durch einen Sprengstoffanschlag zerstört	*The barracks were destroyed by terrorists in a bomb attack*

(Terrorists destroyed it, the bombs were the means)

(d) The distinction between *von* and *durch* is not always consistently upheld in practice
It is often not fully apparent whether one is dealing with the 'agent' or the 'means', and there is considerable hesitation between *von* and *durch*. Helbig and Heinrich (1983:31) point out that 'most native speakers' would accept either alternative in the following cases:

Die Brücke ist von Pionieren/ durch Pioniere gesprengt worden	*The bridge has been demolished by sappers*
Der Baum ist von dem Blitz/durch den Blitz getroffen worden	*The tree has been struck by lightning*

NB: The degree of uncertainty in current usage can be gauged from the fact that in DUDEN (1985:515) we read 'Man kann nicht sagen: *Der Baum ist* **durch den Blitz** *getroffen worden*!' In practice, unless it is <u>absolutely</u> clear that one is dealing with the 'doer' or the 'means', *von* and *durch* are effectively interchangeable in modern German.

(e) A phrase with the preposition *mit* is used to indicate the <u>instrument</u> used to perform an action:

Das Schiff wurde mit einem Torpedo versenkt	*The ship was sunk by a torpedo*

Das Schloß mußte mit einem Hammer   *The lock had to be opened with*
    geöffnet werden   *a hammer*
Dieser Brief ist mit der Hand   *This letter was written by hand*
    geschrieben

NB: *durch* (but never *von*) may replace *mit* when inanimate instruments are involved. Compare the following alternative for the first two examples above:
Das Schiff wurde durch ein Torpedo versenkt

15.4 Alternative passive constructions

Although the passive is widely used in German, particularly in the written language, and it is certainly not to be 'avoided' as a matter of course, as some handbooks suggest, it tends to be less frequent than in English. One reason for this is that we often employ a passive in English in order to put something other than the subject into initial position in the sentence. In German, with its more flexible word-order, this can be done quite simply by shifting the elements round in the sentence, e.g.:

Diesen Roman hat Thomas Mann während   **This novel** *was written by Thomas*
    eines Aufenthaltes in Italien   *Mann during a stay in Italy*
    geschrieben

In German, the object can be placed before the verb and the subject after it without having to resort to a passive construction, as in English. For further details on this, see 21.2.5b.

German also has a wide range of alternative means of expressing passives. The most frequent and useful of these are given in the remainder of this section.

15.4.1 The indefinite pronoun *man*, cf. 5.5.18, is often employed in German if the subject is truly non-specific

English tends naturally to use a passive in such cases:

Man sagt, daß . . .   *It is said that*
Man hatte ihn davor gewarnt   *He had been warned about it*
Das macht man nicht   *That's not done*

15.4.2 A passive construction may be formed using the verbs *bekommen* or *kriegen*

(a) By using this construction the indirect object of a verb governing both a direct and an indirect object may be made the subject of a passive
Cf. 15.1.3b. The English equivalent may be a passive or a construction with *have* and a past participle:

Ich bekomme/kriege das Geld   *I am paid the money regularly/*
    regelmäßig ausgezahlt   *I have the money paid to me*
                                   regularly

Wir haben viel gezeigt bekommen/ gekriegt	*We were shown a lot/We had a lot shown to us*
Sie bekam/kriegte den Schrank frei Haus geliefert	*She had the wardrobe delivered free*

NB: Less commonly, the verb *erhalten* is used in this construction, e.g.: Sie erhielt den Schrank frei Haus geliefert

This construction is chiefly found in spoken German (especially when used with *kriegen*), but it is not infrequent in writing. It may be used with most verbs governing a direct and indirect object (but <u>not</u> with *geben*).

(b) The passive with *bekommen* or *kriegen* is sometimes found with verbs which just govern the dative, e.g.:

Sie bekam gratuliert	*She was congratulated*
Vera bekommt von dir geholfen	*Vera is being helped by you*
Er bekam von niemandem widersprochen	*He was contradicted by nobody*

This usage is still largely restricted to spoken German and not all Germans accept it as standard. It is only possible with verbs which express an action, as in the examples. Thus, it cannot be used with such verbs as *ähneln, begegnen, gefallen, gehören* or *schaden*.

15.4.3 A reflexive verb is a frequent possible alternative to a passive:

Der Schlüssel hat sich gefunden	*The key has been found*
Mein Verdacht hat sich bestätigt	*My suspicions have been confirmed*
Die Startflagge senkt sich	*The starting flag is being lowered*
Wie erklärt sich das?	*How is that explained*

Such reflexive constructions are often found in association with an adverb or adverbial phrase:

Das lernt sich rasch	*That is quickly learned*
Das erklärt sich leicht	*That is easily explained*
Das Buch verkaufte sich in Rekordauflagen	*The book was sold in record numbers*

NB that a reflexive verb is the natural German equivalent of many English passives, e.g.:

sich ärgern	*be annoyed*	sich freuen	*be pleased*
sich schämen	*be ashamed*	sich verbinden	*be associated*

15.4.4 Many phrasal verbs have a passive meaning.

Such phrasal verbs comprise a verbal noun (especially in *-ung*) and a verb which has little real meaning in the context. The following verbs are frequently used to form such complex verb phrases with a passive sense: *erfahren, erhalten, finden, gehen, gelangen, kommen*:

eine große Vereinfachung erfahren (= sehr vereinfacht werden)	*be greatly simplified*

seine Vollendung finden	*be completed*
(= vollendet werden)	
zur Erörterung gelangen	*be discussed*
(= erörtert werden)	
in Vergessenheit geraten	*be forgotten*
(= vergessen werden)	
zur Anwendung kommen	*be used*
(= angewendet werden)	
Unsere Arbeit hat Anerkennung	*Our work was appreciated*
gefunden	
Der Wunsch ging in Erfüllung	*The wish was fulfilled*
Das Stück gelangte/kam zur Aufführung	*The play was performed*

NB: The use of such phrasal verbs is a very characteristic feature of modern formal written German. They have been much criticized by stylists as unnecessarily verbose. However, as DUDEN (1985:496) points out, they have nuances lacking in the simple verb. Thus, for example, *Das Stück gelangte zur Aufführung* strongly emphasizes the start of the action, whilst *Das Stück wurde aufgeführt* simply records that the action took place.

15.4.5 The infinitive with *zu* used after *sein* has passive meaning

Depending on the context, this construction has the sense of *können, müssen* or *sollen* followed by a passive infinitive, cf. 13.2.3:

Die Anträge sind im Rathaus abzuholen	*The applications may/must be collected from the town-hall/ are to be collected from the town-hall*
(= Die Anträge können/müssen im Rathaus abgeholt werden)	
Diese Frage ist noch zu erörtern	*This question must still be discussed/is still to be discussed*
(= Diese Frage muß noch erörtert werden)	
Dieser Text ist bis morgen zu übersetzen	*This text must be translated by tomorrow/This text is to be translated by tomorrow*
(= Dieser Text muß/soll bis morgen übersetzt werden)	

This construction can be turned into an extended adjective using a present participle, e.g. *diese noch zu erörternde Frage*, cf. 13.5.2.

15.4.6 The infinitive with *zu* after a number of other 'semi-auxiliary' verbs has a passive meaning

Depending on the individual verb used, these constructions have the sense of *können* or *müssen* followed by a passive infinitive. They are usually alternatives to the construction with *sein* explained in 15.4.5. See also 13.2.3 for further details:

(a) *bleiben* with a following infinitive expresses necessity:

Vieles bleibt noch zu erledigen	*Much still remains to be done*
(= Vieles muß noch erledigt werden)	

(b) *gehen* **with a following infinitive expresses possibility:**

Das Bild geht nicht zu befestigen   *The picture cannot be secured*
   (= Das Bild kann nicht befestigt werden)

This construction is restricted to informal colloquial speech.

(c) *stehen,* **used impersonally with a following infinitive, expresses necessity**
It is only used with a few verbs, principally *befürchten* and *erwarten*:

Es steht zu befürchten, daß sich   *It is to be feared that these*
   diese Vorfälle häufen   *incidents will occur increasingly*
   (= Es muß befürchtet werden, daß sich
   diese Vorfälle häufen)

(d) *es gibt* **with a following infinitive expresses necessity:**

Es gibt noch viel zu tun   *There's still a lot to be done*
   (= Vieles muß noch getan werden)

15.4.7 *sich lassen* with a following infinitive has a passive sense and expresses possibility,

i.e. it is the equivalent of *können* followed by a passive infinitive. This construction is very frequent in all registers:

Das läßt sich aber erklären   *But that can be explained*
   (= Das kann aber erklärt werden)
Dieses Problem läßt sich leicht lösen   *This problem can be solved easily*
   (= Dieses Problem kann leicht gelöst werden)
Das ließe sich aber ändern   *That might be altered, though*
   (= Das könnte geändert werden)

This construction is often used impersonally:

Hier läßt es sich gut leben   *It's a good life here*
Darüber läßt (es) sich streiten   *We can argue about that*

NB: This construction is normally only possible if the subject is a thing rather than a person. Reflexive *lassen* with a person as subject usually has the sense of 'cause' or 'permit', cf.13.3.1c, e.g.:
   Sie ließ sich die Haare schneiden   *She had her hair cut*
   Sie wollte sich nicht sehen lassen   *She didn't want to show herself*

15.4.8 *gehören* with a past participle has passive force and the sense of obligation or necessity

This construction is used mainly in colloquial German, chiefly in the south:

Dieser Kerl gehört eingesperrt   *That bloke ought to be locked up*
   (= Dieser Kerl sollte eingesperrt werden)

Dem gehört das deutlich gesagt   *He ought to be told that clearly*
  (= Ihm sollte das deutlich gesagt werden)

15.4.9 Adjectives in *-bar* from verbs can be used with *sein* to express a possibility with a passive sense

This usually corresponds to the use of adjectives in *-able/-ible* in English:

Diese Muscheln sind nicht eßbar   *These shellfish are not edible/*
  (= Diese Muscheln können nicht   *cannot be eaten*
  gegessen werden)
Dieses Argument ist nicht widerlegbar   *This argument is irrefutable/cannot*
  (= Dieses Argument kann nicht   *be refuted*
  widerlegt werden)
Das ist einfach nicht machbar mit   *That simply can't be done with a*
  einem solchen Wörterbuch   *dictionary like that*
  (= Das kann man mit einem solchen
  Wörterbuch nicht machen)

Adjectives with the suffixes *-lich* (from some verbs) or *-fähig* (from some verbal nouns) may have similar force:

Seine Antwort war unverständlich   *His answer was incomprehensible/*
  (= Seine Antwort konnte nicht   *could not be understood*
  verstanden werden)
Dieser Apparat ist nicht weiter   *This apparatus cannot be developed*
  entwicklungsfähig   *further*
  (= Dieser Apparat kann nicht weiter
  entwickelt werden)

16 The subjunctive mood

The grammatical category of 'mood' signals our attitude to what we are talking about

If we use the indicative mood, we are presenting something as a fact. If we use the subjunctive, on the other hand, we are characterizing an activity, event or state as unreal, possible or, at best, not necessarily true (hence the old German name of *Möglichkeitsform*). There are other ways of indicating this in German, for example by using one of the 'modal auxiliary' verbs (cf. chapter 17) or an adverb of manner like *vielleicht* 'perhaps', *wahrscheinlich* 'probably' or *vermutlich* 'presumably'. In English, where the subjunctive mood is all but defunct, we are limited to such ways of expressing possibility. But German has retained the subjunctive as a distinct category of the verb, with its own special endings and forms.

However, although many subjunctive forms are widely used in modern German, some forms and usages are effectively restricted to the formal written language, whilst others are nowadays wholly obsolete. There is much uncertainty among even educated native speakers and 'good' writers, so that we are often dealing with tendencies far more than hard and fast grammatical rules, and there is often a gulf between what people think they ought to say or write and their actual usage. In this chapter we concentrate on those usages which are most likely to be encountered in practice or needed when speaking and writing German.

Much has been written on the subjunctive, and no other aspect of German grammar has attracted so much attention from would-be linguistic regulators. Bausch (1979) gives a balanced account of modern usage, Jäger (1970) provides helpful recommendations based on current usage, and Buscha and Zoch (1984) is a detailed survey, with exercises for the foreign learner. Many of our examples have been gleaned from Fernandez-Bravo (1976).

16.1 Forms and tenses of the subjunctive

16.1.1 In English grammars of German, the forms of the German subjunctive are traditionally referred to by the names of the tenses,

i.e. present subjunctive (e.g. *es schlafe*), past subjunctive (e.g. *es schliefe*), perfect subjunctive (e.g. *es habe geschlafen*), etc. However, the use of these forms seldom reflects time differences in the same way as do the apparently corresponding tenses of the indicative. For this reason, almost all recent German grammars, e.g. DUDEN (1984:§253ff.), Engel (1988:418ff.), Schulz/Griesbach (1960:27 and 32–3), etc. nowadays prefer the terms 'Konjunktiv I' and 'Konjunktiv II', not least because this makes it easier to explain how the subjunctive is used, and classify the main forms as follows:

Konjunktiv I:
'present' subjunctive:	*es schlafe*
'perfect' subjunctive:	*es habe geschlafen*
'future' subjunctive:	*es werde schlafen*

Konjunktiv II:
'past' subjunctive:	*es schliefe*
'pluperfect' subjunctive:	*es hätte geschlafen*
'conditional'	*es würde schlafen*

NB: (i) Full details on the conjugation of verbs in the subjunctive are given in 12.5.
    (ii) As explained in 12.5.4, there is no essential difference in meaning between the 'past subjunctive' and the 'conditional' forms. Which one is used depends on the individual verb used and on register.

16.1.2 'Konjunktiv I' and 'Konjunktiv II' have distinct meanings and uses

These have nothing to do with time or tense; what are traditionally called the 'present subjunctive' and the 'past subjunctive' in fact both refer to the present. Compare:

(a) 'present' subjunctive:

Gisela sagte ihrer Mutter, sie **komme** um sechs in Berlin an

What she said was, using the present tense:

Ich komme um sechs in Berlin an.

The major use of the 'present subjunctive', and all the other 'Konjunktiv I' forms, is to mark indirect speech, cf. 16.2.

(b) 'past' subjunctive:

Wenn ich es **wüßte**, **könnte** ich es dir sagen

i.e. if I knew it <u>now</u>, I would be able to tell you
The 'past subjunctive', and all the other 'Konjunktiv II' forms are mainly used to indicate an unreal condition or a possibility, cf. 16.3.

16.1.3 Time differences are shown within both 'Konjunktiv I' and 'Konjunktiv II' by using compound forms.

(a) The 'perfect subjunctive' functions as the past tense of 'Konjunktiv I':

Gisela sagte ihrer Mutter, sie **sei** um sechs in Berlin **angekommen**

What she probably said was, using the past or perfect tense:

Ich kam um sechs in Berlin an *or* Ich bin um sechs in Berlin angekommen

(b) Similarly, the 'pluperfect subjunctive' is effectively the past tense of 'Konjunktiv II':

Wenn ich es **gewußt hätte**, **hätte** ich es dir sagen **können**

i.e. if I had known it <u>then</u>, I would have been able to tell you.

16.2 Indirect speech

16.2.1 In indirect (or 'reported') speech we report what someone said by incorporating it into a sentence of our own rather than quoting it in the original spoken form

In writing, we indicate direct speech (but not indirect speech) by using quotation marks. Compare the following English examples:

Direct speech:	She said, "I have written the letter".
Indirect speech:	She said that she had written the letter.

A number of cues tell us that we are dealing with indirect speech. It is introduced by a verb of saying, the conjunction *that* shows that what follows is dependent on the verb of saying, the pronoun is altered (from first to third person) and the tense is shifted to indicate that the letter had been written <u>before</u> she said she had done it.

In German, instead of shifting the tense, as in English, we can use forms of the subjunctive to mark indirect speech. Compare:

Direct speech:	Sie sagte: „Ich habe den Brief geschrieben".
Indirect speech:	Sie sagte, daß sie den Brief geschrieben **habe**.

Some of the other cues we saw for English may be present in German, too, but:
It is important to realize that Konjunktiv I is often alone sufficient to indicate indirect speech.
There is considerable variation in the use of the subjunctive to mark

indirect speech, and much uncertainty among native speakers. By way of introduction, we summarize the most important modern forms and usages here, indicating the sections where further details are given on the individual variants.

(a) Verb in the third person singular
Original direct speech: **Meine Frau liegt im Krankenhaus**
This is given in indirect speech in one of the following ways:
(i) Konjunktiv I:

Herr Gruber sagte, { seine Frau liege im Krankenhaus
daß seine Frau im Krankenhaus liege

This is the usual form in formal written German, especially if the conjunction *daß* is omitted (16.2.2a), but it is not used in colloquial speech (16.2.5b).
(ii) Konjunktiv II (simple form):

Herr Gruber sagte, { seine Frau läge im Krankenhaus
daß seine Frau im Krankenhaus läge

This is common in spoken German if the simple form of Konjunktiv II is still in current use (16.2.5a), and it is not unusual in writing (16.2.4b).
(iii) Konjunktiv II (*würde*-form)

Herr Gruber sagte, { seine Frau würde im Krankenhaus liegen
daß seine Frau im Krankenhaus liegen würde

This is usual in spoken German if the simple form of Konjunktiv II is obsolete (16.2.5c). It is frowned on (though not unknown) in written usage (16.2.4c).
(iv) Indicative:

Herr Gruber sagte, { seine Frau liegt im Krankenhaus
daß seine Frau im Krankenhaus liegt

This is the most current form in everyday spoken German (16.2.5a), and it is frequent in writing if the conjunction *daß* is present (16.2.4d).

(b) Verb in the third person plural
Original direct speech: **Meine Kinder liegen im Krankenhaus**
This is given in indirect speech in one of the following ways:
(i) Konjunktiv II (simple form)

Herr Gruber sagte, { seine Kinder lägen im Krankenhaus
daß seine Kinder im Krankenhaus lägen

This is the standard form in formal writing according to the 'replacement rule' (16.2.2b). It is also common in speech, as long as the one-word Konjunktiv II form is not obsolete (16.2.5a)

(ii) Konjunktiv II (*würde*-form)

Herr Gruber sagte,   { seine Kinder würden im Krankenhaus liegen
daß seine Kinder im Krankenhaus liegen würden

This is common in spoken German (16.2.5c) and may occur in written German (16.2.4c) if the simple Konjunktiv II form is unusual or (as in the case of weak verbs) identical with the past indicative.

(iii) Konjunktiv I = Indicative

Herr Gruber sagte,   { seine Kinder liegen im Krankenhaus
daß seine Kinder im Krankenhaus liegen

This may occur in written German if the 'replacement rule' is ignored (16.2.4a) and it is the most common form in spoken German (16.2.5a)

16.2.2 The 'standard rules' for the use of the subjunctive in indirect speech in formal written German

All modern grammars of German prescribe the following rules to be observed in the formal written language:

(a) Konjunktiv I should be used to mark indirect speech wherever possible, (i.e. where the forms of Konjunktiv I are different from those of the indicative). The tenses of the indicative in the original direct speech are converted into Konjunktiv I forms according to the following pattern:

Direct Speech		Indirect Speech
present	→	**present subjunctive**
Ich schreibe den Brief		Sie sagte, sie schreibe den Brief
I am writing the letter		*She said she was writing the letter*
future	→	**future subjunctive**
Ich werde den Brief schreiben		Sie sagte, sie werde den Brief schreiben
I shall write the letter		*She said she would write the letter*
past	→	**perfect subjunctive**
Ich schrieb den Brief		Sie sagte, sie habe den Brief geschrieben
I wrote the letter		*She said she had written the letter*
perfect	→	**perfect subjunctive**
Ich habe den Brief geschrieben		Sie sagte, sie habe den Brief geschrieben
I have written the letter		*She said she had written the letter*
pluperfect	→	**perfect subjunctive**
Ich hatte den Brief geschrieben		Sie sagte, sie habe den Brief geschrieben
I had written the letter		*She said she had written the letter*

NB: (i) If the original direct speech was in the pluperfect tense, a complex pluperfect form may be found in the corresponding indirect speech, e.g. *Sie sagte, sie **habe** den Brief* **geschrieben gehabt.**

(ii) If the present tense of the original direct speech refers to the future, cf. 14.2.3, the future subjunctive is often used in indirect speech, e.g.:

Sie heiratet bald   →   Sie sagte, sie werde bald heiraten
She will marry soon   *She said she would marry soon*

würde is often used for *werde* in such 'future-in-the-past' meanings, cf. 16.2.4b.

(b) If the form of Konjunktiv I is the same as that of the indicative, then Konjunktiv II should be used

The principle underlying this 'replacement rule' is that indirect speech should be marked by a distinct subjunctive form if possible. However, for most verbs except *sein*, the only distinct Konjunktiv I forms are those of the third person singular, cf. 12.5.1. The others are identical to those of the indicative and recourse is made to Konjunktiv II to provide a clear subjunctive form, e.g.:

Direct Speech		Indirect Speech
present	→	**past subjunctive**
Wir schreiben den Brief		Sie sagten, sie schrieben den Brief
We are writing the letter		*They said they were writing the letter*
future	→	**conditional**
Wir werden den Brief schreiben		Sie sagten, sie würden den Brief schreiben
We shall write the letter		*They said they would write the letter*
past	→	**pluperfect subjunctive**
Wir schrieben den Brief		Sie sagten, sie hätten den Brief geschrieben
We wrote the letter		*They said they had written the letter*
perfect	→	**pluperfect subjunctive**
Wir haben den Brief geschrieben		Sie sagten, sie hätten den Brief geschrieben
We have written the letter		*They said they had written the letter*

For the examples above, the Konjunktiv I forms *sie schreiben, sie werden schreiben* and *sie haben geschrieben* are not different from those of the indicative, and they are replaced by Konjunktiv II forms.

NB: This replacement rule is most usual in the third person plural. But it is also normal in the second person singular and plural, where the Konjunktiv I forms, e.g. *du machest*, *ihr machet* are widely regarded as artificial. Thus, we usually find *Sie meinten, du kämst* (not: *kommest*) *heute erst um sieben an.*

16.2.3 The 'standard rules' given in 16.2.2 are in practice most closely observed in newspapers

As Konjunktiv I shows a statement to be 'merely reported' without any commitment as to whether it is true or not, it is a handy way for newspapers to indicate what others have said:

Der Bundespressechef verwies darauf, daß in den kommenden Gesprächen noch manches verfeinert werden **könne** (*FAZ*)

The Federal information officer pointed out that some things could be refined in future discussions

Auf seine Eindrücke über den Stand des Bürgerkrieges – der besser **verliefe**, als es die Presse **darstelle**, erklärte Johnson – sollen sich die Beschlüsse stützen (*Welt*)

The decisions ought to be based on his impressions of the state of the civil war – which, Johnson declared, was going better than portrayed by the press

Konjunktiv I can be used on its own to mark reported speech without the need for the other cues (e.g. *He said that . . . , He went on to say that . . .*) which may be necessary in English. The following longer example illustrates the typical exploitation of this possibility in German journalism:

Die Bundesregierung **verhalte** sich „widerrechtlich", wenn sie DDR-Bürgern in ihrer Botschaft Aufenthalt **gewähre**, sagte der Sprecher des Ostberliner Ministeriums am Abend. Diese „grobe Einmischung in die souveränen Angelegenheiten der DDR" **könne** ebenso wie „Kampagnen, die bis zur versuchten Erpressung anderer Staaten ausarten, zu folgenreichen Konsequenzen führen". Bundesdeutsche Medien **führten** eine Kampagne, in die sich Berichten zufolge nun auch das Auswärtige Amt in Bonn **eingeschaltet habe**. (*Süddeutsche Zeitung 8.8.1989*)

Note the alternation of Konjunktiv I and Konjunktiv II forms in accordance with the standard rule and that, even in a main clause without any explicit verb of saying, the subjunctive on its own is enough to signal indirect speech.

16.2.4 Certain deviations from the 'standard rules' are frequently encountered in formal written German

This is especially the case in fiction and outside the field of newpapers and technical language in general.

(a) The 'replacement rule' is not always followed,
i.e. an ambiguous Konjunktiv I form, identical to the indicative, is used:

Die Verfügung des letzten deutschen Kaisers besagte, daß im Ruhrgebiet weder Universitäten noch Kasernen gebaut werden **dürfen** (*v.d. Grün*) (the standard rule would require *dürften*)	*The decree by the last German emperor declared that neither universities nor barracks were allowed to be built in the Ruhr*

An ambiguous form may often be preferred if the 'replacement rule' would involve an archaic Konjunktiv II form, as in the following newspaper example given by Lockwood (1987:272):

Der Unterhändler sagte, er hoffe, daß die Vernunft siege und Verhandlungen **beginnen** (the standard rule would require the obsolete form *begönnen*)	*The negotiator said he hoped that reason would prevail and talks would begin*

(b) Konjunktiv II is used even where a distinct Konjunktiv I form is available,
i.e. in the third person singular of most verbs except *sein*:

Er versicherte widerholt, daß man förmlich dabei in den Herrenreiter hineinsähe (*Mann*) (The standard rule would prescribe the Konjunktiv I form *sehe*)	*He assured me repeatedly that one could really see right down into the jockey* (when he coughed)

Sie sagte, ihr Vater **schliefe** erst gegen morgen richtig ein und **würde** bis neun im Bett bleiben, und sie müsse . . . den Laden aufmachen (*Böll*)	*She said that her father didn't get* *to sleep properly till the morning* *and he would stay in bed till nine* *and that she had to open the shop*

(By the standard rule one would expect *schlafe* and *werde* here)

The following remarks should also be noted in respect of this usage:
(i) Konjunktiv II is in the main typical of less formal language, cf. 16.2.5, but it is by no means uncommon in writing, where Konjunktiv II may alternate randomly with the Konjunktiv I prescribed by the standard rule. There is no difference in meaning between Konjunktiv I and Konjunktiv II when used in indirect speech.
(ii) The *würde*-form of Konjunktiv II (the 'conditional') is commonly used for expected *werde* where the sense is of a 'future-in-the-past':

Er glaubte, er würde schon eine Lösung finden	*He thought he would surely find* *a solution*

(c) The *würde*-form of Konjunktiv II (the 'conditional') is used

Despite being frowned on by purists, who still try to insist on the use of simple forms of Konjunktiv II, the *würde*-form is used in indirect speech in writing, although in general it is more typical of everyday spoken language. It is most common with those strong verbs whose simple Konjunktiv II forms are obsolete (cf. 12.6) or with weak verbs, the Konjunktiv II of which is identical with the past indicative and thus fails to provide a clear subjunctive form to mark indirect speech. It may occur:
(i) for a Konjunktiv II required by the replacement rule (cf. 16.2.2b):

Alle zwei Wochen, erzählt er, würden sie eine Band engagieren (*Zeit*)	*Every two weeks, he tells us, they* *hire a group*
Unrichtig ist ferner, daß diese acht Türken in einer Dachkammer hausen würden (*BILD*)	*It is furthermore incorrect to* *assert that these eight Turks were* *living in an attic*
Sieben Leser gaben an, sie würden regelmäßig Fachzeitschriften lesen (*MM*)	*Seven readers declared that they* *regularly read specialist journals*

(Here the conditional is preferred to the obsolescent *läsen*)

(ii) even where a distinct Konjunktiv I form is available (cf. 16.2.4b):

Sie sagte, sie würde dieses Wörterbuch nie benützen	*She said she never used that* *dictionary*

(Konjunktiv II *benützte* is identical with the past tense. The standard rule would stipulate *benütze*)

Er meinte, dieser Bach würde in den Neckar fließen	*He thought this stream flowed into* *the Neckar*

(The Konjunktiv II form *flösse* is obsolete. The standard rule would require *fließe*)

(d) The indicative is used rather than the subjunctive
In general, the use of the indicative in indirect speech is typical of less

formal registers. However, it is by no means unusual in written German, in particular:

(i) If the indirect speech is in a subordinate clause introduced by the conjunction *daß* after a verb of saying or thinking:

Der Kanzler erklärte, daß er zu weiteren Verhandlungen bereit **ist/war**	*The Chancellor declared that he was ready to enter into further negotiations*
Es wurde erzählt, daß der Verwalter ihnen persönlich das Mittagessen **auftrug** (*Wiechert*)	*It was recounted that the administrator served them lunch in person*

NB: If the main verb is in the past tense, the verb in the subordinate clause is usually in the present (i.e. the tense of the original direct speech), but it may be in the past, with the tense shifted as in English.

Even in written German the indicative is almost as frequent as the subjunctive in these constructions. As other cues are present to show that one is dealing with indirect speech, the subjunctive is unnecessary. However, if the *daß* is omitted, then the subjunctive is essential:

Der Kanzler erklärte, er **sei** zu weiteren Verhandlungen bereit
Es wurde erzählt, der Verwalter **trage** ihnen persönlich das Mittagessen auf

NB: *daß* is optional after verbs of saying or thinking, but it is usually included if the main verb is negative. Thus *Er sagte nicht, daß er sie nach Hause fahren werde* is more usual than *Er sagte nicht, er werde sie nach Hause fahren*.

(ii) After a verb in the first or second person:

Ich sagte ihm, von wo wir gekommen **sind**	*I told him where we had come from*
Ich glaube, der Fluß **ist** hier tief	*I think the river's deep here*
Du meinst wohl, er **ist** nicht krank	*I suppose you think he's not ill*
In deinem letzten Brief hast du mir geschrieben, seine Tochter **studiert** schon vier Semester in Hamburg	*In your last letter you wrote that his daughter had already been studying in Hamburg for four terms*

NB: As Konjunktiv I signals that a statement is 'merely reported' without any commitment on the part of the speaker as to whether it is true or not, it may sound unnatural if used after a verb in the first or second person.

(iii) If the indicative is used in written German in other cases, it sounds colloquial (and may sometimes be used with precisely this stylistic intention):

Manfred sagte, er **wußte** nicht, wo Georg **wohnte**	*Manfred said he didn't know where Georg was living*
(formal written usage: *er wisse nicht, wo Georg wohne*)	
Monika sagte, ihr Vater **will** sie zwingen, Medizin zu studieren	*Monika said her father wanted to make her study medicine*
(formal written usage: *ihr Vater wolle sie zwingen*)	

NB: As DUDEN (1984:§286) makes clear, there is no difference in meaning between the indicative and Konjunktiv I when used in indirect speech.

16.2.5 Indirect speech in spoken German

(a) In everyday colloquial German, either the indicative or Konjunktiv II is used in indirect speech

If the indicative is used, the tense of the original direct speech is normally retained:

Sie hat gesagt, sie **weiß/wüßte** es schon	*She said she knew it already*
Sie hat gesagt, sie **hat/hätte** es verstanden	*She said she had understood it*
Sie hat gesagt, sie **wird/würde** den Brief noch heute schreiben	*She said she'd write the letter today*

There is no distinction in meaning between the indicative and Konjunktiv II, although Konjunktiv II sounds rather less informal and may be preferred in past tense contexts. Konjunktiv II also tends to be used if there is a longer stretch of reported speech covering more than one sentence:

Er sagt, er hat eben einen neuen Wagen gekauft. Der hätte über 80 000 Mark gekostet und hätte eine Klimaanlage	*He says he's just bought a new car. It cost more than 80,000 marks and has got air-conditioning*

(b) Konjunktiv I is not normally used in indirect speech in everyday spoken German

If it is used there it sounds stilted and affected. The only exception is that the forms of the verb *sein* are occasionally encountered. In this case, there often tends to be an implication that the speaker does not believe what was said:

Gertrud hat mir gesagt, sie sei heute krank (implying that she might not have been telling the truth)	*Gertrud told me she was ill*

(c) If Konjunktiv II is used, it is often in the *würde*-form

As explained in 12.5.4, the use of the simple form of Konjunktiv II is restricted to a few common verbs in spoken German. The *würde*-form is thus usual with the weak verbs and those strong verbs whose one-word Konjunktiv II form is felt to be obsolete:

Sie behaupteten, sie würden bei sich alle Westfernsehen gucken (*Bednarz*)	*They claimed that they all watch western television at home*
Er sagte, ich würde zu schnell reden	*He said I talk too fast*
Sie sagte, sie würde diese Zeitschrift jede Woche lesen	*She said she reads this magazine every week*

16.2.6 Indirect questions and commands

(a) Usage in indirect questions follows exactly the same pattern as in indirect statements
(i) In written German Konjunktiv I (or Konjunktiv II, by the 'replacement rule') is used:

Er fragte ihn, wie alt sein Vater sei	*He asked him how old his father was*

Herr Müller fragte sie, ob sie
   Hunger habe
	*Herr Müller asked her if she was
	   hungry*

Sie fragte ihn, ob es seine Eltern
   schon wüßten
	*She asked him whether his parents
	   already knew it*

NB: (i) As in statements, Konjunktiv II is sometimes used even if a distinct Konjunktiv I form is available, e.g. *Er fragte ihn, wie alt sein Vater wäre.*
(ii) The indicative is unusual in indirect questions in written German, even though the conjunction cannot be deleted.

(ii) In spoken German either the indicative or Konjunktiv II is used:

Sie hat ihn gefragt, wie alt sein Vater ist/wäre
Herr Müller hat sie gefragt, ob sie Hunger hat/hätte
Sie hat ihn gefragt, ob es seine Eltern schon wissen/wüßten

(b) Commands are reported in indirect speech by using a modal verb
Konjunktiv I may be used in written German, but Konjunktiv II is quite frequent even where the replacement rule does not apply, and it is the norm in speech.
(i) *sollen* is the verb most frequently used in indirect commands:
Direct commands:

Rufe mich morgen im Büro an! ⎫
Ruft mich morgen im Büro an! ⎭   *Ring me at the office tomorrow*

The corresponding indirect commands:

Herr Hempel sagte ihm, er solle ihn morgen im Büro anrufen
   (in formal written German only)
Herr Hempel sagte ihm, er sollte ihn morgen im Büro anrufen
   (in written or spoken German)
Herr Hempel sagte ihnen, sie sollten ihn morgen im Büro anrufen
   (in written or spoken German, with a plural verb)
(ii) *müssen* may be used to indicate a more forceful command:

Herr Hempel sagte ihm, er müsse/müßte ihn (unbedingt) morgen im Büro anrufen

(iii) *mögen* (nowadays always in the Konjunktiv II form *möchte(n)*) is restricted to very formal usage. It sounds rather less peremptory:

Herr Hempel sagte ihm, er möchte ihn morgen im Büro anrufen

NB: The use of the Konjunktiv I form of *mögen* in indirect commands, e.g. *Sie sagte ihm, er möge zu ihr kommen*, is now obsolete, even in formal written German.

16.3 Conditional sentences

Conditional sentences typically have the following form:

Wenn ich Zeit hätte, käme ich   *If I had time, I would like*
   gern mit   *to come with you*

i.e. a subordinate clause introduced by the conjunction *wenn*, expressing a condition, and a main clause, expressing the consequence.

6.3.1 Konjunktiv II is used in sentences which express unreal conditions

As the most important function of Konjunktiv II in modern German is to signal a hypothetical possibility or a supposition, it is typically used, in both spoken and written German, in sentences which express unreal or unfulfilled conditions.

(a) The simple or compound form of Konjunktiv II is used to express an unreal condition relating to the present moment or the immediate future:

Wenn wir Zeit **hätten, könnten** wir   *If we had time, we would be able to*
   einen Ausflug machen   *go for a trip*
Die Europäer **wären** erleichtert, wenn   *The Europeans would be relieved if*
   England wieder **austreten würde** (*Zeit*)   *England withdrew again*
Wir **würden** es **begrüßen**, wenn Sie uns   *We would welcome it if you could*
   besuchen **könnten**   *come to visit us*
Wenn ich 20 000 Mark im Lotto   *If I won 20,000 marks on the pools*
   gewinnen würde, würde ich sofort   *I would fly to Tenerife right away*
   nach Teneriffa **fliegen**

NB: (i) Konjunktiv II is used in <u>both</u> the *wenn*-clause <u>and</u> the main clause. This is different to English, which uses the past tense in the *if*-clause, and the conditional in the main clause.
(ii) Konjunktiv I is <u>never</u> used in conditional sentences (except in reported speech).

Either the simple form or the compound form (with *würde*) of Konjunktiv II may be used in both the *wenn*-clause and the main clause. Which one is used depends on register and on the individual verb used, as explained in 12.5.4. Stylists have long recommended that sentences with the compound form in <u>both</u> clauses (i.e. with *würde* used twice) should be avoided. However, it is common in speech, e.g.:

Ich würde es für falsch halten, wenn   *I would think it wrong if the*
   die neue Regierung mit einem großen   *new government came to power*
   Programm antreten würde   *with a big programme*

and it is by no means uncommon, though frowned on, in writing, particularly if the simple forms of the verbs involved are obsolete.

(b) The pluperfect subjunctive form of Konjunktiv II is used to express a hypothetical possibility in the past
Note that the pluperfect subjunctive is used in both the *wenn*-clause and the main clause.

Wenn ich es nicht mit eigenen Augen gesehen hätte, hätte ich es nicht geglaubt	*If I hadn't seen it with my own eyes, I wouldn't have believed it*
Wenn wir auf der Autobahn gefahren wären, hätten wir die Fähre rechtzeitig erreicht	*If we had gone on the motorway, we would have reached the ferry in time*
Wenn sie den Zug verpaßt hätte, hätte sie uns sicher angerufen	*If she had missed the train, she would have called us*

NB: (i) Pluperfect forms with *würde*, e.g. . . ., *würde ich es nicht geglaubt haben*, are not unknown, but are in practice uncommon, especially in writing.
(ii) Time differences between the main clause and the *wenn*-clause can be indicated by using appropriate tenses, e.g.:

Ich säße hier nicht auf demselben Stuhl, wenn wir bisher diesen Punkt nicht erreicht hätten (*Zeit*)	*I wouldn't be sitting here in the same chair if we hadn't already reached this point*
Wenn er schuldig wäre, wäre er damals nicht am Tatort geblieben	*If he were guilty, he wouldn't have stayed at the scene of the crime*

(c) Other auxiliary verbs in sentences expressing unreal conditions
(i) The Konjunktiv II of *sollen* is often used in the *wenn*-clause. This is similar to the use of *should* or *were to* in English:

Wenn sie mich fragen sollte, würde ich ihr alles sagen	*If she were to ask me, I would tell her everything*
Wenn ich nach Berlin kommen sollte, würde ich sie sicher besuchen	*If I should get to Berlin, I would certainly go to see her*

Also common, especially in spoken German, is the combination of *sollte* in the *wenn*-clause with a future tense in the main clause:

Wenn ich sie treffen sollte, werde ich dir Bescheid sagen	*If I were to meet her, I'll let you know*

(ii) The Konjunktiv II of *wollen* also occurs frequently in the *wenn*-clause, usually with only a faint suggestion of its basic meaning of 'want, intend':

Wenn du schneller arbeiten wolltest, könntest du mehr verdienen	*If you worked a bit faster you could earn more*
Wie wäre es, wenn wir ihr helfen wollten?	*What about helping her?*

It is particularly common in formal written German if the conjunction *wenn* is omitted (cf. 16.3.3a):

Es würde uns zu lange aufhalten, wollten wir alle diese Probleme ausführlich behandeln	*It would detain us too long if we were to deal in detail with all these problems*

(iii) Especially in south Germany, the Konjunktiv II of *tun* is frequently used in substandard spoken German instead of *würde*:

Wenn ich jetzt losfahren täte, so
    könnte ich schon vor zwölf Uhr
    in Augsburg sein
	If I set off now, I might be in
	Augsburg by twelve

16.3.2 The indicative is used in conditional sentences which express 'open' conditions,

i.e. where there is a real possibility of the conditions being met. These correspond to conditional sentences without *would* in English:

Wenn sie krank ist, muß ich morgen allein kommen	*If she's ill, I'll have to come* *alone tomorrow*
Wenn ich ihr jetzt schreibe, bekommt sie den Brief morgen	*If I write to her now, she'll get* *the letter tommorow*
Wenn wir jetzt losfahren, werden wir schon vor zwölf in Augsburg sein	*If we set off now, we'll be in* *Augsburg by twelve*

With the past tense, the sense is that the conditions have been met:

Wenn meine Eltern mir Geld schickten,
    kaufte ich mir sofort etwas zum
    Anziehen
	If my parents sent me money I
	immediately bought something to
	wear

16.3.3 Alternative forms for conditional sentences

The typical conditional sentence consists of a *wenn*-clause and a main clause, as shown in 16.3. There are a number of possible variations to this pattern, i.e.:

(a) The conjunction *wenn* may be omitted

In this case, the verb in the subordinate clause is moved to first position:

Hätte ich Zeit, käme ich gern mit
Ist sie krank, muß ich morgen allein kommen
Sollte ich nach Berlin kommen, würde ich sie sicher besuchen

This construction is more usually found in formal written German than in everyday speech. It is rare, if not unknown, for the main clause to come first:

Das Bild wäre unvollständig, würden
    nicht die vielen Gruppen erwähnt,
    die den Einwanderern das Leben
    leichter machen (*FR*)
	The picture would be incomplete if
	the many groups were not mentioned
	who make life easier for the
	immigrants

(b) If the *wenn*-clause comes first in the sentence, it may be picked up by *so* or *dann* at the start of the main clause

This 'correlating' *so* or *dann* is optional, but quite common:

Wenn ich Zeit hätte, (so/dann) käme ich gern mit
Wenn ich ihr heute schreibe, (so/dann) bekommt sie den Brief morgen

If anything, *so* is most frequent if *wenn* is omitted , cf. (a) above:

Hätte ich Zeit, (so) käme ich gern mit
Ist sie krank, (so) muß ich morgen allein kommen
Sollte ich nach Berlin kommen, (so) würde ich sie sicher besuchen

(c) The condition may appear in another form than in a *wenn*-clause,
i.e. in an adverb, an adverbial phrase or a relative or other clause. If the
condition is unreal, then Konjunktiv II will be used in the same way as in a
sentence with *wenn*:

Bei dem Wetter wäre ich nicht segeln gegangen	*I wouldn't have gone sailing in that weather*
Sonst würde ich das Fenster nicht aufmachen	*Otherwise I wouldn't open the window*
Unter anderen Umständen wäre ich erfolgreicher gewesen	*In other circumstances I would have been more successful*
Wer diese Entwicklung vorausgesehen hätte, hätte viel Geld verdienen können	*Anyone foreseeing this development would have made a lot of money*

In some sentences the condition may be wholly implicit:

Lieber bliebe ich zu Hause (i.e. wenn ich die Wahl hätte)	*I would rather stay at home*
Ich hätte dasselbe getan (i.e. wenn ich an deiner Stelle gewesen wäre)	*I would have done the same*

(d) Other conjunctions used in conditional sentences
Although *wenn* is the predominant conjunction in conditional sentences,
other conjunctions do occur.
(i) *falls* 'if' is especially frequent in 'open' conditions (cf. 16.3.2). It is
particularly useful if *wenn* is potentially ambiguous (i.e. it could be
understood as 'when' rather than 'if', cf. 19.2.1.). It can be used with an
optional correlating *so*:

Falls ich nach Berlin komme, (so) werde ich sie sicher besuchen	*If I get to Berlin, I'll be sure to call in on her*
Falls sie mich anruft, (so) sage ich dir Bescheid	*If she calls me, I'll let you know*

NB: The phrasal conjunction *im Falle, daß* is an occasional alternative to *falls*.
(ii) *angenommen, daß* . . ., *vorausgesetzt, daß* . . . 'assuming that,
'provided that'. These conjunctions mainly introduce 'open' conditions.
The *daß* is frequently omitted, in which case the following clause has the
word order of a main clause:

Angenommen, er hat den Brief erhalten, ⎫ Angenommen, daß er den Brief erhalten hat, ⎬ wird er bald hier sein	*Assuming he got the letter, he'll be here soon*
Vorausgesetzt, es kommt nichts dazwischen, ⎫ Vorausgesetzt, daß nichts dazwischen kommt, ⎬ ziehen wir im Frühjahr nach Mainz	*Provided that all goes well, we'll be moving to Mainz in the spring*

sofern and *soweit* are also frequently used in the sense of 'if' or 'provided that' in open conditions:

Sofern/Soweit es die Witterungs-
   bedingungen erlauben, findet die
   Aufführung im Freien vor der alten
   Abtei statt

If weather conditions permit, the
performance will take place in the
open air in front of the old abbey

(iii) *selbst wenn, auch wenn, sogar wenn, wenn . . . auch*

All these are equivalents for English 'even if'. Thus, English 'Even if I wrote him today, he wouldn't get the letter until Tuesday', could be given in German in any one of the following ways:

Selbst/Auch/Sogar wenn ich ihm heute schriebe, }
Wenn ich ihm auch heute schriebe,
   würde er den Brief erst Dienstag bekommen

or, with *wenn* omitted, in formal written German only (and commonly with an optional *doch* in the main clause):

Schriebe ich ihm auch heute, würde er den Brief (doch) erst Dienstag bekommen

(iv) *es sei denn, (daß)* . . . 'unless' is chiefly used in 'open' conditions. The *daß* may be omitted, in which case the following clause has the word order of a main clause:

Ich komme gegen zwei Uhr, es sei denn,
  { ich werde aufgehalten
  { daß ich aufgehalten werde

I'll come at about two, unless

I'm held up

wenn . . . nicht is probably the most frequent equivalent for English 'unless'. It is used with open or unreal conditions, in the latter case with Konjunktiv II:

Wenn er nicht bald kommt, wird es zu
   spät sein
Er hätte es nicht gesagt, wenn er
   nicht schuldig wäre

Unless he comes soon, it will be
too late
He wouldn't have said it unless
he was guilty

NB: *außer wenn* can also be used for English 'unless', cf. 19.6.2b.

16.4 Other uses of the subjunctive

16.4.1 The subjunctive in 'as if' clauses

(a) Clauses expressing a hypothetical comparison are most often introduced by the conjunction *als ob* 'as if, as though', with the verb in a form of Konjunktiv II

(i) If the action in the subordinate clause is simultaneous with the action in the main clause, the basic form of Konjunktiv II is used

Er tat, als ob er krank wäre
Das Kind weint, als ob es Schmerzen
   hätte

He acted as if he were ill
the child is crying as if it
is in pain

NB: The compound form of Konjunktiv II (with *würde*) may be used if the simple form is obsolete or unusual, in accordance with the guidelines given in 12.5.4, e.g.:

Mir war, als ob ich in einem riesigen See schwimmen würde	*I felt as if I was swimming in a huge lake*

(The simple form *schwömme* is obsolete)

(ii) If the action in the main clause took place before the action in the main clause, the pluperfect subjunctive is used:

Sie sieht aus, als ob sie seit Tagen nicht gegessen hätte	*She looks as if she hasn't eaten for days*
Er tat, als ob nichts passiert wäre	*He acted as if nothing had happened*

(iii) If the action of the main clause will take place after the action in the main clause, the *würde*-form of Konjunktiv II is used:

Es sieht aus, als ob es regnen würde	*It looks as if it will rain*
Es sah aus, als ob er gleich hinfallen würde	*It looked as if he was about to fall down*

(b) Some alternative forms are possible for these clauses which express unreal comparisons, i.e.:

(i) The *ob* of *als ob* may be omitted, in which case the finite verb follows immediately:

Er tat, als wäre er krank   Es sah aus, als würde er gleich hinfallen
Sie sieht aus, als hätte sie seit Tagen nicht gegessen

Sie sprach Deutsch, als wäre es ihre Muttersprache (*Bednarz*)	*She spoke German as if it was her native language*

This alternative is quite frequent in formal written German, but is used less often than *als ob* in speech.

(ii) *als wenn* or *wie wenn* are sometimes found instead of the more common *als ob*:

Er tat, als wenn/wie wenn er krank wäre
Sie sieht aus, als wenn/wie wenn sie seit Tagen nicht gegessen hätte
Es war ihm, als wenn/wie wenn er hinfallen würde

(iii) Konjunktiv I is sometimes used rather than Konjunktiv II, in written German only, if its form is distinct from that of the present indicative:

Er tat, als ob er krank sei	Es sah aus, als werde er hinfallen

Sie sieht aus, als ob sie seit Tagen nicht gegessen habe

Es klang, als beklage sie sich bei Klaus Buch über Helmut (*Walser*)	*It sounded as if she was complaining to Klaus Buch about Helmut*

There is no difference in meaning between Konjunktiv I and Konjunktiv II in *als ob*-clauses. Konjunktiv I is less frequent than Konjunktiv II even in writing and some Germans even consider it incorrect.

(iv) The indicative is sometimes used rather than Konjunktiv II in colloquial spoken German:

Er tat, als ob er krank war	Es ist mir, als ob ich hinfallen werde

Sie sieht aus, als ob sie seit Tagen nicht gegessen hat

There is no difference in meaning between the indicative and Konjunktiv II in *als ob*-clauses. The indicative is considered incorrect in written German and even in speech it only tends to be more frequent than Konjunktiv II in the present tense. *ob* is never omitted if the verb is in the indicative.

16.4.2 The subjunctive in clauses of purpose

(a) Clauses introduced by *damit* 'so that' occasionally have a verb in the subjunctive

Appropriate tense forms of Konjunktiv I or Konjunktiv II are used without any real difference in meaning:

Er zog sich zurück, damit wir ihn nicht sähen	*He withdrew so that we didn't see him*
Und damit diese Autorität intakt bleibe, wird ihm angeraten, sich möglichst wenig in aktuelle Streitfragen einzumischen (*Zeit*)	*And in order for this authority to remain intact, he is advised to interfere as little as possible in current controversies*

In practice, the subjunctive is only occasionally encountered in *damit*-clauses nowadays. It is restricted to formal (especially literary) German and can sound rather old-fashioned. The indicative is more frequent in all registers, and the modal verbs *können* or *sollen* are often used:

Er zog sich zurück, damit wir ihn nicht sahen/sehen konnten/sehen sollten.

(b) The conjunction *auf daß* 'so that' is sometimes used in formal German as an alternative to *damit*

It has an archaic ring and is almost always followed by a subjunctive (Konjunktiv I or Konjunktiv II):

Der Häuptling eines Eingeborenenstammes verfluchte sie, auf daß ihnen nichts von allem, was sie dem Boden und den Gewässern abgewinnen würden, je zum Nutzen gereiche (*Spiegel*)	*The chief of a native tribe cursed them, that they might never derive any benefit from anything they gained from the earth or the rivers*

16.4.3 Konjunktiv II is very frequent, especially in spoken German, to moderate the tone of an assertion, a statement, a request or a question and make it sound less blunt:

Ich wüßte wohl, was zu tun wäre	*I think I know what's to be done*
Eine Frage hätte ich doch noch (*Th. Valentin*)	*There's one more thing I'd like to ask*
Da wäre er nun aufgewacht (*Dürrenmatt*)	*He seems to have woken up*
Ich würde auch meinen, daß es jetzt zu spät ist	*It seems a little late to me, too*
Diese Sache hätten wir also geregelt	*That would appear to be sorted out*
Das wär's für heute	*I think that's enough for today*
Hätten Sie sonst noch einen Wunsch?	*Is there anything else you would like*

Würden Sie bitte das Fenster
    zumachen?

Would you be so kind as to shut the
    window?

Könnten Sie mir bitte sagen, wie ich
    zum Bahnhof komme?

Could you please tell me how to get
    to the station

16.4.4 Konjunktiv II may be used in time clauses introduced by *bis*, *bevor* or *ehe*

The subjunctive in such clauses is restricted to formal written German and is an optional alternative to the indicative. If it is used, it emphasises that it was still in doubt whether the action or event in question would actually take place:

Sie beschlossen zu warten, bis er käme

They decided to wait till he came

Er weigerte sich, den Vertrag zu
    unterzeichnen, bevor wir ihm weitere
    Zugeständnisse gemacht hätten

He refused to sign the contract
    before we had made further
    concessions

16.4.5 The use of the subjunctive in negative contexts

Konjunktiv II is often used where it is a question of something which was possible, but which in fact did not take place or was not the case. In all these constructions the indicative is usually a possible alternative, especially in speech, but it tends to sound much more definite and less tentative:

(a) After the conjunctions *nicht daß*, *ohne daß* and *als daß*

Nicht, daß er faul wäre, (*or*: ist) aber
    er kommt in seinem Beruf nicht voran

Not that he's lazy, but he's not
    getting on in his profession

Diese Mannschaft ist seit Jahren in
    der Bundesliga, ohne daß sie jemals
    deutscher Meister geworden
    wäre (*or*: ist)

This team has been in the first
    division for years without ever
    winning the championship

Diese Hi-Fi-Anlage ist viel zu teuer,
    als daß ich sie mir leisten
    könnte (*or*: kann)

This stereo system is much too dear
    for me to be able to afford

NB: The set phrase *nicht daß ich (es) wüßte* 'not that I know of' is <u>always</u> used with a subjunctive.

(b) In other subordinate clauses where the main clause and/or the subordinate clause have a negative element

Das bedeutet keineswegs, daß ich mit
    allem zufrieden wäre (*or*: bin)

This in no way means that I'm
    satisfied with it all

Es gibt nichts, was schwieriger wäre
    (*or*: ist), als der Gebrauch des
    Konjunktivs

There's nothing more difficult
    than the use of the subjunctive

nicht eine einzige Großstadt . . ., die
    nicht ihr Gesicht in zwei Jahrzehnten
    gründlich gewandelt hätte (*Zeit*)
    (*hat* would sound much more positive)

not a single city that has not
    changed its appearance totally
    in twenty years

(c) In sentences with *fast* or *beinahe*

In these the pluperfect subjunctive is often used to emphasise that something almost happened, but didn't:

Er wäre (*or*: ist) beinahe hingefallen   *He almost fell down*
Ich wäre (*or*: bin) fast nicht gekommen   *I nearly didn't come*
Wir hätten (*or*: haben) das Spiel   *We almost won the match*
    beinahe gewonnen

16.4.6 The use of the subjunctive in wishes, instructions and commands

(a) Konjunktiv I is used in the third person to express a wish

In practice this usage is largely restricted to set phrases in modern German:

Gott segne dich/dieses Haus!   *God bless you/this house!*
Es lebe die Freiheit!   *Long live freedom!*
Gott sei Dank!   *Thank God!*
Behüte dich Gott!   *God protect you!*

NB: (i) *Behüte dich Gott* is very frequently heard in Bavaria and Austria in the contracted form *Pfiati (Gott)!* 'goodbye'.
(ii) The use of the Konjunktiv I of *mögen* in wishes, e.g. *Möge er glücklich sein!* 'May he be happy!' is now archaic.

(b) A conditional clause with Konjunktiv II is very frequently used to express a wish

The clause may have the form with or without *wenn*, cf. 16.3.3a. One or more of the modal particles *doch*, *nur* or *bloß* is usually inserted, cf. 10.7.7. and 10.26.3:

Wenn er doch nur käme!   *If only he would come!*
Wenn er bloß fleißiger arbeiten würde!   *If only he would work harder!*
Wenn ich bloß/nur/doch zu Hause   *If only I'd stayed at home!*
    geblieben wäre!
Hätte mein Vater doch dieses Haus nie   *If only my father hadn't bought*
    gekauft!   *this house!*
Wenn sie Ihnen das Geld doch bloß   *If only she hadn't given you the*
    geben würde!   *money!*

(c) Konjunktiv I is used in commands in the first person plural,

i.e. as an equivalent to English *let's*:

Na, also, gehen wir ganz langsam   *Well then, let's walk quite*
    (*Fallada*)   *slowly*

Seien wir dankbar, daß nichts passiert ist!	*Let's be thankful that nothing happened*
Also, spielen wir jetzt Karten!	*Well, let's play cards*

NB: *Laß uns/Laßt uns* with a following infinitive is a common alternative to the construction above, e.g. *Laßt uns in den Garten gehen!*

(d) Konjunktiv I is occasionally used for commands or instructions in the third person

man is normally used as a subject in this construction:

Im Notfall wende man sich an den Hausmeister!	*In case of emergency please apply to the caretaker*
Man gebe den Inhalt des Beutels in eine Salatschüssel	*Put the contents of the packet in a salad bowl*

NB: In practice, this usage is increasingly rare. For general instructions, *sollen* is used, e.g. *Im Notfall soll man sich an den Hausmeister wenden*, in recipes and the like the infinitive (cf. 13.3.3a) is now the norm, e.g.: *Beutelinhalt in eine Salatschüssel geben*.

(e) The Konjunktiv I form of *sein* or the *sein*-passive is not uncommon in technical German to express a proposition:

Mein Name sei Gantenbein (*Frisch*)	*Let my name be Gantenbein*
Gegeben sei ein Dreieck ABC	*Given a triangle ABC*
In diesem Zusammenhang sei nur darauf verwiesen, daß diese Hypothese auf Einstein zurückgeht	*In this context we merely wish to point out that this hypothesis goes back to Einstein*
Hier sei nur vermerkt, daß ihm dieses Experiment nie einwandfrei gelungen ist	*Let it just be noted here that he never succeeded in carrying out this experiment to perfection*

NB: In mathematical contexts the indicative is nowadays at least as common as the subjunctive, e.g. *Gegeben ist ein Dreieck ABC*.

16.4.7 The use of the subjunctive in concessive sentences

In concessive sentences corresponding to the English type 'Wherever that may be', 'However he may have done it', etc., cf. 19.5.2, German usually has the indicative nowadays in all registers, e.g.:

Wann sie auch ankommt/ankommen mag ich will sie sofort sprechen	*Whenever she may arrive, I want to see her at once*
Wie schnell er auch lief, der Polizist holte ihn ein	*However fast he ran, the policeman caught him up*
Was auch immer geschieht/geschehen mag, . . .	*Whatever may happen, . . .*

The use of Konjunktiv I in such clauses is now wholly archaic except in the set phrase:

Wie dem auch sei	*However that may be*

17   The modal auxiliaries

The six modal auxiliary verbs *dürfen, können, mögen, müssen, sollen, wollen* are chiefly used to indicate the standpoint of the speaker with regard to what is being said,
i.e. whether he or she regards it as possible, desirable, permissible, etc. In this way, their role is linked to that of the category of mood, cf. 12.1.1c, which is why they are known as 'modal' auxiliaries. In general terms, they are used with other verbs to express ability, possibility, permission, inclination, necessity, obligation, volition, and the like. However, each verb has a wide range of meaning which is not always easy to pin down, and they all have a number of elusive idiomatic uses.

All these verbs have a number of features in common, which are dealt with in 17.1. Each individual verb is then treated, in alphabetical order, in sections 17.2 to 17.7. The conjugation of the modals is given in full in 12.2.3.

The most useful straightforward account of the German modals is that in Helbig & Buscha (1986:131–7). Palmer (1986) is a helpful introduction to the problems associated with mood and modality in language, and has a range of examples from English and German.

17.1 The modal auxiliaries: general comments on form and syntax

17.1.1 The German modal auxiliaries have a full range of tense and mood forms

In this the German modals differ from the English ones (*can, may, must,* etc.), which have at most only a present tense and a past tense (often with conditional meaning). Thus, whilst we tend to think of German *können* as the equivalent of English *can*, it may be used in the future, e.g.:

Ich werde es morgen nicht machen   *I shan't be able to do it tomorrow*
   können

English *can* is impossible here, as it has no future, and we have to fall back on the paraphrase 'be able to'.

This range of possible forms often makes the German modals seem very daunting for the English learner. But they are not difficult to master if the various combinations of tense and mood with a following simple or compound infinitive are treated independently and learned with their usual English equivalents. The examples in sections 17.2 to 17.7 are set out to facilitate this, and by way of illustration we give here examples of the various possible combinations of tense, mood and type of following infinitive with *können*:

(a) present tense + simple infinitive

Sie kann es machen	*She can do it*

(b) present tense + compound infinitive

Sie kann es gemacht haben	*She may have done it*

(c) future tense + simple infinitive

Sie wird es machen können	*She will be able to do it*

(d) past *or* perfect tense + simple infinitive

Sie konnte es machen ⎫ Sie hat es machen können ⎭	*She was able to do it*

(e) past subjunctive + simple infinitive

Sie könnte es machen	*She could/might do it*

(f) past subjunctive + compound infinitive

Sie könnte es gemacht haben	*She might have done it*

(g) pluperfect subjunctive + simple infinitive

Sie hätte es machen können	*She would have been able to do it*

NB: (i) There is no difference in meaning between the past and perfect forms, cf.14.3. In general usage, the past is commoner with most modal verbs, even in spoken German; only with *können, müssen* and *wollen* is the perfect significantly frequent as an alternative to the past.
(ii) The *würde*-form of Konjunktiv II is very rarely used with the modals, cf. 12.5.4.
(iii) The difference in meaning between (f) and (g) with some of these verbs is not always straightforward for English learners, as they often have the same equivalents in English. Details are given with the individual verbs, i.e. *können* 17.3.8, *müssen* 17.5.3b and *sollen* 17.6.5b.

17.1.2 The modal verbs are followed by the bare infinitive, without *zu*

(cf.13.3.1a). As the examples in 17.1.1 show, they may be followed by a simple infinitive or, in some tenses, by the compound infinitive (cf. 13.1.1).

(a) The infinitive is normally placed in final position in the clause, cf. 21.1, e.g.:

Darf ich heute Tennis **spielen**?	*May I play tennis today?*
Ich möchte das Buch gern **lesen**	*I would like to read that book*
Sie könnte morgen **kommen**	*She might come tomorrow*

(b) In compound tenses, the infinitive of the modal verb comes <u>after</u> the dependent infinitive at the end of the clause, cf. 21.1.3a:

Sie wird morgen nicht kommen **können**	*She won't be able to come tomorrow*
Ich habe nach Ulm fahren **müssen**	*I had to go to Ulm*
Sie hätte ihrem Mann doch helfen **sollen**	*She really ought to have helped her husband*

(c) In infinitive clauses with *zu*, the modal verb, preceded by the particle *zu*, comes <u>after</u> the dependent infinitive at the end of the infinitive clause:

Es scheint regnen **zu wollen**	*It looks as if it's going to rain*
Sie gab vor, meine Handschrift nicht lesen **zu können**	*She claimed not to be able to read my handwriting*

(d) In subordinate clauses, the modal verb comes <u>after</u> the dependent infinitive at the end of the clause, cf. 21.1.3b:

Wenn Sie diesen Ring nicht kaufen **wollen**, . . .	*If you don't want to buy this ring, . . .*
Obwohl ich gestern abend ausgehen **durfte**, . . .	*Although I was allowed to go out last night*
Die Frau, die ich besuchen **sollte**, . . .	*the woman I ought to visit*

(e) If a modal verb is used in a compound tense in a subordinate clause, the tense auxiliary *werden* or *haben* comes <u>before</u> the two infinitives, cf. 21.1.3c:

Obwohl ich ihn morgen **werde** besuchen können, . . .	*Although I'll be able to visit him tomorrow*
Es war klar, daß er sich **würde** anstrengen müssen	*It was clear that he would have to exert himself*
Das Buch, das ich **hätte** kaufen sollen, kostete dreißig Mark	*The book I ought to have bought cost thirty marks*
Sie hat mir gesagt, daß sie es **hat** machen müssen	*She told me she had had to do it*

17.1.3 In the perfect tenses, the infinitive of the modal verbs is used, <u>not</u> the past participle, if they are followed by a dependent infinitive,

cf. 13.3.2a:

Wir haben meinen Onkel nicht besuchen **können**	*We weren't able to visit my uncle*
Ich habe es ihr versprechen **müssen**	*I had to promise her*
Sie hätte das Buch lesen **sollen**	*She ought to have read the book*

However, if there is no dependent infinitive, cf. 17.1.4, the past participle is used, e.g. *Ich habe es nicht* **gewollt**.

17.1.4 The omission of the infinitive after the modal verbs

In certain cases the infinitive dependent on a modal verb is left understood and omitted. This is frequent:

(a) With a verb of motion understood
If there is an adverb, an adverb phrase or, very commonly, a separable prefix in the sentence which conveys the idea of movement, a specific verb of motion may be omitted after the modal verbs. This usage is preponderantly colloquial, but it is by no means restricted to the spoken register:

Wo wollen Sie morgen hin?	*Where do you want to go tomorrow?*
Ich will nach Frankfurt	*I want to go to Frankfurt*
Ich sollte zu meinem Onkel	*I ought to go to my uncle's*
Ich könnte heute abend ins Theater	*I could go to the theatre this evening*
Sie will ihm nach	*She wants to go after him*
Er kletterte über die Mauer, aber er konnte nicht zurück	*He climbed over the wall, but he couldn't get back*
Ich möchte jetzt fort	*I'd like to leave now*

(i) The verb understood is usually *gehen, kommen* or *fahren*, as in the above examples, but other verbs may also be omitted as long as the idea of movement is clear from the adverbial or the prefix:

Er wollte über die Mauer [klettern]	*He wanted to climb over the wall*
Die Strömung war so stark, daß er nicht bis ans Ufer [schwimmen] konnte	*The current was so strong that he couldn't swim to the bank*
Er mußte in den Krieg [ziehen] (*Böll*)	*He had to go to the war*

(ii) If the modal is at the end of the clause, a separable prefix will be written together with it:

Mich wundert, daß er um diese Zeit noch hinausdarf (*Th. Valentin*)	*I'm surprised that he's allowed out at this time of night*
Wir werden bald zurückmüssen	*We'll have to get back soon*
Ich glaube, ich werde vorbeikönnen	*I think I'll be able to get past*

(iii) This usage is most usual with simple tense forms (i.e. the present and past, or the past subjunctive), but the future tense of *können* and *müssen* is also found, as in the last two examples. Occasionally, the perfect tenses of *können* and *müssen* are also used with a verb of motion understood:

Er hat ins Geschäft gemußt	*He's had to go to work*
Ich hätte eigentlich hingemußt	*I really ought to have gone there*
Er hätte gestern ins Kino gekonnt	*He could have gone to the cinema yesterday*

(b) With the verb *tun* understood

Das kann ich nicht	*I can't do that*
Das darfst/sollst du nicht	*You mustn't/ought not to do that*
Was soll ich damit?	*What am I supposed to do with it?*
Ich kann nichts dafür	*I can't help it*
Er kann was	*He is very able*

(c) With a verb just mentioned previously understood

This usually corresponds to English usage. *es* may be added, cf. 3.6.2:

Ich wollte Tennis spielen, aber ich konnte/durfte (es) nicht	*I wanted to play tennis, but I couldn't/wasn't allowed to*
Soll ich?	*Shall I?*
Ich versuchte ihn zu überzeugen, aber ich habe (es) nicht gekonnt	*I tried to persuade him, but I couldn't*
Mußt du diesen Brief lesen? –	*Must you read that letter?*
Natürlich muß ich (es)	*Of course I must*

(d) In some idiomatic phrases

Ich kann nicht mehr [weitermachen]	*I can't go on*
Was soll das eigentlich [bedeuten]?	*What's the point of that?*
Sie hat nicht mehr gewollt	*She didn't want to go on*
Er kann mich [am Arsch lecken] (vulg.)	*He can get lost*
Mir kann keiner [was antun]	*No-one can touch me*

17.1.5 The conjugation of the modal verbs is highly irregular

All their forms are given in 12.2.3.

17.2 *dürfen*

17.2.1 *dürfen* is most often used to express permission
(a) In this sense it corresponds to English 'be allowed to' or 'may':

Sie dürfen hereinkommen	{ *They may/can come in* { *They are allowed to come in*
Sie durfte ausgehen, wann sie wollte	*She was allowed to go out when she wanted to*
Endlich durfte er die Augen wieder aufmachen	*At last he could open his eyes again*
Sie wird erst heute nachmittag mit uns spielen dürfen	*She won't be allowed to play with us till this afternoon*

NB: In colloquial English, 'can' is frequently used to express permission. Whilst *können* may be heard in place of *dürfen* in colloquial German, cf. 17.3.5, it is less common in this sense than English 'can'. *dürfen* is by no means uncommon in spoken German, and it lacks the rather affected ring of English 'may'.

(b) Negative *dürfen* has the sense of English 'must not',
i.e. it expresses a prohibition:

Sie dürfen nicht hereinkommen	{ *They mustn't come in* { *They're not allowed to come in*
Aber ich darf mich nicht loben (*Langgässer*)	*But I mustn't praise myself*
Wir dürfen es uns nicht zu leicht machen (*Brecht*)	*We musn't make it too easy for ourselves*

NB: *muß nicht* usually has the meaning 'doesn't have to', 'needn't', cf. 17.5.1c.

Konjunktiv II forms of *dürfen* with a negative may correspond to English 'shouldn't', 'ought not to'. As *dürfen* retains its basic sense of permission, it tends to be rather more incisive than *sollen*, cf. 17.6.5a:

Das dürfte sie doch gar nicht wissen (i.e. it shouldn't be allowed)	*She ought not to know that*
Er hätte so etwas nicht machen dürfen (i.e. someone should have forbidden it)	*He ought not to have done anything like that*

(c) *dürfen* is very frequent in polite formulae in place of *können*
The tone is that of a polite request or a tentative suggestion:

Das darf als Vorteil betrachtet werden	*That can/may be seen as an advantage*
Hierher, wenn ich bitten darf	*This way, if you please*
Bitte, was darf's sein? (in shop)	*What can I get you?*
Der Wein dürfte etwas trockener sein	*The wine could be just a bit drier*
Dürfte ich Sie um das Salz bitten	*Could I ask you to pass the salt*
Wir freuen uns, Sie hier begrüßen zu dürfen	*We are pleased to be able to welcome you here*

With a negative, *dürfen* can be more incisive and more definite than *können*:

Das darf doch nicht wahr sein	*But that can't be true*

17.2.2 *dürfen* can express probability

The Konjunktiv II of *dürfen* expresses a rather higher degree of possibility than *könnte* (i.e. 'a fair likelihood' rather than just 'possibility', cf.17.3.2c). This sense of *dürfen* is very close to that of the future tense with *werden*, cf. 14.4.2, or that of the modal particle *wohl*, cf. 10.35.1:

Das dürfte mein Vater sein	*That will (probably) be my father*
Das dürfte reichen	*That'll be enough*
Es dürfte nicht leicht sein, ihn zu überzeugen	*It won't be easy to persuade him*
Das dürfte ein Vermögen gekostet haben	*That'll have cost a fortune*

17.3 *können*

17.3.1 The most common sense of *können* is to express ability

Its usual English equivalents are 'can' or 'be able to':

Sie kann ihn heute besuchen	*She can/is able to visit him today*
Ich konnte sie nicht besuchen ⎫	⎧ *I couldn't visit her*
Ich habe sie nicht besuchen können ⎭	⎨ *I wasn't able to visit her*
Ich werde sie morgen besuchen können	*I'll be able to visit her tomorrow*
Ich könnte sie morgen besuchen, wenn ich Zeit hätte	*I could visit her tomorrow if I had time*
Ich hätte sie gestern besuchen können, wenn ich Zeit gehabt hätte	*I would have been able to/could have visited her yesterday, if I'd had time*

17.3.2 *können* can express possibility:

(a) The most common English equivalent is 'may':

Das kann sein	*That may be*
Ich kann mich irren	*I may be wrong*
Er kann krank sein	*He may be ill*

(b) *können* is very frequently used with a compound infinitive to express possibility:

Er kann den Schlüssel verloren haben	*He may have lost the key*
Die Straße kann gesperrt sein	*The road may be blocked*
Können sie den Anschluß verpaßt haben?	*Can they have missed the connection?*
Er kann krank gewesen sein	*He may have been ill*

(c) The Konjunktiv II form *könnte* is very frequently employed to denote a remote possibility
(= English 'might, could'):

Sie könnte jetzt in Wien sein	*She could be in Vienna now*
Sie könnten recht haben	*You might/could be right*
Das könnte peinlich gewesen sein	*That might/could be embarrassing*
Wir hätten umkommen können	*We might/could have been killed*
Er könnte krank sein	*He might/could be ill*
Er könnte krank gewesen sein	*He might/could have been ill*

könnte can also be used to express a tentative request (cf. 16.4.3):

Könnten Sie mir bitte helfen?	*Could you please help me?*

17.3.3 The use of *können* to express possibility is limited

Other German equivalents are often necessary for English 'may, might' (or 'can, could' used with a sense of possibility).

(a) *können* can only be used to denote possibility in contexts where it cannot be taken to mean 'be able to'

If there is such risk of possible ambiguity, the adverbs *vielleicht* or *möglicherweise*, or a paraphrase (e.g. *Es ist möglich, daß* . . .) are necessary to denote possibility:

Vielleicht arbeitet er im Garten	*He may be working in the garden*
(Er kann im Garten arbeiten = 'He is able to work in the garden')	
Sie wird mir vielleicht helfen	*She may help me*
(Sie kann mir helfen = 'She is able to help me')	
Repariert er vielleicht den Wagen?	*Can he be mending the car?*
(Kann er den Wagen reparieren? = 'Can he mend the car?')	
Es ist unmöglich, daß er den Wagen jetzt repariert	*He can't be mending the car now*
(Er kann den Wagen nicht reparieren = 'He can't mend the car')	
Vielleicht kommt sie heute abend	*She may come tonight*
(Sie könnte heute abend kommen = 'She would be able to come tonight')	

NB: The use of *mögen* to express possibility (= 'may') is limited in modern German to certain restricted senses in formal written language and to some set phrases, cf. 17.4.2.

(b) With negative *können*, the sense of possibility may be made clear by the addition of *auch*, cf.10.4.1

Alternatively, a different phrasing can be used:

Sie kann auch nicht kommen ⎫ Möglicherweise kommt sie nicht ⎬	*She may not come*
Er kann auch nicht krank gewesen sein ⎫ Vielleicht ist er gar nicht krank gewesen ⎬	*He may not have been ill*

Sie kann das Auto auch nicht gesehen
    haben ⎫
Vielleicht hat sie den Wagen gar
    nicht gesehen ⎬
	She may not have seen the car

Er könnte auch nicht kommen ⎫ Es wäre möglich, daß er nicht kommt ⎬	*He might not come*
(Er könnte nicht kommen = 'He wouldn't be able to come')	

17.3.4 *können* is used in the meaning 'know' of things learnt,

especially languages, other school subjects, the rules of games, etc.:

Er kann Spanisch	*He can speak Spanish*
Kannst du Russisch?	*Do you know any Russian?*

Ich kann die Melodie der
    österreichischen Nationalhymne
    (i.e. I've learnt it)
	*I know the tune of the Austrian
	    national anthem*

Kann der Manfred Skat?	*Does Manfred know how to play Skat?*
Ich kann den Trick	*I know that trick*
(i.e. 'I can do it'. Compare *Ich kenne den Trick* 'I've seen it before')	

17.3.5 *können* is used colloquially for *dürfen* to express permission:

Kann ich hereinkommen?	*Can I come in?*
Du kannst den Bleistift behalten	*You can keep the pencil*

können is less frequent in this sense, even in colloquial German, than is 'can' in English, cf. 17.2.1.

17.3.6 *können* is used less frequently than English 'can' with verbs of sensation

English often employs 'can' with verbs like *see, hear, feel* and *smell* without any real idea of being able. In such contexts *können* is not felt to be necessary in German:

Ich sehe die Kirche	*I can see the church*
Ich höre Musik	*I can hear music*
Sie sahen die Stadt im Tal liegen	*They could see the town lying in the valley*

17.3.7 German equivalents for English 'I couldn't help . . .'

There are a number of alternative possibilities in German for this English construction, e.g., for English *I couldn't help laughing*:

(i) Ich mußte einfach lachen
(ii) Ich konnte nicht anders, ich mußte lachen
(iii) Ich konnte nichts dafür, ich mußte lachen
(iv) Ich konnte nicht umhin zu lachen

Alternative (i) is the simplest and most usual in modern German, although (ii) and (iii) are quite current. Alternative (iv) is now restricted to formal (especially literary) registers.

17.3.8 Combinations of the type *könnte . . . gemacht haben* and *hätte . . . machen können* have quite different meanings in German

The English equivalents for both are 'could have done' or 'might have done'. However, these are ambiguous, and this ambiguity has to be sorted out in order to establish which of the German equivalents is appropriate for the context:

Sie könnte den Brief nicht geschrieben haben	*She couldn't have written the letter*
(i.e. it isn't possible that it was she who wrote it)	
Sie hätte den Brief nicht schreiben können	*She couldn't have written the letter*
(i.e. she wouldn't have been able to)	
Er könnte umgekommen sein	*He might have been killed*
(i.e. it is possible that he was)	
Er hätte umkommen können	*He might have been killed*
(i.e. it was possible, but he wasn't)	

17.4 *mögen*

17.4.1 The most frequently used sense of *mögen* is to express liking

(a) It is most commonly employed in the Konjunktiv II form
The usual English equivalent of *möchte* is 'would like'. It is often linked with the adverb *gern*:

Sie möchte (gern) nach Rom fahren	*She would like to go to Rome*
Ich möchte nichts mehr davon hören	*I don't want to hear any more about it*
Ich möchte ihr Gesicht gesehen haben	*I would have liked to see her face*
Ich möchte nicht, daß er heute kommt	*I wouldn't like him to come today*

NB: Only the simple past subjunctive is used, not the pluperfect subjunctive. For 'I would have liked to read the book', German simply uses *gern* with the pluperfect subjunctive of the verb, i.e. *Ich hätte gern dieses Buch gelesen*.

(b) Other tenses of *mögen* are used in the sense of English 'like', especially with reference to people, places and food:

Sie mag keinen Tee	*She doesn't like tea*
Wir mögen den neuen Lehrer nicht	*We don't like the new teacher*
Ich mag ihn nicht	*I don't like him*
Sie mag ihn gut/nicht leiden	*She's (not) very fond of him*
Er mochte diese Schule nicht	*He didn't like that school*
Sie hat ihn nie gemocht	*She never liked him*

(c) Other tenses of *mögen* are often used in the negative with a dependent infinitive in the sense of 'like, wish':

Wie es im Winter werden soll, daran mag er noch gar nicht denken (*Böll*)	*He doesn't want to think about what it's going to be like in winter*
Ich mag das Wort gar nicht aussprechen	*I don't even like saying that word out loud*

17.4.2 *mögen* sometimes expresses possibility or probability

The use of *mögen* to express possibility is restricted in standard German to formal written registers and set phrases (although it is more widely used in spoken South German). Generally speaking, where it is used it tends to express a rather higher degree of probability than *können*, see 17.3.2–3.

(a) When indicating possibility *mögen* often has a concessive sense,
i.e. there is an expected qualification by a following *aber* (which may or may not be present). This usage corresponds, for instance, to English *That may well be (, but. . . .)*:

Das mag vielen nicht einleuchten, (aber . . .)	*That may not be clear to many, (but . . .)*

Der Leser mag über diese Theorie staunen, (aber. . .)	*The reader may be astonished at this theory (but. . .)*
Für Fremde mochte es ein Streit um Worte sein, in Wirklichkeit verbarg sich aber dahinter mehr	*For strangers it may have been a quarrel over words, but in actual fact this concealed much more*

(b) Other examples of the use of *mögen* to convey probability or possibility
This usage is restricted to formal registers:

Sie mag etwa sechzig sein	*She is perhaps about sixty*
Sie mochte etwa sechzig sein	*She was probably about sixty*
Jetzt mögen über 1000 DDR-Bürger sich in der Botschaft aufhalten (*ARD*)	*There are now probably more than a thousand GDR citizens in the embassy*
ein korrektes, sehr britisches Englisch, das sie in irgendeinem Pensionat gelernt haben mochte (*V. Baum*)	*a correct, very British English, that she had probably learnt in some boarding school*

(c) Set phrases and expressions with *mögen* expressing possibility
These are in more general use:

Das mag (wohl) sein	*That may well be*
Wer mag das (schon) sein?	*Who can that be?*
Wie mag das (nur) gekommen sein	*How can that have happened?*

(d) The Konjunktiv II *möchte* can be used to convey a doubt or a supposition
This is nowadays restricted to a couple of set phrases, where *könnte* is a possible alternative to *möchte*:

Man möchte/könnte meinen, daß. . .	*One might almost think that. . .*
Dabei möchte/könnte man verrückt werden	*It's enough to drive you mad*

17.4.3 The use of *mögen* in concessive clauses,

i.e. in clauses of the type *whatever, however, whoever that may be*, etc., cf. also 19.5.2. This usage is related to that explained in 17.4.2a. In general, *mögen* is optional in such clauses, and the main verb may be used on its own:

Wer er auch sein mag/ist, ich will ihn sprechen	*Whoever he may be, I will speak to him*
Wann er auch ankommen mag/ankommt, ich will ihn sofort sprechen	*Whenever he may arrive, I want to speak to him at once*
Wie schwierig es auch sein mag/ist, ich will es tun	*However difficult it may be, I will do it*
Was auch immer geschehen mag/ geschieht, ich werde hier bleiben	*Whatever happens, I'm going to stay here*

NB: (i) The use of the Konjunktiv I of *mögen* in this construction, e.g.
Was auch immer geschehen möge, is now obsolete, cf. 16.4.7.
(ii) *mögen* is always used in the set phrase:
Wie dem auch sein mag   *However that may be*

17.4.4 The use of *mögen* in wishes and commands

(a) The use of Konjunktiv I of *mögen* to express a wish or a command is restricted to formal German
Even there, it sounds rather stilted or archaic nowadays, cf. 16.4.6a:

Möge er glücklich sein!	*May he be happy!*
Die Herren mögen bitte unten warten	*Would the gentlemen be so kind as to wait downstairs*

b) The subjunctive of *mögen* is sometimes used in indirect commands:

Sagen Sie ihr, sie möchte zu mir kommen	*Ask her to be kind enough to come and see me*
Er sagte mir, ich möchte einen Augenblick auf ihn warten	*He asked me to wait for him a moment*

The Konjunktiv I of *mögen* (e.g.: . . . *sie möge zu mir kommen*) is nowadays rather old-fasioned in indirect commands. In practice, *sollen* or *müssen* are more frequent than *mögen* in indirect commands, cf. 16.2.6b.

17.5 *müssen*

17.5.1 The most frequent meaning of *müssen* is to express necessity or compulsion

(a) The most common English equivalent is 'must, have (got) to'

Wir müssen jetzt abfahren	{ *We must leave now* / *We have (got) to leave now*
Wir werden bald abfahren müssen	*We'll have to leave soon*
Ich mußte um acht abfahren Ich habe um acht abfahren müssen }	*I had to leave at eight*
Ich muß den Brief bis heute abend geschrieben haben	*I'll have to have the letter written before tonight*
Wir mußten die Anträge bis zum 15. Januar abgegeben haben	*We had to have the applications handed in by the 15th of January*
Sie muß sich beeilen, wenn sie den Zug erreichen will	*She'll have to hurry if she wants to catch the train*
Er hat es gut gemacht, das muß man sagen	*He did it well, you have to admit*
Muß das sein?	*Is that really necessary?*
Das muß man gesehen haben	*That's worth seeing*

(b) When *müssen* is used with a passive infinitive or a passive equivalent, 'need' is sometimes a more natural English equivalent:

Das muß gut überlegt werden	*That needs thinking about properly*
Man muß sich um sie kümmern	*She needs looking after*

(c) Negative *müssen* retains the sense of necessity
i.e. it corresponds to English 'needn't' or 'don't have to':

Wir müssen noch nicht gehen	*We needn't go yet* *We don't have to go yet*
Er hat es nicht tun müssen	*He didn't need to/have to do it*
Du mußt nicht hierbleiben, du kannst auch gehen	*You needn't stay here, you <u>can</u> leave*

NB: (i) In practice *nicht brauchen* (see 13.2.3) is rather more frequent than *nicht müssen* in this meaning, e.g. *Du brauchst nicht hierzubleiben*.

(ii) English 'mustn't' expresses a prohibition, and usually corresponds in German to *nicht dürfen*, cf. 17.2.1b. The use of *nicht müssen* in this sense, which is not infrequent in North German speech, e.g. *Sie müssen den Salat nicht im Kühlschrank aufbewahren* 'You mustn't keep the lettuce in the fridge' is a non-standard regionalism.

17.5.2 *müssen* can express a logical deduction

The usual English equivalent is 'must':

Sie spielt heute Tennis, also muß es ihr besser gehen	*She's playing tennis today, so* * she must be better*
Etwas muß passiert sein	*Something must have happened*
Sie muß den Unfall gesehen haben	*She must have seen the accident*

Note that the use of tenses is different in German to that in English when a logical deduction occurs in the context of a narrative in the past:

Draußen stieg jemand, der den
    gleichen Gang haben mußte wie
    Fräulein Gröschel, die Hintertreppe
    hinauf (*E. Fried*)
	Outside, someone who must have
	* had the same gait as Fräulein*
	* Gröschel was coming up the*
	* back stairs*

NB: (i) If, in the context of a particular sentence, *müssen* could be taken to convey necessity where logical deduction is intended, the meaning can be made clear by using the adverb *sicher* rather than *müssen*, e.g.:

Er ist heute sicher in Frankfurt	*He must be in Frankfurt today*

(*Er muß heute in Frankfurt sein* would naturally be taken to mean 'He has to be in Frankfurt today').

(ii) *nicht brauchen* is more usual than *nicht müssen* to query a logical deduction, e.g.:

Er war heute nicht im Büro, aber
    deshalb braucht (rarer: muß) er
    nicht krank zu sein
	He wasn't at the office, but that
	* doesn't necessarily mean that*
	* he's ill*

(iii) A negative logical deduction is expressed by *nicht können* (= English 'can't'):

Sie spielt heute Tennis, also kann sie nicht krank sein	*She's playing tennis today, so she* * can't be ill*

17.5.3 The use of the Konjunktiv II of *müssen*

(a) The Konjunktiv II of *müssen* conveys the idea of a possible compulsion, necessity or logical deduction

(i) This most often corresponds to English 'should, ought to':

Deutschlands Kohle ist teurer, als sie sein müßte (*Zeit*)	*Coal in Germany is dearer than* * it ought to be/should be*
So viel Zeit wie er müßte man haben	*I wish I had as much time as him*
Das müßte reichen	*That ought to be enough*

Jeder müßte einmal auf einem
   Bauernhof gearbeitet haben
	Everyone ought to have worked on
	   a farm at some time

Ich hätte mich vielleicht anders
   ausdrücken müssen
	Perhaps I ought to/should have
	   expressed myself differently

(ii) In such contexts the meaning of *müßte* is very close to that of *sollte*, which also corresponds to English 'should, ought to', cf. 17.6.5. However, they are not interchangeable. Whilst *sollte* always retains the sense of an obligation (often laid on a person by someone else), *müßte* most often conveys the idea of a logical probability or necessity. Compare:

Sie sollte heute im Büro sein	*She ought to be at the office today*
(i.e. she is obliged to if she doesn't want to get wrong with the boss)	
Sie müßte heute im Büro sein	*She ought to be at the office today*
(i.e. I assume that is the most likely place for her to be)	
Das hätte er eigentlich wissen sollen	*He ought to have known that*
(i.e. he was obliged to –it could have stopped him making a mistake)	
Das hätte er eigentlich wissen müssen	*He ought to have known that*
(i.e. I would have thought it was a pretty fair assumption that he did)	

Wo ist der Brief? – Er müßte in
   dieser Schublade sein
	Where's the letter? – It ought
	   to be/should be in this drawer

(A logical deduction; *sollte* would not be possible)	

NB: (i) *müßte nicht* is seldom used as an equivalent of the English negatives 'shouldn't, ought not to'; we usually find *sollte nicht* or *dürfte nicht*, cf. 17.6.5.

(ii) In some contexts *müßte* may correspond to English 'would have to', e.g.:

Da müßtest du den Chef fragen	*In that case you would have* *to ask the boss*

In corresponding negative sentences, Konjunktiv II forms of *nicht brauchen* are more usual than those of *nicht müssen*, cf. 17.5.2, e.g.:

Du hättest nicht hinzugehen
   brauchen, wenn . . .
	You wouldn't have had to go
	   there if . . .

(b) Combinations of the type *müßte . . . gemacht haben* and *hätte . . . machen müssen* have quite different meanings in German

The English equivalent for both is usually 'should/ought to have done', but German makes a clear distinction between these constructions, e.g., for English *He ought to have written the letter yesterday*:

Er müßte den Brief schon gestern geschrieben haben
   (i.e. it is a fair deduction that he did)
Er hätte den Brief schon gestern schreiben müssen
   (i.e. he needed to, but he didn't)

17.6 *sollen*

17.6.1 The most common use of *sollen* is to express an obligation

(a) In the indicative this usually corresponds to English 'be to' or 'be supposed to'

(aside from a few cases where we still use 'shall'):

Um wieviel Uhr soll ich kommen?	*What time am I to/shall I come?*
Ich soll nicht so viel rauchen	*I'm not supposed to smoke so much*
Was soll ich in Greifswald tun?	*What am I (supposed) to do in Greifswald?*
Sie wußte nicht, was sie tun sollte	*She didn't know what to do*
Wir sollten uns gestern treffen	*We were (supposed) to meet yesterday*
Du solltest doch deinem Freund helfen?	*You were (supposed) to help your friend, weren't you?*

(b) The meaning of *sollen* is often close to that of *müssen* (and 'must, have to' is often a possible English equivalent)

However, *sollen* always conveys the idea that some other person is requiring something of one. Compare:

Ich soll hier bleiben (i.e. someone's told me to)	*I am to/have (got) to stay here*
Ich muß hier bleiben (i.e. it is necessary for me to do so)	*I've got to stay here*

(c) Given its basic sense, *sollen* is often used with the force of a command:

Du sollst nicht stehlen (*Bible*)	*Thou shalt not steal*
Du sollst das Fenster zumachen	*(I want you to) shut the window*
Ihr sollt sofort den Saal verlassen	*Everyone has to leave the room immediately*
Das soll dir eine Warnung sein	*Let that be a warning to you*
Er soll sofort kommen	{ *He is to/has got to come at once* / *Tell him to come at once*
Er soll sich in acht nehmen	*Let him watch out*

sollen is the most frequent modal used in indirect commands, cf. 16.2.6b:

Er sagte ihr, sie solle/sollte unten warten	*He told her to wait downstairs*
Ich habe ihm gesagt, er soll seinem Vater helfen	*I told him to help his father*

17.6.2 *sollen* may express an intention or similar:

(a) The usual English equivalents are 'be to', 'be supposed to' or 'be meant to':

Eine zweite Fabrik soll bald hier gebaut werden	*A second factory is to be built here soon*
Soll das ein Kompliment sein?	*Is that meant as a compliment?*
Es sollte eine Überraschung sein	*It was intended to be a surprise*
Was soll das heißen?	*What's that supposed to mean?*
Es soll nicht wieder vorkommen	*It won't happen again*
Das sollst du noch bereuen	*You're going to regret that*

(b) The sense of intention is particularly common in first person plural questions

sollen is here an alternative to *wollen*, although there is a slight difference of meaning, cf. 17.7.1c:

Was sollen wir uns heute in der Stadt ansehen?	*What are we going to look at in town today?*
Sollen wir heute abend ins Kino gehen?	*Shall we go to the cinema tonight?*

(c) The past tense of *sollen* is used in questions to prompt a strong negative or positive reaction, depending on the context
It can sound rather ironic:

Wie sollte ich das wissen?	*How was I (supposed) to know that?*
Sollte das nun fertig sein?	*Is that supposed to be finished (ironic)*
Sollte er wirklich nichts davon wissen?	*Is he really supposed not to know anything about it?*

17.6.3 The past tense of *sollen* can be used to indicate what was destined to happen

This sense is essentially that of a 'future-in-the-past', and 'would' is often a possible English equivalent (though not the only one):

Diese Meinung sollte sie noch oft zu hören bekommen	*She would often hear this opinion again*
Er sollte früh sterben	*He would/was (destined) to die young*
Er sollte niemals nach Deutschland zurückkehren	*He would never return to Germany*

Cf. also the set phrase:

Es hat so sein sollen	*It was meant to be (so)*

17.6.4 *sollen* can be used to express a rumour or report,

i.e. 'It is said that . . .'. In practice, only the present tense of *sollen* is used in this sense, with a compound infinitive to refer to past time if necessary:

Er soll steinreich (gewesen) sein	*He is said to be (have been) enormously rich*
Bei den Unruhen soll es bisher vier Tote gegeben haben (*FAZ*)	*So far four people are reported to have been killed in the course of the riots*
Das soll er gewesen sein?	*Do you mean to say it was him?*
Eine solche Bombe soll die Katastrophe von Lockerbie ausgelöst haben (*ARD*)	*A similar bomb is assumed to have caused the Lockerbie disaster*

17.6.5 The use of the Konjunktiv II of *sollen*

(a) The Konjunktiv II of *sollen* most often conveys the idea of a possible obligation
This is related to its basic sense, see 17.6.1, but in these forms it usually has the clear English equivalents 'should (have)', 'ought to (have)':

Warum sollte ich denn nicht ins Theater gehen?	*Why shouldn't I go to the theatre?*
Das solltest du mal probieren	*You ought just to try that*
Das sollte ihm inzwischen klar geworden sein	*He ought to have realised that by now*
Das hätten Sie mir aber gestern sagen sollen	*You ought to have told me that yesterday*

NB: (i) For the distinction between *sollte* and *müßte* as equivalents of English 'should/ought to', see 17.5.3a.
(ii) For negative 'shouldn't, ought not to', *dürfte nicht* may be used as an alternative to *sollte nicht* in order to emphasise that something ought not to have been allowed, cf. 17.2.1b:

Das dürfte er eigentlich gar nicht wissen	*He really ought not to know that*

(b) Combinations of the type *sollte . . . gemacht haben* and *hätte . . . machen sollen* have quite different meanings in German
The English equivalent for both is usually 'should/ought to have done', but German makes a clear distinction between these constructions, e.g., for English *He ought to have written the letter yesterday*:

Er sollte den Brief gestern geschrieben haben
      (i.e. I would expect him to have done so)
Er hätte den Brief gestern schreiben sollen
      (i.e. he ought to have done, but he didn't)

(c) In questions, *sollte* is often used as an alternative to *können* with no real difference in meaning:

Wie sollte/konnte ich das wissen?	*How could I know that?*
Sollte/könnte es ein Mißverständnis gewesen sein?	*Could it have been a mistake after all?*
Warum sollte/könnte er nicht einmal in London gewesen sein?	*Why shouldn't he have been to London some time?*

(d) The Konjunktiv II of *sollen* is frequently used in conditional and final sentences
(i) Its use in conditional sentences corresponds to that of 'should' or 'were to' in English, cf. 16.3.1c:

Wenn es regnen sollte, so komme ich nicht	*If it should rain, I shan't come*
Sollten Sie ihn sehen, dann grüßen Sie ihn bitte von mir	*If you should see him, please give him my regards*
Falls er wegbleiben sollte, habe ich daran kein Interesse	*If he were not to come, I'm not interested in it any more*

The following usage is idiomatic:

Man sollte meinen, er würde es gern   *One would think he'd be glad*
    tun   *to do it*

(ii) In final clauses, it is a more current alternative to the subjunctive of the main verb which is still occasionally used in formal literary German:

Ich trat zurück, damit sie mich   *I stepped back, so that they*
    nicht sehen sollten (older: sähen)   *shouldn't see me*

The indicative of the main verb is also commonly used in such final clauses, cf. 16.4.2a.

17.7 *wollen*

17.7.1 *wollen* most often expresses desire or intention

This basic meaning of *wollen* is quite wide, and there are a good number of possible English equivalents.

(a) In many contexts it expresses a wish, and corresponds to English 'want (to)', 'wish (to)':

Sie will ihn um Geld bitten   *She wants to ask him for money*
Sie wollte ihn um Geld bitten   ⎫
Sie hat ihn um Geld bitten wollen ⎬   *She wanted to ask him for money*
Hättest du dann kommen wollen?   *Would you have wanted to come*
                                                    in that case
Willst du nicht deinem Vater helfen?   *Don't you want to help your father?*

In this sense, *wollen* is frequently used without a dependent infinitive:

Ich will nur dein Bestes   *I only want what's best for you*
Was wollen Sie von mir?   *What do you want from me?*
Der Arzt will, daß ich mich mehr   *The doctor wants me to take more*
    bewege   *exercise*
Mach, was du willst   *Do what you like*

The sense of 'wish' is most often given by Konjunktiv II:

Ich wollte, ich hätte sie nicht so   *I wish I hadn't offended her like*
    beleidigt   *that*
Ich wollte, ich wäre zu Hause   *I wish I was at home*

(b) *wollen* can express willingness on the part of the subject

It can then correspond to English 'will, would', but it must be carefully distinguished from the future tense:

Willst du mir helfen? –   *Will you help me?*
Ja, ich will dir helfen   *Yes, I will help you*
    The future, i.e. *Wirst du mir helfen – Ja, ich werde dir helfen*, has a more impersonal
    tone and lacks the sense of active willingness on the part of the speaker conveyed by
    wollen.
Er will es nicht zugeben   *He won't admit it*

Mit ihm ist nichts zu wollen	*There's nothing to be done with him*

Ich bat sie, es zu tun, aber sie
   wollte nicht
	*I asked her to do it, but she
	   wouldn't*

Ich will es gern glauben	*I quite believe it*

NB: This use of *wollen* is common in second person questions which have the sense of an insistent request, as in the first example above and the following:

Willst du bitte nochmal nachsehen?	*Will you have another look, please?*

Wollen Sie bitte die Frage
   wiederholen?
	*Will you repeat the question,
	   please?*

The tone of such requests can be moderated by using Konjunktiv II, cf. 16.4.3., e.g. *Würden Sie vielleicht nochmal nachsehen?* which sounds rather less blunt and direct than when *wollen* is used.

(c) *wollen* can express intention.

(i) In such cases it very frequently corresponds to English 'be going to', but *wollen* stresses the notion of intention more forcefully than the future with *werden*:

Wir wollen uns bald einen neuen
   Fernseher anschaffen
	*We're going to buy ourselves a
	   new TV set soon*

The future *Wir werden uns bald einen neuen Fernseher anschaffen* has more the sense of a prediction than a definite intention.

Wie wollen Sie ihm das klarmachen?	*How are you going to explain that to him?*
Was wollen Sie damit sagen?	*What do you mean by that?*
Das will nicht viel sagen	*That doesn't mean much*
Es scheint regnen zu wollen	*It looks as if it's going to rain*

Der Gast wollte gerade aufstehen, als
   der Wirt in der Küchentür erschien
	*The guest was just going to get up
	   when the landlord appeared at the
	   kitchen door*

(ii) In certain contexts, other English equivalents are required:

Sie wollen doch nicht behaupten,
   daß ich es getan habe?
	*Surely you're not trying to say that
	   I did it?*

Ich will sie erst morgen anrufen	*I don't intend phoning her till tomorrow*
eine gewollte Beleidigung	*a deliberate insult*

(iii) Linked to this sense of *wollen* is its use in first person plural questions in the sense of English 'Shall we . . .?':

Wollen wir eine Tasse Kaffee trinken?	*Shall we/Let's have a cup of coffee*
Was wollen wir heute machen?	*What shall we do today?*

NB: *sollen* is an alternative to *wollen* in such constructions, cf. 17.6.2b. However, whilst *wollen* clearly indicates that the speaker is in favour of the proposal, *sollen* leaves the decision entirely to the other person(s).

17.7.2 Used with an inanimate subject, *wollen* has a similar sense to those explained in 17.7.1, but the English equivalent is most often 'need':

Tomaten wollen viel Sonne	*Tomatoes need a lot of sun*
Eine solche Arbeit will Zeit haben	*A piece of work like that needs time*

| Das will gut überlegt werden | *That needs proper consideration* |
| Solche Dolmetscherarbeit will gelernt sein, das darf man mir glauben (*Frisch*) | *Working like that as an interpreter needs to be learnt, believe me* |

In the negative, this use of *wollen* has the sense of English 'refuse':

Der Koffer wollte nicht zugehen	*The suitcase refused to/wouldn't close*
Meine Beine wollen nicht mehr	*My legs won't carry me any further*
Das will mir nicht in den Kopf	*I can't grasp that*

17.7.3 *wollen* can be used in the sense of 'claim', often with the implication that the claim is false

In this sense, *wollen* is most commonly linked with a compound infinitive:

Er will eine Mosquito abgeschossen haben (*Gaiser*)	*He claims to have shot down a Mosquito (type of aeroplane)*
Sie wollen dich in Berlin gesehen haben	*They say they saw you in Berlin*
Zur gleichen Zeit, da ich das Judenauto gesehen haben wollte, . . . (*Fühmann*)	*At the same time at which I said I had seen the car with the Jews, . . .*

The following set phrases are an extension of this sense of *wollen*:

Keiner will es getan haben	*No-one admits doing it*
Ich will nichts gesagt haben	*Go on as if I hadn't said anything*
Ich will nichts gehört/gesehen/ gemerkt haben	*I'll go on as if I hadn't heard/ seen/noticed anything*

18   Verbs: valency

The term 'valency' has been borrowed from chemistry, where the 'valency' of a chemical element determines the number of atoms of that element which are needed to form a compound. In grammar, it is used to refer to the type of construction required by a particular verb (i.e. whether a verb governs the dative, the accusative, the accusative and the dative, etc.). The term 'valency' is widely used in recent German grammars, e.g. DUDEN (1984:1082ff.), Engel (1988:185ff.), Helbig and Buscha (1986:619ff.), etc. Good introductions in English to the notion of valency as applied to German grammar are given in Fox (1990:218ff.) and Herbst *et al.* (1980:142ff.).

In this chapter we first (18.1) explain in full what is meant by 'valency' and then (18.2–18.8) deal with the different valency patterns in detail, with lists of verbs, paying particular attention to those verbs and constructions which are most difficult for the English learner.

Much more extensive detail on the valency of German verbs may be found in two 'valency dictionaries', i.e. Helbig and Schenkel (1978) and Engel and Schuhmacher (1978). In addition, Wahrig (1978) is particularly useful for the foreign learner in that it indicates very clearly the valency of each verb in all its various meanings.

18.1   Valency, complements and sentence patterns

18.1.1 We can classify all the verbs of German in terms of the number and type of the elements which they govern, and this is called the 'valency' of the verb

Different verbs require different types of element in order to construct a grammatical sentence. Thus, *geben* needs a subject (in the nominative), a direct object (in the accusative) and an indirect object (in the dative) in order to form a complete sentence, e.g.:

Gestern hat **mein Vater mir das Geld** gegeben

If we omitted any of these elements, we would not be left with a meaningful sentence.

Other verbs, like *telephonieren*, only need a subject, e.g.:

Ich habe eben telephoniert   *I've just made a phone call*

A large number of verbs, like *schlagen*, require a subject and a direct object (in the accusative), e.g.:

Sie hat **den Ball** geschlagen   *She hit the ball*

A number of verbs require constructions other than with the four cases. For example, very many govern a construction with a particular preposition, like *warten*, e.g.:

Ich habe lange **auf dich** gewartet   *I waited a long time for you*

18.1.2 The elements which are required by a verb in order to construct a complete sentence are called its 'complements'

In German, these are known as *Ergänzungen*. Following Engel (1988:187–98), we can distinguish eight different types of complement used with verbs in German, i.e.:

(a) The subject
This is usually a noun or a pronoun in the nominative case, e.g.:

Der Bäcker trank zu viel   Das hast **du** mir doch versprochen!

Subject complements are treated in detail in 18.2.

(b) The accusative object
This is the direct object of transitive verbs. It is usually a noun or a pronoun (in the accusative), e.g.:

Er trinkt **viel Kaffee**   Sie sah **ihn** in der Stadt

Accusative complements are treated in detail in 18.3.

(c) The dative object
This may be a noun or a pronoun in the dative case, e.g.:

Sie hat **ihrem Sohn** das Geld gegeben   Er nahm **ihr** den Ring

Dative complements are fully dealt with in 18.4.

(d) Genitive objects
This is usually a noun in the genitive case, e.g.:

Sie bedarf **unserer Hilfe**   Er erinnerte sich **des Vorfalls**

Genitive complements are treated in 18.5.

(e) Prepositional objects
The complement has the form of a prepositional phrase, e.g.:

Sie wartete **auf ihre Freundin**   Ich dankte ihr sehr **dafür**

The prepositional complement is fully treated in 18.6, with lists of the prepositions required by particular verbs.

(f) Place complements
A few verbs denoting position have a complement indicating place, e.g.:

Sie wohnte lange **in Hildesheim**   Ich blieb **dort**

Place complements are dealt with in 18.7.1.

(g) Direction complements
A direction complement may occur with verbs of motion, e.g.:

Gestern ging sie **in die Stadt**   Ich folgte ihr **hinein**

Direction complements are treated in 18.7.2.

(h) Predicate complements
A few verbs like *sein*, *werden* and *scheinen* have a predicate complement, usually a noun or pronoun in the nominative case or an adjective, e.g.:

Er ist **ihr Betreuer**   Das Heft ist **teuer**

Predicate complements are treated in 18.8.

18.1.3 Complements are clearly differentiated from adverbials

Besides the complements, which are required by the verb to complete its sense, a German sentence may contain other elements. Compare the following examples:

Mein Vater hat mir **gestern** das Geld gegeben
Heute habe ich Gudrun **in der Stadt** gesehen
Der junge Tenor hat **in Berlin gut** gesungen
Dein Bruder hat **aber tüchtig** gearbeitet

Elements like those in bold provide additional information, often about the time, manner or place of the action or event. Although they may be important in context, they are not an essential component of the sentence in the way that complements are. If they are omitted we are still left with a meaningful sentence, e.g.:

Mein Vater hat mir das Geld gegeben   Ich habe Gudrun gesehen
Der junge Tenor hat gesungen   Dein Bruder hat gearbeitet

The German term for these elements is *freie Angaben*, which gives a clear indication of their function in the sentence. In English they are usually referred to as 'adverbials'. As the examples show, they may be single words (adverbs, modal particles, etc.) or phrases (often with prepositions). They can be freely added to sentences to give extra circumstantial detail, but their selection does not depend on the choice of verb as is the case with complements and they are thus less closely linked to the particular verb.

NB: Although, in general, 'complements' are necessary to construct a complete sentence, whilst 'adverbials' are optional, certain complements of some verbs may be deleted without this resulting in an meaningless sentence. Compare:

Er trinkt **viel Kaffee**   –   Er trinkt
Sie fährt **in die Stadt**   –   Sie fährt

We still have full sentences even though the elements in bold are not present. However, the elements in question, i.e. the accusative object *viel Kaffee* with *trinken* and the directional complement *in die Stadt* with *fahren* are so closely associated with the action of the verb and dependent on it that they must still be considered as complements.

18.1.4 German sentence patterns

Every verb requires one, two or three of the complements listed in 18.1.2 to form a complete clause or sentence. How many there are, and of what type, is determined by the valency of the verb.

There are a limited number of combinations of complements which occur commonly with German verbs, as many verbs have the same valency. In this way, we can say that German possesses a restricted number of possible sentence structure types or 'sentence patterns' (the German term is *Satzbaupläne*).

The most frequently occurring sentence patterns of German are summarized below. More extensive detail may be found in DUDEN (1984:1088–141) and Engel (1988:200–17).

(a) Subject + verb, e.g.:
Mein Vater (subj.) schwimmt gern
This is the simple intransitive pattern.

(b) Subject + verb + accusative object, e.g.:
Sie (subj.) bauten **ein Haus** (acc.)
This is the simple transitive pattern.

(c) Subject + verb + dative object, e.g.:
Der Polizist (subj.) hilft **der alten Frau** (dat.)
Verbs governing the dative are listed in 18.4.1.

(d) Subject + verb + accusative object + dative object, e.g.:
Mein Vater (subj.) schreibt **seinem Freund** (dat.) **einen Brief** (acc.)
This construction is explained in 18.4.2.

(e) Subject + verb + genitive object, e.g.:
Sie (subj.) bedarf **der Ruhe** (gen.)
An uncommon pattern, dealt with in 18.5.1-2.

(f) Subject + verb + accusative object + genitive object, e.g.:
Man (subj.) klagte **ihn** (acc.) **des Diebstahls** (gen.) an
Few transitive verbs also have a genitive object, cf. 18.5.3

(g) Subject + verb + prepositional object, e.g.:
Sie (subj.) suchte **nach ihrem Taschentuch** (prep.)
All verbs taking prepositional objects, including those which also have an
accusative or a dative object, or two prepositional obects, i.e. patterns (h),
(j) and (k) below, are treated in 18.6.

(h) Subject + verb + accusative object + prepositional object, e.g.:
Ich (subj.) konnte **ihn** (acc.) **von der Richtigkeit meiner**
        Auffassung (prep.) überzeugen
i.e. transitive verbs with a further prepositional object.

(j) Subject + verb + dative object + prepositional object, e.g.:
Sie (subj.) dankte **ihm** (dat.) **für seine Mühe** (prep.)

(k) Subject + verb + two prepositional objects, e.g.:
Der Arzt (subj.) hat **aus der Art der Verletzung** (prep.) **auf einen**
        Selbstmordversuch (prep.) geschlossen

(l) Subject + verb + place complement, e.g.:
Das Bild (subj.) hängt **über seinem Arbeitstisch** (place)
This construction is treated in 18.7.1.

(m) Subject + verb + direction complement, e.g.:
Der Junge (subj.) fiel **in den Brunnen** (dir.)
Intransitive and transitive constructions with direction complements, i.e.
patterns (m) and (n), are explained in 18.7.2.

(n) Subject + verb + accusative object + direction complement, e.g.:
Sie (subj) steckte **den Schlüssel** (acc.) **in ihre Tasche** (dir.)

(o) Subject + verb + predicate complement, e.g.:
Helga (subj.) ist **Lehrerin** (pred.) geworden
This construction is dealt with in 18.8.

18.1.5 In order to use a German verb correctly, we have to know its valency,

i.e. the sentence pattern, cf. 18.1.4, in which it is used. As German
sentence patterns are often very different from those required by what may

seem to be an equivalent English verb, it is particularly important to commit German verbs to memory in typical sentences which show the valency of the verb clearly, e.g.:

Das hat er **mir** gestern mitgeteilt	*He informed me of that yesterday*
Ich fürchte **mich vor dem Zahnarzt**	*I'm afraid of the dentist*
Er riet **ihr von dieser Reise** ab	*He advised her against (making) this journey*

NB: A number of verbs, especially the most frequent, are used with different valencies. This is often associated with a difference in meaning, e.g.:

jemanden achten	*respect somebody*
auf jemanden achten	*pay attention to somebody*

Further examples are given in the remainder of this chapter.

18.2 The subject

18.2.1 The majority of verbs in German require a subject complement

(a) If the subject is a noun or pronoun, it is in the nominative case,
cf. 2.1.2. A finite verb agrees with the subject for person and number, cf. 12.1:

Ich reise nach Italien	Das hat uns **die Geschichte** gelehrt
Wer ruft mich?	Kommen **deine Geschwister** morgen?

NB: For the use of *es* as a 'dummy subject' in main clauses in order to permit the real subject to occur later, e.g. **Es** *saß eine alte Frau am Fenster*, see the detailed account in 3.6.5.

(b) If the subject is a clause (whether a *daß*-clause or an infinitive clause), the verb has the form of the third person singular, e.g.:

Daß du hier bist, freut mich	**Dich wiederzusehen**, hat mich gefreut

NB: If such a clause is not in first position in the sentence, it may be anticipated by *es*, e.g. *Es freut mich, daß du hier bist*. This construction is explained in detail in 3.6.6.

18.2.2 A handful of verbs do not require a subject complement.

Most of these verbs express an emotion or sensation. They are used in the third person singular form with an accusative (or sometimes a dative) object, although a few have a prepositional object in addition. Most of these verbs are nowadays restricted to literary registers. We give a selection of those which may still be encountered, together with more currently used equivalents where appropriate:

Mich hungert, dürstet	*I am hungry, thirsty*
(More usual: Ich habe Hunger, Durst)	

Mich friert   *I am cold*
    (More usual: Es friert mich. Or, more colloquially: Ich friere)
Mich wundert, daß . . .   *I am surprised that* . . .
    (This construction is not infrequent in all registers, but there are
    common alternatives, i.e.: Es wundert mich/Ich wundere mich, daß . . .)
Mich/Mir schauderte vor etwas   *I shuddered at sth.*
    (More usual: Es schauderte mich vor etwas)
Mich/Mir ekelte vor etwas   *I was disgusted at sth.*
    (More usual: Es ekelte mich/Ich ekelte mich vor etwas)
Mich/Mir schwindelt   *I feel dizzy*
    (More usual: Mir ist schwindlig)
Mir träumte von etwas   *I dreamt of sth.*
    (More usual: Ich träumte von etwas)
Mir graut vor etwas   *I have a horror of sth.*
    (More usual: Es graut mir vor etwas)
Mir bangt vor etwas   *I am afraid of sth.*
    (More usual: Ich habe Angst vor etwas)

18.2.3 German is less free than English as regards the type of noun which may occur as the subject of the verb

In particular, nouns which, strictly speaking, do not denote the person or thing actually carrying out the action often appear in prepositional phrases rather than as the verb subject in the nominative, as is common in English. The following examples are taken from Hawkins (1986:57-61) who provides more detail on this tendency of German:

In diesem Hotel sind Hunde verboten	*This hotel forbids dogs*
In diesem Zelt können vier schlafen	*This tent sleeps four*
Mit dieser Anzeige verkaufen wir viel	*This advertisement will sell us a lot*
Wir können mit dem Prozeß nicht fortfahren	*The trial cannot proceed*
Damit haben wir den besten Mittelstürmer verloren	*This loses us the best centre-forward*
In Berlin wird es wieder ziemlich heiß sein	*Berlin will be rather hot again*

Logically, 'hotels' do not really 'forbid', 'tents' do not actually 'sleep', 'advertisements' do not do any 'selling', etc., and, in the last example, Berlin is <u>where</u> 'it' is hot rather than a person or thing feeling the heat, and the German construction reflects this more clearly than do the corresponding English sentences.

18.2.4 The impersonal subject *es*

A large number of verbs are exclusively or commonly used impersonally, with the indefinite subject *es*. The *es* is never omitted with these verbs except in the few cases indicated below.

(a) Verbs referring to weather

Es regnet, hagelt, schneit	*It is raining, hailing, snowing*
Es blitzte	*There were flashes of lightening*
Es dämmert	*It is growing light/dusk*

These verbs can only be used impersonally.

(b) Verbs used with impersonal *es* to refer to an indefinite agent

These are verbs which can be used with a specific subject, but are used impersonally if the agent is vague or unknown, e.g.:

(i) Verbs referring to natural phenomena:

Es zieht	*There's a draught*
Es brennt	*Something's burning*
Da riecht es nach Teer	*There's a smell of tar there*

(ii) Verbs denoting noises

Es läutet, klingelt	*Someone's ringing the bell*
Es klopfte an der Tür	*There was a knock at the door*
Es kracht, zischt, knallt	*There is a crashing, hissing, banging noise*

NB: Many other verbs can be used with an impersonal *es* to bring out the idea of a vague, impersonal agent, cf. 3.6.7b.

(c) Verbs denoting sensations and emotions

Many verbs denoting sensations can be used with an impersonal *es* as subject to bring out the idea of an unspecified force causing the sensation. The person involved appears as an accusative object, e.g.:

Es juckt mich	*I itch*
Es überlief mich kalt	*A cold shiver ran up my back*
Es zog mich zu ihr	*I was drawn to her*
Es hält mich hier nicht länger	*Nothing's keeping me here any more*

NB: Some of the verbs which are used without a subject in older German, cf. 18.2.2, are now constructed in this way, e.g. *Es friert mich*, *Es wundert mich*, etc.

(d) Impersonal *es* used with *sein* and *werden* followed by a noun or an adjective.

This usually corrresponds to the English use of *it*, e.g.:

Es ist, wurde spät	*It is, got late*
Es ist dein Vater	*It's your father*

Details of this use of *es* are given in 3.6.1.

NB: See 18.2.5 for the use of e*s ist* in the sense of English 'there is/are'.

(e) The verbs *sein* and *werden* used impersonally with a personal dative and an adjective,
see also 2.5.13:

Es ist mir bange, heiß, kalt, schwindlig, warm, etc.

This *es* may be omitted in non-initial position, e.g.:

Mir ist (es) kalt   Ich merkte, daß (es) mir schwindlig wurde.

(f) Other miscellaneous impersonal verbs and constructions
Many of these are idiomatic and the verbs involved are also used in other constructions with a definite subject. We give a selection of the most common:

Es bedarf noch einiger Mühe (gen.)	*Some effort is still needed*
Es fehlt mir an etwas	*I lack sth.*
Es gefällt mir in Heidelberg	*I like it in Heidelberg*
Es gibt	*There is/are*

The distinction between *es gibt* and *es ist* as equivalents of English 'there is/are is dealt with in 18.2.5.

Es geht	*It can be done; OK (in answer to Wie geht es?)*
Wie geht es Ihnen?	*How are you?*
Es geht um Leben und Tod	*It's a matter of life and death*
Heute geht es nach Freiburg	*We're going to Freiburg today*
Es gilt, etwas zu tun	*The thing is to do something*
Es geschah ihm recht	*It served him right*
Es handelt sich um etwas	*It is a question of sth.*
Es heißt, daß . . .	*It is said that . . .*
Es kommt auf etwas an	*It depends on sth.*
Es kommt zu etwas	*Something occurs*
e.g.: Am Abend kam es zu neuen Zusammenstößen	*There were fresh clashes in the evening*
Es liegt an etwas	*It is due to sth.*
e.g.: Woran liegt es, daß . . .?	*Why is it that . . .?*
Es macht/tut nichts	*It doesn't matter*
Es steht schlecht/besser um ihn	*Things look bad/better for him*
Wie steht es mit ihr?	*How's she doing?*
Es verhält sich so	*Things are like that*
e.g.: Ähnlich verhält es sich an der Universität Münster	*Things are similar at the University of Münster*

(g) Impersonal passive and reflexive constructions, e.g.:

Es lebt sich gut in dieser Stadt   Es wurde im Nebenzimmer geredet

These are treated in 3.6.7, 15.1.5 and 15.4.3.

18.2.5 *es ist/sind* and *es gibt* as equivalents of English 'there is/are'
As the two German equivalents for English 'there is/are' are rarely

interchangeable, English learners often find it difficult to choose the correct one in context.

(a) *es gibt* points to existence as such, without reference to a particular place
It is a real impersonal construction, and the *es* is never omitted.
(i) *es gibt* is typically used in broad, general statements, denoting existence in general without reference to a particular place:

Es gibt Tage, wo alles schiefgeht	*There are days when everything goes wrong*
So etwas gibt es nicht	*There's no such thing*
Es gibt verschiedene Gründe dafür	*There are various reasons for that*
Es hat immer Kriege gegeben (*Valentin*)	*There have always been wars*
Unglückliche gibt es in allen Häusern, in jedem Stand (*Walser*)	*There are unhappy people in every kind of home, in every walk of life*
Urlaub gibt es jetzt sowieso nicht (*Gaiser*)	*In any case there's no leave at the moment*

(ii) *es gibt* is used to point in a general way to permanent existence in a large area (i.e. a city or country):

Es gibt drei alte Kirchen in unserer Stadt	*There are three old churches in our town*
In München gibt es ja so viel zu sehen	*There's so much to see in Munich*
Es dürfte in der Bundesrepublik wenige geben, die so gut wie er informiert sind (*Zeit*)	*There are probably not many people in the Federal Republic who are as well informed as he is*

(iii) *es gibt* is used to record the consequences of some event:

Wenn du das tust, gibt's ein Unglück	*If you do that, there'll be an accident*
Bei den Unruhen soll es bisher vier Tote gegeben haben (*FAZ*)	*It is reported that there have been four killed in the disturbances so far*

NB: In everyday speech in south-west Germany, *es hat* is used instead of *es gibt*. This usage is purely colloquial and regarded as sub-standard.

(b) *es ist/sind* indicates the presence of something at a particular time and place
Essentially, the *es* of *es ist/sind* is merely a 'dummy' subject, allowing the real subject of the verb to occur later in the sentence, and it drops out when it is not in initial position, cf. 3.6.5. Compare:

Es war eine Maus in der Küche	–	In der Küche war eine Maus
There was a mouse in the kitchen		
Es sind zwei Hunde im Garten	–	Zwei Hunde sind im Garten
There are two dogs in the garden		

This is also the case in subordinate clauses, e.g.:

Er hat mir gesagt, daß eine Maus in der Küche sei	*He told me there was a mouse in the kitchen*

Given this, *es ist/sind* is used:

(i) to refer to permanent or temporary presence in a definite and limited place, or temporary presence in a large area, e.g.:

Es war eine kleine Gastwirtschaft im Keller (*Baum*)	*There was a little bar in the cellar*
Schade, daß hier im Haushalt keine Nähmaschine ist (*Fallada*)	*It's a shame there isn't a sewing-machine here in the house*
Es ist irgendjemand an der Tür	*There's someone at the door*
Es waren noch viele Menschen auf den Straßen	*There were still a lot of people in the streets*
Es waren Wolken am Himmel	*There were clouds in the sky*
Es war ein Frühlingsgefühl in der Luft	*There was a feeling of spring in air*

NB: (i) If *es ist/sind* is used in such contexts, the sentence <u>must</u> contain an indication of place. If necessary, *da* must be added, e.g.:

Es ist ein Brief für Sie da	*There's a letter for you*

(ii) *es gibt* may occasionally be used in such contexts. If so, it emphasizes the thing rather than the place and underlines the distinctive character of the thing concerned, e.g.:

In dieser Diele gab es gegenüber der Tür einen offenen Kamin (*Wendt*)	*In this lounge there was an open fireplace opposite the door*

(ii) to record events and when speaking of weather conditions, e.g.:

Letzte Woche war in Hamburg ein Streik	*There was a strike in Hamburg last week*
Im Fernsehen war eine Diskussion darüber (*Valentin*)	*There was a discussion about that on the television*
In Mainz war ein Aufenthalt von fünf Minuten	*There was a five minute stop in Mainz*
Am nächsten Morgen war dichter Nebel	*Next morning there was thick fog*
Gestern war ein Gewitter in Füssen	*There was a thunderstorm in Füssen yesterday*

NB: Usage varies a good deal in this context, and *es gibt* is often used, e.g.:

Letzte Woche gab es einen Streik in Hamburg
In Mainz gab es einen Aufenthalt von fünf Minuten
Gestern gab es ein Gewitter in Füssen

es gibt is particularly frequent when a need is felt to emphasise the exceptional nature of the event or to refer to the future, e.g.:

Es gab eine Explosion in der Fabrik	*There was an explosion in the factory*
Morgen wird es wieder schönes Wetter geben	*It will be fine again tomorrow*

18.3 The accusative object

18.3.1 Transitive verbs govern a direct object in the accusative as one of their complements

With many verbs, the accusative is the only complement apart from the subject, (sentence pattern 18.1.4b), e.g.:

Er schlug **sie**   Christian hat **seine Freundin** besucht
Seine Worte haben **mich** verletzt   Sie hat **den Arzt** gesehen

Other transitive verbs have, in addition, a dative object (sentence pattern 18.1.4d), a genitive object (sentence pattern 18.1.4f), a prepositional object (18.1.4h) or a direction complement (sentence pattern 18.1.4n). Further details about these verbs may be found in the sections dealing with these other complements.

NOTE that the accusative is used with certain time and place phrases, e.g.: Es hat **den ganzen Tag** geschneit (cf. 2.2.5). These are not accusative complements, but adverbials.

18.3.2 If the accusative object is a clause, it may be anticipated by *es* with some verbs

This is the case whether the complement is a subordinate clause or an infinitive clause, e.g.:

Sie sah **es** als gutes Zeichen an, daß keine Leute mehr vorbeikamen
Ich konnte **es** kaum ertragen, ihn so leiden zu sehen

Details on the verbs with which this 'anticipatory' *es* is used are given in 3.6.8.

18.3.3 A handful of verbs are used with <u>two</u> accusatives

(a) The verbs *kosten* and *lehren* have two accusative objects:

Die Reise hat meinen Vater 5000 Mark   *The journey cost my father 5000*
  gekostet   *marks*
Sie hat mich Deutsch gelehrt   *She taught me German*

NB: Especially in colloquial German, both these verbs may be heard with a dative of the person, e.g. *Sie hat mir Deutsch gelehrt, Das hat mir viel Geld gekostet*. This is usually considered substandard, although DUDEN (1985:435) accepts it for *kosten*, as an alternative to the accusative, in figurative contexts, e.g.:
Das kann ihn/ihm das Hals kosten   *that may cost him his life*

(b) The verbs *angehen* and *fragen* may be used with two accusatives
The second accusative is usually an indefinite pronoun, e.g.:

Das geht mich nichts an   *That doesn't concern me*
Hast du ihn etwas gefragt?   *Did you ask him something?*

NB: *Hast du ihm eine Frage gestellt?* 'Did you ask him a question?'

(c) A few verbs have a predicate complement in the accusative,
i.e. an additional element which relates back to the accusative object,
describing or identifying it, e.g.:

Er nannte **mich einen Lügner**	*He called me a liar*

This construction is restricted in German to verbs of calling, i.e. *heißen*,
nennen and *schimpfen*. It is much more common in English, and in most
such cases the German equivalent is either an appositional phrase with *als*
(cf. 2.6) or a prepositional complement introduced by *zu*, e.g.:

Ich sehe es als eine Schande an	*I consider it a shame*
Er bewies sich als Feigling	*He proved himself a coward*
Er machte sie zu seiner Frau	*He made her his wife*
Man erklärte ihn zum Verräter	*He was declared a traitor*

Cf. also:

Wir hielten ihn für einen Idioten	*We considered/thought him an idiot*

18.3.4 A few German transitive verbs have usual English equivalents with rather different constructions, e.g.:

etwas beantragen	*to apply for sth.*
jemanden beerben	*to inherit from sb.*
etwas bezahlen	*to pay for sth.*
etwas dauert mich	*I regret sth.*
etwas ekelt mich	*I am disgusted at sth.*

  (cf. 18.2.2 and 18.6.12a for other constructions with *ekeln*)

etwas freut mich	*I am pleased/glad about sth.*
jemanden/etwas fürchten	*to be afraid of sb./sth.*

18.3.5 Fewer verbs can be used both transitively and intransitively in German than in English

German verbs are often less flexible than their English counterparts and
more frequently restricted to use in certain constructions only. Whereas a
number of German verbs may be used both transitively and intransitively,
e.g.:

Ich brach den Zweig	*I broke the branch*
Der Zweig brach	*The branch broke*

far fewer German than English verbs have this facility, and different
German equivalents are needed for the transitive and intransitive uses of
many English verbs. These different equivalents may take a number of
forms:

(a) The transitive and intransitive uses of some English verbs may correspond to quite different verbs in German, e.g.:

grow

Er züchtet Blumen	*He grows flowers*
Die Blumen wachsen im Garten	*The flowers are growing in the garden*

leave

Sie verließ das Haus	*She left the house*
Ich ließ den Brief auf dem Tisch (liegen)	*I left the letter on the table*
Der Zug ist schon abgefahren	*The train has already left*
Er ging früher als ich (weg)	*He left before me*

open

Ich machte die Tür auf	*I opened the door*
Die Tür ging auf	*The door opened*

(See (c) below for alternative equivalents for English 'open')

(b) The transitive and intransitive uses of some English verbs may correspond to related verbs in German

In particular, the prefix *be-* (cf. 22.4.1) is often used to form transitive verbs from intransitive verbs, although *er-* and *ver-* are also sometimes found, e.g.

answer

Sie beantwortete die Frage	*She answered the question*
Sie antwortete	*She answered*

climb

Ich bestieg den Berg	*I climbed the mountain*
Ich erstieg den Berg	*I climbed the mountain*
Die Maschine stieg	*The plane climbed*

NB: *ersteigen* differs from *besteigen* in making clear that I climbed right to the top of the mountain

sink

Wir versenkten das Schiff	*We sank the ship*
Das Schiff sank	*The ship sank*

(c) Some German verbs require a reflexive pronoun to be used in constructions corresponding to the intransitive use of the English verb

Such verbs require an accusative object, and the reflexive pronoun must be used in this function if there is no other object, e.g.:

change

Das hat nichts geändert	*That has changed nothing*
Das hat sich geändert	*That has changed*

feel

Sie fühlte etwas unter ihren Füßen	*She felt something under her feet*
Sie fühlte sich unwohl	*She felt unwell*

open

Ich öffnete die Tür	*I opened the door*
Die Tür öffnete sich	*The door opened*

(See (a) above for alternative equivalents for English 'open')

turn

Ich drehte das Rad	*I turned the wheel*
Das Rad drehte sich	*The wheel turned*

(d) In some cases a construction with *lassen* is used as the equivalent of an English transitive verb,
i.e. if the German verb in question can only be used intransitively. For this use of *lassen*, see 13.3.1c:

drop

Ich ließ den Stein fallen	*I dropped the stone*
Der Stein fiel	*The stone dropped*

fail

Sie haben den Kandidaten durchfallen lassen	*They failed the candidate*
Der Kandidat ist durchgefallen	*The candidate failed*

(e) In some cases a construction with *sich lassen* is used as the equivalent of an English intransitive,
i.e. if the German verb in question can only be used transitively. For further uses of this construction, see 15.4.7:

Sie hat das Papier geschnitten	*She cut the paper*
Das Papier läßt sich leicht schneiden	*The paper cuts easily*

18.3.6 Verbs used with an accusative reflexive

(a) Many verbs are used with a reflexive pronoun in the accusative case
For the form of the reflexive pronoun, see 3.2. These 'reflexive verbs' fall into two groups:
(i) 'True' reflexive verbs, which cannot be used without the reflexive pronoun. For example:

sich bedanken	*say 'thank you'*	sich beeilen	*hurry*
sich befinden	*be (situated)*	sich benehmen	*behave*
sich eignen	*be suited*	sich erkälten	*catch a cold*
sich verabschieden	*say 'good-bye'*, etc.		

With these verbs, the reflexive pronoun is an integral part of the verb, not a separate complement.
(ii) Transitive verbs used reflexively, cf.:

Das habe ich meinen Bruder gefragt	–	Das habe ich mich gefragt
Ich setzte den Koffer auf den Stuhl	–	Ich setzte mich auf den Stuhl
Ich habe den Hund gewaschen	–	Ich habe mich gewaschen
Ich habe ihn nicht überzeugen können	–	Ich habe mich nicht überzeugen können

In these cases, the accusative object appears as a reflexive pronoun if the action of the verb relates back to the subject.

(b) As English has no comparable reflexive verbs, we find various English equivalents for German reflexive verbs (of both kinds)

Many German reflexives have separate English equivalents, e.g. *sich setzen* 'sit down' (cf. *setzen* 'put'), *sich versprechen* 'make a slip of the tongue' (cf. *versprechen* 'promise'), but the following should be noted:

(i) German reflexive verbs often correspond to English passive constructions, e.g.:

Das hat sich inzwischen aufgeklärt	*That has since been cleared up*
Meine Hoffnung hat sich erfüllt	*My hopes were fulfilled*
Ich habe mich sehr gefreut	*I was very pleased*
Das Problem hat sich gelöst	*The problem was resolved*

Further examples of reflexives used in a passive sense are given in 15.4.3 and 15.4.7.

(ii) German reflexive verbs often correspond to English intransitive verbs, e.g.:

Sie hat sich beeilt	*She hurried*
Der Feind hat sich ergeben	*The enemy surrendered*

Further examples are given in 18.3.5c.

(c) A number of verbs used with a reflexive accusative also have other complements,

e.g. a dative, genitive or prepositional object. They are treated in the sections dealing with these other complements.

NB: For verbs with a reflexive pronoun in the dative case see 18.4.3.

18.4 The dative object

A dative object occurs in three main sentence patterns, i.e.:

  (i) 18.1.4c: Subject + verb + dative object
 (ii) 18.1.4j: Subject + verb + dative object + prepositional object
(iii) 18.1.4d: Subject + verb + accusative object + dative object

The first two of these are treated together in 18.4.1 (for the prepositional objects in relevant cases, see 18.6). The verbs which govern both a dative (indirect) and an accusative (direct) object, are explained in 18.4.2. Verbs with a dative reflexive are dealt with in 18.4.3.

NB: (i) The dative has a wide range of uses in addition to its use with verb complements, cf. 2.5. In particular a 'free' dative can occur with many verbs. As the name indicates, these are not usually regarded as complements since they are not closely linked to the verb.

(ii) The dative object of an active construction can <u>never</u> become the subject of the corresponding passive sentence, cf. 15.1.3:

Man kann **diesem Mann** helfen	– **Diesem Mann** kann geholfen werden
Er gab **ihm** ein Zeugnis	– **Ihm** wurde ein Zeugnis gegeben

18.4.1 Verbs governing the dative

It is helpful to be aware that, with many of these, the dative object is a person who is advantaged or disadvantaged in some way through the action expressed by the verb.

(a) A selection of commonly used verbs governing the dative:
abraten   *advise against*

Sie hat **ihm** von einer Teilnahme abgeraten

She advised him against taking part

ähneln   *resemble, look like*

Er ähnelt **seinem Bruder**

He looks like his brother

antworten   *answer*

Sie hat **mir** geantwortet

She answered me

NB: With *antworten*, the dative is only used to refer to persons, cf:
*Er hat **auf** meinen Brief, meine Frage geantwortet.*

ausweichen   *get out of the way of, evade, avoid*

Er ist **der Gefahr** ausgewichen

He avoided the danger

begegnen   *meet* (by chance)

Ich bin **ihr** in der Stadt begegnet

I met her in town

bekommen   *agree with one* (of food)

Fleisch bekommt **mir** nicht

Meat doesn't agree with me

NB: *bekommen* with an accusative means 'receive', e.g. *Er bekam einen langen Brief von seinem Vater*

danken   *thank*

Ich danke **Ihnen** sehr für Ihre Mühe

I thank you very much for your effort

dienen   *serve*

Er diente **dem König von Italien**

He served the King of Italy

drohen   *threaten*

Sie drohte **dem Jungen** mit einem Stock

She threatened the boy with a stick

einfallen   *occur*

Das ist **mir** nicht eingefallen

That didn't occur to me

sich ergeben   *surrender* (cf. also 18.6.4)

Wir mußten uns **dem Feind** ergeben

We had to surrender to the enemy

folgen   *follow*

Er ist **ihr** ins Exil gefolgt   *He followed her into exile*

NB: *folgen* is used with *auf* (acc.) in the sense 'succeed, come after' e.g. *Auf den Sturm folgten drei sonnige Tage.*

gehorchen   *obey*

Sie gehorcht **ihrem Vater**   *She obeys her father*

gehören   *belong*

Der Mercedes gehört **mir** doch nicht   *But the Mercedes doesn't belong to me*

NB: (i) In the sense 'be part of, be one of', *gehören* is used with *zu*, e.g. *Das Feld gehört zu unserem Garten. Das gehört zu meinen Aufgaben.*
(ii) In the sense 'belong' (i.e. 'be a member of'), *angehören* is used. It also takes a dative, e.g.: *Ich gehöre diesem Verein an.*

gelten   *be meant for, be aimed at, be for*

Gilt diese Bemerkung **mir**?   *Is that comment meant for me?*
Sein letzter Gedanke galt **seinem Volk**   *His last thought was for his people*

gleichen   *be equal to, resemble*

Jeder Tag glich **dem anderen**   *One day was like the next*

gratulieren   *congratulate*

Sie haben **ihr** zum Geburtstag   *They congratulated her on her*
  gratuliert   *birthday*

helfen   *help*

Er half **seinem Vater** in der Küche   *He helped his father in the kitchen*

imponieren   *impress*

Sie hat **ihm** sehr imponiert   *She impressed him a lot*

kündigen   *fire, give notice*

Der Chef hat **ihm** gestern gekündigt   *The boss gave him notice yesterday*

NB: In the sense of 'cancel, terminate (a thing)', *kündigen* is used with an accusative object, e.g. *Er hat den Vertrag gekündigt.*

sich nähern   (elev.) *approach*

Wir näherten uns **der Stadt**   *We approached the city*

nutzen/nützen   *be of use*

Das nutzt **mir** doch gar nichts   *But that's no use to me*

passen   *suit*

Das neue Kleid paßt **dir** gut | *The new dress suits you*

schaden   *harm*

Rauchen schadet **der Gesundheit** | *Smoking is harmful to your health*

schmeicheln   *flatter*

Der Student wollte **dem Professor** schmeicheln | *The student wanted to flatter the professor*

trauen   *trust*

Ich traute **meinen Augen** nicht | *I couldn't believe my eyes*

NB: *mißtrauen* 'distrust' also has a dative object.

trotzen   *defy*

Er trotzte **der Gefahr** | *He defied, braved the danger*

unterliegen   *be defeated by, be subject to*

Er unterlag **seinem Gegner** | *He lost to his opponent*

vertrauen   *have trust in*

jemandem blind vertrauen | *have a blind trust in somebody*

vorbeugen   *prevent, preclude*

Wir taten alles, um **einem Konflikt** vorzubeugen | *We did everything to prevent a conflict*

wehtun   *hurt*

Der Wespenstich hat **ihm** sehr wehgetan | *The wasp sting hurt him a lot*

(b) Most verbs with the meaning 'happen', 'occur' are used with a dative, e.g.:

Es wird **dir** doch nichts geschehen | *But nothing will happen to you*
Was ist **ihm** gestern passiert? | *What happenened to him yesterday?*
So etwas ist **mir** noch nie vorgekommen | *Nothing like that has ever happened to me*

Similarly: *bevorstehen, widerfahren, zustoßen*, etc.

(c) Verbs with certain prefixes usually take a dative,
i.e. those with *bei-, ent-, entgegen-, nach-, wider-, zu-*, e.g.

Er ist **der SPD** beigetreten | *He joined the SPD*
Das entsprach **meinen Erwartungen** | *That came up to my expectations*
Sie kam **mir** entgegen | *She approached me*
Er eilte **ihr** nach | *He hurried after her*
Das Kind widersprach **seiner Mutter** | *The child contradicted its mother*
Er hat **dem Gespräch** zugehört | *He listened to the conversation*

Similarly (among many others):

beistehen	*give support to*	beiwohnen	*be present at*
entsagen	*renounce*	entstammen	*originate from*

also all the verbs prefixed with *ent-* meaning 'escape', i.e.:
entgehen, entfliehen, entkommen, entrinnen, entwischen, etc.

entgegengehen	*go to meet*	entgegenwirken	*counteract*
nachahmen	*imitate*	nachgeben	*give way to*
nachkommen	*follow*	nachlaufen	*run after*
nachstellen	*follow, pester*	nachstreben	*emulate*
sich widersetzen	*oppose*	widerstehen	*resist*
zulaufen	*run up to*	zulächeln	*smile at*
zustimmen	*agree with*	zuvorkommen	*anticipate*

NB: A few verbs with these prefixes have a dative <u>and</u> an accusative object, cf. 18.4.2, e.g.
jemandem etwas beibringen 'teach somebody something', *jemandem etwas zutrauen*
'credit somebody with something'.

(d) The dative object of a few verbs corresponds to the subject of the usual English equivalent, i.e.:

Etwas fällt **mir** auf	*I notice something*
Etwas entfällt **mir**	*I forget something*
Es fällt **mir** leicht, schwer	*I find something easy, difficult*
Etwas fehlt, mangelt **mir** ⎫	
Es fehlt, mangelt **mir** an etwas ⎭	*I lack something*
Etwas gefällt **mir**	*I like something*
Etwas geht **mir** auf	*I realise something*
Etwas gelingt **mir**	*I succeed in something*
Etwas tut **mir** leid	*I am sorry about something*
Das leuchtet **mir** nicht ein	*I don't understand, see that*
Es liegt **mir** viel an etwas	*I am keen on something*
Etwas liegt **mir**	*I fancy something*
Das genügt, reicht **mir**	*I have had enough of that*
Etwas schmeckt **mir**	*I like something* (i.e. food)

18.4.2 Verbs governing a dative and an accusative object

These are transitive verbs with two complements aside from the subject,
i.e. an accusative (direct) object, which is usually is a thing, and a dative
(indirect) object, which is usually a person. It is thus helpful to remember
them as *einem etwas* verbs. The German dative commonly corresponds to
an English prepositional phrase with *to* or *from,* or to an English indirect
object (e.g. *He gave **me** the book*). With many such verbs (e.g. *geben*) the
dative object is obligatory to construct a complete sentence, with others
(e.g. *beweisen*) it may be suppressed in certain contexts.

(a) This set includes verbs of giving and taking (in the widest sense)
The following examples may serve as illustration:

Diese Strecke verlangt den Läufern sehr viel ab	*This stretch demands a lot from the runners*
Die Post hat mir eine Stelle angeboten	*The post-office offered me a job*
Das wollte er (mir) beweisen	*He wanted to prove that (to me)*
Er brachte (ihr) einen Blumenstrauß	*He brought (her) a bunch of flowers*
Ich kann (dir) diesen Roman empfehlen	*I can recommend this novel (to you)*
Das konnte ich seinem Brief entnehmen	*I was able to gather/infer that from his letter*
Er hat dem Lehrer einen Bleistift gegeben	*He gave the teacher a pencil*
Sie will mir jetzt etwas Ruhe gönnen	*She is now willing to let me have some peace and quiet*
Kannst du mir zehn Mark leihen?	*Can you lend me ten marks?*
Wir haben (ihr) die Tasche genommen	*We took the bag (from her)*
Würden Sie mir bitte das Salz reichen?	*Would you pass me the salt, please*
Er hat ihr zum Geburtstag eine Hifi-Anlage geschenkt	*He gave her a stereo system for her birthday*
Ich habe (ihr) das Paket geschickt	*I've sent (her) the parcel*
Du schuldest mir noch hundert Mark	*You still owe me a hundred marks*
Er verkaufte (mir) seinen alten Opel	*He sold (me) his old Opel*
Er konnte ihr diese Bitte nicht verweigern	*He couldn't refuse her this request*
Er zeigte ihr seine Kupferstiche	*He showed her his etchings*

(b) Most verbs involving an act of speaking or communicating are used with a dative and an accusative object

The accusative object is in practice often an indefinite pronoun or a clause. A number may be used just with the accusative or the dative object and with some this may differ from the construction required by the usual English equivalent verb.

(i) Examples of usage:

Wer hat (dir) befohlen, den Hund zu töten?	*Who ordered you to kill the dog?*
Die irakische Regierung erlaubte (der Delegation) die Einreise	*The Iraqi government allowed the delegation into the country*
Das habe ich ihm schon gestern erzählt	*I've already told him that yesterday*
Er hat mir geraten, mein Haus zu verkaufen	*He advised me to sell my house*
Sie hat mir (einen langen Brief) geschrieben	*She wrote me (a long letter)*
Er versicherte mir, daß er alles erledigt hätte	*He assured me he had taken care of everything*
Das wird er (dir) nie verzeihen können	*He'll never be able to forgive you that*

(ii) *glauben* is used with a dative of the person and/or an accusative of the thing, e.g:

Er glaubt **dem Lehrer**	Er glaubt **jedes Wort**
Er glaubt **dem Lehrer jedes Wort**	

NB: *glauben an* (acc.), cf. 18.6.2b, is used for 'believe in', e.g. *Ich glaube an seinen Erfolg.*

(iii) *sagen* is normally used with an optional dative of the person, e.g.:

Was wollen Sie (ihm) sagen?	*What do you want to say (to him)?*

However, in some cases it occurs with *zu*, i.e.:
When introducing direct speech, e.g.:

„Nun komm doch!" sagte sie zu Christian	*"Come along now", she said to Christian*

When addressing oneself, e.g.:

„Wie kannst du das nur machen?" sagte er zu sich selbst.	*"How on earth can you do that?" he said to himself*

(c) With some verbs the German dative and accusative construction differs from the construction used with the corresponding English verb:

Man merkt ihm die Anstrengung an	*One notices the effort he's making*
Sie fügte es dem Brief bei	*She enclosed it with the letter*
Das hat ihm das Studium ermöglicht, erschwert	*That made it possible, difficult for him to study*
Das hat sie mir gestern mitgeteilt	*She informed me of that yesterday*
Das Kind machte mir die Gesten nach	*The child copied my gestures*
Die Polizei konnte ihm nichts nachweisen	*The police couldn't prove anything against him*
Das hat sie mir aber verschwiegen	*She didn't tell me about that, though*
Ich habe ihr wohl zu viel zugemutet	*I probably expected too much of her*
Das hätte ich ihr nicht zugetraut	*I wouldn't have believed her capable of that*

(d) With verbs of sending or transferring a phrase with *an* may be a common alternative to the dative
The effect is to emphasize the recipient rather more strongly, e.g::

Ich habe ein Paket an meinen Vater geschickt
Ich habe einen Brief an meinen Vater geschrieben
Er hat seinen alten Opel an seinen Vater verkauft

18.4.3 Reflexive verbs with a dative

(a) Many verbs governing a dative may be used with a dative reflexive pronoun if the action refers back to the subject, e.g.:
(i) Verbs where the dative is the sole object, cf. 18.4.1:

Ich habe **mir** mehrmals widersprochen	*I contradicted myself a number of times*
Du schadest **dir** mit dem Rauchen	*You're harming yourself by smoking*

(ii) *einem etwas* verbs, cf. 18.4.2

Ich erlaubte **mir**, ihm zu widersprechen	*I allowed myself to contradict him*
Ich muß **mir** Arbeit verschaffen	*I must find work*
Ich habe **mir** zu viel zugemutet	*I've taken on too much*

(b) A few other verbs occur with a dative reflexive pronoun.

These are 'true' reflexive verbs, cf. 18.3.6, where the reflexive pronoun is an integral part of the verb. They all have a further object in the accusative case:

Das habe ich **mir** angeeignet	*I acquired that*
Das habe ich **mir** eingebildet	*I imagined that*
Das verbitte ich **mir**	*I refuse to tolerate that*
Ich habe **mir** vorgenommen, das zu tun	*I have resolved to do that*
Das kann ich **mir** gut vorstellen	*I can imagine that well*
Ich habe **mir** eine Grippe zugezogen	*I contracted flu*

18.5 Genitive objects

Genitive objects occur in two major sentence patterns, i.e.:
 (i) 18.1.4e: Subject + verb + genitive object
(ii) 18.1.4f: Subject + verb + accusative object + genitive object
These are both uncommon nowadays, and all verbs requiring these constructions are restricted to formal written (especially official) German. A few more are used only in set phrases. In listing those verbs which are still encountered with a genitive we give more widely used alternatives wherever possible.

18.5.1 Non-reflexive verbs where the genitive is the only object:

bedürfen   *need* (more common: *brauchen, benötigen*)

Er bedarf meiner Hilfe nicht	*He doesn't need my help*

entbehren   *lack* (more commonly used with an accusative object)

Der Staat konnte eines kraftvollen Monarchen nicht entbehren (*v. Rimscha*)	*The state could not do without a powerful monarch*

gedenken   *remember* (elev. for *denken an* (acc.), with reference to the dead)

Wir gedenken der Opfer des Krieges	*We remember the victims of the war*

harren   *await* (elev. for *warten auf* (acc.), esp. in biblical contexts)

Wir harren einer Antwort (*Zeit*)	*We are awaiting an answer*

18.5.2 Reflexive verbs with a genitive object

In the main, these are 'true' reflexive verbs, cf. 18.3.6, with an accusative reflexive pronoun:

sich annehmen   *look after, take care of* (more usual: *sich kümmern um*)

Er hätte sich dieses Kindes angenommen (*Walser*)	*He would have looked after this child*

sich bedienen   *use* (more usual: *benutzen, gebrauchen, verwenden*)

Auch er hat sich dieses Mannes
    bedient (*Zeit*)

He too made use of this man

sich bemächtigen   *seize* (various alternatives, e.g. *ergreifen, nehmen*)

Sie bemächtigten sich des
    Bürgermeisters von Le Mans (*Zeit*)

They seized the mayor of Le Mans

sich entsinnen   *remember* (more usual: *sich erinnern an* (acc.), see 18.6.2b)

Er entsann sich jenes heißen Tages
    noch recht gut

*He still remembered that hot day
    quite well*

sich erfreuen   *enjoy* (more usual: *genießen, sich freuen über* (acc.))

Sie erfreuten sich des schönen
    Sommerwetters (*OH*)

*They were enjoying the fine
    summer weather*

sich erinnern   *remember* (more usual: *sich erinnern an* (acc.), see 18.6.2b)

Ich erinnere mich bestimmter Details
    noch (*Böll*)

I still remember certain details

sich erwehren   *refrain from* (more usual: *sich wehren gegen*)

Ich konnte mich des Lachens kaum
    erwehren

*I could scarcely refrain from
    laughing*

sich rühmen   *boast about/of* (more usual: *stolz sein über*)

Die meisten Länder Europas rühmen
    sich einer tausendjährigen
    Geschichte (*Haffner*)

*Most European countries can boast
    of a thousand years of history*

sich schämen   *be ashamed of* (more usual: *sich schämen für/wegen*, cf.18.6.5)

Er schämte sich seines Betragens

He was ashamed of his behaviour

sich vergewissern   *make sure* (more usual: *nachprüfen, überprüfen*)

Sie vergewisserte sich der
    Zuverlässigkeit dieses Mannes

*She made sure about this man's
    reliability*

18.5.3 Verbs used with a genitive and an accusative object

anklagen   *accuse* (outside formal legal parlance: *anklagen wegen*)

Man klagte ihn der fahrlässigen
    Tötung an

*He was accused of manslaughter
    through culpable negligence*

berauben   *rob* (more commonly: *einem etwas rauben*)

Er beraubte ihn der Freiheit

He robbed him of his freedom

versichern   *assure* (more commonly: *einem etwas zusichern*)

Ich versichere Sie meines uneingeschränkten Vertrauens	*I assure you of my absolute trust*

The following verbs are used with a genitive in legal language, but with an following clause in everyday speech:

jemanden einer Sache beschuldigen } jemanden einer Sache bezichtigen }	*accuse sb. of sth.*
jemanden einer Sache überführen	*convict sb. of sth.*
jemanden einer Sache verdächtigen	*suspect sb. of sth.*

18.5.4 Set phrases with the genitive

der Gefahr nicht achten	*pay no heed to danger*
jemanden eines Besseren belehren	*teach someone better*
sich eines Besseren besinnen	*think better of something*
jeder Beschreibung spotten	*beggar description*
jemanden des Landes verweisen	*expel someone from a country*
seines Amtes walten	*discharge one's duties*
jemanden keines Blickes würdigen	*not to deign to look at someone*

18.6 Prepositional objects

18.6.1 Many verbs are followed by an object introduced by a preposition

With these, the preposition is wholly idiomatic and determined by the verb. It is not interchangeable with any other preposition and thus does not have its full meaning, but merely serves as a link between the verb and a noun or pronoun. In general, the foreign learner has to treat each combination of verb and preposition separately and remember them as a whole.

The prepositional object may be the only complement aside from the subject, e.g.:

sentence pattern 18.1.4.g: **Das hängt** von ihrem Vorgesetzten ab

A few verbs can have two prepositional objects, e.g.:

sentence pattern 18.1.4k: Der Arzt hat **aus der Art der Verletzung auf einen Selbstmordversuch** geschlossen

Many verbs have an accusative or dative object in addition to the prepositional object, e.g.:

sentence pattern 18.1.4h: Alle haben ihn **für einen Vollidioten** gehalten
sentence pattern 18.1.4i: Er dankte ihm **für seine Mühe**

In the following, we give a selection of common verbs used with prepositions, listed according to the preposition, with an indication of what other objects can or may be used in appropriate cases.

NB: When the prepositional object takes the form of a clause, it is usually anticipated by a prepositional adverb, e.g. *Sie hat ihm* **dafür** *gedankt,* **daß er ihr geholfen hatte**. This construction is explained in detail in 18.6.14.

18.6.2 *an*

an most often occurs with a following dative in prepositional objects, but a few verbs govern *an* with the accusative.

(a) With verbs, *an* (dat.) often conveys the idea of 'in respect of, in connection with', e.g.:

Ich erkannte sie an ihrem knallroten Haar	*I recognised her by her bright red hair*
Er ist an einer Lungenentzündung gestorben	*He died of pneumonia*
Ich zweifele an seiner Ehrlichkeit	*I doubt his honesty*

A selection of other verbs:

arbeiten an	*work at*	mitwirken an	*play a part in*
erkranken an	*fall ill with*	riechen an	*sniff (at)*
gewinnen an	*gain (in)*	teilnehmen an	*take part in*
(e.g.: an Bedeutung gewinnen)		verlieren an	*lose (some)*
hängen an	*cling, stick to*	(e.g. an Boden verlieren)	
leiden an	*suffer from*		

sich an jemandem/etwas freuen	*take pleasure in sb./sth.*
(Cf.: *sich freuen auf* (acc.) 'look forward to' (18.6.3a), *sich freuen über* 'be glad/ pleased about (18.6.9))*	
jemanden an etwas hindern	*prevent sb. from (doing) sth.*
Es fehlt mir an etwas	*I lack sth.* (cf. 18.4.1d)
Es liegt mir viel an etwas	*I am very keen on sth.* (cf. 18.4.1d)
sich an etwas orientieren	*orientate oneself by sth.*
etwas an jemandem rächen	*avenge sth. on sb.*
sich an jemandem für etwas rächen	*take revenge on sb. for sth.*

(b) *an* + accusative is used with a few verbs, most of which denote mental processes, e.g.:

Du erinnerst mich an ihn	*You remind me of him*
Ich erinnere mich an ihn	*I remember him* (cf. 18.5.2)
Ich glaube an den Fortschritt	*I believe in progress* (cf. 18.4.2b)

Similarly:

denken an	*think of*	sich gewöhnen an	*get used to*

18.6.3 *auf*

With verbs *auf* is usually found with an accusative, but a very few verbs govern *auf* with a dative.

(a) *auf* + accusative is the most common preposition in prepositional objects in German, e.g.:

Ich werde auf deine Kinder aufpassen	*I'll mind your children*
Er drängte seine Gläubiger auf Zahlung	*He was pressing his creditors for payment*
Seine Bemerkung bezog sich auf dich	*His comment related to you*
Das läuft auf das gleiche hinaus	*It amounts to the same thing*
Er wies (mich) auf die Schwierigkeiten hin	*He pointed the difficulties out (to me)*

A selection of further verbs:

achten, achtgeben auf	*pay attention to*	pochen auf	*insist on*
sich berufen auf	*refer to*	schimpfen auf/über	*curse about*
sich beziehen auf	*refer to*	schwören auf	*swear on/by*
sich erstrecken auf	*extend to*	sich spezialisieren auf	*specialize in*
folgen auf (cf. 18.4.1a)	*follow*		
		sich stützen auf	*lean, count on*
sich freuen auf (cf. 18.6.1a)	*look forward to*	sich verlassen auf	*rely on*
		sich verstehen auf	*be expert in*
sich gründen auf	*be based on*	(jdn) verweisen auf	*refer (sb.) to*
hoffen auf	*hope for*	versichten auf	*do without*
sich konzentrieren auf	*concentrate on*	warten auf	*wait for*
lauern auf	*lie in wait for*	zählen auf	*count on*
pfeifen auf (coll.)	*not care less about*	zurückkommen auf	*come back to, refer to*
reagieren auf	*react to*		

Es kommt (mir) auf etwas an	*Sth. matters (to me)*
etwas auf etwas beschränken	*limit/restrict/confine sth to sth*
sich auf etwas beschränken	*limit oneself to sth./be limited to sth.*
etwas auf etwas zurückführen	*put sth down to sth*

(b) *auf* + dative occurs with a few verbs which convey very clearly the idea of not moving, e.g.:

Er beharrte auf seiner Meinung	*He didn't shift from his opinion*
Ich bestehe auf meinem Recht	*I insist on my right*

NB: *bestehen aus* 'consist of' (18.6.4), *bestehen in* 'consist in' (18.6.6b).

Other verbs used with *auf* + dative all mean 'rest on, be based on', i.e. *basieren, beruhen, fußen auf.*

NB, however, *sich gründen auf* (**acc.**) 'be based on', e.g. *Der Vorschlag gründet sich auf diese Annahme.*

18.6.4 *aus*

aus usually has the meaning 'of', 'from' in prepositional objects, e.g.:

Ihr Essen bestand aus trockenem Brot	*Their food consisted of dry bread*

Other verbs:

etwas aus etwas entnehmen, ersehen   *infer, gather sth. from sth.*

NB: *entnehmen* (but not *ersehen*) may alternatively be constructed with
 a dative, e.g. *Ich entnehme (aus) ihrem Brief, daß Sie das Geschäft aufgeben wollen*

sich aus etwas ergeben   *result from sth.*

NB: *sich in etwas* (acc.) *ergeben* 'submit to sth.' (cf. 18.6.6b),
 sich jemandem/etwas (dat.) *ergeben* 'surrender to sb./sth.' (cf. 18.4.1a)

etwas aus etwas folgern, schließen   *conclude sth. from sth.*

18.6.5 *für*

für usually has the meaning 'for' in prepositional objects, e.g.:

Ich habe ihm für seine Mühe gedankt	*I thanked him for his trouble*
Ich habe mich für den Audi entschieden	*I decided on the Audi*
Ich halte deine Freundin für hochbegabt	*I consider your friend to be very gifted*

Other verbs:

sich (bei jemandem) für etwas bedanken	*give thanks for sth. (to sb.)*
sich für etwas begeistern	*be enthusiastic about sth.*
sich für jemanden/etwas eignen	*be suitable for sb./sth.*

NB: *sich eignen zu/als* 'be suitable as'

sich für jemanden/etwas interessieren   *be interested in sb./sth.*

NB: Non-reflexive *interessieren* may be used with *für* or *an* (dat.), e.g. *Er hat sie für das/an
 dem Unternehmen interessiert.*

sich für jemanden/etwas schämen   *be ashamed of sth./for sb.*

NB: *sich (wegen) jemandes/etwas* (gen.) *schämen* (cf.18.5.2) 'be ashamed of sb./sth.', *sich
 vor jemandem schämen* 'be ashamed in front of sb.' (cf.18.6.12a).

für jemanden/etwas sorgen   *take care of/look after sb./sth.*

NB: *sich um jemanden/etwas sorgen* 'be worried about sb./sth.'.

18.6.6 *in*

in, with verbs, is more frequently used with a following accusative, but a
few verbs have *in* with a dative.

(a) *in* + accusative, e.g.:

Sie willigte in die Scheidung ein	*She agreed to the divorce*
Er verliebte sich in sie	*He fell in love with her*

Other verbs:

jemanden in etwas einführen	*introduce sb. to sth.*
sich ergeben in	*submit to* (cf. 18.6.4)
sich fügen in (elev.)	*bow to*
sich mischen in	*meddle in*
sich vertiefen in	*become engrossed in*

(b) *in* + dative occurs with very few verbs, i.e.:

Meine Aufgabe besteht in der Erledigung der Korrespondenz (cf. also 18.6.3b and 18.6.4)	*My duties consist in dealing with the correspondence*
Ich habe mich nicht in ihr getäuscht	*I was not mistaken in (my judgement of) her*

18.6.7 *mit*

mit usually has the sense of 'with' in prepositional objects, e.g.:

Sie hat mit ihrer Arbeit angefangen	*She made a start on her work*
Willst du bitte damit aufhören?	*Please stop doing that*
Ich mußte mich mit einer sehr geringen Summe abfinden	*I had to be satisfied with a very small sum*
Sie hat ihm mit der Faust gedroht	*She threatened him with her fist*
Ich habe gestern mit ihm telephoniert	*I spoke to him on the telephone yesterday*

Other verbs:

sich befassen mit *deal with*	übereinstimmen mit *agree with*
sich begnügen mit *be satisfied with*	sich unterhalten mit *converse with*
sich beschäftigen mit *occupy o.s. with*	vergleichen mit *compare with*
rechnen mit *count on*	sich verheiraten mit *marry*
sprechen mit *speak to/with*	versehen mit *provide with*
(or: jemanden sprechen)	zusammenstoßen mit *collide with*

18.6.8 *nach*

(a) *nach* often has the sense of English 'after', 'for' with verbs of calling, enquiring, longing, reaching, etc., e.g.:

Haben Sie sich nach seinem Befinden erkundigt?	*Have you enquired how he is?*

COMPARE: *Ich erkundigte mich über den neuen Film* 'I enquired about the new film'.

Plötzlich griff das Kind nach der Katze	*Suddenly the child made a grab for the cat*
Sie schrie nach ihrem Cousin	*She yelled for her cousin*
Ich telephonierte nach einem Arzt	*I rang for a doctor*

Other verbs:

fragen nach	*ask after, for*	sich sehnen nach	*long for*
NB: *fragen über*	'ask about'	streben nach	*strive for*
hungern nach	*hunger after, for*	suchen nach	*search for*
rufen nach	*call after, for*	verlangen nach	*ask, long for;*
sehen nach	*look after*		*crave*

(b) *nach* often has the sense of English 'of' with verbs of smelling, etc., e.g.:

Es riecht nach Teer	*It smells of tar*
Es schmeckte nach Fisch	*It tasted of fish*

Similarly *duften nach*, *stinken nach*, etc.
Cf. also *Es sieht nach Regen aus* 'It looks like rain'.

18.6.9 *über*

In prepositional objects *über* is always followed by an accusative.

(a) *über* corresponds to English 'about' with verbs of saying, etc., e.g.:

Ich habe mich sehr über sein Benehmen geärgert	*I was very annoyed at his behaviour*
Sie mußte lange darüber nachdenken	*She had to think it over for a long time*
Ich sprach gestern mit dem Chef über diese Bewerbung	*I talked to the boss about this application yesterday*

A large number of verbs are used with *über* in this sense. A few others may be noted here:

sich bei jemandem über etwas beklagen, beschweren	*complain to sb. about sth.*
sich über jemanden/etwas freuen (Cf. also 18.6.2a)	*be pleased about sth.*
jemanden über etwas informieren	*inform sb. about sth.*
(*einem etwas mitteilen* has the same meaning, cf. 18.4.2c)	
über jemanden/etwas spotten	*mock sb./sth.*
sich täuschen über etwas	*be mistaken about sth.*
(For *sich täuschen in*, see 18.6.6b)	
über etwas urteilen	*judge sth.*
sich über jemanden/etwas wundern	*be surprised at sb./sth.*

NB: A few verbs, i.e. *denken, erzählen, hören, lesen, sagen, schreiben, sprechen, wissen* may be used with *über* or *von* in the sense of 'about'. *über* tends to refer to something more extensive than *von*, e.g.:

Was denken Sie darüber?	*What is your view of that?*
Was denken Sie von ihm?	*What do you think of him?*
Er wußte viel über Flugzeuge	*He knew a lot about aeroplanes*
Er wußte nichts von ihrem Tod	*He knew nothing of her death*

(b) Other verbs used with *über* (acc.)

es über sich bringen, etwas zu tun	*bring o.s. to do sth.*
sich über etwas hinwegsetzen	*disregard sth.*
über etwas verfügen	*have sth. at one's disposal*

18.6.10 *um*

um with verbs usually has the sense of 'concerning', 'in respect of', e.g.:

Sie hat sich um ihre Schwester in Dresden geängstigt	*She was worried about her sister in Dresden*
Es handelte sich um eine Wette (cf. 18.2.4f)	*It was a question of a bet*
Ich kümmerte mich um meine Enkelkinder	*I took care of my grandchildren*

Other verbs:

sich um etwas bemühen	*take trouble over sth.*
jemanden um etwas bemühen	*trouble sb. for sth.*
jemanden um etwas beneiden	*envy sb. sth.*
(zu Gott) um etwas beten	*pray (to God) for sth.*
jemanden um etwas betrügen	*cheat sb. out of sth.*
jemanden um etwas bitten, ersuchen (elev.)	*ask sb. for sth., request sth. from sb.*
jemanden um etwas bringen	*make sb. lose sth.*
Es geht um etwas (cf. 18.2.4f)	*Something is at stake*
um etwas kämpfen	*fight for sth.*
um etwas konkurrieren	*compete for sth.*
um etwas kommen	*lose sth., be deprived of sth.*
sich um jemanden/etwas sorgen	*be worried about sth.*
um Geld spielen	*play for money*
um etwas streiken	*(go on) strike for sth.*
sich um/über etwas streiten	*argue about/over sth.*
sich an jemanden um etwas wenden	*turn to sb. for sth.*

18.6.11 *von*

With verbs, *von* usually has the sense of English 'of' or 'from', e.g.:

Ich will dich nicht von der Arbeit abhalten	*I don't want to keep you from your work*
Wir müssen davon ausgehen, daß . . .	*We must start by assuming that . . .*
Ich muß mich von meinem Kollegen distanzieren	*I have to dissociate myself from my colleague*
Das Kind träumte von einer schönen Prinzessin	*The child was dreaming of a beautiful princess*

Other verbs:

Etwas hängt von jemandem/etwas ab	*Something depends on sb./sth.*
jemandem von etwas abraten	*advise sb. against sth.*

von etwas absehen	*refrain from sth., disregard sth.*
jemanden von etwas befreien	*liberate sb. from sth.*
sich von etwas erholen	*recover from sth.*
von etwas herrühren	*stem from sth.*
jemanden von etwas überzeugen	*convince sb. of sth.*
jemanden von etwas verständigen	*inform sb. of sth.*
von etwas zeugen	*show, demonstrate sth.*

NB: For *von* and *über* in the sense of 'about' with verbs of saying, see 18.6.9a.

18.6.12 *vor*

With verbs, *vor* is always used with the dative.

(a) *vor* is typically used with verbs of fearing, etc., often corresponding to English 'of', e.g.:

Ich ekele mich vor diesen großen Spinnen	*I have a horror of these big spiders*
Er fürchtete sich vor dem Rottweiler	*He was afraid of the Rottweiler*
Er warnte mich vor dem Treibsand	*He warned me about the quicksand*

Other verbs:

sich vor jemandem/etwas ängstigen (cf. also 18.6.10)	*be afraid of sb./sth.*
Angst vor jemandem/etwas haben	*be afraid, scared of sb./sth.*
sich vor etwas drücken (coll.)	*dodge sth.*
vor jemandem/etwas erschrecken	*be scared by sb./sth.*
sich vor jemandem/etwas hüten	*beware of sb./sth., be on one's guard against sb./sth.*
sich vor jemandem schämen	*be ashamed in front of sb.*
(see 18.6.5 for other constructions with *sich schämen*)	
sich vor etwas scheuen	*be afraid of, shrink from sth.*

(b) *vor* often corresponds to English 'from' with verbs of protecting, etc., e.g.:

Sie bewahrte ihn vor der Gefahr	*She protected him from danger*
Sie flohen vor der Polizei	*They fled from the police*

Other verbs:

jemanden vor jemandem/etwas beschützen, beschirmen (elev.)	*protect sb. from sb./sth.*
jemanden vor etwas retten	*save sb. from sth.*
sich vor jemandem/etwas verbergen	*hide from sb./sth.*

18.6.13 *zu*

(a) *zu* commonly corresponds to English '(in)to' with verbs of empowering, leading, persuading, etc.

All these verbs are transitive, i.e. they have an accusative object besides the prepositional object with *zu*, e.g.:

Er ermutigte sie zum Widerstand	*He encouraged them to resist*
Er trieb sie zur Verzweiflung	*He drove her to despair*
Er überredete mich zu einem Glas Wein	*He talked me into having a*
	glass of wine
Er zwang mich zu einer Entscheidung	*He forced me into a decison*

A selection of further verbs used with this construction:

autorisieren	*authorise*	herausfordern	*challenge*
berechtigen	*entitle*	nötigen	*invite*
bewegen (cf. 12.6)	*induce*	provozieren	*provoke*
einladen	*invite*	veranlassen	*cause*
ermächtigen	*empower*	verführen	*seduce*

(b) A number of other verbs have a prepositional object with *zu*, e.g.:

Das hat zu seinem Erfolg sehr beigetragen	*That contributed a lot to his success*
Sie entschloß sich zur Teilnahme	*She decided to take part*
Ich rechne, zähle ihn zu meinen Freunden	*I count him among my friends*

Other verbs:

jemanden zu etwas bestimmen	*designate sb. as sth.*
jemanden zu etwas bringen	*get sb. to (do) sth.*
es zu etwas bringen (cf. 3.6.11)	*attain sth.*
zu etwas dienen	*serve as sth.*
sich zu etwas eignen	*be suitable as sth.*
(for *sich eignen für*, see 18.6.5)	
zu etwas führen	*lead to sth.*
zu etwas gehören	*be part of sth., be one of sth.*
(for *gehören* + dative, see 18.4.1a)	
jemandem zu etwas gratulieren	*congratulate sb. on sth.*
	(e.g. birthday, anniversary)
zu etwas neigen	*tend to sth.*
zu jemandem/etwas passen	*go with sb./sth.*

e.g. *Das neue Kleid paßt zu deinen roten Schuhen*. Compare *Das paßt mir nicht* 'That doesn't suit me', see 18.4.1a.

jemandem zu etwas raten	*advise sb. to (do) sth.*
sich zu etwas verhalten	*stand in a relationship to sth.*

e.g. *Drei verhält sich zu sechs wie fünf zu zehn.*

jemandem zu etwas verhelfen	*help sb. to (do) sth.*

18.6.14 If a prepositional object takes the form of a clause, it is usually anticipated by a prepositional adverb,

i.e. the form *da(r)*+preposition, cf. 3.5. The prepositional object may be a subordinate clause (usually introduced by *daß*), or an infinitive clause with *zu*, e.g.:

Sie hat ihm **dafür** gedankt, **daß er ihr geholfen hatte**
Ich verlasse mich **darauf, daß er alles arrangiert**

Er hinderte mich **daran, den Brief zu schreiben**
Ich verlasse mich **darauf, ihn zu Hause zu finden**

This use of the prepositional adverb is optional with some verbs, e.g.:

Ich ärgerte mich (**darüber**), daß er so wenig getan hatte
Sie haben (**damit**) angefangen, die Ernte hereinzubringen

A selection of common verbs with which the prepositional adverb <u>may</u> be omitted in this way:

abhalten von	sich ekeln vor	sich hüten vor
abraten von	sich entscheiden für	klagen über
achtgeben auf	sich entschließen zu	raten zu
anfangen mit	sich erinnern an	sich scheuen vor
(sich) ärgern über	fragen nach	sich schämen über
aufhören mit	sich freuen auf	sich sehnen nach
aufpassen auf	sich freuen über	sorgen für
beginnen mit	sich fürchten vor	sich sorgen um
sich beklagen über	glauben an	sich streiten über
sich bemühen um	hindern an	träumen von
sich beschweren über	hoffen auf	überzeugen von
bitten um	sich wundern über	urteilen über
sich einigen über	zweifeln an	

In addition, the prepositional adverb may be omitted with all the transitive verbs governing *zu* treated in 18.6.13a.

NB that, with the above verbs, it is never incorrect to include the prepositional adverb. If it is used, it tends to throw rather more emphasis on the following clause. In practice, it is more commonly included than omitted in written German, whilst its omission is more typical of more colloquial registers.

18.7   Place and direction complements

18.7.1   A few verbs denoting position have a complement indicating place,

e.g. (sentence pattern 18.1.4k):

Sie wohnte lange **in der Pfeilgasse**	*She lived a long time in the Pfeilgasse*
Der Brief befand sich **dort**	*The letter was there*
Er übernachtete **in einer Gaststätte**	*He spent the night in a pub*
Sie hielt sich **in Hamm** auf	*She stayed in Hamm*

The place complements often have the form of a prepositional phrase or an equivalent word.

These place complements are essential to complete the meaning of the sentences, which would be ungrammatical without them. Thus, *Sie wohnte lange* or *Der Brief befand sich* are meaningless without the addition of the place phrase. Their function in the sentence is thus quite different from that of adverbials, cf. 18.1.3, which may have the same form but lack the close link with the verb and simply add extra information to the sentence. Compare the function of the phrases used in the examples above with their function when used with other verbs, which do not denote position:

Die Kinder spielten **in der Pfeilgasse**	*The children were playing in the Pfeilgasse*
Dort habe ich sie gestern gesehen	*I saw her there yesterday*
Am Abend hat er **in einer Gaststätte** gegessen	*That night he ate in a pub*
Sie starb **in Hamm**	*She died in Hamm*

These sentences would be quite grammatical without the place phrases, the function of which is adverbial, i.e. they give us a bit more information. They may be important in context, but they are not essential.
Common verbs which require place complements are:

sich aufhalten	*stay*	stattfinden	*take place*
bleiben	*stay, remain*	stehen	*stand*
hängen	*hang*	übernachten	*spend the night*
leben	*live*	sich verlieren	*get lost*
liegen	*lie, be lying*	wohnen	*live, dwell*
parken	*park*	zelten	*camp*
sitzen	*sit*		

18.7.2 Verbs which denote motion may occur with a direction complement

We find such complements:
(i) with intransitive verbs (sentence pattern 18.1.4l):

Gestern fuhr sie **nach Italien**	*She went to Italy yesterday*
Der Junge fiel **hinein**	*The boy fell in*

(ii) with transitive verbs (sentence pattern 18.1.4m):

Ich stürzte mich **darauf**	*I leapt upon it*
Sie legte das Buch **auf den Tisch**	*She put the book on the table*

The direction complement usually takes the form of a prepositional phrase or an equivalent word (e.g. a compound with *da(r)-*, cf. 3.5, or *hin-/her-*, cf. 7.3).

Like place complements, direction complements are not adverbial. They have a similar close link with the meaning of the verb and are often essential to complete the meaning of the sentence. Thus, *Gestern fuhr sie* and *Sie legte das Buch* are meaningless without the direction complements.

In principle, we may say that <u>all</u> verbs of motion may be used with a direction complement, although it may be suppressed in certain contexts with some of these verbs.

18.7.3 The distinction between place and direction complements and adverbials is particularly important in relation to word order

As place and direction complements have a particularly close link with the verb, they tend to come last in the clause, cf. 21.8.1.

18.8 Predicate complements

A very few verbs have a predicate complement, which normally takes the form of either a noun or pronoun in the nominative case or an adjective (sentence pattern 18.1.4n):

Er ist **mein Freund**	*He is my friend*
Das Buch ist **rot**	*The book is red*
Sie scheint auch **eine solche**	*She seems to be a person like that, too*
Sie wurde **blaß**	*She went pale*

The complement describes the subject or identifies it more closely. The verb may be seen as linking the subject with the complement and these verbs are known as 'copula' (i.e. 'linking' verbs).

The following verbs are used with a predicate complement:

bleiben	*remain*	scheinen	*seem*
heißen	*be called*	werden	*become*
sein	*be*		

19 Conjunctions

In this chapter we deal first with the coordinating conjunctions (19.1), then the subordinating conjunctions, arranged according to their meanings (19.2-7).

19.1 Coordinating conjunctions

Coordinating conjunctions link main clauses. They are followed by main-clause word order, i.e. the verb does not go to the end of the clause they introduce, cf. 21.1.1c, e.g.:

Er ist gestern abend angekommen, aber ich **habe** ihn noch nicht gesehen

Most of them can also link single words or phrases, e.g.:

Ich finde diese Compact-Disc schön, aber etwas zu teuer

A few, like *sowie*, are only used in this way, i.e. they cannot link clauses.

German has the following coordinating conjunctions, which are all treated in this section:

aber	*but*	nämlich	*as*
allein only	*but*	oder	*or*
bald . . . bald	*now . . . now*	sondern	*but*
beziehungsweise	*or*	sowie	*as well as*
denn	*as*	sowohl als/wie	*as well as*
doch	*but*	teils . . . teils	*partly . . . partly*
entweder . . . oder	*either . . . or*	und	*and*
jedoch	*but*	weder . . . noch	*neither . . . nor*

19.1.1 *aber, allein, doch, jedoch* 'but'

(a) *aber* is the usual equivalent of English 'but':

Er runzelte die Stirn, aber sie sagte noch nichts
He frowned, but she still didn't say anything

NB: (i) For the distinction between *aber* and *sondern* as the equivalent of English 'but', see 19.1.4.
(ii) For the use of *aber* with *zwar* in the preceding clause, see 19.5.1d.

(b) allein, doch and *jedoch* are mainly literary alternatives to *aber*
(i) *allein* usually introduces a restriction which is unwelcome or unexpected, e.g.:

Ich hatte gehofft, ihn nach der Sitzung zu sprechen, allein er war nicht zugegen	*I had hoped to speak to him after the meeting, but he wasn't present*

(ii) Examples of the use of *doch* and *jedoch* as conjunctions. *jedoch* is rather more emphatic:

Der Lohn ist karg, doch man genießt die abendlichen Stunden (*Jens*)	*The wages are meagre, but one enjoys the evening hours*
Im allgemeinen war er kein guter Schüler, jedoch in Latein war er allen überlegen	*In general he was not a good pupil, but he was better than any in Latin*

(c) *aber, doch* and *jedoch* are also used as modal particles or adverbs with much the same sense as when they are used as conjunctions
(For *aber*, see 10.1.2, for *doch*, see 10.7.1).
(i) As modal particles or adverbs (= English 'though', 'however'), they form part of the clause rather than introduce it, giving a different word order, as the following alternatives to the sentences in (a) and (b) above show:

Er runzelte die Stirn, sie aber sagte noch nichts ⎫
Er runzelte die Stirn, sie sagte aber noch nichts ⎭
Der Lohn ist karg, doch genießt man die abendlichen Stunden ⎫
Der Lohn ist karg, man genießt doch die abendlichen Stunden ⎭
. . ., in Latein jedoch war er allen überlegen ⎫
. . ., in Latein war er jedoch allen überlegen ⎭

Note that, in such constructions the second clause may lack an introductory conjunction. The effect of these alternatives is to highlight the contrast rather more strongly.
(ii) Where two verbs have the same subject, *aber* is commonly used in this way, being placed after the second verb:

Er runzelte die Stirn, sagte aber noch nichts	*He frowned, but still said nothing*

NB: Further uses of *aber* and *doch* as modal particles are explained in 10.1 and 10.7 respectively.

19.1.2 *denn, nämlich* 'as', 'because'

(a) *denn* expresses cause or reason:

Der Tote konnte nicht identifiziert werden, denn er hatte keine Ausweispapiere bei sich	*The dead man could not be identified because he was not carrying any identity papers*

Note carefully that *denn*, like the rather old-fashioned English 'for', is a coordinating, <u>not</u> a subordinating conjunction. It introduces a main clause, with the verb in second position. A *denn*-clause can never begin a sentence.

NB: (i) *denn* is no longer frequent in spoken German, and *weil* is often heard in its stead as a coordinating conjunction, followed by a main clause, even though this usage is universally regarded as substandard, cf. 19.3.1c.
(ii) For the uses of *denn* as a modal particle, see 10.6.

(b) A clause with *nämlich* is a useful common alternative to a main clause with *denn* (or a subordinate clause with *weil*, cf. 19.3.1).
nämlich is always placed within the clause, after the verb, e.g.:

Er konnte sie nicht verstehen, er war nämlich taub	*He couldn't understand her, as he was deaf*

19.1.3 *oder, beziehungsweise* 'or', *entweder . . . oder* 'either . . . or'

(a) *oder* is the usual equivalent for English 'or':

Dieses Modell kann mit Benzin- oder Dieselmotor geliefert werden	*This model can be supplied with a petrol engine or a diesel engine*
Morgen können wir zu Hause bleiben, oder wir können einen Spaziergang machen, wenn du willst	*Tomorrow we can stay at home, or we can go for a walk if you want to*
Wir können in Heidelberg oder in Mannheim umsteigen	*We can change trains in Heidelberg or Mannheim*
Sie wollten das Haus aus- oder umbauen	*They wanted to extend or alter the house*

NB: (i) As with English 'or', the alternatives linked by *oder* can be exclusive (one or the other, but not both) or inclusive (i.e. 'and/or', as in the last example above). In order to stress that exclusion is meant, *aber* may be added to *oder*, cf. 10.1.2, e.g.:
Wir können in Heidelberg, oder aber (auch) in Mannheim umsteigen.
Alternatively, *beziehungsweise* or *entweder . . . oder* can be used to signal exclusion, cf. (b) and (c) below.
(ii) *oder* should not be used in cases where 'or' is preceded by a negative in English, cf.19.1.6b.

(b) *beziehungsweise* may be used to make it clear that we are dealing with mutually exclusive alternatives
In writing, *beziehungsweise* is usually abbreviated to *bzw.*:

Sie haben lange in Deutschland gewohnt, bzw. sie haben dort oft Urlaub gemacht	*They lived a long time in Germany, or (else) they often took their holidays there*
Es kostet 300 Mark, bzw. 250 Mark mit Rabatt	*It costs 300 marks, or 250 marks with the discount*

beziehungsweise was originally restricted to formal registers, but it is now common both in speech and writing.

(c) *entweder . . . oder* 'either . . . or' signals mutually exclusive alternatives

It is thus an alternative to *beziehungsweise*:

Entweder du leihst mir das Geld, oder ich gebe den Plan auf	*Either you lend me the money or I'll give up the plan*

NB: (i) Rather less commonly, *entweder* may be immediately followed by the verb, e.g. *Entweder leihst du mir das Geld, . . .*
(ii) If *entweder . . . oder* link two third person singular subjects, the verb has the singular form, e.g. *Entweder Klaus oder Peter **wird** kommen*. In other cases the verb agrees with the nearer subject, e.g *Entweder er oder ich **werde** ihr das Geld geben*.

19.1.4 *sondern* 'but'

(a) *sondern* contradicts a negative, correcting an erroneous assumption, e.g.:

Er ist nicht reich, sondern arm	*He is not rich, but poor*
Wir sind nicht ins Kino gegangen, sondern wir haben im Garten gearbeitet	*We didn't go to the cinema, but worked in the garden*

(b) *aber* may be used after a negative, but does not imply an exclusive contrast,
i.e. both the linked elements may be valid, e.g.:

Er ist nicht reich, aber ehrlich (i.e. he is <u>both</u> 'not rich' <u>and</u> 'honest')	*He is not rich, but honest*

(c) *nicht nur . . . sondern auch* corresponds to 'not only . . . but also':

Er ist nicht nur reich, sondern auch großzügig	*He is not only rich, but generous, too*
Sie besorgt nicht nur ihren Haushalt, sondern sie ist auch berufstätig	*She doesn't only run the household, she's got a job, too*

NB: (i) If two subjects are connected by *nicht nur . . . sondern auch*, the verb agrees with the nearer one, e.g. *Nicht nur er, sondern auch ich bin dagegen*.
(ii) Initial *nicht nur* is followed immediately by the finite verb, e.g. *Nicht nur hat Helmut kräftig mitgeholfen, sondern Franziska hat auch ihren Teil dazu beigetragen*.

19.1.5 *und* 'and'; *sowie, sowohl . . . als/wie* 'as well as'

(a) *und* is the common equivalent for English 'and':

Angela und Gudrun wollen auch kommen	*Angela and Gudrun want to come too*
Einer der Verdächtigen durchbrach eine Straßensperre und konnte erst nach einer Verfolgungsjagd . . . gestoppt werden (*NZZ*)	*One of the suspects broke through a road block and could only be stopped after a chase*

NB: For the use of a clause with *um . . . zu* as a stylistic alternative to *und*, see 13.2.5a.

(b) *sowie, sowohl . . . als/wie* 'both . . . and', 'as well as' are frequent stylistic alternatives to *und*
They are particularly common in written German, if they are by no means

unknown in the spoken language. They emphasize the connection between the elements more than *und*. All are often used with a following *auch*, e.g.:

Dürrenmatt hat sowohl Dramen als/wie (auch) Kriminalromane geschrieben	*Dürrenmatt has written both plays and detective novels*

sowie puts rather more stress on the second element, e.g.:

Dürrenmatt hat Dramen sowie (auch) Kriminalromane geschrieben

NB: If *sowohl . . . als/wie* or *sowie* link two singular subjects, the verb usually has a plural ending, but the singular is also acceptable, e.g.: *Sowohl sein Vater wie seine Mutter waren* (or: *war*) *dagegen.*

19.1.6 *weder . . . noch* 'neither . . . nor'

(a) Examples of the use of *weder . . . noch*:

Er liest weder Bücher noch Zeitungen	*He reads neither books nor newspapers*
Ich habe weder seinen Brief bekommen, noch habe ich sonst von ihm gehört	*Neither have I received his letter, nor have I heard from him in any other way*

NB: (i) If *weder . . . noch* connects two singular subjects, the verb can have a singular <u>or</u> a plural ending, e.g. *Weder er noch sie wußte(n) davon.*
(ii) *noch* cannot be used on its own, without a preceding *weder*, see (b) below .

(b) A common alternative to *weder . . . noch* is to use *und auch nicht/kein*. This is often felt to be less clumsy and more natural, especially in spoken German:

Er liest keine Bücher und auch keine Zeitungen.
Ich habe seinen Brief nicht bekommen, auch habe ich nicht sonst von ihm gehört.

und auch nicht/kein is used where English has simple 'nor' (i.e. without a preceding 'neither', e.g.:

Sie hat mir noch nicht geschrieben, und ich erwarte auch nicht, daß ich bald von ihr höre	*She hasn't written to me yet, nor do I expect to hear from her soon*

und auch nicht/kein should also be employed where *or* in English is preceded by a negative, e.g.:

Ich höre die Nachrichten im Radio nicht und kaufe auch keine Zeitungen	*I don't listen to the news on the radio or buy newspapers*

19.1.7 Less frequent coordinators

(a) *bald . . . bald* 'one moment . . . the next, now . . . now'
This form is mainly found in formal written German. *bald* is followed
immediately by the verb in both clauses, e.g.:

Bald weinte das Kind, bald lachte es	*One moment the child was crying, the next it was laughing*

(b) *teils . . . teils* 'partly . . . partly'

Wir haben unseren Urlaub teils in Italien verbracht, teils in der Schweiz	*We spent our holiday partly in Italy, partly in Switzerland*
teils heiter, teils wolkig	*cloudy with sunny intervals*

When used to link clauses, *teils* is followed immediately by the verb:

Teils war man sehr zuvorkommend, teils hat man mich völlig ignoriert	*Sometimes people were very helpful, at others I was completely ignored*

NB: (i) If *teils* links two (or more) singular subjects, the verb has the singular ending, e.g
Teils sein Einfluß, teils seine Herkunft hat ihm diese Stellung verschafft.
(ii) *teils, teils* is frequent in colloquial speech in response to a question, e.g.:

Waren auch nette Leute da? Teils, teils	*Were there nice people there? – Some were, some weren't*
Wie geht es dir? – Teils, teils	*How are you? – So-so*

19.2 Conjunctions of time

A list of the main conjunctions referring to time in German:

als	*when*	seit(dem)	*since*
bevor, ehe	*before*	sobald, sowie	*as soon as*
bis	*until, till; by the time*	solange	*as long as, while*
indem (obs.)	*as*	sooft	*as often as, whenever*
indes, indessen (obs.)	*while, whilst*	während	*while, whilst*
kaum daß	*hardly, scarcely*	wenn	*when (ever)*
nachdem	*after*	wie	*as*

Notes on some of these conjunctions are given in the remainder of this
section.

19.2.1 *als, indem, wann, wenn, wie* 'when', 'as'

(a) Clauses introduced by *als* refer to a <u>single</u> occurrence or state in the past
It may correspond to English 'when' or 'as', e.g.:

Als ich in Passau ankam, habe ich sie auf dem Bahnsteig gesehen	*When I arrived in Passau, I saw her on the platform*
Als ich weiterging, wurde ich immer müder	*As I went on, I grew more and more tired*

Als ich jung war, habe ich gern   *When I was young I liked reading*
   Karl May gelesen   *Karl May*

NB: (i) A main clause following an *als*-clause is not infrequently introduced by a correlating *da*, e.g. *Als ich in Passau ankam,* **da** *habe ich sie auf dem Bahnsteig gesehen.* This *da* is always optional.
(ii) *da* is a literary (and rather old-fashioned) alternative to *als*, e.g.:
Die Sonne schien an einem wolken-   *The sun was shining in a cloudless*
   losen Himmel, da er seinen   *sky as/when he left his home*
   Heimatort verließ (*Dürrenmatt*)   *village*

(b) *wie* may be used for 'when' with a verb in the present tense referring to a past action,

i.e. with a 'historic' present, cf. 14.2.4. In such cases, *wie* is an alternative to *als*, e.g.:

Als/Wie ich das Fenster öffne,   *As/When I opened the window,*
   schlägt mir heftiger Lärm entgegen   *I was confronted by an*
                                intense noise

NB: The use of *wie* in place of *als* with a <u>past</u> tense is common in colloquial spoken German, especially in the south, e.g. *Wie ich in Passau ankam, . . .* This usage is considered substandard.

(c) *wann* is used in questions

wann is an interrogative adverb (= 'when?'), cf. 7.6.1a. As such, it is used to introduce questions in direct speech:

Wann kommst du heute abend nach Hause?

or in indirect speech:

Er fragte mich, wann ich heute abend nach Hause komme

(d) *wenn* introduces clauses referring to the present, the future, or repeated actions in the past:

Ich bringe es, wenn ich morgen   *I'll bring it when I drop by*
   vorbeikomme   *tomorrow*

It often conveys the sense of English 'whenever', e.g.:

Er empfand eine Art Ekel, wenn er   *He felt a kind of disgust when(ever)*
   daran dachte, mit wieviel Vergangen-   *he thought about how full of the*
   heit er schon angefüllt war (*Walser*)   *past he was*

Note the use of *wenn*, not *als*, to refer to a future-in-the-past:

Ich wollte zu Hause sein, wenn   *I wanted to be at home when Karl*
   Karl ankam   *arrived*

NB: (i) For the use of *wenn* in a conditional sense (i.e. = 'if'), see 16.3.
(ii) A main clause following a *wenn*-clause is not infrequently introduced by *dann*. This *dann* is always optional, e.g.:
Wenn das Wasser ausgelaufen ist,   *When the water has run out, the*
   (dann) schließt sich die Klappe   *valve shuts off automatically*
   automatisch

(e) *indem* 'as'

indem can only link simultaneous actions, e.g.:

Er erzählte seine Geschichte, indem er nach jedem Satz pausierte	*He told his story, pausing after every sentence*

NB: This use of *indem*, where, as the example shows, the *indem*-clause may correspond to an English participial phrase, is now obsolete and should be avoided by the foreign learner, cf. 13.7.3a. In modern German, *indem* is only used in the sense of English 'by + . . . ing', see 19.6.3.

(f) Equivalents of English 'when' introducing relative clauses,

e.g. *zu einer Zeit, wo* . . . 'at a time when . . .'.
Usage in such constructions is explained fully in 5.4.7b.

19.2.2   *bevor, ehe* 'before'; *bis* 'until, till', 'by the time'

NB: For the occasional use of the subjunctive in clauses introduced by these conjunctions, see 16.4.4.

(a) *bevor* is the usual equivalent of English 'before':

Ich will das Fenster reparieren, bevor ich in Urlaub gehe	*I want to fix the window before I go on holiday*

(b) *ehe* is a rather literary and elevated alternative to *bevor*:

Es bestand, ehe die Erde geschieden war von den Himmeln (*Heym*)	*It existed before the earth was separated from the heavens*

NB: Both *bevor* and *ehe* may be strengthenend by a preceding *noch* to give the sense of English 'even before', e.g. *Noch bevor/ehe sie zurückkam,* . . . 'Even before she got back . . .'.

(c) *bis* has two main English equivalents.
(i) 'until, till', e.g.:

Ich warte hier, bis du zurückkommst	*I'll wait here till you get back*

(ii) 'by the time (when)', e.g.:

Bis du zurückkommst, habe ich das Fenster repariert	*I'll have fixed the window by the time you get back*

NB: For the use of the perfect tense here, see 14.3.4.

(d) German equivalents for English 'not . . . before', 'not . . . until'
(i) The most serviceable equivalent is *erst* . . . *wenn/als*, e.g.:

Ich will erst nach Hause gehen, wenn Mutter wieder da ist	*I don't want to go home before/until mother gets back*
Das Kind hörte erst zu weinen auf, als es vor Müdigkeit einschlief	*The child didn't stop crying until it was so tired that it fell asleep*

(ii) *nicht* . . . *bevor* (or *ehe*) and *nicht* . . . *bis* are only used if the clause with *bevor* or *bis* expresses a condition. In this case an additional, redundant *nicht* is often added in the *bevor* or *bis*-clause, e.g.:

Bevor er sich (nicht) entschuldigt hatte, wollte sie das Zimmer nicht verlassen	*She didn't want to leave the room before he had apologised*
Du darfst nicht gehen, bis du (nicht) deine Hausaufgaben fertig hast	*You can't go out until you've finished your homework*

NB: DUDEN (1985:489f.) states that an additional *nicht* may only be used if the subordinate clause comes first. However, this ruling is not always followed in practice.

19.2.3 *kaum daß* and alternatives

(a) The phrasal conjunction *kaum daß* is sometimes used for English 'hardly/scarcely . . . when', 'no sooner . . . than':

Kaum daß wir das Wirtshaus erreicht hatten, begann es zu regnen	*We had hardly reached the inn when it began to rain/No sooner had we . . . when it began to rain*

(b) A more frequent alternative to *kaum daß* is to use two main clauses, the first introduced by *kaum*, the second by *so* or *da*:

Kaum hatten wir das Wirtshaus erreicht, so/da begann es zu regnen

A further possible variant is to use *kaum . . . als*, e.g.:

Kaum hatten wir das Wirtshaus erreicht, als es zu regnen begann

19.2.4 *nachdem* 'after'

In modern German, *nachdem* is almost exclusively used in a temporal sense (= 'after'), e.g.:

Die Probleme häuften sich, nachdem wir die Grenze passiert hatten	*The problems mounted up after we had crossed the frontier*

NB: (i) *nachdem* is sometimes used in a causal sense, as an alternative to *da* (= 'as, since', cf.19.3.1), e.g.:

Er mußte zurücktreten, nachdem ihm verschiedene Delikte nachgewiesen wurden	*He had to resign, as various offences had been proved against him*

This usage is now restricted to south Germany and Austria.

(ii) For *je nachdem* 'according as', see 19.6.5.

19.2.5 *seit, seitdem* 'since'

seit was formerly restricted to colloquial registers, but it is probably more frequent than *seitdem* nowadays, even in writing. Examples:

Seitdem er sein Haus verkauft hat, wohnt er in einem Hotel	*Since he sold his house, he's been living in a hotel*

Seit ich warte, sind mindestens dreißig Leute 'reingegangen (*Fallada*)	*Since I've been waiting, at least thirty people have gone in*

NB: For the use of tenses in sentences with *seit(dem)*, see 14.2.2 and 14.3.3a.

19.2.6 *sobald* 'as soon as', *solange* 'as long as', *sooft* 'as often as'

Note that none of these conjunctions is normally followed by *als* or *wie*. They are always spelled as single words, cf. 23.2.3.

(a) *sobald*

Das tat sie auch, sobald sie wieder nach Hause kam	*She did that, too, as soon as she got home again*

NB: *sowie* is commonly used for *sobald* in colloquial registers, e.g.:
Das tat sie auch, sowie sie nach Hause kam.

(b) *solange*
(i) *solange* may be used to refer purely to time, e.g.:

Wir haben gewartet, solange wir konnten	*We waited as long as we could*
Solange ich ihn kenne, haben wir uns nie gestritten	*We have never quarrelled as long as I've known him*

NB: The sense of *solange* may approach that of *seit(dem)*, as in the second example, and tense use is similar, cf. 14.2.2 and 14.3.3a.

(ii) It may also have a conditional sense (= 'provided that', cf.16.3.3d), e.g.:

Solange er sein Bestes tut, bin ich zufrieden	*As long as he does his best, I shall be satisfied*

NB: (i) The conjunction *solange* must be distinguished from the phrase *so lange* 'so long', e.g.:

Du hast uns **so lange** warten lassen, daß wir den Zug verpaßt haben	*You kept us waiting so long that we missed the train*
So lange er auch wartete, es kam kein Zug mehr	*However long he waited, no more trains came*

(ii) The final *-e* of *solange* is sometimes dropped, especially in speech.

(c) *sooft* may correspond to English 'as often as' or 'whenever':

Du kannst kommen, sooft du willst	*You can come as often as you want to*
Sooft er kam, brachte er uns immer Geschenke mit	*Whenever he came, he always brought us presents*

NB: Equivalents for 'whenever' used in a concessive sense are given in 19.5.2.

19.2.7 *während* 'while, whilst' and alternatives

(a) *während* is the most usual equivalent of English 'while, whilst', either to

express time or a contrast (i.e. = 'whereas'):

Die Zollprobleme löste Boris, während wir in Urlaub waren (*Bednarz*)	*Boris solved the problems with the customs while we were on holiday*
Ich lese gern lange Romane, während mein Bruder nur kurze Krimis liest	*I like reading long novels, whilst my brother only reads short detective stories*

NB: *noch während* is used for 'even as/whilst', e.g. *Noch während sie schlief* . . . 'Even as she slept . . .'

(b) *indes* and *indessen* are alternatives to *während* in both senses
They are restricted to rather old-fashioned literary styles:

Du kannst mich füttern, indes ich die Ente rupfe (*Langgässer*)	*You can feed me while I'm plucking the duck*

NB: *indessen* is frequently used as an adverb (= 'meanwhile').

(c) *wohingegen* is a common alternative to *während* to signal a contrast
It emphasizes the contrast rather more strongly, e.g.:

Er ist sehr zuvorkommend, wohingegen sein Bruder oft einen recht unfreundlichen Eindruck macht	*He is very obliging, whilst/whereas his brother often makes a very unpleasant impression*

19.3 Causal conjunctions

The following conjunctions signal a cause or a reason and are dealt with in this section:

da	*as, since*	weil	*because*
nun (da/wo)	*now that, seeing that*	zumal	*especially as*
um so mehr als	*all the more because*		

19.3.1 *da* and *weil*

(a) The distinction between *da* and *weil* parallels almost exactly that between English 'as (or 'since') and 'because':

Ich mußte zu Fuß nach Hause gehen, weil ich die letzte Straßenbahn verpaßt hatte	*I had to walk home because I had missed the last tram*
Da du sowieso zur Post gehst, kannst du diesen Brief für mich einwerfen	*As/Since you're going to the post-office anyway, you can post this letter for me*

(b) A *weil*-clause may be anticipated by *darum*, *deshalb* or *deswegen* in the preceding main clause:

Er konnte darum/deshalb/deswegen nicht kommen, weil er krank war	*He wasn't able to come because he was ill*

This is particularly common in spoken German. The effect is to give greater emphasis to the reason given in the *weil*-clause.

(c) In colloquial German *weil* is frequently heard with a main clause word order,

i.e. with the finite verb second rather than at the end of the clause:

Du mußt langsam sprechen, weil der versteht nicht viel	*You'll have to speak more slowly because he doesn't understand a lot*

This usage, though very common, is universally regarded as substandard, and it is quite unacceptable in written German. In effect, *weil* is coming to be used as a coordinating conjunction in place of *denn* in such cases, cf. 19.1.2.

(d) *denn* and *nämlich* are also used to indicate a cause or a reason,
i.e. in the sense of English 'because'. They are, however, <u>coordinating</u> conjunctions, used with main clause word-order, cf. 19.1.2.

19.3.2 *nun* (*da/wo*) 'now that', 'seeing that'

(a) *nun da* is the most widely used equivalent for these English conjunctions:

Nun da wir alle wieder versammelt sind, können wir das Problem weiter besprechen	*Seeing/Now that we're all gathered together again, we can carry on talking about the problem*

(b) Simple *nun* is occasionally found in formal written registers:

Nun alles geschehen ist, bleibt nur zu wünschen, daß . . . (*FAZ*)	*Now that everything has been done, one can only wish that . . .*

(c) There are a number of further alternatives to *nun da*,
i.e. *nun wo, wo . . . (doch), da . . . nun (mal)*. In the main, these are more typical of colloquial registers:

Nun wo du sowieso in die Stadt fährst, kannst du uns wohl mitnehmen, oder?	*Seeing as you're going into town anyway, you'll be able to take us with you, won't you?*
Ich muß es wohl tun, wo ich es dir doch versprochen habe	*I'll have to do it, seeing that I promised you*
Da er das nun (mal) schon weiß, (so) muß ich ihm wohl das weitere erzählen	*Seeing that he already knows that, I'll have to tell him the rest*

19.3.3 Other causal conjunctions

(a) *zumal* is a stronger alternative to *da*, corresponding to English 'especially as'
It is still used sometimes with a following *da*, but this is no longer essential:

Sie wird uns sicher helfen, zumal (da) sie dich so gern hat	*She's sure to help us, especially as she's so fond of you*

Mehr verriet sie nicht, zumal es
    Stiller gar nicht wunderte, warum sie
    dieses Bedürfnis hatte (*Frisch*)
	She didn't reveal any more,
	    especially as Stiller was not
	    at all surprised why she felt this
	    need

(b) *um so mehr als/da/weil* correspond to 'all the more because':

Ich freute mich um so mehr über
    seinen Erfolg, als er völlig
    unerwartet war
	I was all the more pleased about
	    his success because it was totally
	    unexpected

Das hätte schlimme Folgen haben
    können, um so mehr als sie schwanger
    war
	That could have had serious
	    consequences, all the more because
	    she was pregnant

A similar construction with *um so . . . als* (or *da/weil*) can be used with other adjectival or adverbial comparatives, e.g.:

Die Sache ist um so dringlicher,
    als/da die Iraker den Ölhahn
    zudrehen könnten
	The matter is all the more urgent
	    because the Iraqis could turn off
	    the oil tap

19.4 Conjunctions of purpose and result

The following final and consecutive conjunctions are treated in this section:

als daß	*for . . . to*
damit, auf daß	*so that, in order that*
so daß, derart daß	*so that, such that*

NB English learners should be careful to distinguish between the final and consecutive senses of English 'so that', i.e.:
> (i) Final 'so that' expresses purpose and is an alternative to 'in order that'. The usual German equivalent is *damit*, cf. 19.4.1.
> (ii) Consecutive 'so that' expresses a result. It has the sense of '(in) such (a way) that' and corresponds to German *so daß*, cf. 19.4.2:

19.4.1 Clauses of purpose

(a) *damit* is the most widely employed conjunction introducing clauses of purpose (so-called 'final' clauses):

Diese Tüte ist aus Papier, damit sie
    nicht aus Kunststoff ist
	This bag is made of paper so that
	    it shouldn't be made of plastic

Er sprach sehr laut, damit ihn auch
    diejenigen verstehen konnten, die
    in den hinteren Reihen saßen
	He spoke very loud, so that the
	    people sitting in the back rows
	    could hear him, too

NB: (i) The verb in *damit*-clauses is usually in the indicative in modern German. For the occasional use of the subjunctive, see 16.4.2a.
> (ii) An infinitive clause with *um . . . zu* is to be preferred to a subordinate clause with *damit* if the subjects of the two clauses are the same, cf. 13.2.5a. Thus one usually says *Ich bin gekommen, um dir zu helfen* rather than *Ich bin gekommen, damit ich dir helfen kann*.

(iii) Negative final clauses are sometimes introduced by 'lest' in formal English. In such cases German uses *damit . . . nicht*:

Er half ihr, damit sie nicht noch einmal durchfiel	*He helped her lest she fail again*

(b) *auf daß* is a rather old-fashioned sounding alternative to *damit*

It is still sometimes used for stylistic effect and is always followed by a subjunctive, cf. 16.4.2b:

. . . schenke du ihr ein reines Herz, auf daß sie einstmals eingehe in die Wohnungen des ewigen Friedens (*Th. Mann*)	*give her a pure heart, so that she may some day enter into the dwellings of eternal peace*

(c) Simple *daß* is sometimes used for *damit* in colloquial German:

Ich mache dir noch ein paar Stullen, daß du unterwegs auch was zu essen hast	*I'll make you a couple of sandwiches so that you've got something to eat on the journey*

19.4.2 Clauses of result

(a) *so daß* is the most widely used conjunction introducing clauses of result (so-called 'consecutive' clauses):

Sein Bein war steif, so daß er kaum gehen konnte	*His leg was stiff, so that he could hardly walk*
Das Wetter war schlecht, so daß wir wenig wandern konnten	*The weather was bad, so that we couldn't do much hiking*
Er schob den Ärmel zurück, so daß wir die Narbe sehen konnten	*He pushed his sleeve back, so that we were able to see the scar*

NB: In the last example, *damit wir die Narbe sehen konnten* would imply that he did it with the express purpose that we should see the scar. As *so daß* is used, we are only dealing with a (perhaps unintentional) result of his action.

(b) In clauses with adjectives or adverbs, the *so* may precede the adjective

Many consecutive clauses contain adjectives or adverbs, as in the first two examples in (a) above, and these have an alternative phrasing with *so* preceding the adjective, cf. similar constructions in English e.g.:

Sein Bein war so steif, daß er kaum gehen konnte	*His leg was so stiff that he could hardly walk*
Das Wetter war so schlecht, daß wir wenig wandern konnten	*The weather was so bad that we weren't able to do much hiking*

(c) *derart* and (in some contexts) *dermaßen* are rather more emphatic alternatives to *so* in consecutive sentences:

Er fuhr so/derart/dermaßen langsam, daß Frieda uns leicht einholte	*He drove so slowly that Frieda caught us up easily*

Es hat so/derart/dermaßen geregnet, daß wir schon Montag nach Hause gefahren sind	*It rained so much that we came home as early as Monday*

NB: *dermaßen* is only possible if some idea of quantity is involved. Thus, in the following sentence, only *derart* can substitute for *so*:
Er hat den Ärmel derart zurückgeschoben, daß wir die Narbe sehen konnten.

19.4.3 The conjunction *als daß* is used only after adjectives modifed by *zu, nicht genug* or *nicht so*.

The equivalent English sentences usually have an infinitive with *for*, e.g.:

Er ist zu vernünftig, als daß ich das von ihm erwartet hätte	*He's too sensible for me to have expected that of him*
Es ist noch nicht so kalt, als daß wir jetzt schon die Heizung einschalten müßten	*It's not so cold for us to have to turn the heating on yet*
Das Kind ist nicht alt genug, als daß wir es auf einer so langen Reise mitnehmen könnten	*The child is not old enough for us to be able to take it with us on such a long journey*

NB: (i) If the subject of the two clauses is the same, an infinitive clause with *um . . . zu* will be used, cf. 13.2.5a.
(ii) Konjunktiv II, particularly of a modal verb, is commonly used in *als daß* clauses, cf. 16.4.5a.
(iii) In everyday speech, simpler constructions will usually be preferred to sentences with *als daß*, e.g. *Es ist noch nicht so kalt, also brauchen wir die Heizung noch nicht einschalten.*

19.5 Concessive conjunctions

In this section we deal first (19.5.1) with the various German equivalents for English '(al)though', then (19.5.2) with those forms which correspond to English 'however', 'whatever', 'where(so)ever' and the like. Conditional concessive conjunctions (i.e. = English 'even if') are treated in 16.3.3d.

19.5.1 German equivalents for English '(al)though'

(a) *obwohl* is the commonest concessive conjunction in current usage:

Obwohl es sehr spät war, habe ich weitergearbeitet	*Although it was very late, I carried on working*

NB: (i) If the *obwohl*-clause comes first, the contrast can be emphasized by using *so . . . doch* in the main clause, e.g:

Obwohl ich unterschrieben hatte, **so** blieb sie **doch** sehr skeptisch	*Although I had signed, she still remained very sceptical*

(ii) Less commonly, the contrast may be stressed by putting the verb second in the following main clause, e.g.:

Obwohl er mein Vetter ist, ich **kann** nichts für ihn tun	*Although he is my cousin, I can't do anything for him*

(b) Alternatives to *obwohl* in formal German

The following are found mainly in written registers, roughly in descending order of frequency:

obgleich   obschon   wenngleich   wiewohl   obzwar

obschon is used particularly by Swiss writers, e.g.:

Ivy hatte drei Stunden lang . . . auf mich eingeschwätzt, obschon sie wußte, daß ich grundsätzlich nicht heirate (*Frisch*)	*Ivy had kept on at me for three hours although she knew I shan't get married on principle*

(c) *trotzdem* is sometimes used as a conjunction in the sense of 'although':

Trotzdem ich mich auf alle mögliche Weise anstrengte, ernst zu sein, kam das Lachen stoßweise immer wieder (*Rilke*)	*Although I made every possible effort to be serious, the laughing kept coming back spasmodically*

This use of *trotzdem* as a conjunction is primarily colloquial, and many stylists consider it unacceptable in writing. However, both DUDEN (1985:665f.), which cites the example above, and Engel (1988:728f.) state that it can no longer be regarded as incorrect.

(d) A frequent and useful alternative means of expressing concession is a construction with *zwar . . . aber,*

i.e. with two main clauses. The first one contains the particle *zwar*, cf. 10.36.1, and the second is introduced by *aber*, e.g.:

Der Aufsatz ist **zwar** ganz gut, **aber** ich muß dazu sagen, daß . . .	*Although the essay is quite good, I have to say that . . .*

19.5.2 Concessive clauses of the type 'however', 'whoever', 'whenever', etc.

(a) The most common structure for this type of concessive clause in German is to use one of the interrogative pronouns (cf. 5.3) or adverbs (cf. 7.6.1) with the particle *auch* later in the clause:

Wer er **auch** ist, ich kann nichts für ihn tun	*Whoever he may be, I can do nothing for him*
Wann sie **auch** ankommt, ich will sie sofort sprechen	*Whenever she may arrive, I want to speak to her straight away*
Wohin sie **auch** geht, ich werde ihr folgen	*Wherever she may go, I shall follow her*
Wo er sich **auch** zeigte, er wurde mit Beifall begrüßt	*Wherever he showed himself, he was greeted with applause*

NB: (i) The modal verb *mögen* is often used in these clauses, e.g. *Wer er auch sein mag, . . .*, etc., cf. 17.4.3.
(ii) In modern German, the indicative mood is used in clauses of this type. The subjunctive can now sound rather affected, except in the set phrase *Wie dem auch sei* 'However that may be', cf. 16.4.7.

(iii) As the examples show, a main clause following these concessive clauses usually has normal word order, with the verb second, cf.21.2.2d.

(iv) *auch* may be strengthened by adding *immer*, e.g. *Wo er sich auch immer zeigte,* . . .. Alternatively, *immer* may be used on its own. It always follows the interrogative, e.g.: *Wo immer er sich zeigte* . . .

(b) For English 'however' followed by **an adjective or an adverb, German** uses *so/wie . . . auch*

(i) Some examples:

So/Wie gescheit er **auch** sein mag, für diese Stelle paßt er nicht	*However clever he may be, he's not right for this job*
So/Wie teuer das Bild **auch** ist/sein mag, ich will es doch kaufen	*However dear the picture is, I'm still going to buy it*
So/Wie schnell er **auch** lief, die Polizei holte ihn doch ein	*However fast he ran, the police still caught up with him*

(ii) Similarly *sosehr . . . auch* is usual for 'however much', e.g.:

Sosehr ich es **auch** bedaure, es wird mir nicht möglich sein	*However much I might regret it, it just won't be possible*

(iii) *noch so* can be used in a concessive sense with a following adjective, cf. the following alternative for the first example under (i) above:

Er mag **noch so** gescheit sein, für diese Stelle paßt er nicht.

Also:

Es mögen sich noch so viele Leute beschweren, es wird nichts geschehen	*However many/No matter how many people complain, nothing will happen*

(c) For 'whatever' followed by a noun, German uses *was für (ein)* or *welcher . . . auch*:

Was für Schwierigkeiten du **auch** hast, es ist der Mühe wert	*Whatever difficulties you may have, it's worth the trouble*
. . . diese Vorgänge, von **welcher** Seite man sie **auch** betrachtet (*SZ*)	*these events, from whatever side one considers them*
aus **welchem** Land **auch immer**	*from whatever country*
aus **welchem** Grund **auch immer**	*for whatever reason*

19.6 Conjunctions of manner and degree

A full list of the main conjunctions of manner and degree is given below. Further information may be found in the remainder of this section or where indicated.

als	*than*	nur daß	*only that*
als ob/wenn	*as if* (cf. 16.4.1)	ohne daß	*without + . . . ing*
(an)statt daß	*instead of* (cf.13.2.5c)	sofern	*provided that*
außer daß	*except that*	soweit	*as/so far as*
außer wenn	*except when*	wie	*as, like*
dadurch daß, indem	*by + . . . ing*		
insofern (als), insoweit (als), *inasmuch as, (in) so far as*			
je . . . um so/desto (cf. 8.2.7) *the more . . . the more*			
je nachdem (ob/wie) *according to, depending on*			

19.6.1 *als* and *wie* are used to introduce comparative clauses,

cf. 8.2.1 and 8.2.3, e.g.:

Wir fahren schneller, als du denkst	*We're travelling faster than you think*
Der Vortrag war nicht so interessant, wie ich erwartet hatte	*The lecture was less interesting than I had expected*

19.6.2 *außer daß* and *außer wenn*

(a) *außer daß* corresponds to English 'except that':

Ich habe nichts herausfinden können, außer daß er erst im April zurückkommt	*I didn't find anything out, except that he's not coming back till April*

NB: An infinitive clause with *außer . . . zu* can be used if the subjects of the two clauses are the same, cf. 13.2.5d.

(b) *außer wenn* often corresponds to English 'except when', but in many contexts 'unless' is a possible (or the only) equivalent:

Wir gingen oft im Gebirge wandern, außer wenn es regnete	*We often used to go hiking in the mountains, except when/unless it was raining*
Du brauchst die Suppe nicht zu essen, außer wenn du sie wirklich magst	*You don't need to eat the soup, unless you really like it*

NB: (i) *es sei denn(, daß)* 'unless' is often a possible alternative to *außer wenn*, cf. 16.3.3d, but *wenn . . . nicht*, which can also often mean 'unless', may have a different meaning in some contexts. Compare:

Du brauchst die Suppe nicht zu essen, wenn du sie wirklich nicht magst	*You needn't eat the soup if you really don't like it*

(ii) Especially in colloquial speech, *außer* may occur for *außer wenn*. It is followed by normal word order, with the verb second, e.g.:

Sonntags arbeite ich im Garten, außer meine Mutter kommt zu Besuch	*On Sundays I work in the garden, unless my mother comes to visit us*

19.6.3 *dadurch daß* and *indem* have instrumental meaning

Their usual English equivalent is *by* followed by the *ing*-form of the verb, cf. also 13.7.2a, e.g.:

Er hat sich dadurch gerettet, daß er aus dem Fenster sprang
Er hat sich gerettet, indem er aus dem Fenster sprang
   He saved himself by jumping out of the window
Man kann dadurch Unfälle vermeiden helfen, daß man die Verkehrsvorschriften beachtet
Man kann Unfälle vermeiden helfen, indem man die Verkehrsvorschriften beachtet
   One can help to avoid accidents by observing the highway code

NB: This is the only current use of *indem* in modern German. Its use in time clauses, cf. 19.2.1e, is now obsolete.

19.6.4 *insofern (als), insoweit (als), sofern, soweit*

These are all quite close in meaning, but they are not interchangeable in all contexts.

(a) *insofern (als)* and *insoweit (als)* correspond to English '(in) so/as far as' or 'inasmuch as/in that', e.g.:

Ich werde dir helfen,
    insofern (als) ich kann/
    insoweit (als) ich kann
	I'll help you in so far as I'm
	    able to

insofern and *insoweit* may be placed within a preceding main clause, in which case they must be used with a following *als*, e.g:

Diese Verhandlungen werden insofern/
    insoweit schwierig sein, als es sich
    um einen ausgesprochen heikles
    Problem handelt
	These negotiations will be
	    difficult, inasmuch as/in that
	    we're dealing with an extremely
	    tricky problem

(b) *soweit* is most often used in the sense of '(in) so/as far as'

In this sense it is an alternative to *insofern/insoweit (als)*, e.g.:

Ich werde dir helfen, soweit ich kann	*I'll help you in so far as I'm able to*

Soweit ich die Lage beurteilen kann,
    muß ich ihm recht geben
	In so far as I can judge the
	    situation, I've got to admit
	    he's right

It may sometimes be used with a conditional sense, and thus be an alternative to *sofern*, cf. (c) below, e.g.:

Soweit/Sofern noch Interesse besteht,
    wollen wir schon morgen damit
    anfangen
	Provided there's still interest,
	    we're going to make a start
	    tomorrow

NB: With the verb *wissen*, *soviel* is commonly employed for English 'as far as', e.g. *soviel ich weiß* 'as far as I know'.

(c) *sofern* usually has a clear conditional sense,

i.e. it corresponds to English 'provided that' or 'if', cf. 16.3.3d:

Sofern wir es im Stadtrat durchsetzen
    können, wird die neue Straße bald
    gebaut
	Provided (that)/If we can get it
	    through the town council, the new
	    road will soon be built

19.6.5 *je nachdem* 'according to', 'depending on'

je nachdem is normally used with a following *ob* or an interrogative, e.g.:

Je nachdem ob es ihm besser geht oder
    nicht, wird er morgen verreisen
	Depending on whether he's better or
	    not, he'll leave tomorrow

Je nachdem wann wir fertig sind,
    werden wir hier oder in der Stadt
    essen
	Depending on when we get finished,
	    we'll eat here or in town

Je nachdem wie das Wetter wird, werden wir am Montag oder am Dienstag segeln gehen	*According to what the weather is like, we'll go sailing on Monday or Tuesday*

NB: *je nachdem* often occurs in isolation, e.g.:

Kommst du morgen mit? – Na, je nachdem	*Are you coming tomorrow? – It depends.*

19.6.6 *nur daß* 'only (that)'

In der neuen Schule hat er sich gut eingelebt, nur daß seine Noten etwas besser sein könnten	*He's settled down well at his new school, only his marks could be a bit better*

NB: Especially in spoken German, a construction with main clauses will often be preferred to the conjunction *nur daß*, e.g. . . . , *nur könnten seine Noten etwas besser sein.*

19.6.7 *ohne daß* 'without'

ohne daß must be used for English 'without' followed by an *ing*-form if the two clauses have a different subject, e.g.:

Er verließ das Zimmer, ohne daß wir es merkten	*He left the room without us noticing*
Sie haben mir sofort geholfen, ohne daß ich sie darum bitten mußte	*They helped me immediately without my having to ask them*

NB: (i) If the subjects are the same, an infinitive clause with *ohne . . . zu* may be used for English 'without' + *ing*, cf. 13.2.5b.
(ii) The subjunctive is often used in *ohne daß* clauses, cf. 16.4.5a.

19.7 Conditional conjunctions

The following conjunctions are used to introduce conditional clauses in German. They are all dealt with in 16.3 (especially 16.3.3):

angenommen, daß	*assuming that*	vorausgesetzt, daß	*provided that*
es sei denn, daß	*unless*	wenn	*if*
falls/im Falle, daß	*if*		

20 Prepositions

This chapter deals with all the prepositions of German, ordered according to the case they govern, i.e. the accusative (20.1), the dative (20.2), the dative or the accusative (20.3) and the genitive (20.4). The final section (20.5) deals with the German equivalents for English 'to', which poses particular difficulties.

In the sections dealing with German prepositions, all the main literal and figurative senses of each preposition are treated together, with an indication where necessary of where further information may be found in other parts of the book. Note that the use of prepositions in time phrases is fully treated in 11.6, the use of prepositions after adjectives in 6.6, after verbs in 18.6, the contraction of some prepositions with the definite article (e.g. *am, ins*, etc.) in 4.1.1b, and the use of the prepositional adverb (e.g. *darauf, damit*, etc.) in 3.5.

Schmitz (1964) is an extremely useful introduction to the use of prepositions in German, specifically written for the foreign learner, and several examples have been taken from it.

20.1 Prepositions taking the accusative

Six common prepositions are used with the accusative in modern German:

bis	für	ohne
durch	gegen	um

The following are less frequent. They are treated together in 20.1.7:

à	eingerechnet	pro
betreffend	per	wider

20.1.1 *bis*

bis is <u>never</u> followed by an article (or any determiner). It is used on its own only with names, adverbs and some time words. Otherwise it has another preposition with it, which determines the case.

(a) Referring to place, *bis* means 'as far as', '(up) to'
(i) *bis* with names, etc., used without an article:

403

Ich fahre nur bis Frankfurt	*I'm only going as far as Frankfurt*
Bis dahin gehe ich mit	*I'll go that far with you*
bis hierher und nicht weiter	*so far and no further*

(ii) If the following noun has an article, an appropriate preposition must follow, usually the appropriate equivalent of English 'to', cf. 20.5:

Wir gingen bis zum Waldrand	*We went as far as the edge of the forest*
Sie ging bis zur Tür	*She went up to the door*
Sie ging bis an die Tür	*She went right up to the door*
Wir fuhren bis an die Grenze	*We went as far as/up to the border*
. . . standen sie im Wasser bis an die Knöchel (*H.Mann*)	*They were standing in water up to their ankles*
(cf. Sie standen in Wasser bis über die Knöchel)	
bis hin zu den Warzen im Gesicht (*Borst*)	*right down to the warts on his face*
Er stieg bis aufs Dach	*He climbed right onto the roof*
bis über die Ohren verschuldet	*up to one's ears in debt*

(iii) With names of towns, cities and countries, *bis* or *bis nach* can be used. The latter is rather more emphatic:

Wir fahren bis (nach) Freiburg, von Köln bis (nach) Bonn	
Alexander der Große drang bis nach Indien vor	*Alexander the Great advanced as far as India*

(b) Referring to time, *bis* means 'until, till',

cf.11.6.4. If the noun has a determiner, *zu* is inserted, e.g.:

bis zum Abend, bis zum 4. Mai, bis zu seinem Tod, bis zu diesem Augenblick

NB: (i) *erst* is used for 'not until', e.g. *Er kommt erst am Montag*, cf. 10.12.1.
(ii) In a few phrases, *bis zu* is used with no following article, e.g. *bis zu Beginn des Weltkrieges, Kinder bis zu zwölf Jahren*.
(iii) In some instances, *bis* may be followed by other prepositions in time phrases, e.g. *bis auf weiteres* 'until further notice', *bis vor zehn Tagen, bis in den Herbst hinein*, cf. 11.6.4.
(iv) *bis* is frequently used in colloquial leave-taking phrases, e.g. *Bis gleich! Bis bald! Bis morgen! Bis nächste Woche!*

(c) *bis auf* (+ acc.) means 'down to (and including)' or 'all but, except':

Die Kabinen waren mit 447 Passagieren bis auf das letzte Klappbett belegt (*Zeit*)	*With 447 passengers, the cabins were full down to the last folding bed*
Die Insassen kamen alle um bis auf drei	*All but three of the passengers were killed*

NB: *bis auf* may be ambiguous in some contexts. Thus, *Der Bus war bis auf den letzten Platz besetzt* could mean 'The bus was full down to the last seat' or 'The bus was full except for the last seat'.

20.1.2 *durch*

(a) *durch* means 'through', referring to place:

Sie ging durch die Stadt	*She went through the city*
Er atmete durch den Mund	*He was breathing through his mouth*
mitten durch den Park (cf. 7.2.3)	*through the middle of the park*

durch is often strengthened by adding *hindurch*, cf. 7.3.4, e.g.:

Wir gingen durch den Wald hindurch	*We went (right) through the forest*

It can also be used for English 'across', especially with a preceding *quer* to give the sense of 'crosswise, diagonally':

Wir wateten (quer) durch den Fluß	*We waded across the river*

(b) *durch* can also be used for English 'throughout'
(i) This is its usual sense when it refers to time, in which case it may be strengthened by adding *hindurch*, e.g.:

durch viele Generationen (hindurch)	*throughout many generations*

(ii) *hindurch* can be used without a preceding *durch* for 'throughout' after an accusative phrase of time with *ganz*, cf. 11.4.1:

den ganzen Winter hindurch	*throughout the winter*
die ganze Nacht hindurch	*throughout the whole night*

NB: A phrase with *ganz* and an appropriate preposition is needed to give the sense of English 'throughout' referring to place, e.g.:

im ganzen Land	*throughout the country*
durch die ganze Stadt	*throughout the town*

(c) *durch* is used to express means.
(i) It introduces the agent (animate or inanimate) or means through whom or which an action is carried out, e.g.:

Mein Onkel hatte mich durch seinen Sohn/durch ein Telegramm gewarnt	*My uncle had warned me through his son/by a telegram*
Durch harte Arbeit hat er sein Ziel erreicht	*He attained his aim by (means of) hard work*
Er ist durch einen Unfall ums Leben gekommen	*He was killed through an accident*
durch seine eigene Schuld	*through his own fault*
durch Zufall habe ich erfahren, daß . . .	*I learnt by chance that . . .*

NB: (i) This use of *durch* corresponds to its use for *by* in passive sentences, cf. 15.3.
   (ii) Whilst *durch* indicates the means, *mit* is used for the instrument used to carry out an action, e.g. *Er hat sie mit einem Messer getötet*, cf. 20.2.5b.

(ii) *durch* used in this sense can be the equivalent of English *by* used with a verbal noun:

die Annahme des Kaisertitels durch den König	*the assumption of the title of emperor by the king*
die Erfindung des Verbrennungsmotors durch Benz und Daimler	*the invention of the internal combustion engine by Benz and Daimler*

(iii) The use of *durch* with a verbal noun often corresponds to English *by* + . . . *ing*-form, cf. 13.7.2a:

durch Betätigung des Mechanismus	*by activating the mechanism*

(iv) The prepositional adverb *dadurch* is often used in the sense of 'thereby':

Was willst du dadurch erreichen?	*What do you hope to gain by that?*
Meinst du, dadurch wird alles wieder gut?	*Do you think that will make everything all right again?*

NB: For the compound conjunction *dadurch, daß*, see 19.6.3.

20.1.3 *für*

(a) *für* corresponds to English 'for' in a wide range of senses,
i.e. where 'for' has the meaning of 'on behalf of' and the like, e.g.:

Er hat viel für mich getan	Das wäre genug für heute
Das war sehr unangenehm für mich (cf. 6.5.1)	Das ist kein Buch für Kinder
	Ich habe es für zehn Mark gekriegt
Für einen Ausländer spricht er recht gut Deutsch	

NB: (i) *für* is used idiomatically in:

ein Sinn, ein Beispiel für etwas	*a sense, an example of sth.*

(ii) Where English 'for' expresses purpose, its usual German equivalent is *zu*, see 20.2.9d.

(b) *für* is used to indicate a period of time,
e.g. *für sechs Wochen* 'for six weeks'. For this, and other German equivalents for English 'for' referring to time, see 11.6.5.

20.1.4 *gegen*

(a) Referring to place or opposition, *gegen* means 'against':

Er warf den Ball gegen die Mauer	*He threw the ball against the wall*
gegen den Strom schwimmen (in literal and figurative senses)	*swim against the current*
Er verteidigte sich gegen seine Verleumder	*He defended himself against the people who were slandering him*
Ich bin gegen diesen Plan	*I am against this project*

The prepositional adverb *dagegen* is very frequent to indicate opposition, e.g.:

Hast du was dagegen, wenn wir früher anfangen?	*Do you have any objection to us starting earlier?*

NB: Note the different usage between German and English in:

Ich brauche Tabletten gegen Kopfschmerzen	*I need tablets for a headache*

(b) *gegen* can indicate direction
It then often corresponds to 'into':

Er fuhr gegen einen Baum	*He drove into a tree*

NB: (i) Note the difference from English usage in the following phrase:
etwas gegen das Licht halten   *hold sth. up to the light*
(ii) The use of *gegen* with the points of the compass is now old-fashioned. For older (and literary) *gegen Norden fahren* one finds **nach** *Norden fahren* in most modern usage.

(c) *gegen* can express a contrast (= 'contrary to', 'compared with'):

Ich handelte gegen seinen Befehl	*I acted against/contrary to his orders*
gegen alle Erwartungen	*against/contrary to all expectations*
Gegen meine Schwester bin ich groß	*I'm tall compared with my sister*
gegen früher	*compared with formerly*

(d) *gegen* can be used in the sense of '(in exchange/return) for'

Er gab mir das Geld gegen eine Quittung	*He gave me the money in exchange for a receipt*
Ich tauschte meinen Kuli gegen einen Filzstift	*I exchanged my ball-point for a felt-tip*

(e) *gegen* can express approximation (= 'about'):

Es waren gegen (or: etwa, or: an die) 500 Zuschauer im Saal	*There were about 500 spectators in the hall*

(f) *gegen* is used after a number of nouns and adjectives,
cf. also 6.6.1. These mainly involve a mental attitude 'towards' something or someone, e.g.:

die Abneigung gegen *aversion for*	die Grausamkeit gegen *cruelty towards*
der Haß gegen *hatred of*	das Mißtrauen gegen *distrust of*
argwöhnish gegen *suspicious of*	gesichert gegen *secure against*
gleichgültig gegen *indifferent to*	
seine Pflicht gegen seine Eltern	*his duty towards his parents*
sein Verhalten gegen seinen Chef	*his attitude to(wards) his boss*
rücksichtslos/rücksichtsvoll gegen	*(in)considerate towards*

NB: With these, *gegenüber* is a frequent possible alternative to *gegen*, see 20.2.4d, and a number of adjectives may be followed by *zu* or *gegen*, cf. 20.2.9g.

(g) Referring to time, *gegen* means 'about', 'towards,
e.g. *Sie kam gegen Abend, gegen vier Uhr an.* For this usage, see 11.6.6.

20.1.5 *ohne*

The use of *ohne* corresponds almost exactly to that of English 'without', e.g.:

Das tat er ohne mein Wissen   Er geht selten ohne Hut
Das haben wir ohne große Schwierigkeiten erledigt

NB: (i) *ohne* is used with no determiner in many contexts where English has an indefinite article or a possessive, cf. 4.10.3b.
(ii) Note the idiomatic use of *ohne* on its own in colloquial speech:
Der Wein ist nicht ohne   *The wine's got quite a kick*
Er ist gar nicht so ohne   *He's got what it takes*
(iii) For the use of *ohne* in infinitive clauses (i.e. *ohne . . . zu*), see 13.2.5b, for the compound conjunction *ohne daß*, see 19.6.7.

20.1.6 *um*

(a) Referring to place, *um* means 'round', 'about' :

Wir standen um den Teich   *We were standing round the pond*
Er kam um die Ecke   *He came round the corner*
Sie sah um sich   *She looked round (in all directions)*
Er hat gern viele Mädchen um sich *He likes having a lot of girls
                                    about him*

um is often strengthened by adding *rund, rings* or *herum* (cf. 7.3.4b), e.g.:

Wir standen rings/rund um den Tisch *or* um den Tisch herum
Er kam um die Ecke herum   Sie sah um sich herum

(b) *um* means 'at' with clock times, but 'about' with other time expressions, cf. 11.6.10 for more details.

Ich komme um zwei Uhr   Um halb sieben ist sie in Augsburg

In the sense of 'about', it may be strengthened by adding *herum*:

um Weihnachten (herum)   um 1870 (herum)

NB: For the use of *um* as an adverb in other approximations (e.g. *um die vierzig ausländische Gäste*), see 9.1.7.

(c) *um* is used to denote the degree of difference.
This often corresponds to English 'by':

Ich werde meinen Aufenthalt um zwei   *I shall extend my stay by two days*
    Tage verlängern
Sie hat sich um 20 Mark verrechnet   *She was 20 marks out in her
                                        calculations/accounts*
um die Hälfte mehr   *half as much again*
eine Erweiterung der EWG um England   *an expansion of the EEC by the
    und andere EFTA-Länder (SZ)   inclusion of England and the
                                        other EFTA countries*

When *um* is used in this sense with a comparative adjective and a measurement phrase, cf. 8.2.3c, an alternative to *um* is simply to put the measurement phrase in the accusative case, cf. 2.2.5b:

Er ist (um) einen Kopf größer als ich   *He's taller than me by a head*

(d) *um* can convey the idea of 'in respect of', 'concerning'
This usage is particularly common when *um* is used to introduce the prepositional object of verbs, cf. 18.6.10, but it also occurs in other constructions, especially after some nouns and adjectives, e.g.:

der Kampf ums Dasein	*the struggle for existence*
Er tat es nur um das Geld	*He only did it for the money*
um Geld schreiben	*write (asking) for money*
Ich habe mit ihm um 500 Mark gewettet	*I bet him 500 marks*
Er wandte sich an mich um Rat	*He turned to me for advice*
Es ist schade um den Verlust	*It's a pity about the loss*
Es steht schlecht um ihren Bruder	*Her brother's in a bad way*
ein Streit um etwas	*an argument about sth.*
die Sorge um ihren Sohn	*the concern for her son*
die Angst ums Leben	*fear for one's life*
Es war etwas Besonderes um diese Landerziehungsheime (*K. Mann*)	*There was something special about these boarding-schools*
Es ist recht still um ihn geworden	*You don't hear anything about him now*

An idiomatic use:

Auge um Auge, Zahn um Zahn   *an eye for an eye, a tooth for a tooth*

(e) The prepositional adverb *darum* is also used in the meaning 'therefore', 'that's why'
It is an alternative to *deshalb*.

Darum habe ich nicht schreiben können	*That's why I couldn't write*
Sie hatte eine Panne, darum ist sie so spät gekommen	*She had a breakdown, that's why she was so late coming*

20.1.7 Some less frequent prepositions governing the accusative

(a) *à* is used in the sense of 'at' (i.e. @), with prices:

Zehn Paar Schuhe à 150 Mark

This usage is now rather old-fashioned, and *zu* is now more frequent than *à*, cf. 20.2.9h.

(b) *betreffend* 'with regard to' is used mainly in commercial German
It is an alternative to *betreffs* (+ gen.) and may procede or follow the noun it governs:

betreffend Ihr Schreiben vom 23. Mai, . . . }
Ihr Schreiben vom 23. Mai betreffend, . . . }

(c) *eingerechnet* 'including' is limited to commercial language
It follows the noun it governs:

meine Unkosten eingerechnet   *including my expenses*

(d) *per* 'per', 'by' is used principally in commercial German, but it is not unknown in colloquial speech
When used with a means of transport it is an alternative to more usual *mit*, cf. 20.2.5b:

per Post (= mit der Post) *by post*	per Bahn (= mit der Bahn) *by rail*
per Luftfracht *by air*	per Einschreiben *by recorded mail*
per Adresse (p.A.) *c/o*	per Anhalter fahren *to hitchhike*
mit jemandem per du sein	*be on first-name terms with sb.*
Sie bezahlen erst per 31. Dezember	*You do not pay until December 31st*
Die Waren sind per 1. Februar bestellt	*The goods are ordered for February 1st*

(e) *pro* 'per' is mainly used in commercial German, but it is not uncommon in the spoken language
A common alternative is *je*, cf. 9.4.1:

Die Pfirsiche kosten 80 Pfennig pro Stück	*The peaches cost 80 pfennigs each*
Was ist der Preis pro Tag?	*What is the cost per day?*
zwanzig Mark pro Person	*twenty marks per person*
Unsere Reisekosten betragen 3000 Mark pro/je Vertreter pro/je Monat	*Our travel expenses average 3000 marks per representative per month*

(f) *wider* 'against' is an obsolete alternative to *gegen*
It is occasionally found in elevated registers, but most frequently in a few set phrases:

Diese Unterlassung relativiert alle markigen Worte wider den Terrorismus (*Zeit*)	*This omission qualifies all the vigorous speeches against terrorism*
wider (alles) Erwarten	*against (all) expectations*
wider Willen	*against my (his, her, etc) will*
wider besseres Wissen	*against my (etc) better judgement*
Das geht mir wider den Strich	*That goes against the grain*

20.2 Prepositions taking the dative

Nine common prepositions are used only or chiefly with a following dative:

aus	gegenüber	seit
außer	mit	von
bei	nach	zu

The following are less frequent, and are treated together in 20.2.10:

ab	entsprechend	nebst
binnen	fern	zufolge
dank	gemäß	zuliebe
entgegen	(mit)samt	zuwider
	nahe	

20.2.1 *aus*

(a) The basic sense of *aus*, referring to place, is 'out of'.

(i) = 'out of':

Er kam aus dem Haus	*He was coming out of the house*
Ich sah aus dem Fenster	*I looked out of the window*
(or: zum Fenster hinaus)	
Er trank aus einer Tasse	*He was drinking out of a cup*
Sie ging mir aus dem Weg	*She avoided me*
aus der Mode kommen/sein	*go/be out of fashion*
aus der Übung kommen	*get out of practice*

(ii) Given its basic sense, *aus* is used for English 'from' with reference to places one has been 'in', with the idea of origin. Its opposite is *in* (+acc.). *von*, on the other hand (cf. 20.2.8a), is used for 'from' with reference to places one has been 'at', i.e. it expresses the idea of direction. Its opposite is *zu*.

Er kommt aus Hamburg	*He comes from Hamburg*

i.e. *Er wohnt <u>in</u> Hamburg. Er kommt von Hamburg* means 'He is travelling from Hamburg (on this occasion).

aus dieser Richtung	*from that direction*

cf. *in diese(r) Richtung* 'in that direction'.

Dieser Schrank ist aus dem 18. Jahrhundert	*This cupboard is from the 18th century*

i.e. it was made <u>in</u> the 18th century

ein Mädchen aus unserer Klasse	*a girl from our class*

i.e. she is <u>in</u> our class

(b) *aus* denotes 'made of' referring to materials:

Die Kaffeekanne war aus Silber	*The coffee pot was made of silver*
aus Holz, Stahl, Eisen	*made of wood, steel, iron*
ein Kleid aus Wolle	*a woollen dress*

NB also *bestehen aus* 'consist of', cf. 18.6.4.

(c) *aus* is used to denote a cause, a reason or a motive:

Sie tat es aus Dankbarkeit, aus Mitleid, aus Überzeugung	*She did it out of gratitude out of sympathy, from conviction*
Ich weiß es aus (der) Erfahrung	*I know it from experience*
Ich frage nur aus Interesse	*I'm only asking out of interest*
aus Furcht vor, Liebe zu etwas	*for fear, love of sth.*

| aus diesem Grund(e) | *for that reason* |
| aus sich heraus | *of one's own accord* |

NB: For the distinction between *aus* and *vor* (+ dat.) to indicate cause, see 20.3.15d.

(d) some idiomatic uses:

aus erster Hand	*at first hand*
Daraus werde ich nicht klug	*I can't make it out*
Aus dir wird nichts werden	*You'll never come to anything*

20.2.2 *außer*

(a) *außer* usually expresses a restriction (= 'except (for)', 'besides'):

Niemand hat ihn gesehen außer dem Nachtwächter	*No-one saw him except for the night-watchman*
Niemand wird es machen können außer mir	*No-one will be able to do it except for me*
Ich konnte nichts sehen außer Straßenlichtern	*I couldn't see anything besides street-lights*
Sie kommt jeden Tag außer dienstags	*She comes every day except Tuesdays*

NB: It is possible to use *außer* with the same case as the word to which it refers back, rather than with the dative, and the following are quite acceptable alternatives to the examples above:
Ich konnte **nichts** sehen außer **Lichter**
Niemand wird es machen können außer **ich**
In such cases, *außer* is, in effect, being used as a conjunction rather than a preposition.

(b) *außer* is used in the meaning 'out of', 'outside'
This meaning is mainly found in set phrases, in most of which *außer* is used without a following article:

Die Maschine ist außer Betrieb	*The machine is out of service*
außer Dienst (a.D.)	*retired*
außer der Reihe	*out of turn, sequence*
außer Kontrolle sein/geraten	*be/get out of control*
etwas außer acht lassen	*disregard sth.*
Ich war außer mir	*I was beside myself*
Aber dies war etwas, was ganz außer seiner Macht lag (*Musil*)	*This was something which lay quite outside his power*

Similarly:

außer Atem *out of breath*	außer Gefahr *out of danger*
außer Reichweite *out of range*	außer Sicht *out of sight*
außer Übung *out of practice*	außer Zweifel *beyond doubt*

NB: (i) In one or two obsolescent phrases *außer* is used with a genitive, notably in *außer Landes gehen* 'leave the country'. More usual for this would be *ins Ausland gehen*, or simply *auswandern*.
(ii) With verbs of motion, *außer* is used with the accusative, although this is only obvious in those rare cases where a determiner or an adjective is used, e.g. *etwas außer jed**en** Zweifel setzen*.

20.2.3 *bei*

(a) Referring to place, *bei* usually corresponds to English 'by' or 'at'
(i) In this sense it is rather less precise than *an* (+ dat.), cf. 20.3.2a, meaning 'in the vicinity of' rather than 'adjacent to'.

Er stand bei mir (= Er stand in meiner Nähe)	*He was standing by/near me*
Bad Homburg liegt bei Frankfurt	*Bad Homburg is by/near Frankfurt*
(dicht) bei der Kirche	*(right) by the church*
Ich habe ihn neulich beim Fußballspiel gesehen	*I saw him recently at the football match*
Er saß beim Feuer	*He was sitting by the fire*

NB: *bei* is always used with battles, e.g. *die Schlacht bei Hastings*

(ii) Used with reference to people, it usually means 'at (the house of)'. It is also used to indicate place of employment:

Sie wohnt bei ihrer Tante	*She lives at her aunt's*
Ich habe dieses Fleisch beim neuen Metzger gekauft	*I bought this meat at the new butcher's*
Sie arbeitet bei der Post, bei Bayer	*She works at the post-office, at Bayer's*
bei uns	*at our house*
bei uns in der Fabrik	*at our works*

NB: Unlike French *chez*, *bei* can never be used to indicate motion <u>to</u> somebody's house, cf. *Sie geht zu ihrer Tante* 'She's going to her aunt's house'.

(iii) It can also be used in a number of extended senses with reference to people. This often corresponds to English 'with':

Bei ihm kann man nie sicher sein	*You can never be sure with him*
Das hat ihm bei den Amerikanern sehr geschadet	*That did him a lot of harm with the Americans*
Ich habe mich bei ihm entschuldigt, beschwert	*I apologized, complained to him*
Er hat großen Einfluß beim Minister	*He has a lot of influence with the minister*
Mathe haben wir bei Frau Gerstner	*We have Frau Gerstner for maths*
Hast du deinen Ausweis bei dir/dabei?	*Have you got your identity-card on you?*
Bei Goethe liest man . . .	*In Goethe's works one reads . . .*

(b) *bei* is frequently used to indicate attendant circumstances.
This usage has a wide range of English equivalents, i.e.:
(i) It can mean 'in view of', 'with', etc., e.g.:

Bei seinem unzuverlässigen Charakter muß man vorsichtig sein	*In view of his unreliable character you have to be careful*
bei den immer steigenden Preisen	*in view of the constantly rising prices*
Bei diesem Gehalt kann ich mir keinen neuen Wagen leisten	*With this salary I can't afford a new car*
Bei all seinen Verlusten bleibt er ein Optimist	*Despite all his losses he remains an optimist*

(ii) It can mean 'on the occasion of', 'at'. This sense is related to its use in time expressions, cf. 11.6.3:

bei dieser Gelegenheit	*on this occasion*
bei dem bloßen Gedanken	*at the very thought*
Sie erblaßte bei der Nachricht	*She turned pale at the news*
Acht Menschen kamen bei diesem . . . Verkehrsunfall ums Leben (*FAZ*)	*Eight people were killed in this road accident*
bei Vollbeschäftigung	*in the case of full employment*
bei diesem Anblick	*at the sight of this*
bei einem Glas Wein	*over a glass of wine*

Similarly:

bei der Arbeit *at work*	beim Fußball *when playing football*
bei Tisch *at table*	bei seinem Tod *at his death*
bei schönem Wetter *if it's fine*	bei diesen Worten *at these words*

NB: Either *bei* or *auf* are used for English 'at', referring to formal occasions, functions and the like, e.g.:

Ich habe sie bei/auf ihrer   *I met her at their wedding*
    Hochzeit kennengelernt

The difference of meaning is often slight, cf. 20.3.4b, but in general *bei* points more clearly to the <u>time</u>, rather than the <u>place</u>, of the event in question.

(iii) *bei* is used with the infinitive or other verbal nouns in the sense of English 'on + . . . -ing' or a subordinate time clause, cf. 13.4.3a and 13.7.2d. This usage is particularly frequent in non-literary written German, but it is in no way restricted to this register:

beim Schließen der Türen	*on shutting the doors*
beim Besteigen des Turmes	*on/when ascending the tower*
beim Schlafen, Essen	*whilst sleeping, eating*
bei seiner Ankunft	*on arrival/when he arrived*
bei näherer Überlegung	*on closer consideration*
bei unserer letzten Zusammenkunft	*when we last met*

(c) Some idiomatic uses of *bei*:

Sie war bei guter/schlechter Laune	*She was in a good/bad mood*
Sie nannte mich beim Vornamen	*She called me by my first name*
Sie nahm mich beim Wort	*She took me at my word*
Sie nahm mich bei der Hand	*She took me by the hand*

20.2.4 *gegenüber*

(a) The position of *gegenüber*
(i) *gegenüber* always follows a pronoun, e.g.:

Sie saß mir gegenüber   *Ihr gegenüber stand ein alter Herr*

(ii) *gegenüber* may come before or after a noun. It tends to follow words denoting people, otherwise it is commoner for it to precede, e.g.:

Alten Menschen gegenüber soll man   *One ought always to be ready to*
    immer hilfsbereit sein   *help old people*
    (Rather less common: *Gegenüber alten Menschen* . . .)

Gegenüber dem Rathaus liegt ein
   Krankenhaus
   (Rather less common: *Dem Rathaus gegenüber* . . .)

Opposite the town-hall there is a
   hospital

(b) Referring to place, *gegenüber* means 'opposite':

Ich saß ihr gegenüber
Ich wohne gegenüber dem Krankenhaus

I was sitting opposite her
I live opposite the hospital

NB: (i) In this sense, *gegenüber* is often used with a following *von*, especially in colloquial spoken German, e.g. *Ich saß gegenüber von ihr. Ich wohne gegenüber vom Krankenhaus.*
     (ii) *schräg gegenüber* means 'almost (i.e. diagonally) opposite'.
     (iii) *gegenüber* is often used on its own, as an adverb, e.g. *Sie wohnt gegenüber; das Haus gegenüber; die Leute von gegenüber.*

(c) *gegenüber* can express a comparison (= 'compared with')

gegen, cf. 20.1.4c, or *neben*, cf. 20.3.10d, are possible alternatives to *gegenüber* used in this sense:

Gegenüber meiner Schwester bin ich
   groß
gegenüber dem Vorjahr

I'm tall compared with my sister

compared with last year

(d) *gegenüber* often has the sense of 'in relation to', in respect of', 'towards':

die Politik der USA gegenüber Rußland
Erhards Hilflosigkeit gegenüber
   Positionskämpfen und taktischen
   Finten (*Zeit*)
Er konnte seiner Frau gegenüber ein
   Gefühl von unbezahlten Schulden nicht
   loswerden (*V. Baum*)

the policy of the USA towards Russia
Erhard's helplessness in the face of
   jockeying for position and tactical
   subterfuges
He could not get rid of a feeling of
   unpaid debt towards his wife

In this sense, *gegenüber* is particularly common after nouns and adjectives, where it is an (often more common) alternative to *gegen*, cf. 20.1.4f, or, in some cases, *zu*, cf. 20.2.9g:

Er handelte durchaus gerecht mir
   gegenüber (or: gegen mich)
Seine Güte mir gegenüber (or: zu mir)
   war rührend

He acted absolutely fairly towards
   me
His kindness towards me was touching

Similarly:

das Mißtrauen gegenüber/gegen
eine Pflicht gegenüber/gegen
gleichgültig gegenüber/gegen
rücksichtsvoll/-los gegenüber/gegen
freundlich gegenüber/zu

distrust of
a duty towards
indifferent towards
(in)considerate to
kind to(wards)

20.2.5 *mit*

(a) In most of its uses *mit* corresponds to English 'with':

Er kam mit seiner Freundin	*He came with his girlfriend*
ein Paar Würstchen mit Kartoffelsalat	*a pair of sausages with potato salad*
Mit ihr spiele ich oft Tennis	*I often play tennis with her*
Was ist mit dir los?	*What's up with you?*
mit großer Freude	*with great pleasure*
mit meinem Bruder zusammen	*together with my brother*

(b) *mit* indicates the instrument with which an action is performed
(i) In most cases, this usage of *mit* corresponds to English 'with':

Er schrieb mit einem Filzstift	*He wrote with a felt-tip*
Er hat sie mit einem Messer getötet	*He killed her with a knife*

(ii) However, German usage is sometimes at variance with English:

mit Tinte schreiben	*write in ink*
mit leiser Stimme	*in a low voice*
mit der Maschine schreiben	*type*

(iii) This is notably the case where a means of transport is involved, where German has *mit* for English 'by':

mit der Bahn/dem Zug	*by rail/train*	mit dem Auto	*by car*
mit dem Flugzeug	*by plane*	mit dem Schiff	*by boat*
mit der Post	*by post*	mit Luftpost	*by airmail*
Ich bin mit dem Fahrrad gekommen		*I came by bike/on a bike*	

NB: Whereas *mit* indicates the <u>instrument</u>, the <u>means</u> by which an action is carried out is usually given by *durch*, cf. 20.1.2c

(c) *mit* is common in phrases involving parts of the body, where English does not have a preposition or uses a simple verb:

Sie hat mich mit dem Fuß gestoßen	*She kicked me*
mit den Achseln zucken	*shrug one's shoulders*

(d) Selected common idiomatic uses of *mit*:

mit vierzig Jahren	*at the age of forty*
mit der Zeit	*in (the course of) time*
etwas mit Absicht tun	*do sth. on purpose*
mit anderen Worten (m.a.W.)	*in other words*
Her damit! (coll.)	*Give it here!*
Schluß damit!	*That's enough!*

NB: For the use of *damit* as a conjunction (= 'so that'), see 19.4.1a.

20.2.6 *nach*

(a) *nach* is used in the sense of English 'to',
cf. also 20.5.3. This usage is restricted to the following contexts:

(i) Neuter names of countries and towns used without an article:

Er ging nach Amerika, nach Irland, nach Bacharach

NB: *in* is used with names of countries (mainly masculine and feminine) which always have an article, cf. 4.5.1, e.g. *Sie ging in die Schweiz.*

(ii) Points of the compass used without an article:

Wir fuhren nach Norden, Süden, Westen, Osten

NB: If an article is present, *in* is used, e.g. *Wir fuhren in den sonnigen Süden.*

(iii) With adverbs of place:

Sie ging nach oben, nach unten, nach vorne, nach rechts, links

NB also *nach Hause gehen* 'go home'.

(iv) Colloquial north German usage, where *nach* is often used in place of *zu, an, auf* or *in*, e.g.:

Ich gehe nach (standard German: zu) meiner Schwester
Wir gingen nach dem (standard German: auf den, an den, zum) Bahnhof

This usage is generally considered to be a non-standard regionalism, although it is sometimes used by writers from North Germany.

(b) *nach* can be used in standard German in the sense of 'towards', 'in the direction of'
It is frequently strengthened by adding *hin*, cf. 7.3.3, e.g.:

Er bewegte sich langsam nach der Tür	*He moved slowly towards the door*
Ich sah nach der Tür (hin)	*I looked in the direction of the door*
Er richtete seine Schritte nach der alten Brücke	*He turned his steps towards the old bridge*
Als ich nach dem Dorf (hin) eilte, . . .	*As I was hurrying towards the village, . . .*
nach allen Seiten (hin)	*in all directions*

NB: *auf . . . zu* is a rather more frequent equivalent for English 'towards', cf. 20.3.5a.

(c) Referring to time, *nach* means 'after',
e.g. *nach vier Uhr, nach dem Sommer*, etc. Full details are given in 11.6.8. The prepositional adverb *danach* is commonly used in the sense of 'after' or 'later', cf. 11.7.4b.

(d) *nach* can be used in the sense of 'according to', 'judging by':

Nach meiner Uhr ist es schon halb elf	*According to/By my watch, it's already half past ten*
Nach meiner Rechnung sind wir ihr noch 1000 Mark schuldig	*According to my calculations we still owe her 1000 marks*
nach dem Testament ihres Vaters	*under her father's will*
nach italienischer Art	*in the Italian manner*
nach allem, was ich höre	*according to all that I hear*
nach Ansicht meines Bruders	*in my brother's view*
nach einem Bild von Rubens	*after a picture by Rubens*

Das habe ich nach dem Gedächtnis gezeichnet	*I drew it from memory*
nach meinem Geschmack	*according to my taste*
etwas nach dem Gewicht verkaufen	*sell sth by weight*
nach besten Kräften	*to the best of one's ability*
nach Wunsch	*just as I (he, she, etc.) wanted*
je nach den Umständen	*depending on the circumstances*

When used in this sense, *nach* may sometimes follow the noun. In general, this is usual only with certain nouns (most of which it may precede or follow), and in the meaning 'judging by':

allem Anschein nach	*to all appearances*
diesem Bericht nach	*according to this report*
(in less formal language usually: *nach diesem Bericht*)	
dem Gesetz nach	*according to the law*
(in less offical language usually: *nach dem Gesetz*)	
der Größe nach	*according to size*
(also commonly: *nach der Größe*)	
meiner Meinung nach	*in my opinion*
(also: *nach meiner Meinung*)	
Ich kenne sie nur dem Namen nach	*I only know her by name*
immer der Nase nach	*straight ahead*
der Reihe nach	*in turns*
Ihrer Aussprache nach kommt sie aus Schwaben	*Judging by her pronunciation she comes from Swabia*

NB: A number of other prepositions are used with the meaning 'according to' in formal registers, i.e. *entsprechend, gemäß, laut,* and *zufolge.* The use of these is dealt with in 20.2.10e.

20.2.7 *seit*

seit is used exclusively with reference to time, in the meaning of English 'since' (e.g. *seit dem achtzehnten Jahrhundert*) or 'for' (e.g. *Ich warte seit einer halben Stunde auf meine Schwester*). Its usage is dealt with fully in 11.6.9. For the use of tenses with *seit* phrases, see 14.2.2 and 14.3.3a.

20.2.8 *von*

(a) *von* is used to indicate direction 'from' a place
(i) In this sense, *von* is the opposite of *zu*, which indicates direction towards, cf. 20.2.9. For the difference between *von* and *aus* as equivalents of English 'from', see 20.2.1a:

Ich fuhr von Frankfurt nach München	*I travelled from Frankfurt to Munich*
Sie bekam einen Brief von ihrer Mutter	*She received a letter from her mother*
Sie kommt von ihrer Schwester	*She's coming from her sister's*
Ich wohne zehn Minuten vom Bahnhof (entfernt)	*I live ten minutes from the station*
Die Blätter fallen von den Bäumen	*The leaves are falling from the trees*

(ii) In this sense, *von* may, optionally, be strengthened by adding *aus* after the noun, e.g.:

Von meinem Fenster (aus) kann ich die Paulskirche sehen	*I can see St Paul's church from my window*
Wir sind von Madrid (aus) mit der Bahn nach Barcelona gefahren	*We travelled by train from Madrid to Barcelona*

(iii) *von . . . aus* occurs in a few idiomatic constructions:

Er war von Haus aus Lehrer	*He was originally a teacher*
von mir aus	*as far as I'm concerned*
von Natur aus	*by nature*
Das ist von Grund aus falsch	*That is completely wrong*

(b) *von* also usually has the sense of 'from' referring to time
In this case it is often strengthened by *an* following the noun, e.g. *von neun Uhr an*. Full details are given in 11.6.11.

(c) *von* is used to introduce the agent in passive constructions
Full details on the use of *von* with the passive, and on the distinction between *von* and *durch* as equivalents of English 'by' are given in 15.3.

(d) A phrase with *von* is often used in place of a genitive,
i.e. for English 'of', e.g. *ein Ereignis von weltgeschichtlicher Bedeutung*. This usage is fully treated in 2.4.

(e) *von* has a wide range of figurative uses
(i) It corresponds to English 'of' in the sense of 'on the part of':

Das war sehr nett, liebenswürdig, vernünftig von ihr	*That was very nice, kind, sensible of her*
Das war doch dumm von mir	*That was silly of me, wasn't it?*
Es ist nicht recht von ihm	*It's not right of him*
Er tat es von selbst	*He did it of his own accord*

(ii) A selection of other common idiomatic uses of *von*:

Das ist nicht von ungefähr passiert	*It didn't happen by accident*
Das kommt vom vielen Trinken	*That comes of drinking so much*
Das kommt davon	*That's what comes of it*
Sie ist von deutschen Eltern	*She was born of German parents*
Das gilt nicht von ihm	*That's not true of him*
Ich kenne sie nur vom Sehen	*I only know her by sight*
von Sinnen sein	*be out of one's mind*
von ganzem Herzen	*with all one's heart*
Da fällt mir ein Stein vom Herzen	*That's a load off my mind*

20.2.9 *zu*

(a) *zu* expresses direction.
As such it is a common equivalent for English 'to', particularly:

(i) For going to a person('s house):

Er ging zu seinem Onkel, zu Müllers, zum Frisör.

NB: For <u>at</u> (a person's house), *bei* is used, see 20.2.3.

(ii) For going to a place or an occasion:

Dieser Bus fährt zum Bahnhof	*This bus goes to the station*
Ich ging zur Kirche und wartete dort auf sie	*I went to the church and waited for her there*
Wir machten einen Ausflug zum Dorf	*We went on an outing to the village*
Ich war auf dem Weg zu einem einsamen Tal	*I was on my way to a secluded valley*
Wir gingen zum Marktplatz	*We went to the market place*
Sie kehrte zu ihrer Arbeit zurück	*She returned to her work*
Der Rauch stieg zur Decke	*The smoke rose to the ceiling*
eine Expedition zum Mond	*an expedition to the moon*
Wir gingen zusammen zur Bibliothek	*We went to the library together*
Ich muß heute noch zur Post	*I've got to get to the post-office today*
Sie geht morgen zu einem Kongreß	*She's going to a conference tomorrow*

NB: (i) *zu* is the opposite of *von*, cf. 20.2.8a and puts the emphasis on the general direction rather than reaching the destination. For the distinction between it and the more specific prepositions *an, auf* or *in* (with the accusative), see 20.5.

(ii) *zu* is often used in conjunction with *hin*, cf. 7.3.3, e.g. *Dieser Pfad führt zum Wald* (*hin*). *Sie ging zur Post* (*hin*). *Er blickte zur Decke* (*hin*). The effect is to emphasize the destination or the distance to be covered.

(iii) In some idiomatic phrases:

Sie sah zum Fenster, zur Tür hinaus	*She looked out of the window, the door*
sich zu Tisch setzen	*sit down at table* (for a meal)
Setzen Sie sich doch zu uns!	*Do come and join us*

(b) *zu* may sometimes refer to a place,

i.e. with the meaning of English 'at' or 'in'. This sense of *zu* was formerly common, especially with names of towns, but it is now only used in elevated styles, as modern German prefers *in*:

J.S.Bach wurde zu (usually: in) Eisenach geboren	*J.S.Bach was born in Eisenach*
der Dom zu Köln (more usually: der Kölner Dom)	*Cologne cathedral*

However, *zu* still occurs in this sense in some set phrases, e.g.:

zu Hause	*at home*
zu beiden Seiten	*on either side*

(c) *zu* is used in certain time expressions

It usually corresponds to English 'at', e.g. *zu Ostern, zu dieser Zeit*. Full details are given in 11.6.13.

(d) *zu* is the usual equivalent of English 'for' to express purpose
(i) Examples of this usage:

der Mut zu einer Entscheidung	*the courage for a decision*
zu diesem Zweck	*for this purpose*
Das ist kein Anlaß zur Klage	*That is no cause for complaint*
Was gibt es heute zum Nachtisch?	*What's for dessert today?*
Stoff zu einem neuen Anzug	*material for a new suit*
Zum Geburtstag hat er mir eine Uhr geschenkt	*He bought me a watch for my birthday*
Wir hatten keine Gelegenheit zu einem Gespräch	*We didn't have a chance for a talk*

NB: The prepositional adverb *dazu* is commonly used in the sense of 'for that purpose', e.g. *Dazu soll man ein scharfes Messer gebrauchen.* Cf. also *Wozu?* 'To what purpose?', 'What for?', see 7.6.1d.

(ii) In this sense, *zu* is very common with an infinitive used as a noun, or with other verbal nouns, where English uses *for + . . . ing* or an infinitive with *to*, e.g.:

Wozu gebraucht man dieses Messer? – Zum Kartoffelschälen.	*What do you use this knife for? – For peeling potatoes/To peel potatoes*
Hier gibt es viele Möglichkeiten zum Schilaufen	*There are lots of possibilities for skiing here*
Ich sage dir das zu deiner Beruhigung	*I'm telling you this to reassure you*

NB: More details on this usage are given in 13.4.3b and 13.7.2b. It is particularly frequent in written non-literary German, but by no means confined to that register.

(iii) In certain contexts, this sense of *zu* approaches that of *als*, i.e. 'by way of', 'as':

Er murmelte etwas zur Antwort	*He muttered something by way of reply*
Er tat es mir zu Gefallen	*He did it as a favour to me*

Similarly:

zur Abwechslung *for a change*	zum Andenken an *in memory of*
zum Beispiel *for example*	ihr zu Ehren *in her honour*
zur Not *if necessary, at a pinch*	zum Scherz *as a joke*
zum Spaß *as a joke*	zur Strafe *as a punishment*
	zum Vergnügen *for pleasure*

(e) In some contexts *zu* can indicate a result or an effect
The English equivalent is most often 'to':

Seine Rede hatte eine politische Krise zur Folge	*His speech resulted in a political crisis*
Zu meinem Erstaunen hat sie das Examen bestanden	*To my surprise she passed her finals*

Similarly:

zu meinem Ärger	*to my annoyance*
zu meiner Befriedigung	*to my satisfaction*
zu meiner großen Freude	*to my great pleasure*
Es ist zum Lachen, zum Heulen, zum Verrücktwerden	*It is laughable, enough to make one weep, enough to drive one mad*

NB: *zu* commonly occurs in this sense in the prepositional object of a number of verbs, see 18.6.13a.

(f) *zu* can express a change of state
This usage is associated with a small number of verbs or nouns with appropriate meanings:

Sie wählten ihn zum Präsidenten	*They elected him President*
Er wurde zum Major befördert	*He was promoted to major*
Ich habe ihn mir zum Feind gemacht	*I've made an enemy of him*
Ich habe es mir zur Regel gemacht, dies zu tun	*I've made it a rule to do this*
etwas zu Brei kochen	*cook sth. to a pulp*

Similarly with *bestimmen* 'destine to be', *degradieren* 'demote', *ernennen* 'appoint', *krönen* 'crown', *weihen* 'ordain', etc. and the nouns *die Beförderung* 'promotion', *die Ernennung* 'appointment', *die Wahl* 'election', etc.

NB: *werden* 'become' is used with a following *zu* if it involves a change of state, e.g.:

Die Felder waren zu Seen geworden	*The fields had turned into lakes*
Es wurde zur Mode	*It became a fashion*
Das ist mir zur Gewohnheit geworden	*That has become a habit of mine*
Dieser Prozeß wurde zu einer Qual für ihn (*V. Baum*)	*This trial became a torment for him*

However, with nouns denoting professions or types of person, *werden* is used without *zu*, e.g. *Er wurde Lehrer, Katholik, Kommunist*, etc.

(g) *zu* can express a mental attitude <u>towards</u> someone or something
(i) This is frequent with adjectives, cf. 6.6.1, e.g.:

Sie war sehr freundlich zu mir	*She was very kind to me*

Similarly:

frech zu *impudent towards*	gut zu *good, kind to*
(un)höflich zu *(im)polite to*	nett zu *nice to*
respektvoll zu *respectful to*	unfreundlich zu *unkind to*

(ii) Also with a number of nouns, e.g.:

Wir haben freundliche Beziehungen zu Müllers	*We're on friendly terms with the Müllers*
ihre Einstellung zur Wieder – vereinigung	*her attitude to reunification*
aus Freundschaft zu ihr	*out of friendship for her*

seine Liebe zu ihr	*his love for her*
das Verhältnis des Einzelnen zum Staat	*the relationship of the individual to the state*

NB: *gegen* (cf. 20.1.4f) and *gegenüber* (cf. 20.2.4d) are also used to denote attitude towards or relations with someone or something. Whether *gegen* or *zu* occurs depends largely on the particular noun or adjective, though *gegen* tends to occur with those which denote hostile attitudes, *zu* with those which denote friendly attitudes. A few adjectives may be used with either, e.g.:

gerecht zu/gegen *fair, just to*   grausam zu/gegen *cruel to*
hart zu/gegen   *hard towards*
gegen is used with some nouns although the related adjective has *zu*:
die Frechheit, Gerechtigkeit, Grausamkeit, Härte, (Un)höflichkeit gegen jdn.
gegenüber is a common alternative to *gegen* or *zu* with most adjectives or nouns which occur with these prepositions.

(h) Uses of *zu* with numbers
(i) To indicate price or measure:

10 Stück Seife zu je 2 Mark	*10 pieces of soap at 2 marks each*
5 Päckchen Kaffee zu hundert Gramm	*5 hundred gram packs of coffee*
zum halben Preis	*at half price*

Also with fractions, etc.:

zur Hälfte, zum Teil, zu einem Drittel fertig
(ii) With the dative of the cardinal or the stem of the ordinal to indicate groups, e.g *zu zweien, zu zweit*, cf. 9.1.4b.
(iii) With the declined ordinal number for 'first(ly)', 'secondly', etc., e.g. *zum ersten, zum zweiten*, etc., cf. 9.2.3.

(j) Selected idiomatic uses of *zu*:

Die Haare standen mir zu Berge	*My hair stood on end*
jemanden zum besten haben	*make a fool of somebody*
zu Boden fallen	*fall to the ground*
sich (dat.) etwas zu eigen machen	*adopt sth.*
zu Ende gehen	*draw to a close*
jemanden zu Fall bringen	*bring somebody down*
zu Fuß	*on foot*
Der Wein geht zur Neige	*The wine is running out*
jemanden zu Rate ziehen	*ask somebody's advice*
jemanden zur Rechenschaft ziehen	*call somebody to account*
zur Sache kommen	*come to the point*
der Schlüssel zur Wahrheit	*the key to the truth*
jemandem zur Seite stehen	*give somebody one's support*
jemandem etwas zur Verfügung stellen	*put sth. at somebody's disposal*
zur Welt kommen	*be born*

20.2.10 Less frequent prepositions taking the dative

(a) *ab* 'from' was originally restricted to commercial and official German, but it is now quite common in colloquial registers

(i) Referring to place, it is an alternative to *von*, but emphasizes the starting point rather more strongly:

Ab Jericho folgten wir einer langen Kolonne israelischer Touristenbusse (*Zeit*)	*From Jericho we followed a long convoy of Israeli tourist buses*
Dieser Sondertarif gilt ab allen deutschen Flughäfen	*This special fare applies from all airports in Germany*
ab Fabrik	*ex works*

(ii) Referring to time, it is an alternative to *von . . . an*, cf. 11.6.11. If it is used without a following article (as is usually the case, cf. 4.10.3c), it may take the dative or, rather more frequently, the accusative:

ab neun Uhr, ab heute	*from nine o'clock, from today*
ab sofort	*with immediate effect*
ab ersten (erstem) Mai	*from the first of May*
ab nächste(r) Woche	*from next week*
ab meinem 21. Lebensjahr	*from the age of 21*

(b) *binnen* indicates a period of time (= 'within')

It is mainly used in formal registers to avoid the potential ambiguity of *in*, cf. 11.6.7c:

binnen drei Jahren	*within three years*
binnen kurzem	*shortly*

In elevated literary usage it may still occasionally be found with a following genitive:

binnen eines Jahres (more usual: binnen einem Jahr)	*within a year*

(c) *dank* 'thanks to'

It is mainly found in formal German and is often used with a genitive, especially with a following plural noun:

dank seinem Einfluß/seines Einflusses	*thanks to his influence*
dank seiner Sprachkenntnisse (*Goes*)	*thanks to his knowledge of languages*

(d) *entgegen* 'contrary to' may precede or follow the noun

The position before the noun is rather more frequent:

entgegen allen Erwartungen (less commonly: allen Erwartungen entgegen)	*contrary to all expectations*

(e) *entsprechend, gemäß, laut, zufolge* 'according to'

These prepositions are used chiefly in formal German. They all mean 'according to', as does the more frequent *nach*, see. 20.2.6d, but they are not interchangeable in all contexts:

(i) *entsprechend* means 'in accordance with'. It may precede or (more commonly) follow the noun:

unseren Anordnungen entsprechend	*in accordance with our instructions*

(ii) *gemäß* usually follows the noun, but occasionally precedes it. It has the sense of 'in accordance with':

Die Maschine wurde den Anweisungen gemäß in Betrieb gesetzt	*The machine was put into operation in accordance with the instructions*

NB: The use of *gemäß* with a genitive, which is occasionally heard in spoken German, is considered substandard.

(iii) *laut* introduces a verbatim report of something said or written. It is commonly used without a following article, cf. 4.10.3:

Laut Berichten soll Saddam Hussein neue Verhandlungen vorgeschlagen haben	*According to reports Saddam Hussein has proposed fresh negotiations*
laut Gesetz	*according to the law*
laut Helmut Kohl	*according to Helmut Kohl*

If the following noun has an article (or an adjective) with it, it is often in the genitive rather than the dative:

laut des Berichtes/dem Bericht aus Bonn	*according to the report from Bonn*
laut neuer/neuen Berichte(n)	*according to recent reports*
laut ämtlichem Nachweis/ämtlichen Nachweises	*according to an official attestation*

(iv) *zufolge* follows the noun. In accepted usage it indicates a consequence:

Dem Vertrag zufolge werden nun große Mengen von Rohöl geliefert	*In accordance with the contract large quantities of crude oil are now being delivered*

It is also used where there is no sense of a consequence or a result. This usage has been frowned on by purists, but it is very widespread:

unbestätigen Berichten zufolge	*according to unconfirmed reports*
einem Regierungssprecher zufolge	*according to a government spokesman*

NB: The use of *zufolge* with a following noun in the genitive, e.g. *zufolge des Vertrages*, is now obsolete and *infolge* (+ gen.) is used in its stead.

(f) *fern* 'far from' is restricted to elevated registers

More common usage is *fern von* or *weit von*. *fern* occasionally follows the noun:

Sie blieben fern der Heimat	*They remained far from home*
Europa liegt immer noch fern dem britischen Horizont (*Zeit*)	*Europe is still far removed from British horizons*

(g) *mitsamt* and *samt* mean 'together with'

They are restricted to elevated styles. The usual equivalent for 'together with' is *zusammen mit*, or often simply *mit*:

Das große Krögersche Haus stand mitsamt seiner würdigen Geschichte zum Verkaufe (*Th. Mann*)	*The great Kröger house, together with its stately history, was up for sale*

(h) *nahe* 'near (to)' is used chiefly in formal registers:

ein altes Haus nahe dem freien Feld *an old house near the open field*
  (*FR*)

When used in an abstract sense it commonly follows the noun:

Sie war der Verzweiflung nahe *She was close to despair*

(j) *nebst* 'together with', 'in addition to' is used mainly in formal registers:

Sie hatten das Haus nebst Obstgarten *They had rented the house together*
  gemietet *with the orchard*

(k) *zuliebe* 'for the sake of' follows the noun it governs:

Ich habe es meiner Mutter zuliebe *I did it for my mother's sake*
  getan
Dir zuliebe gibt es Spargel *Just for you, we're having asparagus*
wahrscheinlich dem Wald zuliebe *probably for the sake of the forest*
  (*Walser*)

(l) *zuwider* 'contrary to' follows the noun it governs
It is an emphatic alternative to *gegen* in formal registers:

Karl handelte seinem Befehl zuwider *Karl acted contrary to his order*

20.3 Prepositions taking the accusative <u>or</u> the dative

Ten prepositions govern the accusative <u>or</u> the dative, i.e.:

an	in	unter
auf	neben	vor
entlang	über	zwischen
hinter		

We first give general rules governing the use of the two cases with these prepositions (20.3.1), and then deal with the individual prepositions. For the commoner ones (i.e. *an, auf, in, über, unter* and *vor*) the use with the accusative and the dative is treated separately.

20.3.1 These prepositions govern the accusative if they express movement in a particular direction, but the dative if they express rest in a particular place, e.g.:

Ich hänge das Bild an **die** Wand *I'm hanging the picture on the wall*
Das Bild hängt an **der** Wand *The picture is hanging on the wall*
Wir gingen in dies**es** Zimmer hinein *We went into this room*
Wir essen in dies**em** Zimmer *We eat in this room*

However, there are instances where the choice of case is less obvious, or where there are fluctuations in usage, i.e.:

(a) Even if movement is involved, the dative is still used as long as there is no movement in relation to the person or thing denoted by the following noun:

Er ging neben seiner Frau *He was walking next to his wife*
Er ging zwischen seinen Eltern *He was walking between his parents*
    (His position is constant in relation to his wife or his parents)
Ein Flugzeug kreiste über der Stadt *A plane was circling over the town*
    (Though it was moving, it stayed over the town)

Usage where two prepositional phrases occur in the same sentence with a verb of motion follows the basic rule, e.g.:

Elke legte sich auf eine Bank im Schatten hin
    (Elke is moving in relation to the bench, but the bench is not moving in respect of the shadow)

(b) The dative is normal in conjunction with all verbs of arriving, appearing and disappearing:

Sie kamen sie am Bahnhof an *They arrived at the station*
Wir trafen in der Hauptstadt ein *We arrived in the capital*
Sie kehrten in einer Gaststätte ein *They turned in at an inn*
Sie landeten auf dem Mond *They landed on the moon*
Er kroch unter dem Tisch hervor *He crept out from under the table*
Sie erschien hinter der Theke *She appeared behind the counter*
Der Reiter verschwand hinter dem Berg *The horseman disappeared behind the hill*

Sie verbarg sich unter der Decke *She hid under the sheet*

NB: In a few contexts with verbs of disappearing the idea of movement in a particular direction may be so strong that the accusative is used, e.g. *Er verschwand über das Dach.*

(c) In a few cases, these prepositions are used with the accusative after a simple verb, but with the dative after a related prefixed verb:

(an/fest)binden *tie, fasten*
Das Pferd war an einen Baum gebunden
Das Pferd war an einem Baum an-/festgebunden
(vor)fahren *drive (up)*
Der Wagen fuhr vor den Bahnhof
Der Wagen fuhr vor dem Schloß vor
(auf)hängen *hang (up)*
Sie hängte das Bild an die Wand
Sie hängte das Bild an der Wand auf
sich (fest)klammern *cling to*
Er klammerte sich an sie
Er klammerte sich an ihr fest
sich (nieder)legen, -setzen *lie, sit down*
Sie legte/setzte sich auf die Bank
Sie legte/setzte sich auf der Bank nieder
(auf)schreiben *write (down)*
Ich schrieb ihre Adresse in mein Notizbuch
Ich schrieb ihre Adresse in meinem Notizbuch auf

(d) Usage with verbs with the prefix *ein-*
(i) These verbs are often used in conjunction with *in*, which is then most usually followed by the accusative:

Sie stieg in **den** Zug ein
Ich trug den Namen in mein**e** Liste ein
Wir weihten ihn in **das** Geheimnis ein
Er wickelte sich in ein**e** Reisedecke ein

(ii) The accusative is used even in the *sein*-passive, although here usage may be variable:

Er war in ein**e** Reisedecke eingehüllt
Sein Name war in **die/der** Liste eingetragen

(iii) *sich einschließen* is used with the accusative or the dative, depending on whether the actual movement is emphasized:

Sie schloß sich in ihr/ihrem Zimmer ein

(iv) *sich einfinden, einkehren* and *eintreffen* are followed by a preposition with the dative, as they denote arrival, cf. (a) above.

(e) Some further difficult cases after certain verbs

With some of the verbs below usage may fluctuate, depending on how the native speaker envisages the action. We give the commoner usage in all cases:

(i) The dative is usual in conjunction with the following verbs:

anbringen *fix*   drucken *print*
befestigen an *fasten*   notieren *note*

(ii) The accusative is usual in conjunction with the following verbs:

anbauen an *build on to*   sehen, schauen *look*
anschließen an *add on to*   stützen auf *support on*
gebeugt über *bent over*   verteilen *distribute*
grenzen an *border on*   vertieft in *engrossed in*
kleiden in *clothe in*   verwickelt in *involved in*
münden in *flow into*

(f) In conjunction with a few verbs, the dative and the accusative may have different meanings:
aufnehmen
The accusative implies complete acceptance, the dative that the acceptance is less permanent:

Er ist in den Chor aufgenommen worden   *He was admitted into the choir*
Ich wurde in seiner Familie sehr   *I was amiably received in his*
　　freundlich aufgenommen   　　*family*

einführen
If there is an idea of direction, the accusative is used, whereas the dative puts the stress on the place:

Waren in ein Land einführen   *import goods into a country*
　　(i.e. **nach** Italien)

Er will die Sitte in diesem Land
  einführen
  (i.e. **in** Italien, dort)

He wants to introduce the custom
in that country

halten
If the gesture is emphasized, the accusative is used, if the position, the dative:

Er hielt das Buch in die Höhe   *He held the book up in the air*
Er hielt das Buch in der Hand   *He held the book in his hand*

klopfen
In general, the accusative is usual with *klopfen*, but in the context of knocking on doors, etc., the dative can be used if the emphasis is on the place rather than the action:

Ich klopfte an die Tür, auf den Tisch   *I knocked on the door, the table*
Da klopfte es an der Haustür   *There was a knock at the front door*
  (i.e. the front door rather than somewhere else)

schreiben
The accusative is used when talking about the actual action of writing, the dative if the place where something is written down is foremost:

Er schrieb es in sein Heft   *He wrote it (down) in his notebook*
In seinem Brief schreibt er, daß . . . *He writes in his letter that . . .*

(g) In contexts where there is no reference to place, these prepositions are used only or predominantly with one of the two cases
In such uses, *auf* and *über* are used with the accusative, the others chiefly with the dative. This is particularly evident:
(i) Where these prepositions are used to refer to time, cf. 11.6.
(ii) Where they are used in prepositional objects, cf. 18.6, with adjectives, cf. 6.6, and in other contexts where they are not being used in their literal senses.

20.3.2 *an* (+ dative)

(a) The underlying sense of *an* with the dative is 'on (the side of)'

It thus contrasts with *auf* (+ dat.), which means 'on (top of)'. Given this basic sense, *an* (+ dat.) can correspond to English 'on', or, if the person or thing is not actually touching, 'at' or 'by'. See 20.2.3a for the distinction between *an* (+ dat.) and *bei* in the sense of 'at':

Das Bild hing an der Wand   *The picture was hanging on the wall*
am Berg   *on the mountain(side)*
  (cf. *auf dem Berg* 'on the mountain-top')
An der Grenze wird kontrolliert   *There's a check at the border*
Wir warteten an der Bushaltestelle   *We were waiting at/by the bus-stop*
am Fluß   *on the river(side)*
  (cf. *auf dem Fluß* 'on the river' (i.e. in a boat))

Bonn liegt am Rhein	*Bonn is on the Rhine*
Wir standen an der Kirche	*We were standing by the church*
Ich stand am Fenster	*I was standing by/at the window*
Sie wohnt am See	*She lives by the lake*

an (+ dat.) is also used for 'on (the underside of)':

Die Lampe hängt an der Decke	*The lamp is hanging from the ceiling*
am Himmel	*in the sky*
(cf. *im Himmel* 'in heaven')	

NB: (i) In older German, *an* was commonly used in the sense of 'down on', and this is still apparent in phrases like *am Boden, an der Erde* 'on the ground', where *auf* is a possible alternative. Cf. also *am Strand* 'on the beach', *am Ufer* 'on the bank', etc.
(ii) With a following *hin*, cf. 7.3.3, *an* can express movement alongside:
Sie gingen an der Mauer hin   *They were walking along the wall*
(iii) *an* (+ dat.) . . .*vorbei* means 'past', e.g.:
Wir gingen an seinem Haus vorbei   *We walked past his house*
(iv) For *an* (+ dat.) . . . *entlang*, see 20.3.6d.

(b) *an* (+ dat.) is used with academic and similar institutions at which a person is employed:

Sie lehrt an der Universität Augsburg	*She teaches at the University of Augsburg*
Er ist Intendant am Staatstheater	*He is director at the State Theatre*
Er ist Lehrer am Städtischen Gymnasium	*He is a teacher at the city secondary school*
Er ist Pfarrer an der Peterskirche	*He is the pastor at St Peter's*

(c) *an* (+ dat.) is used in a number of time expressions, especially with nouns denoting days,
e.g. *am Dienstag, am 31. August*. Full details are given in 11.6.1.

(d) *an* (+ dat.) is used with many nouns, adjectives and verbs meaning 'in respect of', 'in connection with':

ein großer Aufwand an Energie	*a great expenditure of energy*
Der Bedarf an Arbeitskräften verringert sich	*The demand for labour is decreasing*
Wir haben mehrere Millionen Mark an Aufträgen vorliegen	*We have several million marks worth of orders on the books*
Sie hat etwas Eigenartiges an sich	*There's something strange about her*
Das Schönste an der Sache ist, daß . . .	*The best thing about it is that . . .*
Sie waren siebzig an der Zahl	*They were seventy in number*
Was das Leben an Freuden bietet	*What kinds of pleasures life offers*
Es fehlt ihm nur an Mut	*He only lacks courage*
Sie ist noch jung an Jahren	*She is still young in years*
Das Land ist arm, reich an Bodenschätzen	*The country is poor, rich in natural resources*

an (+ dat.) is particularly frequent to indicate the feature by which one recognizes or notices something:

Ich bemerkte an seinem Benehmen, daß . . .	*I noticed from his behaviour that . . .*
Sie erkannte ihn an seinen Bart	*She recognized him by his beard*

NB: For further details of the use of *an* in this sense with adjectives, see 6.6.1, with verbs in prepositional objects, see 18.6.2a.

(e) *an* (+ dat.) indicates a partially completed action:

Sie strickt an einem Pullover	*She's knitting a pullover*
Er arbeitet an seiner Dissertation	*He's working on his thesis*

(f) Other uses of *an* (+ dat.)

(i) *am* is used to form the superlative of adverbs and predicate adjectives, e.g. *am schönsten, am einfachsten*, cf. 8.3.1.
(ii) In colloquial north German *am* is used with the infinitive to express a continuous action, e.g. *Sie ist am Schreiben*, cf. 14.6.2c.

20.3.3 *an* (+ accusative)

(a) *an* (+ acc.) is used to indicate direction in all cases where rest is expressed through *an* (+ dat.)
(i) It most often corresponds to English 'to' (cf. 20.5.1c) or 'on':

Sie hängte ein Bild an die Wand	*She hung the picture on the wall*
Wir gingen an die Kirche	*We went to the church*
Sie fuhr an die Küste	*She drove to the coast*

Similarly:

Ich ging ans Fenster, an die Tür, an seinen Platz
Er kam an die Bushaltestelle, an den Waldrand
(ii) The idea of right up to somebody or something can be indicated by adding *heran*, cf. 7.3.4b, e.g.:

Sie trat an mich, an den Tisch heran	*She walked up to me, to the table*

an occurs commonly with the person to whom one addresses something:

Er richtete diese Frage an mich	*He addressed this question to me*
eine Bitte an den Bundeskanzler	*a request to the Federal Chancellor*
Ich werde mich an ihn um Rat wenden	*I shall turn to him for advice*

(b) *an* (+ acc.) is commonly used with nouns from verbs which take a dative, cf. 18.4:

die Anpassung an die neuen Verhältnisse	*adaptation to new circumstances*
sein Befehl an die Truppen	*his order to the troops*

Similarly:

eine Antwort an mich	ein Bericht an die Akademie
viele Grüße an Onkel Robert	die Kriegserklärung an Japan

der Verkauf des Hauses an meinen Sohn   sein Vermächtnis an seine Tochter
der Verrat von Geheimnissen an den Feind

NB: For the use of *an* (+ acc.) in this sense with verbs in place of a dative, see 18.4.2d.

(c) *an* (+ acc.) is used to indicate indefinite quantity,

e.g. *Er verdient an die 5000 im Monat.* For this usage, and alternatives to it, see 9.1.7a.

(d) Some idiomatic uses of *an* (+ acc.):

etwas ans Licht, an den Tag bringen	*bring sth. to light*
an (und für) sich	*actually*
die Erinnerung an seine Jugend	*the memory of his youth*
der Glaube an den Sieg	*the belief in victory*

NB: For the use of *an* (+ acc.) in prepositional objects with verbs denoting mental processes, see 18.6.2b.

20.3.4 *auf* (+ dative)

(a) The basic meaning of *auf* (+ dat.) is 'on (top of)'
For the distinction between this and *an* (+ dat.), see 20.3.2a.

Das Buch liegt auf dem Tisch	*The book is lying on the table*
Sie sind auf dem Mond gelandet	*They landed on the moon*
Die Katze spielt auf dem Rasen	*The cat is playing on the lawn*
auf dem Weg nach Stuttgart	*on the way to Stuttgart*

(b) *auf* (+ dat.) is used for English 'at' or 'in' in some contexts.
(i) For formal occasions, e.g. weddings, conferences, parties, etc.:

Ich traf sie auf einem Empfang	*I met her at a reception*
Wir lernten uns auf ihrer Hochzeit kennen	*We met at their wedding*
Sie ist auf einer Tagung	*She's at a conference*

NB: *bei* is a common alternative to *auf* in this sense, but there may be a slight difference in meaning, cf. 20.2.3b.

(ii) With a restricted number of nouns, where usage differs from English:

Die Schafe sind auf der Wiese	*The sheep are in the meadow*
Er ist auf seinem Zimmer	*He is (up) in his room*
auf dem Feld	*in the field*
auf dem Land(e)	*in the country*
Die Kinder spielten auf der Straße	*The children were playing in the street*

NB: *in* (+ dat.) is used to refer to a particular street, e.g. *Wir wohnen in der Schillerstraße.* *Das Unglück ereignete sich in unserer Straße.*

Similarly:

auf dem (Bauern)hof *on the farm*	auf ihrer Bude *in her digs*
auf dem Flur *in the (entrance-)hall*	auf dem Gang *in the corridor*

auf seinem Gut *on his estate*   auf dem Hof *in the yard*
auf der Toilette *on the toilet*

(iii) With certain public buildings and places. This usage is restricted to a small number of nouns, and with some *auf* is now obsolescent, especially in less formal registers. In this case, the preposition which is more frequently used nowadays is given in brackets:

auf dem Bahnhof (an)   auf dem Markt(platz)
auf der Bank (in)   auf der Post
auf der Bibliothek (in)   auf dem Rathaus (in)
                                                         auf der Universität (an)

(c) Some idiomatic uses of *auf* (+ dat.)

blind auf einem Auge   *blind in one eye*
Das hat nichts, viel auf sich   *There's nothing, a lot to that*
etwas auf dem Herzen haben   *have sth. on one's mind*
auf der Jagd sein   *be hunting*
auf der anderen Seite   *on the other hand*
auf der Stelle   *immediately*
auf dem Trockenen sitzen   *be out of money*

20.3.5 *auf* (+ accusative)

(a) *auf* (+ acc.) is used to indicate direction in cases where rest is expressed through *auf* (+ dat.),
cf. 20.3.4:
(i) *auf* (+ acc.) usually corresponds to English 'on(to)':

Sie legte das Buch auf den Tisch   *She put the book on the table*
Die Katze sprang auf das Dach   *The cat leapt onto the roof*

(ii) Where German uses *auf* (+ dat.) for English 'at' or 'in', *auf* (+ acc.) usually corresponds to English 'into' or 'to':

Wir gingen auf das Feld   *We went into the field*
Er ging auf sein Zimmer   *He went (up) to his room*
Er geht auf die Toilette   *He's going to the toilet*

NB: This use of *auf* (+ acc.) is rather restricted in modern German. More details are given in 20.5.1b.

(iii) *auf* (+ acc.) . . . *zu* commonly indicates direction (i.e. = 'towards'):

Sie kam auf mich zu   *She came towards me/approached me*
Sie ging auf die Tore des Friedhofs zu *She went towards the cemetery gates*

(b) *auf* (+ acc.) indicates a period of time extending from 'now',
e.g. *Ich fahre auf vier Wochen in die Schweiz.*
Full details of this usage are given in 11.6.2.

NB: (i) The prepositional adverb *darauf* is used in the sense of 'after', cf. 11.7.4b, e.g. *am Tag darauf* 'the day after'.
(ii) *auf* (+ acc.) is similarly used to indicate a distance from here, e.g.:
Kurven auf fünf Kilometer   *bends for 5 kilometres*

(c) *auf* (+ acc.) is used after a large number of adjectives and verbs,
e.g.: *Sie ist neidisch auf ihn. Ich wartete vor dem Bahnhof auf sie.*
For the use of *auf* with adjectives, see 6.6.1, with verbs in prepositional
objects, see 18.6.3a.

(d) *auf* (+ acc.) can denote 'in reponse to', 'as a result of'
In this sense it is often strengthened by a following *hin*, cf. 7.3.3c:

Auf meine Bitte (hin) hat er die Sache für sich behalten	*At my request he kept the matter to himself*
Er hat sofort auf meinen Brief hin gehandelt	*He acted immediately following my letter*

Similarly:

auf Anfrage	*on application*
auf meine Empfehlung (hin)	*on (the strength of) my recommendation*
auf ihre Initiative	*following her initiative*
auf einen Verdacht hin	*on the strength of a suspicion*
auf Wunsch, auf meinen Wunsch (hin)	*by request, at my request*
daraufhin	*as a result, thereupon*

(e) Other uses of *auf* (+ acc.)
(i) with languages:

Sie hat mir auf deutsch geantwortet	*She answered me in German*

NB: *in* (+ dat.) is also used, especially with extended phrases:

Er hält seine Vorlesungen in/auf deutsch	*He gives his lectures in German*
Er sagte es in gebrochenem Deutsch	*He said it in broken German*
Wie heißt das in Ihrer Sprache?	*What's that called in your language?*

(ii) to form absolute superlatives, cf. 8.3.3:

Das hat mich aufs angenehmste überrascht	*That surprised me in a very pleasant way*

(iii) Some common idiomatic expressions with *auf*:

jemanden auf den Arm, auf die Schippe (N.Ger.) nehmen	*pull somebody's leg*
etwas auf die lange Bank schieben	*put sth. off*
auf den ersten Blick	*at first sight*
Das kommt, läuft auf dasselbe hinaus	*It comes to the same thing*
auf jeden Fall, auf alle Fälle	*in any case*
auf keinen Fall	*on no account*
auf eigene Gefahr	*at one's own risk*
auf eigene Kosten	*at one's own expense*
jemandem auf die Nerven gehen, auf den Wecker gehen, fallen	*get on somebody's nerves*
Das geht auf meine Rechnung	*This one's on me*
auf diese Weise (also: in dieser Weise)	*in this way*

20.3.6 *entlang*

In all its senses, *entlang* corresponds to English 'along'. There is considerable variation in its use, both in respect of its position and the use of cases with it. However, predominant usage in modern German makes it appropriate to deal with it under the prepositions which govern a dative to express position, but an accusative to express movement, as follows:

(a) To indicate position alongside an extended object, *entlang* <u>precedes</u> a noun in the dative:

Wir warnen vor einer Politik der gebrannten Erde entlang der Grenze (*ND*)	*We are warning them against a scorched earth policy along the frontier*
die Männer, die entlang der Küchenwand saßen (*Welt*)	*the men sitting along the kitchen wall*
Pappeln standen entlang der Bahnlinie	*Poplars stood along the railway line*

(b) To indicate movement alongside an extended object (or down the middle of, for instance, roads or rivers) *entlang* <u>follows</u> a noun in the accusative:

Sie hastete den Flur entlang bis zum Ende des Ganges (*Johnson*)	*She hurried along the entrance-hall to the end of the corridor*
Sie laufen die Feldwege entlang (*Strittmatter*)	*They ran along the tracks through the fields*
. . . der schwarze Hausdiener, der den Pfad entlang auf das Haus zukommt (*Grzimek*)	*the black servant who is coming along the path towards the house*

(c) Variations in the use of *entlang*

Although modern usage of *entlang* usually follows the pattern given in (a) and (b) above, a number of variant constructions are possible which are equally permissible and still encountered.

(i) In written German, *entlang* is occasionally used with a following genitive to express position:

die Pioniere, die entlang des ganzen Weges Aufstellung genommen hatten (*ND*)	*the pioneers who had lined up along the whole of the way*

(ii) *entlang* is sometimes used with a preceding dative to express movement or position:

Wir flogen gar nicht der Küste entlang (*Frisch*)	*We were not flying along the coast at all*
die Straße, die Mussolini der Küste entlang gebaut hat (*Grzimek*)	*the road which Mussolini built along the coast*

(iii) *entlang* with a preceding accusative occasionally refers to position rather than movement:

Flaschen und Gläser standen die lange Tafel entlang (*Welt*)	*Bottles and glasses were standing along the long table*

(d) *an* (+ dat.) *entlang* is a common alternative to simple *entlang*
It can be used with reference to position or movement alongside an extended object, but not usually for 'down the middle' of roads, rivers, etc.:

Da gab es an der nördlichen Friedhofs – mauer entlang den Bittweg (*Grass*)	*Along the north wall of the cemetery was the Bittweg*
Er steuerte am Ufer entlang, bis die Stelle gefunden war (*Frisch*)	*He steered along the bank until he had found the spot*

(e) Alternatives to *entlang* in the meaning 'along'
(i) *längs*, cf. 20.4.3, only expresses position. It governs a following genitive or (less commonly) a dative, e.g *längs der Küste, längs des Flusses/dem Fluß*.
(ii) *an* (+ dat.) *hin* can be used to refer to movement alongside something, especially when one is very close to it or in contact with it:

Sie ging an der Mauer hin	*She went along the wall*
Er rutschte am Boden hin	*He slid along the floor*

20.3.7 *hinter*

(a) *hinter* is used almost exclusively with reference to place and usually corresponds to English 'behind'
(i) Used with a following dative, *hinter* indicates position:

Der Wagen steht hinter der Garage	*The car is behind the garage*
Jetzt haben wir das Schlimmste hinter uns	*Now we've got the worst behind us*
100 Kilometer hinter der Grenze	*100 kilometres beyond the border*

(ii) Used with a following accusative, *hinter* indicates direction:

Er fuhr den Wagen hinter die Garage	*He drove the car round the back of the garage*
Sie trieben ihn hinter die Kirche	*They drove him round the back of the church*

(b) To indicate movement in relation to another person or thing, *hinter* is used with a following *her*,
cf. also 7.3.3b. The noun is always in the dative:

Er rannte hinter ihr her	*He was running after her*
Ich ging hinter meinen Eltern her	*I was walking behind my parents*
Sie riefen hinter ihr her	*They called after her*
Sie schickten einen Boten hinter ihm her	*They sent a messenger after him*

(c) *hinter* is used in a few idiomatic expressions:

Ich konnte nicht dahinter kommen	*I couldn't get to the bottom of it*
Es muß etwas dahinter stecken	*There must be something in it*
jemanden hinters Licht führen	*lead somebody up the garden path*
Schreib dir das hinter die Ohren!	*Will you get that into your thick head!*

20.3.8 *in* (+ dative)

(a) The basic sense of *in* (+ dat) is 'in(side)'
(i) Examples of use (cf. also (iii) below):

Sie ist im Haus, im Freien, in der Kirche, im Kino, in der Stadt, im Wald, im Tal, in ihrem Zimmer	*She is in the house, in the open air, in the church, in the cinema, in town, in the forest, in the valley, in her room*
Die Milch ist im Kühlschrank	*The milk is in the refrigerator*
Sie sind in Bremen, in Deutschland, in der Schweiz, im Ausland	*They are in Bremen, in Germany, in Switzerland, abroad*
Die Sonne geht im Westen unter	*The sun sets in the west*

(ii) In colloquial German *in* is often strengthened by adding *drin*:

Die sind in der Hütte drin	*They're inside the hut*

(iii) In a few cases, German usage is at variance with English, e.g.:

Ihr Büro ist im vierten Stock	*Her office is on the fourth floor*
Das habe ich im Fernsehen gesehen, im Radio gehört	*I saw it on the television, heard it on the radio*

In particular, German uses *in* with reference to buildings and the like, where English can often use 'at' or 'in', depending on the sense:

Die Kinder sind heute in der Schule	*The children are at school today*
Meine Eltern sind in der Kirche	*My parents are at church*
Elke ist im Kino, im Theater, in einem Konzert, im Rathaus, in der Bibliothek	*Elke is at the cinema, at the theatre, at a concert, at the town-hall, at the library*

(b) *in* (+ dat.) indicates a period of time
e.g. *In drei Wochen sind wir wieder da.* Full details are given in 11.6.7.

(c) Some common idiomatic expressions with *in* (+ dat.):

in der Absicht, etwas zu tun	*with the intention of doing something*
im allgemeinen	*in general*
Ist dein Chef im Bilde?	*Is your boss in the picture?*
im Durchschnitt	*on average*
nicht im geringsten/entferntesten	*not in the slightest*
in (or: bis zu) einem gewissen Grad(e)	*to a certain extent*
in dieser Hinsicht	*in this respect*
in gewissem Maße	*to a certain extent*
in dieser Weise (also: auf diese Weise)	*in this way*
in diesem Zusammenhang	*in this context*

20.3.9 *in* (+ accusative)

(a) *in* (+ acc.) is used to indicate direction in cases where rest is expressed through *in* (+ dat.),
cf. 20.3.7a.

(i) It thus often corresponds to English 'into':

Sie ging ins Haus, in die Kirche,	*She went into the house, the church,*
in den Wald, in das Tal,	*the forest, the valley,*
in ihr Zimmer (hinein)	*her room*
Ich habe die Milch in den	*I put the milk in the refrigerator*
Kühlschrank gestellt	

NB: With *Richtung* the accusative or the dative are equally acceptable alternatives, e.g. *in diese/dieser Richtung.*

(ii) It is a common equivalent of English 'to', if, on arrival, one will be *in* the place concerned, cf. 20.5.1a:

Sie ging in ein Konzert, ins Kino,	*She went to a concert, to the cinema,*
in den vierten Stock	*to the fourth floor*
Wir sind in die Schweiz, ins Ausland gefahren	*We went to Switzerland, abroad*
Die Kinder gehen heute in die Schule	*The children are going to school today*
Die Kinder gehen in die Schule	*The children go to school*

(b) Other uses of *in* (+ acc.)

(i) *ins* is common in phrasal verbs with a following infinitive and *geraten* and *kommen*, e.g. *Der Wagen kam ins Gleiten*, cf. 13.4.3c.

(ii) Some frequent idiomatic phrases with *in* (+ acc.):

Der Vorteil springt ins Auge	*The advantage is obvious*
sich in Bewegung setzen	*begin to move*
etwas in Gebrauch nehmen	*put sth. into use*
mit jemandem ins Gespräch kommen	*get into conversation with sb.*
aus dem Französischen ins Deutsche übersetzen	*translate from French into German*
sein Schäfchen ins Trockene bringen	*see oneself all right*
die Verhandlungen in die Länge ziehen	*drag the negotiations out*
in die Luft gehen	*hit the roof*
Ich muß den Aufsatz noch ins Reine schreiben	*I've still got to make a fair copy of the essay*

20.3.10 *neben*

(a) *neben* is most often used with reference to place
It usually corresponds to English 'next to' or 'beside':
(i) Used with a following dative, *neben* indicates position:

Die Blumen standen neben dem Schrank	*The flowers were next to the cupboard*
Das Geschäft ist neben dem Verkehrsverein	*The shop is next to the tourist information office*
Er saß neben seiner Frau	*He was sitting next to his wife*

(ii) Used with a following accusative, *neben* indicates direction:

Er stellte die Blumen neben den Schrank (hin)	*He put the flowers (down) next to the cupboard*
Er setzte sich neben seine Frau (hin)	*He sat down next to his wife*

(b) To indicate movement in relation to another person or thing, *neben* is used with a following *her*,
cf. also 7.3.3c. The noun is always in the dative:

Er ging neben seiner Frau her	He was walking by the side of his wife

(c) *neben* (+ dat.) can be used in the sense of 'besides', 'apart from'
Its sense is close to that of *außer*, cf. 20.2.2a:

Neben zwei Franzosen waren alle Anwesenden aus Deutschland	Apart from two Frenchmen all those present were from Germany

(d) *neben* (+ dat.) can be used to express a comparison
It is a common alternative to *gegen* or *gegenüber*, cf. 20.2.4c:

Neben ihrer Mutter ist sie groß	She's tall compared with her mother

(e) The prepositional adverb *daneben* is frequently used with verbs to express the idea of failing to hit a target
It is usually interpreted as a separable prefix and written together with the verb:

Er hat danebengeschossen	He shot wide of the mark
Sie hat sich danebenbenommen	She behaved quite abominably

20.3.11 *über* (+ dative)

With a dative, *über* is used exclusively with reference to position. It usually corresponds to English 'over', 'above' or, in certain contexts, 'across':

Das Bild hängt über meinem Tisch	The picture hangs over my desk
Briançon liegt 1400 Meter über dem Meeresspiegel	Briançon lies 1400 metres above sea level
Der Baum lag mir (quer) über dem Weg	The tree lay across my path
Er wohnt über der Grenze	He lives over/across the border
Sie wohnt über dem See	She lives across/beyond the lake

20.3.12 *über* (+ accusative)

(a) *über* (+acc.) indicates movement <u>over</u> a person or object
It may correspond to English 'above', 'over', 'across' or 'beyond'.
(i) Some typical examples of use:

Sie hängte das Bild über meinen Tisch	She hung the picture over/above my desk
Wir gingen über die Straße	We crossed the road
die neue Brücke über den Inn	the new bridge over/across the Inn
Wir ruderten über den See	We rowed across the lake
Der Baum fiel uns (quer) über den Weg	The tree fell across our path
Er ist über die Grenze geflüchtet	He fled over the border
Tränen liefen ihm über die Wangen	Tears ran over his cheeks
Es lief mir eiskalt über den Rücken	An ice-cold shiver went down my back

Rather more idiomatic:

Der Kaiser herrschte über viele Länder	*The emperor ruled over many countries*

(ii) If the movement involved is parallel to a surface, *über* (+ acc.) is frequently strengthened by adding *hin*, cf. 7.3.3a:

Die Wildenten flogen über den See (hin)	*The wild ducks were flying over the lake*

(iii) *über* (+ acc.) corresponds to English 'via':

Wir sind über die Schweiz nach Italien gefahren	*We drove to Italy via Switzerland*
Dieser Zug fährt nach Mannheim über Heidelberg	*This train goes to Mannheim via Heidelberg*

(iv) *über* (+ acc.) can also be used in more abstract senses of 'above' or 'beyond'. In some contexts it is strengthened by adding *hinaus*:

Diese Aufgabe geht über meine Fähigkeiten (hinaus)	*This task goes beyond my capabilities*
Das geht über menschliches Verständnis hinaus	*That goes beyond human understanding*
über alle Maßen	*beyond measure*
Er liebt die Ruhe über alles	*He likes quiet above all things*
darüber hinaus	*over and above that*

(b) *über* (+ acc.) occurs in a few time expressions in the sense of 'over':

Sie ist über Nacht, übers Wochenende geblieben	*She stayed overnight, over the weekend*
über kurz oder lang	*sooner or later*

It can be used <u>after</u> the noun to emphasize duration:

`Sie blieb die ganze Nacht über	*She stayed the whole night*
Den ganzen Sommer über gingen wir aufs Land	*We went to the country for the whole of the summer*
Tagsüber hat es geregnet	*It rained during the day*

(c) *über* (+ acc.) has the sense of 'over', 'more than' with quantities, e.g. *Es hat über tausend Mark gekostet. Kinder über zehn Jahre*, etc. See 9.1.7c for further details of this usage and the distinction between the adverbial and prepositional usage of *über* with quantities.

(d) *über* (+ acc.) is used in the sense of 'about', 'concerning':

seine Ansicht über eine mögliche Wiedervereinigung	*his views concerning a possible reunification*
ein Buch über die europäischen Vögelarten	*a book about European bird species*
meine Freude über ihren Erfolg	*my delight at her success*
in Verzweiflung über etwas	*in despair about sth.*
Er beschwerte sich über den kaputten Fernsehapparat	*He complained about the broken television set*
Sie war ärgerlich über ihn	*She was annoyed at him*

NB: This usage is particularly frequent with adjectives, see 6.6.1, and in the prepositional object of verbs of saying, etc., see 18.6.9a.

(e) Some common idiomatic phrases with *über* (+ acc.):

alle Zweifel über Bord werfen	*cast all doubts overboard*
etwas über den Haufen werfen	*throw sth. out*
über Leichen gehen	*be totally ruthless*
über jeden Zweifel erhaben	*beyond all shadow of a doubt*

20.3.13 *unter* (+ dative)

(a) With reference to place, *unter* (+ dat.) corresponds to English 'under(neath)', 'beneath', 'below'

(i) Some typical examples of usage (literal and figurative):

Manfred lag unter dem Tisch	*Manfred was lying under(neath) the table*
200 Meter unter dem Gipfel	*200 metres below the summit*
Das Land steht unter Wasser	*The land is under water*
Den Ring fanden sie unter dem Brunnen	*They found the ring under the well*
unter Tage	*below ground/underground (of miners)*
Sie trug die Tasche unter dem Arm	*She was carrying her bag under her arm*
unter dem Schutz der Dunkelheit	*under cover of darkness*
unter Zwang handeln	*act under duress*
jemandem den Boden unter den Füßen wegziehen	*take the ground from under somebody's feet*

(ii) *unter* (+ dat.) is a common equivalent for English 'among(st)',

Es gab Streit unter den Kindern	*There was quarrelling among the children*
Hier bist du unter Freunden	*You're among friends here*
Ich fand das Rezept unter meinen Papieren	*I found the prescription among my papers*
Es waren viele Ausländer unter den Zuschauern	*There were a lot of foreigners among the spectators*
unter uns gesagt	*between ourselves*
unter vier Augen	*in private*
unter anderem (u.a.)	*amongst other things*

NB: *zwischen* can also correspond to English 'among', cf. 20.3.17a. It is preferred if *unter* could be understood to mean 'under', cf.:

Das Haus steht unter Bäumen	*The house stands under some trees*
Das Haus steht zwischen Bäumen	*The house stands amongst some trees*

(b) *unter* (+ dat.) is used to indicate circumstances:

unter diesen Umständen	*under these circumstances*
unter allen Umständen	*in any case*
unter den größten Schwierigkeiten	*with the greatest difficulty*
unter dieser Bedingung	*on this condition*
unter diesem Vorwand	*on this pretext*
Sie starb unter großen Schmerzen	*She died in great pain*
Er gestand unter Tränen	*He confessed amid tears*
unter Vorspiegelung falscher Tatsachen	*on false pretences*
. . . und unter wachsendem Hallo wurde auch dies bestätigt (*Th.Mann*)	*and amid the growing uproar this too was confirmed*

(c) *unter* **(+ dat.) has the sense of 'under', 'below' with reference to quantity,**

e.g. *Es hat unter tausend Mark gekostet. Kinder unter zehn Jahre*, etc. See 9.1.7c for further details of this usage and the distinction between the adverbial and prepositional usage of *unter* with expressions of quantity.

20.3.14 *unter* (+ accusative)

(a) *unter* **(+ acc.) is used almost exclusively to indicate direction in cases where position is given by the use of** *unter* **(+ dat.),**
i.e. where English has 'under(neath)', 'below', 'among':

Manfred kroch unter den Tisch	*Manfred crawled under the table*
Sie steckte die Tasche unter ihren Arm	*She put her bag under her arm*
Er tauchte den Kopf unter das Wasser	*He dipped his head under the water*
Wir gingen unter die Brücke hindurch	*We walked under the bridge*
Sie ging unter die Menge	*She went among the crowd*

(b) Some common idiomatic expressions with *unter* **(+ acc.):**

jemanden unter die Arme greifen	*come to somebody's assistance*
sein Licht unter den Scheffel stellen	*hide one's light under a bushel*
etwas unter den Tisch fallen lassen	*let sth. go by the board*
seine Tochter unter die Haube bringen	*marry one's daughter off*

20.3.15 *vor* (+ dative)

(a) With reference to place, *vor* **(+ dat.) means 'in front of', 'ahead of':**

Das Auto steht vor der Garage	*The car is in front of the garage*
Der Himalaja lag vor uns	*The Himalayas lay before us*
Ich habe noch einen weiten Weg vor mir	*I've still got a long way ahead of me*
vor ihm in einiger Entfernung	*some distance ahead of him*
vor Gericht erscheinen	*appear in court*
Die Insel liegt vor der deutschen Ostseeküste	*The island lies off the Baltic coast of Germany*

(b) To indicate movement in relation to another person or thing, *vor* **(+ dat.) is used with a following** *her*, cf. also 7.3.3b:

Vor uns her fuhr ein roter BMW	*A red BMW was driving along ahead of us*

(c) *vor* **is used in time expressions with the sense of 'ago' or 'before',**
e.g. *vor zwei Jahren, vor Ostern*. For details, see 11.6.12.

(d) *vor* **can be used to indicate cause or reason**
In this sense, *vor* (+ dat.) normally occurs without a following article:

Man konnte vor Lärm nichts hören	*You couldn't hear anything for the noise*

Ich war außer mir vor Entzücken	*I was beside myself with delight*
Ich konnte vor Aufregung nicht einschlafen	*I couldn't sleep with the excitement*
Vor Nebel war nichts zu sehen	*You couldn't see anything for the fog*
Sie gähnte vor Langeweile	*She yawned from boredom*
Sie warnte mich vor dem Hund	*She warned me of the dog*
Gott bewahre mich vor meinen Freunden!	*God protect me from my friends*
blaß vor Furcht, gelb vor Neid	*pale with fear, green with envy*

NB: (i) In contrast to *aus*, cf. 20.2.1c, which points to a voluntary cause or reason, *vor* (+ dat.) always expresses a cause which is <u>involuntary</u>.
(ii) This use of *vor* (+ dat.) is very common with adjectives, cf. 6.6.1, and in the prepositional object of verbs, see 18.6.12.

(e) Some common expressions with *vor* (+ dat.):

Da hatte ich einfach ein Brett vor dem Kopf	*My mind simply went blank*
Sie hatte immer dieses Ziel vor Augen	*She always had this aim in sight*

20.3.16 *vor* (+ accusative)

(a) *vor* (+ acc.) is used almost exclusively to indicate direction in cases where position is given by *vor* (+ dat.):

Ich fuhr den Wagen vor die Garage	*I drove up in front of the garage*
Sie stellte sich vor mich	*She stood in front of me*
Alle traten vor den Vorhang	*Everyone stepped out in front of the curtain*
Die Sache kommt vor Gericht	*The case is coming to court*

(b) *vor sich hin* has the meaning of 'to oneself', cf. 7.3.5b, e.g.:

Sie las vor sich hin	*She was reading to herself*
Ich murmelte etwas vor mich hin	*I muttered something to myself*

20.3.17 *zwischen*

(a) *zwischen* is used with reference to place or time in the sense of English 'between'
(i) *zwischen* (+ dat.) indicates position:

Ich saß zwischen dem Minister und seiner Frau	*I was sitting between the minister and his wife*
Das Geschäft liegt zwischen dem Kino und der Post	*The shop is between the cinema and the post-office*
Die Tagung fand zwischen dem 4. und dem 11. Oktober statt	*The conference took place between the 4th and the 11th of October*
zwischen den Zeilen lesen	*read between the lines*

zwischen can also correspond to English 'among(st)' if more than two objects are involved, (cf. also 20.3.13a):

Pilze wuchsen zwischen den Bäumen	*Toadstools were growing among(st) the trees*

(ii) *zwischen* (+ acc.) indicates direction:

Ich setzte mich zwischen den Minister und seine Frau	*I sat down between the minister and his wife*
Wir legen die Tagung zwischen den 4. und den 11. Oktober	*We are putting the conference between the 4th and the 11th of October*

(b) To indicate movement in relation to another person or thing, *zwischen* is used with a following *her*, cf. also 7.3.3b. The noun is always in the dative:

Ich ging zwischen meinen Eltern her	*I was walking between my parents*

(c) *zwischen* (+ dat.) has the sense of 'between' with reference to quantity, e.g. *Kinder zwischen dem 10. und dem 15. Lebensjahr*. See 9.1.7c for further details of this usage and the distinction between the adverbial and prepositional usage of *zwischen* with expressions of quantity.

20.4 Prepositions taking the genitive

The prepositions governing the genitive fall into three main groups, i.e.:
(i) Four common prepositions, dealt with in 20.4.1:

(an)statt	trotz	während	wegen

These are normally used with the genitive in formal German, but are often found with a dative in colloquial speech.
(ii) Eight prepositions expressing place relationships, dealt with in 20.4.2:

außerhalb	oberhalb	beiderseits	unweit
innerhalb	unterhalb	dieseits	
		jenseits	

These are often used with a following *von* rather than a genitive.
(iii) A large number of prepositions with rather specialized meanings which are hardly used outside very formal (often official) styles. They are listed and explained in 20.4.3.

20.4.1 The four common prepositions which govern the genitive

(a) *(an)statt* **'instead of'**
(i) Examples of *statt* with a following genitive:

Statt eines Fernsehers hat sie sich eine neue Stereoanlage gekauft	*Instead of a television she bought herself a new stereo system*
Statt eines Briefes schickte er ihr eine Postkarte	*Instead of a letter he sent her a postcard*
statt dessen	*instead (of that)*

(ii) *(an)statt* can be used as a conjunction rather than a preposition, i.e. as an alternative to *und nicht*. If this is so, the case of the following noun is governed by its relationship to the verb, e.g.:

Ich besuchte meinen Onkel statt (= und nicht) meinen Bruder	*I visted my uncle instead of my brother*
Ihr Haus hat sie mir statt (= und nicht) ihm vermacht	*She left her house to me instead of to him*

statt is always used in this way if it links prepositional phrases:

Ich schreibe jetzt mit einem Flizstift statt mit einem Füller	*I write with a felt-tip now instead of with a fountain-pen*

NB: (i) The longer form *anstatt* is less frequent; it occurs chiefly in formal written German.
(ii) *anstelle von* is a common alternative to *(an)statt*:

Wir gebrauchen jetzt Margarine anstelle von Butter	*We use margarine instead of butter now*

(iii) For the use of *(an)statt . . . zu* and the conjunction *(an)statt daß* see 13.2.5c.

(b) *trotz* 'despite', 'in spite of':

Wir sind am Sonntag nach Eulbach gewandert trotz des starken Regens	*We walked to Eulbach on Sunday despite the heavy rain*

NB: Dative forms are fixed in the adverb *trotzdem* 'nevertheless' and the phrase *trotz alledem* 'for all that'. For the use of *trotzdem* as a conjunction, see 19.5.1c.

(c) *während* 'during':

Während ihres Studiums in Frankfurt hat sie in der Stadtmitte gewohnt	*During her studies in Frankfurt she lived in the city centre*
Sie hat während der Vorstellung geschlafen	*She slept during the performance*

NB: Unlike English 'during', *während* cannot be used to express duration as such with nouns like *Abend, Nacht, Tag* or *Jahr*. Compare:

am Abend, am Tag, in der Nacht	*during the evening, during the day, during the night*

(d) *wegen* 'because of', 'for the sake of'
(i) *wegen* normally precedes the noun it governs, but it may follow in elevated styles:

Wir konnten wegen des Regens nicht kommen	*We couldn't come because of the rain*
Er mußte wegen zu schnellen Fahrens eine Geldstrafe bezahlen	*He had to pay a fine because he had been driving too fast*
. . . um mich der Eindeutigkeit wegen zu wiederholen	*to repeat myself for the sake of clarity*

(ii) *wegen* is sometimes used in the sense of 'about', 'concerning':

Wegen deiner Reise muß ich noch mit der Astrid sprechen	*I've still got to talk to Astrid about your trip*

(iii) The combination *von* (+ gen.) *wegen* is used in a few set phrases, i.e.:

von Amts wegen	*ex officio*

| von Berufs wegen | *by virtue of one's profession* |
| von Rechts wegen | *legally, by rights* |

(iv) The combination *von wegen* (+ dat.) is common in colloquial German to mean 'because of' or 'concerning'. It is regarded as substandard:

| Jetzt hört mir nur auf von wegen | *For goodness' sake stop talking* |
| Idealismus (*Th. Valentin*) | *about idealism* |

It is very frequent in isolation to challenge a previous statement:

| Also, heute abend bezahlst du alles – | *So, you're paying for everything* |
| Von wegen! | *tonight – No way!* |

NB: For the forms of personal pronouns with *wegen* (*meinetwegen, ihretwegen*, etc.), see 3.1.1d.

(e) (*an*)*statt, trotz, während* and *wegen* are commonly used with a dative in everyday colloquial speech, e.g.:

Ich konnte wegen dem Regen nicht kommen
Während dem Mittagessen hat sie uns etwas über ihren Urlaub erzählt

This usage is regarded as substandard, but it is by no means unknown in writing, especially to avoid the use of the genitive of the personal pronouns, cf. 3.1.2, to avoid consecutive genitives in -(*e*)s, cf. 2.3.2a or to achieve a particular stylistic effect, e.g:

Langsam fahren – wegen uns! (on a road sign outside a Kindergarten)
trotz dem Rollen des Zuges (*Th. Mann*)
Freies Denken statt starrem Lenken (slogan on an election poster)

(f) (*an*)*statt, trotz, während* and *wegen* may be followed by a dative, even in formal written German, in two types of construction, i.e.:
(i) if they are followed by a plural noun which is not accompanied by a declined determiner or adjective:

| während fünf Jahren | wegen ein paar Hindernissen |

(ii) if the noun they govern is preceded by a possessive genitive:

| während Vaters kurzem Urlaub | wegen des Kanzlers langem Schweigen |

NB: (i) The dative may be used in similar contexts with those of the less common prepositions which are asterisked in the list in 20.4.3.
(ii) *während* may be followed by a dative relative pronoun, e.g.:
die Reise, während der wir so viel Schönes sahen.

20.4.2   The eight prepositions denoting position

(a) Meaning and use of these prepositions
(i) *außerhalb* 'outside' and *innerhalb* 'inside', 'within' can be used with reference to place or time:

Sie wohnt außerhalb der Stadt	*She lives outside the city*
Das liegt außerhalb/innerhalb meines	*That lies outside/within my*
Fachgebietes	*specialist field*

Das kann sie außerhalb der Arbeitszeit erledigen	*She can finish that outside working hours*
Ich verbrachte den ganzen Tag innerhalb des Lagers	*I spent the whole day inside the camp*
Das wird innerhalb eines Jahres geändert werden	*That will be changed within a year*

NB: *außerhalb* and *innerhalb* only denote rest, cf. *Wir gingen aus der Hütte hinaus, in die Hütte hinein* 'We went outside, inside the hut'.

(ii) *oberhalb* 'above' and *unterhalb* 'below', 'underneath' are more specific in meaning than *über* and *unter*:

Oberhalb der Straße war ein Felsenvorsprung	*Above the road there was a rocky ledge*
Ich habe mich unterhalb des Knies verletzt	*I injured myself below the knee*
der Rhein oberhalb/unterhalb der Stadt Basel	*the Rhine above/below Basle*

(iii) *beiderseits* 'on both sides of', *diesseits* 'on this side of, *jenseits* 'beyond', 'on the other side of':

beiderseits der Landstraße	*on both sides of the road*
dieseits, jenseits der niederlän- dischen Grenze	*on this side, the other side of the Dutch border*

NB: *hinter* is more commonly used for 'beyond' than *jenseits*, especially in everyday German, e.g. *Das Dorf liegt hinter der Grenze, hinter Hannover.*

(iv) *unweit* 'not far from':

Wir standen auf einer Höhe unweit des Dorfes	*We were standing on a hill not far from the village*

NB: *unfern*, with the same meaning as *unweit*, is now obsolete. It could be used with the genitive or the dative.

(b) All these prepositions are frequently used with a following *von* rather than the genitive.

(i) This usage is especially frequent in colloquial German and it is by no means unknown in the written language, although the genitive is usually felt to be preferable there:

Sie wohnt außerhalb von der Stadt
Innerhalb von einem Jahr wird alles anders werden
Jenseits von der Grenze standen vier Vopos
ein Dorf unweit von Moskau (*Bednarz*)

(ii) The use of *von* is the norm even in written German in those contexts where the common prepositions taking the genitive may be used with a dative, cf. 20.4.1f, e.g. *innerhalb von drei Jahren.*

(iii) These prepositions may be used with a dative relative pronoun, e.g.:

die Zone, innerhalb der Autos verboten sind (less frequent: innerhalb deren)	*the zone within which cars are prohibited*

20.4.3 Other prepositions governing the genitive

The large number of other prepositions with the genitive are only
encountered in formal written German, the majority in official and
commercial language. Outside this register, they can sound very stilted.
Many of them were originally adverbs, participles or phrases which have
come to be used as prepositions, and similar new ones are constantly
entering the language. With this proviso, the following list is as complete as
possible.

NB: The prepositions asterisked in this list may be used with a dative in the same contexts as
with the common prepositions, cf. 20.4.1f.

abseits 'away from'
Unser Haus liegt abseits der Hauptstraße
**abzüglich* 'deducting', 'less'
abzüglich der Unkosten
anfangs 'at the beginning of'
anfangs dieses Jahres (or with the accusative: *anfangs nächsten Monat*)
angesichts 'in view of'
angesichts der gegenwärtigen massenhaften Auswanderung von DDR-Bürgern (*Spiegel*)
anhand 'with the aid of', 'from'
anhand einiger Beispiele
> It is still sometimes spelled *an Hand*, and is often used with *von* e.g. *anhand von einigen Beispielen*.
anläßlich 'on the occasion of'
anläßlich seines siebzigsten Geburtstages
anstelle 'in place of'
anstelle einer Antwort
> It is still occasionally spelled *an Stelle*, and is often used with *von* e.g.: *anstelle von einer Antwort*.
aufgrund 'on the strength of'
aufgrund seiner juristischen Ausbildung
> It is perhaps more frequently spelled *auf Grund*, and is often used with *von*, e.g.: *aufgrund von diesen Erkenntnissen*.
**ausschließlich* 'exclusive of'
die Miete ausschließlich der Heizungskosten
behufs 'for the purpose of'
behufs einer Verhandlung
betreffs, bezüglich 'with regard to'
betreffs, bezüglich Ihres Angebotes

NB: These prepositions are restricted to officialese. In everyday German, the usual
equivalent for 'with regard to' 'in respect of' is *was etwas/jemanden betrifft/anbelangt*.

eingangs 'at the beginning of'
eingangs dieses Jahres
eingedenk 'bearing in mind'
eingedenk seiner beruflichen Fehlschläge
> *eingedenk* may also follow the noun.
**einschließlich* 'including'
einschließlich der Angehörigen (*SZ*)
**exklusive* 'excluding'
exklusive Versandkosten

fernab 'far from'
fernab des Lärms der Städte
gelegentlich 'on the occasion of'
gelegentlich seines Besuches
halber (following the noun) 'for the sake of':
der Wahrheit halber

NB: (i) *halber* is compounded with a few nouns to form adverbs e.g. *sicherheitshalber* 'for safety's sake', *vorsichtshalber* 'as a precaution', *spaßeshalber* 'for a joke'.
(ii) When used with a personal pronoun, *halber* appears as *-halben* and is compounded with forms of the pronoun in *-t*, e.g. *meinethalben* 'for my sake' 'for all me', see 3.1.1d.

hinsichtlich 'with regard to'
hinsichtlich Ihrer Anfrage
infolge 'as a result of'
infolge der neuen Steuergesetze
    infolge is quite frequently used with *von*, e.g.: *infolge von meiner Erkrankung*.
***inklusive** 'including'
inklusive Bedienung
inmitten 'in the middle of'
inmitten üppiger Blütenpracht (*HA*)
kraft 'in virtue of'
kraft seines Amtes
längs 'along(side)'
längs des Flusses
    längs is also (less frequently) used with a dative, e.g. *längs dem Fluß*.
links 'on/to the left of'
links der Donau
***mangels** 'for want of'
Freispruch mangels Beweises
***mittels** 'by means of'
mittels eines gefälschten Passes

NB: *vermittels* is a less frequent alternative to *mittels* with the same meaning.

namens 'in the name of'
Ich möchte Sie namens unseres Betriebes einladen
ob 'on account of'
die Besorgnisse des sowjetischen Staatspräsidenten ob der deutschen Frage (*Zeit*)

NB: *ob* with a following dative in the meaning 'above' is now only found in place names, e.g. *Rothenburg ob der Tauber, Österreich ob der Enns*.

rechts 'to/on the right of'
rechts der Isar
seitens 'on the part of'
seitens der Bezirksverwaltung
seitlich 'to/at the side of':
seitlich der Hauptstraße
um . . . willen 'for the sake of'
um meiner Mutter willen

NB: *um . . . willen* forms compounds with special forms of the personal pronouns, e.g. *um meinetwillen*, cf. 3.1.2d.

unbeschadet 'without prejudice to' occasionally follows the noun:
unbeschadet seiner berechtigten Ansprüche
ungeachtet 'notwithstanding'
ungeachtet dieser Lage auf dem Weltmarkt
NB: *ungeachtet* occasionally follows the noun. *unerachtet*, with the same
        meaning, is obsolescent.
vermöge 'by dint of'
vermöge seines unermüdlichen Fleißes
vorbehaltlich 'subject to'
vorbehaltlich seiner Zustimmung
zeit 'during' is only used in set phrases with *Leben*
zeit seines Lebens
zugunsten 'for the benefit of'
eine Sammlung zugunsten der Opfer des Faschismus
__zuzüglich__ 'plus'
Es kostet 2000 Mark zuzüglich der Versandkosten
__zwecks__ 'for the purpose of'
Er besuchte sie zwecks einer gründlichen Erörterung der Situation

20.5 German equivalents for English 'to'

English 'to' has various possible German equivalents depending on
context and the use of each of these is summarized in this section. Fuller
details and further examples may be found in earlier sections under the
relevant German prepositions.

20.5.1 *an, auf* or *in* (+ accusative) are frequent equivalents for 'to'

The basic rule is that the same preposition is used with the accusative to
indicate direction which one uses with the dative to express position 'in' or
'at' the place concerned. Thus:

(a) *in* (+ accusative) is used for going 'to' places which one will then be
inside, i.e. *in* (+ dative):

Sie ging ins Büro, ins Dorf, ins Kino, in die Kirche, in ein Museum, ins Restaurant, in die
        Schule, in die Stadt, in den Zoo, etc.

Ich gehe in die Kirche   *I am going to church*
        (i.e. to a service. If one is just going up to the church, one says *Ich gehe an die Kirche*
        or *Ich gehe zur Kirche*)

NB: For *in* with names of countries, see 20.5.3.

(b) *auf* (+ accusative) is used for going 'to' certain places and events,
presence 'at' which is denoted by *auf* (+ dative)
(i) This use of *auf* is fixed with a number of nouns:

Die Schafe gingen auf die Wiese   *The sheep went into the meadow*
Wir fuhren aufs Land   *We went into the countryside*
Die Kinder gingen auf die Straße   *The children went into the street*

Similarly:

auf den Berg *up the mountain*	auf ihre Bude *to her digs*
auf den (Bauern)hof *to the farm*	auf den Gang *into the corridor*
auf den Flur *into the (entrance-)hall*	auf den Hof *into the yard*
auf sein Gut *to his estate*	auf die Jagd gehen *go hunting*
auf die Toilette *to the toilet*	

With all these, *auf* (+ dative) is used to denote presence 'in' or 'on' them, cf. 20.3.4b.

(ii) *auf* (+ accusative) is also sometimes used for going 'to' formal occasions (e.g. weddings, conferences, parties, etc.):

Sie ging auf einen Empfang, auf eine Hochzeit, auf eine Party, auf eine Tagung

NB: Although *auf* (+ dative) (or *bei*, cf. 20.2.3b) is still currently used to denote presence 'at' such functions, cf. 20.3.4b, *zu* is more frequent than *auf* (+ acc.) for going 'to' them, especially in less formal registers.

(iii) *auf* (+ accusative) is sometimes used for going 'to' certain public buildings:

Sie ging auf den Bahnhof, auf die Bank, auf die Bibliothek, auf den Markt(platz), auf die Post, auf das Rathaus, auf die Universität

NB: With most of these words, *auf* now tends to occur only in more formal registers, both with the accusative to indicate direction and with the dative to indicate presence 'in' or 'at' the place concerned, (cf. 20.3.4b). *zu* is regularly used in its place, although *an* (+ accusative) is frequent with *Universitat*.

(c) *an* is used to express direction 'to' a precise spot or objects which extend lengthways (i.e. rivers, shores, etc.)
an expresses movement to a point adjacent to the object concerned. One is then *an* (+ dative) that point, i.e. 'at' it, cf. 20.3.2a, e.g.:

Er ging an den Tisch	→	Er steht an dem Tisch
Sie kam an die Bushaltestelle	→	Sie traf ihn an der Haltestelle
Sie ging an die Grenze	→	An der Grenze wurde kontrolliert
Wir fahren an das Meer	→	Wir verbringen unseren Urlaub am Meer

Similarly:

Sie geht ans Mikrophon, an ihren Platz, an die Straßenkreuzung, an die Tür, an die Tafel, an die Stelle, wo der Tote aufgefunden wurde
Sie gingen an den Fluß, an die Mosel, an den Strand, an den See, an die Theke, an den Zaun

Er eilte ans Fenster	Er ging an die Kasse
Wir kamen an die Front	Sie ging ans Ufer

20.5.2 *zu* commonly has the meaning of English 'to'.

(a) *zu* is used in many contexts rather than the more precise prepositions *an*, *auf* and *in* treated in 20.5.1
It is rather vaguer than these three prepositions and tends to emphasize

general direction rather than reaching the objective. It is particularly frequent in colloquial registers.

(i) *zu* is used rather than *in* if one is just going up to the place involved, but not necessarily going inside, or to emphasize the general direction rather than reaching the place:

Ich ging zum neuen Kino und wartete auf ihn
Die Straßenbahn fährt zum Zoo

(ii) *zu* is in practice more common than *auf* in current usage with reference to functions and public buildings:

Er geht zu einem Empfang, zu einer Tagung, zu einer Party
Wir gehen zum Bahnhof, zur Bank, zur Post, zum Rathaus, zur Universität

(iii) *zu* may be used rather than *an* if the emphasis is on general direction rather than arriving adjacent to the place concerned:

Ich begleitete sie zur Fabrik   Er ging zum Fenster, zur Tür
Sie ging zu ihrem Platz   Er schlenderte zur Theke

(b) *zu* is always used with reference to people,
i.e. going up to someone or to their house or shop:

Sie ging zu ihrem Onkel, zu ihrer Freundin
Er ging zu Fleischers, zu seinem Chef
Wir gehen zum Bäcker frische Semmeln kaufen

20.5.3 Equivalents for English 'to' with geographical names

(a) *nach* is used with neuter names of continents, countries and towns which are used without an article, cf. 20.2.6a:

Wir fahren nach Amerika, nach Frankreich, nach Duisburg

(b) *in* (+acc.) is used with names of countries, etc. which are used with an article
The majority of these are feminine, but a few are masculine, neuter or plural, cf. 4.5.1:

Sie reist morgen in die Schweiz, in den Jemen (or nach Jemen), in das Elsaß, in die USA.

(c) Various prepositions are used with other geographical names.
In particular *in, an* or *auf* (+ acc.) are used in the same way as with other nouns, cf. 20.5.1, depending on whether one will be *in, an* or *auf* (+ dat.) on arrival:

Wir fahren in die Alpen, in den Harz
Wir gingen auf den Feldberg, auf die Jungfrau
Wir wollen im Sommer an den Bodensee, an die Riviera fahren

21 Word order

German word order is rather more flexible than English word order, as it does not need to show what are the subject and the object(s) of the verb. In a sentence like *My father lent our neighbour the old lawn-mower* we cannot move the elements round without changing the meaning of the sentence. Compare this with German, where there are numerous possible positions for the elements concerned, e.g.:

(i) *Mein Vater hat unserem Nachbarn den alten Rasenmäher geliehen*
(ii) *Unserem Nachbarn hat mein Vater den alten Rasenmäher geliehen*
(iii) *Den alten Rasenmäher hat mein Vater unserem Nachbarn geliehen*
(iv) *Mein Vater hat den alten Rasenmäher unserem Nachbarn geliehen*

The various permutations do not change the basic meaning of the sentence, rather they give a slightly different emphasis to each of the elements. Sentence (iv), for example, stresses who is being lent the lawn-mower. Whilst in English we only know who is doing what to whom from the word order, this is shown in German by case endings, and the word order can be employed for other purposes, particularly to indicate the relative importance of the elements in context.

In this way, many aspects of German word order are as much a matter of tendency as of strict rule. It is important to be aware of what elements have a fixed place within the clause (especially the verb), and also of where variations are possible or grammatical and how they mark meaning and emphasis within the clause.

It should be noted that we usually speak of word-order, but what we are dealing with is as often as not a phrase of some kind rather than a 'word'. For example, a time adverbial has a particular place in the clause, irrespective of whether it is a single word, like *heute*, a phrase like *den ganzen Tag* or a prepositional construction like *am kommenden Dienstag*. In order to cover all these possibilities, it is useful to refer to the various 'bits' of the clause whose position we are explaining as 'elements'.

A great deal has been written on German word-order. The account given here draws in particular on the very full treatments in Engel (1988:303-55), Heidolph et al. (1981:702-64) and Hoberg (1981). Kirkwood (1969) provides an invaluable comparison of word order in German and English, and Fox (1990:244-56) gives a useful outline in English of the principles of German word order.

453

21.1 Clause structure and the position of the verb

A fundamental feature of German word order is that the various parts of the verb (i.e. the finite verb, any infinitives or past participles, and separable prefixes) have a fixed position in the clause and this forms a framework for the clause as a whole.

21.1.1 There are three types of basic clause structure in German

The finite verb has a different fixed position in each of these, i.e.:

(a) Main clause statements: the finite verb is the second element
Only one element can normally come in initial position before the finite verb in these clauses. This element may be the subject, but it is quite frequently another word or phrase, or a subordinate clause, cf. 21.2. Any other bits of the verb complex are then in final position, i.e. an infinitive or past participle in a compound tense or with one of the modal or other auxiliary verbs, or a separable prefix, e.g.:

Initial position	Verb^1	Other elements	Verb^2
Helga	kommt	eben aus der Bäckerei	
Morgen	muß	ich mit dem Zug nach Trier	fahren
Dann	blickte	sie zum Fenster	hinaus
In der Stadt	habe	ich eine neue Compact-Disc	gekauft
Als er klein war,	hat	er oft mit Werner	gespielt

NB: (i) Exceptions to the rule that the verb must be the second element are explained in 21.2.2.
(ii) The order of infinitives and participles at the end of the clause when there is more than one of these is explained in 21.1.3.
(ii) Indirect speech clauses with the *daß* omitted, cf. 16.2, have the same structure as main clause statements, e.g.:
Er hat gesagt, sie **dürfe** heute nicht bleiben

(b) Questions and commands: the finite verb is the first element
As in main clause statements, any other parts of the verb are in final position. In certain types of question, the verb is preceded by an interrogative word or phrase (e.g. *was, was für ein . . .,* etc.):

	Verb^1	Other elements	Verb^2
	Kommt	sie bald?	
	Mußt	du schon	gehen?
	Hat	dich Peter schon	gesprochen?
	Fangen	Sie sofort	an!
	Paß	doch an der Kreuzung	auf!
Was	hast	du da schon wieder	angestellt?
Welches Buch	sollen	wir zuerst	lesen?
Was für eine Stadt	ist	Bochum?	

NB: Conditional clauses with no conjunction, cf. 16.3.3a, and comparative clauses introduced by *als*, cf. 16.4.1b, have a similar structure, with the finite verb in first position, e.g.:
Hätte ich Zeit, so würde ich gern mit Ihnen nach Italien fahren.
Es war mir, als **wäre** ich hoch in der Luft.

(c) Subordinate clauses: the finite verb is the <u>final</u> element

The clause is introduced by a conjunction in first position. Other parts of the verb usually come immediately before the finite verb at the end of the clause (for details, see 21.1.3), e.g.:

	Conjunction	Other elements	Verb²	Verb¹
Ich konnte es nicht,	weil	ich gestern krank		war
Der Mann,	der	in der Ecke allein		steht
Weißt du,	ob	sie eine neue Bluse	gekauft	hat?
Hast du ihr gesagt,	daß	sie den Brief sofort	schreiben	soll?
Bist du sicher,	daß	er morgen		kommt?

NB: (i) Non-finite clauses with a participle or an infinitive with *zu* have a similar structure, with the verb last, e.g.:
Den Schildern **folgend**, fanden sie das Krankenhaus (*Walser*)
eine Betonburg, wie von einem anderen Stern in diesen Wald **gefallen** (*Walser*)
Gibt es eine Möglichkeit, ihm zu **helfen**?
(ii) Exclamations introduced by an interrogative word may have the form of questions or subordinate clauses, e.g.:
Wie der Chef darüber geschimpft **hat**!   <u>or</u>:   Wie **hat** der Chef darüber geschimpft!

21.1.2 A characteristic feature of all clause types in German is that most or all of the other elements in the sentence are sandwiched between the various parts of the verb in main clauses or the conjunction and the verb in subordinate clauses

This construction is often referred to as the 'verbal bracket' (in German *Verbklammer* or *Satzklammer*). This 'bracket' forms a basic fixed framework for German clauses and we can relate the order of all the other elements in the clause to it. Many of the examples in 21.1.1 illustrate this construction, and further examples are given below:

Initial position	Bracket¹ [	Other elements	Bracket²]
Heute	darf	sie mit uns ins Kino	kommen
Ich	habe	sie zufällig in der Stadt	gesehen
Ich	komme	morgen gegen zwei Uhr noch einmal	vorbei
	Darf	sie heute mit uns ins Kino	kommen?
	Hast	du sie zufällig in der Stadt	gesehen?
	Komm	doch morgen gegen zwei Uhr noch einmal	vorbei!
. . .,	ob	sie heute mit uns ins Kino	kommen darf
. . .,	weil	ich sie heute zufällig in der Stadt	gesehen habe
. . .,	daß	du morgen gegen zwei Uhr noch einmal	vorbeikommst

Notes on the structure of the 'verbal bracket':

(a) Only in main clause statements is there one (and <u>only</u> one) element lying outside the 'bracket', in initial position

This is called the *Vorfeld* in German; its use is explained in 21.2.

(b) All other elements (and this means <u>all</u> elements in questions, commands and subordinate clauses) are placed within the 'bracket'

In German, this is called the *Mittelfeld*. The order of elements in the *Mittelfeld* is exactly the same for all clause types; it is explained in 21.3 – 21.8.

(c) In main clauses with simple verbs in the simple tenses (i.e. the present or the past) there is no closing 'bracket'
This applies equally to statements, questions or commands, e.g.:

Ich **komme** morgen um zwei Uhr.
Kommst du morgen um zwei Uhr?
Komm doch morgen um zwei Uhr!

It is still helpful to refer to the elements after the finite verb as the *Mittelfeld*, as their order is exactly the same as in clauses where there is a second, closing 'bracket', e.g. *Ich **komme** morgen um zwei Uhr **vorbei***, etc.

(d) It is sometimes possible to place elements <u>after</u> the closing bracket,
i.e. after the part of the verb which is in final position. This is equally true of main and subordinate clauses, e.g.:

Ich rufe an **aus London**   Will er dich morgen sehen **in seinem Büro**?
Er hat gesagt, daß er mich morgen sehen möchte **in seinem Büro**

This position is called the *Nachfeld* in German. The possibility of placing elements in the *Nachfeld* is explained in section 21.9.

21.1.3 If there is more than one part of the verb in final position in the clause, they occur in a fixed order

(a) In main clauses (statements, questions and commands), the auxiliary verb comes after the full verb, e.g.:

	Finite verb	Other elements	Full verb	Auxiliary verb
Ich	**werde**	es ihr doch	**sagen**	**müssen**
Sie	**hat**	ihn voriges Jahr	**schwimmen**	**gelehrt**
	Ist	dir das schon	**erklärt**	**worden**?
	Soll	dieser Brief heute noch	**geschrieben**	**werden**?

(b) In subordinate clauses the finite verb usually comes after all infinitives and participles, which have the same order as in main clauses, e.g.:

	Conj.	Other elements	Full verb	Aux. verb	Finite verb
	Da	ich sie zufällig	**gesehen**		**habe**, . . .
. . . ,	**daß**	er mir das Geld	**leihen**		**wird**
. . . ,	**daß**	sie mit uns ins Kino	**gehen**		**darf**
. . . ,	**wie**	sie den Brief	**fallen**		**ließ**
Das Haus,	**das**	sie	**verkaufen**		**sollte**, . . .
. . . ,	**daß**	mir das schon	**erklärt**	**worden**	**ist**
Der Brief,	**der**	heute noch	**geschrieben**	**werden**	**muß**

(c) If both the full verb and the non-finite auxiliary verb are infinitives, the finite verb comes before them at the end of the clause,
cf. also 13.3.2d and 17.1.2e, e.g.:

	CONJ.		FINITE AUXILIARY	FULL VERB INFINITIVE	AUXILIARY INFINITIVE
Ich weiß,	**daß**	ich es bald	**werde**	**erledigen**	**müssen**
der Brief,	**den**	sie	**hat**	**fallen**	**lassen**
das Haus,	**das**	sie	**hätte**	**verkaufen**	**sollen**,. . .

21.1.4 Coordinated clauses have the same structure

This applies to all coordinated clauses, in particular those linked by one of the coordinating conjunctions such as *aber*, *oder* and *und* (see 19.1).

(a) In coordinated main clause statements, the verb is in second position in both

(i) Examples of this construction:

Zu Hause **schreibt** Mutter Briefe, und Vater **arbeitet** im Garten
Am Abend **blieb** ich in meinem Zimmer, aber ich **konnte** nicht arbeiten
Du **kannst** mit uns ins Kino kommen, oder du **kannst** zu deiner Freundin gehen

(ii) If the subject of clauses linked by *sondern* or *und* is identical, it may be omitted ('understood'), e.g.:

Wir **gingen** nicht ins Kino, sondern **arbeiteten** im Garten
Jürgen **kam** um vier Uhr in Soest an und **ging** sofort zu seiner Tante

(iii) If the second clause has another element in initial position, however, the subject <u>must</u> be inserted (in the *Mittelfeld*) and may <u>not</u> be omitted. This is a common error for English learners, as in English the subject may still be understood even if another element precedes the verb. Compare:

Ich schrieb ein paar Briefe, und dann ging **ich** zu meiner Tante	*I wrote a few letters and then went to my aunt's*

(iv) An element other than the subject in initial position may be understood in second and subsequent following coordinated clauses if it is to be emphasized that it applies there equally. The following clauses then begin with the verb, and the subject is repeated after it, e.g.:

Schon im April demonstrierten die Bauern, blockierten sie Straßen in Ost-Berlin und protestierten sie vor der Volkskammer (*Zeit*)	*As early as April the farmers demonstrated, blocked streets in East Berlin and protested in front of the Volkskammer*

    (Here, the phrase *Schon im April* is taken to apply to all three coordinated clauses)

However, if the connection is felt to be less strong, the second clause has its own initial element (most commonly the subject). In practice this is more usual, especially outside formal written German:

Am Abend blieb ich zu Hause, und meine Schwester ging ins Kino	*That night I stayed at home and my sister went to the cinema*

(b) The verb is in final position in all parallel subordinate clauses linked by coordinating conjunctions

(i) Examples of this construction:

Ich weiß, daß sie gestern krank **war** und daß ihr Mann deswegen zu Hause geblieben **ist**	*I know that she was ill yesterday and that her husband stayed at home because of that*
Wenn deine Familie dagegen **ist** oder wenn du keine Zeit **hast**, dann wollen wir den Plan fallen lassen	*If your family is against it or you don't have time, then we'll drop the plan*

(ii) If the two clauses have compound tenses with the same auxiliary, it may be omitted in the first one, e.g:

Nachdem ich Tee getrunken und eine Weile gelesen **hatte**, machte ich einen kurzen Spaziergang	*After I had had tea and read for a while, I went for a short walk*

NB: There is normally no comma between linked subordinate clauses, cf. 23.5.1b.

21.2 Initial position in main clauses: the *Vorfeld*

21.2.1 In main clause statements <u>one and only one</u> element precedes the finite verb, cf. 21.1.1a, e.g.:

Mein Bruder räumte das Frühstücksgeschirr auf
Diesen schönen Mercedes habe ich vor ein paar Wochen gebraucht gekauft
In drei Stunden kommen wir in Moskau an

This structure of main clause statements is quite different to English, where the subject <u>must</u> come before the finite verb, as this is the only way we have of recognising the subject. And there is no restriction in English on other elements occurring in front of the verb as well, e.g.:

Then she typed the letter
Then, reluctantly, she typed the letter
Then, reluctantly, once she had shut the window, she typed the letter

In the corresponding German sentences, all but one of these elements must be transposed to another position, e.g (among other possible permutations):

Dann tippte sie den Brief
Widerwillig tippte sie dann den Brief/ Sie tippte dann widerwillig den Brief
Nachdem sie einmal das Fenster zugemacht hatte, tippte sie dann widerwillig den Brief/ Dann tippte sie widerwillig den Brief, nachdem sie das Fenster zugemacht hatte

Failure to observe the 'verb second' rule in main clauses is a very characteristic error in the German of English learners.

21.2.2 Constructions where more than one element may precede the finite verb

There are a few possible exceptions to the strict 'verb second' rule in main clauses. In the main, they are only apparent exceptions in constructions of a rather special kind, i.e.:

(a) interjections, the particles *ja* and *nein* and names of persons addressed
These are regarded as standing outside the clause proper. They are placed before the initial element and followed by a comma, e.g.:

Ach, es regnet schon wieder   Du liebe Zeit, da ist sie auch
Ja, du hast recht   Nein, das darfst du nicht
Karl, ich habe dein Buch gefunden   Lieber Freund, ich kann nichts dafür

(b) some parenthetical words and phrases
(i) These are normally words or phrases used to link what follows with what has just been said or the general context. They are similarly regarded as standing outside the clause. The most frequent are:

das heißt (d.h.)	*that is (i.e.)*	sehen Sie, siehst du	*d'you see*
im Gegenteil	*on the contrary*	so	*well now, well then*
kurz, kurzum, kurz gesagt,		unter uns gesagt	*between ourselves*
kurz und gut	*in short*	weiß Gott	*Heaven knows*
mit anderen Worten	*in other words*	wie gesagt	*as I said*
nun, na	*well*	wissen Sie, weißt du	*you know*

Examples:

Also, wir wollen jetzt zu Mittag essen   Kurzum, die Lage ist nun kritisch
Wissen Sie, ich habe sie nie richtig kennengelernt

(ii) A few such words or phrases can be used <u>either</u> parenthetically, like the group above, <u>or</u> (rather more commonly) on their own in initial position as an integral part of the clause, e.g.:

Er ist unzuverlässig.   *He is unreliable.*
    Zum Beispiel, er kommt immer spät ⎫
    Zum Beispiel kommt er immer spät ⎬   *For instance, he always comes late*

The following may be used in this way:

zum Beispiel	*for instance*	natürlich	*of course*
erstens, zweitens, etc. (cf. 9.2.3)		offen gesagt	*to be frank*
first, secondly, etc.			

(c) A few adverbs and particles may be used together with another element in initial position, i.e.:

Daran **allerdings** sind nicht nur die   *To be sure, not only the mystific-*
    Mystifikationen schuld (*Hildesheimer*)   *ations are to blame for that*
Am Ende **freilich** ist etwas Unerwar-   *To be sure, at the end something new*
    tetes und etwas Neues da (*Borst*)   *and unexpected was there*

Selbst in den Chroniken der Städter **schließlich** hat sich die Stadt als revolutionäre Neuheit in die Feudalwelt gestellt (*Borst*)	*After all, even in the chronicles of the burghers the city appears as a revolutionary innovation in feudal society*

The following adverbs may be used in this way:

also *thus*	immerhin *all the same*
allerdings *to be sure, admittedly*	wenigstens *at least*
freilich *to be sure, admittedly*	sozusagen *so to speak*
höchstens *at most*	übrigens *incidentally*

Alternatively, these may also occur on their own in initial position in the usual way, e.g.:

Allerdings sind nicht nur die Mystifikationen daran schuld

NB: The function of these adverbs and particles approaches that of a coordinating conjunction in such constructions, and the conjunctions *aber*, *doch* and *jedoch* have a similar flexibility in their positioning, cf. 19.1.1c.

(d) Some clause types are similarly seen as standing outside the clause proper and are followed by another element before the finite verb, i.e.
(i) a *was*-clause which relates to the following clause as a whole, e.g:

Was so wichtig ist, das Buch verkauft sich gut	*What is so important, the book is selling well*

(ii) most concessive clauses, cf. 19.5.2, e.g.:

Es mag noch so kalt sein, die Post muß ausgetragen werden
Wer er auch ist, ich kann nichts für ihn tun
Wie schnell er auch lief, der Polizist holte ihn ein

(e) Two (or more) elements of the same kind may occur together in initial position if they complement or extend one another.
In effect they are being visualised as a single entity. This is most frequent with adverbials of time and place, e.g.:

Gestern um zwei Uhr wurde mein Mann operiert
Auf dem alten Marktplatz in der Marburger Stadtmitte findet diese Woche
    ein Fest statt
Gestern abend in Leipzig fand eine große Demonstration statt

(f) A highlighted element may occur in isolation from the clause.
It is usually picked up by a pronoun or the like in initial position in the clause proper, e.g:

Nach Kanada auswandern, das haben sie ja immer gewollt
Die Gudrun, der traue ich ja alles zu
Der Nachbar, der hat uns ja immer davon abhalten wollen
Als ich davon hörte, da war es schon zu spät
Mit Andreas, da wird es bald Ärger geben

This construction is typical of everyday colloquial language and is rarely encountered in formal writing.

NB: Alternatively, the highlighted element may be placed <u>after</u> the clause, with a pronoun, etc. within the clause referring forward to it, e.g. *Der traue ich doch alles zu, der Gudrun. Es wird da bald Ärger geben, mit dem Andreas.*

21.2.3 Many types of element may occur in initial position.

The subject is often the most natural element to occur in initial position, and it has been estimated that some two thirds of main clause statements in German begin with the subject (cf. Engel 1988:331), e.g.:

Sie hat gestern eine neue Stelle gefunden
Der Sohn von deinem Freund will in Kiel Jura studieren

However, it would be quite wrong to see the order *subject + finite verb* as the 'normal' order in German (as it is in English) and thereby imply that it is in some way 'abnormal' for another element to occur in initial position. Almost all types of element except the negative *nicht* and the modal particles (cf. chapter 10) may quite naturally come first in a main clause. Time and place adverbials (cf. (b) below) are particularly favoured in initial position. We give below examples of most of the elements, aside from the subject, which are commonly employed at the beginning of a main clause. The reasons determining the selection of element to appear in first position are explained in 21.2.4:

(a) an accusative or dative object
This is occasionally a pronoun, more usually a noun phrase:

Ihn/Den kann sie überhaupt nicht leiden
Ihm war das Bett viel zu klein
Deinen Bruder sehe ich nur selten
Ihrem Mann habe ich nicht helfen können

(b) an adverbial (a single adverb or a phrase):

Trotzdem werde ich mich nicht um diese Stelle in Gelsenkirchen bewerben
Zum Glück bin ich ziemlich langsam um die Ecke gefahren

Time and place adverbials are especially frequent in initial position:

Gestern ist sie ihrem Chef im Freibad begegnet
In Mannheim gibt es ein ausgezeichnetes Stadttheater

(c) another complement of the verb,
i.e. a genitive object, a prepositional object, a place or direction complement or a predicate complement, cf. 18.2.2:

An diesen Vorfall/Daran konnte ich mich aber nicht erinnern
Ins Theater/Dahin komme ich jetzt nur sehr selten
Ein guter Kerl ist er trotz alledem

(d) a prepositional phrase qualifying a noun later in the clause:

Auf Elke habe ich einen besonderen Wut

(e) the non-finite part of a compound tense
This construction gives particularly strong emphasis to the verb:

Anzeigen wird sie ihn (*Fallada*)
Gesehen habe ich ihn noch nie, bloß von ihm gehört

(f) a noun belonging with a quantifying determiner later in the clause
This construction is primarily colloquial and gives particular emphasis to the noun:

Arzt braucht er keinen mehr (cf. Er braucht keinen Arzt mehr)
Menschen sind um diese Zeit wenige unterwegs (*Gaiser*)

Occasionally this construction is found with other adjectives, e.g.:

Beweise hat er äußerst triftige gebracht

(g) part of a verb phrase:

Sehr leid hat es mir getan
Zur Abstimmung ist dieser Vorschlag nicht gekommen

(h) a subordinate clause:
This may be a finite or non-finite clause

Als sie mich rief, spielte ich gerade Klavier
Den Schildern folgend, fanden sie das Krankenhaus (*Walser*)
Ihr Geld zu leihen, habe ich doch nie versprochen

The clause in initial position may be a *daß*-clause which is the subject of the main verb, e.g.:

Daß sie das Examen nicht bestanden hat, erstaunt mich nicht

NB: In colloquial speech a pronoun or similar in initial position is often elided, cf. also
3.1.1.b, e.g:
(Das) weiß ich nicht   (Da) kann man nichts machen

21.2.4 The element in initial position functions as the 'topic' of the clause,

i.e. it is that element which we put first in order to say something further about it, e.g.:

Der Kranke hat die ganze Nacht nicht geschlafen
     (Information is being given about the patient)
In Frankfurt findet jedes Jahr die internationale Buchmesse statt
     (We are being told what happens in Frankfurt)
In diesem Zimmer kannst du dich nicht richtig konzentrieren
     (We are given information about this room)
In zwei Tagen wird die Reparatur fertig sein
     (We are informed about what will be happening in two days)

These examples show that whatever is in first position (whether the subject or not) operates as a starting point for the clause. We put it first because it is the thing about which we wish to give our listener some piece of new information.

Further details on the element in the *Vorfeld*:

(a) The element in initial position is often known or familiar to both the speaker and the listener
A clause often starts off with something which is 'known' in this way, and some piece of new information is given about it later in the clause. This is shown by the examples above. Cf. also:

Trotz des Poststreiks ist der Brief rechtzeitig angekommen
   (You knew about the postal strike, but it's news to you that the letter still got there on time)
An den meisten deutschen Gymnasien ist Englisch die erste Fremdsprache
   (You are aware of German schools but this is something you didn't know about the curriculum)

The fact that a clause often begins with an element which is known and familiar to both speaker and listener is a reason why time phrases are so frequently used in initial position.

(b) The element in initial position often refers back to something just mentioned
Very often we want to pick up something which has just been referred to and give further information about it. The element in the *Vorfeld* frequently takes up a preceding word or phrase, especially in continuous texts or dialogue:

Wir haben ihn im Garten gesucht, aber **im Garten** war niemand zu sehen
Ich sehe ihn oft. **Seinen Bruder** aber sehe ich jetzt recht selten
Ich war drei Wochen auf Sylt. – **Darum** siehst du auch so gut aus.

The answer to a question often repeats an element in the question and gives the answer later in the clause. Compare:

Was ist gegen Kriegsende geschehen?	–	**Gegen Kriegsende** wurden viele Städte zerstört
Wann wurden diese Städte zerstört?	–	**Diese Städte** wurden gegen Kriegsende zerstört

(c) The element in initial position is seldom the main piece of new information in the clause.
This follows from what has been said in (a) and (b) above. Most main clauses begin with something familiar and the new information appears later. Thus, the following sentences sound, at best, rather odd, because they start off with an important piece of new information:

?? In einem kleinen Dorf in Böhmen ist Stifter im Jahre 1805 geboren
?? Ein neues Schloß kaufte dieser Mann gestern

?? Scharlachrot ist ihr neues Kleid
Wann wurden viele deutsche Städte zerstört? –
   ?? Gegen Kriegsende wurden viele deutsche Städte zerstört

NB: These examples also show that it is not true that 'any' element may be used in initial
   position in German 'for emphasis', as is often asserted. The first element is the 'topic'
   of the clause and the strongest emphasis is normally on the most important piece of
   new information later in the clause, cf. 21.3.1a.

(d) In many clauses, the subject may not be suitable for use in initial position

The subject is often a natural choice as 'topic' of a clause, cf. 21.2.3.

(i) However, if the subject imparts new information, it may be rather more
natural to begin with something 'known' and delay the subject until later in
the clause, according to the principle explained in (c) above, e.g.:

Vor deiner Tür steht doch **ein neues Auto**	*But there's a new car by your front door*
(With strong emphasis on the surprise at seeing the new car)	
Da ist doch **niemand**	*Nobody's there, though*
(*Niemand ist doch da* sounds very unusual)	
Über die Bedingungen des israelischen Truppenrückzugs sollen nächste Woche in der libanesischen Hauptstadt **Verhandlungen** stattfinden (*Zeit*)	*There are to be negotiations next week in the Lebanese capital about the conditions for Israeli troop withdrawals*
(*Verhandlungen* is the most important piece of new information; it would sound rather odd to begin the sentence with it)	
Zwei Tage darauf wurde gegen die Streikenden **Militär** eingesetzt (*Brecht*)	*Two days later the military was deployed against the strikers*

(ii) In particular, the subject is rarely employed in initial position with
verbs of happening (as the event is usually the main new information), cf.
also 21.5.4, e.g.:

Gestern ereignete sich **ein schwerer Unfall** in der Kärntner Straße

(iii) A 'dummy subject' *es* (cf. 3.6.5) is often employed to allow the subject
to occur later in the clause and give it heavier emphasis as important new
information, e.g.:

Es kamen viele Gäste	*There were many guests*
Es möchte Sie jemand am Telephon sprechen	*There's sombody who wants to speak to you on the telephone*

NB: *da* is a common alternative to *es* in this function in colloquial speech.

(e) As almost any element can occur in the *Vorfeld* in German, we can change the 'topic' of the sentence quite easily

This follows from the explanations in (a) to (c) above. The following
examples show how we can alter the emphasis of the clause by changing the
element in initial position. The element we select to occur in first position
depends on precisely how we want to present the information and what we
assume the listener already knows:

(i) If we say:

Das Konzert findet heute abend im Rathaus statt

the listener knows that there is a concert on, and we are telling him or her where it is.
(ii) On the other hand, if we say:

Heute abend findet ein Konzert im Rathaus statt

we are telling the listener what's happening tonight. We are assuming that he or she doesn't know that there's a concert on in the town-hall, and we are giving him or her this information. We can begin with *heute abend*, because that is information which the speaker and the listener share.
(iii) Finally, if we say:

Im Rathaus findet heute abend ein Konzert statt

we are telling the listener something about the town-hall, i.e. that there's a concert on there tonight.

21.2.5 Some English equivalents for German constructions with an element other than the subject in initial position

The ease with which German can move an element into initial position to serve as the 'topic' of the clause is not shared by English, where the subject <u>must</u> occur immediately (or almost immediately) before the finite verb. For this reason, if we need to make something other than the subject the 'topic' of a main clause in English we must have recourse to more complex constructions for which German has no need. For example:

(a) English often uses 'cleft sentence' constructions which are not necessary in German
To bring an element other than the subject into first position English often places it in a clause of its own, usually with *it* and the verb *be*. In German, we merely need to put the relevant element in initial position, e.g.:

Erst gestern habe ich es ihr gesagt	*It was only yesterday that I told her*
Dort habe ich sie getroffen	*It was there that I met her*
Über diese Werkstatt habe ich mich doch beschweren wollen	*It was that garage I was wanting to complain about, though*
Weil sie oft schwimmt, ist sie fit	*It's because she swims a lot that she's fit*
Was man sagt, zählt	*It's what you say that counts*

There are numerous variations on this construction, all with simpler equivalents in German, e.g.:

Diesen Wagen da muß ich kaufen	*That's the car I've got to buy*
Dort/Hier wohnt sie	*That/This is where she lives*

Das meine ich (auch)	*That's what I mean*
Zu diesem Schluß gelangt Heidemann in seiner neusten Arbeit	*This is the conclusion reached by Heidemann in his latest work*
So macht man das	*That's the way to do it*
Dann ist es passiert	*That's when it happened*
Dem gehört es	*That's whose it is*
Im Frühjahr ist es hier am schönsten	*Spring is when it's loveliest here*

With the exception of the type *Er war es, der mich davon abhielt*, cf. 3.6.4, cleft sentence constructions sound unnatural in German and should be avoided.

(b) English often uses a passive where an active is possible or preferable in German

A common reason for using a passive in English is to allow what would normally be the object of the verb to occur in initial position, as the subject. Although passives are by no means unusual in German, the active construction, with the object in first position, is often preferred, cf. also 15.4. For example:

Diesen Roman hat Thomas Mann während eines Aufenthaltes in Italien geschrieben	*This novel was written by Thomas Mann during a stay in Italy*
Meinem Vater hat der Chef sehr freundlich gratuliert	*My father was congratulated by the boss in a very kind manner*
Auf diese Worte müssen nun Taten folgen (*Zeit*)	*These words must now be followed by deeds*

(c) English uses a construction with *have* and a participle which has no direct correspondence in German

This is essentially a device to bring the relevant element to the beginning of the sentence by making it the subject of *have*. In German all that is necessary is to put the element concerned into initial position, e.g.:

In diesem Buch fehlen zwanzig Seiten	*This book has (got) twenty pages missing*
In diesem Wald haben voriges Jahr viele Nachtigalle genistet	*This wood had a lot of nightingales nesting in it last year*
Ihm wurde eine Golduhr gestohlen	*He had a gold watch stolen*
Ihnen wurden die Fenster eingeworfen	*They had their windows smashed*

21.3   The order of elements in the central portion of the clause: general

21.3.1   Most of the elements in all types of clauses in German occur within the verbal 'bracket',

i.e. in the so-called *Mittelfeld*, as explained in 21.1.2. The relative order of these elements is the same for <u>all</u> clause types, i.e. for main clause statements, questions and commands as well as for subordinate clauses. Compare:

Gestern hat	[er auf der Terrasse vergeblich auf das Mädchen] gewartet
Hat	[er auf der Terrasse vergeblich auf das Mädchen] gewartet?
..., ob	[er auf der Terrasse vergeblich auf das Mädchen] gewartet hat

This order is determined chiefly by two underlying principles, viz.:

(a) Elements which are more heavily stressed and convey important new information tend to follow elements which are less stressed
Cf. also 21.2.4. The elements in the *Mittelfeld* are normally placed in order of increasing importance, passing from the known to the unknown, with the element nearest the end of the bracket carrying the greatest emphasis.

NB: In speech emphasis through word order may be strengthened, or overridden, by vocal stress. Thus, in writing, the dative object may be given prominence by placing it after the accusative object, e.g.:
Er hat sein ganzes Vermögen seinem Neffen vermacht
In speech, the same effect may be achieved, with the more usual order, by vocal emphasis, e.g.:
Er hat **seinem Neffen** sein ganzes Vermögen vermacht

(b) Elements which are more closely linked to the verb tend to come after elements with a less strong link
Thus, verb complements usually appear immediately before the final 'bracket'. And direct objects, if they are nouns, normally come after the indirect objects whose link with the verb is less 'direct'.

21.3.2 The 'basic' order of elements within the *Mittelfeld*

In general, the elements between the verbal brackets tend most commonly to occur in the order given below, which reflects the general principles given above. Fuller details are given on the individual groups of elements in sections 21.4 – 21.8:

NB: This account is intended as a general guideline to help the English speaking learner. The order of these elements is very much a matter of 'tendency' rather than 'rule' and a good deal of variation is possible, especially for reasons of emphasis, as is explained in later sections. It is good practice, when reading or listening to German, to note any variations from this order and attempt to establish the reasons for it.

(a) pronouns
Cf. 21.4. If there are two or more pronouns, they are placed in the order:

(i) personal pronouns before demonstrative pronouns, e.g.:
Gestern ist **ihm das** eingefallen

(ii) nominative + accusative + dative, e.g.:
Sie sagte, daß **sie es ihm** erzählen würde

(b) noun subject
Cf. 21.5, e.g.:

Wenn ihm **der Lehrer** bei der Vorbereitung zur Prüfung hilft, dann . . .

(c) dative noun
Cf. 21.5, e.g.:

Wenn der Lehrer **meinem Sohn** bei der Vorbereitung zur Prüfung hilft, dann, . . .

(d) most adverbials
Cf. 21.6. Most adverbials (whether words or phrases) – with the exception of adverbials of manner, cf. (g) below –usually occur after the dative noun, but before the accusative noun, e.g.:

Der Lehrer hat dem Schüler **trotz seiner Bedenken** eine gute Note gegeben
Er wollte seiner Frau **zum Geburtstag** etwas Ungewöhnliches schenken

The relative order of adverbials if more than one is present in the clause is explained in 21.6.2.

(e) accusative noun
Cf. 21.5, e.g:

Ferdinand hat in London **einen schönen neuen Anzug** gekauft

(f) negatives
i.e. *nicht* and similar words, as long as they negate the whole clause, cf. 21.7, e.g.:

Sie hat ihren Onkel **nicht** um Geld bitten wollen

(g) adverbials of manner
cf. 21.6., e.g.:

Wir haben ihm **herzlich** für seine Mühe gedankt

(h) other verb complements
cf. 21.8. This group includes all verb complements aside from the subject and the accusative and dative objects, cf. 18.1.2, e.g.:

Wir haben ihm herzlich **für seine Mühe** gedankt
The table opposite gives examples for the order of elements in the *Mittelfeld* as outlined above.

21.4 The place of the pronouns

21.4.1 Pronouns usually follow immediately after the finite verb or the conjunction.

(a) Pronouns refer to persons and things already mentioned or known to the

Table 21.1 A 'basic' order for the elements in German sentences

Vorfeld	Bracket¹	Pronouns N A D	Noun Subject	Dative Noun	Most Adverbials	Accusative Noun	nicht	Adverbials of manner	Complements	Bracket²
Gestern	hat	ihm	mein Vater		am Lagerfeuer	ein Märchen				erzählt
	Hat	sie es ihm			schon					gegeben?
'..'	weil		der Lehrer	dem Schüler					für seine Hilfe	gedankt hat
Sie	will			den Kindern	jetzt	die Geschenke				bringen
	Haben	sie			trotzdem	das Angebot	nicht			angenommen?
	Soll	er Ihnen				das Geld	nicht			bringen?
'..'	da		mein Freund		oft		nicht	vorsichtig		fährt
Trotzdem	möchte	mich	der Chef					höflich	nach Berlin	schicken
Wir	wurden				nachher			schnell	daran	erinnert
Dann	hat	sie				das Tuch			in ihre Tasche	gesteckt

speaker and listener. They typically occupy the least prominent position in the *Mittelfeld*

They thus usually precede all other elements, e.g.:

Gestern hat **ihn** mein Mann in der Stadt gesehen
Hat **ihn** dein Mann gestern in der Stadt gesehen?
Da **ihn** mein Mann gestern in der Stadt gesehen hat, . . .

Er fragte, ob **mir** der Wein geschmeckt hätte	*He asked if I had enjoyed the wine*
Dann hat **es** mein Bruder meinem Vater gegeben	*Then my brother gave it to my father*
Dann hat **mir** mein Bruder den Brief gegeben	*Then my brother gave me the letter*

(b) The only exception to the general rule given in (a) above is that a pronoun (or pronouns) may precede or follow a noun subject

In general it is perhaps rather more common for them to come first, but the following are quite usual and acceptable alternatives to the first three examples in (a) above:

Gestern hat mein Mann **ihn** in der Stadt gesehen
Hat dein Mann **ihn** gestern in der Stadt gesehen?
Da dein Mann **ihn** gestern in der Stadt gesehen hat, . . .

(c) The pronoun does more usually follow the noun subject if the endings do not show nominative and accusative case unambiguously, e.g:

Gestern hat meine Mutter sie in der Stadt gesehen	*My mother saw her in town yesterday*
Da das Mädchen sie in der Stadt gesehen hat, . . .	*As the girl saw her in town yesterday . . .*
Da meine Brüder sie in der Stadt gesehen hatten, . . .	*As my brothers saw them in town yesterday . . .*

(d) If there are two pronoun objects, it is rather more usual for them to follow the subject, e.g.:

Weil der Lehrer **es ihnen** gezeigt hat, . . .	*Because the teacher has shown it to them*

Nevertheless, other orders are also quite possible, e.g.:

Weil **es** der Lehrer **ihnen** gezeigt hat, . . .
Weil **es ihnen** der Lehrer gezeigt hat, . . .

21.4.2 Personal pronouns precede other pronouns

Thus, *er, dir, Ihnen, ihm*, etc. (and *man*) come before demonstrative pronouns such as *der, das, dieser*, etc., irrespective of case, e.g.:

Wollen Sie **die** gleich mitnehmen?	*Do you want to take those away with you?*
Hat ihn **dieser** denn nicht erkannt?	*Didn't that person recognise him, then?*
Eben hat sie mir **das** gezeigt	*She's just shown me that*

21.4.3 If more than one personal pronoun is present in the clause, they appear in the order *nominative* + *accusative* + *dative*:

Da **sie dich ihm** nicht vorstellen wollte, . . .	*As she didn't want to introduce you to him*
Hast **du es uns** nicht schon gesagt?	*Haven't you already told us that?*
Gestern hat **er sie ihm** gegeben	*He gave them to him yesterday*
Heute will **sie ihm** helfen	*She's going to help him today*
Heinz hat **es mir** gezeigt	*Heinz showed it to me*

This order is relatively fixed. The only common variation on it is that the pronoun *es*, in the reduced form *'s*, often follows a dative pronoun in colloquial speech, e.g. *Heinz hat **mir's** gezeigt.*

21.4.4 The position of the reflexive pronoun *sich* is the same as that of any other personal pronoun,

i.e. it occupies the same place as any other accusative or dative personal pronoun, e.g.:

Gestern hat **sich** der Deutsche über das Essen beschwert
Gestern hat **sich** jemand darüber beschwert
Gestern hat er **sich** darüber beschwert
Er hatte es **sich** (dat.!) so vorgestellt
Er hat **sich** (acc.!) mir vorgestellt

However, it is occasionally placed after a noun subject, e.g.:

Gestern hat der Deutsche **sich** über das Essen beschwert

And very occasionally, it may occur later in the clause, e.g:

Gestern hat der Deutsche über das Essen **sich** beschwert

In general, this is only possible in the case of 'true' reflexive verbs used with an accusative reflexive, cf. 18.3.6a.

21.5 The position of the noun subject and accusative and dative objects

21.5.1 The usual order for the noun subject and objects in the *Mittelfeld* is *nominative* + *dative* + *accusative*

This group of elements includes not only noun phrases in the nominative, accusative or dative case but also indefinite pronouns such as *etwas, jemand, niemand, nichts, keine, viel(e)*, etc. As the table in 21.3.2. shows, they usually follow personal and demonstrative pronouns (but see 21.4.1b for certain exceptions) and come before other verb complements.
For the position of adverbials in relation to them, see 21.6.1.
Examples of this ordering:

Gestern hat **jemand meinem Vater eine Kettensäge** geliehen
Warum hat **Manfred seiner Freundin nichts** gebracht?

Ich weiß, daß **mein Freund seiner Frau diese Bitte** nicht verweigern konnte
Heute hat **der Chef den Mitarbeitern** für ihre Mühe gedankt

Variations on this order are not uncommon, but usually involve special circumstances of some kind, as explained in 21.5.2 – 21.5.4.

21.5.2 The dative object may follow the accusative object if it is felt to be more important in context and needs to be emphasised more strongly

In practice this ordering gives considerable emphasis to the dative object and it is used sparingly, especially in cases of giving 'things' to 'persons', e.g.:

Er hat sein ganzes Vermögen **seinem**   *He left his whole fortune to his*
  Neffen vermacht   *nephew*
    (Here we already know about the fortune, what is news is who he left it to)
Er stellte seinen Neffen **dem Pfarrer**   *He introduced his nephew to the*
  vor   *parson*
    (Who the nephew was introduced to is being regarded as more important than who was being introduced to the parson)
. . . , als mein Vater gestern diese   *When my father told this remarkable*
  merkwürdige Geschichte **einem ihm**   *story yesterday to a gentleman whom*
  völlig unbekannten Herrn erzählte   *he didn't know at all*
    (The dative object is indefinite and thus previously unknown to the listener, whereas 'this story' must have been mentioned before)
Er hat sein Glück **seiner Karriere**   *He sacrificed his happiness to*
  geopfert   *his career*
    (Compare the different emphasis in *Er hat seiner Karriere sein ganzes Glück geopfert*)

21.5.3 A dative object referring to a thing usually follows an accusative object referring to a person

In such cases it is rarely possible for the dative object to come first, e.g.:

Sie überantworteten die Verbrecher   *They delivered up the criminal to*
  der Justiz   *justice*
Sie haben den armen Jungen **der**   *They exposed the poor boy to*
  Lächerlichkeit preisgegeben   *ridicule*

21.5.4 The noun subject may come after an accusative and/or a dative object (and other elements) if it constitutes the major piece of new information

Cf. also 21.2.4d. In practice the subject is in such cases usually a noun with an indefinite article or no article or an indefinite pronoun:

Glücklicherweise wartet nun in Wien an   *Luckily there is a cafe waiting for*
  jeder Ecke **ein Kaffeehaus** (*S. Zweig*)   *you on every corner in Vienna*

Nun begrüßte den Dirigenten und den Virtuosen **lautes Händeklatschen** (*G. Kapp*)	*Now the conductor and the virtuoso were met with loud applause*
Gestern hat meinen Bruder Gott sei dank **niemand** gestört	*Thank goodness nobody disturbed my brother yesterday*
Er wußte, daß dieser Gruppe **etwas Unangenehmes** bevorstand	*He knew that something unpleasant was in store for this group*

Occasionally a subject with a definite article will be placed late in the clause if it needs strong emphasis, e.g.:

Die Tatsache, daß der EG unausweich- lich 1994 **das Geld** ausgeht (*Zeit*)	*The fact that the EEC's money will inevitably run out in 1994*

The late position of an indefinite subject is almost regular with verbs of happening and the like, and it is also very frequent in passive sentences, e.g.:

Er wußte, daß seinem Chef **eine große Ehre** zuteil geworden war	*He knew that a great honour had been bestowed on his boss*
Zum Glück ist meinem Bruder da **nichts** passiert	*Luckily nothing happened to my brother*
Deshalb können den Asylanten **keine Personalausweise** ausgestellt werden	*For this reason no identity cards can be issued to the asylum-seekers*

21.6 The place and order of adverbials

An 'adverbial' may be a single word (e.g. *trotzdem*, *heute*), or a phrase with or without a preposition (e.g. *den ganzen Tag, mit großer Mühe*), cf. section 18.1.3. This difference in form has no effect on word order.

The placing of adverbials is perhaps more flexible than that of any other element in the clause. This reflects their general freedom of occurrence as elements optionally added to give additional circumstantial information. In this section we deal first with the placing of adverbials in relation to other elements (chiefly the noun subject and objects), and then explain the ordering of adverbials in cases where more than one is present in the clause.

21.6.1 The placing of adverbials in relation to the noun subject and objects

As shown in the table in 21.3.2, most adverbials are usually placed after a noun subject and dative object, but before an accusative object, e.g.:

Ich weiß, daß er dem Jungen **nach der Stunde** das Buch zurückgegeben hat
Jürgen hat sich **trotz dieser Schwierigkeiten** ein Haus bauen lassen
Wir konnten unseren Kindern **leider** nicht helfen
Es hat **im amerikanischen Außenministerium** einen Personalwechsel gegeben

However, a number of refinements are necessary to this general guideline, notably because the position of adverbials in relation to noun subjects and objects depends largely on their relative importance in the clause. Specifically, that element appears later in the clause which needs to be emphasised most strongly or conveys the most important new information. Thus:

(a) Unemphatic adverbs (usually single words) may precede the noun subject and/or the dative object
This applies in particular to modal particles and to adverbs which indicate the attitude of the speaker, cf. 21.6.2a, e.g. *bestimmt, sicher, vielleicht, wahrscheinlich*, etc. Unstressed short adverbs like *da, dort, hier, gestern, heute, morgen, dann, damals, daher* also often occur early in the clause, immediately after the personal pronouns, e.g.:

Sie wird es **wohl** ihrem Mann sagen	*She'll probably tell her husband*
Er wird **doch** meiner Schwester helfen können, oder?	*He will be able to help my sister, won't he?*
Ich weiß, daß sie es **sicher** meinem Vater empfehlen wird	*I know she'll be sure to recommend it to my father*
Sie ist **heute** ihrem Freund nach Bonn gefolgt	*She followed her boy-friend to Bonn today*
Hat sie **damals** ihrem Großvater die ganze Geschichte erzählt?	*Did she tell her grandfather the whole story at that time?*

In most of the above cases the adverb may follow the noun subject or object, which will then carry rather less emphasis, e.g.:

Sie wird es ihrem Mann **wohl** sagen
Er wird meiner Schwester **doch** helfen können
Hat sie ihrem Großvater **damals** die ganze Geschichte erzählt?

Such permutation is, however, scarcely possible in the following, where the noun subject or object is indefinite and thus clearly the vital piece of new information:

Das hat **bisher** keiner gemerkt	*Nobody's noticed it up to now*
Da war **doch** niemand	*Nobody was there, though*
Ich bin **da** einem Freund von deinem Bruder begegnet	*I ran into a friend of your brother's there*

Compare the effect of the different position of *gestern* in the following sentences:

Das hat **gestern** ihr Kollege meinem Verlobten erzählt
    (who was told is the point at issue)
Das hat ihr Kollege **gestern** meinem Verlobten erzählt
    (who did the telling is seen as relatively unimportant)
Das hat ihr Kollege meinem Verlobten **gestern** erzählt
    (prominence is given to the time when the fiancé was told)

(b) The order of adverbials and noun objects (accusative or dative) most

frequently depends on the emphasis they require in the context of the overall sense of the sentence
The element which is seen as more important comes later. Compare the following:

Sie haben Fußball **im Park** gespielt
    (This tells us <u>where</u> they were playing)
Sie haben im Park **Fußball** gespielt
    (This tells us <u>what</u> they were playing)
Er hat diesen neuen Wagen **im Sommer** gekauft
    (The stress is on <u>when</u> he bought the new car)
Er hat im Sommer **diesen neuen Wagen** gekauft
    (The new car itself is the most important piece of information)

It must be noted that, although from a grammatical point of view there is flexibility here, in that either order is acceptable, in a particular context only one may be appropriate. Thus, in answer to the question *Wann hat er diesen neuen Wagen gekauft?* one would most naturally use the first of the alternatives above.

(c) Adverbials of manner follow the noun objects
(and, for that matter, all other adverbials, cf. 21.6.2). This is because they usually convey the most important new information, e.g.:

Meiner Meinung nach hat das Quartett dieses Stück **viel zu schnell** gespielt	*In my opinion the quartet played the piece much too fast*
Er warf den Ball **sehr vorsichtig** über den Gartenzaun	*He threw the ball very carefully over the garden fence*

21.6.2 The relative order of adverbials

(a) If a clause contains more than one adverbial, they most frequently occur in the following order:
(i) adverbials expressing an attitude.
This group includes all the modal particles, cf. chapter 10, and other adverbials which express some attitude on the part of the speaker towards what is being said, e.g. *angeblich, bekanntlich, hoffentlich, leider, sicher, vermutlich, wahrscheinlich, zum Glück, zweifellos*, etc., e.g.:

Sie wollte **doch** vor zwei Uhr in Magdeburg sein
Er ist **vielleicht** schon am Montag abgereist

(ii) time adverbials (cf. chapter 11).
These may give information about

<u>when</u> an even occurs, e.g. *bald, voriges Jahr, am kommenden Sonntag*.
<u>how often</u>, e.g. *jeden Tag, stündlich*.
<u>its duration</u>, e.g. *lange, seit Montag, ein ganzes Jahr*.
If more than one time adverbial occurs in the clause, they will be placed in the order given above. Within these categories the general precedes the particular, e.g. *jeden Tag um vier Uhr.*

Examples:

Sie ist **vor zwei Tagen** trotz des Regens nach Reutte gewandert
Die Streikenden blieben **vier Stunden lang** vor dem Rathaus versammelt

(iii) adverbials expressing reason or cause.
This is a rather disparate group of adverbs and phrases which indicate:

a condition, e.g. *gegebenenfalls, bei schlechtem Wetter*, etc.
a reason, e.g. *wegen des Unfalls, aus diesem Grunde*, etc.
a consequence, e.g. *folglich, zu unserem Erstaunen*, etc.
a purpose, e.g. *dazu, zur Durchsicht, zu diesem Zweck*, etc.
a concession, e.g. *dennoch, jedoch, trotz des schlechten Wetters*, etc.

The passive agent introduced by *von* or *durch*, cf. 15.3, also occurs in this position.
Examples:

Sie hat den Brief **trotzdem** mit der Maschine geschrieben
Der Brand wurde **von der freiwilligen Feuerwehr** schnell gelöscht

(iv) instrumental adverbials,
i.e. those indicating the instrument with which an action is carried out, e.g. *mit einem Messer, mit der Kettensäge*. Other phrases introduced by the prepositions *mit* or *ohne* also occur in this position, as do adverbials expressing a 'point of view', e.g. *finanziell* 'from a financial point of view'.
Examples:

Der Oberst hat sie **mit dem Beil** in der Küche erschlagen
Er ist gestern **ohne Hut** im Wald herumgelaufen

(v) place adverbials, e.g.:

Der Oberst hat sie mit dem Beil **in der Küche** erschlagen
Ich habe bis 18. Uhr **im Büro** gearbeitet

NB: Place adverbials must be distinguished from place and direction complements, see (c) below.

(vi) manner adverbials,
i.e. those which indicate <u>how</u> an action is carried out. This group includes most adverbs from adjectives, cf. 7.1.2 and 7.4. Adverbs of manner are almost always the final element in the clause before the complement, e.g.:

Sie ist heute mit ihrem Porsche **viel zu schnell** in die Kurve gefahren
Der Vorschlag wurde von den Anwesenden **einstimmig** angenommen

(b) The order given in (a) above is not absolute and is subject to variation for reasons of emphasis
As in the case of the relative order of adverbials and the noun subject and objects, this variation follows the general principle given in 21.3.1a, in that an adverbial can be given more or less emphasis by being placed later or earlier in the clause. This often depends on what is regarded as the main

new information in context, e.g.:

Paula ist zum Glück **gestern** nicht zu schnell gefahren
Paula ist gestern **zum Glück** nicht zu schnell gefahren

> The adverbial in bold is made rather more prominent in each case by being placed later. Note that the manner adverbial, as the major information, is the last element in both cases.

Viele deutsche Städte wurden gegen Kriegsende **von den Alliierten** zerstört
Viele deutsche Städte wurden von den Alliierten **gegen Kriegsende** zerstört

> Placing the time adverbial after the *von*-phrase in the second example gives it particular prominence, possible in reply to a question about <u>when</u> it happened.

Sie hat sehr lange **dort** auf ihre Mutter gewartet
Sie hat dort **sehr lange** auf ihre Mutter gewartet

> Although time adverbials usually precede place adverbials, they
> may follow if it is felt necessary to give them particular prominence. Note that the prepositional object, as a complement, always follows both adverbials.

(c) The order of adverbials is given in many handbooks as *time – manner – place*. This is misleading as it confuses adverbials and complements

As shown in (a) above, the main categories of adverbials occur in the order *time – place – manner*, e.g.:

Der junge Tenor hat gestern in Berlin gut gesungen
Die Kinder wollten heute auf der Wiese ungestört spielen

Elements indicating place and direction at the end of the *Mittelfeld*, immediately before the final part of the verb, are complements of the verb, not adverbials, cf. 21.8.1. These complements follow <u>all</u> adverbials, including those of manner, e.g.:

Paula ist gestern viel zu schnell **in die Kurve** gefahren
Andreas wollte gestern mit seiner Freundin gemütlich **nach Freising** wandern
Sie hat die schöne Vase sehr vorsichtig **auf den Tisch** gestellt
Müllers wohnen einsam **in einem großen Haus im Wald**
Astrid lag erschöpft **auf dem Couch**
Sie sind gestern wegen des schlechten Wetters widerwillig **zu Hause** geblieben

All the elements in bold in the above examples are <u>complements</u>, not adverbials. They are either direction complements depending on verbs of motion or place complements depending on verbs of position. They complete the sense of the verb, as explained in 18.1, where the difference between adverbials and complements is made clear. Complements are much more closely linked to the verb than adverbials, which simply give additional circumstantial information, and thus, following the principle given in 21.3.1b, they are placed at the end of the *Mittelfeld*.

21.7 The position of *nicht* and other negative elements

For the use of *nicht* and *kein* in negation, see 5.5.16b. Other negative
elements like *nie* 'never' and *kaum* 'hardly, scarcely' occupy much the
same position in the clause as *nicht*, and the following account applies
equally to them.

21.7.1 If *nicht* is used to negate the content of the clause as a whole it follows all objects and adverbials (<u>except</u> those of manner) and precedes adverbs of manner and all verb complements

Nicht is itself in essence an adverb of manner, and this determines its
position in the clause if it relates globally to the whole action of the clause.
However, it usually precedes other manner adverbials.
Thus:

(a) *nicht* **follows any noun objects,** e.g.:

Er hat seinen Zweck nicht erwähnt	*He didn't mention his purpose*
Er hat mir das Buch nicht gegeben	*He didn't give me the book*
Verkaufe die Bücher nicht!	*Don't sell the books*
Ich weiß, daß sie ihren Bruder gestern nicht gesehen hat	*I know she didn't see her brother yesterday*

However, *nicht* precedes objects used with no article which are part of the
verb phrase, e.g.:

Sie hatte damals nicht Klavier gespielt	*She didn't play the piano then*

(*Klavier spielen* is essentially a fixed phrase, cf. 21.8.2)

(b) *nicht* **follows all adverbials except those of manner,** e.g.:

Sie haben sich seit langem nicht gesehen	*They haven't seen each other for a long time*
Den Turm sieht man von hier aus nicht	*You can't see the tower from here*
Ich wollte es ihr trotzdem nicht geben	*I didn't want to give it to her all the same*
Das ist mir in diesem Zusammenhang nicht aufgefallen	*That didn't occur to me in that context*
Wir sind wegen des Regens nicht nach Füssen gewandert	*We didn't walk to Füssen because it was raining*
Sie haben gestern nicht gut gespielt	*They didn't play well yesterday*
Ich weiß es nicht ausführlich	*I don't know it in detail*

(c) *nicht* **precedes verb complements,**
i.e. those verb complements with the exception of the subject and the
accusative and dative objects which are dealt with in 21.8.

Sie sind gestern nicht nach Aalen gefahren	*They didn't go to Aalen yesterday*
Sie legte das Buch nicht auf den Tisch	*She didn't put the book on the table*

Wir konnten uns nicht an diesen Vorfall erinnern	*We couldn't remember the incident*
Er blieb nicht in Rostock	*He didn't stay in Rostock*
Sie ist sicher nicht dumm	*She's certainly not stupid*
Sie war heute nicht im Büro	*She wasn't at the office today*

NB: *nicht* may follow prepositional objects or place and direction complements if it is relatively unstressed and the complement itself is to be given prominence. Compare:

Das kann ich doch *nicht* von ihm verlangen	*I can't ask that of him*
Das kann ich doch von *ihm* nicht verlangen	*I can't ask that of him*

21.7.2 If *nicht* applies to one particular element in the clause rather than the clause as a whole, then it precedes that element

As *nicht* in such cases only applies to part of the clause, this is often referred to as 'partial' negation, in contrast to the 'global' negation treated in 21.7.1. The sense is thus usually 'not <u>that</u> one, but another one':

Sie hat mir nicht das Buch gegeben (i.e. not the book, but something else)	*She didn't give me the <u>book</u>*
Sie sind nicht am Freitag nach Teneriffa geflogen (i.e. not on Friday, but some other day)	*They didn't fly to Tenerife on Friday*
Nicht mir hat er das Buch gegeben, sondern meiner Schwester	*It wasn't me he gave the book to, it was my sister*

NB: The stressed element may also appear on its own in initial position, with the *nicht* later in the clause, e.g. *Mir hat er das Buch nicht gegeben.* This is the norm if the contrast is implicit, i.e. if there is no following *sondern* clause.

Unstressed *nicht* is often used in this way in tentative or rhetorical questions or exclamations, e.g.:

Hast du nicht die Königin gesehen?	*Didn't you see the Queen?*
War nicht dein Vater eigentlich etwas enttäuscht?	*Wasn't your father really a bit disappointed?*
Was du nicht alles weißt!	*Don't you know a lot!*

21.8 The position of complements

The 'complements' of the verb are those elements which are most closely linked with it in a sentence, or 'governed' by it, cf. 18.1. Of the complements of the verb, the subject and the accusative and dative objects, whether pronouns or nouns, have their own position within the clause, cf. 21.4 – 21.5. The other complements, following the general principle given in 21.3.1b, invariably come towards the end of the *Mittelfeld*, immediately before the bits of the verb in final position. This position for the complements is relatively fixed, irrespective of emphasis, and only very exceptionally are they found earlier in the clause.

21.8.1 The following complements are placed at the end of the *Mittelfeld*:

(a) genitive objects
cf. 18.5, e.g.:

, . . . weil der Verletzte dringend **eines Arztes** bedurfte	*. . . because the injured man needed a doctor urgently*

(b) prepositional objects
cf. 18.6., e.g.:

Nun wird er sich sicher **um seine beiden Kinder** kümmern können	*Now he will certainly be able to look after his two children*
Sie hat in der Ankunftshalle lange **auf ihren Mann** gewartet	*She waited for her husband in the arrivals hall for a long time*
Wir haben uns vorgestern lange und ausführlich **darüber** unterhalten	*We talked about it in detail for a long time the day before yesterday*

(c) place complements with verbs of position,
in particular with verbs like *sich aufhalten, sich befinden, bleiben, liegen, sitzen, stehen* and *wohnen*, cf. 18.7.1, e.g.:

Er befand sich plötzlich **in einem dunklen Saal**	*He suddenly found himself in a dark room*
Er wollte unter keinen Umständen **in Wuppertal** bleiben	*He didn't want to remain in Wuppertal under any circumstances*
Sie haben lange **in dieser Hütte** gewohnt	*They lived in that hut for a long time*

(d) direction complements with verbs of motion,
cf. 18.7.2, e.g.:

Warum hat Peter den Stein plötzlich **in den Bach** geworfen?	*Why did Peter suddenly throw the stone in the water?*
Sie ist mit ihrem Porsche zu schnell **in die Kurve** gefahren	*She took the bend too fast in her Porsche*
Wir möchten nächste Woche kurz **nach Emden zu meinen Eltern** fahren	*We want to go to my parents' in Emden next week*

NB: Such place and direction complements as given in (c) and (d) above must be carefully distinguished from place adverbials, cf. 21.6.2.

(e) the predicate complement of copular verbs,
i.e. *sein, werden, bleiben, scheinen, heißen*, cf. 18.8. This complement may be a noun or an adjective, e.g.:

Herbert war immerhin längere Zeit **der beste Schüler in unserer Klasse**	*All the same, Herbert was top of our class for a long time*
Sie wurde plötzlich **blaß**	*She suddenly turned pale*
Dann scheinen mir diese Bedingungen jedoch **etwas hart**	*In that case these conditions seem rather hard to me, though*

21.8.2 The noun portions of phrasal verbs also come in the last position in the *Mittelfeld*

Such extended verb phrases usually consist of a noun (often with no article) or an infinitive or other verbal noun used in a set phrase with a verb, e.g. *Abstand halten, Abschied nehmen, ins Rollen geraten, zur Kenntnis nehmen*, etc., cf. 4.3.3. In respect of their position in the clause such noun portions of phrasal verbs are rather similar to separable prefixes, and they could be considered as constituting the final portion of the verb bracket rather than as elements within the clause.

Examples:

Er hat sie durch seine Unvorsichtig-keit **in die größte Gefahr** gebracht	*He brought her into very great danger through his carelessness*
Ich habe ihr alle meine Bücher **zur Verfügung** gestellt	*I put all my books at her disposal*
Gestern hat uns der Minister von seinem Entschluß **in Kenntnis** gesetzt	*The Minister informed us of his decision yesterday*
Sein Chef hat ihn vorige Woche sehr **unter Druck** gesetzt	*The boss put him under a lot of pressure last week*
Ich merkte, wie der Wagen langsam **ins Rollen** kam	*I noticed the car slowly starting to roll forwards*

21.9 The placing of elements <u>after</u> the final portions of the verb

As a general rule, the last element in a German clause is the final 'bit' of the verb, whether this is a separable prefix, an infinitive or a past participle (in main clause staements, questions and commands) or the finite verb (in subordinate clauses). This is the second part of the verbal 'bracket', as explained in 21.1.2.

However, there are a number of cases where an element may be placed <u>after</u> this final bracket. This construction is known as *Ausklammerung* in German, and it has been noted that it is becoming increasingly frequent in the modern language. It was probably always quite common in colloquial registers, but it is nowadays used much more regularly in the formal written language. Nevertheless, there are clear limitations on *Ausklammerung*, and the following sections give details about where it is possible or acceptable.

21.9.1 It is usually preferable not to enclose subordinate clauses within the verbal bracket even in formal written German

(a) One clause will usually be finished off, with its closing bracket, before another is begun

(i) In the following pair of examples, the second alternative, though not ungrammatical, would be regarded as rather clumsy nowadays:

Ich konnte den Gedanken nicht loswerden, daß wir ihn betrogen hatten
Ich konnte den Gedanken, daß wir ihn betrogen hatten, nicht loswerden

(ii) A relative clause may be separated from the noun it refers to in order to avoid enclosing it, e.g.:

Und wie dürfte man eine Zeitung verbieten, die sich wiederholt und
    nachhaltig für die Wahl der staatstragenden Partei eingesetzt hat?
    (*Spiegel*)

Enclosing the relative clause, though quite grammatical, would result in an unwieldy sentence, e.g.:

Und wie dürfte man eine Zeitung, die sich wiederholt und nachhaltig für
    die Wahl der staatstragenden Partei eingesetzt hat, verbieten?

(iii) Sentences with clauses enclosed within one another and a cluster of verbs at the end (so-called *Schachtelsätze*) can be cumbersome and are best avoided. For this reason DUDEN (1985:587) regards the second of the following sentences as clearly preferable in modern German:

Er hätte ihr, da die Kleiderstoffe am Donnerstag, obwohl dieser Tag als
    Termin festlag, nocht nicht eingefärbt waren, wenigstens Nachricht geben
    müssen.
Da die Kleiderstoffe am Donnerstag noch nicht eingefärbt waren, obwohl
    dieser Tag als Termin festlag, hätte er ihr wenigstens Nachricht geben
    müssen.

(b) Infinitive clauses are not usually enclosed
Cf. also 13.1.3, e.g.:

Sie haben beschlossen zu warten	*They decided to wait*
Sie haben beschlossen, vor dem Rathaus zu warten	*They decided to wait in front of the town hall*
Er hat versucht, sein Geschäft zu verkaufen	*He tried to sell his shop*
Er hat große Opfer gebracht, um dir zu helfen	*He made great sacrifices to help you*

(i.e. not: *Sie haben zu warten beschlossen*, etc.)

NB: (i) A simple infinitive with *zu* is occasionally enclosed by a verb with a separable prefix, e.g. *Sie fing **zu weinen** an* (but, more usually: *Sie fing an **zu weinen***)
(ii) Certain 'semi-auxiliary' verbs regularly enclose a dependent infinitive clause, e.g. *Das hat sie uns **zu verstehen** gegeben*. Full details of the verbs used in such constructions are given in 13.2.3.

21.9.2 Comparative phrases introduced by *als* or *wie* are not usually enclosed

(a) This is almost always the case if the *als* or *wie* phrase is the second

element in a comparison, e.g.:

Gestern haben wir einen besseren Wein getrunken als diesen	*Yesterday we drank a better wine than this one*
Ich wußte, daß sie ebenso ärgerlich war wie ich	*I knew she was just as annoyed as me*

(b) However, comparative phrases with *wie* (= 'like', 'as') **may be enclosed**
This is essentially optional, e.g.:

ein Mann, der **wie ein Italiener** aussah ⎫
ein Mann, der aussah **wie ein Italiener** ⎬   *a man who looked like an Italian*

Nevertheless, enclosing is quite frequent within longer clauses, especially in the written language, e.g.:

da . . . die Orangen und Zitronen von den Kindern **wie Schneebälle** über die Gartenmauern geworfen wurden (*Andres*)

21.9.3 Other elements may sometimes be placed after the verbal bracket

There are three main reasons for such *Ausklammerung*, i.e.:
(i) to emphasise the element placed last, e.g.:

Du hebst das auf **bis nach dem Abendessen** (*V.Baum*)

(ii) as an afterthought, e.g.:

Ich habe sie doch heute gesehen **in der Stadt**

(iii) In order not to overstretch the verbal bracket, e.g.:

Seitdem Rodrigue seine Chronik begonnen hatte, freute er sich darauf, sie zu beschließen **mit der Darstellung der Regierung dieses seines lieben Schülers und Beichtkindes**

Ausklammerung is encountered under the following conditions:

(a) Adverbials which have the form of prepositional phrases are commonly excluded for the reasons given above, e.g.:

Vieles hatte Glum schon gesehen **auf seinem Weg von seiner Heimat bis über den Rhein hinweg** (*Böll*)
Hallo, ich rufe an **aus London** (*Telecom advert*)

In general, such exclusion is rather more typical of colloquial German than the formal written language. However, *Ausklammerung* is by no means uncommon in writing, especially if the prepositional phrase is lengthy or if a further clause (usually a relative clause) depends on the element excluded, e.g.:

Von hier aus konnte man noch wenig sehen **von der kleinen Stadt**, die am anderen Ufer im Nebel lag

(b) The only complement of the verb (cf. 18.1.2) which may regularly be excluded in standard German is a prepositional object, e.g.:

Er hätte das merken können **an den gelegentlichen Rückblicken und dem Arm,**
    der entspannt auf der freien Vorderlehne lag (*Johnson*)
Du solltest dich nicht zu sehr freuen **auf diese Entwicklung**

NB: As Engel (1988:316) points out, not all prepositional objects can be excluded in this way. For example, a sentence like *Ich habe vor dem Bahnhof gewartet* **auf meine Freundin** is unacceptable to many native speakers. As no clear rules can be given for which prepositional objects can be excluded and which not, it is advisable for the English learner to avoid such constructions in cases of doubt.

Other verb complements (e.g. the verb subject, the accusative and dative objects, place and direction complements) are not usually excluded in standard German, although *Ausklammerung* of lengthy elements is occasionally encountered in the written language, cf. the following example from Engel (1977:233):

Wir haben aus Steuergeldern gebaut **Wohnungen für nahezu zwanzigtausend Menschen**

Otherwise, such exclusions are restricted to substandard colloquial speech (and then only nouns, never pronouns), e.g.:

Gestern habe ich gesehen **Manfred Schuhmacher und Angela Hartmann**

(c) Exclusion of simple adverbs is common in colloquial speech, but rare in formal written German, e.g.:

Bei uns hat es Spätzle gegeben **heute**   Sie sollen leise reden **hier**
Ich bin nach Trier gefahren **deshalb**   Hat es euch gefallen **dort**?

22 Word formation

Knowing how complex words are made up in German is an invaluable aid in extending the foreign learner's vocabulary. The importance of being able to deduce the meaning of a whole word from its parts or to recognise patterns like *Dank – danken – dankbar – Dankbarkeit – Undankbarkeit* cannot be overestimated. Such series of related words are often much more transparent in German than English, with its mixed vocabulary, as we see when we compare the above with English *thanks – to thank – grateful – gratitude – ingratitude.*

This chapter deals with the most common and productive means of word formation in modern German. A short general introduction to the methods of word formation is given in 22.1, then the main individual parts of speech are treated in turn, i.e. the nouns (22.2), adjectives (22.3) and verbs (22.4 – 22.7). Fleischer (1974) gives extensive coverage to all aspects of the topic and his material has been widely drawn on here.

22.1 Methods of word formation

22.1.1 Complex words are formed from simpler words in three main ways, i.e.:

(a) by means of a prefix or a suffix
In general, prefixes and suffixes do not occur as words in their own right, but are only used with root-words to form other words, e.g.:
(i) Prefixes:

die Sprache → die **Ur**sprache

schön → **un**schön

stehen → **be**stehen

besser → **ver**bessern

(ii) Suffixes:

gemein → die Gemein**heit**

bedeuten → die Bedeut**ung**

der Freund → freund**lich**

denken → denk**bar**

der Motor → motor**isier**en

die Kontrolle → kontroll**ier**en

NB: Prefixes are most often used to create nouns from nouns, adjectives from adjectives or verbs from other verbs or from nouns and adjectives. Suffixes are most common to make nouns from adjectives or verbs or adjectives from nouns or verbs; they are little used in the formation of verbs.

485

(b) by means of vowel changes

These vowel changes are often associated with particular suffixes, but they sometimes occur on their own. We find the following types of vowel changes in word formation:

(i) Umlaut, e.g.:

der Arzt → die Ärztin	der Bart → bärtig
der Druck → drücken	scharf → schärfen

(ii) Ablaut, i.e. vowel changes like those used to form the tenses of strong verbs, cf. 12.1.2. In general, Ablaut is restricted in word formation to strong verb roots, e.g.:

aufsteigen → der Aufstieg	werfen → der Wurf
beißen → bissig	schließen → schlüssig

NB: These vowel changes, especially Ablaut, are barely still productive (cf.22.1.2) in modern German.

(c) by forming compound words

In compounding, a new word is made up from two (or more) existing words, e.g.:

der Staub + saugen → der Staubsauger	der Rat + das Haus → das Rathaus
hell + blau → hellblau	die Brust + schwimmen → brustschwimmen

Sometimes there is a linking element (German *Fugenelement*) between the two words, e.g.:

der Bauer + der Hof → der Bauernhof	das Land + der Mann → der Landsmann

The ease with which compounds may be formed is a distinctive and characteristic feature of German (and, for that matter, all the Germanic languages), compared to, say, French, Italian or Russian, and the extensive use of compounds is a typical feature of modern German, especially in technical registers.

NB: A distinction is usually made between word formation by 'derivation', i.e. by using prefixes, suffixes or vowel changes, and by 'compounding', which involves juxtaposing independent words.

22.1.2 If new words are still being created by a particular word formation pattern, that pattern is termed 'productive'.

For example, the suffix *-bar* is very commonly employed to make adjectives from nouns (= English *-able, -ible*, cf. 22.3.1a), and new words in *-bar* are regularly encountered, or, as Bergenholtz & Mugdan (1979) put it, *Solche Wörter sind jederzeit bildbar*.

On the other hand, although many abstract nouns from adjectives are found with the suffix *-e*, and Umlaut of the vowel where possible, e.g.:

groß – die Größe   gut – die Güte   hoch – die Höhe   lang – die Länge

this pattern is no longer productive. No new nouns are being created by this means and the pattern is 'unproductive'. Naturally, many of the words which were formed according to this pattern at a time when it was productive remain in the language.

In the later sections of this chapter we shall deal in the main with those types of word-formation which are still productive in modern German but attention will also be paid to those which, although no longer productive, still account for a significant number of words in the modern language.

22.2 The formation of nouns

22.2.1 Noun derivation by means of suffixes

The following suffixes are commonly found in noun derivation, although not all of them are fully productive. It should be noted that most noun suffixes are associated with a particular gender, see 1.1.

(a) *-chen, -lein* (neuter)
These suffixes are very productive and used to form diminutives from nouns, and the vowel of the stressed syllable usually has Umlaut if possible.

die Karte *card* → das Kärtchen *little card* die Stadt → das Städtchen *little town*
das Auge → das Äuglein *little eye*   das Buch → das Büchlein *little book*

-chen is the commoner in standard German, *-lein* being used principally with words ending in *-ch*, *-g* or *-ng*, in a few set words (like *Fräulein*) and in archaic or poetic language. It was originally south German, but, in practice, colloquial south German speech now uses other related forms from the local dialects, e.g. *-li* (Switzerland), *-(e)le* (Baden), *-la* (Franconia), *-(er)l* (Austria and Bavaria).

NB: (i) Nouns ending in *-e* or *-en* drop this before *-chen* and *lein*, e.g. *der Kasten → das Kästchen → die Pflanze das Pflänzchen*.
(ii) The double diminutive *-elchen* is sometimes used in North German speech with words ending in *-ch* or *-g*, e.g. *das Buch → das Büchelchen*.
(iii) There is no Umlaut in many recent derivations with *-chen*, in particular with names, e.g. *Kurtchen, Tantchen*.
(iv) In some cases, derivations with both *-chen* and *-lein* from the same root are used in standard German with a difference in meaning, e.g. *Fräulein* 'girl', *Frauchen* 'mistress' (e.g. of a dog), *Weibchen* 'female' (of an animal), *Weiblein* 'little woman'.
(v) In substandard colloquial speech, *-chen* is sometimes added to plurals in *-er*, e.g. *Kinderchen*.

(b) *-e* (feminine)
(i) Nouns in *-e* from verbs may denote an action or an instrument. The latter is still productive, especially in technical registers, e.g:

pflegen → die Pflege *care*   absagen → die Absage *refusal*
bremsen → die Bremse *brake*   leuchten → die Leuchte *light*

(ii) Nouns in *-e* from adjectives denote a quality. The vowel has Umlaut if possible. This pattern is no longer productive, having been replaced by *-heit* or *-(ig)keit*, see (e) below:

groß → die Größe *size*   stark → die Stärke *strength*

(c) *-ei, -erei* (feminine)
These suffixes are productive and are used to form nouns from verbs or from other nouns.
(i) Nouns in *-erei* from verbs are mainly pejorative, indicating a repeated, irritating action:

fragen → die Fragerei   *lots of annoying questions*

The basis may be a whole phrase, e.g.:

Rekorde haschen → die Rekordhascherei *record hunting*

-ei is used in the same sense from verbs in *-eln* and *-ern*:

lieben → die Liebelei *flirtation*

(ii) Nouns in *-ei* from nouns denote the place where something is done. The basis is often a noun in *-er*:

die Auskunft → die Auskunftei *information bureau*
der Bäcker → die Bäckerei *bakery*

The associated forms *-elei* and *-erei*, used with a noun base, have pejorative meanings of various kinds:

Fremdwörter → die Fremdwörtelei *using (too) many foreign words*
die Sklave → die Sklaverei *slavery*

(d) *-er, -ler, -ner* (masculine)
These productive suffixes are used to derive nouns from verbs or nouns. The root vowel occasionally has Umlaut, though this is rare with recent formations:
(i) Most nouns in *-er* from verbs denote the person who does something. They often indicate a profession:

einbrechen → der Einbrecher *burglar*   lehren → der Lehrer *teacher*
schreiben → der Schreiber *writer*   betteln → der Bettler *beggar*

The base may be a whole phrase:

einen Auftrag geben → der Auftraggeber *client, customer*

(ii) *-ler* (less commonly *-ner*) is used to derive nouns from other nouns to indicate the person who does something. Some are pejorative:

die Kunst → der Künstler *artist*   der Sport → der Sportler *sportsman*
die Wissenschaft → der Wissenschaftler *scientist*
der Profit → der Profitler *profiteer*   das Bühnenbild → der Bühnenbildner *stage designer*

NB: In some cases -*er* is used rather than -*ler* to form nouns from other nouns, e.g.:
   die Eisenbahn → der Eisenbahner *railway worker*
   die Taktik → der Taktiker *tactician*

(iii) Some nouns in -*er* from verbs denote the instrument used to perform the action:

bohren → der Bohrer *drill*   empfangen → der Empfänger *receiver*

The base is very often a whole phrase, especially in technical language:

Staub saugen → der Staubsauger *vacuum cleaner*

(iv) Nouns in -*er* from place names designate the inhabitants:

Frankfurt → der Frankfurter   Hamburg → der Hamburger
Wien → der Wiener   Österreich → der Österreicher

Some of these are rather irregular, e.g.:

Hannover → der Hannoveraner   Zürich → der Zürcher

(e) -*heit*, -(*ig*)*keit* (feminine)

These suffixes are used productively to form abstract nouns from adjectives denoting a quality:

bitter → die Bitterkeit *bitterness*   gleich → die Gleichheit *similarity*
eitel → die Eitelkeit *vanity*   heftig → die Heftigkeit *violence*
geschwind → die Geschwindigkeit *speed*   genau → die Genauigkeit *precision*

NB: The distribution of the forms -*heit*, -*keit* and -*igkeit* is not wholly regular. In general, -*heit* is the most common form. -*keit* is used with adjectives ending in -*bar*, -*ig*, -*lich* and -*sam* and with <u>most</u> in -*el* and -*er* (but not all, cf. *die Dunkelheit, die Sicherheit*). -*igkeit* is used with adjectives ending in -*haft* and -*los* (e.g. *die Glaubhaftigkeit*) and a few others.

(f) -*in* (feminine)

The productive suffix -*in* forms nouns denoting the feminine of most persons and many animals. The root vowel usually has Umlaut:

der Arzt → die Ärztin *lady doctor*   der Fuchs → die Füchsin *vixen*

NB: For the use of these feminine forms denoting professions in modern German, see 1.1.4a.

(g) -*ling* (masculine)

This productive suffix is used to form nouns from verbs or adjectives.
(i) Nouns in -*ling* from verbs denote persons who are the object of the verbal action:

prüfen → der Prüfling *examinee*   strafen → der Sträfling *prisoner*

(ii) Nouns in -*ling* from adjectives designate persons possessing that quality, often (but not always) with a pejorative sense:

feige → der Feigling *coward*   fremd → der Fremdling *stranger*

NB: Similar formations denoting plants and animals are common, e.g. *der Grünling* 'greenfinch', but they are no longer productive.

(h) *-nis* (neuter or feminine)

Nouns in *-nis* are abstract nouns from verbs or adjectives. Those from verbs (which often have irregular forms or use the past participle as a base) often denote the result of the verbal action. The suffix is no longer productive:

ersparen → das Ersparnis *savings* gestehen → das Geständnis *confession*
erkennen → die Erkenntnis *recognition* erleben → das Erlebnis *experience*
finster → die Finsternis *darkness* geheim → das Geheimnis *secret*

(i) *-schaft* (feminine)

The productive use of this suffix is to form nouns from other nouns designating a collective or a state:

der Student → die Studentenschaft *student body*
der Freund → die Freundschaft *friendship*

NB: Other derivational patterns with *-schaft*, i.e. from adjectives (e.g. *die Schwangerschaft* 'pregnancy') or from participles (e.g. *die Errungenschaft* 'achievement') are no longer productive.

(j) *-tum* (neuter)

-tum is used productively in modern German with nouns referring to persons to form nouns denoting institutions, collectives or characteristic features:

der Papst → das Papsttum *papacy*
der Beamte → das Beamtentum *civil servants*
der Deutsche → das Deutschtum *German ethos*

(k) *-ung* (feminine)

This is the most frequent productive suffix used to form nouns from verbs which refer to the action indicated by the verb, e.g.:

bedeuten *mean* → die Bedeutung *meaning* bilden *form* → die Bildung *formation*
landen *land* → die Landung *landing* töten *kill* → die Tötung *killing*

22.2.2 Noun derivation by means of prefixes

All these prefixes except *Ge-* are usually stressed. The gender of nouns with prefixes is the same as that of the root noun, with the exception of those in *Ge-*, which are neuter if they result from productive derivation, cf. 1.1.8c.

(a) *Erz-*
= 'arch-', 'out and out':

der Bischof → der Erzbischof *archbishop*
der Gauner → der Erzgauner *out and out scoundrel*

(b) *Ge-*

Nouns in *Ge-* (often with the suffix *-e* in addition) can be formed from verbs or from other nouns in modern German:

(i) Nouns in *Ge-* from verbs denote a repeated or protracted activity. They often have a pejorative sense, like nouns in *-erei*, cf. 23.2.1, to which *Ge-* is often an alternative:

laufen → das Gelauf(e) *running about, bustle* (esp. to no real purpose)
schwätzen → das Geschwätz(e) *idle talk, gossip*

(ii) Nouns in *Ge-* from other nouns are collectives. The root vowel has Umlaut if possible (and *-e-* changes to *-i-*):

der Ast → das Geäst *branches*   der Berg → das Gebirge *mountain range*

(c) *Grund-*

= 'basic', 'essential':

die Tendenz → die Grundtendenz *basic tendency*

(d) *Haupt-*

= 'main':

der Bahnhof → der Hauptbahnhof *main station*

(e) *Miß-*

Miß- designates an opposite or a negative, sometimes with a pejorative sense:

der Brauch → der Mißbrauch *misuse*   der Erfolg → der Mißerfolg *failure*

NB: *Fehl-* is nowadays probably more productive than *Miß-* in modern German to express an opposite or a negative, e.g.
die Einschätzung → die Fehleinschätzung *false estimation*

(f) *Mit-*

= *co-*, etc.:

der Arbeiter → der Mitarbeiter *colleague, collaborator*
der Reisende → der Mitreisende *fellow traveller*

(g) *Nicht-*

= *non-*:

der Raucher → der Nichtraucher *non-smoker*

(h) *Riesen-*

Riesen- is particularly common in colloquial speech with an augmentative sense:

der Erfolg → der Riesenerfolg *enormous success*

NB: Colloquial German is rich in other augmentative prefixes, e.g.:
Superhit, Spitzenbelastung, Bombengeschäft, Heidenlärm, Höllendurst, Mordsapparat, Topmanager, etc.

(j) *Rück-*

This prefix occurs with many nouns related to verbs in *zurück-*:

die Fahrt → die Rückfahrt *return journey* (cf.: *zurückfahren*)

NB: *Zurück-* is usually retained with nouns in *-ung* from verbs, cf. *zurückhalten* → *die Zurückhaltung*.

(k) *Un-*
= opposite, abnormal:

die Ruhe → die Unruhe *unrest*   das Wetter → das Unwetter *bad weather*
der Mensch → der Unmensch *inhuman person*   die Summe → die Unsumme *vast sum*

(l) *Ur-*
= 'original':

die Sprache → die Ursprache *original language*

22.3 The formation of adjectives

22.3.1 Adjective derivation by means of suffixes

(a) *-bar*
This very productive suffix forms adjectives from verbs with the sense of English *-able, -ible*, e.g.:

brauchen → brauchbar *usable*   essen → eßbar *edible*

NB: Adjectives in *-bar* are a frequent alternative to passive constructions, cf. 15.4.9.

(b) *-(e)n, -ern*
These suffixes are formed from nouns denoting a material. The adjective indicates that the qualified noun is made from that material. The form *-ern* is normally associated with Umlaut if possible:

das Gold → golden *golden*   das Holz → hölzern *wooden*
das Silber → sibern *silver*   der Stahl → stählern *steel*

NB: Note the difference between adjectives in *-(e)n* or *-ern* and those in *-ig* from the same noun, e.g. *silbern* '(made of) silver', *silbrig* 'silvery' (i.e. like silver), cf. (d) below.

(c) *-haft*
Adjectives formed from nouns with the suffix *-haft* indicate a quality like the person or thing denoted by the noun, e.g.:

der Greis → greisenhaft *senile*   der Held → heldenhaft *heroic*

(d) *-ig*
This is a common and productive suffix, often associated with Umlaut. It is mainly used to form adjectives from nouns:
(i) with the idea of possessing what is denoted by the noun, e.g.:

das Haar → haarig *hairy*   der Staub → staubig *dusty*

(ii) indicating a quality like the person or thing denoted by the noun:

die Milch → milchig *milky*   der Riese → riesig *gigantic*

NB: Adjectives in -*ig* are frequently formed from whole noun phrases, e.g. *blauäugig* 'blue-eyed', *heißblütig* 'hot-blooded'.

(iii) indicating duration (from time expressions):

zwei Stunden → zweistündig *lasting two hours*

NB: Note the difference in meaning between adjectives from time expressions in -*ig* (which express duration) and in -*lich* (which express frequency), see also (f) below. Compare *zweistündig* with *zweistündlich* 'every two hours'.

(iv) -*ig* is used to form adjectives from adverbs, e.g.:

dort → dortig   hier → hiesig   heute → heutig
morgen → morgig   ehemals → ehemalig   sonst → sonstig

(e) -*isch*
This is a common and productive suffix, used mainly to form adjectives from nouns. Its chief uses are:
(i) to form adjectives from proper names and geographical names:

Homer → homerisch *Homeric*   Europa → europäisch *European*
Sachsen → sächsisch *Saxon*   England → englisch *English*

(ii) to form adjectives which indicate a quality like that of the person or thing denoted by the noun. These are often pejorative:

der Held → heldisch *heroic*   der Wähler → wählerisch *fastidious*
das Kind → kindisch *puerile*   der Herr → herrisch *imperious*

Compare the clearly pejorative *bäuerisch* 'boorish' with the neutral *bäuerlich* 'rustic'.
(iii) to form adjectives from foreign words:

die Biologie → biologisch *biological*   die Mode → modisch *fashionable*
die Musik → musikalisch *musical*   der Nomade → nomadisch *nomadic*

(f) -*lich*
A common suffix with a wide range of functions. Adjectives formed with -*lich* often have Umlaut:
(i) Adjectives from nouns in -*lich* indicate a relationship to that person or thing, or indicate the possession of the quality denoted by it:

der Arzt → ärztlich *medical*   der Preis → preislich *in respect of price*
der Fürst → fürstlich *princely*   der Tod → tödlich *fatal, deadly*

NB This is the only use of -*lich* which is still productive in modern German.

(ii) Adjectives in -*lich* from time expressions denote frequency:

zwei Stunden → zweistündlich *every two hours*

NB: For the difference between adjectives in -*ig* and -*lich* from time expressions, see (d) above.

(iii) Adjectives in *-lich* from verbs indicate ability:

bestechen→ bestechlich *corruptible*   verkaufen→ verkäuflich *saleable*

NB: This use of *-lich* is no longer productive, having been replaced by *-bar*, see (a) above

(iv) Adjectives in *-lich* from other adjectives usually indicate a lesser degree of the relevant quality:

rot→ rötlich *reddish*   klein→ kleinlich *petty*
krank→ kränklich *sickly*   arm→ ärmlich *shabby; humble*

(g) *-los*

*-lo*s is used to form adjectives from nouns and corresponds to English *-less*:

die Hoffnung → hoffnungslos *hopeless*   die Wahl → wahllos *indiscriminate*

(h) *-mäßig*

This is very productive in modern German, especially in formal registers, to derive adjectives from nouns:

(i) with the sense of 'in accordance with':

die Gewohnheit → gewohnheitsmäßig *habitual*
der Plan → planmäßig *according to plan*

NB: *-gemäß* is often an alternative to *-mäßig* in this sense, but it is rather less common, e.g.
      plangemäß, ordnungsgemäß.

(ii) with the sense of 'in respect of something':

der Instinkt → instinktmäßig *instinctive*
der Verkehr → verkehrsmäßig *relating to traffic*

(iii) with the sense of 'like someone or something':

der Fürst → fürstenmäßig *princely*
das Lehrbuch → lehrbuchmäßig *like a textbook*

(j) *-sam*

This suffix is barely productive in modern German. Adjectives in *-sam* have two main sources:

(i) from verbs (especially reflexive verbs), expressing a possibility or a tendency:

sich biegen → biegsam *flexible*   sparen → sparsam *thrifty*

(ii) from nouns, indicating a quality:

die Furcht → furchtsam *timid*   die Gewalt → gewaltsam *violent*

22.3.2 Adjective derivation by means of prefixes

These prefixes are usually stressed, although *un-* may not be in some words. They are all used to form adjectives from other adjectives.

(a) *erz-, grund-, hoch-*

These prefixes all have intensifying meaning, with *erz-* mainly used with a rather negative sense, whereas *grund-* and *hoch-* tend to be more positive.

Both *erz-* and *grund-* are rather limited in use:

reaktionär → erzreaktionär *very reactionary*
ehrlich → grundehrlich *thoroughly honest*
verschieden → grundverschieden *totally different*
begabt → hochbegabt *highly talented*
intelligent → hochintelligent *very intelligent*

(b) *un-*

Like English *un-*, it negates and/or produces an opposite meaning:

artig → unartig *naughty*   vorsichtig → unvorsichtig *incautious*
wahrscheinlich → unwahrscheinlich *improbable*

NB: (i) Where an adjective already has a simple word as an antonym (e.g. *klug* vs. *dumm*), the form in *un-* gives a negative rather than an opposite. Thus whilst *dumm* means 'stupid', *unklug* means 'not clever'.
(ii) In general, only adjectives with a positive meaning can form an opposite with *un-*. Thus, whilst *unschön* (← *schön*) is fairly common, one does not find *unhäßlich* (← *häßlich*).

(c) *ur-*

ur- with adjectives usually intensifies the sense:

alt → uralt *very old*   komisch → urkomisch *very comical*
Sometimes, it gives the idea of 'original' or 'typical':

deutsch → urdeutsch *typically German*

22.4 The formation of verbs: inseparable prefixes

Verbs may be formed from nouns, adjectives or other verbs by means of the prefixes *be-*, *emp-*, *ent-*, *er-*, *ge-*, *ver-* and *zer-*. They are termed 'inseparable' prefixes because they always remain attached to the root. They are always unstressed, whereas separable prefixes are stressed, cf. 22.5.

Many patterns of word-formation with inseparable prefixes are common or productive, and the most important are given in the following sections, arranged according to the individual prefixes.

NB: Some prefixes, e.g. *durch-*, *über-*, *um-*, *unter-*, may be separable or inseparable. They are treated in 22.6.

22.4.1 *be-*

With a very few exceptions, verbs with the prefix *be-* are transitive.

(a) *be-* is commonly and productively used to make intransitive verbs transitive,

cf. 18.3.5b. The simple intransitive verb may be used with a dative object

or a prepositional object, which becomes the accusative object of the verb
with *be-*, e.g.:

jemanden bedienen *serve sb.* (cf. jemand**em** dienen)
eine Frage beantworten *answer a question* (cf. **auf** eine Frage antworten)

(b) *be-* used with transitive verbs can change the action to a different object:

jemanden mit etwas beliefern *supply sb. with sth.*
(cf. etwas an jemanden liefern *deliver sth. to sb.*)

(c) *be-* is used to make verbs from nouns with the idea of providing with something
In some cases the suffix *-ig-* is added:

das Wasser → bewässern *irrigate*   der Reifen → bereifen *put tyres on*
die Nachricht → benachrichtigen *notify*

(d) *be-* is used to make verbs from adjectives with the sense of giving someone or something that quality
In some cases the suffix *-ig-* is added:

feucht → befeuchten *moisten*   frei → befreien *liberate*
gerade → begradigen *straighten*

22.4.2 *ent-*

(a) Verbs in *ent-* formed from verbs of motion have the idea of escaping or going away
What is being escaped from usually appears as a dative object with these
verbs, cf. 18.4.1c, e.g.:

gleiten → jemandem entgleiten *slip away from sb.* (e.g. glass from hand)
laufen → jemandem/etwas entlaufen *run away/escape from sb./sth.*
reißen → jemandem etwas entreißen *snatch sth. from sb.*

(b) Verbs in *ent-* from nouns, adjectives or other verbs often have the sense of removing something
This sense of *ent-* often corresponds to the English prefixes *de-* or *dis-*:

das Gift → entgiften *decontaminate*   der Mut → entmutigen *discourage*
scharf → entschärfen *tone down*   spannen → entspannen *relax*

NB: The prefix *emp-* is a variant form of *ent-* used before some roots beginning with *f*, e.g.
    empfehlen, empfinden.

22.4.3 *er-*

(a) Verbs in *er-* formed from other verbs often express the achievement or conclusion of an action:

bitten → erbitten *get (sth.) by asking for it*   schießen → erschießen *shoot (sb.) dead*

A distinctive and productive use of *er-* is to form verbs from verbs or nouns with the idea of acquiring something by the action expressed by the simple verb or implied in the noun, cf. *erbitten* above and the following:

arbeiten → Er hat etwas **er**arbeitet *He got sth. by working for it*
die List → Er hat etwas **er**listet *He got sth. through cunning*

NB: A few verbs in *er-* from other verbs point to the start of an action, e.g. *erklingen* 'ring out', *erbeben* 'tremble'.

(b) Verbs in *er-* formed from adjectives express a change of state,
i.e. either intransitive verbs with the idea of becoming sth., or transitive verbs with the idea of making somebody or something have the quality expressed by the adjective, e.g.:

blind → erblinden *become blind*   rot → erröten *turn red, blush*
frisch → erfrischen *refresh (sb./sth.)*   leichter → erleichtern *make (sth.) easier*

22.4.4 *ver-*

This is the most widely used of these prefixes, and it has a range of different uses. The following are the most frequent or productive:

(a) Many verbs in *ver-* formed from other verbs express the idea of finishing or 'away':

blühen → verblühen *fade* (of flowers)   brauchen → verbrauchen *use up, consume*
hungern → verhungern *starve to death*   klingen → verklingen *fade away* (of sounds)

(b) A number of verbs in *ver-* formed from other verbs convey the notion of 'wrongly' or 'to excess'

biegen → verbiegen *bend out of shape*   lernen → verlernen *unlearn, forget*
salzen → versalzen *put too much salt in sth.*

Some reflexive verbs in *ver-* have the idea of making a mistake, e.g.:

fahren → sich verfahren *get lost, take a wrong turning*
wählen → sich verwählen *misdial*

A few verbs in *ver-* are opposites, e.g.:

achten → verachten *despise*   kaufen → verkaufen *sell*

(c) Verbs in *ver-* formed from adjectives often express a change of state
As with *er-*, cf. 22.4.3, these may be intransitive verbs with the idea of becoming sth., or transitive verbs with the idea of making somebody or something have the quality expressed by the adjective, e.g.:

arm → verarmen *become poor*   stumm → verstummen *become silent*
einfach → vereinfachen *simplify*   länger → verlängern *make (sth.) longer*

A number of verbs in *ver-* from nouns have a similar meaning, e.g.:

das Unglück → verunglücken *have an accident*
der Sklave → versklaven *enslave*

(d) Many verbs formed from nouns with *ver-* convey the idea of providing with something:

das Glas → verglasen *glaze*   das Gold → vergolden *gild*
der Körper → verkörpern *embody*   der Zauber → verzaubern *enchant*

22.4.5 *zer-*

Verbs in *zer-*, which are usually formed from other verbs, always convey the notion of 'in pieces', e.g.:

beißen → zerbeißen *bite into pieces*   brechen → zerbrechen *smash*
fallen → zerfallen *distintegrate*   streuen → zerstreuen *scatter, disperse*

22.5 The formation of verbs: separable prefixes

22.5.1 Separable prefixes: general

Most separable prefixes also exist as independent words, usually as prepositions, nouns, adverbs or adjectives. Thus, they are not just used in word formation, as the inseparable prefixes dealt with in 22.4 are, and their meanings in both uses are often closely related. The following points relate to all separable prefixes, including the variable prefixes dealt with in 22.6 when they are used separably:

(a) In main clauses (statements, questions or commands), the prefix is placed at the end of the clause
It thus forms the second part of the 'verbal bracket', cf. 21.1.2, e.g.:

ausgehen: Sie geht heute mit meinem Bruder **aus**
ablehnen: Lehnen Sie mein Angebot **ab**?
aufhören: Hören Sie sofort damit **auf**

(b) Separable prefixes join with the finite verb at the end of a subordinate clause, e.g.:

Sie hat gesagt, daß sie heute abend mit meinem Bruder **aus**geht

(c) Separable prefixes are joined to the non-finite forms of verbs,
cf. also 12.2.2j and 13.1.3. The prefixes precede the *ge-* of the past participle and the *zu* of the extended infinitive, the whole being written as a single word, e.g.:

Infinitive *ausgehen*   Inf. with *zu*: *auszugehen*
Present participle: *ausgehend*   Past participle: *ausgegangen*

(d) Double prefixes, i.e. separable prefixes added to verbs with an inseparable prefix
With these, the separable prefix is treated as such and detached from the verb in the same way as for verbs with a simple prefix, e.g.:

anerkennen *acknowledge*:

Ich erkenne seine Leistungen **an** . . .,	um seine Leistungen **an**zuerkennen
Wenn ich seine Leistungen **an**erkenne	Seine Leistungen werden **an**erkannt

Similarly:

anvertrauen *entrust*	**aus**verkaufen *sell out*
beibehalten *retain*	**vor**enthalten *withhold*

(e) Separable prefixes are always stressed, e.g.:

'angeben, vor'aussagen, hin'ausgehen, 'anerkennen, 'teilnehmen

(f) Separable prefixes used in initial position in a statement are written separately from the verb, e.g.:

Fest steht, daß . . .	*It is certain that . . .*
Hinzu kommt, daß . . .	*Add to this the fact that . . .*

22.5.2 Simple separable prefixes

The majority of these derive from prepositions or adverbs and their meanings are often transparent. The examples below illustrate some common and productive patterns of derivation.

NB: Prefixes from prepositions expressing direction (e.g. *ab-, an-, auf-*, etc.) frequently have a less transparent or figurative sense because direction can be indicated by using a prefix with *her-* or *hin-*, cf. 7.3.4.

(a) *ab-*
(i) = 'away':

abfahren *depart, leave*	**ab**fliegen *take off*

(ii) = 'down':

absteigen *get down*	**ab**setzen *put, set down*

(iii) indicating finishing, achieving or completing an action:

abdrehen *switch off*	**ab**laufen *wear out* (i.e. shoes)

(b) *an-*
(i) with the idea of approaching:

ankommen *arrive*	**an**reden *address (sb.)*

(ii) indicating the start of an action, or doing sth. partially:

andrehen *switch on*	**an**brennen *catch fire, get scorched*

(c) *auf-*
(i) = 'up' or 'on'

aufbleiben *stay up*	**auf**setzen *put on* (e.g. hat, water)

(ii) with the idea of a sudden start:

auflachen *burst out laughing*	**auf**klingen *ring out*

(d) *aus-*
= 'out', often pointing to the completion of an action:

ausbrennen *burn out*   **aus**dorren *dry up*

(e) *ein-*
ein- is related to the preposition *in* and frequently conveys the idea of becoming accustomed to something:

einfahren *run in* (i.e. new car)   sich **ein**leben *settle down*

(f) *los-*
Most often with the meaning of beginning something:

losgehen *set off; start*   **los**reißen *tear off, away*

(g) *mit-*
Usually with the idea of accompanying or cooperating:

mitgehen *go with sb.*   **mit**arbeiten *cooperate*

(h) *vor-*
(i) with the idea of going forward or preceding:

vorgehen *go ahead; be fast* (clock)   **vor**stoßen *push forward; attack*

(ii) with the idea of demonstrating something:

vorlesen *read out aloud*   **vor**machen *show sb. how to do sth.*

(j) *weg-*
= 'away':

wegbleiben *stay away*   **weg**laufen *run away*

NB:*fort-* is a possible, if rather less frequently used alternative to *weg-* with some verbs, e.g. *fortbleiben, fortlaufen*.

(k) Other simple prefixes are less frequent or no longer productive:
Selected examples:

bei-:	**bei**treten *join* (e.g. club)	**bei**tragen *contribute*
da-:	**da**bleiben *stay on/behind*	**da**stehen *stand there*
dar-:	**dar**stellen *portray, depict, represent*	
fehl-:	**fehl**gehen *miss one's way*	**fehl**greifen *miss one's hold*
inne-:	**inne**haben *occupy* (position)	**inne**halten *pause*
nach-:	**nach**ahmen *imitate*	**nach**gehen *follow*
nieder-:	**nieder**brennen *burn down*	**nieder**lassen *lower, let down*
zu-:	**zu**drehen *turn off* (tap)	**zu**steigen *get on, board* (train)

22.5.3 Compound separable prefixes

(a) A number of compound elements, mostly deriving from adverbs, have come to be used widely as separable prefixes with a number of verbs
Selected examples:

dabei- (indicating proximity):   **dabei**stehen *stand close by*

daneben- (indicating missing sth.):	**daneben**schießen *miss* (a shot)
davon- (meaning 'away'):	**davon**eilen *hurry away*
dazu- (indicating an addition):	**dazu**kommen *be added*
empor- (meaning 'upwards'):	**empor**blicken *look up*
entgegen- (meaning 'towards'):	**entgegen**nehmen *receive, accept*
überein- (indicating agreement):	**überein**kommen *agree*
voraus- (= 'in advance'):	**voraus**sagen *foretell, predict*
vorbei-, vorüber- (= 'past')	**vorbei**gehen *pass*

NB: *vorbei-* is generally commoner than *vorüber-*, especially in spoken registers, except when referring to time, e.g. *Der Winter ging vorüber.*

zurück- (= 'back')	**zurück**fahren *drive back, return*
zusammen- (= 'together' or 'up')	**zusammen**rücken *move together*
	zusammenfalten *fold up*

NB: (i) Compound prefixes of direction formed with *hin-* and *her-* are treated fully in 7.3.4.
(ii) A few other compound elements, e.g. *drauf-, hintan-, vorweg-, zuvor-* are used with one or two verbs only, for instance *hintansetzen* 'put last', *vorwegnehmen* 'anticipate'.

(b) Compound prefixes consisting of a preposition with *einander*

Compounds of a preposition with *einander* (cf. 3.2.7) are written together with the verb if the whole can be understood as expressing a single concept, e.g.:

Ich habe die Bücher aufeinandergelegt	*I stacked the books*
aneinandergrenzende Grundstücke	*adjacent plots of land*
Es hat sich gezeigt, daß die Meinungen hierüber auseinandergehen	*It has become evident that opinions differ about this*

However, if genuine reciprocity is involved (i.e. = 'each other'), or if the compound with *einander* is the equivalent of an adverb, it is written as a separate word, e.g.:

Wir haben aneinander gedacht	*We thought of each other*
Die beiden Läufer sind nacheinander gestartet	*The two runners set off one after the other*

22.5.4 A large number of nouns, adjectives, adverbs, participles and infinitives are used as separable prefixes,

e.g. *statt*finden 'take place':

Es findet heute im Saal **statt**	Da es heute im Saal **statt**findet, . . .
Es hat gestern **statt**gefunden	

(a) Many of these are unique combinations with a single verb, e.g.:
(i) with a noun:

teilnehmen (an D) *participate* (*in*)	**acht**geben (auf A) *pay heed* (*to*)

(ii) with an adjective:

liebgewinnen *grow fond of*	**offen**lassen *leave open*

(iii) with an adverb:

fernsehen *watch television*   **schwarz**arbeiten *moonlight*

(iv) with a participle:

gefangennehmen *take prisoner*   **verloren**gehen *get lost*

(v) with an infinitive:

kennenlernen *meet, get to know*   **spazieren**gehen *go for a walk*

NB: Some verbs look as if they have prefixes, but they are formed from compound nouns and the first element does not separate, e.g. *frühstücken* 'breakfast': *Ich frühstücke, habe gefrühstückt*, etc.
Similarly:
frohlocken (elev.) *rejoice*   handhaben *manipulate*
liebkosen *caress*   langweilen *bore*
wetteifern *compete*

(b) These elements are treated as separable prefixes if the resulting combination has a distinctive new meaning

This is illustrated by the examples in (a) above. On the other hand, if the element concerned and the verb retain their literal meanings, they are not written together and the element is not treated as a separable prefix. In such cases, the element concerned and the verb are stressed separately. Compare:

Er hat mir 'weitergeholfen   *He went on helping me*
Ich werde dir 'weiter 'helfen   *I shall help you again*
Sie hat es mir 'leichtgemacht, die   *She made it easy for me to get the*
   Stelle zu bekommen   *   job*
Das hat sie mir sehr 'leicht ge'macht   *She made that very easy for me*
'fallenlassen   *drop* (figuratively, i.e. plan, member of team, remark)
'fallen 'lassen   *drop* (literally, i.e. book, plate, cup, etc.)
'stehenbleiben   *stop*
'stehen 'bleiben   *remain standing*

NB: Compounds of *sein* and *werden* are written together only in their non-finite forms, e.g.:
dasein: wenn wir da sind <u>but</u> Wir sind dagewesen
loswerden: wenn ich es los werde <u>but</u> um es loszuwerden

(c) A few verbs are still in the process of developing into true separable verbs

This results in a number of uncertainties and anomalies with the following verbs:

(i) *radfahren* 'cycle' and *maschineschreiben* 'type'
With these verbs the prefix is still spelled as a noun, with a capital letter, when it is separated, e.g.:

Wir wollen radfahren   Wir sind radgefahren   Da ich gern radfahre, . . .
Ich habe früher nicht maschinegeschrieben   ein maschinegeschriebener Brief
BUT: Ich fahre gern **Rad**   Ich schreibe nicht **Maschine**

NB: *maschineschreiben* is only used intransitively, and in practice *tippen* is much more frequent for 'type'.

(ii) *notlanden* 'make a forced landing'
This is generally an inseparable verb, e.g. *Wir notlandeten*. However, the past participle and extended infinitive have the forms *not*gelandet and *not*zulanden.
(iii) With a number of verbs the noun or adverb is still always treated as a separate element, although it occupies the position of a separable prefix in the clause, cf. also 23.2.1, e.g.:

auswendig lernen *learn by heart*	jdm Bescheid sagen *inform sb.*
Bescheid wissen *be informed*	Klavier spielen *play the piano*
sich satt essen *eat one's fill*	Schach spielen *play chess*
Schi laufen *ski*	Schlittschuh laufen *skate*

(d) A number of compounds are restricted to the infinitive or the infinitive and the past participle.
This type of defective compound verb is particularly frequent in technical German.
(i) infinitive only, e.g.:

brustschwimmen *swim breast-stroke*	kettenrauchen *chain-smoke*
segelfliegen *glide*	wettlaufen *race*

(ii) infinitive and past participle only, e.g.:

seiltanzen *walk the tightrope*	uraufführen *perform for the first time*

22.6 The formation of verbs: variable prefixes

A small number of prefixes can form both separable and inseparable verbs. As a rule, the verb is separable if the prefix is stressed, if it is inseparable, it is unstressed.

22.6.1 *durch-*

This prefix always has the idea of *through*, whether separable or inseparable.

(a) A few compounds with *durch-* are only inseparable, i.e.:

durch'leben *experience*	durch'löchern *make holes in*
durch'denken *think through*	

NB 'durchdenken is also found with identical meaning, but it is less common

(b) A large number of compounds with *durch-* are only separable, e.g.:

'durchblicken *look through*	'durchfallen *fall through; fail*
'durchführen *carry out*	'durchhalten *hold out, survive*
'durchkommen *get through, succeed*	'durchkriechen *crawl through*
'durchrosten *rust through*	'durchsehen *look through*

(c) Many verbs form separable <u>and</u> inseparable compounds with *durch-*
The separable compounds always mean 'right the way through'. The inseparable verbs emphasize penetration without necessarily reaching the other side. However, the distinction may be fine, especially with verbs of motion, e.g.:

Er eilte durch die Vorhalle durch	*He hurried through the vestibule*
Er durcheilte die Vorhalle	*He hurried across the vestibule*
Er ritt durch den Wald durch	*He crossed the forest on horseback*
Er durchritt den Wald	*He rode through the forest*

Similarly:

durchbrechen *break through*	durchdringen *penetrate*
durchfahren *travel through*	durchlaufen *run through*
durchreisen *travel through*	durchschauen *see through*
'durchsetzen *carry through*	durch'setzen *infiltrate*
durchstoßen *break through*	durchwachen *stay awake*

22.6.2 *hinter-*

(a) All the commonly used compounds of *hinter-* are inseparable, e.g.:

hinter'gehen *deceive*	hinter'lassen *leave, bequeathe*
hinter'legen *deposit*	hinter'treiben *foil, thwart*

(b) Separable compounds with *hinter-* are restricted to substandard regional speech, e.g.:

'hintergehen *go to the back*

22.6.3 *miß-*

(a) *miß-* is generally inseparable.
It has two main senses, i.e.:
(i) opposite, e.g.:

mißachten *despise, disdain*	mißtrauen *distrust*

(ii) badly, wrongly, e.g.:

mißdeuten *misinterpret*	mißhandeln *ill-treat*

(b) With a few verbs the prefix may be treated as separable in the past participle and the infinitive with *zu*,
e.g. *mißgeachtet, mißzuachten*, cf.13.1.3. These forms are alternatives to the regular inseparable forms *mißachtet, zu mißachten* and are generally less frequent, with the exception of *mißverstehen*, where the stress is always on the prefix (i.e. *'mißverstehen*) and the extended infinitive normally has the form *mißzuverstehen*.

22.6.4 *über-*

(a) A few compounds with *über* are only separable
They are all intransitive and have the literal meaning 'over', e.g.:

'überhängen *overhang* 'überkippen *keel over*
'überkochen *boil over*

(b) A large number of compounds with *über-* are only inseparable
They are all transitive and have a variety of meanings, i.e.:

(i) repetition: über'arbeiten *rework* über'prüfen *check*
(ii) more than enough: über'fordern *overtax* über'treiben *exaggerate*
(iii) failing to notice: über'hören *fail to hear* über'sehen *overlook*
(iv) 'over': über'denken *think over* über'fallen *attack*

(c) Many verbs form separable <u>and</u> inseparable compounds with *über-*.
The separable compounds are mostly intransitive. They all have the literal meaning *over*. The inseparable verbs are mostly transitive, with a more figurative meaning, e.g.:

	Separable	**Inseparable**
überfahren	*cross over*	*knock down*
überführen	*transfer*	*convict*
übergehen	*turn into sth.*	*leave out*
überlaufen	*overflow; desert*	*overrun*
überlegen	*put sth. over sb./sth.*	*consider*
übersetzen	*ferry over*	*translate*
überspringen	*jump over*	*skip*
übertreten	*change over*	*infringe*
überziehen	*put on*	*cover*

22.6.5 *um-*

(a) A large number of compounds in *um-* are only separable
The majority express the idea of turning or changing a state, e.g.:

'umblicken *look round* 'umbringen *kill*
'umdrehen *turn round* 'umfallen *fall over*
'umschalten *switch* 'umsteigen *change* (trains, etc.)

(b) Many compounds in *um-* are only inseparable.
They all express encirclement or surrounding, e.g.:

um'armen *embrace* um'fassen *embrace, encircle*
um'geben *surround* um'ringen *surround*
um'segeln *sail round, circumnavigate* um'zingeln *surround, encircle*

(c) Many verbs form separable <u>and</u> inseparable compounds in *um-*
The difference in meaning corresponds to that given in (a) and (b) above, e.g.:

	Separable	Inseparable
umbauen	*rebuild*	*enclose*
umbrechen	*break up*	*set* (i.e. type)
umfahren	*run over, knock down*	*travel round*
umgehen	*circulate*	*avoid*
umreißen	*tear down*	*outline*
umschreiben	*rewrite*	*paraphrase*
umstellen	*rearrange*	*surround*

22.6.6 *unter-*

(a) A large number of compounds in *unter-* are only separable
They generally have a literal meaning, i.e. 'under', e.g.:

'unterbringen *accommodate*   'untergehen *sink, decline*
'unterkommen *find accommodation*   'untersetzen *put underneath*

(b) Many compounds in *unter-* are only inseparable
They have a variety of meanings, i.e.:
(i) less than enough:

unter'bieten *undercut*   unter' schätzen *underestimate*
unter'schreiten *fall short*   unter'steuern *understeer*
(ii) 'under':

unter'drücken *suppress; oppress*   unter'liegen *be defeated*
unter'schreiben *sign*   unter'stützen *support*
(iii) other, miscellaneous meanings:

unter'bleiben *cease*   unter'brechen *interrupt*
unter'lassen *refrain from*   unter'laufen *occur*
unter'richten *teach*   unter'sagen *forbid, prohibit*
unter'suchen *investigate*

(c) Many verbs form separable <u>and</u> inseparable compounds with *unter-*
The separable verbs are mostly intransitive and have the meaning 'under'.
The inseparable compounds are all transitive. Most have a more figurative meaning, e.g.:

	Separable	Inseparable
unterbinden	*tie underneath*	*prevent*
untergraben	*dig in*	*undermine*
unterhalten	*hold underneath*	*entertain*
unterlegen	*put underneath*	*underlay*
unterschieben	*foist*	*insinuate*
unterschlagen	*cross* (e.g. legs)	*embezzle*
unterstellen	*keep, store*	*assume*
unterziehen	*put on underneath*	*undergo*

22.6.7 *voll-*

(a) Many verbs form compounds with *voll-* which are only separable
They all have the meaning 'full', e.g.:

'vollbekommen *manage to fill*
'vollschreiben *fill with writing*

'vollstopfen *cram full*
'volltanken *fill up* (car)

(b) A few compounds with *voll-* are only inseparable
Most of these are words of formal registers with the meaning 'complete', 'finish' or 'accomplish', e.g.:

voll'bringen *achieve, accomplish*
voll'führen *execute, perform*
voll'ziehen *execute, carry out*

voll'enden *complete*
voll'strecken *execute, carry out*

22.6.8 *wider-*

(a) *wider-* is in most cases used to form inseparable verbs, e.g.:

wider'legen *refute*

wider'stehen *resist*

(b) Only two verbs in *wider-* are separable, i.e.:

'widerhallen *echo, reverberate*

'widerspiegeln *reflect*

22.6.9 *wieder-*
One verb prefixed with *wieder-* is inseparable, i.e.:

wieder'holen *repeat*

All other verbs in *wieder-* are separable, e.g.:

'wiederkehren *return*

'wiederkriegen *get back*

22.7 Verb formation by means other than by prefixes

Prefixation, as dealt with in 22.4–22.6, is by far the most productive means of deriving verbs. Nevertheless, a few other derivational patterns are frequent or productive enough to deserve mention.

22.7.1 Verbs meaning 'cause to do' have often been formed from strong verbs by means of vowel change

This pattern is no longer productive, but its results are still common. In general, a transitive weak verb has been formed from an intransitive strong verb, e.g.:

ertrinken *drown* (intr.) → ertränken *drown* (trans.)
fallen *fall* → fällen *fell*
sitzen *sit* → setzen *set*
springen *jump* → sprengen *blow up*

22.7.2 Verbs in *-eln*, usually with Umlaut, express a weakened form of an action:

husten *cough*   → hüsteln *cough slightly*
lachen *laugh*   → lächeln *smile*
streichen *stroke*   → streicheln *stroke gently, caress*

Some such verbs have a pejorative sense, e.g.:

tanzen *dance*   → tänzeln *mince*

This formation is still productive and may be based on nouns or adjectives as well as on other verbs, e.g.:

der Schwabe *Swabian*   → schwäbeln *talk like a Swabian*
fromm *pious*   → frömmeln *affect piety*

22.7.3 The suffix *-ieren* is chiefly and productively employed to form verbs from foreign roots

The source of most verbs in *-ieren* (and its derivatives *-isieren* and *-ifizieren*) is French or Latin. Some have entered German directly from French verbs in *-er*, e.g. *arranger* → *arrangieren*. Others have been formed in German from foreign roots, e.g. *Tabu* → *tabuisieren* and a very few have been created from German roots, e.g. *der Buchstabe* → *buchstabieren*.

23   Spelling and punctuation

A few aspects of German spelling and punctuation cause difficulty, either because the rules are different to those for English, or because they can be ambiguous in certain contexts and difficult to apply, or because there are inexplicable irregularities and anomalies. A selection of these problematic points is dealt with in this chapter, following the guidelines laid down in DUDEN (1985:314ff., 385ff. & 785ff.). The rulings given there are accepted as authoritative throughout Germany, and variations in the other German-speaking countries are insignificant.

23.1 The use of capitals

The basic rules are:
(i) The first word in a sentence or a line of poetry is written with an initial capital letter (as in English).
(ii) All nouns are written with an initial capital letter, e.g.:

der Sack   die Schwierigkeit   das Bürgertum   die Pfirsiche

(iii) All other words begin with a small letter.
There are a number of exceptions and anomalies to these rules which are explained in this section.

23.1.1 Other parts of speech used as nouns are written with an initial capital letter, e.g.:

beim Lesen   das Für und Wider   das Ich   das Entweder-Oder
eine Drei   ein Drittel   die Vorbeigehenden   Bekanntes
alles Gute   nichts Schlechtes (cf. 6.4.6)
der Erste unter Gleichen *first among equals*

There are several inconsistencies in the application of this rule, as there may be doubts as to whether the word is really being used as a noun, i.e.:

(a) Adjectives used as nouns are written with an initial small letter in a number of set phrases
Some frequent examples:

im allgemeinen *in general*   auf dem laufenden bleiben
beim alten bleiben *remain as it was*   *keep up-to-date*

509

jemanden zum besten haben *have sb. on*
durch dick und dünn *through thick and thin*
in großen und ganzen *in general*
von klein auf *from childhood*
vor kurzem *recently*
seit kurzem/langem *for a short/long time*

alles mögliche *everything possible*
aufs neue *afresh*
des öfteren *frequently*
im stillen *in secret*
bei weitem *by far*
im wesentlichen *essentially*

(b) Adjectives are spelled with an initial small letter if a preceding (or following) noun is understood, e.g.:

Das rote Kleid hat mir nicht gepaßt, ich mußte das blaue nehmen
Es ist wohl das schnellste von diesen drei Autos

(c) Most indefinite determiners and adjectives are always written with a small letter,
cf. 5.5. This applies in particular to the following:

ähnlich* *similar*	bestimmt* *definite*	gewiß* *certain*	verschieden *various*
ander *other*	derartig* *suchlike*	gleich *same*	weiter* *further*
beide *both*	einzeln *individual*	nächst *next*	
beliebig *any*	folgend *following*	übrig *remaining*	

NB: Those marked with an asterisk do have a capital after *alles* and *nichts*, e.g. *alles Weitere*, *nichts Derartiges*.

(d) Usage with geographical and other proper names
(i) Adjectives forming part of geographical or other names referring to something unique have an initial capital letter, e.g.:

das Schwarze Meer *the Black Sea*
das Auswärtige Amt *Foreign Office*
Karl der Erste *Charles the First*
die Französische Revolution   *the French Revolution*

das Neue Testament *New Testament*
der Eiserne Vorhang *Iron Curtain*
die Olympischen Spiele *Olympic Games*

NB: The following, and others like them, are not names of unique things, and they are spelled with a small letter:
die goldene Hochzeit *golden wedding*   der schwarze Markt *black market*

(ii) Indeclinable adjectives in *-er* from the names of towns and countries have an initial capital, e.g.:

der Kölner Dom   die Berliner Straßen   das Wiener Rathaus

(iii) Adjectives formed from proper names with the suffix *-isch* (or *-sch*) have a capital letter when they refer directly to the person concerned, but a small letter if they mean 'in the manner of'. Compare the following pairs:

die Einsteinsche Relativitätstheorie	*Einstein's theory of relativity*
einsteinsche Theorien	*theories like those of Einstein*
das Elizabethanische England	*Elizabethan England*
(i.e. during the reign of Elizabeth I)	
das elizabethanische Drama	*Elizabethan drama*
(i.e. drama written during her reign, but she was not the author)	
die Platonischen Schriften	*Plato's writings*
die platonische Liebe	*platonic love*

(e) Usage with *deutsch* and other adjectives of nationality

(i) Adjectives of nationality are written with a capital letter when used as a noun to refer to the language or the school subject (cf.6.4.7a), e.g.:

Er kann kein Wort Deutsch	Mein Deutsch ist schlecht
Das ist (kein) gutes Deutsch	im heutigen Deutsch
Wir haben Deutsch in der Schule	Ich habe eine Drei in Deutsch

Sie spricht, kann, lernt, liest (kein, gut) Deutsch, Russisch, Englisch
Das Buch ist in Deutsch und Englisch erschienen
Sie hat das Buch aus dem Französichen ins Deutsche übersetzt

der/die Deutsche 'German' (cf. 6.4.4) is also spelled with a capital letter, e.g.:

Ich kenne viele Deutsche	wir Deutschen
Was ißt ein Deutscher am liebsten?	Ist sie Deutsche?

(ii) When used as adjectives they have a small letter, e.g.:

das deutsche Volk	ein deutsches Lied	italienische Weine
die deutsche Bundesrepublik	ein britisches Schiff	

NB: This runs counter to English usage, which requires a capital letter (*the German people, Italian wines, a British ship*, etc.). Only in names (cf. (d) above) is a capital used in German, e.g. *die Deutsche Bundesbahn*.

(iii) They have a small letter when used as the equivalent of an adverb, e.g.:

Der Minister hat mit ihr deutsch gesprochen
Redet sie jetzt deutsch oder niederländisch?

Er denkt sehr deutsch	*He thinks in a very German way*
Wenn ich deutsch reden soll, . . .	*If I'm to speak plainly*

They are also spelled with a small letter when used with the preposition *auf*, as the whole is seen as having adverbial force, e.g.:

Wie sagt man das auf deutsch?	*How do you say that in German?*
Sie hat es mir auf spanisch erzählt	*She told it me in Spanish*

(f) Superlatives are spelled with a small letter if they are used with *sein* as the equivalent of a form with *am*, cf. 8.3.1, e.g.:

Es ist das beste (= am besten), wenn wir ihr alles sagen
  (Compare *das Beste, was ich je gegessen habe*)

Similarly with other adjectives which can have an absolute sense:

Es ist das richtige (= richtig), ihr alles zu sagen
  (Compare *Tue das Richtige!*)

23.1.2 Nouns used as other parts of speech are written with a small letter, i.e.:

(i) nouns used as prepositions, cf. chapter 20, e.g.:

angesichts   kraft   mittels   statt   trotz

NB: Some prepositions from complex phrases have alternative spellings, i.e. *anhand/an Hand, anstelle/an Stelle, aufgrund/auf Grund*

(ii) nouns used as adverbs, cf. 11.5.2 and 11.7, e.g.:

morgen	heute abend	von morgens bis abends
kreuz und quer	anfangs	

(iii) nouns used in indefinite expressions of number, e.g.:

ein bißchen   ein paar (see 5.5.7, cf. *ein Paar* 'a pair')

(iv) nouns used as predicate adjectives with *sein*, i.e.:

Mir ist angst (BUT: Ich habe Angst)	*I am afraid*
Sie ist schuld daran	*It's her fault*
Es ist schade	*It's a pity/It's too bad*

(v) nouns used as separable prefixes (cf. 22.5.4), e.g.:

achtgeben *pay attention*	Es tut jemandem leid *sb. is sorry*
stattfinden *take place*	teilnehmen *participate*
jemandem wehtun *hurt sb.*	

(vi) In a number of other set phrases with verbs the noun does not have a capital, i.e.:

außer acht lassen	*leave out of account*
sich in acht nehmen	*take care*
recht/unrecht haben	*be right/wrong*

23.1.3 Capitalisation with pronouns and related forms

(a) All forms of the 'polite' second person pronoun *Sie* and the related possessive are spelled with a capital letter,
cf. 3.1.1 and 3.3, e.g. *Sie, Ihnen, Ihre Frau*, etc.

(b) Forms of the other second person pronouns, *du* and *ihr*, are spelled with a capital letter in letter-writing,
cf. 3.3, e.g.:

Ich danke Dir recht herzlich für Deinen Brief
Wir wollen Euch zu Eurer Verlobung gratulieren

23.2 One word or two?

The general rule is that compounds are written as a single word if they are felt to be a single concept. On the other hand, where the individual words are still felt to retain full meaning, they are written separately. The word stress often gives a clue to this, as a true fused compound only has one main stress, whereas separate words are still stressed independently. Compare:

'gut 'schreiben *write well*	'gutschreiben *credit*
'so 'weit *so far*	'soweit *on the whole*
'stehen 'lassen *leave standing*	'stehenlassen *leave untouched*

(This is similar to English, cf. *'black 'bird* and *'blackbird*).

However, even this is not a wholly reliable guide, and in practice there is much uncertainty, variation and inconsistency in the matter of writing single or separate words. DUDEN (1985:781) recommends that one should continue to write words separately in all cases of doubt.

We deal here with selected important groups of words where clear indications can be given.

23.2.1 preposition + noun

(a) These are written separately if the words concerned are still felt to have independent meanings, e.g.:

in Frage kommen, stehen, stellen	in/außer Kraft treten, sein
nach Hause gehen, zu Hause sein	zu Ende gehen
mit Bezug auf	unter Bezug auf
zur Zeit	

NB: In Austria and Switzerland *zurzeit* is accepted.

(b) In some cases the words are still written separately, but the noun has a small letter,
cf. also 24.1.1a, e.g.:

von seiten   in betreff   in bezug auf   bei weitem

(c) In several such combinations the meanings of the individual components are no longer perceived as independent
They are thus written together, e.g.:

beiseite (stehen)	instand (setzen)
zugrunde (gehen, richten)	infolge
inmitten	zustande (bringen)

NB: Those of the above which are used with verbs are not usually written together with the verb, although they occupy the position of a separable prefix in the clause, cf. 23.5.4c. Nevertheless, the participles and derived nouns are written as single words, e.g. *die instandgesetzte Maschine, der zugrundeliegende Gedanke, das Zugrundegehen, die Instandsetzung*, etc.

23.2.2 Combinations of a noun or an adverb with a participle or an adjective are often written together

The following general principles apply:

(a) Established combinations with a noun as first element are normally written together, e.g.:

ein aufsehenerregendes Ereignis	*a sensational occurrence*
das bahnbrechende Werk	*the pioneering work*

(i) Further examples of established compounds :

herzerquickend *heart-warming*   himmelschreiend *outrageous*
vertrauenerweckend *inspiring confidence*   zeitraubend *time-consuming*

(ii) Compounds which involve suppressing a preposition are always written together, e.g.:

staubbedeckt *covered with dust*   freudestrahlend *beaming with joy*
   (= mit Staub bedeckt)   (= vor Freude strahlend)

(iii) If the noun is qualified, e.g. by an adjective, it is written separately, e.g.:

ein heimliches Grauen erregender Anblick
ein unser aller Herz erquickendes Wort

(b) Occasional combinations with an adverb as first element may be written together or separately, e.g.:

ein reichgeschmücktes Haus   or   ein reich geschmücktes Haus
der hellstrahlende Stern   or   der hell strahlende Stern
ein weichgekochtes Ei   or   ein weich gekochtes Ei

Which is preferred depends on whether the writer perceives the meanings as as a new whole or as still distinct.

NB: A number of adverbs are <u>never</u> compounded as they are always perceived as retaining a distinct meaning. They include *eben, fast, gerade, kaum, soeben,* e.g.:
   das soeben erschienene Buch   ein fast vergessener Autor

(c) Established combinations with an adverb as first element are normally written together when they are used with a following noun, but less usually after the verb *sein*
Thus:

eine leichtverdauliche Speise   <u>but:</u>   die Speise ist leicht verdaulich
der schwerverletzte Mann   <u>but:</u>   der Mann war schwer verletzt

However:
(i) They are written separately if the adverb is qualified, e.g.:

eine sehr leicht verdauliche Speise   ein sehr schwer verletzter Mann

(ii) Such combinations are always written together, even after *sein*, if they have a figurative sense or a generic sense, referring to a whole class of people or things, e.g.:

Das Angebot ist freibleibend   *The offer is subject to alteration*
Das Kind ist minderbegabt   *The child is less gifted*

23.2.3 Compound adverbs with *so-, wie-* and *wo-*

Note the difference between the following pairs:

sobald *as soon as* (cf. 19.2.6a)   so bald *so soon*
solange *as long as* (cf. 19.2.6b)   so lange *so long*

sooft *as often as* (cf. 19.2.6c)	*so oft so often*
wieweit *to what extent*	*wie weit how far, what distance*
woanders *elsewhere* (cf. 7.2.5d)	*wo anders? where else?*
womöglich *possibly*	*wo möglich if possible*

NB: (i) The consecutive conjunction *so daß* 'so that', cf. 19.4.2, is always spelled as two words in standard German usage, although *sodaß* is accepted in Austria and Switzerland.
(ii) For the spelling of forms with *-viel* and *-wenig*, e.g. *soviel, wieviel, zuwenig*, etc. see 5.5.25f..

23.2.4 Some further problematic instances regarding the spelling of compounds are dealt with in other sections, i.e.:

(i) For forms with *irgend-*, e.g. *irgendwelcher, irgend jemand*, see 5.5.11.
(ii) The spelling of prefixed verbs is treated in 22.5.4.

23.3 *ss* or *ß*?

23.3.1 It is the predominant usage to distinguish in writing between -*ss*- and -*ß*- (referred to as *eszet* or *scharfes s*)

The distinction is now universally observed in Germany and Austria; only in Switzerland is no distinction made and -*ss*- used in all cases. Foreign learners are strongly recommended to follow the majority practice and use *ß* in appropriate contexts.

(a) *ß* is used in the following contexts:
(i) before consonants, e.g.:

du läßt, ihr laßt, er wußte, wir mußten, der größte, etc.

(ii) at the end of a word or part of a compound, e.g.:

das Faß, der Fuß, der Fluß, der Haß, der Maß, groß, gewiß, daß, etc.
das Flußbett, flußabwärts, haßerfüllt, der Großbuchstabe, etc.

(iii) between vowels <u>if</u> the preceding vowel is long, e.g.:

die Buße, die Füße, die Maße, die Grüße, beißen, größer, etc.

(b) *ss* is used between vowels if the preceding vowel is short, e.g.:

die Flüsse, ein gewisser, lassen, müssen, wissen, das Wasser, etc.

23.3.2 The rules given in 23.3.1 above are applied without exception.

This means that -*ss*- and -*ß*- alternate in the declension of many words with a short vowel, depending on whether a vowel, a consonant or the end of the word follows, e.g.:

lassen, ich lasse <u>but</u> du läßt, wir ließen
müssen <u>but</u> ich muß, ich mußte

wissen <u>but</u> ich weiß, ihr wißt, ich wußte, gewußt
ein gewisser Herr <u>but</u> gewiß
der Fluß, das Faß <u>but</u> die Flüsse, die Fässer

NB: (i) A few personal names are spelled with a final -*ss*, e.g.:
Günther Grass, Theodor Heuss, Richard Strauss (<u>but</u> Johann Strauß), Carl Zeiss
(ii) *ß* is in principle only a lower case letter and *SS* should be used in its place when
capitals are required, e.g. FRANKFURTER STRASSE, ICH WEISS ALLES, ICH
MUSS, etc.

23.4.   Other miscellaneous points concerning spelling

23.4.1 Nouns in -*ee* and -*ie* do not add an extra -*e* in forming the plural, even if the plural ending is pronounced as a distinct syllable, e.g.:

der See, die Seen [ze:ən]   das Knie, die Knien [kni:ən]
die Industrie, die Industrien [industr:ən]

Similarly in verb forms, cf. 12.2.2d:

knien [kni:ən] *knee*   wir schrien [ʃʀi:ən] *we cried*

23.4.2 Double vowels are simplified under Umlaut, e.g:
(i) in plural forms (cf.1.2.2d): der Saal *room* → die Säle
(ii) in diminutive forms (cf. 22.2.1a):

das Paar *pair*→ das Pärchen   das Boot *boat*→ das Bötchen

23.4.3 Sequences of three identical consonants in compound words

(a) If a vowel follows, one consonant is deleted, e.g.:

das Bett + das Tuch→ das Bettuch   still + legen→ stillegen
rollen + die Läden→ die Rolläden   brennen + die Nessel→ die Brennessel
das Schiff + die Fahrt → die Schiffahrt
i.e. <u>not</u>: das Betttuch, stilllegen, etc.

(b) However, if a further consonant follows, all three are retained, e.g.:

das Fett + der Tropfen → der Fetttropfen
das Bett + die Truhe → die Betttruhe

23.5 The use of the comma

The basic rule for the use of the comma in German is that every clause within a sentence should begin and end with a comma
In this way, the comma in German is used to mark off grammatical units, <u>not</u> to signal a pause when speaking.
This rule includes <u>all</u> types of clauses, i.e.:

(i) main clauses linked by a coordinating conjunction, cf. 19.1, e.g.:

Mein Vater arbeitet im Garten, und meine Mutter fährt in die Stadt
Er runzelte die Stirn, aber sie sagte nichts
Er konnte nicht identifiziert werden, denn er hatte keine Papiere bei sich

(ii) subordinate clauses introduced by a conjunction, cf. 19.2ff., e.g.:

Er fragte, ob ich morgen nach Halberstadt fahren wollte
Weil ich morgen arbeiten muß, werde ich keine Zeit haben

(iii) subordinate clauses not introduced by a conjunction, e.g.:

Sie sagte, sie habe diesen Mann nie vorher gesehen
Unsere Lage wäre unmöglich gewesen, hätte Erich diesen Plan nicht
    ausgedacht

(iv) non-finite subordinate clauses, cf. 13.2 and 13.6:

Ich habe sie dringend gebeten, uns morgen zu helfen
Ich bin doch nur gekommen, um meinen alten Freund Peter wiederzusehen
Einmal in Zürich angekommen, mußte er sich sofort bei der Polizei anmelden

Major exceptions to this rule and areas of doubt and difficulty are
explained in the remainder of this section.

NB: This rule means that, unlike English, adverbs and adverbial phrases within the
sentence are <u>never</u> separated off by commas. Compare:

Er konnte ihr jedoch helfen   *He was, however, able to help her*
Bitte bringen Sie mir wenn   *Bring me a newspaper, if possible,*
    möglich eine Zeitung   *please*

23.5.1 Clauses linked by *und* or *oder*

**(a) Main clauses joined by *und* or *oder* do not have a comma if the subject of
the second clause is understood,**
i.e. if the subject is omitted because it is the same as that of the first clause,
e.g.:

Er kam herein und sah seine Frau in der Ecke sitzen
Mein Vater geht ins Theater oder besucht ein Konzert

**(b) Parallel subordinate clauses linked by *und* or *oder* do not have a comma
between them,** e.g:

Er sagte, daß ich sofort kommen müßte und daß er mir etwas sehr Wichtiges
    zu berichten hätte
Sie wird nicht kommen, weil sie nicht kann oder weil sie einfach keine
    Lust hat

23.5.2 Deviations from the basic rule in infinitive clauses with *zu*

Like other subordinate clauses, infinitive clauses with *zu* are usually separated off by commas, e.g.:

Sie beschloß, den Betrag möglichst bald zu überweisen, und ging am
    nächsten Morgen zur Bank

There are a few exceptions to this general rule, i.e.:

(a) No comma is used if the clause consists simply of the infinitive with *zu*,
e.g.:

Sie beschloß zu warten   Ich hoffte zu gewinnen

Compare:

Ich hoffte, in der nächsten Runde zu gewinnen

NB: A comma is necessary with compound infinitives, e.g. *Sie glaubten, gesiegt zu haben.*

(b) No comma is used if the infinitive clause is conflated with the clause on which it depends,
cf. 13.2.2e, e.g.:

Das bleibt noch abzuwarten
Diesen Vorgang wollen wir zu erklären versuchen

(c) No comma is used if the infinitive clause is the subject of the finite verb
Cf. 13.2.1, e.g.:

So etwas zu erlauben ist unerhört

(d) No comma is used after certain verbs even if the infinitive clause contains other elements
This is particularly the case with some of the 'semi-auxiliary' verbs dealt with in 13.2.3 and a few others. With these, the infinitive clause is felt to form a single unit with the main verb and a comma is seen as unnecessary, e.g.:

Ich brauche heute nicht ins Geschäft zu gehen
Du hast dir jetzt die Hände zu waschen
So ein Apparat ist in London nicht mehr zu bekommen
(i) This is always the case with the following semi-auxiliary verbs:

brauchen   haben   pflegen   scheinen   sein   vermögen
(ii) With a number of verbs the use of a comma is optional <u>if</u> they have no objects or adverbs with them, e.g.:

Sie hörte auf(,) mich zu belästigen
Sie versuchte(,) ihn telephonisch zu erreichen

This applies to the following:

anfangen	bitten	fürchten	versprechen	wagen
aufhören	denken	glauben	verstehen	wissen
beginnen	drohen	hoffen	versuchen	wünschen

NB: No comma is used if parts of these verbs enclose the dependent infinitive, cf. 13.2.3, e.g.:
Ich habe ihm zu helfen versprochen
Ich weiß, daß er sein Geschäft zu verkaufen versucht

23.5.3 Longer participial clauses are separated by commas from the remainder of the sentence, e.g.:

Später wanderte er, ein altes Lied summend, durch den Garten
Einmal in seiner Heimatstadt angekommen, ging er sofort zum Haus, wo seine
    Großmutter gewohnt hatte

Commas are also used with absolute phrases (cf. 2.2.6), e.g.:

Der Polizist trat ins Zimmer, einen Revolver in der Hand

NB: Short phrases, especially those which simply consist of a participle, are not separated by commas if they are felt to be an integral part of the clause, e.g.:
Das Kind lag weinend im Bett   Sie kam lachend auf mich zu
Es war im Grunde genommen bloß ein Scherz

23.5.4 Interjections, exclamations, explanatory phrases, phrases in apposition and parenthetical words and phrases which are seen as separate from the clause are normally divided from it by commas, e.g.:

Ach, kannst du morgen wirklich nicht zu uns kommen?
Kurz und gut, die Lage ist kritisch
Wissen Sie, ich kann Ihnen da leider nicht mehr helfen
Sohn eines reichen Gutsbesitzers, hat er in seiner Eigenschaft als
    Reserveoffizier mit den Regeln des Ehrenhandels Bekanntschaft geschlossen
Das macht, grob gerechnet, vierzig Prozent von unserem Absatz aus
Ich habe jetzt, wie gesagt, keine Zeit dazu
Wir wurden durch Herrn Meiring, den Direktor des Instituts, aufs
    herzlichste empfangen

NB: Comparative phrases introduced by *als* or *wie* (cf. 21.9.2) are not normally separated off by commas, e.g.:
Sie ist jetzt wohl größer als ihre ältere Schwester
Dieser Mann sah aus wie ein Schornsteinfeger

23.5.5 Two or more adjectives qualifying a noun are divided by commas if they are of equal importance.
i.e. if they could, alternatively, be linked by *und*, e.g.:

gute, billige Äpfel (i.e. the apples are good <u>and</u> cheap)

But no comma is used if the second adjective is felt to form a single idea with the noun, e.g.:

gute englische Äpfel (i.e. English apples which are good)

In practice, this rule is not always followed consistently (no more than the similar rule in English is) and many German writers use no commas in any series of adjectives.

23.6 Other punctuation marks

23.6.1 The semi-colon is in practice little used in German

In general, the comma or full stop is preferred, as appropriate. In particular, a comma tends to be used between two main clauses not linked by a conjunction, e.g.:

Gehe in die Stadt und kaufe Mehl, unterdessen heize ich schon den
     Backofen an

23.6.2 A colon, not a comma, is used when direct speech is introduced by a verb of saying, e.g.:

Dann sagte sie: „Ich kann es nicht"

23.6.3 The first of a set of inverted commas is placed <u>on</u> the line, not above it

This applies both to single and double inverted commas, e.g.:

Dann sagte sie: „Ich kann ihn überhaupt nicht verstehen"
Er fragte mich: „Kennen Sie Brechts Stück ‚Mutter Courage und ihre Kinder'?"

23.6.4 The use of the exclamation mark

(a) The exclamation mark is used after interjections and exclamations, e.g.:

Ach!   Donnerwetter!   Pfui Teufel!   Guten Tag!

(b) Commands are followed by an exclamation mark:

Komm sofort zurück!   Seid doch vorsichtig, Kinder!
Hören Sie sofort auf!   Einsteigen und die Türen schließen!

Standard usage has traditionally required the use of the exclamation mark with commands in German, but this rule is not always followed nowadays, and many Germans prefer to use a full stop, especially if the command is not felt to be particularly forceful.

(c) An exclamation mark is used after the words of address at the beginning of a letter, e.g.:

Sehr geehrter Herr Dr. Fleischmann!   Liebe Petra!

This traditional usage is now being rapidly supplanted by the use of the comma, as in English. However, if a comma is used, a capital is not used for the first word of the letter proper, as, strictly speaking, it is not the beginning of a sentence, e.g:

Lieber Martin,
es hat uns sehr gefreut, wieder mal von Dir zu hören. . . .

BIBLIOGRAPHY AND REFERENCES

We give below all the major works which were consulted during the preparation of the revised edition, together with those books and articles on more specialised topics which are cited in the text. Reference is made to them where appropriate by giving author, year of publication and page number(s) in the conventional way, e.g. Engel (1988: 477–82).

Admoni, Wladimir (1970) *Der deutsche Sprachbau*. 3rd. ed. Beck: München.

Agricola, Erhard et al. (eds.) (1977) *Wörter und Wendungen*. 8th ed. Bibliographisches Institut: Leipzig.

Andersen, Paul Kent (1990) 'Typological approaches to the passive'. In: *Journal of Linguistics* 26, pp. 189–202.

Ballweg, Joachim (1988) *Die Semantik der deutschen Tempusformen*. Schwann: Düsseldorf.

Bausch, Karl-Heinz (1979) *Modalität und Konjunktivgebrauch in der gesprochenen deutschen Standardsprache. Sprachsystem, Sprachvariation und Sprachwandel im heutigen Deutsch*. Teil I. Hueber: München.

Bergenholtz, Henning (1985) 'Kasuskongruenz der Apposition'. In: *Beiträge zur Geschichte der deutschen Sprache und Literatur* 107, pp. 21–44.

Bergenholtz, Henning & Joachim Mugdan (1979) *Einführung in die Morphologie*. Kohlhammer: Stuttgart.

Berger, Dieter (1982) *Fehlerfreies Deutsch*. 2nd. ed. Dudenverlag: Mannheim.

Bresson, Daniel (1988) *Grammaire d'usage de l'allemand contemporain*. Hachette: Paris.

Buscha, Joachim (1988) 'Die Funktionen der Pronominalform *es*'. In: *Deutsch als Fremdsprache* 25, pp. 27–33.

Buscha, Joachim & Irene Zoch (1984) *Der Konjunktiv*. Enzyklopädie: Leipzig.

Buscha, Joachim & Irene Zoch (1988) *Der Infinitiv*. Enzyklopädie: Leipzig.

Butt, John & Carmen Benjamin (1988) *A New Reference Grammar of Modern Spanish*. Edward Arnold: London.

Clyne, Michael (1984) *Language and Society in the German-speaking Countries*. CUP: Cambridge.

Collinson, W. E. (1953) *The German Language Today. Its Patterns and Historical Background.* Hutchinson's University Library: London.

Curme, George O. (1922) *A Grammar of the German Language.* Macmillan: New York.

Dal, Ingerid (1962) *Kurze deutsche Syntax auf historischer Grundlage.* Niemeyer: Tübingen.

Dickens, Eric (1990) *German for University Students.* Acme Publications: Stoke-on-Trent.

Dieling, Klaus & Fritz Kempter (1989) *Die Tempora.* 2nd. ed. Enzyklopädie: Leipzig.

Dückert, Joachim & Günter Kempcke (1984) *Wörterbuch der Sprachschwierigkeiten. Zweifelsfälle, Normen und Varianten im gegenwärtigen deutschen Sprachgebrauch.* Bibliographisches Institut: Leipzig.

DUDEN (1976–81) *Das große Wörterbuch der deutschen Sprache.* 6 vols. Dudenverlag: Mannheim.

DUDEN (1984) *DUDEN Band 4. Grammatik der deutschen Gegenwartssprache.* 4th. ed. by Günther Drosdowski et al. Dudenverlag: Mannheim.

DUDEN (1985) *DUDEN Band 9. Richtiges und gutes Deutsch.* 3rd. ed. by Dieter Berger, Günther Drosdowski et al. Dudenverlag: Mannheim.

Eggeling, H. F. (1961) *A Dictionary of Modern German Prose Usage.* Clarendon Press: Oxford.

Eisenberg, Peter (1986) *Grundriß der deutschen Grammatik.* Metzler: Stuttgart.

Eisenberg, Peter & Alexander Gusovius (1985) *Bibliographie zur deutschen Grammatik 1965–1983.* Gunter Narr Verlag: Tübingen.

Engel, Ulrich (1977) *Syntax der deutschen Gegenwartssprache.* Erich Schmidt: Berlin.

Engel, Ulrich (1988) *Deutsche Grammatik.* Groos: Heidelberg.

Engel, Ulrich & Helmut Schuhmacher (1976) *Kleines Valenzlexikon deutscher Verben.* Narr: Tübingen.

Farrell, R. B. (1977) *Dictionary of German Synonyms.* 3rd. ed. CUP: Cambridge.

Fernandez-Bravo, Nicole (1976) *Histoire du discours indirect allemand de Grimmelshausen à nos jours.* Centre Universitaire du Grand Palais: Paris.

Fleischer, Wolfgang (1974) *Wortbildung der deutschen Gegenwartssprache.* 3rd. ed. Bibliographisches Institut: Leipzig.

Fourquet, Jean (1952) *Grammaire de l'allemand.* Hachette: Paris.

Fox, Anthony (1990) *The Structure of German.* Clarendon Press: Oxford.

Freund, Folke & Birger Sundqvist (1988) *Tysk grammatik.* Natur och Kultur: Stockholm.

Glück, Helmut & Wolfgang Werner Sauer (1990) *Gegenwartsdeutsch.* Metzler: Stuttgart.

Götze, Lutz & Ernest W. B. Hess-Lüttich (1989) *Knaurs Grammatik der deutschen Sprache*. Knaur: München.

Graustein, Gottfried et al. (eds.) (1984) *English Grammar. A University Handbook*. 4th. ed. Enzyklopädie: Leipzig.

Gregor, Bernd (1983) *Genuszuordnung. Das Genus englischer Lehnwörter im Deutschen*. Niemeyer: Tübingen.

Griesbach, Heinz (1986) *Neue deutsche Grammatik*. Langenscheidt: München, Wien, Zürich.

Griesbach, Heinz & Dora Schulz (1960) *Grammatik der deutschen Sprache*. Hueber: München.

Grimm, Hans-Jürgen (1986) *Untersuchungen zum Artikelgebrauch im Deutschen*. Enzyklopädie: Leipzig.

Grimm, Hans-Jürgen (1987) *Lexikon zum Artikelgebrauch*. Enzyklopädie: Leipzig.

Hartwig,, Heinz (1985) *Besseres Deutsch — größere Chancen*. Heyne: München.

Hawkins, John A. (1986) *A Comparative Typology of English and German*. Croom Helm: London & University of Texas: Austin.

Heidolph, Karl Erich, Walter Flämig & Wolfgang Motsch (eds.) (1981) *Grundzüge einer deutschen Grammatik*. Akademie-Verlag: Berlin.

Helbig, Gerhard (1976) *Probleme der deutschen Grammatik für Ausländer*. Enzyklopädie: Leipzig.

Helbig, Gerhard (1988) *Lexikon deutscher Partikeln*. Enzyklopädie: Leipzig.

Helbig, Gerhard & Joachim Buscha (1986) *Deutsche Grammatik. Ein Handbuch für den Ausländerunterricht*. 9th. ed. Enzyklopädie: Leipzig.

Helbig, Gerhard & Gertraud Heinrich (1972) *Das Vorgangspassiv*. Bibliographisches Institut: Leipzig.

Helbig, Gerhard & Wolfgang Schenkel (1978) *Wörterbuch zur Valenz und Distribution deutscher Verben*. 4th. ed. Bibliographisches Institut: Leipzig.

Herbst, Thomas, David Heath & Hans-Martin Dederding (1980) *Grimm's Grandchildren. Current Topics in German Linguistics*. Longman: London.

Hoberg, Ursula (1981) *Die Wortstellung der geschriebenen deutschen Gegenwartssprache. Untersuchungen zur Elementenfolge in einfachen Verbalsatz*. Heuber: München.

Jäger, Siegfried (1970) *Empfehlungen zum Gebrauch des Konjunktivs*. Schwann: Düsseldorf.

Judge, Anne & Frank Healey (1985) *A Reference Grammar of Modern French*. Rev. ed. Edward Arnold: London.

Jung, Walter (1966) *Grammatik der deutschen Sprache*. Bibliographisches Institut: Leipzig.

Kirkwood, Henry W. (1969) 'Aspects of Word-order and its Communicative Function in English and German'. In: *Journal of Linguistics* 5, pp. 85–107.

Köpcke, Klaus-Michael (1982) *Untersuchungen zum Genussystem der deutschen Gegenwartssprache.* Niemeyer: Tübingen.

Lamprecht, Adolf (1977) *Grammatik der englischen Sprache.* 5th. ed. Cornelsen-Velhagen & Klasing: Berlin.

Latzel, Sigbert (1977) *Die deutschen Tempora Perfekt und Präteritum. Eine Darstellung mit Bezug auf Erfordernisse des Faches "Deutsch als Fremdsprache".* Hueber: München.

Lockwood, W. B. (1987) *German Today. The Advanced Learner's Guide.* Clarendon Press: Oxford.

Marx-Moyse, Janine (1983) *Untersuchungen zur deutschen Satzsyntax. 'Es' als vorausweisendes Element eines Subjektsatzes.* Steiner: Wiesbaden.

Palmer, Frank Robert (1986) *Mood and Modality.* CUP: Cambridge.

Pfeffer, J. Alan (1984) *Studies in Descriptive German Grammar.* Groos: Heidelberg.

Rowley, Anthony (1988) 'Zum Genitiv des ganz besonderen Typ'. In: *Muttersprache* 98, pp. 58–68.

Schanen, François and Jean-Paul Confais (1986) *Grammaire de l'allemand. Formes et fonctions.* Nathan: Paris.

Schmitz, Werner (1964) *Der Gebrauch der deutschen Präpositionen.* Hueber: München.

Sommerfeldt, Karl-Ernst (ed.) (1988) *Entwicklungstendenzen in der deutschen Gegenwartssprache.* Bibliographisches Institut: Leipzig.

Sommerfeldt, Karl-Ernst & Herbert Schreiber (1977) *Wörterbuch zur Valenz und Distribution deutscher Adjektive.* 2nd. ed. Bibliographisches Institut: Leipzig.

Sommerfeldt, Karl-Ernst & G. Starke (eds.) (1988) *Einführung in die Grammatik der deutschen Gegenwartssprache.* Bibliographisches Institut: Leipzig.

Swan, Michael (1980) *Practical English Usage.* OUP: Oxford.

Ulvestad, Bjarne & Henning Bergenholtz (1983) ' "Es" als "Vorgreifer" eines Objektsatzes'. Teil II.' In: *Deutsche Sprache* 11, pp. 1–26.

Wahrig, Gerhard (ed.) (1978) *dtv-Wörterbuch der deutschen Sprache.* dtv: München.

Wegener, Heide (1985) *Der Dativ im heutigen Deutsch.* Narr: Tübingen.

Weydt, Harald et al. (1983) *Kleine deutsche Partikellehre.* Klett: Stuttgart.

Zifonun, Gisela (1986) *Vor-Sätze zu einer neuen deutschen Grammatik.* Narr: Tübingen.

Sources

The examples illustrating points of grammar and usage have been drawn from a wide range of sources and registers, spoken as well as written. Many of the unattributed examples which are new to this revised edition have been simplified or amended from modern texts, from phrases and sentences heard in conversation or on radio or television, etc., and in large number from the computerised corpus of modern spoken and written German held at the Institut für deutsche Sprache in Mannheim. Longer examples quoted verbatim have been attributed wherever possible, and the following sources have provided such material.

(a) Authors

A. Andersch	M. Frisch	U. Johnson	E. M. Remarque
V. Baum	G. Gaiser	E. Jünger	R. M. Rilke
K. Bednarz	A. Goes	A. Kolb	H. von Rimscha
H. Böll	M. von der Grün	E. Langgässer	J. Roth
K. H. Borst	B. Grzimek	S. Lenz	E. Strauß
W. Brandt	S. Haffner	H. Mann	E. Strittmatter
B. Brecht	St. Heym	K. Mann	Th. Valentin
A. Döblin	W. Hildesheimer	Th. Mann	M. Walser
F. Dürrenmatt	M. Horbach	R. Musil	I. Wendt
H. Fallada	K. Jaspers	Th. Pinkwart	E. Wiechert
E. Fried	W. Jens	Th. Plievier	C. Zuckmayer
			St. Zweig

(b) Newspapers

Quotations from newspapers or periodicals are attributed by means of abbreviations or shortened forms of their titles as follows:

BILD	BILD-Zeitung	NZZ	Neue Zürcher Zeitung
FAZ	Frankfurter Allgemeine Zeitung	OH	Odenwälder Heimatzeitung
FR	Frankfurter Rundschau	Spiegel	Der Spiegel
HA	Hamburger Abendblatt	SZ	Süddeutsche Zeitung
MM	Mannheimer Morgen	Welt	Die Welt
ND	Neues Deutschland	Zeit	Die Zeit

(c) Broadcast sources

i.e. the following radio and television stations in the Federal Republic: ARD, NDR, SWF, WDR, ZDF.

German word index

The indexes comprise a German word-index, an English word-index and a topic index. The German word-index contains all those words about which specific information is given, but does not include all words in lists (e.g. the irregular and strong verbs in 12.6). The English word-index gives all those English words whose German equivalents are specifically explained. All references are to sections.

NB: A hyphen indicates a suffix or a prefix, e.g. *er-, -ung.*

English word index

The indexes comprise a German word-index, an English word-index and a topic index. The German word-index contains all those words about which specific information is given, but does not include all words in lists (e.g. the irregular and strong verbs in 12.6). The English word-index gives all those English words whose German equivalents are specifically explained. All references are to sections.

NB: A hyphen indicates a suffix or a prefix, e.g. *er-, -ung.*

about 11.6.6, 11.6.10b, 18.6.9a, 20.1.4e, 20.1.6, 20.3.12d, 20.4.1d
above 20.3.11/12, 20.4.2
according to 19.6.5, 20.2.6d, 20.2.10e
across 20.3.11/12
admittedly 10.3, 10.14.1
after 11.6.8, 11.7.4b, 18.6.8a, 19.2.4, 20.2.6c
after all 10.29
against 20.1.4a
ago 7.3.5e, 11.6.12, 20.3.15c
ahead of 20.3.15
all 5.5.1, 5.5.23
all but 20.1.1c
all right 10.30.4
all the same 10.2, 10.14, 10.18
along 20.3.2a, 20.3.6
already 10.30.1
although 19.5.1
among(st) 20.3.13a, 20.3.14a, 20.3.17a
and 19.1.5
answer 18.3.5b
any 4.9.7, 5.5.10b, 5.5.12, 5.5.14b, 5.5.26
anyhow 10.20.2, 10.32.1
anyone/-body 5.5.5c, 5.5.11d
anything 5.5.10a
anything at all 5.5.11
anyway 10.9, 10.27, 10.31
anywhere 7.2.5
apart from 20.3.10c
around 11.6.10b
as 13.4.3a, 19.1.2, 19.2.1, 19.3, 20.2.9b
as a result of 20.3.5d
as far as 20.1.1a
as if 16.4.1
as long as 19.2.6
as often as 19.2.6
as soon as 19.2.6
assuming that 16.3.3d
as well as 19.1.5b
at 11.6.3, 11.6.10a, 20.1.6b, 20.1.7a, 20.2.3, 20.2.9b, 20.3.2, 20.3.4b, 20.3.8a, 20.5.1

at all 10.32.1
at any rate 10.20.1
at least 8.3.4b, 10.20.1

be able to 17.3.1
be allowed to 17.2.1a
because 19.1.2, 19.3.1
because of 20.4.1d
before 11.7.4a, 19.2.2
not before 10.12.1, 19.2.2d
be going to 17.7.1c
behind 20.3.7
below 20.3.13, 20.3.14a, 20.4.2
be meant to 17.6.2a
beneath 20.3.12a, 20.3.14a, 20.4.2
beside 20.3.10a
besides 13.2.5d, 20.2.2a, 20.3.10c
be supposed to 17.6.1a, 17.6.2a
be to 17.6.1a, 17.6.2a
between 20.3.17
beyond 20.3.12a, 20.4.2a
(a) bit 5.5.10c
boil 12.6
both 5.5.3
both . . . and 19.1.5b
bottom 7.2.2
but 10.1.2, 19.1.1, 19.1.4
by 11.6.4, 20.1.2c, 20.1.6c, 20.1.7d, 20.2.3, 20.2.5b, 20.3.2
by . . . ing 13.7.2a, 19.6e, 20.1.2c
by the time (when) 19.2.2c
by the way 10.33
by way of 20.2.9d

can 17.2.1a, 17.3.1, 17.3.3, 17.3.5, 17.3.6, 17.5.2
change 18.3.5c
claim 17.7.3
climb 8.3.5b
come 13.7.5b
compared with 20.1.4c, 20.2.4c, 20.3.10d
concerning 18.6.10, 20.1.6d, 20.3.12d, 20.4.1d
in connection with 18.6.2, 20.3.2d
contrary to 20.1.4c, 20.2.10d
could 17.3.2c, 17.3.3

de- 22.4.2b
despite 20.4.1b
depending on 19.6.5
different(ly) 7.4.3c, 7.4.4
dis- 22.4.2b
down 7.3.5a
down to 20.1.1c
drop 18.3.5d
during 20.4.1c

each 5.5.12, 5.5.14, 9.4.1
each other 3.2.7
either . . . or 19.1.3
else 7.4.3
elsewhere 7.2.5d
escape 18.4.1c
especially as 19.3.3a
even 8.2.3d, 10.4.5, 10.19.5
even as 19.2.7a
even if 16.3.3d
even so 10.18
-ever 19.5.2
every 5.5.12, 5.5.14
everybody/-one 5.5.12, 5.5.13
everywhere 7.2.5
exactly 10.8.3
except 13.2.5d, 20.1.1c, 20.2.2a
except that 19.6.2a
except when 19.6.2b
extremely 8.3.2

fail 18.3.5
feel 13.7.5a, 17.3.6, 18.3.5c
(a) few 5.5.7, 5.5.8, 5.5.25
find 13.7.5c
first 9.2.2a, 9.2.3
for (conj) 19.1.2a
for (prep) 11.4.1, 11.6.5, 11.6.9, 13.2.5e, 18.6.5, 20.1.3, 20.1.4d, 20.2.9d
for . . . ing 13.4.3b, 13.7.2b, 20.2.9b

535

Topic index

The indexes comprise a German word-index, an English word-index and a topic index. The German word-index contains all those words about which specific information is given, but does not include all words in lists (e.g. the irregular and strong verbs in 12.6). The English word-index gives all those English words whose German equivalents are specifically explained. All references are to sections.

NB: A hyphen indicates a suffix or a prefix, e.g. *er-*, *-ung*.